P9-APA-220

VOCATIONAL PSYCHOLOGY

McGRAW-HILL SERIES IN PSYCHOLOGY

Consulting Editors

NORMAN GARMEZY, RICHARD L. SOLOMON, LYLE V. JONES, HAROLD W. STEVENSON

ADAMS, *Human Memory*

BEACH, HEBB, MORGAN, AND NISSEN, *The Neuropsychology of Lashley*

VON BÉKÉSY, *Experiments in Hearing*

BERKOWITZ, *Aggression: A Social Psychological Analysis*

BERLYNE, *Conflict, Arousal, and Curiosity*

BLUM, *Psychoanalytic Theories of Personality*

BROWN, *The Motivation of Behavior*

BROWN AND GHISELLI, *Scientific Method of Psychology*

BUTCHER, *MMPI: Research Developments and Clinical Applications*

COFER, *Verbal Learning and Verbal Behavior*

COFER AND MUSGRAVE, *Verbal Behavior and Learning: Problems and Processes*

CRAFTS, SCHNEIRLA, ROBINSON, AND GILBERT, *Recent Experiments in Psychology*

CRITES, *Vocational Psychology*

DAVITZ, *The Communication of Emotional Meaning*

DEESE AND HULSE, *The Psychology of Learning*

DOLLARD AND MILLER, *Personality and Psychotherapy*

EDGINGTON, *Statistical Inference: The Distribution-free Approach*

ELLIS, *Handbook of Mental Deficiency*

EPSTEIN, *Varieties of Perceptual Learning*

FERGUSON, *Statistical Analysis in Psychology and Education*

FORGUS, *Perception: The Basic Process in Cognitive Development*

FRANKS, *Behavior Therapy: Appraisal and Status*

GHISELLI, *Theory of Psychological Measurement*

GHISELLI AND BROWN, *Personnel and Industrial Psychology*

GILMER, *Industrial Psychology*

GRAY, *Psychology Applied to Human Affairs*

GUILFORD, *Fundamental Statistics in Psychology and Education*

GUILFORD, *The Nature of Human Intelligence*

GUILFORD, *Personality*

GUILFORD, *Psychometric Methods*

GUION, *Personnel Testing*

HAIRE, *Psychology in Management*

HIRSCH, *Behavior-genetic Analysis*

HIRSH, *The Measurement of Hearing*

HURLOCK, *Adolescent Development*

HURLOCK, *Child Development*

HURLOCK, *Developmental Psychology*
JACKSON AND MESSICK, *Problems in Human Assessment*
KARN AND GILMER, *Readings in Industrial and Business Psychology*
KRECH, CRUTCHFIELD, AND BALLACHEY, *Individual in Society*
LAZARUS, *Patterns of Adjustment and Human Effectiveness*
LAZARUS, *Psychological Stress and the Coping Process*
LEWIN, *A Dynamic Theory of Personality*
LEWIN, *Principles of Topological Psychology*
MAHER, *Principles of Psychopathology*
MARX AND HILLIX, *Systems and Theories in Psychology*
MESSICK AND BRAYFIELD, *Decision and Choice: Contributions of Sidney Siegel*
MILLER, *Language and Communication*
MORGAN, *Physiological Psychology*
NUNNALLY, *Psychometric Theory*
RETHLINGSHAFER, *Motivation as Related to Personality*
ROBINSON AND ROBINSON, *The Mentally Retarded Child*
SCHERER AND WERTHEIMER, *A Psycholinguistic Experiment on Foreign Language Teaching*
SHAW AND WRIGHT, *Scales for the Measurement of Attitudes*
SIDOWSKI, *Experimental Methods and Instrumentation in Psychology*
SIEGEL, *Nonparametric Statistics for the Behavioral Sciences*
STAGNER, *Psychology of Personality*
TOWNSEND, *Introduction to Experimental Methods for Psychology and the Social Sciences*
VINACKE, *The Psychology of Thinking*
WALLEN, *Clinical Psychology: The Study of Persons*
WARREN AND AKER, *The Frontal Granular Cortex and Behavior*
WATERS, RETHLINGSHAFER, AND CALDWELL, *Principles of Comparative Psychology*
WINER, *Statistical Principles in Experimental Design*
ZUBEK AND SOLBERG, *Human Development*

John F. Dashiell was Consulting Editor of this series from its inception in 1931 until January 1, 1950. Clifford T. Morgan was Consulting Editor of this series from January 1, 1950 until January 1, 1959. Harry F. Harlow assumed the duties of Consulting Editor from 1959 to 1965. In 1965 a Board of Consulting Editors was established according to areas of interest. The current board members are Richard L. Solomon (physiological, experimental), Norman Garmezy (abnormal, clinical), Harold W. Stevenson (child, adolescent, human development), and Lyle V. Jones (statistical, quantitative).

VOCATIONAL PSYCHOLOGY

The Study of Vocational Behavior and Development

JOHN O. CRITES

Professor of Psychology, University of Iowa

McGraw-Hill Book Company

New York St. Louis San Francisco London
Sydney Toronto Mexico Panama

ACKNOWLEDGMENTS

Grateful acknowledgment is hereby made to the authors and publishers for permission to quote from the following:

Table 8-1, p. 329, is reprinted from p. 7, *The Meaning of Work and Retirement, by* E. A. Friedmann and R. J. Havighurst, by permission of The University of Chicago Press. Copyright © 1954 by The University of Chicago Press.

Figure 5-5, p. 175, is reproduced from Figure 4, p. 97, in *Psychological Studies of Human Development,* ed. by Raymond G. Kuhlen and George G. Thompson. Copyright 1952 by Appleton-Century-Crofts, Inc. Reprinted by permission.

The quotation on p. 28 is from p. 62, *The Psychology of Human Differences,* 3d ed., by L. E. Tyler. Copyright 1965 by Appleton-Century-Crofts, Inc. Reprinted by permission.

Table 5-1, p. 157, is from pp. 376–382, *Youth: The Years from Ten to Sixteen,* by Arnold Gesell et al. Copyright © 1956 by Gesell Institute of Child Development, Inc. Reprinted by permission of Harper & Row, Publishers, Incorporated.

Tables 12-1 and 12-6, pp. 533 and 563, are from Figure 77, p. 638, and Figure 76, p. 622, in *Industrial Sociology,* by D. C. Miller and W. H. Form. Copyright 1951. Reprinted by permission of Harper & Row, Publishers, Incorporated.

The quotation on p. 80 is from p. 660, *Industrial Sociology,* by D. C. Miller and W. H. Form. Copyright 1951. Reprinted by permission of Harper & Row, Publishers, Incorporated.

Table 11-1, p. 481, is from p. 243, *Job Satisfaction,* by R. Hoppock. Copyright 1935. Reprinted by permission of Harper & Row, Publishers, Incorporated.

VOCATIONAL PSYCHOLOGY

Copyright © 1969 by McGraw-Hill, Inc. All rights reserved. Printed in the United States of America. No part of this publication may be reproduced, stored in a retrieval system, or transmitted, in any form or by any means, electronic, mechanical, photocopying, recording, or otherwise, without the prior written permission of the publisher.

Library of Congress Catalog Card Number 69–14485

13780

1 2 3 4 5 6 7 8 9 0 MAMM 7 6 5 4 3 2 1 0 6 9

158.6
C86V

To My Family

143744

PREFACE

There were three major reasons why this book was written. First, there was what appeared to be a need for an up-to-date review and synthesis of research and theory in the field of vocational psychology, which was not otherwise available. Not only are the two major texts in the field, Roe's *Psychology of Occupations* (1956) and Super's *Psychology of Careers* (1957), over a decade old, but both of them are more surveys than they are critical analyses of the literature on vocational behavior and development. Thus, a primary purpose of this book has been to appraise and evaluate empirical studies and theoretical statements in the field to determine, by certain generally accepted criteria of sound methodology and principles of scientific explanation, what reliable behavioral laws apply to vocational phenomena and how useful contemporary conceptual schemata are in accounting for them.

A second reason for writing the book was that, in the author's opinion, the units of analysis used in the earlier texts were not the most appropriate which might have been selected. As will be discussed at greater length in Chapter 1, Roe organized her book around the occupation, classified by field and level, as the unit of analysis, whereas Super used a combined developmental-factorial framework, in which the main focus was upon the course and correlates of stages in the work life. Neither of these schemata emphasizes vocational *behavior,* however, although it would seem to be the most psychologically meaningful unit of analysis for studying both occupational differences and career patterns. Accordingly, this book has been divided into two main parts, one on vocational choice and the other on vocational adjustment, which are assumed to be the behavioral units of analysis of greatest importance and interest in vocational psychology.

Still another reason for writing this book was to further codify and define vocational psychology as a field of scientific inquiry. Despite the fact that a large body of research and theory on vocational behavior and development has accumulated during the past half century or more, it has been disparate and unintegrated, having been the product of several disciplines, each with a unique orientation. Moreover, vocational psychology has never been clearly differentiated from vocational guidance and counseling; yet if there is to be a science of vocational behavior, it must be distinguished from the art of assisting individuals to choose and adjust to vocations. This is not to say that the one does not have implications for the other, but only that the two encompass essentially different substantive areas (see Chapter 1). The subject matter covered in this book is, therefore, that of vocational psychology, not of vocational counseling.

Throughout the book, the frame of reference adopted in organizing and analyzing and interpreting this subject matter has been strongly influenced by what have become known as the "behavior theoretic" and "logical positivist" points of view in psychology. To some vocational psychologists, raised in the tradition of "dustbowl empiricism," with its largely atheoretical and pragmatic emphases, this orientation may seem unfamiliar, and to some experimental psychologists, with their training and background in the laboratory, it may appear inappropriate. Hopefully, however, both will be convinced, as they read this book, that such concepts and principles as "operational definitions," "functional relationships," and "intervening variables," to mention a few, are as applicable in the study of vocational behavior as they are in the study of other behaviors. Indeed, it can be argued that they are necessary, as the *sine qua non* of systematic knowledge, to further the development of vocational psychology as a science by clarifying what is known and by identifying what is not known.

The plan of the book, which is outlined in detail in Chapter 1, has followed this principle. Both within and between chapters, an attempt has been made to explicate the meaning of concepts by specifying the procedures used to measure them, to classify variables by type (stimulus, organismic, or response) and delineate the relationships among them (S-R, O-R, etc.), and to juxtapose theory and research so that the status of each might be meaningfully assessed. Previously unpublished data on the vocational choices of college male and female freshmen are reported in Chapter 4; a new diagnostic system for problems in vocational choice is presented in Chapter 7; and suggestions for further research based upon the studies reviewed in earlier chapters are discussed in Chapter 13. At the graduate level, the text has been used, supplemented by readings in primary sources, in a one-semester course on vocational psychology, but at the undergraduate level it might better be assigned on a two-semester basis, the first covering vocational choice and the second vocational adjustment.

This book is dedicated to my wife Jane, sons John and Jerry, and parents Orr and Ora, all of whom, each in his or her unique way, have made it possible for me to write it. In addition, however, there are many others who, by their interest or encouragement, advice or criticism, have contributed significantly to it. As mentor, colleague, and friend, Donald E. Super introduced me to vocational psychology and, by his example as a leader in the field, stimulated me to pursue a career in it which has resulted in this book. My colleagues in the department of psychology at the University of Iowa, notably Harold P. Bechtoldt, Gustav Bergmann, Leonard D. Goodstein (now at the University of Cincinnati), Dee W. Norton, and the late Kenneth W. Spence, through their writings and in countless discussions, have clarified and refined my thinking on many complex methodological and theoretical issues. The students in my course on vocational choice and adjustment have corrected numerous errors of both form and content in earlier drafts of the book and have tried it out in similar courses they have taught, giving me the benefit of their students' reactions to it. And I am indebted to the many secretaries and typists who have labored long and hard on the manuscript over the past eight years: Mrs. Marjorie Miller, Mrs. Shirley Fawcett, Mrs. Beverly Judgins, Miss Eleanor Barker, Miss Linda Moel, and Mrs. Sharon Hammond.

Had it not been for a leave of absence during the academic year of 1966–1967, however, this book would still be unfinished. I am particularly grateful to Dr. Anne Roe, then director of the Center for Research in Careers, Harvard University, for inviting me to join the staff as a visiting research associate and for providing me with the time and resources to finish writing Chapters 1, 2, 11, 12, 13, and 14. I also wish to express my appreciation to the Graduate College of the University of Iowa for a research professorship during the fall semester of 1964, which gave me an opportunity to write most of the chapters in Part II.

Finally, it is a pleasure to acknowledge the work of the many authors cited and quoted in the book; in each instance, references to them and the publishers are given in the text and bibliography.

John O. Crites

If I did not work,
these worlds would perish . . .

BHAGARAD-GITA

CONTENTS

I
INTRODUCTION

1

THE FIELD OF VOCATIONAL PSYCHOLOGY

In the latest edition of the *Dictionary of Occupational Titles,* published in 1966 by the U.S. Department of Labor, there are listed over 21,000 titles of different occupations. Yet, despite the fact that vocational psychologists compiled the dictionary, this occupational title is not included in it! Similarly, in books (Anastasi, 1964) and pamphlets (American Psychological Association, 1963) on the fields and specialties of psychology, there is no mention of vocational psychology as a distinct discipline. The reason for these omissions is not that vocational psychology is not a field of study, but that it has not been formally recognized as such. Because it developed out of a strong applied tradition, dating back to the decade prior to World War I, vocational psychology has usually been associated with, if not subsumed by, vocational guidance and, more recently, counseling psychology. That vocational psychology is not *necessarily* related to these applied areas, however, is well documented by its long and distinguished record of scientific contributions. What these are, and, more generally, what constitutes the field of vocational psychology are the topics of this chapter. It is divided into three sections: (1) a brief history of vocational psychology; (2) the subject matter of vocational psychology; and (3) fields related to vocational psychology. The overall plan of the book, based upon the definition of vocational psychology which is derived from the discussion of its history and subject matter, is then presented.

A BRIEF HISTORY OF VOCATIONAL PSYCHOLOGY

An historical knowledge of a field provides insights into its present concerns and interests, its problems and shortcomings, its dimensions and depths. Brayfield (1961, p. 43) observes: "I believe that knowledge of our intellectual antecedents may bring to light important research leads or hypotheses, that it will enhance our discrimination of current important contributions, and finally, that one of the joys of scholarship comes from the feeling of continuity with the past—in short, that a historical feel lends added significance and effectiveness to our daily efforts." He also notes "our lack of historical sophistication." Certainly, histories of psychology have been written, notably those of Boring (1942; 1950) and Murphy (1949), as have histories of vocational guidance (Brewer, 1942; Borow, 1964b; Williamson, 1964), but there is no history which deals specifically with the field of vocational psychology.[1] Our purpose here, then, is to provide such a history, to present an overview of the development of vocational psychology as a field of scientific inquiry. The account is brief. It does not pretend to be comprehensive and thoroughly documented. Rather, it is an outline of (1) some of the notable events which have highlighted the progress of research in vocational psychology; (2) the activities and contributions of current programs of research on vocational behavior and development; and (3) the major trends which have characterized research and theory in vocational psychology.

Notable Events in Vocational Psychology

It is always difficult, if not impossible, to identify, much less agree upon, starting points in history. To date the beginning of psychology from Fechner's work in psychophysics would be to ignore the philosophical *Zeitgeist* of the previous century, from which he inherited the intellectual underpinnings for the experimental rather than mentalistic study of sensory phenomena, were it not that his rigorous investigations "laid the foundation for the new [scientific] psychology and still lie at the basis of its methodology" (Boring, 1950, p. 275). Similarly, to start the history of vocational psychology from 1909, when Parson's classic book *Choosing a Vocation* was published, would be to disregard the contributions of Galton (1883), Cattell, J. M. (1890), and Binet and Henri (1895) to the emerging mental-testing movement and to overlook books by Munsterberg (1899), *Psychology and Life,* and by Richards, L. S. (1881), *Vocophy,* in which he advocated the use of phrenology as an aid in career choice, were it not that it was Parsons who laid the conceptual cornerstones for what became the major research orientation in vocational psychology for more than 30 years. We shall start our chronology of vocational psychology with Parsons, therefore, but with cognizance of Boring's (1950, p. 275) observation that "nothing is new at its birth."

1909 Frank Parsons died the year before his book appeared, but his ideas have lived on to be some of the most in-

[1] For a personal account of the field's history and development by one of its pioneers, see Kitson (1958). Also of historical interest is Hollingworth's (1931) early textbook, *Vocational Psychology and Character Analysis.*

fluential ones ever voiced in the field of vocational psychology. He was a practitioner, a service-oriented counselor of youth, not a hard-headed scientist, and thus it is somewhat ironic that his impact on vocational research has been every bit as great as it has been on vocational counseling and guidance. In brief, he formulated a conceptual model of the individual's relationship to occupations based upon the assumption that adjustment to the world of work is a function of the agreement between the individual's capacities and characteristics, on the one hand, and the demands of the occupation, on the other (see Chapter 3).

1917 With the active involvement of the United States in World War I, there developed the need to select men for service in the Army and to assign them to duties appropriate to their abilities. Under the leadership of Robert M. Yerkes, the first paper-and-pencil tests of intelligence—the Army Alpha (a verbal test) and the Army Beta (a nonverbal test)—were administered on a large-scale basis. In all, 18,423 men took these tests, and from the data thus gathered reported in the *Memoirs of the National Academy of Sciences* (Yerkes, 1921), the first analyses of occupational differences in intelligence were conducted (see Chapter 2).

1927 This was a banner year in the history of vocational psychology, in that three landmark contributions were made. First, pursuing the research on interest measurement initiated in 1915 by James Burt Miner, Bruce V. Moore, and Walter V. Bingham at the Carnegie Institute of Technology, Edward K. Strong, Jr., at Stanford University, published the first edition of the Strong Vocational Interest Blank (SVIB) and launched a long and distinguished career of research on interests, choice, satisfaction, and related vocational phenomena. Second, at the same time Strong was beginning his studies of interests, Elton Mayo and his colleagues at the Harvard School of Business Administration joined with George A. Pennock and C. E. Snow, engineers at the Hawthorne Plant of the Western Electric Company, to conduct the single most influential program of research on the productivity of workers ever known in industry. The findings and reflections of these investigators gave birth to what has come to be known as the "human relations" point of view. (For a detailed discussion, see Chapter 9.) Finally, it was also in this year that Clark L. Hull, later to become renowned as a learning theorist at Yale University, conceived his prophetic idea to build a "forecasting" machine for predicting an individual's probable success in every possible occupation he might enter. Some prototypic machines were actually built, but it has not been until recently, since the advent of high-speed electronic data processing, that serious efforts have been made to implement Hull's idea in practice (cf. Cooley, 1964a; Shartle, 1964).

1931 Established during a period of increasing economic dislocation and growing unemployment, the Minnesota Employment Stabilization Research Institute (MESRI) initiated the first programmatic study of vocational choice and adjustment which was designed to make comprehensive analyses of large numbers of workers over a span of several years. Under the direction of the Committee on Individual Diagnosis and Training, which included such pioneer vocational psychologists as Donald G. Paterson, John G. Darley, Beatrice J. Dvorak, and Marion R. Trabue, this project pursued three objectives: "(1) to test various methods of diagnosing the vocational aptitudes of unemployed workers; (2) to provide a cross-section of the basic re-education problems of the unemployed; and (3) to demonstrate methods of re-education and industrial rehabilitation of workers dislodged by industrial changes" (Paterson & Darley, 1936, p. iii). To accomplish these goals MESRI constructed new tests of vocational capabilities and made comparisons (1) between the early and late unemployed and (2) between the late unemployed and the employed, in order to determine which psychological and social characteristics differentiated these various groups of workers. The results from these initial studies were later replicated on a portion of the original as well as new samples in the years from 1939 to 1942 (Yoder, Paterson, Heneman, Stone, et al., 1948).

1933 In this year, Congress passed the Wagner-Peyser Act, which authorized the organization of the United States Employment Service (USES). Created in order to stabilize the imbalance between labor supply and demand, the USES was to act as a "clearing house" through which persons seeking employment could locate job openings that were suited to their talents and through which employers could recruit the best-qualified applicants for positions in their establishments (Stead & Masincup, 1941). Accordingly, approximately 25,000 employers and more than 100,000 employees were surveyed to: (1) gather occupational information from extensive and comprehensive job analyses; (2) develop measures of proficiency and potentiality; (3) establish job equivalence schedules for the transfer of skills; (4) write job descriptions and compile a *Dictionary of Occupational Titles* (DOT); (5) collect data on the occupational capabilities of youth in cooperation with the American Youth Commission; (6) organize Community Research Centers; and (7) devise a coding system of entry jobs (Part IV of the DOT) (Stead & Shartle, 1940; Shartle, Dvorak, et al., 1943; Shartle, Dvorak, Heinz, et al., 1944). Today, this work is being carried on by the Functional Occupational Classification Project, which has just recently completed a revision of the DOT (see Chapter 2).

1941 With the bombing of Pearl Harbor and the active involvement of the United States in World War II, one era in the history of vocational psychology came to an end, and another began. Confronted with the problems of selecting and classifying men for duty in the armed services on a scale never before known, vocational psychology "grew up" almost overnight. A revised point of view on the relation of man to work emerged which was to have far-reaching implications for the subsequent development of the field. With the use of the relatively new technique of factor analysis in the construction of tests and evaluation of success criteria, it was found that "rather than the 10, or even 20, traits which many psychologists regarded as the maximum number of important independent traits only a few years ago, the number is almost certainly 50 or even 100, or even larger" (Flanagan, 1947, p. 241). This finding, combined with the observation that there is "a high degree of specificity among the requirements for various types of activities" (Flanagan, 1947, p. 244), led to a shift in emphasis from the requirements of the job, which had characterized much of the research conducted in the prewar period, to the characteristics of the individual. What had been called the Matching Men and Jobs approach in the 1930s gave way to what became known as Trait and Factor theory in the 1940s (Guilford, 1948).

1951 At the passing of the midcentury mark, an event took place which changed the face of vocational psychology. It was at this time that Eli Ginzberg, an economist of Freudian persuasions, and a group of co-workers at Columbia University published their catalytic book, *Occupational Choice,* which had two almost immediate effects. First, it presented an explicit *theory* of career decision making which represented a revolutionary departure from the "dustbowl empiricism" of MESRI and the methodological-statistical focus of the military psychology program. And, second, it conceptualized vocational choice as a *developmental* process which spanned the years from late childhood to early adulthood, rather than as a point-in-time event, which, according to earlier formulations, occurred usually at the end of high school. The impact which Ginzberg's work has had on vocational psychology can be documented not only by the number of "theories" which have appeared in the past decade, over 15 at last count, but also by its emphasis upon the developmental nature of vocational choice. To Ginzberg the study of choice was only a part, albeit an important one, of the more general problem of the conservation of human resources, and so, after having made an analysis of choice which was sufficient for his purposes, he has followed his interest in economics elsewhere (e.g., Ginzberg & Berman, 1963). He has left behind, however, a legacy of provocative, but largely untested, hypotheses which should occupy the research endeavors of vocational psychologists for many years to come.

These years—1909, 1917, 1927, 1931, 1933, 1941, and 1951—stand out, then, in the history of vocational psychology as denoting its most significant events in research and theory. They can be broadly grouped into three eras, each of which represents a stage in the development of vocational psychology as a field of scientific inquiry: The first might be called the *observational,* which embraced the period from Parsons and his precursors to World War I, when knowledge of vocational behavioral phenomena was largely qualitative; the second would be the *empirical,* which spanned the years between the two world wars, when variables were quantified and empirical laws were established; and the third might be termed the *theoretical,* which characterizes the present concern of the field with formulating and testing hypotheses. In the not too distant future we may envision still another era, best described as *experimental,* in which our research will be conducted in the laboratory as well as in the field (see Chapter 13).

Programs of Research in Vocational Psychology

Before 1950, there were very few of what might be called "programs" of research in vocational psychology. In addition to MESRI and the programs associated with the two world wars, the only other research of comparable proportions was conducted by the National Institute of Industrial Psychology in England (Hunt, E. G., & Smith, G., 1945; Marcrae, Jennings, & Stott, 1937; Stott, 1936; 1956). Since 1950, however, an increasing number of studies have been the product of long-term research projects. There are at least two reasons for this trend: First, Ginzberg's proposition that vocational choice is a developmental process has stimulated a more extensive use of longitudinal designs in the study of career decision making, and these are not only broader in scope than cross-sectional investigations, but they require greater personnel and financial resources over longer periods of time for their completion. And, second, during the past decade, support for such comprehensive programs of research, from both private and public sources, has increased tremendously. Borow (1960) and Holland (1964b) have described most of these programs of research in vocational psychology in considerable detail; consequently, only general summaries of their major purposes and activities will be given here.

The Career Pattern Study (CPS). Under the direction of Donald E. Super at Teachers College, Columbia University, this 20-year longitudinal survey of the vocational development of adolescents and young adults is the oldest among the current programs of research in vocational psychology, having been formally initiated in 1951, after some preliminary conceptualization in 1949 and 1950. The theoretical framework of CPS has been built primarily upon concepts and principles from general developmental psychology and self theory (see Chapter 3). In brief, the central proposition which CPS is designed to test is that vocational development is a process of acquiring, clarifying, and implementing a self-concept through preparation for and participation in the world of work. A large amount of data, from interviews and archival records as well as standardized tests, have been collected on a relatively few Subjects, who have been assiduously followed up, so that, contrary to most studies of this type, the attrition rate has been very low. Because CPS is a longitudinal project, only preliminary data are available from it. When it is completed, its findings will be reported in a series of monographs, with such titles as "Self-concepts in Vocational Development" and the "Patterning of Careers."

The Harvard Studies of Career Development (HSCD) and the Center for Research in Careers (CRC). Stimulated by Ginzberg's conceptualizations of vocational choice and by Super's work in the Career Pattern Study, David V. Tiedeman launched a series of studies on career development in 1952, as part of the training program in guidance at the Harvard Graduate School of Education, which have dealt with almost every aspect of how and why adolescents choose occupations as they do. To describe the work of HSCD, we can divide it into three phases, according to the emphases which have predominated: In the first, "method called the tune," as Tiedeman and O'Hara (1960) put it, with the generalization of Fisher's two-group discriminant function analysis to the *k* group case and the application of multivariate statistical methods to problems of choice and classification; in the second, the focus shifted from methodology to theory construction as an attempt was made to apply concepts drawn from Erikson's ego psychology and current existential formulations to the process of decision making; and, in the third, which has recently started (summer, 1966), energies are being directed toward the establishment of a computer-based "information system for vocational decisions" which can eventually be used by students at the secondary school level to assist them in their choices.

Overlapping this research of HSCD, and to a certain extent embracing it since 1963, has been the work of the Center for Research in Careers (CRC), under the direction of Anne Roe. One of the main purposes of CRC has been to complement HSCD and to broaden its scope: Roe has further developed and tested her hypotheses about familial influences upon the formation and development of choice and interests; studies of the careers of women, a largely neglected area of research heretofore, have been made; and visiting research associates—vocational psychologists from other institutions—have been given the opportunity to pursue their own research interests. Thus, CRC in conjunction with HSCD has carried on one of the most varied and vigorous programs of research which the field of vocational psychology has known.

Holland's Research at the National Merit Scholarship Corporation and the American College Testing Program. It is probably significant that the research program of John L. Holland does not have a formal name or title, such as CPS or HSCD, for his work reflects an orientation and direction of inquiry which is difficult to label. It is more idiosyncratic than the others because it has largely been the inductive outgrowth of "his experience as a counseling and clinical psychologist and his development of an inventory to assess personality by means of occupational titles" (Holland, 1964b, p. 272), rather than the deductive formulation of concepts and hypotheses which has characterized the research of Super and Tiedeman, in particular. Accordingly, Holland has concentrated his efforts upon the prediction of such variables as vocational choice, occupational membership, and the work history, and "theory building is regarded as a means to this end" (Holland, 1964b, p. 272). This approach is well illustrated by two large-scale longitudinal studies in which he classified college students according to a personality typology he formulated (see Chapter 3) and then compared the various types on a host of aptitude, demographic, educational, social, and vocational variables. In fact, it is characteristic of Holland's research that it involves analyses of data on a large number of variables obtained from a large number of Subjects.

The Minnesota Studies in Vocational Rehabilitation (MSVR). This program of research differs from the others in vocational psychology in two respects: First, it has focused primarily upon the vocational behavior of disabled workers, although it has compared them with normals; and, second, it has dealt exclusively with vocational adjustment rather than vocational choice phenomena. Its inception dates from 1959, although it was preceded by a 2-year study of the placement problems of the disabled. A variety of studies were completed between 1959 and 1963, some titles of which are: "A Study of Referral Information," "A Follow-up Study of Placement Success," "A Survey of the Physically Handicapped in Minnesota," and "Attitudinal Barriers to Employment." Since 1964, however, when the MSVR group published a paper entitled "A Theory of Work Adjustment," the orientation of the project has become less applied and more theoretical. This change in emphasis has involved, first, the measurement of the principal concepts in the theory, which include the capacities, needs, satisfaction, and satisfactoriness of the worker (whether he is disabled or not); and, second, the empirical evaluation of hypotheses deduced from the theory. According to Betz et al. (1966), the direction of MSVR in the future will be much like it has been in the recent past (since 1964): Follow-up studies will be conducted; better controls will be used; old measures will be refined and new ones constructed; and the theory of work adjustment will be further tested, and revised or not, as the findings indicate.

The Vocational Development Project (VDP). In contrast to the other contemporary programs of research in vocational psychology, this one was established initially in order to construct and standardize an objective measure of vocational development, which, unlike the interview-based indices of vocational maturity devised by CPS, could be administered economically to large samples. Accordingly, the writer (Crites, 1961b; 1965) developed what has become known as the Vocational Development Inventory (VDI), which consists of two parts, the Attitude Scale and the Competence Test. With these measures of choice attitudes and competencies, it is the plan of VDP to study, both cross-sectionally and longitudinally, the dispositional response tendencies and cognitive variables which are involved in the vocational decision-making process. To do this, it is necessary not only to conduct field studies, in which the psychometric characteristics of the VDI as a measure of the dependent variables of interest can be ascertained, but also to conduct laboratory experiments, in which independent variables can be manipulated under highly controlled conditions. In contrast to the other programs of research, VDP is more strongly committed to the experimental investigation of vocational behavior and development, the intention being to isolate the stimulus conditions which are functionally related to these phenomena, so that theory construction might become more rigorous and systematic.

These are only a few of the programs of research which have been established in the past 15 years. Others which should be mentioned include the following: the Center for Research on Occupational Planning at the University of Oregon; the Cornell University Studies of Job Satisfaction; the Center for Interest Measurement at the University of Minnesota (Campbell, 1964); Gribbons and Lohnes's (1966a) project on Readiness for Vocational Planning at Regis College; Davis's, J. A. (1964; 1965) survey of vocational aspirations at the National Opinion Research Center of the University of Chicago; and Project Talent at the American Institutes for Research (Flanagan & Dailey, 1960; Flanagan, Dailey, Shaycoff, Gorham, Orr, & Goldberg, 1962). Most of these are described in detail in subsequent chapters on the topics with which they deal.

Trends in the History of Vocational Psychology

If we attempt to gain an overview of the notable events and programs of research which have marked the development of vocational psychology as a field of study, three historical trends can be extrapolated: (1) the Matching Men and Jobs approach, which since World War II has been called Trait and Factor theory; (2) the Psychodynamics of Vocational Behavior point of view; and (3) Vocational Development theory. Each of these is briefly summarized with reference to Figure 1-1, where it can be seen that since 1950 the first two orientations have blended into the third, which is the predominant one in vocational psychology today.

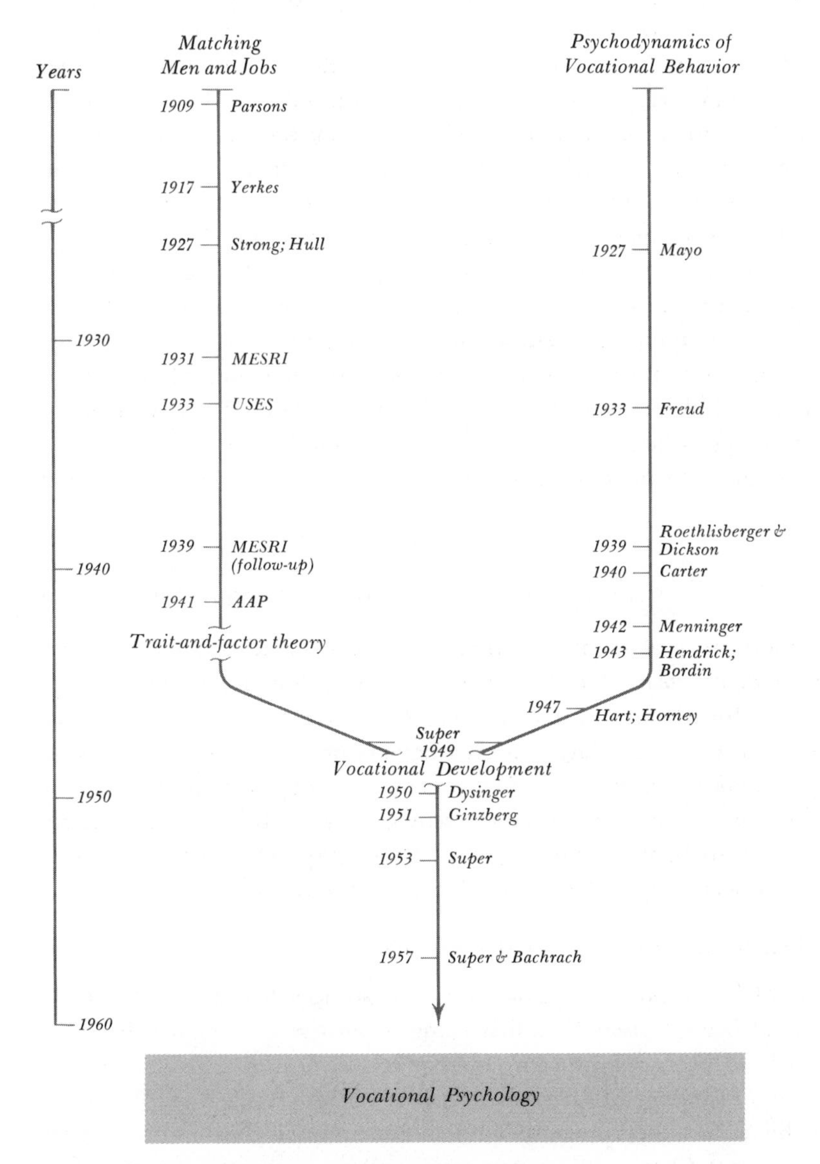

Figure 1-1. Historical trends in vocational psychology.

The Matching Men and Jobs approach began shortly after the turn of the twentieth century, reached its peak of influence and popularity during the Depression and World War II, and went into an incipient decline during the postwar period. It has recently regained some of its former vitality through association with the concepts of developmental psychology, but its essence remains unchanged. It postulates that individuals differ in their psychological traits, that occupations differ in their requirements, and that realistic vocational choice and optimal vocational adjustment are functions of the agreement between traits and requirements. In contrast, the Psychodynamics of Vocational Behavior point of view proposes that drives and desires, rather than attributes and characteristics, are the salient variables in choosing a vocation and adjusting to work. Stemming primarily from the Freudian and neoanalytic writers, the need theorists, and the phenomenologists, this viewpoint uses such concepts as sublimation, ego functions, need hierarchies, and the self to explain why people behave vocationally as they do. The third, and most recent, trend in the history of vocational psychology has been toward a synthesis of the earlier orientations into a comprehensive Vocational Development theory, based upon the assumptions of differential and dynamic psychology. All the major theories in the field today have, as one of their basic propositions, stated in one way or another that the vocational behavior of the individual develops as he grows older. We shall encounter these three orientations in many places throughout this book and shall describe them in greater detail as we do.

THE SUBJECT MATTER OF VOCATIONAL PSYCHOLOGY

Implicit in the history of vocational psychology is a definition of the subject matter with which it deals; but, in order to organize this subject matter in a meaningful way for discussion, its definition must be made more explicit. To do this, some of the existing classification schemata or taxonomies of the literature of vocational psychology are first reviewed, and their limitations are noted. Then, a new schema is proposed, which provides the basic outline for the remainder of the book. A computerized "bibliographic" program for rapid access to the subject matter of vocational psychology is also described.

Classification Schemata for Vocational Psychology

Three kinds of classification schemata for the subject matter of vocational psychology have been devised. The first comes from the ways in which theory and research have been organized in textbooks on vocational psychology. In her book, *The Psychology of Occupations,* Roe (1956) classified studies of occupational differences according to her two-dimensional classification system for occupations (see Chapter 2). For example, all the research she could find on vocational counselors was summarized and discussed along with that on other occupations, such as social work and occupational therapy, which were in the same field. Many studies were not concerned with occupational groups, however, and consequently Roe had to include separate chapters on such topics as studies of occupational choice and progress in the occupation. In his book, *The Psychology of Careers,* Super (1957) encountered the same problem but solved it in a different way. He adopted a developmental framework for one major part of the book, in which he described the various stages in vocational development from "Adolescence as Exploration: Developing a Self-concept" to "The Years of Decline: Adjustment to a New Self," and a factorial approach for the other, in which he reviewed the research on the trait-and-factor, familial, economic, and other correlates of vocational development. Supplementary chapters dealt with the nature of work and implications and applications. Commenting upon such approaches as these to classifying the subject matter of vocational psychology, Borow (1964a, p. 371) has observed that: "Tables of contents of books of readings and of textbooks on occupational behavior represents a step toward classification, but each reflects the special discipline and orientation of the compiler or author and, hence, lacks catholicity." Thus, Roe focused upon occupational differences and Super upon the process of vocational development.

The second type of classification schema for vocational theory and research stems from an effort to develop a bibliographic system for vocational psychology. As part of a larger project on classifying the literature in counseling psychology, Kirk (1958) formulated an outline of "vocational development" designed to encompass the "Literature pertinent to [the] process of adjusting to [the] world of work." Certain categories in the outline, however, do not appear to bear any relationships to each other, nor is the rationale for their selection clear. Furthermore, they are not explicitly defined, and at least one, viz., "work attitudes," occurs twice in the system. Another bibliography, which was prepared specifically for vocational psychology and which, hence, is more comprehensive and detailed than Kirk's, has been described by Giele and Roe (1964) and Goodman (1966). In the more recent version of the system, the main breakdown is called the "Principal Subjects Index" and has such divisions as people and work (work adjustment, attributes of occupations and persons in them, industrial psychology); career-relevant general development and adjustment (physical and mental aspects); and sociology of role and status (family, women's roles, minority groups, social class, etc.). These and related topical headings cover most of the literature relevant to vocational psychology, but the system is less useful than it might otherwise be, because the categories are only partly behavioral ones, a shortcoming which will be discussed at greater length later on.

The third approach to classifying the subject matter of vocational psychology represents a deliberate attempt to formulate a "taxonomy of occupational research." Borow (1964a) has proposed the categories listed in Table 1-1, which he calls "research issues." For many purposes, this taxonomy is an excellent one: it indicates, for example, the range and diversity of topics covered by vocational psychology as well as some of their interrelationships. It does have shortcomings, however, the major one being the same as that of the Principal Subjects Index already mentioned. Borow (1964a, pp. 371–372) comments upon it as follows: "Grouping research activities in any field of study by means of generic labels [as in his taxonomy] . . . presents a special problem. The items to be categorized are not the objects or events in a science, but, instead, classes of overlapping activities which form the map of the research field. Hence, the rules of scientific classification do not wholly apply and cannot be fully satisfied."

A Behavioral Taxonomy for Vocational Psychology

If these classification schemata are taken as a starting point, with an appreciation of their merits and an awareness of their limitations, it may be possible to develop a taxonomy which is more directly relevant to the "objects and events" of vocational psychology as a science. But, first, definitions of what these objects and events are must be formulated:

1. Given the meanings of certain terms, *vocational psychology can be defined as the study of vocational behavior and development.* By "vocational behavior" is meant all the responses the individual makes in choosing and adjusting to an occupation. In other words, his vocational behavior is distinguished from his other behavior, in that the stimulus which evokes it is occupational rather than physical or social (Brown, J. S., 1961; Underwood, 1966). The term *occupational* in this context should be interpreted broadly to refer to all the various aspects of the world of work, e.g., labor-market conditions as well as automation and retirement plans, rather than just a circumscribed set of job duties and tasks. Also, it should be noted that, for purposes of clarity, "occupational" is used to designate only stimulus variables whereas "vocational" is used to denote only response variables. Thus, we shall speak of *occupational* analysis and measurement, for example, but of *vocational* choice and adjustment, the referrent for the former being the occupation and for the latter the behavior of the individual.

2. Another distinction which should be made is that between *choice* and *adjustment.* Although it is not sufficient, the most convenient criterion for differentiating these two kinds of vocational behavior is occupational entry. Vocational choice typically takes place before an individual enters the world of work, whereas vocational adjustment cannot occur until he does. There are some instances, however, in which vocational choices must be made after a

***Table 1-1. Categories in Borow's Taxonomy of Occupational Research** (1964a)*

Concept formulation and theory construction	Worker socialization processes
Observation mode (experimental or naturalistic)	Modification of vocational development
Life stage	Worker satisfaction
Role and situs	Social psychology of work behavior
Expressive and stylistic traits	Social correlates of occupation
Motivational traits	Individual career patterns
Personality configurations	Biography of occupation
Prediction and assessment methodology	Occupational mobility
Prediction technology	Occupational demography
Criterion development	Work adjustment of disadvantaged groups
Improvement of worker proficiency	Work and leisure analysis
	Occupational counseling technology

person is employed full-time. For this reason, entry is not a sufficient criterion for discriminating choice and adjustment behaviors, but it applies in most cases.

3. Finally, vocational behavior is either *developmental* or *nondevelopmental*. Because not all vocational behavior develops as the individual grows older, the basic unit of study in vocational psychology is taken to be vocational behavior, rather than the process of vocational development, as some would contend (e.g., Field, Kehas, & Tiedeman, 1963). The latter is considered to be a construct which is inferred from the systematic changes that can be observed in vocational behavior over time (see Chapter 5). These definitions of vocational behavior and development, choice and adjustment, and the distinction made between "occupational" and "vocational" provide a first approximation to a general taxonomy of the "objects and events" of vocational psychology.

Two problems remain to be solved, however, before this taxonomy can be used. First, where does the vast literature on occupations and occupational differences in traits and factors fit into it? As has been noted, this problem has been handled in different ways (Roe, 1956; Super, 1957), and none of them is wholly satisfactory. In fact, there may be no ideal solution, but one possibility which appears to have some promise follows from the distinction just made between the terms *occupational* and *vocational*. Occupations were defined as stimulus variables, and not as response or behavioral variables. Consequently, they should not be included in the taxonomy of a field which studies behavioral variables. The study of occupations might better be referred to as "occupationology," in order to distinguish it from vocational psychology.

This would not mean, however, that the two areas are not closely related. To the contrary, occupationology, which encompasses such subject matter as occupational analysis, classification, and measurement, occupational demography, and occupational information, can be considered one of the foundations of vocational psychology (see Chapter 2). Similarly, differential psychology, which is the study of individual differences in traits and factors (Anastasi, 1958; Tyler, 1965), is another foundation of vocational psychology, primarily because such variables as aptitudes, interests, and personality have been found to be more highly related to vocational behavior than any others. Finally, the analysis of occupational differences, which derives from a combination of differential psychology and occupationology, is a third foundation of vocational psychology. This field might be described more accurately, however, as the study of the *correlates of occupational membership*. The members of an occupational group are compared either with other occupational groups or with an occupationally unselected reference group, and differences in traits and factors are observed. Defined in this way, it is clear that occupational differences are *not* vocational behavior, i.e., responses to occupational stimuli, and consequently are not part of the subject matter of vocational psychology.

The second problem in making the proposed taxonomy operational is to devise some sort of system for categorizing the literature in vocational psychology, so that the work which has been done on vocational behavior and development, whether it be empirical, methodological, or theoretical, can be organized in a meaningful way for review and discussion. An essential classificatory dimension for such a system, which was not used in the previously described schemata, although it was implicit in Borow's, is whether an article is empirical or nonempirical. By an "empirical" article is meant a report in which *quantitative data* are presented. They need not to have been statistically analyzed nor scaled, but they do need to have been quantified in some manner. Thus, categorical data on the number of high school seniors who have and have not made a vocational choice would be empirical, by this criterion, whereas career-pattern thema extrapolated from work-history data (e.g., Super, 1954) would be nonempirical.

Articles classified as empirical would most certainly include many which not only reported data, but which also dealt with theory and methodology, if for no other reason than to state hypotheses or to define variables. The nonempirical articles, however, would report no data; they would be exclusively "think pieces." As such, they might be statements of theory, conceptualizations of variables, proposals of new methodologies, or reviews of the literature. Case studies would also be classified as nonempirical. The reason for suggesting this categorization of the subject matter in vocational psychology as empirical or nonempirical is to have a basis for drawing conclusions about (1) what reliable knowledge there is on vocational behavior and development and (2) the extent to which it confirms theory.

A Computerized Bibliography for Vocational Psychology

For many practical purposes, it is not sufficient to classify the literature in vocational psychology solely according to the empirical-nonempirical dichotomy. Other breakdowns are needed for the everyday use of the reference system, such as the following: (1) journals versus books; (2) published versus unpublished materials; (3) cross-sectional versus longitudinal studies; (4) American versus foreign studies; and (5) indexes for authors, measures of variables, characteristics of Subjects, occupational groups, etc. From some of the recent work which has been done on information retrieval (Borow, 1962; 1963; Bodin, 1963; Garvey & Griffith, 1963), the writer has developed a computerized bibliography for vocational psychology which lists references for any one, or combination, of these entries. For example, it is possible to print out, in a matter of minutes, all the foreign, cross-sectional studies of the vocational choices of tenth-grade females published in journals, arranged alphabetically by author.

FIELDS RELATED TO VOCATIONAL PSYCHOLOGY

A field of study is defined not only by what it is but also by what it is not. There are several disciplines which are closely related to vocational psychology, and it is important to identify both the areas of communality and the areas of dissimilarity among them. The fields with which vocational psychology overlaps the most are (1) industrial psychology, (2) occupational sociology, and (3) vocational guidance. Each of these is briefly defined, and empirical estimates of their percentages of overlap with vocational psychology are made.

Industrial Psychology

Traditionally, the field of industrial psychology, from its formal inception with the publication of Hugo Munsterberg's *Psychology and Industrial Efficiency* in 1913 to the recent emergence of consumer psychology as a distinct area of activity and study, has had a strong applied character, although, as Haire (1959, p. 49) points out, its roots are in the academic disciplines of differential, experimental, motivational, and social psychology. Haire goes on to identify three traditions within industrial psychology, which, he says, have relatively distinct conceptual bases, in that they are concerned with essentially different problems: *Personnel psychology* has focused upon the problems of selecting, training, and promoting employees and, to a lesser extent, executives; *human engineering* has dealt with the problems of optimally relating men to machines; and *industrial social psychology* has concentrated upon the motivation of the worker and his relationship to the work group and environment. To these might be added the current interests in management psychology (Haire, 1964) and organizational psychology (Bass, 1965), but the definition of industrial psychology has not changed substantially over the years (Viteles, 1932, p. 55; Gilmer, 1966, p. 11). Textbooks in the field typically cover such topics as job analysis and job requirements, personnel testing, performance appraisal, measurement of attitudes and morale, motivation and job satisfaction, equipment and work design, and accidents and safety (Tiffin & McCormick, 1965). Of these, the greatest overlap with vocational psychology is in the following: motivation, satisfaction, and success (performance appraisal). Approximately 40 percent of the literature on these topics can be cross-classified as relevant to both industrial and vocational psychology.[2]

The interest of the two fields in these variables, however, is essentially different. The industrial psychologist approaches their study to solve the problems of the workaday world, usually in order to achieve the most efficient operation possible of a business or industrial enterprise, whereas the vocational psychologist analyzes them to learn about the behavior and development of the individual in adjusting to work. Because of this difference in orientation and purpose, industrial and vocational psychologists may interpret the same data in quite different ways.

Occupational Sociology

Sociologists are not agreed upon what constitutes occupational sociology. Some make distinctions between this field of study and industrial sociology, which is usually conceived of as more inclusive, and some do not; and others call it the sociology of work, which implies a somewhat different focus. Here is a sampling of the various ways in which this field has been defined.[3]

> An industrial sociology signifies the body of knowledge which would record and organize experience in human association in the industrial community [Van Kleeck, 1946, p. 501].

> The field of industrial sociology . . . is concerned with the application or development of principles of sociology relevant to the indus-

[2] Percentage of overlap was computed by determining how many articles classified in the field of vocational psychology, in proportion to the total, might also be classified in related fields. The classifications were based solely upon the writer's knowledge of these fields. Independent classifications of the same references by others in occupational sociology and industrial psychology, as well as vocational psychology, should be made in order to corroborate the percentages.

[3] For additional definitions and discussions of occupational sociology, see Moore, W. E. (1947) and Smigel (1954).

> trial mode of production and the industrial way of life [Moore, 1948, p. 383].[4]
>
> The field of industrial sociology may be conveniently defined as the study of: (1) *work groups and work relations,* (2) *the role the worker plays in work groups,* and (3) *the social organization of work plant society*... [Miller & Form, 1951, p. 16; italics in original].
>
> The sociology of work will be treated primarily as *the study of those social roles which arise from the classification of men by the work they do* [Caplow, 1954, p. 4; italics in original].

Topics found in industrial or occupational sociology textbooks include the following: occupational mobility, measurement of occupational status, social adjustment of the worker, occupation and family, and social organization of the work plant.

The variables in which both occupational sociology and vocational psychology are interested, and for which there is approximately 30 percent overlap in subject matter, are career patterns, prestige and status of occupations, vocational aspiration and choice, and occupational roles. The basic units of analysis in studying these phenomena, however, are essentially different in the two fields: In occupational sociology, the unit of analysis is the occupation as a social institution, whereas in vocational psychology, it is the vocational behavior of the individual as a prospective or actual worker.

Vocational Guidance

The official definition of vocational guidance formulated by the National Vocational Guidance Association in 1937 was that it is "the process of assisting the individual to choose an occupation, prepare for it, enter upon and progress in it." To place a greater emphasis upon the psychological nature of vocational choice, Super (1951b, p. 92) has suggested that this definition be revised to indicate that vocational guidance is "the process of helping a person to develop and accept an integrated and adequate picture of himself and of his role in the world of work, to test this concept against reality, and to convert it into a reality, with satisfaction to himself and benefit to society." Whichever way it is defined, it is clear that vocational guidance is a facilitative process, a service rendered to the individual to aid him in choosing and adjusting to an occupation. It is *not* the science of studying how and why he behaves vocationally as he does, although this knowledge may be used in guiding and counseling him. In other words, vocational guidance is *applied* vocational psychology.

[4] See the discussion of this definition by several leading industrial sociologists in the same article for different points of view.

This distinction has not usually been made, since historically the field of vocational psychology grew out of the practice of vocational guidance. It seems desirable to differentiate between them, however, if vocational psychology is to become firmly established as the science of vocational behavior and development—unconfounded with the purposes and procedures of vocational guidance, which is still largely an *art*. There is one important area of overlap (approximately 10 percent) which should be mentioned. To the extent that vocational guidance, as a stimulus variable or treatment condition, is functionally related to vocational behavior, then it falls within the purview of vocational psychology as a field of study. But, since the literature on vocational guidance, which is almost as extensive as that in vocational psychology, is beyond the scope of this book, no attempt will be made to review it in this context.

Summary

Figure 1-2 summarizes the relationships of vocational psychology to (1) industrial psychology, (2) occupational sociology, and (3) vocational guidance. The

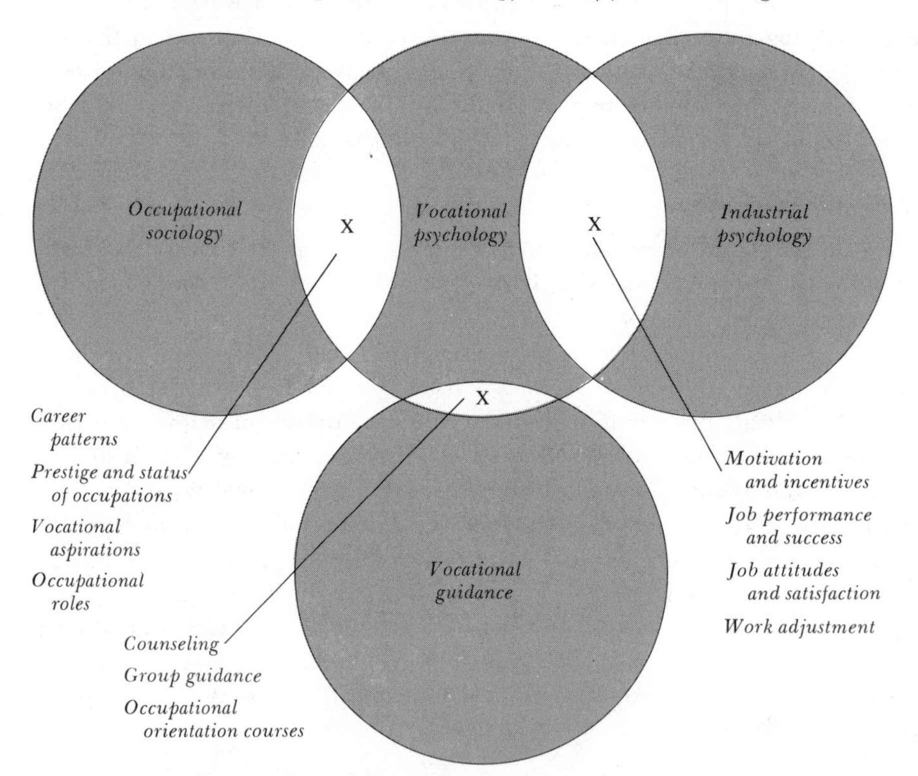

Figure 1-2. Relationships of industrial psychology, occupational sociology, and vocational guidance to vocational psychology.

congruence of the circles represents the estimated percentages of overlap among the four fields, and the lists of variables within the overlapping areas indicates the subject matter which they have in common. What the figure does not reveal, however, are the different emphases of the fields, which, in brief, are as follows: *vocational psychology*—the study of the individual's vocational behavior and development through the years of choice and adjustment; *industrial psychology*—the application of psychological knowledge to the solution of personnel, human engineering, and social problems in the world of work; *occupational sociology*—the analysis of occupations and work as social institutions; and *vocational guidance*—the process or program of assistance designed to aid the individual in choosing and adjusting to a vocation.

PLAN OF THE BOOK

The organization of the book follows the discussion of the history and subject matter of vocational psychology which was presented in this chapter. The major portions of the book, Part II ("The Process of Vocational Choice") and Part III ("The Dynamics of Vocational Adjustment"), have been constituted by using occupational entry as the criterion for differentiating the two broadest classes of vocational behavior—choice and adjustment. The distinction between vocational behaviors which are developmental and those which are nondevelopmental has been maintained by separate chapters in each of these parts, namely, "The Development of Vocational Choice" (Chapter 5) and "Developmental Aspects of Vocational Adjustment" (Chapter 12). The other two main sections of the book are the introductory and concluding ones: Part I includes this chapter, "The Field of Vocational Psychology," and the next chapter, "The Foundations of Vocational Psychology," in which relevant knowledge for the study of vocational behavior from differential psychology, occupationology, and occupational differences is summarized. Part IV is designed to provide an overview of vocational psychology based upon the review and discussion of research and theory presented in the other parts of the book. Chapter 13, "Research in Vocational Psychology," deals with the questions of what we know and what we do not know about vocational behavior and development, and Chapter 14, "Theory Construction in Vocational Psychology," evaluates the present status of conceptualization and explanation in the field and suggests some possible new directions for the future.

Because of the voluminous literature of vocational psychology, not to mention the closely related fields of industrial psychology and occupational sociology, it would have been virtually impossible to review, much less reference, all the materials which have accumulated on vocational behavior and development. Nor would it have been desirable. Some articles are old, others are methodologically unsound, and still others are inadequate for one reason or another. Consequently, certain discriminations were made in selecting the literature to be included in the book.

Studies from the early years of vocational psychology have largely been omitted, not only because many of them are dated today, but also because most of them were relatively unsophisticated methodologically, and it is often difficult to draw any justifiable conclusions from them. The exceptions are those studies which can be considered "classics" because they opened up an area of research or contributed reliable knowledge on a problem. These have been summarized in detail. So have recent studies, if they have been particularly outstanding. Where several investigations have dealt with the same (or a closely related) phenomenon, either they have been reviewed as a group or the better ones among them have been singled out for a more intensive analysis. Where research is scarce on a problem, all the pertinent studies have usually been discussed, with critiques of those which are faulty in design and/or conclusions. When space did not permit the discussion of an article, but it seemed likely it might be of interest to someone working in the area, it was listed in the bibliography, which is as complete as possible through December 31, 1966. Finally, the literature on special groups of workers, viz., women, Negroes and other minorities, the handicapped, the disadvantaged, and the aged, has not been included for two reasons: First, it is a disparate body of knowledge, which does not meaningfully lend itself to any one organizational scheme and hence is better treated separately; and, second, it is marked by many lacunae in both research and theory, which indicate that it is not ready for review at this time.[5]

[5] Some studies of Negroes and older workers are reported in Chaps. 6 and 12, in order to examine race and age as correlates of vocational behavior, but they are not treated as special groups of workers per se.

2
THE FOUNDATIONS OF VOCATIONAL PSYCHOLOGY

In Chapter 1, three foundations of vocational psychology were identified: differential psychology, occupationology, and occupational differences. These three substantive areas, when related to each other in Parson's model of vocational decision making, have largely constituted what has been called the Matching Men and Jobs approach, which dominated the field of vocational psychology until approximately 1950. The purpose of this chapter is to review and evaluate the present status of the subject matter of this approach and to draw conclusions about its role in contemporary research and theory on vocational behavior and development. The chapter is divided into three parts, corresponding to the foundations of vocational psychology previously mentioned: (1) individual differences in traits and factors (differential psychology); (2) occupational analysis, classification, and measurement (occupationology); and (3) occupational differences in traits and factors (correlates of occupational membership).

INDIVIDUAL DIFFERENCES IN TRAITS AND FACTORS

The field which studies individual differences in traits and factors is differential psychology. It addresses itself to such questions as: "What is the nature and extent of such differences? What can be discovered about their causes? How are the differences affected by training, growth, physical conditions? In what manner are the differences in various traits related to one another, or organized?" (Anastasi, 1958, pp. 1–2). Individual differences in behavior, both human and infrahuman, are a matter of everyday observation, and they were recognized many centuries ago when Plato wrote in the *Republic* that "no two persons are born exactly alike," but they were not scientifically investigated until the latter half of the nineteenth century. Francis Galton, usually considered to be the "father" of differential psychology, was influenced by

Darwin's work on evolution and became interested in the inheritance of specific capacities for different kinds of work and the appraisal of intelligence, on which he published two books, *Hereditary Genius* and *Inquiries into Human Faculty and Its Development,* in 1870 and 1883, respectively. He also pioneered the development of correlational analysis, which was later refined mathematically by one of his students, Karl Pearson, as a method for expressing the degree of relationship between two variables. It was not until the advent of the mental-testing movement in the early 1900s, however, that differential psychology was given the impetus which has made it a viable field of scientific inquiry.

Today, differential psychology encompasses a wide range of subject matter on individual and group differences in aptitudes, interests, personality, constitution, heredity, physique, sex, age, race, and culture (Anastasi, 1958; Guilford, 1959; Tyler, 1965). Of these traits and factors, however, aptitudes, interests, and personality have been more extensively studied in relation to vocational behavior and development than any of the others. Accordingly, the discussion which follows deals only with these variables. Its purpose is to provide a general overview of the work which has been done on the definition, dimensions, and development of these behaviors. It does not present detailed documentation of conclusions, nor a discussion of measuring instruments, both of which can be found elsewhere (Anastasi, 1958; Super & Crites, 1962; Tyler, 1965). It closes with an evaluation of differential psychology as a foundation of vocational psychology.

Aptitudes

The *definition* of aptitude has been beset by so many conceptual and semantic ambiguities and confusions that there is considerably less than general agreement on its meaning. Some consensus has been reached, however, on certain differentia of the concept which are specified by the operations used to measure it as compared with those for closely related behaviors. Super and Crites (1962, p. 73) have proposed that *ability* be used as a generic term which embraces both aptitude and proficiency or skill. The latter denotes "the degree of mastery already acquired in an activity," as typically measured by achievement and job-knowledge tests, whereas the former refers to specific, factorially unitary behaviors which facilitate the learning of a task and which are relatively constant over time. In other words: "If a test's function is to record present or past accomplishment, what is measured may be called achievement [or proficiency or skill]. If we wish to make inferences concerning future learning, what is measured is thought of as aptitude" (Test Service Bulletin, 1956, p. 2).

A further distinction has also frequently been made between "general" and "special" aptitudes: "One kind of aptitude test, usually some combination of verbal and numerical and/or abstract reasoning measures, is sometimes called an intelligence test; more properly, in educational settings, it is called a scholastic aptitude test" (Test Service Bulletin, 1956, p. 2). In short, general aptitude, or intelligence, can be defined as a composite of special aptitudes. What the structure of this composite is, however, has been the problem of innumerable factor analyses of intelligence during the past half century.

The *dimensions* of aptitude which have been identified through factor analysis have varied from one or two to as many as 120, depending largely upon the statistical methodology which has been used and, to a lesser extent, upon the variables which have been measured. Spearman's (1904) pioneer work on both the measurement of intelligence and the development of factorial procedures led him to conclude that all intellectual behaviors have in common a single general factor *g*; but, in addition, each behavior is also loaded on relatively specific factors *s*. In his later research, he recognized that there might be still other factors, such as *p* ("perseveration"), *o* (oscillation), and *w* (will), of intermediate generality, i.e., group factors more general than *s* but less so than *g*, which were essentially nonintellective in nature (cf. Wechsler, 1950). Thurstone (1938) challenged this conceptualization of intelligence with his studies of the "primary" mental abilities, which, he contended, were relatively independent group factors, viz., *V* (verbal comprehension), *N* (number), *S* (space), *P* (perceptual speed), *W* (word fluency), *M* (rote memory), and *I* (induction). In other words, he argued, as had some others before him (e.g., Kelley, 1928), that Spearman's *g* is of negligible significance as a dimension of intelligence or general aptitude. Guilford's (1959) current program of research on what he calls the "structure of intellect" reflects Thurstone's orientation, in that he hypothesizes only group factors in the composition of ability.

Juxtaposed to this viewpoint, however, is the so-called "hierarchical" model of intelligence which has been proposed by Vernon (1950) and other British psychologists. It is depicted graphically in Figure 2-1, where it can be seen that

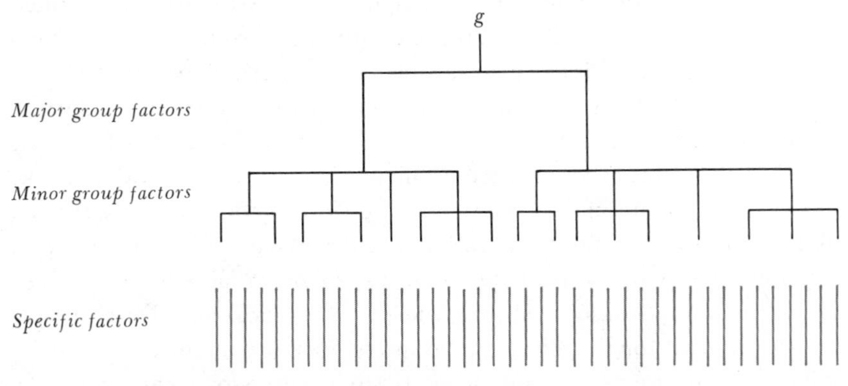

Figure 2-1. A hierarchical model of intelligence. *(After Vernon, 1950, p. 22.)*

intelligence is regarded as consisting of different levels of factors, each being more general than the ones below it. With the possible exception of the Guilford-Zimmerman Aptitude Survey (GZAS), most of the multifactor aptitude batteries which have been constructed in the last 20 to 25 years, e.g., the General Aptitude Test Battery (GATB), Differential Aptitude Tests (DAT), Flanagan Aptitude Classification Tests (FACT), etc., fit this model rather closely: their subtests contribute both unique and common variance to the measurement of aptitudes, the average intercorrelations being in the .40s and .50s (American Personnel and Guidance Association, 1958).

Many issues raised by these opposing points of view are still unresolved, primarily because of the great variety of methods which can be used in factor analyses, but, as the following discussion of the development of aptitudes suggests, the hierarchical model may emerge as the most useful one for conceptualizing the dimensions of aptitude.

The *development* of aptitudes has been assumed theoretically, if not unequivocally established empirically, since Binet and Simon (1915) adopted the "age scale" model for the measurement of intelligence. Tyler (1965, p. 62) comments that:

> One obvious fact that gave psychologists a means of attacking the intelligence-testing problem is that in an absolute sense children become more intelligent as they grow older. . . . What Binet and his successors tried to work out was a pool of items, questions, and tasks that sampled mental abilities typical of the various age levels.

The curve which intelligence follows as the individual develops, however, has still not been conclusively determined. At first, it was thought that the asymptote in mental maturation was reached in midadolescence, but, in recent years, largely as a result of the findings of Bayley (1955), it has been extended to at least the mid-twenties and possibly even later in life.

Garrett (1946) has proposed that, concurrent with these changes in degree of intelligence, there are changes in its composition or structure. His "differentiation" hypothesis on the development of intelligence states that "intelligence changes in its organization as age increases from a fairly unified and general ability to a loosely organized group of abilities or factors" (Garrett, 1946, p. 373). In other words, he would maintain that the hierarchy of abilities shown in Figure 2-1 would become more differentiated as the individual grows older: In childhood, intelligence is largely a general factor, but in adulthood it consists of group and specific factors as well. Garrett cites evidence from several studies in support of his hypothesis, but there are also findings which are nonconfirmatory (Anastasi, 1958). One of the critical problems in such research is to control for the effects of variations in test content and difficulty when different age groups are compared. Despite methodological weaknesses in some of the research which has been reported, however, Burt (1954, p. 85) is of the opinion that there is enough reliable data to conclude that "between late infancy and early adolescence, there is a definite increase in specialization in ability."

Interests

There is no one generally accepted conceptual *definition* of interests, but several, each of which emphasizes a slightly different aspect of this trait.[1] In the first comprehensive review of interests, of which there have been several over the years (e.g., Berdie, 1944a; 1960; Carter, 1944; Darley & Hagenah, 1955; Super, 1949), Fryer (1931, p. 348) distinguished between "subjective" interests, or *feelings* of pleasantness and unpleasantness, and "objective" interests, or observable *reactions* to these experiences, but defined both as "acceptances or rejections of stimulation." Strong has reflected a similar interpretation in these two definitions of interests:

> Interest is present when we are aware of an object or, better still, when we are aware of our set or disposition toward the object. We like the object when we are prepared to react toward it; we dislike the object when we wish to let it alone or get away from it [1943, p. 7].
>
> What are interests? . . . They remind me of tropisms. We go toward liked activities, go away from disliked activities [1960, p. 12].

Because interests have been viewed in this way, viz., as dispositional response tendencies, it is not surprising that they have been generally classed as motivational variables, since at least one of the attributes of the latter is their "directional" nature (Melton, 1941). Strong (1955, p. 142) reasons that:

> Interest scores measure a complex of liked and disliked activities selected so as to differentiate members of an occupation from nonmembers. Such a complex is equivalent to a "condition which supplies stimulation for a particular type of behavior," i.e., toward or away from participation in the activities characteristic of a given occupation. Interest scores are consequently measures of drives.

Similarly, Darley and Hagenah (1955, p. 191) propose that "interests reflect, in the vocabulary of the world of work, the value systems, the needs, and the motivations of individuals." Super and Crites (1962, p. 410) have taken a broader view, concluding from the accumulated research on interests that they are "the product of interaction between inherited neural and endocrine factors, on the one hand, and opportunity and social evaluation on the other."

[1] For a brief historical survey of the development of concepts of interest, as well as an appraisal of recent influences, see Gaddis (1959).

The *dimensions* of interests have been investigated in a number of studies, and there is fairly close agreement in their results, at least on what appear to be the major interest factors. In one of the first factor analyses which was done with the Strong Vocational Interest Blank (SVIB), Thurstone (1931) extracted four factors: Science, People, Language, and Business. Strong (1943) subsequently obtained essentially these same factors, with the addition of a bipolar one, which he called Things versus People, and a further division of Business into System and Contact. Cottle (1950) analyzed the Kuder Preference Record, Bell Adjustment Inventory, and Minnesota Multiphasic Personality Inventory, as well as the SVIB, and, although the relationships between the interest and personality inventories were negligible (as will be discussed later), the factors which emerged from the intercorrelations of the Kuder and SVIB were similar to those obtained by Thurstone and Strong.

Other studies of the Kuder and of values (Lurie, 1937; Brogden, 1952), as measured by the Allport-Vernon Study of Values or similar instruments, have yielded findings generally consistent with those reported for the SVIB, the major differences being in the identification of aesthetic factors, i.e., interest in artistic and musical activities, which are not well represented in the latter. The most wide-ranging study of the dimensions of interests, which has as yet been completed, was conducted by Guilford, Christensen, Bond, and Sutton (1954), who administered 100 ten-item scales to a sample of approximately 1,300 Air Force enlisted men and officers. Of the large number of factors which were found (24 for airmen, 23 for officers), eight were clearly representative of vocationally relevant interests: Scientific, Social-welfare, Mechanical, Outdoor, Clerical, Business, Aesthetic-expression, and Aesthetic-appreciation. Super and Crites (1962, pp. 383–384) have synthesized the results of these various factor analyses into the following dimensions of interests: scientific, social-welfare, literary, material, systematic, contact, and aesthetic.

The *development* of interests was, at one time, thought to be largely capricious and unorderly (Lehman & Witty, 1929), but, as Super and Crites (1962) have pointed out, this conclusion was based upon the stability of *expressed* interests, which, it is true, fluctuate considerably from one occasion to another. The accumulated findings on *inventoried* interests, however, as assessed by such instruments as the SVIB and Kuder, indicate that there are only slight changes in interests with increasing age and that most of these occur during adolescence. Strong (1943) has reported that two-thirds of what change does take place in interests is between ages 15 and 18, the other third being between ages 18 and 25, so that by early adulthood they have developed about as much as they ever will. The possible exception is social-welfare interests, which may continue to crystallize until about age 25, but even these are usually emergent as secondary patterns somewhat earlier. Similarly, studies of the Kuder have established that, although there may be some change in the ranks of interests in high and low patterns during the adolescent years, the patterns remain relatively stable (Mallinson & Crumrine, 1952).

Nevertheless, Tyler (1955; 1959a; 1964) has argued that significant developments in interests do occur, not only in childhood and early adolescence, but also in adulthood. She found that there is a definite tendency for interests to be based more and more upon both "likes" and "dislikes," rather than just likes, as the individual grows older. Such a trend would appear to contradict the evidence on the stability of interests, particularly in adulthood, were it not that different patterns of likes and dislikes can produce the same kind of overall interests. Thus, Strong (1943) has reported that as many as 40 percent of the responses to a SVIB scale can change on test and retest without appreciably lowering its stability coefficient, because one change cancels out another, and the scoring weights sum to essentially the same total. Furthermore, Tyler (1959a) has noted that a person may acquire new likes and/or dislikes without affecting his more general interests, if they are not weighted for a particular scale. In short, because of the peculiarities of interest inventories, especially the SVIB, it is possible for likes and dislikes to change but for interests to stay the same.

Personality

The *definition* of personality within the trait-and-factor frame of reference is quite different from the definitions found in most other theories of personality (Hall & Lindsey, 1957). Probably the most articulate and comprehensive trait-and-factor conception of personality, although it is certainly not the only one (e.g., Allport, 1937; 1966; Cattell, R. B., 1946; Eysenck, 1947; 1953), has been formulated by Guilford (1959, p. 5), who starts with the basic proposition that: *"An individual's personality ... is his unique pattern of traits"* (italics in original). He then defines a "trait" as *"any distinguishable, relatively enduring way in which one individual differs from others"* (italics in original). Traits, in turn, are organized into more inclusive classes called *modalities.* Included among the latter are aptitudes, attitudes, interests, morphological and physiological characteristics, needs, and temperament attributes. In other words, for Guilford "personality" is a global concept which embraces all these various traits, but he is careful to point out that it is not simply their sum total.

He considers the organization or patterning of the traits to be the central consideration in defining personality. And this patterning is revealed by means of factor analysis. Through the use of this method, according to Guilford, it is possible to obtain a parsimonious, yet comprehensive, description of personality. He rejects the idiographic approach of Allport, which attempts to define each individual's personality in terms of a unique combination of "trait-names," as well as the typologies, at the other extreme, which obscure discernible individual differences in common traits. Based upon the assumption that "Factor theory and methods seem ideally suited for the purpose of discovering psychologically meaningful and useful dimensions in the personality sphere," Guilford's (1959, p. 94) approach to the definition and measurement of personality well represents the trait-and-factor point of view in both differential and vocational psychology. It should be noted, however, that there are differences of opinion concerning how inclusive the concept of personality should be. Most trait-and-factor theorists would define personality more narrowly than Guilford to include needs and temperament, and possibly attitudes, but not aptitudes, interests, and organismic modalities.

The *dimensions* of personality, much as in the case of aptitudes, have been conceptualized with different theoretical models. One of these is the "factorial" model, which has been explicated primarily by Guilford (1959). He begins with the assumption that traits are properties of persons, not of behavior. That is, traits are inferred from behavior: a person is considered to be gregarious (trait), for example, if he talks a great deal in conversations with others (behavior). He calls these behaviors *trait indicators,* which, in turn, are typically quantified by tests, although they may also be measured by rating scales and other methods of systematic observation. In deriving the factorial model of the dimensions of personality, the next step is to intercorrelate the tests and then factor-analyze the resulting matrix. The expectation is that, by following this procedure, it will be possible to identify common factors, each made up of several tests or trait indicators, which "represent" primary personality traits or dimensions.

Guilford (1959, p. 99) points out that the factorial model may need to be supplemented by the other major model which has been used in trait-and-factor theories of personality, the "hierarchical" model, because "This one applies better to the single personality whereas the factor model applies better to populations of persons and populations of measuring instruments." The hierarchical model for personality is much like that for aptitudes shown in Figure 2-1. Its base is what Guilford calls the "specific-action" level, with higher-order levels being more generalized personality traits. The main difference between the factorial and hierarchical models, then, is that the latter provides for broader, more inclusive clusters or classes of traits, and, to this extent, it is not only more intuitively satisfying, but it may also have greater subsumptive and predictive value in studying the dimensions of personality.

The *development* of personality has been of little interest to most trait-and-factor theorists. Their concern has been almost exclusively with its *description,* Guilford's (1959, p. 30) viewpoint being, for example, that problems of how personality develops cannot be adequately investigated until it has been thoroughly described. There have been some longitudinal studies of personality development, however, which are important to discuss, if not to indicate what is known about the changes which occur in traits and factors with age, then to reveal what is not known. Bloom (1964) has synthesized and classified most of this literature according to the following categories: (1) the observed correlations between personality measures on test and retest; (2) the theoretically expected correlations on the basis of an age curve of development, when it is assumed the tests are perfectly reliable; and (3) the estimated correlations, corrected for the unreliability of the tests. In 10 different studies 38 correlation coefficients were found, and of these *r*'s, 25 were significantly different, at either the .05 or .01 levels, from the theoretically expected values. The former ranged from .32 to .82, whereas the latter ranged from .75 to .97. From these findings Bloom (1964, p. 176) concludes that:

> In most cases, the correlations reported are significantly below the estimated values based on an age curve of development.... In seeking an explanation for the relatively low level of stability for the self-report personality instruments, we are struck by the susceptibility of these instruments to conscious as well as unconscious distortion by the examinee. We are led to the conclusion that it is unlikely that the stability of personality can be determined with any degree of precision by these instruments.

That distortion or dissimulation contributes to instability in personality inventory scores may well be true, but this does not necessarily mean that these measures are of no value in studying the development of personality. If nothing else, they indicate that test-taking response sets, to the extent that they are "personality" variables, change over time. But, more importantly, they pose again the problem of how to determine the stability of instruments which measure variables in which there are individual differences in rates of development. Until the variance attributable to this phenomenon can be independently defined from that contributed by errors of measurement, it seems more justifiable to conclude that the present evidence on the development of personality is inconclusive than that personality inventories are too inaccurate to assess change.

Interrelationships of Aptitudes, Interests, and Personality

A considerable amount of research has been devoted to the interrelationships of (1) aptitudes and interests, (2) interests and personality, and, to a lesser extent, (3) aptitudes and personality. There is little or no research, however, in which all three variables have been studied simultaneously. No attempt will be made here to review this literature in detail, since this has been done elsewhere (e.g., Roe, 1956; Super & Crites, 1962), but rather only to indicate what general conclusions can be drawn:

1. *Aptitudes and interests.* It can be said that the relationships between general and special aptitudes, on the one hand, and interests, on the other, are usually quite low, being mostly in the ± .20s, with only an occasional coefficient as high as .40. When the rank orderings of cognate special aptitudes and interests have been studied *intra*individually, the *rho*'s are somewhat higher, averaging .46, but the range of individual differences in aptitude-interest congruency is considerable, extending from −.57 to 1.00 (Wesley, Corey, & Stewart, 1950).

2. *Interests and personality.* Although much has been made of the hypothesis that interests and personality are closely related (e.g., Darley & Hagenah, 1955; Roe, 1956), the relationship between these variables is about of the same magnitude as that between aptitudes and interests. From a review of most of the studies which have been conducted on the interest-personality relationship, Super and Crites (1962, p. 409) have concluded that: "Personality adjustment in the sense of feelings of adequacy and security has not been shown to be related to interest patterns, but social adjustment does appear to be." The latter refers to studies such as Darley and Hagenah's (1955), in which they found that the Social Adjustment score of the Minnesota Personality Scale significantly differentiated individuals with business-contact and social-service interests from those with other types of interests, the former being the better adjusted socially. That a "social" factor is related to differential interest patterning is generally consistent with Roe's (1957; Roe & Siegelman, 1964) hypothesis that a major orientation in life activities toward "nonpersons" determines the kinds of interests which an individual develops.

3. *Aptitudes and personality.* Much the same must be concluded about the relationship of aptitudes to personality as for the other variables, despite the widespread contention, particularly among clinical psychologists, that they are systematically associated (Wechsler, 1950). Not only are the findings over many years largely negative for individual measures of intelligence (Rabin, 1945; Rabin & Guertin, 1951; Guertin, Frank, & Rabin, 1956; Guertin, Rabin, Frank, & Ladd, 1962), but also for group tests (e.g., Brower, 1947; Winfield, 1953; Panton, 1960). Thus, it would appear that, although there are some scattered low-to-moderate interrelationships among them, for both theoretical and practical purposes, aptitudes, interests, and personality can be considered relatively independent behaviors.

Differential Psychology as a Foundation of Vocational Psychology

There is no denying the very real contribution differential psychology has made to the description of variables which are highly salient for the study of vocational behavior and development. As was apparent in the preceding discussion, differential psychology has accumulated a large fund of data on the definition, dimensions, and, to a lesser extent, development of aptitudes, interests, and personality. But, as Anastasi (1948) has pointed out, this "factuo-descriptive" approach of differential psychology has neglected the principles of behavior. She observes that "The trait investigator has usually asked: '*What* is the organization of behavior?' or '*What* are the traits into which the individual's behavior repertory groups itself?' rather than asking, '*How* does behavior become organized?' and '*How* do psychological traits develop?' " (Anastasi, 1948, p. 128; italics in original). Similarly, Tyler (1959b) has expressed some disenchantment with differential psychology because of its almost exclusive emphasis upon dimensions or trait continua. She comments that: "Little by little, evidence has been accumulating that some of the crucial defining features of psychological individuality are to be found in two aspects of experience and behavior that are not easily expressed as dimensions and that can best be thought of as *dis*continuous" (Tyler, 1959b, p. 77). She is referring here to what she calls *choice* and *organization,* the former being the courses of action the individual selects and the latter the patterns of behavior in which he engages.

Neither of these shortcomings means that differential psychology no longer has any usefulness as a foundation for vocational psychology. It does—but in a way different from that of the past. As the subsequent chapters on vocational choice and adjustment will bring out, the hierarchical model of traits "fits" the data on vocational behavior better than any other, and it may also provide a conceptual framework for the differentiation which occurs in vocational behavior as the individual develops. In other words, much as with the development of aptitudes, this model projected over time may best describe the course which vocational development takes. Also, differential psychology provides data on what might be thought of as the "limiting" variables which circumscribe the possibilities open to the individual as he makes vocational choices and adjustments (Tyler, 1959b). These include not only aptitudes, interests, and personality, but also sex, race, disabilities, etc. Finally, it is conceivable that differential psychology may be synthesized with both developmental and experimental psychology to provide a more comprehensive foundation for vocational psychology than ever before (see Chapters 3 and 13).

OCCUPATIONAL ANALYSIS, CLASSIFICATION, AND MEASUREMENT

This topic is part of the broader area of "occupationology," which, as was mentioned in the previous chapter, also encompasses occupational demography, which is largely the survey and analysis of past, present, and future labor-market conditions, and occupational information, which is the publication and dissemination of facts on the nature and prospects of employment in different occupations. In contrast, occupational analysis, classification, and measurement pertain to the procedures which are used to determine the content of occupations, however this may be defined, and the schemata and scales which have been developed to group similar occupations together or to rank them along some continuum. In other words, through occupational analysis, classification, and measurement, occupations are quantified so that (1) they may be compared with each other and thereby establish their similarities and differences and so that (2) they may be related to other variables of interest.

Occupational Analysis

To indicate what is meant by "occupational analysis" it is necessary first to distinguish among three terms, which are sometimes erroneously used interchangeably: position, job, and occupation. Shartle (1959, p. 23) defines these terms as follows:

> *Position:* a group of tasks performed by one person. There are always as many positions as there are workers in a plant or office.
>
> *Job:* a group of similar positions in a single plant, business establishment, educational institution, or other organization. There may be one or many persons employed in the same job.
>
> *Occupation:* a group of similar jobs found in several establishments.

As is apparent from their definitions, there is an underlying continuum of increasing generality from position, through job, to occupation. The personnel psychologist is primarily concerned with positions and jobs, because of his role in appraising and selecting workers for a particular employer, whereas the vocational psychologist is basically interested in occupations, as a broad class of stimulus variables which elicit vocational behavior irrespective of specific situations. Thus, the former speaks of "position analysis" and "job analysis," and the latter refers to "occupational analysis."

Another distinction which should also be made is between "occupational analysis" and "time-and-motion study." In the latter, "occupational movements are broken down in order to determine the fewest and simplest movements necessary to do the job and the time required for each movement" (Gilmer, 1966, p. 297). More specifically, "In motion study, elemental motions of the job are identified, with the view toward developing improved methods of performing the job. In time study, the time spent in performing each element is determined, with the view toward the development of standard times for total operation" (Tiffin & McCormick, 1965, p. 65). In contrast, occupational analysis has been defined as "a systematic method of obtaining information that is focused primarily on the ... work environment in which persons are found, rather than on a study of persons themselves" (Shartle, 1964, pp. 285–286).

Actually, it would be more accurate to say that occupational analyses can be made with three major methods, each of which focuses upon a slightly different aspect of work.[2] The first is what might be called the traditional or *standard approach* to occupational analysis. It is best illustrated by the work of the USES in compiling data for the definitions of occupations which are listed in Volume I of the *Dictionary of Occupational Titles* (DOT) (all editions; see discussion that follows). The initial phase in the process is for field job analysts to observe workers directly while they are performing the duties and tasks of a position or job (as the case may be). They record their observations on job-analysis forms and descriptions of the "work performed" in positions and jobs throughout the country are then collated and edited, in order to extrapolate the duties and tasks which they have in common. From these, which are, in effect, *occupational* analyses, the definitions for the DOT are written.

The DOT definition for OCCUPATIONAL ANALYST, for example, is as follows:

> Collects, analyzes, and develops occupational data concerning jobs, job qualifications, and worker characteristics to facilitate personnel, administrative, or information functions in private, public, or governmental organizations.... Studies jobs being performed and interviews workers and supervisory personnel to ascertain physical and mental requirements of jobs in relation to materials, products, procedures, subject matter, and services involved. Writes job descriptions, specifications, detailed analysis schedules, and narrative and statistical reports.... Conducts related occupational research, utilizing publications, professional and trade associations, and other media to verify or standardize data.... May write descriptions or monographs of jobs, processes, and industrial patterns or trends for publication [DOT, 1965, Vol. I, p. 394].

It should be understood that, since this definition is based upon a composite of nationwide position and job analyses, it is unlikely that any one person would perform all these duties and tasks. Having such a composite for an occupation, however, is essential in the study of vocational behavior, particularly before the individual enters the world of work, when his choice options are not positions and jobs, at least not until very late in the decision-making process, but rather the more broadly defined concept of occupations.

[2] For a somewhat different survey and evaluation of occupational analysis methods see Neff (1966), who discusses four approaches: mental testing, job analysis, work-sample, and situational.

The second method of occupational analysis is known as the *critical-incident technique*. Whereas the standard approach is designed to provide a description of *all* the work which is performed in an occupation, this technique was conceived to yield data *only* on those behaviors which are essential to the *successful* performance of a position, job, or occupation. The terms *incident* and *critical* are defined by Flanagan (1954, p. 327), who is largely responsible for conceiving this technique, as follows:

> By an incident is meant any observable human activity that is sufficiently complete in itself to permit inferences and predictions to be made about the person performing the act. To be critical, an incident must occur in a situation where the purpose or intent of the act seems fairly clear to the observer and where its consequences are sufficiently definite to leave little doubt concerning its effects.

What is meant by a critical incident can be grasped more concretely from the sample form shown in Figure 2-2, which can be used by an interviewer in collecting data on behaviors considered to be necessary for success in a work activity. An illustrative answer to the first question might be: "One of the

"Think of the last time you saw one of your subordinates do something that was very helpful to your group in meeting their production schedule." (Pause till he indicates he has such an incident in mind.) "Did his action result in increase in production of as much as one per cent for that day?—or some similar period?"

(If the answer is "no," say) "I wonder if you could think of the last time that someone did something that did have this much of an effect in increasing production." (When he indicates he has such a situation in mind, say) "What were the general circumstances leading up to this incident?"________________

"Tell me exactly what this person did that was so helpful at that time."________

"Why was this so helpful in getting your group's job done?"________________

"When did this incident happen?"________________________

"What was this person's job?"________________________

"How long has he been on this job?"________________________

"How old is he?"________________________

Figure 2-2. Form for collecting critical incident data. *(From Flanagan, 1954, p. 342.)*

put-in coil assembly girls suggested a change in the assembly procedure which allowed the group to produce 15 percent more per unit of time." Critical-incident analyses have been made of numerous occupations, including several of flying specialties as part of the Aviation Psychology Program (Miller, N. E., 1947; Wickert, 1947), civilian airline pilots (Gordon, J., 1949; 1950), dentists (Wagner, 1950), bookkeepers (Nevins, 1949), psychology instructors (Smit, 1952), sales clerks (Folley, 1953), store managers (Andersson & Nilsson, 1964), and others (Flanagan, 1954). Parenthetically, it should be mentioned that the critical-incident technique can be applied in the study of problems other than occupational analysis, such as the definition of emotional immaturity (Eilbert, 1953) and the determination of test weights (Wagner, 1951).

The third major type of occupational analysis involves the identification and definition of *worker functions*. The rationale for this approach can be briefly summarized as follows:

> In order to understand the work performed on a job it is necessary to understand that what gets done is quite distinct from what the worker does, and both relate to a specific content [Fine & Heinz, 1958, p. 180].
>
> The worker functions are intended to answer the question "What does the worker do on the job?" as opposed to the question, "What gets done on the job?" [Fine, 1955, p. 66].

Thus, worker functions are contrasted with job content and are described by a different language:

> The means for expressing these functions are work-action verbs in gerund form defined in terms of (1) the variety or range of tasks occurring in the work action; (2) the objectives of the over-all work action; (3) the machines, tools, and equipment involved and (4) the materials, substances, or services worked on [Studdiford, 1951, p. 38].

Worker function descriptions of occupations indicate *what* gets done, *how* it gets done, and *why* it gets done, as in this example:

> CATALOGER (library) 100.388. catalog librarian; descriptive cataloger. Compiles information on library materials, such as books and periodicals, and prepares catalog cards [*what*] . . . to identify materials and to integrate information into library catalog [*why*]. . . . Verifies author, title, and classification number [*how*]. . . . [DOT, 1965, Vol. I, p. xv].

All worker functions can be classified according to the degree that occupations require performance at different levels of complexity in relation to *data*, *people*, and *things*. The levels for each of these classes of worker functions are listed in Table 2-1. To illustrate how an occupation can be described in terms of these hierarchies, consider what the CATALOGER does: As his occupational analysis indicates, he functions at a moderate level of complexity in relation to data (compiling) but has no significant relationships to people and things. Obviously, drawing this inference from the description of his occupation necessitates making a judgment and raises the question of how reliably this can be done. Fine (1955) has reported that the average percentages of agreement among four judges in rating worker functions for 100 occupations were 59 percent, 66 percent, and 88 percent for data, people, and things, respectively. It would appear, therefore, that this approach to occupational analysis yields relatively reliable information on worker functions and their levels of complexity.

The Dictionary of Occupational Titles (DOT). The worker-function approach to occupational analysis was developed as part of the USES Functional Occupational Classification Project, which was initiated in 1950 to revise the second edition of the DOT. As has been mentioned, this dictionary and its predecessor, which was published in 1939, as well as certain supplementary materials, such as Part IV for entry occupations, had been compiled using the standard type of occupational analysis. Several shortcomings in this methodology, however, accentuated the need for a new system of occupational definition and classification:

> (*a*) Fluctuations in labor market conditions indicated the desirability of occupational classifications that could be responsive to shortages and surpluses of labor supply; (*b*) dual classification structures for use with entry and nonentry workers created problems of filing and training that could be eliminated if a single system were devised to assist the functions of both placement and counseling; (*c*) certain classification inconsistencies and other weak spots existed in the available classification structures; and (*d*) the classification systems in use did not systematically reflect those aptitudes and other worker

Table 2-1. Levels of Complexity of Worker Functions for Data, People, and Things *(DOT, 1965, Vol. I, p. xviii)*

Data (*4th digit*)	*People* (*5th digit*)	*Things* (*6th digit*)
0 Synthesizing	0 Mentoring	0 Setting-up
1 Coordinating	1 Negotiating	1 Precision Working
2 Analyzing	2 Instructing	2 Operating-controlling
3 Compiling	3 Supervising	3 Driving-operating
4 Computing	4 Diverting	4 Manipulating
5 Copying	5 Persuading	5 Tending
6 Comparing	6 Speaking-signaling	6 Feeding-offbearing
7 No significant relationship	7 Serving	7 Handling
8 No significant relationship	8 No significant relationship	8 No significant relationship

> traits that bear significant relationships to job success and satisfaction [U. S. Department of Labor, 1956, p. iv].

Accordingly, not only was the worker-function concept originated, but also research was initiated on determining the worker traits which are required to perform the functions of an occupation. In 1956, the first results of this program were published under the title, "Estimates of Worker Trait Requirements for 4,000 Jobs," which reported the ratings for a representative sample of DOT occupations on each of six trait components: Training Time, Aptitudes, Temperaments, Interests, Physical Capacities, and Working Conditions. The definitions of these variables and the ways in which they are scaled are given in Table 2-2. To illustrate their application in the analysis of an occupation, the trait estimates for ACCOUNTANT, GENERAL are listed in Table 2-3.

Much as the reliability of the worker-function ratings had to be established, so too the reliability of worker-trait ratings, and their relationships to selected criterion variables, had to be demonstrated. One of the critical decisions which had to be made before any extensive rating could be undertaken was whether judgments of traits based upon *descriptions* of occupations were as reliable as those derived from direct *observations* of work being performed. If the indirect ratings could be used, it would greatly simplify the task of rating many thousands of occupations which would otherwise have to be observed. Two studies have indicated that ratings of aptitudes, physical capacities, and working conditions from descriptions were essentially as reliable as ratings from observations and that both kinds of ratings could be made by independent judges with an acceptably high percentage of agreement (Trattner, Fine, & Kubis, 1955; Newman & Fine, 1957). In a third study, which attempted to replicate these findings for temperaments, it was found, however, that adequate reliability could be attained only if this component was defined as a trait required by occupations, rather than as a characteristic of workers (Boling & Fine, 1959). It was concluded that "defining 'temperaments' in terms of the kinds of situations to which workers must adjust may be an effective first step toward a more adequate criterion for measuring personality concomitants of successful job adjustment" (Boling & Fine, 1959, p. 108).

Still another study was addressed to the related, but nevertheless distinct, problem of whether estimated worker-trait requirements can be said to constitute a "scalable domain" (Mosel, Fine, & Boling, 1960). In other words, "do such commonly used requirements as Verbal Ability and Motor Speed represent unidimensional attributes on which jobs can be placed in an unambiguous rank order?" (Mosel et al., 1960, p. 156). With Guttman's (1950) Index of Reproducibility and Jackson's (1949) Plus Percentage Ratio, it was found that interests are the most scalable of the worker traits, temperaments next, and aptitudes least. In other words, the latter two components are quasi-scales,

***Table 2-2. Definitions of Worker Trait Requirements** (U.S. Department of Labor, 1956)*

TRAINING TIME

GED	G	GENERAL EDUCATIONAL DEVELOPMENT
Levels 1	E	
2	D	
3		
4		
5		
6		
7		
SVP	S	SPECIFIC VOCATIONAL TRAINING
0—Over 10 years	V	
8—4–10 years	P	
7—2–4 years		
6—1–2 years		
5—6 months–1 year		
4—3–6 months		
3—30 days–3 months		
2—Short demonstration–30 days		
1—Short demonstration only		
	G	INTELLIGENCE
	V	VERBAL
	N	NUMERICAL
APTITUDES	S	SPATIAL
1—Upper 10%	P	FORM
2—Upper ⅓ less 1	Q	CLERICAL
3—Middle ⅓		
4—Lower ⅓ less 5	K	MOTOR COORDINATION
5—Lowest 10%	F	FINGER DEXTERITY
	M	MANUAL DEXTERITY
	E	EYE-HAND-FOOT COORDINATION
	C	COLOR DISCRIMINATION

which do not permit an unambiguous ranking of occupations, but they may still correlate with other variables, and hence be useful in this sense.

Finally, an investigation of the relationship between worker function and trait ratings, on the one hand, and the Minnesota Occupational Ratings Scales (MORS), on the other, showed that the two systems of rating occupations agreed to a considerable degree, the median intraclass *r*'s for functions and

	1 VARIETY AND CHANGE
	2 REPETITIVE, SHORT CYCLE
	3 UNDER SPECIFIC INSTRUCTIONS
	4 DIRECTION, CONTROL, PLANNING
	5 DEALING WITH PEOPLE
TEMPERAMENTS	6 ISOLATION
	7 INFLUENCING PEOPLE
	8 PERFORMING UNDER STRESS
	9 SENSORY OR JUDGMENTAL CRITERIA
	0 MEASURABLE OR VERIFIABLE CRITERIA
	X FEELINGS, IDEAS, FACTS
	Y SET LIMITS, TOLERANCES OR STANDARDS
	1 THINGS AND OBJECTS
	2 BUSINESS CONTACT
	3 ROUTINE CONCRETE
	4 SOCIAL WELFARE
INTERESTS	5 PRESTIGE
	6 PEOPLE, IDEAS
	7 SCIENTIFIC, TECHNICAL
	8 ABSTRACT, CREATIVE
	9 NONSOCIAL
	0 TANGIBLE, PRODUCTIVE SATISFACTION
PHYSICAL CAPACITIES	1 STRENGTH
S—Sedentary	2 CLIMBING-BALANCING
L—Light	3 STOOPING-KNEELING
M—Medium	4 REACHING-HANDLING
H—Heavy	5 TALKING-HEARING
V—Very heavy	6 SEEING
	1 INSIDE-OUTSIDE
	2 COLD
WORKING CONDITIONS	3 HEAT
I—Inside	4 WET-HUMID
O—Outside	5 NOISE-VIBRATION
B—Both	6 HAZARDS
	7 FUMES, ODORS, ETC.

traits with cognate MORS abilities being .82 and .61, respectively, with four raters and 37 occupations (Fine, 1957). A study by Norton (1962), in which the ratings of 70 workers in 54 different occupations were compared with the trait estimates, would generally support this study, although there was some disagreement between the two sets of ratings, possibly because workers tend to upgrade the requirements of their jobs. Of the differences between the

Table 2-3. Worker Trait Estimates for the Occupation of ACCOUNTANT, GENERAL *(U.S. Department of Labor, 1956, p. 1)*

Line No.	11
DOT job title	Accountant, general
Vol. II code	0–01.20
Part IV code	0–7.11
Training time	GED SVP 6 8
Aptitudes	GVN SPA KFM EC 121 542 444 55
Temperaments	1 2 3 4 5 6 7 8 9 0 X Y 4 0
Interests	1 2 3 4 5 6 7 8 9 0 1 2
Physical capacities	1 2 3 4 5 6 S 4 6
Working conditions	1 2 3 4 5 6 7 I
Industry code	695
OAP no.	5
OOH page	
Line no.	11

ratings of aptitudes, educational level, and training, for example, 87 percent were due to the workers' rating these traits at higher levels. The empirical evidence for the reliability and usefulness of the worker function and trait ratings, then, is largely favorable and provides the necessary foundation for the occupational classification system which has been built upon it (see following discussion).

The Occupational Outlook Handbook (OOH). Like the DOT, the *Occupational Outlook Handbook,* which was first published in 1949 and which is now revised every two years, contains descriptions of a large segment of the occupations found in the American economy, but, in addition, it reports data on occupations and the world of work which are not covered by the DOT. For each of the occupations it describes, the OOH provides the following information: nature of the work, where employed, training and other qualifications, employment outlook, earnings and working conditions, and where to go for more information. Occupations are classified in the OOH in two ways: (1) by level and field and (2) by major industry. There is also a general discussion of occupational trends and prospects which treats such topics as: Employment in Major Occupational and Industrial Groups, Changes in Occupational and Industrial Employment, Projected Occupational Opportunities, Division of Labor by Age and Sex, Future Working Population, Unemployment and Education, and Earnings of Occupational Groups. Summaries of what is known about each of these aspects of the world of work will not be given here, not only because they are readily available in the OOH, but also because they need to be revised practically every year.The most significant finding of the analyses conducted for the OOH has been the rapidly changing nature and composition of occupations in recent years. And, the prospect for the future is that they will continue to change at the same, or even an accelerated, rate.

Other Kinds of Occupational Analysis. Brief mention should be made of two other approaches to occupational analysis, one psychological and the other sociological, which have not been as extensively used as those already discussed, but which have considerable promise for future research, in that they yield data of an unique kind. The psychological analysis of occupations was first proposed by Segal (1954, p. 111), who pointed out the lack of data on "the personality needs gratified by a particular occupational outlet [and] the socially defined role of the worker in the community, i.e., the status value of the job." It remained for Walsh (1959), however, to carry out one of the few analyses of this kind which has been done. From the DOT, a plant's job descriptions for managerial positions, and personal knowledge of specific jobs, he extracted statements of occupational duties and tasks which could be classified by judges as potentially satisfying eight needs selected from Murray's (1938) theory of personality: achievement, affiliation, autonomy, change, dominance, exhibition, nurturance, and order. Descriptions of occupations based upon these needs were then written, so that they could be related to the cognate scales on the Edwards Personal Preference Schedule (EPPS). For 96 male college students, the correlations between "liking" for occupations which might satisfy a particular need and scores on the corresponding EPPS need scale were significant six out of eight times, the r's ranging from .18 to .49. Walsh (1959) concluded that his results supported Segal's proposal for "need" analyses of occupations as one which might have potential heuristic value.

The sociological analysis of occupations is closely related to the psychological, but focuses more upon work as a "way of life" (Cohen, A., 1964; Danskin, 1955; 1956). Overs and Deutsch (1966, p. 711) note that it is "generally characterized by an examination of role identities, role conflicts, cultural pressures, patterns of beliefs, values and cognitive orientations, occupational associations, informal work groups, occupational socialization and social changes in occupations." Over 796 sociological studies of occupations have been reported in books, articles, dissertations, and theses (Overs & Deutsch, 1966), and many of these have been abstracted or summarized (Danskin, 1955; 1956). They vary in quality and reliability, as Cohen (1964) has pointed out, but, if they are considered as "survey" research (see Chapter 13), which identifies variables of interest and suggests hypotheses for more rigorous testing, then they may provide much needed psychosocial information about occupations (Samler, 1961).

Occupational Classification

Once occupations have been analyzed and described, the next step is usually to classify them according to their similarities and differences. To clarify the meaning of occupational "classification," it should be distinguished, in the first instance, from occupational "measurement," but this is difficult to do without qualifications, because of the varying definitions which have been given to these terms in psychology (Campbell, N. R., 1938; Stevens, 1951; Torgerson, 1958). The issue is whether classification can be considered measurement or not. For theoretical and research purposes, however, the more important consideration would seem to be that a classification schema or system can be treated as a variable. Occupations can be grouped according to their distinguishing characteristics, and then the groups can be related to other variables.

There are numerous attributes of occupations, and the workers in them, by which they can be classified. Only a few of these have been selected for discussion, and, with one exception (industries), they are the ones which appear to be most salient psychologically. They are: (1) aptitudes, (2) interests, (3) personality, (4) worker functions, (5) industries, and (6) occupational life spans.

Aptitudes. Both general and special aptitudes have been used in the classification and measurement of occupations, but in different ways. As will be discussed, general aptitude has usually been thought of as a "levels" variable, along which occupations are ranked according to the intelligence they require or the average intelligence of their members. In contrast, special aptitudes have typically been employed as a "fields" variable, into which occupations are classified on the basis of the *patterns* of aptitudes that characterize them. This approach is exemplified by the work of Paterson, Gerken, and Hahn (1953) in their revision of the Minnesota Occupational Rating Scales (MORS). These scales were constructed to provide estimates of the levels of seven "abilities" or aptitudes required by each of 432 occupations. The aptitudes which were rated were the following: academic, mechanical, social, clerical, musical, artistic, and physical. With the exception of musical and artistic aptitudes, the levels were defined as *A,* top decile; *B,* 76th to 90th percentiles; *C,* 26th to 75th percentiles; and *D,* 1st to 25th percentiles. For musical and artistic aptitudes, the ranges at the upper levels were more restricted, e.g., Level *A* equaled 97th to 99th percentiles, in order to reflect the greater amounts of these talents which are demanded by some occupations.

Judges rated each occupation on each aptitude, and 214 patterns for the 432 occupations were obtained. Of these, 137 were unique, and 77 included from 2 to 18 occupations each. Paterson and his associates also classified the occupations according to patterns of academic aptitude at each level but did not extend this system to include all the aptitudes. Table 2-4 lists the aptitude patterns for eight occupations at the *A* level of academic aptitude to illustrate this grouping procedure.

Interests. Although the factor analyses of interests reviewed earlier in this chapter suggest several possible classification schemata for occupations (Vernon, 1949), very little work has been done on using them for this purpose (Holland, Krause, Nixon, & Trembath, 1953). Roe (1956) has utilized the findings on interest "types" in her two-dimensional system for classifying occupations, which is presented below, but the most extensive research on this problem has been conducted by Holland (1966a), who has developed an empirically

Table 2-4. Aptitude Patterns for 18 Occupations at the A Level of Academic Aptitude *(Paterson, Gerken, & Hahn, 1953, p. 43)*

Number and name of occupation	*Ac.*	*Me.*	*So.*	*Cl.*	*Mu.*	*Ar.*	*Phy.*
JOBS REQUIRING "A" ACADEMIC ABILITY							
1. Accountant	A			A			
3. Actor, highest type	A		B				
5. Advertising expert	A		B				
13. Architect	A	A				A	
16. Arranger of music, symphony	A			B	A		
18. Astronomer	A	B		B			
24. Banker, large bank	A		B	A			
25. Banker, small town	A		B	A			
40. Broker, loan	A		B	B			
43. Broker and promoter	A		A	B			
57. Chemist	A	B					
75. Composer, classical	A				A		
77. Concert artist	A				A		
82. Conductor, symphony orchestra	A		B		A		
92. Dentist, great	A	A	B				
98. Designer, machinery	A	A					
101. Designer, stage	A	A				A	
110. Druggist	A						

based schema in which occupations (or choices) are classified according to interest hierarchies or patterns. Measuring interests with his Vocational Preference Inventory (VPI), which elicits an individual's likes and dislikes for a variety of occupations scored on six keys (Realistic, Intellectual, Social, Conventional, Enterprising, and Artistic), he computed the average score on each of these scales for a large number of college students (5,600 males, 5,560 females) grouped by their vocational choices. Thus, he obtained a VPI interest profile for the 152 males in the sample who had chosen mechanical engineering, for example, by determining their scores on the six VPI scales and then ranking these from high to low. Next, he constituted classes, named after the VPI scales, by grouping together all the interest profiles which had the same scale ranked first. These were then ordered within classes by the second and third ranked scales, so that there resulted the occupational classification systems, one for men and one for women, as illustrated in Table 2-5.

In three further analyses, Holland found that (1) the occupational classes differed significantly, according to theoretical expectations, on 24 life-goal, competency, and personal-trait variables, (2) the vocational choice groups differed significantly on the appropriate VPI scales, and (3) the women's clas-

Table 2-5. Classification of Occupations by Interests *(From Holland, 1966a, pp. 281–282)*

Occupational choice	*VPI Code*	*N*
REALISTIC ORIENTATION		
Men		
Forestry	123	105
Architecture	126	83
Women (none)		
INTELLECTUAL ORIENTATION		
Men		
Botany	213	12
Electrical engineering	215	259
Women		
Mathematics, statistics	234	54
Medicine	236	79
SOCIAL ORIENTATION		
Men		
Counseling & guidance	356	36
Clinical psychology	362	42
Women		
Secretarial science	346	267
Nursing	362	301

NOTE: Because of space limitations, all the choices classified by Holland according to all six of the personality orientations in his typology have not been reproduced here, but they can be found in his article describing the system.

sification schema could be refined, so that their choices were more evenly distributed across the occupational categories. These findings support Holland's interest classification system for occupations as one which is objective and potentially useful in the analysis of vocational choices and occupational differences. As he cautions, however, it should be kept in mind that the system was derived from the *choices* of college students, rather than the occupations of employed adults, and consequently may be more applicable to the former than the latter.

Personality. Although Holland (1966a) and Roe (1956) *assume* that interests are personality variables, broadly defined, the only strictly personality-based system of occupational classification has been proposed by Brender (1960). His "fundamentum divisionis" is the dimension of intrinsic-extrinsic rewards which can be gained from work. "Intrinsic rewards may be defined as those satisfactions inherent in an occupation, which are unique to the work activities of that occupation, or to a small family of occupations related in that respect" (Brender, 1960, pp. 96–97). For example, an intrinsic reward in the occupation of WRITER would be the satisfaction derived from gratifying a need for *verbal expression.* In contrast, extrinsic rewards are associated with such aspects of work as opportunity for advancement, rate of advancement, salary, status, and prestige. These kinds of satisfactions are found in many occupations.

Brender does not enumerate all the possible categories of intrinsic rewards into which occupations might be classified, but he does give examples of how a few occupations might be classified, in order to illustrate the principles of the system. Using the letters *ir* to denote "*i*ntrinsic *r*eward," he analyzes the satisfactions which might be inherent in the occupation of CLINICAL PSYCHOLOGIST as follows (Brender, 1960, pp. 98–99):

> (a) Opportunity to assist in the healing of others, which places the occupation—along with medicine, dentistry, osteopathy, podiatry and chiropractic—in the palliative category, i.e., "*ir*-palliative mental, reproductive. . . .
> (b) Opportunity to teach the skills of the occupation to others, which places the occupation, together with all other research specialties, in the inquisitive (or interrogative, or investigative) category, i.e., "*ir*-investigative, scientific, social, applicative (or applied), behavioral, creative.

Brender does not report any empirical data on his system, and, as both he and Warnath (1960), who has commented upon it, point out, it is still incomplete conceptually. It does appear to have promise, however, as one of the few attempts which have been made to analyze occupations in terms of personality (see Segal, 1954; Walsh, 1959) and then to classify them accordingly.

Worker Functions. The classification of occupations by worker functions is based upon the occupational-analysis method described in the previous section. Each occupation in the DOT is assigned a six-digit code number. The first three digits classify the occupations into broad categories, divisions, and groups, whereas the last three digits correspond to the levels of complexity in relation to data, people, and things which are required by the duties and tasks of an occupation. Table 2-6 outlines this coding system and also provides an example of how the occupation of COUNSELING PSYCHOLOGIST (045.108) is coded. In Volume II of the DOT, it is classified by this number in two ways: First, it is listed in the overall Occupational Group Arrangement of Titles and Codes by the entire six-digit number. Thus, it is grouped into a "job family" which follows the 045.088 occupations (e.g., PSYCHOLOGIST, DEVELOPMENTAL) and which precedes the 045.118 occupations (e.g., DIRECTOR OF GUIDANCE IN PUBLIC SCHOOLS). Second, it is classified by the last three digits into one of 22 Areas of Work, which cut across the major three-digit categories. The Areas of Work are further divided into several specific worker-trait groups. The Counseling, Guidance, and Social Work area, for example, is broken down into (1) Social Science, Psychological, and Related Research, (2) Guidance and Counseling, and (3) Interviewing, Information-Giving, and Related Work. The occupations in a given worker-trait group are highly similar with respect to both functions and qualifications. For each group, Volume II gives (1) Work Performed, (2) Worker Requirements, (3) Clues for Relating Applicants and Requirements, and (4) Training and Methods of Entry, as well as a Qualifications Profile for (*a*) General Educational Development, (*b*) Specific Vocational Preparation, (*c*) Aptitudes, (*d*) Interests, (*e*) Temperament, and (*f*) Physical Demands.[3]

Industries. There are three industrial classification systems by which occupations have been classified. The best known and most widely used of these is the Standard Industrial Classification schema (U. S. Bureau of the Budget, 1957), which consists of nine major divisions and 79 major groups. The former are Agriculture, Forestry, and Fisheries; Mining; Contract Construction; Manufacturing; Transportation, Communication, and Other Public Utilities; Wholesale and Retail Trade; Finance, Insurance, and Real Estate; Services; Government; and Nonclassifiable Establishments. These divisions and the groups are further subdivided, so that approximately 1,500 industries are covered by the system. The Census Classification is a condensation of the Standard Industrial Classification, the 79 major groups having been reduced to 13 major groups, with only 145 further breakdowns as compared with an original total of 500. The system which is probably the most useful for the classification of

[3] For a critical appraisal of the FOCP classification system, see Walther (1960).

Table 2-6. An Outline of the New DOT Coding System for Occupations

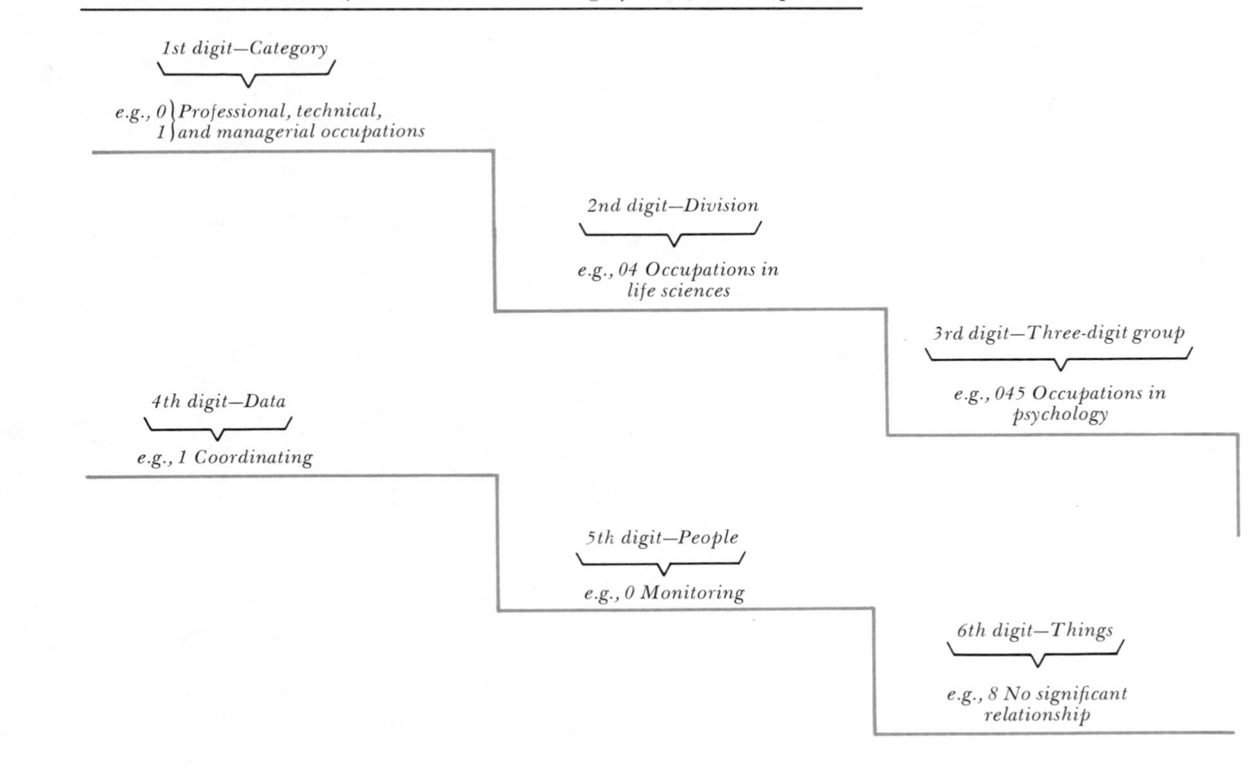

occupations, as contrasted with those which are more appropriate for industries alone, is the Industry Arrangement of Titles in Volume II of the DOT. In this listing, each industry is defined in terms of the occupations which comprise it, and the occupations are arranged in alphabetical order, within industries, by the titles given in Volume I. Like the other industrial classification systems, however, this one also suffers from the shortcoming that many occupations may be found in more than one industry. In other words, the classes of these systems are not mutually exclusive, and consequently they are extremely difficult to use in statistical analyses of relationships to other variables, a problem which will be discussed at greater length in the next section on occupational measurement.

Occupational Life Spans. Another attribute of occupations by which they can be classified is what Super (1957) has termed their "life spans." The life span of an occupation is defined by the period of time which elapses between *entry* and *leaving,* each of which can be "early," "normal," or "late." Early entry would occur upon termination of the minimal formal education required by an occupation; normal entry would follow completion of formal education or brief preliminary work experience; and late entry would come after prolonged specialized training or substantial work experience in another (presumably related) occupation. Similarly, early leaving would be defined as retirement from an occupation while still capable of working in other occupations; normal leaving, as termination at the typical retirement age; and late leaving, as continued work beyond the usual age of retirement in most occupations. The possible combinations of early-normal-late entry and leaving make nine categories into which occupations can be classified. Super (1957, p. 56) has illustrated the use of the system by classifying a few selected occupations, but he has not reported any empirical work on it, such as reliability and relationships to other variables. Examples of some of the occupations which appear to have markedly different life spans are: theatre usher (early-entry, early-leaving); accountant (normal-entry, normal-leaving); and judge (late-entry, late-leaving). Because of the use of the time dimension as one of the criteria of classification in this system, it would seem to be particularly appropriate for research on vocational development.

Comment. Each of these occupational classification systems has its own merits and shortcomings, some of which have been mentioned in summarizing them, but two additional comments should be made. First, no one of the systems is comprehensive enough and so thoroughly studied that it is generally applicable as a method for classifying occupations. Rather, each should be selected for a specific purpose. For example, if a research problem involves the relationship of aptitudes to vocational choice, then the MORS would probably be the most appropriate system for categorizing the latter, whereas if the variable being studied is interests rather than aptitudes, then Holland's schema would most likely be used. Second, depending upon which system is selected for an analysis, different results may be obtained. Remstad and Rothney (1958) classified data on choice in relation to occupation entered and father's occupation according to three different systems and found different results in each instance. They concluded that:

> It has been shown here that the type of classification system used can definitely alter the results of a study in which the occupation of a subject is one of the variables. With a little experimentation one could easily find a classification which did a better job "proving" a hypothesized relationship, if the researcher were trying to establish one. The researcher should, however, consider several classification systems and report the differences so that his readers may judge which is most suitable [Remstad & Rothney, 1958, p. 472].

We can agree with this conclusion in general, adding only that, if possible, the classification system which is used in a study should be selected also for theoretical reasons, so that whatever findings are obtained with it can be more meaningfully interpreted.

Occupational Measurement

Occupational measurement differs from occupational classification, in that it involves the ordering of occupations along some dimension according to the postulates of scaling (Guilford, 1954). Smith, M. (1935) has discussed these and other psychometric methods which are applicable to the measurement of occupations, and Osgood and Stagner (1941) have illustrated the use of a gradient scaling technique with a small sample of occupations. Most approaches to occupational measurement have been less refined and sophisticated, however, than the procedures outlined by these investigators. The typical occupational scale has been based either upon a researcher's best judgment of what the ranking should be or upon the judgments of a group of Subjects, which has usually been selected more because of its availability than its representativeness and expertise. The consequence has been certain anomalies in most occupational scales which have led Caplow (1954) and others to raise the question: Is there a *single* occupational hierarchy? The answer to this question should become apparent as the various kinds of occupational scales which have been constructed are reviewed. These include: (1) socioeconomic scales; (2) prestige scales; (3) an intelligence scale; and (4) a behavior-control scale. In addition, a study of the interrelationships of several different occupational scales is summarized. Finally, two multidimensional measurement systems for occupations are presented and evaluated.[4]

Socioeconomic Scales. Caplow (1954, p. 31) notes that one of the first socioeconomic occupational scales was conceived of by William C. Hunt in 1897 for use by the U. S. Bureau of the Census. His schema consisted of four levels: proprietor, clerical, skilled, and laboring. This early work by Hunt was carried on in the Bureau by Caroll D. Wright and eventually resulted in the widely used scale developed by Edwards, A. M. (1943), an outline of which is presented in Table 2-7. The rationale for the scale is explicated by Edwards, A. M. (1943, p. 179) as follows:

> It is evident that each of these groups represents not only a major segment of the nation's labor force, but, also, a large population group with a somewhat distinct standard of life, economically, and, to a considerable extent, intellectually and socially. In some measure, also, each group has characteristic interests and convictions as to numerous public questions—social, economic, and political. Each of them is thus a really distinct and highly significant social-economic group.

Caplow (1954, pp. 42–43) points out that underlying Edwards's scale, as well

Table 2-7. Socioeconomic Scale of Occupations *(Edwards, A. M., 1943)*

1. Professional persons
2. Proprietors, managers, and officials
   - 2*a*. Farmers (owners and tenants)
   - 2*b*. Wholesale and retail dealers
   - 2*c*. Other proprietors, managers, and officials
3. Clerks and kindred workers
4. Skilled workers and foremen
5. Semiskilled workers
6. Unskilled workers
   - 6*a*. Farm workers
   - 6*b*,*c*. Laborers, except farm
   - 6*d*. Servant classes

[4] A topic which might have been included here, had space permitted, is occupational stereotypes—the ways in which persons perceive occupations and the attributes they ascribe, more or less accurately, to their members. For those interested in this problem, see: Beardslee and O'Dowd (1961; 1962); Dipboye and Anderson (1961); Gonyea (1961; 1963; Gonyea & Lunneborg, 1963); Grunes (1956; 1957); McGill (1931); Mead, M., and Metraux (1957); Osipow (1962); Stagner (1950); Ulrich, Hechlik, and Roeber (1966); and Walker (1958). Of related interest are the early studies of photographs of workers by Child (1936); Gahagen (1933); Landis and Phelps (1928); and Viteles and Smith (1932).

as others which purport to assess socioeconomic level through the ranking of occupations, are five assumptions:

1. White-collar work is superior to manual work.
2. Self-employment is superior to employment by others.
3. Clean occupations are superior to dirty ones.
4. The importance of business occupations depends upon the size of the business, but this is not true of agricultural occupations.
5. Personal service is degrading, and it is better to be employed by an enterprise than to be employed in the same work by a person.

Caplow criticizes these assumptions, not only because they lead to inconsistencies in ranking occupations, particularly in the middle range of the hierarchy, but, more importantly, because they are based upon "half-truths." He argues, for example, that typists may rank higher in social status than machine operators, but not higher than tool-and-die makers, who enjoy a high level of economic well-being as well as social influence. In other words, Caplow's point is that no one criterion of socioeconomic status is sufficient to order occupations consistently from the top to the bottom of the scale.

In addition to Edwards's scale, other socioeconomic rankings of occupations have been devised by Sims (1928; 1952), Goodenough and Anderson (1931), Kefauver, Noll, and Drake (1932), Beckman (1934), Taussig (1939), and Centers (1949), all of which are based upon one or more of the aforementioned assumptions and are biased accordingly. Probably the best and most thoroughly studied socioeconomic scale is the one originally constructed by Warner, Meeker, and Eells (1949) for their analyses of social class, and subsequently revised by Hamburger (1958) as part of his doctoral dissertation in the Career Pattern Study. The scale was initially developed from Edward's ranking of occupations, with some modifications, e.g., a distinction was made between large and small proprietors on the basis of the monetary value of a business, but it was felt that still further changes were necessary, and the scale was expanded to provide for ratings of skill along a 7-point continuum within each level. The final Warner version of the scale is shown in Table 2-8, where it can be seen that many of the inconsistencies which have plagued other socioeconomic scales, such as no differentiation among farmers at high and low levels, have been eliminated. Hamburger (1958) has refined this schema even further to reflect amount of responsibility, levels of education and skill, and behavior control, as well as social status and economic reward. Because the scale in its present form is based upon so many rating factors, it meets most of the objections raised by Caplow. If it has a weakness, it is that only a few occupations have actually been rated by it. Hamburger (1958) has reported high interjudge agreement in using the scale, however, so presumably an investigator could measure additional occupations with acceptable reliability.

Table 2-8. Socioeconomic Scale of Occupations *(Warner et al., 1949)*

Rating assigned to occupation	*Professionals*	*Proprietors and managers*	*Businessmen*
1	Lawyers, doctors, dentists, engineers, judges, high school superintendents, veterinarians, ministers (graduated from divinity school), chemists, etc. with post-graduate training, architects	Businesses valued at $75,000 and over	Regional and divisional managers of large financial and industrial enterprises
2	High school teachers, trained nurses, chiropodists, chiropractors, undertakers, ministers (some training), newspaper editors, librarians (graduate)	Businesses valued at $20,000 to $75,000	Assistant managers and office and department managers of large businesses, assistants to executives, etc.
3	Social workers, grade school teachers, optometrists, librarians (not graduate), undertaker's assistants, ministers (no training)	Businesses valued at $5,000 to $20,000	All minor officials of businesses
4		Businesses valued at $2,000 to $5,000	
5		Businesses valued at $500 to $2,000	
6		Businesses valued at less than $500	
7			

Clerks and kindred workers, etc.	*Manual workers*	*Protective and service workers*	*Farmers*
Certified public accountants			Gentleman farmers
Accountants, salesmen of real estate, of insurance, postmasters			Large farm owners, farm owners
Auto salesmen, bank clerks and cashiers, postal clerks, secretaries to executives, supervisors of railroad, telephone, etc., justices of the peace	Contractors		
Stenographers, bookkeepers, rural mail clerks, railroad ticket agents, sales people in dry goods store, etc.	Factory foremen, electricians, plumbers, carpenters (own business), watchmakers	Dry cleaners, butchers, sheriffs, railroad engineers and conductors	
Dime-store clerks, hardware salesmen, beauty operators, telephone operators	Carpenters, plumbers, electricians (apprentice), timekeepers, linemen, telephone or telegraph, radio repairmen, medium-skill workers	Barbers, firemen, butcher's apprentices, practical nurses, policemen, seamstresses, cooks in restaurant, bartenders	Tenant farmers
	Moulders, semi-skilled workers, assistants to carpenter, etc.	Baggage men, night policemen and watchmen, taxi and truck drivers, gas station attendants, waitresses in restaurant	Small tenant farmers
	Heavy labor, migrant work, odd-job men, miners	Janitors, scrub-women, newsboys	Migrant farm laborers

Prestige Scales. In comparing and contrasting socioeconomic and prestige occupational scales, Caplow (1954, p. 39) points out that: "In the sociological literature, prestige is not exactly the same thing as status or social position, and may perhaps best be said to represent the subjective value granted to the perceived cluster of habits, objects, and expectations associated with the statuses of a given position." He doubts, however, that respondents to either type of scale make this distinction, and he is probably correct, as a perusal of the instructions for typical prestige scales will bring out.

In what has been credited as the first of this kind of scale ever developed, Counts (1925) asked a heterogeneous sample of 93 students and 19 textile workers to rank 45 occupations according to their "social standing." Similarly, Hartmann, G. W. (1934) instructed his 450 Subjects to rank 25 occupations in the order of their "admiration" for them. And, more recently, Hatt (1950) told his nationwide survey sample of 2,930 to rate 88 occupations on a 6-point scale of the "standing" of the occupations. Other scales, for both occupations-in-general (Sims, 1928; Anderson, W. A., 1934; Coutu, 1936; Smith, M., 1943; Welch, 1948; and Stubbins, 1950) and women's occupations (Menger, 1932; Stevens, R. B., 1940; Baudler & Paterson, 1948; and Tuckman, 1950), have utilized much the same instructional set, the essence of which is to order occupations along a dimension ambiguously defined as "standing." Which occupations are selected to be ordered has not been systematically determined. Most investigators have merely reported how many occupations they used, with no statement of why they were chosen, the only exceptions being studies of intra-occupational specialties in the fields of medicine by Hartmann, G. W. (1936) and psychology by Granger (1959) and Porter, T. L., and Cook (1964). In an investigation of the prestige of industries, as contrasted with occupations, Brayfield, Kennedy, and Kendall (1954) administered a list of 29 industries to 120 college students and asked them to rank them "according to what you think their social standing is in your community or state." Using a longer list of industries ($N = 52$), Campbell, R. E. (1960) had his Subjects (360 college juniors and seniors) rate each industry on a 5-point scale (e.g., 1 = "This industry has excellent prestige") and then constituted a rank order from the mean values of the ratings. He found that there was only moderate agreement (*rho*'s = .47 for men, .55 for women) between the two procedures.

The major finding which has emerged from studies with most of these prestige scales is that the occupational hierarchy they measure is remarkably stable over time and highly generalizable across age, sex, racial, and cultural groupings:

1. Deeg and Paterson (1947) replicated Count's original study, the only difference being a reduction in the number of occupations from 45 to 25 in order to simplify the ranking task, and obtained a *rho* of .97 between the two scales.

2. Tuckman (1958) has reported that, in making prestige rankings, there is little difference among scales which provide (1) only the occupational title, (2) only an occupational description, or (3) a combined title and description, the pairwise *rho*'s being .94, .97, and .97, respectively.

3. Lehman and Witty (1931a) asked a large sample of school-age boys ($N = 13{,}346$) and girls ($N = 13{,}532$) to select the three occupations, out of a list of 200, which they believed were most respected and found only negligible differences between age groups and between the sexes. Their younger and older Subjects agreed on physician, banker, and minister as the three most respected occupations, although the percentages increased with age; similarly, boys and girls concurred on these occupations, differing only in the choice of highly sex-typed occupations, such as aviator and elementary school teacher.

4. Rose and Wall (1957) compared the rankings of 15 occupations by 68 Negro high school students in a Southern town with those in the studies by Counts and by Deeg and Paterson and concluded that they were, at least superficially, quite similar. They contend, however, on the basis of supplementary interview data, that there are, nevertheless, racial differences in the *reasons* why Negro children make the same rankings as whites; but they did not collect comparison data on the latter.[5] Consequently, they do not know that white children *actually* rank occupations for different reasons. On the basis of present evidence, the most parsimonious conclusion which can be drawn from their study is that there are very few racial differences in the scaling of occupational prestige. Much the same can be said for the differences between cultures and nations (Kunde & Dawis, 1959; Thomas, R. M., & Soeparman, 1963).

Three studies of the correlates of prestige scales have established that they are related to (1) income, (2) psychoses, and (3) intelligence:

1. Clark, R. E. (1953) obtained a *rho* of .85 between a prestige ranking of 17 occupations and their median incomes as calculated from 1940 census data. Instead of actual income, Folsom and Sobolewski (1957) asked students to judge the income of 26 occupations and also to rank them on a prestige scale. For 42 high school sophomores, the *rho* was .74, and for 47 seniors it was .64. The agreement between the two groups for each of the rankings was high, the *rho* for prestige being .99 and for income .93.

2. Clark, R. E. (1953) also determined the rank-order correlation between the prestige of occupations and the age-adjusted psychosis rates for their mem-

[5] Gunn (1964) has reported a content analysis of the reasons first through twelfth graders give for their prestige rankings of occupations, but she did not analyze them for racial differences. She found that the reasons change, but evidently the rankings do not. Simmons, D. D. (1962), for example, obtained a *rho* of .86 between the rankings of fourth graders and those in the Deeg-Paterson study. For an analysis of the prestige rankings of retarded students, see Rusalem and Cohen (1964).

bers, and he found that the *rho* was −.75. In other words, the incidence of psychoses was less, the higher the prestige level of the occupations. Clark enumerates several reasons why this relationship may exist: (*a*) It may be the result of the selective factors which affect occupational entry and membership and which may be associated with psychoses; (*b*) it may be a function of direct and indirect differentials in occupationally derived experiences, e.g., hazards, roles, working conditions, class mores, etc.; and (*c*) it may be attributable to some third variable which is simply related to both occupational prestige and psychosis rates. Clark discounts the plausibility of the latter explanation, but does not offer any evidence in support of the others. Thus, about all that can justifiably be concluded from his study is that prestige and psychoses are highly negatively associated.

3. Canter (1956) correlated the Counts (1925), Deeg and Paterson (1947), Hatt (1950), and Welch (1948) scales with rankings based upon the median and mean intelligence scores of occupations computed by Harrell and Harrell (1945) and Stewart (1947) from the World War II AGCT data. The *rho*'s were very high, ranging from .89 to .96. Canter (1956, p. 259) concluded from these findings that "judges' perceptions of intelligence of personnel in occupational groups may be a dominant factor leading to judgments of social status of occupations."

Intelligence Scales. Although the evidence just cited indicates a strong relationship between occupational prestige and intelligence, only one scale has been developed for the ranking of occupations according to their intellectual requirements. As part of his first study of the gifted, Terman (1925) asked F. E. Barr to construct an intelligence scale for occupations, which he did by having 30 judges rate 100 "representative" occupations with respect to the "grade of intelligence which each was believed to demand." The occupations ranged from "hobo" and "garbage collector" at the lower end of the scale to "inventive genius" and "surgeon" at the upper end. In commenting upon the scale, Terman (1925, p. 69) concluded that:

> It has been found that different judges agree fairly closely in rating the intellectual demands of occupations by this scale. It can not be claimed that the Barr Scale values correspond exactly to the facts, but they unquestionably approximate the facts more closely than would the judgments of any one individual.

Some empirical support for this statement comes from a study by Lorge and Blau (1942), in which they correlated the Barr Scale with Army Alpha scores for 44 occupations, based upon data compiled by Fryer (1922). The *rho* was .76, which indicates a high relationship between rated and measured occupational intelligence, but not as high as might have been expected. If a choice had to be made between the two scales, the one derived from the actual intelligence scores of the members of occupational groups would be preferred.

Behavior-control Scale. A persistent problem in the construction of occupational scales has been the inconsistent ranking of occupations in the middle range of the hierarchy. Caplow (1954, p. 41) has illustrated this difficulty with the rankings of farmer, electrician, and insurance agent in the Counts, Deeg and Paterson, Goodenough and Anderson, Sims, and Edwards scales, all of which are different. To eliminate such inconsistencies he has proposed an occupational scale of behavior control, which he defines as "the status of the individual in the typical situations elicited by his occupational role, vis-à-vis his clients, customers, subordinates, superiors, pupils, passengers, or indeed whatever other persons he normally meets in the course of his occupational duties" (Caplow, 1954, p. 55). Thus, in some occupations, such as business executive, the primary focus of the work activity is the control and direction of subordinates' behavior, whereas in others, such as street cleaner and ditch digger, little or no control is exerted over even one's own behavior. Caplow had five raters judge the degree of behavior control involved in each of the 45 occupations in Counts's prestige scale and found that the resulting ranking was remarkably consistent, particularly in the troublesome middle range. There were only 3 out of 19 occupations at this level which received higher or lower ratings than the others. In contrast, the percentages of reversals for the same occupations rated on responsibility, nature of work, formal education, training, authority, class attributes, and income were much higher. Of the scales which have been proposed to measure occupational attributes, then, one of the most promising is Caplow's behavior-control scale. It warrants much wider use in research on vocational behavior than it has received.

Interrelationships of Scales. To determine how highly interrelated occupations scaled on different dimensions are, Stefflre (1959) had 59 female and 62 male high school juniors rank 20 occupations on 10 factors. These were as follows: (1) the occupation of their choice; (2) social standing (prestige); (3) altruism (value to the community); (4) behavior control; (5) required education; (6) job freedom; (7) required intelligence; (8) monetary return; (9) security; and (10) self-realization (interest in and satisfaction derived from work). The occupations selected for the rankings were those which "seemed to be important in vocational guidance in the geographic area of the study" (Stefflre, 1959, p. 435), e.g., accountant, carpenter, farmer, lawyer, physician, truck driver, etc. From the ranked occupations, median intercorrelations (type of coefficient not specified) were calculated for males and females separately, and then centroid factor analyses were performed on the two matrices. In the analysis for males, the first factor represented 86 percent of the total variance, and in the analysis for females, it accounted for 90 percent. The only scale which did not load appreciably on this general factor was job freedom, which appeared to consist almost wholly of unique variance. These findings led Stefflre (1959, p. 437) to conclude that "high school students are either unable to clearly distinguish the various bases for the social status which they grant to occupations, or that all of the elements postulated as being important in status are in fact highly associated with each other." Both of these alternatives are probably correct: if status determinants are closely related, as is most likely the case, then it would be difficult to discriminate among them, irrespective of whether the judge is a high school student or an older person.

Multidimensional Systems. With the possible exception of the revised Warner scale, which provides for skill gradations within socioeconomic levels, all the occupational scales considered thus far have been unidimensional. There are at least two systems for quantifying occupations, however, one being an elaboration and extension of the other, which are multidimensional. The original scheme was proposed by Roe (1954), as a convenient framework for organizing the research on occupational differences, and was subsequently modified by Moser, H. P., Dubin, and Shelsky (1956). It is this latter version, as revised slightly by Roe (1956), which will be described

It consists of two dimensions. The vertical axis is divided into six levels or degrees of (1) responsibility, (2) capacity, and (3) skill. Roe (1956) states that responsibility is the primary criterion for designating the level of occupations, but it has to be supplemented with capacity and skill differentiations, particularly in the middle and lower ranges of the scale. Thus, most of the skilled, semiskilled, and unskilled occupations can be graded on the amount of training and experience they require, but not necessarily on the extent of responsibility they entail for materials and personnel. The horizontal axis is based upon interest factors, but, as Roe (1956, p. 145) points out, is not identical with them. The criterion for classifying occupations along this dimension is the primary focus of the work activity, which may be upon (1) personal interactions, (2) physical activities, or (3) knowledge of the world and the works of man. Roe (1956) delineates eight activity categories or groups: I. Service; II. Business Contact; III. Organization; IV. Technology; V. Outdoor; VI. Science; VII. General Cultural; and VIII. Arts and Entertainment. Originally, she cross-classified about 450 occupations by levels and groups, most of them being those listed in the MORS, but recently she has updated and increased the number by classifying all the occupations in the 1966 edition of the *Occupational Outlook Handbook,* a total of 649 occupations.

The groups dimension has usually been treated as a classificatory variable, but Roe (1956, pp. 144–145) has always viewed it as a scale: "Groups are so arranged that, with one exception, contiguous ones are more closely related than noncontiguous ones. . . . The arrangement should be thought of as circular, that is, Group VIII is related to Group I as well as to Group VII." Until recently, there were no empirical data to support this hypothesis, but there is some evidence now, although it is not conclusive, that the groups are ordered on a continuum:

1. Crites (1962a) instructed 100 male and female college and graduate students to rank the Groups by the normalized-rank method (Guilford, 1954) according to the extent that they require "relationships with people as ends in themselves as the primary work activity." The scale which resulted was anchored by Social Service at the upper extreme, followed by General Cultural, Business Contact, Organization, and Arts and Entertainment. At the lower end, Outdoor, Science, and Technology clustered together, being undifferentiable in terms of their focus upon personal interactions. In short, Crites confirmed the scalability of some of the groups, but in a different order and over a less extensive range than proposed by Roe.

2. Jones, K. J. (1965) factor-analyzed the paired comparisons of occupations representative of the eight groups, which were made by 50 summer high school students. He found that the groups were in the hypothesized order, with the exception of Arts and Entertainment, which fell between Service and Business Contact rather than between General Cultural and Service.

3. In the most comprehensive investigation thus far, Roe, Hubbard, Hutchinson, and Bateman (1966) analyzed the shifts in occupational changes from one group to another for 804 men who had been followed up for periods as long as 22 years. They predicted that, if the "neighboring" hypothesis of circularly ordered groups is plausible, then "changes [in occupations] should most often be within the same Group, next most often within contiguous Groups, and least often between the most widely separated Groups." In general, their findings supported this expectation, but they were able only partially to meet the conditions specified by Guttman (1954) as necessary for the groups to be considered a true "circumplex."[6]

The second multidimensional system, which has been devised by Super (1957), who has suggested that a third dimension be added to Roe's levels and groups.[7] This would be Enterprise, or industry, as defined by the Standard Industrial Classification Manual. The Enterprises listed in it are: Agriculture

[6] Although Osipow (1966) did not directly test the circumplex hypothesis, he did find that the first and second choices of 193 male and 182 female college freshmen, when classified within Roe's system, tended to fall in the same or adjacent categories, the implication being that related categories were ordered properly.

[7] Glick (1965b) has modified Super's system by using slightly different names for some categories and adding categories on the Enterprise dimension, but, in effect, it is essentially the same. He reports normative data on the system for 690 college graduates but no findings on interjudge agreement or overlap of categories.

and Forestry; Mining; Construction; Manufacture; Trade; Finance; Transportation; Services; and Government. Super argues that this dimension is necessary in order to provide a full description or taxonomy of occupations in the world of work. A civil engineer, for example, would be cross-classified not only by level (Professional and Managerial, regular) and group (Science), but also by the industrial setting in which he works, such as Construction or Government.

Whether any real advantages are gained from this innovation, however, has not as yet been determined. Super gives only a few examples of the system and reports no empirical data on it. Furthermore, he assumes that the Enterprise dimension is independent of the others, but this would seem to be a tenuous assumption to make. Not only are there occupations which are unique to certain enterprises, but there are enterprises (e.g., services) which largely overlap with certain groups. If there is some value in using Enterprise as a dimension for classifying or measuring occupations, then it would seem to be more consistent methodologically and conceptually to assign occupations to levels and groups *within,* rather than across, enterprises. In other words, make a separate levels and groups classification for each enterprise, and thus eliminate the problem of related dimensions.

Occupational Analysis, Classification, and Measurement as a Foundation of Vocational Psychology

The analysis, classification, and measurement of occupations is an essential substantive foundation for the study of vocational behavior and development. As the principal stimulus variables to which the latter are related, occupations must in some way be quantified: first, analysis and description and, then, classification and measurement are the procedures by which this is done. As later discussions will bring out, research on both vocational choice and vocational adjustment phenomena necessitates the use of occupational classification schemata and rating scales (see Chapters 4, 6, 7, 10, and 11).

OCCUPATIONAL DIFFERENCES IN TRAITS AND FACTORS

From the era of the Minnesota Stabilization Research Institute during the Depression years to approximately midcentury, when Ginzberg's (1951) developmental theory of vocational choice was published, the cornerstone of vocational psychology was the study of occupational differences in traits and factors. This research orientation grew naturally out of the confluence of differential psychology and occupationology and provided the practical knowledge which was so badly needed to "match men and jobs." In the search for occupational differences, many traits and factors were investigated. Of these, the ones which yielded the greatest number of differences between occupations, and which are reviewed here, were aptitudes, interests, and personality variables. Studies of occupational differences in these three traits and factors are discussed under the following topics: (1) rationale for studies of occupational differences; (2) methodology of studies of occupational differences; (3) results of studies of occupational differences; and (4) the study of occupational differences as a foundation of vocational psychology.

Rationale for Studies of Occupational Differences

The logic for studies of occupational differences in traits and factors has been more implicitly assumed than explicitly formulated. It is no more sophisticated than the old adage that "birds of a feather flock together" (Darley & Hagenah, 1955, p. 19). The "birds" are workers, the "feathers" are traits and factors, and "flock together" refers to membership in an occupational group. The underlying assumption is that, *if* birds of a feather flock together, *then* different "flocks" will have different "feathers," or, stated more formally, different occupational groups will have different traits and factors. Seldom has the question been asked concerning *why* some do and some do not. The question has been raised, however, concerning whether the members of an occupational group resemble each other in their traits and factors before they "flock together" or whether they resemble each other because of their association within the same occupation *after* they enter it.

Answers to this question vary: Some maintain that traits and factors are well developed prior to occupational entry and change very little as the result of job experiences, whereas others argue that the occupation has a significant effect upon the worker's psychological characteristics. Commenting upon interests, for example, Darley and Hagenah (1955, p. 18) state that: "The individual's occupational interests are well determined before job experience. Interest measurement merely translates existing motivations and satisfactions into the vocabulary of the world of work." In contrast, Super (1957) describes the changes which occur, particularly in the self-concept, well into the individual's work life, until approximately age 35. Unfortunately, the issue cannot be settled at present, because the relevant long-term developmental data are not available. Extrapolating from what findings have accumulated (Bloom, 1964), however, it is most likely that occupational membership differentially affects traits and factors, changing personality characteristics the most, interests next, and aptitudes the least.

Methodology of Studies of Occupational Differences

Occupational differences in aptitudes, interest, and personality have been studied in two ways: The first method is simply to compare the average scores (usually means) of the members of an occupation on some measure of traits and factors with the scores for an unselected base or norm group, usually the one on which the test or inventory was standardized. To the extent that the average of the occupational group varies from the central tendency of the reference group, the former is said to "differ" from the latter in the measured trait or factor. Given differences along several dimensions, an occupation can then be described on a so-called "psychograph," such as the one depicted in Table 2-9.[8] The second method of establishing occupational differences is to

Table 2-9. Illustrative Psychograph for an Occupation

Job: Power Machine Operator

	1	*2*	*3*	*4*	*5*	*Remarks*
1. Energy		X				
2. Rate of discharge			X			
3. Endurance		X				
4. Control	X					
5. Coordination A				X		
6. Coordination B					X	
7. Initiative		X				
8. Concentration			X			
9. Distribution (of attention)			X			
10. Persistence			X			
11. Alertness		X				
12. Associability		X				
13. Visual discrimination				X		
14. Auditory discrimination	X					
15. Tactual discrimination	X					
16. Kinaesthetic discrimination			X			
17. Space Perception				X		
18. Form Perception		X				
19. Accuracy			X			
20. Visual Memory		X				
21. Auditory Memory	X					
22. Kinaesthetic Memory		X				
23. Understanding		X				
24. Understanding Q	X					
25. Observation			X			
26. Planfulness		X				
27. Intelligence	X					
28. Intellect	X					
29. Judgment	X					
30. Logical analysis	X					
31. Language ability	X					
32. Executive	X					

[8] For discussions of the psychograph and its rationale, see Otis and Smith (1934), Trabue (1934), Rothe (1951a), and Fine (1958).

compare two or more occupations with each other. Sometimes the comparison has been on just one variable, such as intelligence in the analyses of the data from the two World War testings, but more typically it has been on several, particularly since the advent of the multifactor tests in the late 1940s.

Until recently, the analysis of occupational differences on more than one dimension presented some complex problems in assessing profile (psychograph) similarity (e.g., Cronbach & Gleser, 1953; DuMas, 1949) and was usually done visually rather than statistically. Appropriate statistical designs for such comparisons have now been developed (Block, Levine, & McNemar, 1951; Rulon, Tiedeman, Langmuir, & Tatsuoka, 1967), but, with only a few exceptions, they have not been used extensively (see discussion to follow). It would be possible to combine the two methods of analyzing occupational differences in the same study, so that an occupation might be described with reference to both other occupations and a general group; however, to the knowledge of the writer, this has not been done.

Sampling procedures in studies of occupational differences have generally been poor: they have been more a function of expediency than design. The typical sample has consisted of a small group of workers who were tested for some other purpose, usually selection, and who may or may not be representative of others in the same occupation in another part of the country. Furthermore, the work they do has seldom been described (the "Normative and Validity" section in *Personnel Psychology* is a notable exception), so that their "occupation" is known by title only and, consequently, is largely useless for comparative purposes. Still another deficiency in sampling has been the selection of occupations for comparison which are often so similar in content and requirements that it would be very difficult to differentiate the traits and factors of their members.

The most serious methodological problems in studies of occupational differences have arisen, however, in the statistical analyses which have been conducted. Foremost among these has been the violation of the homogeneity of variance assumption which underlies the *t*, critical ratio, and *F* tests and which has frequently led to the interpretation of results as being more significant than they really are (Lindquist, 1953). Another error has been the running of *t* tests on more than one variable without first making an overall *F* test and thus obtaining significant differences between some group means which may have been a function of chance sampling fluctuations rather than systematic trends in the data. Finally, it has been the rare study of occupational differences which has controlled for between-group variations in extraneous variables. As a consequence, it is usually unknown whether to attribute differences between occupations to the dissimilarity of their members on the trait or factor on which they have been compared or to some other variable which has been left uncontrolled. Because of these methodological shortcomings of occupational-difference studies, extreme caution must be exercised in drawing conclusions from their results.

Results of Studies of Occupational Differences

No attempt will be made here to review in detail each study which has been done on occupational differences. Rather, the focus of this discussion is upon summarizing what can be considered the reliable knowledge which these studies have yielded. There are at least three ways in which the findings for such a summary can be organized and presented: The first is exemplified by Roe's (1956) review, in which she classified studies according to her two-dimensional system of occupational measurement (see preceding discussion), e.g., all studies of Service occupations were summarized in Group I at their appropriate levels. This approach highlights the occupation as the unit of analysis, rather than traits and factors. The second is illustrated by Super and Crites's (1962) review of vocational tests, in which occupational differences on each test are discussed. In this case, the test is the unit of analysis, not the traits and factors it measures. The third is represented by Stewart's (1947) analysis of the AGCT data from World War II, in which she ordered occupational groups along the intelligence continuum, from high to low, according to their mean test scores. Because this approach is more *behavioral* than the others, focusing upon the trait and factors as the unit of analysis, and because it makes apparent the similarities as well as differences which exist among occupations, it was followed in collating the results of the occupational-difference studies which are discussed here under the headings of (1) aptitudes, (2) interests, and (3) personality.

Aptitudes. Data on occupational differences in *general* aptitude, or intelligence, are available from both World Wars as well as other sources and have been analyzed by several investigators (Yerkes, 1921; Fryer, 1922; Fryer & Sparling, 1934; Cattell, R. B., 1934; Harrell & Harrell, 1945; Stewart, 1947). Because the results from World War II are not only more recent, but also more extensive, i.e., based upon larger numbers of Subjects and occupations, they are cited here:

1. Harrell and Harrell (1945) have reported the mean AGCT scores for 18,782 Army Air Force enlisted men, who, as civilians, were engaged in 74 different occupations, the *N*'s for which ranged from 21 to 856. They found that the occupations could be ranked consistently by their means, but that significant differences occurred between them only within the range of approximately ± 10 occupations.

2. In a further analysis of these same data, Christensen (1946) determined the confidence intervals within which the "true" means of the occupations would fall 99 times out of 100, thus providing a baseline for identifying those

occupations with little or no overlap of their score distributions. There were only a few of these, as Caplow (1954, p. 38) notes:

"Examining the figures [confidence intervals], we find that such differences do exist but only between widely separated occupational levels. Thus the five occupations of accountant, pharmacist, watchmaker, carpenter, and farmer represent a genuine rank order in AGCT scores, and cover the range from 82.7 to 128.1 with only a few small gaps. On the other hand, none of the adjacent pairs of occupations in the list can be significantly differentiated."

3. Much the same conclusion can be drawn from Stewart's (1947) analysis of AGCT scores for 81,553 Army enlisted men in 227 occupations. She found that these occupations were distributed on the intelligence continuum as shown in Table 2-10, but that they overlapped considerably, with the occupations at the lower extreme being more variable in their scores. Thus, upon close examination of the evidence, it would appear that most occupations are more similar than they are different in the general aptitude or intelligence of their members.

With respect to occupational differences in *special* aptitudes, the accumulated research findings lead to a conclusion similar to that for general aptitude. For many years, the USES has pursued the early work on identifying differential aptitude patterns for occupations, which was initiated by such investigators as Trabue (1933), Hoppock (1934), Segel (1934), Dodge (1935), Dvorak (1935), and Stead and Shartle (1940), but its research program, which has largely involved establishing occupational aptitude patterns (OAPs) for the General Aptitude Test Battery (GATB), has met with only moderate success. Certainly, there are some OAPs which significantly discriminate not only between occupations but also between more and less successful workers within occupations. As Super (1958, p. 30) has incisively pointed out, however, the data in support of many of the GATB OAPs leave much to be desired. Less than half (44 percent) of them are based upon empirical results, but, more importantly, the *N*'s for most of the occupational groups are quite small. Since the primary statistic used in constituting OAPs has been tetrachoric correlation, and since its sampling error is large for small *N*'s, little confidence can be had in OAPs derived from such samples. Much the same can be said about the findings from Barnette's (1951a; 1951b) studies of engineers and Thorndike, R. L., and Hagen's (1959) follow-up of World War II aviation cadets. From his recent review of the validity of occupational aptitude tests, Ghiselli (1966, p. 111) has summarized the situation as follows:

> Two properties of the organization and grouping of jobs seem clear. First of all, in terms of their requirements jobs are not organized into clear-cut and separate groups.... Second, jobs which superficially appear to be similar in terms of nature of work may have quite different ability requirements, and jobs which appear to be quite different may have very similar requirements.

Table 2-10. Occupations Classified by AGCT Scores *(Stewart, 1947, p. 17)*

-2.5σ 85.3	-2.0σ 89.9	-1.5σ 94.5	-1.0σ 99.1	$-.5\sigma$ 103.7
Teamster	Marine fireman	Tractor driver	Welder, electric arc	Not elsewhere classified
Miner	Laundry machine operator	Painter, general	Plumber	Machinist's helper
farm worker	Laborer	Foundryman	Switchman, railway	Foreman, labor
Lumberjack	Barber	Animation artist	Machine operator	Locomotive fireman
	Shoe repairman	Hospital orderly	Hammersmith	Entertainer
	Jackhammer operator	Baker	Student, high school, agricultural	Meat cutter
	Groundman, Telephone, Telegraph, or power	Packer, supplies	Automotive mechanic	Student, high school, vocational
	Section hand, railway	Sewing machine operator	Blacksmith	Cabinetmaker
		Truck driver, heavy	Welder, acetylene	Airplane engine mechanic
		Painter, automobile	Bricklayer	Heat treater
		Hoist operator	Blaster or powderman	Fire fighter
		Construction machine operator	Small craft operator	Engineering aide
		Horsebreaker	Lineman, power	Construction equipment mechanic
		Tailor	Packing case maker	Optician
		Stonemason	Carpenter, general	Packer, high explosives
		Crane operator	Pipe fitter	Petroleum storage technician
		Upholsterer	Electric truck driver	Pattern maker, wood
		Cook	Highway maintenance man	Electrician, automotive
		Concrete-mixer operator	Automobile serviceman	Coppersmith
		Truck driver, light	Rigger	Ship fitter
		Stationary fireman	Woodworking machine operator	Sheet metal worker
		Warehouseman	Chauffeur	Electroplater
		Gas and oil man	Motorcyclist	Instrument repairman, electrical
		Forging-press operator	Burner, acetylene	Steam fitter
		Longshoreman		Diesel mechanic
		Well driller		Carpenter, ship
				Bandsman, snare drum
				Lithographic pressman
				Electric motor repairman
				Shop maintenance mechanic
				Job pressman
				Riveter, pneumatic
				Power shovel operator
				Photographic technician, aerial
				Brakeman, railway
				Automobile body repairman
				Tire rebuilder
				Utility repairman
				Boilermaker
				Foreman, automotive repair shop
				Salvage man
				Structural steel worker
				Welder, combination
				Welder, spot
				Seaman
				Engineman, operating
				Foreman, construction
				Millwright

Why are the findings on special aptitude patterns for occupations so inconclusive and variable? Undoubtedly, one reason is that the data have been less than adequate—small *N*'s, few cross-validations, biased sampling of occupational groups—but, more than this, there may be another reason which has nothing to do with methodological considerations. Implicit in the research of

Mean *108.3*	*+.5 σ* *112.9*	*+1.0 σ* *117.5*	*+1.5 σ* *122.1*	*+2.0 σ* *126.7*	*+2.5 σ* *131.3*
Carpenter, heavy construction	Switchboard installer, telephone, and telegraph, repairman	Bookkeeper, general	Writer	Accountant	
Dispatcher, motor vehicle	Cashier	Chief clerk	Student, civil engineering	Student, mechanical engineering	
Gunsmith	Stock record clerk	Stenographer	Statistical clerk	Personnel clerk	
Musician, instrumental	Clerk, general	Pharmacist	Student, chemical engineering	Student, medicine	
Tool maker	Radio repairman	Typist	Teacher	Chemist	
Nurse, practical	Purchasing agent	Draftsman	Lawyer	Student, electrical engineering	
Photographer, portrait	Survey and instrument man	Chemical laboratory assistant	Student, business or public administration		
Photolithographer	Physics laboratory assistant	Draftsman, mechanical	Auditor		
Rodman and chainman, surveying	Stock control clerk	Investigator	Student, dentistry		
Airplane fabric and dope worker	Manager, production	Reporter			
Multilith or multigraph operator	Boilermaker, layer-out	Tool designer			
Shipping clerk	Radio operator	Tabulating machine operator			
Printer	Linotype operator	Addressing-embossing machine operator			
Steward	Student, mechanics	Traffic rate clerk			
Foreman, warehouse	Salesman	Clerk-typist			
Bandsman, cornet or trumpet	Athletic instructor	Postal clerk			
Instrument repairman, non-electrical	Store manager	Bookkeeping machine operator			
Boring mill operator	Installer-repairman, telephone and telegraph	Meat or dairy inspector			
Projectionist, motion picture	Motorcycle mechanic	Photographic laboratory technician			
Dental laboratory technician	Dispatcher clerk, crew	Teletype operator			
Laboratory technician, V-mail or microfilm	Tool dresser	Student, sociology			
Foreman, machine shop	File clerk				
Stock clerk	Embalmer				
Painter, sign	Brake inspector, railway				
Machinist	Airplane and engine mechanic				
Photographer, aerial	Shop clerk				
Engine lathe operator	Artist				
Parts clerk, automotive	Band leader				
Cook's helper	Photographer				
Railway mechanic, general	Geologist				
Office machine serviceman	Airplane engine service mechanic				
Student, high school, commercial	Cable splicer, telephone and telegraph				
Electrician, airplane	Surveyor				
Student, manual arts	Student, high school, academic				
Policeman	Blueprinter or photostat operator				
Sales clerk					
Electrician					
Lineman, telephone and telegraph					
Watch repairman					
Receiving or shipping checker					
Car mechanic, railway					
Toolroom keeper					
Refrigeration mechanic					
Camerman, motion picture					
Telephone operator					
Hatch tender					

special aptitudes has been the assumption that *all* occupational groups should differ from each other *regardless* of their general aptitude levels. In other words, the expectation has been that high-level occupations on the intelligence continuum, for example, such as accountant and lawyer, would have differential aptitude patterns, as would other occupations at the middle and lower levels. That this assumption may be untenable, however, is well illustrated by the data in Table 2-11, which comes from the manual (1966, p. 5–44) for the Differential Aptitude Tests (DAT). It reveals that the special aptitudes measured by this battery manifest differential patterns, i.e., variability in scores from one subtest to another, only for occupations which are in the middle range of general aptitude. Thus, Supervisors-Foremen, who are within one-half sigma of the mean in Stewart's (1947) Army data (Table 2-10), have several high and low points on the DAT (e.g., CSA, high; Sent., low), whereas the profiles of Engineers and Laborers, who are at the upper and lower extremes of intelligence, respectively, are considerably flatter (i.e., have less score scatter). In short, possibly because the *g* factor in ability is more prominent than group factors at the high and low levels of intelligence, occupational differences in special aptitudes may be found only at the middle level of intelligence, and then only between quite dissimilar occupations.

Interests. The extent to which occupational groups differ in their interests is largely a matter of the point of reference which is used to compare and con-

Table 2-11. Percentile Equivalents of Average Scores on the DAT for Students Tested in 1947 and Classified by Their Occupational Fields in 1955 *(DAT Manual, p. 5–44)*

		Percentiles							
Group	*N*	*VR*	*NA*	*AR*	*SR*	*MR*	*CSA*	*Spell.*	*Sent.*
MEN									
Engineers	22	84	89	86	81	86	74	79	81
Draftsmen	21	47	47	50	67	53	61	44	51
Technicians	49	42	45	45	48	53	51	37	34
Businessmen	21	57	58	54	36	45	64	58	55
Salesmen	39	56	49	58	50	52	55	55	49
Clerks	46	39	41	46	50	43	45	47	46
Supervisors-foremen	21	43	44	43	52	46	69	48	35
Factory workers	37	43	27	34	52	54	28	29	32
Building tradesman	21	32	33	45	50	38	43	35	27
Laborers	24	38	21	28	29	35	32	36	25
Students (current)	107	76	74	72	62	63	68	72	76
Military personnel	132	67	67	63	64	64	58	64	66
WOMEN									
Teachers	49	81	84	81	74	71	73	72	82
Nurses	28	78	75	73	77	64	58	70	66
Stenographers	126	58	56	54	52	52	61	67	56
Clerks	198	46	45	48	48	49	52	46	40
Housewives	277	57	50	55	59	58	52	54	52

trast them. In the process of constructing interest scales for women's occupations, Strong (1943, Chapter 21) became aware of the fact that different women-in-general groups yielded different occupational keys. That is, the correlations among the scales were different when the composition of the base group was changed. Pursuing the study of this phenomenon in the preliminary work on the 1938 revision of the SVIB, Strong was able to demonstrate that the more *dissimilar* the point-of-reference group is in skill level and socioeconomic status, the more *similar* occupations at the same level and status are in their interests. [See Darley and Hagenah (1955, pp. 23–24) for an excellent discussion of this finding.] For example, if the men-in-general group is representative of the average semiskilled worker, then the occupations of accountant and engineer will be more alike in their interests than if the men-in-general group is typical of business and professional workers. This relationship between occupational level and interest differentiation posed the further problem, first identified by Darley (1941), of what the lower limits of occupational differences in interests are. In other words, at which level can occupational groups no longer be differentiated from men in general? Research by Clark, K. E. (1961; Clark, K. E., & Campbell, 1965) has established that the interests of several semiskilled occupations can be contrasted with those of a tradesmen-in-general group, but below this level little differentiation can probably be made between occupations. The measurement of preferences for different job duties and tasks, however, such as precise-approximate, sedentary–bodily active, routine-varied, appears possible at the unskilled level (Long, 1952).

Yet even when an appropriate reference group for differentiating the interests of occupations is used, the similarities among occupational groups are much greater than the dissimilarities. Strong (1943, p. 46) has pointed out that: "Because research regarding interests has been so largely concerned with group differences, it has not been realized that likenesses among the interests of individuals are far more striking than differences. All groups so far studied agree very well in their interests." The common impression that occupations differ markedly in interests has probably stemmed from the fact that interest inventories, particularly the SVIB, have been designed to capitalize upon what differences there are among occupations, not to reflect their similarities. As was mentioned previously in the discussion of the dimensions of interests, there are only a few factors which discriminate between occupations, and the most prominent of these is the bipolar one of Things versus People. Clark, K. E., and Campbell (1965) have reported that the lower-level, nonprofessional occupations assessed by the Minnesota Vocational Interest Inventory (MVII) are also well represented by a "bipolar" dimension, anchored at one end by a cluster of "white-collar, clerical" jobs (e.g., retail sales clerk, stock clerk, printer) and at the other by a cluster of "blue-collar, mechanical" jobs (e.g., truck mechanic, sheet-metal worker, plumber). Within the clusters, the interest scales are intercorrelated approximately .60, and between the clusters the correlation is −.72. If these *r*'s were corrected for unreliability, they would be high enough that any one of the MVII scales could be substituted for all of the others, with very little loss of information. Thus, the weight of the evidence indicates that, at both the professional-managerial and skilled-semiskilled levels, there are only a few occupational differences in interests.

Personality. One of the most venerable, but least well-substantiated, hypotheses in vocational psychology has been that occupations differ in the personalities of their members. The reason that this hypothesis has been so viable is probably twofold: First, widely held cultural stereotypes of occupations, such as the meek accountant and the aggressive salesman, tend to support its credibility; and, second, *some* significant differences between occupations on measures of personality have been found. As with studies of occupational differences in aptitudes and interests, however, those of personality indicate that occupations are much more similar than they are different. In summarizing the accumulated research through approximately 1960, Super and Crites (1962, pp. 516–517) observe that: "Although it has been assumed that there should be linear correlations between certain personality traits and adjustment in some occupations—for example, social dominance and selling, submissiveness and bookkeeping, introversion and research or writing—such relationships have in fact been found in very few occupations." This conclusion has been documented with reviews of studies in which both objective and projective tests of personality have been used (Super, 1949; Roe, 1956; Super & Crites, 1962). For example, with respect to research on the Minnesota Multiphasic Personality Inventory (MMPI), Super and Crites (1962, p. 536) state that: "Occupational differences are either nonexistent or, when present, questionable because of too few cases and too great variation within groups. . . ." Similarly, regarding the Edwards Personal Preference Schedule (EPPS), they note that "there is no knowledge of which patterns are related to either occupational field or level. . . ." (Super & Crites, 1962, p. 555). Negative findings have also been typical with the Rorschach. From an analysis of several occupational groups, Rieger (1949) concluded that they could not be characterized by any one Rorschach pattern of response, as did Roe (1953a) concerning the scientists she studied (see Chapter 10). More recently, Roe and Mierzwa (1960, p. 287) have pointed out again that studies of occupations with the Rorschach are "exploratory or discouraging, and anyway few in number."

Why is it that the evidence for the "occupational personality" hypothesis is not more positive? The most parsimonious, and probably the most likely, explanation is, of course, that there is no systematic relationship between personality and occupational membership. What few significant differences have been found can be attributed to chance factors or sampling errors. Even if it is argued that there is a low-order association between personality and occupation, it is specific to only certain measuring instruments and certain occupational groups and has little or no generality and hence negligible theoretical relevance. It seems much more reasonable to abandon the hypothesis, therefore, than to persist in rationalizing the large number of studies which have failed to support it. Drawing this conclusion should not be interpreted to mean, however, that personality is not related to other vocational behaviors. In Chapters 6 and 8, evidence will be presented and discussed which indicates that personality bears relationships, albeit complex ones, to both vocational choice and adjustment.

Occupational Differences in Traits and Factors as a Foundation of Vocational Psychology

Implicit in the foregoing discussion of the research on occupational differences in aptitudes, interests, and personality has been the conclusion that this approach to the analysis and understanding of vocational behavior has little to offer. Not only is it conceptually barren, but it has been predicated upon what the empirical evidence has shown to be a largely false premise: that occupations are more different than they are alike. In fact, the contradictory of this proposition is more often true, and for good reason, when the formation and nature of occupational groups are analyzed. Not only do individuals choose occupations for myriad reasons, but occupations select individuals for at least as many considerations (Blau, Gustad, Jessor, Parnes, & Wilcock, 1956; see Chapter 3). There are very few uniform standards or criteria for occupational membership which are applicable to more than a handful of occupations. The only qualifying trait and factor which might be singled out is a minimum degree of intelligence for some of the higher-level occupations, but even this requirement fluctuates from time to time, with the pressures of supply and demand, so that there is often considerable within-group variability in even such select occupations as accountant, engineer, and lawyer (Stewart, 1947).

It is not really surprising, therefore, that the heterogeneity of the workers within most occupational groups on measures of traits and factors like aptitudes, interests, and especially personality is so great that it, in effect, cancels out most of the differences between the groups. It cannot be denied, however, that there are some real (statistically significant) differences which exist between some occupations. To take cognizance of these and their possible value in the study of vocational behavior and development, but also to put them in proper perspective as a foundation of vocational psychology, it is proposed that occupational differences in traits and factors be considered simply as *correlates of occupational membership*. In other words, it would be understood that the workers of a few occupational groups, but not necessarily most, have certain distinctive traits and factors and that allowance should be made for them, either as independent or control variables, in designing research on choice and adjustment phenomena associated with the occupations under study.

II
THE PROCESS OF VOCATIONAL CHOICE

3
THEORIES OF VOCATIONAL CHOICE

In this chapter, we shall review some of the theories of vocational choice which have been formulated to explain *how* individuals choose occupations and *why* they select and eventually enter different occupations. The theories can be broadly classified as nonpsychological, psychological, and general. Within each of these classifications, the theories can be further differentiated according to their major characteristics and emphases. The discussion which follows considers the nonpsychological theories of vocational choice first, then summarizes the psychological theories, and concludes with a survey of the general theories. Evaluations of the theories will be made in Chapter 14, after the research on vocational choice and adjustment which is relevant to them has been reviewed.

NONPSYCHOLOGICAL THEORIES OF VOCATIONAL CHOICE

The nonpsychological theories of vocational choice are those which attribute choice phenomena to the operation of some system which is external to the individual. In other words, in these theories the condition or characteristics of the individual, e.g., his intelligence, interests, personality traits, are *not* considered to be either directly or indirectly (as mediating variables) related to choice. The individual enters an occupation solely because of the operation of environmental factors. There are three types of such factors which may determine his course of action: (1) chance or contingency factors, (2) the laws of supply and demand, and (3) the folkways and institutions of society. The theories which deal with the effects of each of these factors upon choice are the accident, economic, and sociological theories of vocational choice, respectively.

The Accident Theory of Vocational Choice

The accident theory of vocational choice is largely a popular theory: it is the layman's explanation of how he entered his occupation. In answer to the question "How did you happen to become what you are?" he responds: "It was an accident" or "It was just by chance." By "accident" or "chance," he means that he did not *deliberately* intend to enter his present occupation. It came about as the result of a series of unforeseen circumstances or events. More formally, "chance" refers to experiences "which are unplanned so far as the individuals themselves are concerned" (Miller, D. C., & Form, 1951, p. 661), or it means "an unplanned exposure to a powerful stimulus" (Ginzberg et al., 1951, p. 19). According to these definitions, chance experiences would include the unexpected inheritance of a large sum of money, the outbreak of a war and compulsory military service, the contraction of a serious disease, or the failure of a business venture due to depressed economic conditions. In other words, chance factors are the fortuitous, unplanned, unpredicted events which affect a person's vocational choice.

They are to be distinguished from "contingency" factors which are predictable and which can be taken into consideration when the individual plans his vocational future. Such characteristics and conditions of the individual as his intelligence and socioeconomic status are contingency rather than chance factors, because their relationships to vocational choice are known (Chapter 6). Other contingency factors include the availability of appropriate training facilities to prepare for an occupation, the extent of familial financial support during the period of training, the prospects for admission to a training institution, and the anticipated occupational opportunities available after training is completed. Even the individual's future job assignments, rate of advancement, and time of retirement can be predicted with fair accuracy, *if* data on these variables in his occupation have been gathered. In fact, Super (1957, p. 278) goes as far as to say that: "Given sufficient knowledge, there is no such thing as chance." His qualification that there be "sufficient knowledge," however, is exactly the criterion which differentiates chance and contingency factors; the former are unpredictable precisely because nothing is known about them. Consequently, it would seem parsimonious to retain both concepts.

Some social scientists have proposed that the accident theory of the layman is a plausible explanation of vocational choice. Two occupational sociologists, Miller, D. C., and Form (1951, p. 660), analyzed the occupational backgrounds of a large number of young people and concluded that:

> One characteristic is outstanding in the experience of most of the case histories that have been cited. In their quest of a lifework there has been a vast amount of floundering, and chance experiences appear to have affected choices more than anything else. No single motivating influence underlies the majority of the choices made. It is the compounding of various experiences and influences which has finally crystallized into a *wish* for a certain occupation. Chance ex-

> periences undoubtedly explain the process by which most occupational choices are made.

Caplow (1954, p. 214), another sociologist, places a greater emphasis upon the role of other factors in vocational choice (see the section on sociological theories in this chapter), but he also observes: "Then too, error and accident often play a larger part than the subject himself is willing to concede." Thus, accident theory is an explanation of vocational choice phenomena which has gained considerable acceptance among laymen and theorists alike and which needs to be evaluated for its usefulness as a theory.[1]

Economic Theories of Vocational Choice

Whereas the accident theory of vocational choice begins with the individual and examines the chance factors which influence his selection of an occupation, economic theories start with a consideration of the distribution of workers in various occupations of the economy and attempt to explain why they differ in the numbers of individuals which choose and enter them. It is a well-established economic fact that some occupations are more heavily populated than others. For example, of the total male civilian labor force in 1950, 38.6 percent were either craftsmen or operatives, whereas only 7.3 percent were professionals (Thomas, L. G., 1956, p. 35). How can these discrepancies between occupations be accounted for? What factors affect the choices of individuals in the labor market so that they decide to enter some occupations more often than others? This is the problem with which economic theories of choice have dealt over the years.

The classical economists of the eighteenth century, led by Smith, Senior, and Mill, maintained that it is the "net advantage" which accrues to the individual from entering an occupation which is the determining factor in his choice. Adam Smith (1937, p. 99) expressed this viewpoint as follows:

> The whole of the advantages and disadvantages of the different employments of labour and stock must, in the same neighborhood, be

[1] In discussing accident theories of vocational choice, Ginzberg et al. (1951, p. 18) state:

> A related contention [to accident theory] argues that valid generalizations can only be derived from statistical analyses of the decisions of large numbers of individuals. Such an approach implicitly denies that it is possible to assess the multitudinous factors that affect the decision-making of specific individuals. Statistical analyses can only contribute to an understanding of broad tendencies that result from the discrete actions of large numbers of people.

As Tiedeman (1952) has correctly pointed out, however, statistical analyses of vocational choice are not evidence for or against any theory, but only *methods* for summarizing and drawing inferences from data.

> either perfectly equal or continually tending to equality. If, in the same neighborhood, there was any employment evidently either more or less advantageous than the rest, so many people would crowd into it in the one case, and so many would desert it in the other, that its advantages would soon return to the level of the other employments. This at least would be the case in a society where things were left to follow their natural course, where there was perfect liberty, and where every man was perfectly free both to choose what occupation he thought proper, and to change it as often as he thought proper. Every man's interest would prompt him to seek the advantageous, and to shun the disadvantageous employment.

In other words, given complete freedom of choice, which is the basic assumption upon which this theory rests, the individual selects that occupation which he thinks will bring him the greatest advantages. He weighs and balances the merits and shortcomings of the available "employments" and chooses the one with the greatest net advantage to him. Traditionally, net advantage has been interpreted to mean the best income or wage: workers enter those occupations which pay the most and avoid those which pay the least. The occupations which pay the most are those which have scarcities of labor, and those which pay the least are those which have surfeits of labor. Thus, there emerges the classical economic principle that the occupational distribution of workers in the labor market is a function of supply and demand as reflected in income differentials between occupations.

As has been mentioned, classical theory assumes that the individual has perfect freedom of choice, that there are no restrictions upon his selection of an occupation. That this assumption finds only scant support in real labor markets, however, has been pointed out by neoclassical economists who have attempted to apply the traditional theory to present-day conditions. When freedom of choice exists, the distribution of workers and income in occupations should be equal, or at least show a tendency toward equality, since movement of workers into undersupplied, well-paid occupations should have the effect of raising wages in surfeited, poorly paid occupations. But this has not happened: the occupational distribution of workers and income is not equal.

Clark, H. F. (1931) has argued that there are two factors which have produced inequalities between occupations in the modern economy and which have made classical theory inapplicable today. One of the factors is the ignorance on the part of the individual about the relative advantages and disadvantages of different occupations. According to Clark, the individual cannot make a free choice of an occupation, because he lacks the necessary information about the alternatives which are available to him. In other words, his choice is determined not only by supply and demand in the labor market, as proposed by classical theory, but also by what he knows about occupations.

The other factor which restricts freedom of choice is the cost of the prerequisite training to qualify for occupations which demand higher-level skills. Because many individuals do not have the financial resources to pursue the technical training or higher education necessary for work at the skilled level or above, the possible number of occupations from which they can choose is limited to those at the lower skill levels. Clark identifies two factors, then, which operate to influence vocational choice in addition to the supply-and-demand variables posited by classical theory: (1) the individual's information about occupations and (2) the cost of education and training.

Because of some of the apparent difficulties encountered by classical theory in accounting for vocational choices solely by the principle of supply and demand, recent theorists have followed Clark's lead and have emphasized other factors as the significant ones in determining the distribution of workers in occupations. A few have accepted accident theory as a partial explanation of occupational selection. For example, Parnes (1954, p. 156) has concluded from the results of a study by Myers and Schultz that "fully a third [of the sample workers] had not 'chosen' the job in any real sense, but had either drifted into it or had taken it because they could find no other." Some have observed that individuals choose an occupation primarily because of their desire for security and sustained employment rather than because one job offers more attractive wages as compared with another. Others have said that choices are based upon ignorance, as Clark maintained, or "personal reasons," or irrational considerations made out of habit rather than deliberate calculation. Most contemporary economic theorists, however, regardless of their orientation and the specific factors which they consider important in choice determination, endorse the proposition that the selection of an occupation is a function of a number of variables, not just labor supply and demand or income differentials. Illustrative of this current emphasis is L. G. Thomas's (1956) analysis of (1) income, (2) occupational appeal (prestige), and (3) occupational qualifications (worker traits) in relation to the occupational distribution. On the assumption that these three variables are independent of each other, he proposes that they are the major determinants of vocational choice.

Although economic theorists agree that choice depends upon the operation of several factors in the labor market, they disagree on whether classical theory is consistent with such a proposition. The predominant position, which is based upon the interpretation of classical theory as encompassing only the law of supply and demand, is that it fails to account adequately for the data on occupational distribution and labor movement. Rottenberg (1956, p. 184; italics in original) points out, however, that: "the early economists said that it was '*the whole of the advantages and disadvantages*' in an employment that would be equal.... They did *not* say *wages* are equal in all employments."

From this statement of classical theory, which greatly increases its comprehensiveness, Rottenberg argues that it includes all factors which influence choice rather than only relative occupational incomes. Also, he makes the observation relevant to Clark's formulation, that classical theory was intended to apply only to *ideal* labor markets, not real markets in which the classical economists recognized that there are certain restrictions upon the individual's freedom to choose an occupation. Rebuttals to Rottenberg's defense of classical theory (Lampman, 1956; Lester, 1956) have dealt with certain minor points in his argument, but none of them has questioned his central thesis that the "whole of the advantages and disadvantages" of an occupation includes not only wages but also other factors. Given this interpretation of classical theory, it probably best represents, as a sort of synthesis, the various economic theories of vocational choice which have been formulated.

Cultural and Sociological Theories of Vocational Choice

According to industrial and occupational sociologists, the major factor in the determination of an individual's vocational choice is the impact of the culture and society in which he lives upon the goals and objectives he learns to value. In selecting an occupation, the individual is more or less directly influenced by several social systems, as shown in Figure 3-1 and as described by Super and Bachrach (1957, p. 104) as follows:

> The individual confronted with . . . choice decisions may be viewed as occupying the center of several concentric circles which represent the social systems with which he interacts. These systems are instrumental in his decisions and choices. The outer circle represents general American cultural variables (free enterprise, American democracy, Western values, American mores). Moving inward we come to the subcultural forces which exert themselves on the individual (class values, attitudes, customs). The next circle represents community variables (peer relationships, ethnic groupings, religious influences, social contacts). Finally, most directly impinging on the individual are the organizational settings in which he is operating at any given time: his home, school, family, church, and so on.

Each of these levels of culture and society affects the individual's vocational choice in a somewhat different way and in varying degrees of importance (Lipsett, 1962).

Culture. The broad cultural milieu in which a person is raised has the least direct effect upon his specific vocational decisions, such as choice of high school curriculum or place of work, but it does have a pervasive influence upon his freedom to choose. In the highly formalized and institutionalized cultures of

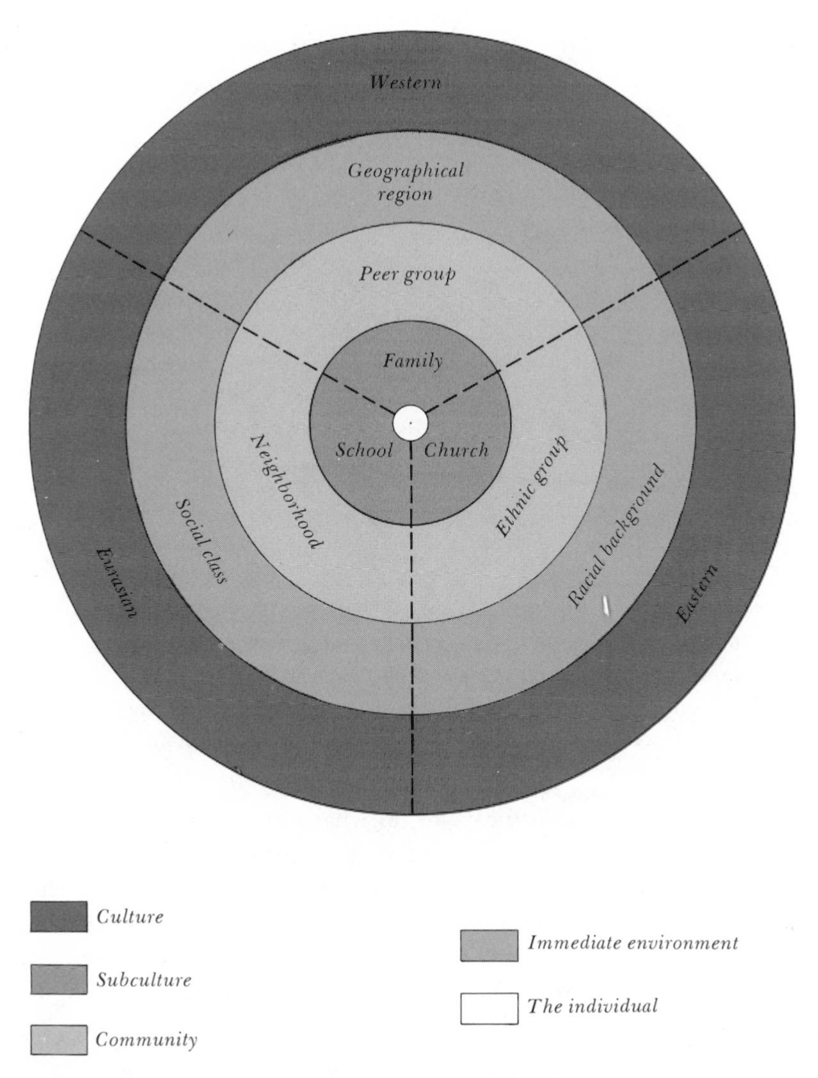

Figure 3-1. Cultural and social systems hypothesized to be related to vocational choice.

the Middle and Far East, there has traditionally been little or no freedom of vocational choice.[2] Much as the woman's marriage is arranged for her by the family, the man's career is chosen for him by his father. Although there are some variations, the son usually follows the occupation of his father, whether

[2] Koyama (1931) notes, however, that in the modern era there are fewer hereditary occupations in Japan than ever before, and this trend has most likely been accelerated since the end of World War II with the Americanization of many aspects of the Japanese economy and culture.

the socioeconomic position of the family is high or low. In Russia, where the state controls the economy and hence the distribution of workers in occupations, the individual has little to say about the career he wants to follow. Young people are assigned to schools and training programs in accordance with their talents and skills. The state decides for the individual what he will be and do. Similarly, in England at the age of 11 the school child takes a series of tests which will determine whether he will be admitted to an academic school or whether he will have to attend a vocational school. If he is fortunate enough to have ability above a certain cutoff point, he has the opportunity to obtain a higher education and most likely to enter one of the professions. If he falls below the critical score on his tests, however, he knows he will probably have to pursue a career in the less prestigeful and less remunerative lower-level occupations.

In the United States, the freedom to choose one's work is considerably greater than it is in many other countries and cultures, but it is not as great as the so-called "tradition of opportunity" would imply. As Chinoy (1952, p. 453) notes:

> The United States is widely pictured as the "land of promise," where golden opportunities beckon to everyone without regard to his original station in life. The Horatio Alger sagas of "little tykes who grow into big tycoons," it is asserted, "truly express a common-place of American experience."

In actuality, there is far less opportunity to do what one wants in the world of work than such success stories might suggest. The consequence is that the credo of the culture finds tenuous confirmation in the experiences of the marketplace. The hope of "getting ahead" only too often leads to vocational choices which are unrealistic in terms of opportunities for employment and advancement. Thus, the culture promises greater freedom of choice than it provides.

Subculture. Within a culture, there are several subcultures which impinge upon vocational decision making. The most important of these is the social class to which an individual belongs. Based largely upon the principal breadwinner's source and amount of income, social-class position comes to bear upon a person's vocational choice in many ways. In general, the individual learns that certain kinds of work are more socially desirable than others. If he lives in a neighborhood on the "right side of the tracks" in a relatively new house with three or more bedrooms, and if his father wears a business suit to work and drives his own late model car, then he most likely has acquired the attitude that clean, white-collar, mental work is preferable to dirty, blue-denim, manual work. He tends to eliminate as career alternatives occupations which his counterpart on the "wrong side of the tracks" considers possible vocations.

According to some sociological theories, the individual's social-class consciousness, the identification he develops with the group of which he is a member (Centers, 1949), is directly related to the vocational aspirations he sets for himself (Sewell, Haller, & Straus, 1957). Hollingshead (1949, p. 285) writes:

> The pattern of vocational choices corresponds roughly with the job patterns associated with each class in the adult's work world. Therefore, we believe that the adolescent's ideas of desirable jobs are a reflection of their experiences in the class and family culture complexes.

Similarly, Lipset, Bendix, and Malm (1962, p. 303) conclude:

> The importance of family background for the education and careers of [young people] is seen in the characteristic cumulation of advantages and disadvantages. Vocational advice from many sources is more often given to those individuals whose families can afford to keep them in school. It also seems to be more realistic and helpful than such advice as is given to the children of working-class parents. The effect of these and other background factors may be discerned in an individual's choice of his first job.

Community. Closer to the everyday experiences of the individual than either the culture in which he lives or the social class of which he is a member are his ethnic group, if he belongs to a distinct one, his neighborhood, and his peers. Particularly his peers, his age-mates in the neighborhood and school, may often have a profound effect upon his vocational choice. McGuire and Blocksma (1953, p. 8) have identified three clusters of age-mate roles which may influence a young person's vocational decision making: First, there is the "top crowd," which comes primarily from the higher social strata and which includes the "wheels" of the peer culture, their "spokes" or followers, and the "brains," who are respected for their intellectual prowess but not genuinely accepted as in-group members. Most of the top crowd plan to obtain a college education and enter a professional or managerial-level occupation. Second, there are the "outsiders" who are largely from the "common man" class and who have little connection with the school and its activities, other than through athletics. This group wants "out of school" as soon as possible and rejects further education in favor of work or marriage. Finally, there are the "outcasts," a group which is comprised of the "drips" and "dopes," who strive to be in the top crowd but seldom gain more than marginal membership, and the "wild ones," who are "getting a reputation" by breaking school and societal rules and regulations. The members of this group typically drop out of school and enter the service, flounder from one job to another, or take up a life of crime.

These peer groups and the roles they impart are related to the social-class structure, but it is possible for an individual to move across class lines and join the group of another social stratum. Depending upon the role which he plays and the status which he attains in his peer group, he may learn the attitudes and values of a social class different from his own. If this happens, then his vocational choice may be much more a function of his age-mate associations than his social-class affiliation (Hollingshead, 1949). For example, an upper-class "wheel" may become an "outcast" and enlist in the Army rather than go to college, or a lower–middle-class "brain" may excel in school and adopt the ambitions of the "top crowd" for a professional career.

School. Next to the family, probably the most important agent of socialization, and of *vocationalization* (Crites, 1958), is the school. Through the school, as Miller and Form (1951) note, the individual acquires a system of values which directly influences his vocational choice. Sometimes the values he learns facilitate his decision making, as when he attempts to plan for the future rather than letting it take care of itself, but other times they pose conflicts, as when he aspires to a socially approved higher-level occupation but lacks the ability to qualify for it. The educational system also presumably influences the individual's vocational choice because it limits the choice he makes. Caplow (1954, p. 216) observes that it does this in two ways: "first, by forcing the student who embarks upon a long course of training to renounce other careers which also require extensive training; second, by excluding from training and eventually from the occupations themselves those students who lack either the intellectual qualities (such as intelligence, docility, aptitude) or the social characteristics (such as ethnic background, wealth, appropriate conduct, previous education) which happen to be required." In so limiting the individual's choices, the school exerts another influence upon his decision making: it provides him with a structure which supports him and gives him direction while he is deliberating about his future. Ginzberg et al. (1951, pp. 204–205) draw attention to the school's "specified curriculum embracing certain areas of choice, its technique of grading the work of students, the formal prerequisites which it lays down for promotion and graduation, [and] the prizes which it awards." Thus, through its organization, the time schedule it sets, and the values it transmits, the school may become an important determinant of vocational choice.

Family. Several vocational psychologists have suggested that the family plays a fundamental part in the shaping of vocational choices (Friend & Haggard,

1948; Ginzberg et al., 1951; Super, 1953), but only recently has there been an articulate and comprehensive statement of what the possible relationships of family factors to choice are. The hypothesized relationships, as outlined by Roe (1957; Roe & Siegelman, 1964), are depicted in Figure 3-2. Within the family circle, the psychological atmosphere may vary between being warm and being cold, depending upon the parents' attitudes toward their children. The predominant attitudes they may express are (1) acceptance, (2) concentration, or (3) avoidance, with the variations of each of these indicated in the "circumplex," i.e., casual acceptance, loving acceptance, overprotective concentration, etc. If the attitudes of the parents are warm and accepting, Roe predicts that their children will develop a major orientation of moving toward others and choose occupations which involve contact with people as the primary

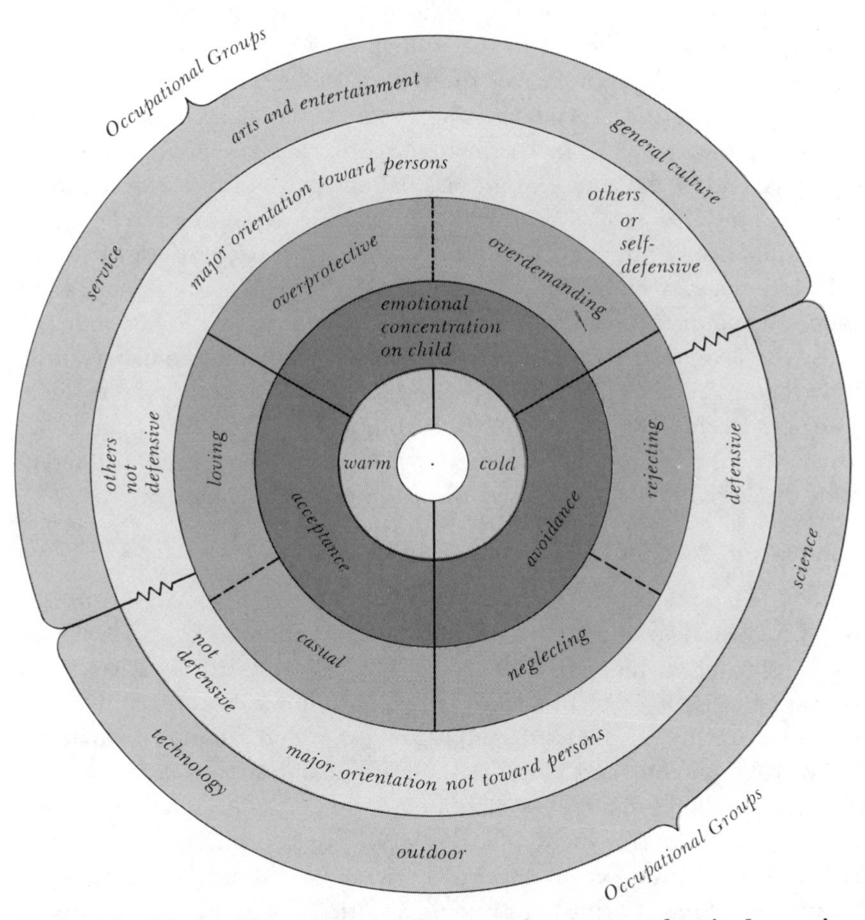

Figure 3-2. Relationships among family atmosphere, parental attitudes, major orientation toward persons, and vocational choice as proposed by Roe (1957, p. 216).

focus of their work. Examples of such occupations are those in the social-service and business-contact fields. If the attitudes of the parents indicate an emotional concentration upon their children, Roe states that their orientation may be more toward persons than not, but that they will choose occupations which minimize close contacts with others, such as those in the arts and entertainment and general cultural fields. Finally, if the parents avoid their children, either through rejection or neglect, Roe proposes that the children will develop a major orientation toward activities which do not involve others and will choose occupations in the technology, outdoor, and scientific fields.

PSYCHOLOGICAL THEORIES OF VOCATIONAL CHOICE

In contrast to the emphasis of nonpsychological theories of vocational choice upon the circumstances external to the individual which determine his selection of an occupation, psychological theories of choice focus more upon the individual per se as the crucial variable in the vocational decision-making process. These theories have in common the assumption that the individual has some freedom in the choice of an occupation, i.e., he can exert at least a modicum of control over his vocational future, whereas the nonpsychological theories do not accord him this latitude. This is not to say, however, that the psychological theories maintain that vocational choice is a capricious affair and cannot be predicted. Rather, they posit that choice is determined, but primarily by the characteristics or functioning of the individual and only indirectly by the environment in which he lives. There are four major types of psychological theories of choice, (1) trait-and-factor, (2) psychodynamic, (3) developmental, and (4) decision-making, each of which emphasizes a different aspect of the individual's behavior as the basic factor in choice.

Trait-and-factor Theories of Vocational Choice

Based upon the psychology of individual differences and the analysis of occupations (Chapter 2), trait-and-factor theories of vocational choice emphasize the relationship of an individual's personal characteristics to his selection of an occupation. The logic of this viewpoint is as follows: because individuals differ in their aptitudes, interests, and personalities and because occupations require varying amounts and kinds of these traits and factors, different individuals choose to enter different occupations. In his early formulation of what has become trait-and-factor theory, Parsons (1909, p. 5) explicated a three-step process through which a person goes in choosing a vocation: "(1) a clear understanding of [himself], [his] aptitudes, abilities, interests, ambitions, resources, limitations, and their causes; (2) a knowledge of the requirements and conditions of success, advantages and disadvantages, compensation, opportunities, and prospects in different lines of work; and (3) true reasoning on the

propositions as the conceptual keystones of their theory of vocational development, Bordin et al. have delineated and defined the dimensions shown in Table 3-1 as the ones which are salient in the choice of an occupation. To illustrate the application of this scheme, the occupations of accounting, social work, and plumbing have been analyzed within it. As can be seen from the entries in columns III through VII, these particular occupations can be clearly differentiated from each other with respect to the degree they satisfy certain needs, the mechanisms involved, and the nature and expression of the gratifications. Bordin et al. point out that their system applies only to individuals who have a fairly high degree of freedom in their choices. In other words, they are not constrained in their decision making by external forces, e.g., economic, cultural, and geographic conditions and limitations, and therefore can express their personalities in their career choices.

A different emphasis in psychoanalytic conceptions of vocational choice comes from ego psychology, which, since the appearance of the writings of Hartmann, H. (1945) and others, has been increasingly recognized as directly relevant to the analysis and understanding of decision-making processes. The role which the ego may play in the selection of an occupation was first explicated by Ginzberg et al. (1951), who attempted to relate such ego functions as (1) reality testing, (2) delay of immediate gratifications, (3) means-end cognizance, and (4) future-time orientation to vocational development. According to their formulation, the adolescent must have an accurate appraisal of his capabilities, his strengths and weaknesses, so that he can set attainable goals for himself. He must "reality-test" his plans against an objective evaluation of his personal and environmental resources for implementing them. Because vocational plans are generally long-range in nature, covering a period of years, it is necessary for the individual to develop a differentiated time perspective, so that he can distinguish between the "right now" and the future in outlining steps which will lead him to his goals. Furthermore, he must follow the "reality principle," rather than the "pleasure principle," and postpone the immediate gratification of needs in order to attain his objectives. In short, to make a realistic vocational choice, the individual must be able to bring the future into the psychological present, consider the advantages and disadvantages of alternative courses of action, commit himself to one of the alternatives, and then control his behavior sufficiently to implement the alternative he selected.

Need Theories of Vocational Choice. Whereas psychoanalytic explanations of vocational choice focus upon the defense mechanisms of the individual in the selection of an occupation, need theories of choice give primary attention to the desires and wants which stimulate the individual to prefer one occupa-

Table 3-1. An Analysis of the Need-gratifying Activities and Aspects of Accounting (A), Social Work (S), and Plumbing (P) by Bordin, Nachman, and Segal *(1963, pp. 111–112)*

I. Dimension	*II. Occupation*	*III. Degree of involvement*	*IV. Instrumental mode*	*V. Objects*	*VI. Sexual mode*	*VII. Affect*
NURTURANT	A	0*				
Feeding	S	3	Material and psychological supplies	Needs of clients	F	R
	P	0				
	A	1	Financial advice and safeguards	Client's financial affairs	M	A
Fostering	S	3	Encouragement and protection	Client's growth and health	F	R-A
	P	0				
ORAL AGGRESSIVE	A	0				
Cutting	S	1	Words	Client's resistance	F	I
	P	1	Lathes, gouges, clippers	Pipes	M	I
	A	0				
Biting-devouring	S	0				
	P	1	Wrenches, pliers	Pipes	M	I
MANIPULATIVE	A	0				
Physical	S	0				
	P	2	Pipes, valves	Steam, water pressure	M	A
	A	3	Advice, recommendation	Business and government policy	M	A
Interpersonal	S	2	Provocation, influence, seduction	Feelings and attitudes of client	F	I
	P	0				
SENSUAL	A	0				
Sight	S	0				
	P	0				
	A	0				
Sound	S	0				
	P	0				
	A	0				

Touch	S	0				
	P	1	Hands-smoothing-sculpturing	Joints	M	A
ANAL	A	2	Recommendations re investment	Fortunes of clients	O	A
Acquiring	S	1	Efforts to equalize distribution	Wealth of society	F	R
	P	0				
Timing-ordering	A	3	Systems, audits	Financial policy	O	A
	S	1	Records, budgets	Own work, lives of clients	O	A
	P	0–1	Calculating costs, estimating	Materials	M	A
	A	2	Prevent waste, encourage saving	Money of client	O	I
Hoarding	S	0				
	P	2	Prevention of blockage-expulsion	Waste–actual anal products	O	R
	A	2	Systems to combat disorder	Financial affairs of business	O	R
Smearing	S	0				
	P	2	Hands, trowels	Pastes, greases	O	A
GENITAL	A	0				
Erection	S	0				
	P	0–1	Hands-tools	Faucets-fixtures	M	I
Penetration	A	0				
	S	0				
	P	1	Reaming, coupling	Pipes, joints	M	I
	A	0				
Impregnation	S	1	Prevention or encouragement	Family planning, marital counseling	F	I-R
	P	0				
	A	0				
Producing	S	1	Giving or withholding	Babies for adoption	F	I
	P	0				
EXPLORATORY	A	2	Audits to detect fraud	Financial behavior of others	O	A
Sight	S	2–1	Visual investigation	Homes of clients	O	A
	P	2	Detecting leaks and blockage	In pipes and water systems	O	A
	A	0				

Table 3-1. An Analysis of the Need-gratifying Activities and Aspects of Accounting (A), Social Work (S), and Plumbing (P) by Bordin, Nachman, and Segal *(Continued)*

I. Dimension	*II. Occupation*	*III. Degree of involvement*	*IV. Instrumental mode*	*V. Objects*	*VI. Sexual mode*	*VII. Affect*
Touch	S	0				
	P	1	Hands-to determine shapes	Where can't see	O	A
Sound	A	1	Questioning	Financial statement of clients	O	A
	S	2	Questioning	Private life of clients	O	I
	P	1	Detecting leaks and disturbances	Sound of running water	O	I
FLOWING-QUENCHING	A	0				
	S	0				
	P	3	Arranging of pipes, valves	Flow of fluids, waste products	M	I
EXHIBITING	A	0				
	S	0				
	P	0				
RHYTHMIC MOVEMENT	A	0				
	S	0				
	P	1	Hands, tools, physical movement	Pipes	O	I

* Degree of involvement: 0 = no significant involvement, 1 = peripheral importance, 2 = secondary importance, 3 = primary importance. Sexual mode: M = masculine, F = feminine, O = not sex linked. Affect: A = affect experienced, R = reaction formation, I = isolation.

tion to another. Probably the most prominent need theory of vocational choice is the one formulated by Roe (1956; 1957; Super & Bachrach, 1957) from her studies of the personality development of eminent scientists (see Chapter 10).[4] In her theory, Roe (1957) begins with the individual's early psychosocial experiences, particularly in the family, and traces their effects upon the formation of needs and the patterning of psychic energy. The way in which the individual learns to more or less automatically (unconsciously) satisfy his needs determines which of his special abilities, interests, and attitudes he will follow and develop. Needs which the parents fill routinely as they appear have little effect upon the factors which determine an individual's vocational behavior, but needs which they satisfy (1) only minimally or (2) with delay become unconscious motivators and directly influence the individual's preferences for activities which involve working with things or with people and which are the basis for vocational choice.

The specific needs which Roe (1956) relates to vocational choice are those defined by Maslow (1954) in his theory of personality. These needs are arranged in a hierarchy of prepotency, since the higher-order needs (understanding, beauty, self-actualization) only become effective after the lower-order needs (food, safety, love) have been satisfied. In modern society, of course, most of the lower-order needs are satisfied for most people most of the time, so that it is the higher-order needs which play a significant part in the motivation of vocational behavior. In particular, it is the need for self-actualization which seems to be of paramount importance. Roe (1956, p. 29) maintains that this need is central in the choice of a vocation, since: "All that a man *can* be he *must* be if he is to be happy." Roe does not relate specific needs to specific occupations or groups of occupations; rather, she points out how any occupation may serve to satisfy needs at a given level. This aspect of her theory is not generally recognized, however, because in her development of a classification scheme for occupations (Roe, 1954) and in other presentations (Roe, 1962), she writes or talks about motivation and personality in relation to occupational *field*. Actually, her theory, and the evidence she cites in support of it (Centers, 1948), pertains to the relationship between *levels* of needs and occupations, not between *kinds* of needs and occupations.

Self Theories of Vocational Choice. Before discussing the self in relation to choice, it is necessary first to know what is meant by the term *self,* which has several different definitions, depending upon the frame of reference used. In sociological terminology, the self is what the person *is* (Sarbin, 1954, p. 244), which consists of two components: the "I" and the "me." The "I" refers to

[4] For other need theories of vocational choice, see Hoppock (1957); Merwin and Di Vesta (1959); and Walsh (1959).

the individual's personal characteristics as he sees them, whereas the "me" reflects the reactions of others to the individual (Mead, G. H., 1934). Psychoanalytic theory distinguishes between the self and the ego, the former being the object which the latter perceives (Symonds, 1951). Trait-and-factor psychology defines the self as the aggregate or composite of the individual's typical reaction patterns, such as dominance, cooperativeness, introversion, etc. (Guilford, 1959). In contrast, phenomenological theory states that the self is functional as well as structural and that it motivates the individual to action and organizes his perceptions of himself and the environment (Combs & Snygg, 1959). According to this viewpoint, which is probably the most widely accepted one, the self "includes those aspects of the perceptual field to which we refer when we say 'I' or 'me' " (Combs & Snygg, 1959, p. 43), and the self-concept consists of these percepts organized into various dimensions, metadimensions, and systems, each of which defines a different aspect of personality structure and functioning. Thus, submissiveness might be one of the dimensions of the self-concept, self-esteem one of its metadimensions, and regnancy one of the metadimensions of a self-concept system (Super, Starishevsky, Matlin, & Jordaan, 1963).

The self influences vocational choice, because, as Super (1951b, p. 88) has put it: "The choice of an occupation is one of the points in life at which a young person is called upon to state rather explicitly his concept of himself, to say definitely 'I am this or that kind of person!' " Throughout his life the individual plays a variety of roles which provide him with an opportunity to discover who he is and what he wants to be. In play and work activities, he tries out his abilities and evaluates them against his accomplishments and the reactions of others. He finds that he does some things well and gains a sense of satisfaction from them: "These successes tend to develop in him a picture of himself as one who writes well or as one who is always on time, and these numerous little specific pictures of aspects of oneself begin to add up, in due course, to a picture of the self" (Super, 1951b, p. 88). As the individual grows older, he integrates the various pictures he has of himself into a consistent self-concept, which he strives to preserve and enhance through all his activities, but particularly through his occupational activities. He attempts to select an occupation which will be compatible with his self-concept and which will allow him to make it a reality by permitting him to play the role he wants to play.

Super, Starishevsky, Matlin, and Jordaan (1963) have further elaborated upon the process whereby the self is related to vocational behavior by enumerating and describing (1) how the self-concept is formed, (2) how it is translated into occupational terms, and (3) how it is implemented in the individual's work life. Five aspects of the evolution of the self-concept are identified: (*a*) exploration, (*b*) differentiation, (*c*) identification, (*d*) role playing, and (*e*) reality testing. Particular attention is given to exploration, which is the first phase in the formation of the self-concept and which is critical to its being meaningfully related to appropriate occupational roles. A model is presented by which the individual's "psychtalk," the adjectives he uses to describe himself, can be translated into "occtalk," the terms he employs to describe occupations. The congruence between the self-concept and the chosen occupation is determined by the degree of comparability among the descriptive statements assigned to the two referents (see Chapter 6).

Tiedeman and his associates (Tiedeman & Pandit, 1958; O'Hara & Tiedeman, 1959; Kibrick & Tiedeman, 1961; Tiedeman & O'Hara, 1963) have also related the self to vocational choice, but have used an approach somewhat different from Super's. They have emphasized the formation of the self in relation to educational experiences more than Super has, and they have conceived of the self as the individual's evaluation rather than perception of himself, which continually changes as he progresses from one educational or vocational "position" to another. In explicating their point of view, O'Hara and Tiedeman (1959, p. 292) write as follows: "The process of occupational choice may be characterized as that of developing a vocational identity. The 'Self' is the central concern of identity. The concepts of identity and self are intuitively satisfying means of attributing motivation for occupational choice to the person choosing." Thus, according to Tiedeman, self and vocational development interact and affect each other as the individual copes with the problems of pursuing a course of training or deciding upon a career.

To illustrate this interaction Tiedeman and O'Hara (1963) have analyzed the cases of four boys, based upon interview data, who are in various stages of vocational development. The concepts which they use for the analyses come primarily from Erikson's (1959) work on the relationship of identity to the life cycle. Thus, they trace the career decision-making process through such periods of developmental crisis as basic trust, autonomy, initiative, industry, and identity formation. They also discuss the "interpenetration of awareness gained from experiencing life's discontinuities" which characterizes each boy's vocational behavior. What they mean by this concept is not explicitly stated, but it apparently refers to the transitional points between the stages of the vocational and life cycles and to the contingencies which obtain between them.[5] In other words, a "discontinuity" may arise, for example, when a vocational decision must be postponed until the outcomes of an educational endeavor are known. Tiedeman and O'Hara (1963, p. 66) have charted many of these discontinuities as they occur in both educational and vocational develop-

[5] See also Tiedeman (1965) for a discussion of "discontinuity" in another context.

ment, and they indicate when decisions must be considered, when problems may exist, and when the discontinuities begin and end.

Developmental Theories of Vocational Choice

Most trait-and-factor and psychodynamic theories of vocational choice have assumed that choice takes place at a given point in time rather than over a period of time.[6] In contrast, developmental explanations of choice propose that the decisions involved in the selection of an occupation are made at a number of different points in the individual's life and that they constitute a continuous process which starts in childhood and ends in early adulthood. This conception of vocational choice as a developmental process had its origin in the early work of Carter (1940) on the formation of interest patterns in adolescence, which, he concluded, are solutions to the problems of "growing up." According to Carter, interest patterns are designed to assist the individual to fit himself, with his biological attributes, into somewhat rigid social structures or institutions. He acquires interest patterns through his identification with some respected person or group. Many times the identification and the resulting interest pattern are appropriate, and the individual makes a good adjustment, but sometimes they are inappropriate, and he finds it necessary to discard or modify his interest pattern in order to solve the practical problems of everyday living. In Carter's formulation, the trial-and-error process of developing an interest pattern is one which progresses from the less mature fantasy solutions of late childhood to the more mature realistic solutions of youth and adulthood.

Ginzberg's Theory. Much as Carter concluded that interests change and develop with increasing age, so current theories of vocational development postulate that choice behaviors mature as the individual grows older (Dysinger, 1950; Beilin, 1955). The theory formulated by Ginzberg et al. (1951), which they derived from interviews with adolescent boys and girls (see Chapter 5), consists of three propositions about the developmental nature of vocational choice. First, they point out that, contrary to the traditional conception of choice as a single event in time, their data indicate that it is a process which spans the entire period of adolescence, from approximately age 10 to age 21. Second, this process is largely irreversible—once launched upon a particular course of action, such as training for a specific job, an individual finds it increasingly difficult to change his goals as time passes. He is restricted more and more by his previous decisions, expenditures of effort and money, and commitments of time. As a result, the single most important factor in his voca-

[6] The theory of Bordin, Nachmann, and Segal (1963) is a notable exception.

tional choice becomes the inertia of the decision-making process itself. And, third, the process ends in a compromise between an individual's needs and the realities which impinge upon him. Even for those who are in extremely favorable reality circumstances, Ginzberg maintains that vocational choice involves *some* element of compromise, some concession to the limitations of environmental conditions.

Ginzberg relates ego functioning (see foregoing discussion) and development to the choice process by identifying some of the tasks which face the adolescent in deciding upon a vocation, by specifying the pressures which make the accomplishment of these tasks difficult, and by describing the supports which are available to withstand the pressures. Table 3-2 presents the various problems, ego functions, pressures, and supports which the selection of a career involves. The problems are those which arise in the formulation of a satisfactory vocational plan. They encompass the steps which are necessary to establish and realize future career goals. They draw upon such ego functions as reality testing, differentiation of the present from the future, inhibition of behavior, and facility in adjusting needs and reality through compromise. The pressures

Table 3-2. A Conceptual Schema of Vocational Choice in Adolescence *(Ginzberg et al., 1951, p. 27 et passim)*

Problem	*Function*	*Pressure*	*Support*
To determine freedom in occupational choice by enlarging knowledge or self and world	Reality testing	Immediate gratification of impulses growing out of general maturation, such as emerging sex needs in adolescence	Internal: Values and goals make it possible to relate present activities to future
To distinguish between present, near future, and distant future	Sharpening of time perspective	Time: necessity to make decisions	Prospects of realizing future goals
To postpone current gratifications	Delaying capacity	Parental aspirations and ambitions	Minimum gratification of present needs
To set realizable goals and to choose suitable approaches for their attainment	Ability to compromise	Motivation: work orientation versus pleasure orientation	External: educational system, which sets up intermediate goals; parental guidance; identification with parent

are those which emerge as a result of the individual's general development and maturation. Adolescence is a time when sexual impulses awaken and the need for peer-group associations increases; it is a time when parental aspirations and strictures become more burdensome and restrictive; it is a time when the necessity to make decisions weighs heavily upon the neophyte adult; and it is a time when conflicts between the security of childhood and the responsibilities of adulthood make the young person ambivalent about the satisfactions he seeks in work. In fact, the opposing motivations to work and to pleasure are often so strong that they would be unresolvable were it not that both internal and external supports are available to assist the adolescent in postponing immediate gratifications and in working toward the realization of his vocational plans in the future.

Super's Theory. Whereas Ginzberg and his associates drew upon the concepts of psychoanalytic ego psychology to construct a developmental theory of vocational choice, Super has utilized principles from differential and phenomenological psychology to describe and explain the choice process. Super (1953) based the first formulation of his theory upon the 10 propositions listed in Table 3-3, which reflect his use of the trait-and-factor approach (propositions 1, 2, and 3), his application of self theory (propositions 8, 9, and 10), his interpretation of choice as a developmental phenomenon (propositions 4, 5, and 6), and his association with the vocational guidance movement (proposition 7).[7] He places even more emphasis than Ginzberg upon vocational choice as a process and suggests that the term *development* be used "rather than 'choice,' because it comprehends the concepts of preference, choice, entry, and adjustment" (Super, 1953, p. 187). He introduced the concept of vocational maturity to denote the individual's degree of development from the time of his early fantasy choices in childhood to his decisions about retirement from work in old age (Super, 1955). As the individual matures vocationally, he passes through a series of life stages, each of which corresponds to some phase in the development of his self-concept (Super, 1957). In adolescence, for example, the individual elaborates upon and clarifies the concept of himself he formed during childhood, and he begins to translate his self-concept into vocational terms through his aspirations, preferences, and work values. To the extent that he successfully copes with the developmental tasks of a life stage, the individual can be considered as more or less vocationally mature. (For a more extended discussion of life stages and vocational maturity, see Chapter 5.)

[7] Throughout his writings on vocational development, Super deals with the problems of guiding and counseling individuals who are making choices as well as the task of formulating a theory of how and why they make them as they do. There is no necessary connection between the two, however, although the latter can be applied in accomplishing the former (see Chapter 1).

Table 3-3. Propositions in Super's Theory of Vocational Development *(1953, pp. 189–190)*

1. People differ in their abilities, interests, and personalities.
2. They are qualified, by virtue of these characteristics, each for a number of occupations.
3. Each of these occupations requires a characteristic pattern of abilities, interests and personality traits, with tolerances wide enough, however, to allow both some variety of occupations for each individual and some variety of individuals in each occupation.
4. Vocational preferences and competencies, the situations in which people live and work, and hence their self-concepts, change with time and experience (although self-concepts are generally fairly stable from late adolescence until late maturity), making choice and adjustment a continuous process.
5. This process may be summed up in a series of life stages characterized as those of growth, exploration, establishment, maintenance, and decline, and these stages may in turn be subdivided into (*a*) the fantasy, tentative, and realistic phases of the exploratory stage, and (*b*) the trial and stable phases of the establishment stage.
6. The nature of the career pattern (that is, the occupational level attained and the sequence, frequency, and duration of trial and stable jobs) is determined by the individual's parental socioeconomic level, mental ability, and personality characteristics, and by the opportunities to which he is exposed.
7. Development through the life stages can be guided, partly by facilitating the process of maturation of abilities and interests and partly by aiding in reality testing and in the development of the self-concept.
8. The process of vocational development is essentially that of developing and implementing a self-concept: it is a compromise process in which the self-concept is a product of the interaction of inherited aptitudes, neural and endocrine makeup, opportunity to play various roles, and evaluations of the extent to which the results of role playing meet with the approval of superiors and fellows.
9. The process of compromise between individual and social factors, between self-concept and reality, is one of role playing, whether the role is played in fantasy, in the counseling interview, or in real-life activities such as school classes, clubs, part-time work, and entry jobs.
10. Work satisfactions and life satisfactions depend upon the extent to which the individual finds adequate outlets for his abilities, interests, personality traits, and values; they depend upon his establishment in a type of work, a work situation, and a way of life in which he can play the kind of role which his growth and exploratory experiences have led him to consider congenial and appropriate.

Tiedeman's Theory. Following Ginzberg's and Super's emphasis upon vocational choice as a process which proceeds through several stages, Tiedeman (1961; Tiedeman & O'Hara, 1963) has attempted to clarify and specify what the series of decisions is which an individual makes in the course of his career development. Tiedeman begins his analysis by dividing the overall process of vocational decision making into two periods and then continues by delineating stages within each period. First, there is a period of anticipation or preoccupation which has four stages: exploration, crystallization, choice, and clarification. During the exploratory stage, the individual becomes familiar with and considers the alternatives which are available to him. Then, in the crystallization stage, he accepts some of the alternatives as feasible or realizable ones and rejects others as inappropriate or unobtainable. Next, in the choice stage, he decides upon which alternative he wants to select and follow. Finally, during the clarification stage, he works out in detail how he will implement his choice. Secondly, there is the period of implementation and adjustment, which follows the clarification stage of the anticipation period and which encompasses three additional stages—induction, reformation, and integration. The succession of these stages represents a progressive realization of the individual's goals as he enters and advances in his chosen position.

The mechanisms by which the individual progresses through these several periods and stages of the choice process are (1) differentiation and (2) integration. Differentiation refers to discriminations among the stimuli which impinge upon the individual, including his cognitions and ideas as well as external events, whereas integration involves the extrapolation of the whole from the parts. At each stage of the decisional sequence, there is a continuous interaction between differentiation and integration, and, although there may be regressions at given points in the process, its overall thrust is forward, i.e., a best-fit function for the process in relation to time would presumably be linear. Differentiation and integration are also the mechanisms of self-development, which Tiedeman and O'Hara (1963, p. 46) see as the more encompassing process: "Career development then is self development viewed in relation with choice, entry, and progress in educational and vocational pursuits."

In addition to the developmental theories of Ginzberg, Super, and Tiedeman, there have been other formulations and speculations about how vocational choices are made over periods of time, but they have been generally less articulate and comprehensive. They have made some distinctive contributions to an understanding of choice as a process, however, and consequently they should be mentioned. Dysinger (1950), for example, in addition to outlining stages in vocational development which parallel those of Ginzberg, has emphasized the idea that negative decisions play an extremely important part in the individual's progress toward the choice of an occupation (see the discussion of the "exclusion process" in Chapter 5). Furthermore, he has focused attention upon the fact that the making of a vocational choice is not necessarily a good criterion of whether an individual is developing normally in his vocational planning, since some individuals make their choices prematurely. In a similar effort to provide a developmental model for vocational choice, Beilin (1955) has attempted to demonstrate how developmental principles, such as the preeminence of behaviors at certain points in an individual's life, levels of maturity, differentiation and integration of behavior, etc., apply to the analysis of changes in vocational behavior with increasing age.[8]

Decision Theories of Vocational Choice

Another variety of psychological theories of vocational choice, and the last type considered here, is that which utilizes decision models to conceptualize the choice process. Although theories of decision making have been formulated in economics and related areas (Edwards, W., 1954), it has only been during the past decade and a half that they have gained currency in psychology and even more recently in vocational psychology. That their applicability to various kinds of problems in information processing, games and statistical decisions, and, particularly, vocational choice is meaningful and useful has been increasingly recognized (Edwards, W., 1961; Girshick, 1954; Simon, 1955). The three theories of vocational choice which have stemmed from this relatively recent interest in decision making are summarized in this section.[9]

Although cast more in terms of the counseling than the choice process, a model of decision making proposed by Gelatt (1962) has implications for conceptualizing vocational choice within a decision-theory framework and has served as a point of reference for other analyses. He takes as his starting point two characteristics which he states all decisions possess: (1) there is an individual who is required to make a decision, and (2) there are two or more courses of action from which he must select one on the basis of information he has about them. The decision may be either terminal (final) or investigatory (calling for additional information). "The investigatory decision becomes a cycle, involving information gathering and decision making, until a terminal decision is made. The terminal decision may also suggest a cycle, since the outcome of such a decision may yield additional information which would serve to modify the result of the terminal decision" (Gelatt, 1962, p. 241). This possibility of indeterminacy or delay in the decisional sequence is represented in Figure 3-3 by the "looping" of Investigatory Decisions back through Method of Investigation to Data, where the process can be repeated until a terminal decision is reached. The central component in the process is the strategy which is used to consider and choose among possible courses of action. As the diagram shows, three steps are involved: (1) the estimation of the probabilities of success associated with the outcomes of alternative courses of action, (2) the

[8] For additional theoretical statements about vocational choice, see Caplan, Ruble, & Segal (1963); Fletcher (1966); Simons (1966); and Stefflre (1966). For commentaries on the major developmental theories of vocational choice, see Bachrach (1957); Borow (1960); and Holland (1964b).

[9] For related treatments of decision making within the context of guidance, see Katz, M. (1963; 1966); also, see Hills (1964) for a discussion of decision making and college choice.

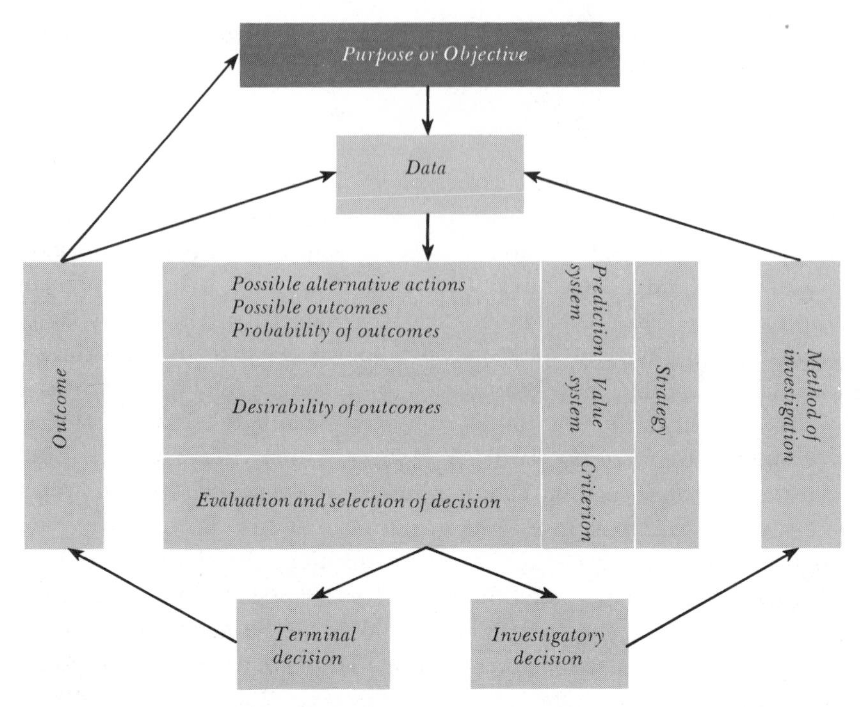

***Figure 3-3. The vocational decision-making process as conceptualized by Gelatt** (1962, p. 242).*

desirability of these outcomes as determined by the individual's value system, and (3) the selection of a course of action by application of an evaluative criterion.

A more complex conceptualization of the decision-making process, which relates it to a general theory of choice behavior, has been outlined by Hilton (1962) as depicted in Figure 3-4. He describes the "flow" which takes place in this model as follows:

> The decision-making process is initiated by some input from the environment. . . . If, when dissonance is tested, the input has raised dissonance above the tolerable level, the person examines his premises. . . . If his premises can be changed to accommodate the input, he makes the change, and the revised set of premises are tested for dissonance. . . .
>
> If the person finds that his premises cannot be revised, he searches for possible alternations in his behavior, one of which may be implied by the environmental input. He selects an alternative and tests the tentative plan for dissonance. If the dissonance is now below threshold he *makes a decision* to accept the tentative plan and ad-

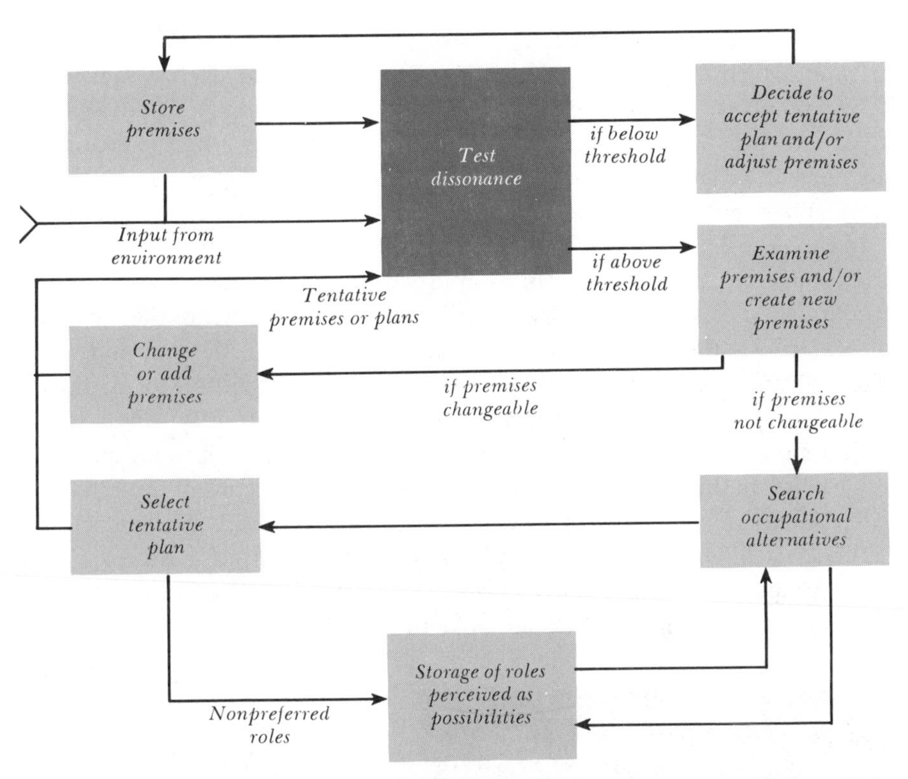

***Figure 3-4. The vocational decision-making process as schematized by Hilton** (1962, p. 295).*

> justs his premises accordingly. If, when tested, the dissonance is still above threshold, he repeats the process, either revising his premises or trying another behavioral alternative [Hilton, 1962, p. 296; italics in original].

The principal variable in this process, cognitive dissonance, is defined differently by Hilton than by Festinger (1957), who introduced the concept. The former "perceives efforts to reduce dissonance as preceding and facilitating decision-making" (Hilton, 1962, p. 296), whereas the latter states that dissonance always follows choice. James (1963) has pointed out that, by definition, dissonance is a *post*-choice behavior and has suggested that the concept of conflict be substituted in Hilton's scheme as a more appropriate one than dissonance.

Neither Gelatt nor Hilton deal directly with the decision-making process in relation to the overall course of vocational development, although a connection between the two is implied in both their models. In an analysis of this relationship, Hershenson and Roth (1966, p. 368) have projected two trends over time, which they hypothesize follow from vocational decisions made at different points in the individual's work life: "First, the range of possibilities available to him is narrowed. Second, those possibilities which remain are strengthened. Eventually, through the process of successively narrowing alternatives and strengthening the remaining ones, the individual arrives at his career choice." These two trends are represented graphically in Figure 3-5, where "range of choices" is shown as approaching an asymptote at unity and "certainty of the choice made" at infinity. In other words, as the range of choices narrows, the certainty of the choices increases. Hershenson and Roth (1966, p. 369) note further that: "the psychological magnitude of a disconfirmatory experience must exceed the area under the 'certainty' curve at the time it occurs for it to be significant enough to throw the choice into question. Thus earlier in the decisional process, a less significant event may have a greater impact on an individual's career decisional process." There may also be individual differences in the shapes of the trends. Thus, for a person who makes a sudden, defensive choice, in order to have an occupational "label" or "identity," the curves might look more like those in Figure 3-6.

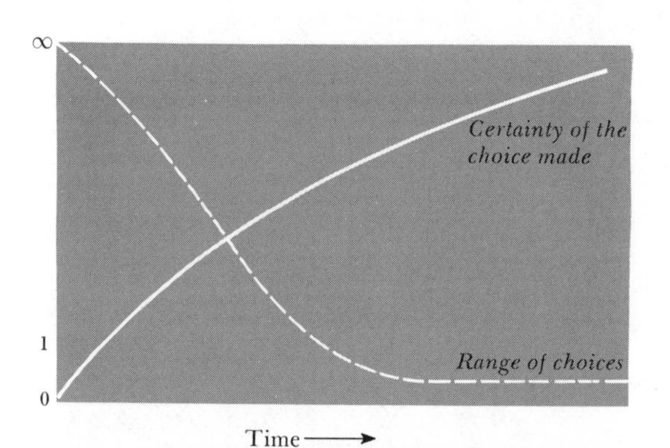

Figure 3-5. Normal development of the decision-making process. *(From Hershenson & Roth, 1966, p. 369.)*

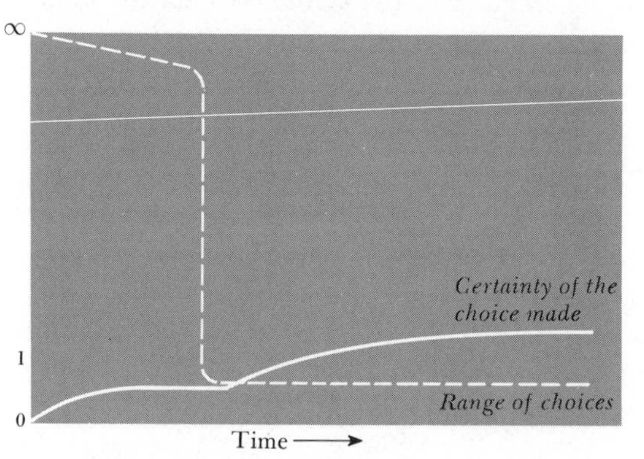

Figure 3-6. Defensive development of the decision-making process. *(From Hershenson & Roth, 1966, p. 370.)*

GENERAL THEORIES OF VOCATIONAL CHOICE

As is apparent from a consideration of the theories of vocational choice which have been reviewed, good arguments can be made for the influence of several variables upon an individual's selection of an occupation. In other words, it seems unreasonable to try to account for individual differences in vocational choice by positing only one related factor, although this would be desirable from the standpoint of constructing as parsimonious a theory as possible. In recognition of the fact that many factors may affect choice, several general theories of vocational choice have been formulated in recent years which attempt to outline how these factors interact to determine the individual's preferences for occupations and how they impinge upon the occupation's selection of individuals. The first theory presented here resulted from the combined efforts of a group of economists, psychologists, and sociologists (Blau, Gustad, Jessor, Parnes, & Wilcock, 1956), who met one summer in an interdisciplinary seminar on vocational choice sponsored by the Social Science Research Council. The second theory emerged from the Arden House Conference on scientific careers and vocational development theory and represents the contributions of 12 psychologists, a natural scientist, a mathematician, and an economist (Super & Bachrach, 1957). And, the third theory is the product of a psychologist (Holland, 1966b) who has attempted to relate environmental variables to various aspects of vocational decision making and achievement by utilizing concepts drawn from both personality and developmental psychology.

An Interdisciplinary Conception of Vocational Choice

Addressing themselves to the central problem in explaining vocational choice, i.e., "Why do people enter different occupations?", Blau et al. (1956) have constructed what they call a "conceptual framework" (rather than "theory") which is based upon principles and empirical investigations from three different scientific disciplines: economics, psychology, and sociology. They start with the observation that occupational entry is *not* determined solely by the individual's preferences, although these constitute one important factor in employment and placement. Rather, occupational entry results from the interaction of the two processes of (1) vocational choice and (2) occupational selection. The process of vocational choice involves a compromise (cf. Ginzberg et al., 1951) between the individual's hierarchy of preferences and his hierarchy of expectations. He prefers or values some occupations more than others, but he also appraises his chances of entering them. He may realize that he has very little chance of entering his most preferred occupations, and consequently he compromises between aspiration and reality and settles for one of his less preferred occupations. Much like the choice process, occupational selection also necessitates compromise between hierarchies of preferences and expectations, the difference being that the hierarchies consist of individuals rather than occupations. In choice, the individual compromises between preferred and expected occupations, whereas in selection the occupation compromises between ideal and available workers.

The factors which Blau et al. see as the determinants of occupational choice, selection, and entry are listed in Table 3-4. The dotted line in the table distinguishes between the factors which are operative at the time an individual enters an occupation and those which are influential earlier in the choice and selection processes. With respect to the former, there are eight immediate determinants of entry which interact to produce the individual's and the occupation's hierarchies of preferences and expectations (Boxes 1 and I). Two of these determinants are complementary or parallel in the individual and the occupation: (1) the individual's technical qualifications and the occupation's performance requirements and (2) the individual's social-role characteristics, such as veteran status, religious background, social class, ethnic-group membership, etc., and the occupation's acceptance or rejection of candidates with these characteristics. The immediate determinants vary in nature between individuals and between occupations to the extent that individuals differ in their sociopsychological attributes and occupations differ in their socioeconomic organizations. Thus, the technical qualifications and functional requirements which determine entry into accounting may be quite different from those which affect entry into farming, because accountants have a higher general level of knowledge and a lower rate of labor turnover than farmers (Stewart, 1947; *Occupational Outlook Handbook,* 1966).

The factors shown below the dotted line (Boxes 3 and III) in Table 3-4 are the antecedent conditions which produce, through personality development and historical change, the immediate determinants of occupational entry. This distinction between past and present influences upon choice and selection reflects the assumption by Blau et al. (1956, p. 532) that: "Occupational choice is a developmental process that extends over many years. . . ." Choices change as the individual develops and as the occupational structure undergoes modifications and reorganizations. Within the limits set by his native endowment, the individual responds to the social structure within which he lives, particularly the family unit and the educational system, and forms various typical reaction patterns, which together constitute his personality. As he makes decisions about occupations at various points in his life, his personality influences his thinking about staying in or dropping out of school, following one course of study or another in high school and college, and applying for a position with Company X instead of Company Y. Similarly, the interaction of social institutions with technological advancements affects the composition

***Table 3-4. The Process of Vocational Choice and Personnel Selection as Conceptualized by Blau et al.** (1956, p. 534)*

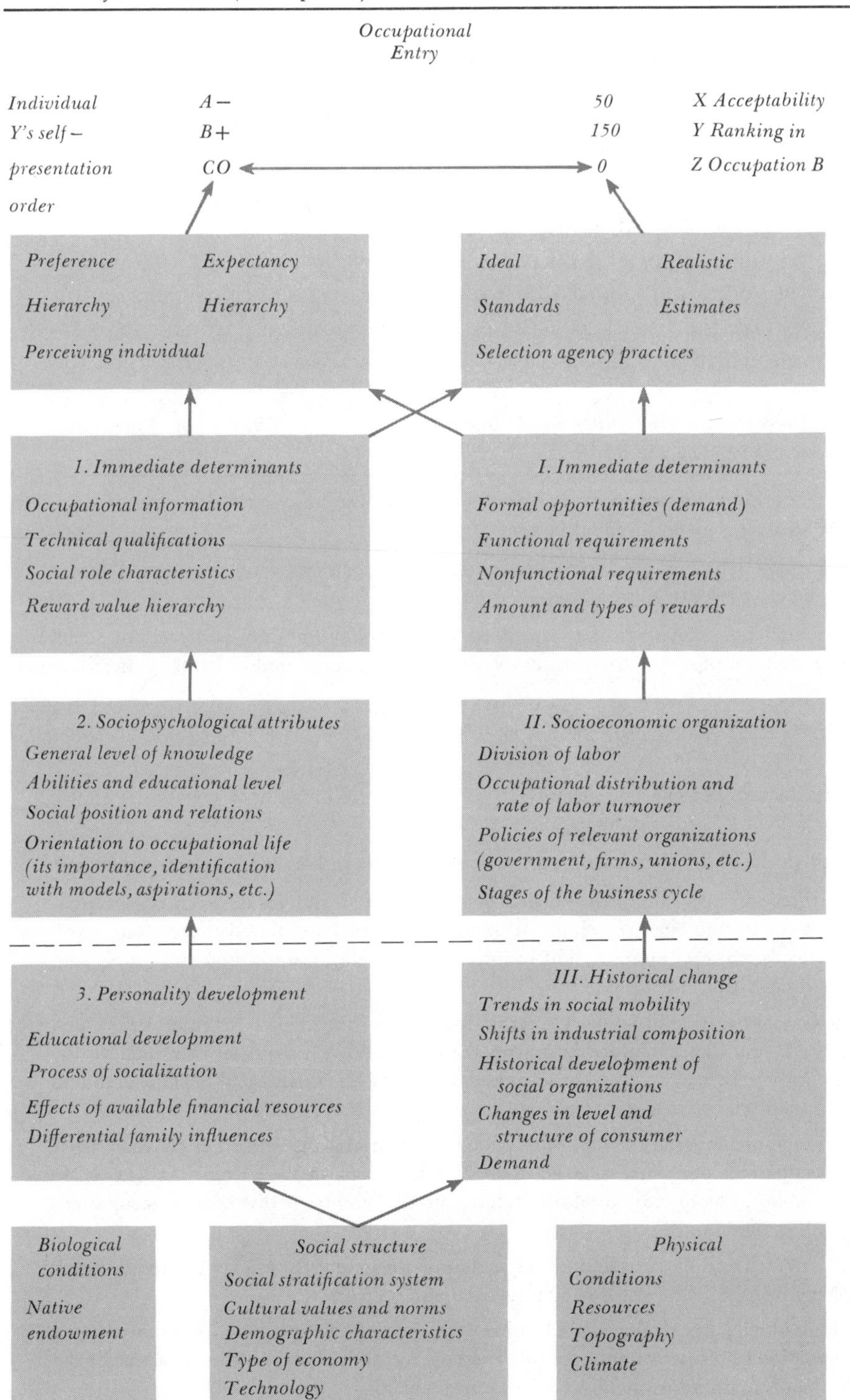

and nature of occupations and brings about changes in them over periods of time which are reflected in their demands and rewards for individuals with certain qualifications.

A General Developmental Interpretation of Vocational Choice

From the Arden House conference on vocational development theory, at which trait-and-factor, sociological, and psychodynamic explanations of choice making were presented, Super and Bachrach (1957) have formulated a comprehensive theory of vocational choice which draws upon contributions from several areas. They state the theory in a series of 12 propositions, which are paraphrased or quoted in Table 3-5. This theory places a heavy emphasis upon the

Table 3-5. Propositions in Super and Bachrach's General Theory of Vocational Development *(1954, pp. 118–120)*

1. Vocational choice is a process, which takes place over an extended period of time, rather than at a given moment in time.
2. As a process, which encompasses a series of related decision events, vocational choice fits a discernible pattern and hence is predictable.
3. Vocational choice involves "a compromise between or synthesis of personal and social factors, self-concept and reality, newly learned responses and existing patterns of reacting."
4. "Self-concepts begin to form prior to adolescence, become clearer in adolescence, and are translated into occupational terms in adolescence."
5. Reality factors become increasingly important as determinants of vocational choice as the individual grows older.
6. An individual's identifications with his parents directly influence his vocational choice.
7. "The direction and rate of the vertical movement of an individual from one occupational level to another are related to his intelligence, parental socioeconomic level, status needs, values, interests, skill in interpersonal relationships, and the supply and demand conditions in the economy."
8. "The occupational field which the individual enters is related to his interests, values, and needs, the identifications he makes with parental or substitute role models, the community resources he uses, the level and quality of his educational background, and the occupational structure, trends, and attitudes of his community."
9. Individuals are generally *multipotential* enough in their abilities and other characteristics and occupations are usually broad enough in the scope of their duties and tasks "to allow some variety of individuals in each occupation and some diversity of occupations for each individual."

10. and 11. Work and life satisfactions depend upon the extent to which an individual can implement his self-concept through his occupational role.

12. An individual's work may provide him with a means to integrate or maintain the organization of his personality. In other words, the activity of work may be one of the individual's main adjustment or defense mechanisms.

developmental nature of work-related decision making and uses the developmental framework of life periods or stages to describe the various phases in the selection of an occupation and to specify the cultural and social, trait, and psychodynamic factors which influence the choice process from childhood to late adulthood.

Central to Super and Bachrach's formulation is the concept of vocational developmental tasks. At each stage in the individual's vocational development, there are certain tasks which society, as represented primarily by the parents and the educational system, expect him to accomplish. For example, in early adolescence at the time the young person enters high school, he has the task of deciding upon his course of study for the next 3 or 4 years, a choice which has implications not only for his short-term success and satisfaction in high school, but also for his eventual adjustment to an occupation after entry into the world of work. To the extent that an individual accomplishes the vocational tasks which confront him in an earlier stage of his development, he will be successful with the tasks which he encounters in a later stage. In other words, success (or failure) with earlier tasks leads to success (or failure) with later tasks, and *normal* vocational development is defined as a series of tasks which are successfully performed by the individual at the appropriate time in his development.

The basic assumption which underlies Super and Bachrach's theory is that vocational development is a special aspect of general development and that the factors which affect vocational development change and interact with each other much as vocational behavior changes and interacts with them. In other words, vocational development is a dynamic process which parallels, influences, and is modified by emotional, intellectual, and social development. As a consequence, the expectation is that vocational development follows the same principles and patterns as other developmental processes (Beilin, 1955). Super and Bachrach (1957, p. 119) write that: "Biological, psychological, economic, and sociological factors combine to affect the individual's career pattern. Now one aspect of behavior, then another, is preeminent throughout the span of development."

A Typological Theory of Vocational Choice

Stated in somewhat oversimplified form, the central idea of Holland's theory is the old notion that "birds of a feather flock together." He has considerably refined this principle, however, from the way in which it was originally formulated by the MESRI vocational psychologists and states it more articulately in the following series of propositions (Holland, 1966b, pp. 9–12):

1. In our culture, most persons can be categorized as one of six types—Realistic, Intellectual, Social, Conventional, Enterprising, and Artistic.

2. There are six kinds of environments: Realistic, Intellectual, Social, Conventional, Enterprising, and Artistic.
3. People search for environments and vocations that will permit them to exercise their skills and abilities, to express their attitudes and values, to take on agreeable problems and roles, and to avoid disagreeable ones.
4. A person's behavior can be explained by the interaction of his personality pattern and his environment.

The six personality types and corresponding environments have been given operational definitions in terms of Holland's (1958) Vocational Preference Inventory (VPI), Astin and Holland's (1961; Astin, 1963) Environmental Assessment Technique, and other procedures, so that the relationships between the two variables might be studied empirically.

Figure 3-7 summarizes the main part of Holland's theory and also illustrates its application to an individual with a Realistic personality. His *range* of vocational choices, given his personality type, is limited to one, or possibly some combination, of the six occupational environments. His *level* of choice is determined by two factors: (1) the level of his intelligence and (2) the level of his self-evaluation, which is based upon "one's status needs, and perception of level of competence and potential competence, and the self-estimate of one's worth with respect to others" (Holland, 1959, p. 38). The individual selects an occupation (unbroken line between "Realistic" environment and "person") in terms of his self-knowledge and occupational knowledge, which vary in quantity and quality from one environment to another (broken lines labelled "K-1" through "K-5," where "5" indicates most information). Because his personality is of the Realistic type and because his level of actual and estimated performance is "2," his vocational choice is in the Realistic environment at the second level.

Holland introduces the concept of development into his theory by means of the individual's life history, which he defines as "a particular pattern of living," in the Adlerian sense of life style. The individual's life history can be traced over time by identifying the interactions he engages in with different environments as he grows up. These environments include: his parents and siblings, peers, schools, churches and other institutions, colleges, and, eventually, work situations. To the extent that the individual's personality "fits" the environment, his development is considered to be more or less stable. "In short, personal stability is the outcome of passing through a series of consistent environments that foster and strengthen one's ability to cope with the world in an integrated way. Instability, in contrast, results from living in a succession of inconsistent environments that create and perpetuate inaccurate, contradictory self-concepts and conflicting ineffective coping behavior" (Holland, 1966b, p. 84).

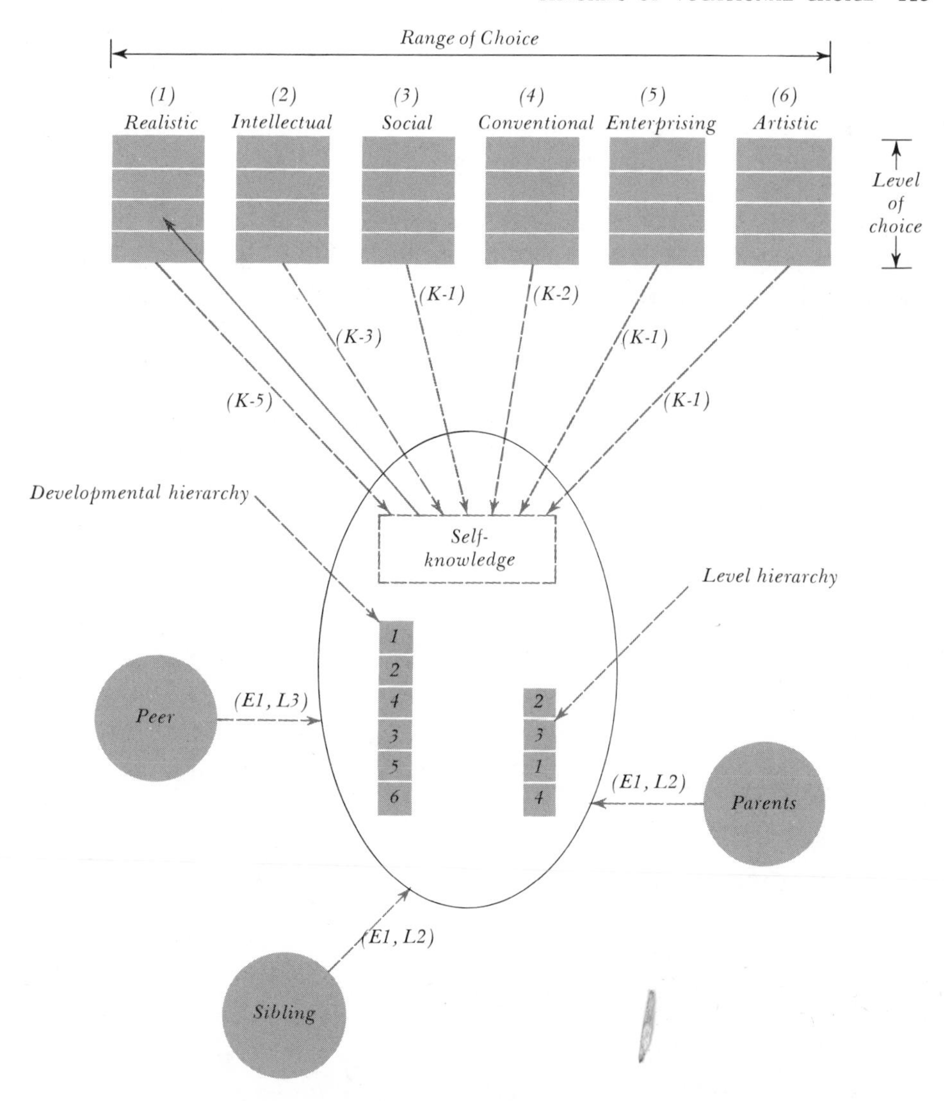

Figure 3-7. Factors in Holland's** (1959, p. 42) **theory of vocational choice.

The concepts of *consistent* and *inconsistent* are defined in terms of the similarity (intercorrelation) of the primary and secondary personality types or environmental models. For example: the Social and Enterprising types are correlated .36 and therefore are consistent with each other, but the Conventional and Artistic types, which are correlated −.09, are inconsistent. Similarly, interactions between personality and environment may be *congruent* or *incongruent,* depending upon whether they belong to the same type and model or not. Thus, if an Intellectual individual is in an Intellectual environment, the interaction would be congruent, but if he were in an Enterprising environment, the interaction would most likely be incongruent. Holland also uses the concepts of *homogeneity* and *heterogeneity* to describe personality-environmental interactions: the greater the magnitude of the difference between the highest and the lowest scores for a type or model, the greater the homogeneity of the personality or environment. It follows from the possible combinations of these personality-type and environmental-model interactions that *consistent, congruent,* and *homogeneous* pairings of the individual and his environment are most conducive to (1) more stable vocational choice, (2) greater vocational achievement, (3) higher academic achievement, (4) better maintenance of personal stability, and (5) greater satisfaction (Holland, 1966b, pp. 73–78).

4

THE NATURE OF VOCATIONAL CHOICE

The purpose of this chapter is to clarify what the nature of vocational choice is by proposing some answers to such questions as the following: What are the characteristics of vocational choice behavior? How can choice be distinguished from closely related concepts, such as vocational preference and aspiration? How can choice be defined operationally? What are the necessary conditions for making a choice? How can choice be measured, and what are the psychometric characteristics of the techniques which are used? How do individuals differ in their choices? To answer these questions, the discussion which follows is organized into four topics: (1) concepts of vocational choice, (2) definitions of vocational choice, (3) measures of vocational choice, and (4) individual differences in vocational choice.

CONCEPTS OF VOCATIONAL CHOICE

Depending upon the frame of reference used in a theory and the assumptions about human behavior which underlie it, there are different ways of conceptualizing vocational choice. Not all theories view choice from the same perspective or standpoint. How they differ in their concepts of choice is our concern in this section, which deals with five questions about the nature of vocational choice behavior: Is it systematic or chance? Is it conscious or unconscious? Is it rational or emotional? Does it represent a compromise or synthesis of desires and realities? And, is it an event or a process?

Vocational Choice: Systematic or Chance Behavior?

It is a basic assumption of all but one of the theories of vocational choice that the individual *systematically* chooses the occupation he intends to enter. Only accident theory posits that he chooses randomly or by *chance*. The distinction here between systematic and chance is a crucial, but often unclear, one in the analysis of choice behavior. By "systematic behavior" most theories mean that individuals or organisms react differentially to the stimuli which impinge upon them. Neither do they respond uniformly to all stimuli, nor do they respond the same way to one stimulus as it changes from occasion to occasion. In other words, discriminations are made in responses to stimuli with different attributes. Systematic behavior can be predicted from a knowledge of the stimulus conditions which preceded or accompanied the individual's responses, whereas chance behavior cannot be so predicted. For example, from knowledge of an individual's social class we can predict, within certain limitations of error, what the level of his vocational choice most likely is, because individuals at different social strata tend to choose occupations at a level consistent with their status and background (see Chapter 6).

What accident theory fails to recognize is that vocational choice is a *response* and that, as such, it is lawfully related to such stimuli as social class. One reason for this failure to conceptualize choice as a response is the confusion which often exists in the definition of responses and stimuli. For example, these concepts have typically been defined as follows: "A response is an observable change in behavior, this change being an activity effected by muscles or glands. An event which elicits a response has come to be known as a stimulus. No adequate general definition of a stimulus can be given without reference to the occurrence of a response" (Underwood, 1949, p. 1).[1] Brown, J. S. (1961) has criticized defining response and stimulus in this way, however, for two reasons: First, he points out that we can measure all kinds of environmental events which are external to and independent of the behavior of individuals and organisms, including such conditions and factors as natural phenomena, social institutions, and the reactions of others. He suggests that we call these various events *physical incidents.* Second, he argues that a stimulus is simply a physical incident which bears some relationship to a response but is not defined in terms of the latter. He writes:

> The assertion that a stimulus must be defined in terms of a response stems from the fact that responses are involved in the process of attaching the name stimulus to a given physical incident. But *the inherent physical properties of such a physical incident are not defined by appeal to responses, but by reference to physical measurements* [Brown, J. S., 1961, p. 11; italics in original].

This distinction which Brown makes between response and stimulus serves to clarify the definition of vocational choice as a response. An individual does

[1] In a recent revision of his text, *Experimental Psychology,* Underwood (1966, p. 11) has changed this definition of a stimulus and no longer stipulates that it must be defined with reference to a response. He states only that: "A stimulus is always some form of physical energy . . ." and, as such, may or may not be related to responses.

not select or enter an occupation indiscriminately, as accident theory proposes. Rather, he makes a definite, selective response which is distinguishable from his other responses and which is related to independently definable physical incidents known as stimuli. The evidence for this conclusion is reviewed in detail in Chapter 6. Suffice it to say here that it supports the concept of vocational choice as systematic behavior.

Vocational Choice: Conscious or Unconscious Behavior?

Given that vocational choices are responses which are lawfully related to stimuli, the next question which is usually asked about the nature of choice is whether it is conscious or unconscious. By "conscious" or "unconscious" is meant whether an individual is *aware* of the experiences which he has had. As Adams, J. K. (1957) has pointed out, however, in a review of laboratory studies of behavior without awareness, it is extremely important to specify what type of experience is referred to and what the conditions were which produced the experience. Adams identifies four referents for the awareness of an individual and concludes that only one of them has been well established empirically. The referents are: (1) the responses which an individual makes; (2) the relation of his responses to some antecedent or contingent event; (3) the context in which his responses occur; and (4) the differences which exist between stimuli. Although the last definition of awareness, i.e., knowing whether stimuli differ, has the most experimental evidence to support it as a reliable phenomenon, definitions (1) and (2) are the ones which are typically used in analyzing vocational choice. Does the individual know at the time he is deciding upon (response) a vocation that this is what he is doing? And, does he know what the factors (stimuli) are which have influenced or produced his choice? Answers to these questions vary considerably between the different theories of vocational choice.

Traditional trait-and-factor theory maintains that vocational choice is largely a conscious, cognitive problem-solving process. According to this viewpoint, confronted with the necessity of choosing an occupation, an individual consciously proceeds to make an analysis of his vocational assets and liabilities, accumulates information about occupations, and arrives at a decision, through what Parsons (1909) has called "true reasoning." The assumption is that the individual knows both what he is doing and why he is doing it and that he uses this information in selecting an occupation. Similarly, ego psychology suggests that the individual is conscious of his vocational choice and his reasons for it. Ginzberg et al. (1951), for example, place a heavy emphasis upon the ego functions in the process of vocational decision making. In their theory, they state that the individual consciously sets the goals he wants to attain in the future and tests them against the realities of his physical and psychological environment. Once his goals are established as realistic ones, he relates his present activities and efforts to them (means-end cognizance) and then, following the reality principle, he delays the gratification of his present needs in order to fulfill his long-term objectives. Throughout this process, the individual is aware of his behavior and its consequences.

Proponents of more motivation-oriented conceptions of vocational choice, particularly those who follow orthodox psychoanalytic interpretations of behavior (e.g., Brill, 1949; Menninger, K. A., 1942), challenge the proposition that choice is conscious. They claim that this is a naïve hypothesis which fails to take into account the extremely complex nature of motives which develop from so many experiences that the individual is unable to comprehend them, much less integrate them and relate them to his vocational behavior. In answer to the observation that, when questioned, young people can cite their reasons for choosing an occupation, they reply, as Forer (1953, p. 361) does in the following passage, that:

> Primary reasons for selecting a particular vocation are unconscious in the sense that when the individual is pressed to elaborate beyond the superficial rationalizations of economic advantage and opportunity, he is forced to admit that he does not know why; he simply has to build bridges or can't stand paper work. These activities have immediate appeal or distaste for him. We are saying that interests and preferences have unconscious roots.

In traditional psychoanalytic theory, the primary sources of motivation—the life and death instincts—are unconscious. The individual is aware of them, as they would be expressed in his vocational choice, only through their transformations by sublimation, reaction formation, projection, and the other defense mechanisms. Consequently, in most instances, his knowledge of his behavior is superficial, and he has no awareness of the why and wherefore of his actions, including his vocational choice.

Midway between these extreme positions, that vocational choice is either conscious or unconscious, is Super's (1957) interpretation within the framework of developmental theory. He maintains that to make a choice the individual must be aware of himself and be able to relate himself consciously to occupations. This does not mean, however, that he is necessarily aware of the factors or processes which have produced his particular self-concept. Super (1957, p. 284) notes that vocational development involves an interaction among many individual and environmental factors and that often it is late in the process before the individual realizes what kind of person he is becoming and what kind of occupation he wants to enter:

> When intra-individual interaction takes place or intrudes upon consciousness, it is synonymous with self-exploration. When individual-

> environmental interaction takes place on the conscious level, it involves reality testing. In both instances the self-concept is developing. But interaction is not always at the conscious level. Much of it takes place without verbalization, without awareness on the part of the experiencing individual of what is taking place.

Thus, Super concludes that the individual is more or less conscious of his vocational decision making, depending upon the stage of his development.

Empirical evidence on whether vocational choice is conscious or unconscious is limited to one study of a largely informal and impressionistic nature which was conducted by Kline and Schneck (1950). These investigators used a method called the "hypnotic scene visualization" technique to determine what the unconscious choices and motivations were of four people who were undergoing either vocational counseling or psychotherapy. After they had reached a satisfactory induction level in hypnosis, the Subjects were given the following instructions by the investigators: "I'm going to count from one to five and when I reach five you will be able to visualize a scene involving an occupation for which you have a real interest, even though this interest may be unknown to you now" (Kline & Schneck, 1950, p. 5). The responses of the four Subjects to these instructions indicated that three of them had conscious choices which disagreed with their unconscious choices and that all of them were unaware of the motivations for their choices. In one case, a young man who was majoring in psychology saw himself in the "hypnotic scene visualization" as a famous lawyer who saves an innocent man from going to jail. In another case, a young woman who was failing as an actress visualized herself under hypnosis as a fashion designer. These reports, in combination with theoretical considerations based upon psychoanalytic and projective psychology, led Kline and Schneck to the conclusion that vocational choice may be more a matter of primary perceptual impulses, which are unconscious, rather than apperceptive processes, which are always conscious.

It is difficult to resolve the issue of whether vocational choice is conscious or unconscious, because empirical data are not only scarce, but also inadequate. The study of Kline and Schneck is certainly novel and provocative, but it is hardly conclusive. They studied only four Subjects, and each of these was in treatment for a more or less serious psychological problem. It is quite possible that the high incidence of discrepancies between conscious and unconscious choices in this group of clients reflects their problems and would not be typical of nonclients who are not experiencing difficulties in their vocational decision making and planning. Until more definitive studies are available, it seems wise to reserve judgment about the role of consciousness in choice and simply suggest possible lines of further investigation. One of these might be a replication of Kline and Schneck's study on nonclients, and another might be an analysis of how aware individuals are of their choices at different points in their vocational development. Research on the latter might be particularly fruitful, since, as Super (1957) has observed, it seems reasonable that the individual would become increasingly aware of his vocational choices, and his motivations for them, as he grew older and responded more and more to the expectation that he select and prepare for a life's work. What we may eventually find is that (1) prior to adolescence vocational choices are largely unconscious and (2) during adolescence they are mostly conscious, except for those individuals who are less well adjusted.

Vocational Choice: Rational or Emotional?

Closely related to the problem of whether vocational choice is conscious or unconscious is the question of whether choice is rational or emotional. To be "rational" means to base decisions upon logical and realistic considerations. The rational person "thinks through" a problem by surveying the various alternative solutions which are feasible, projecting into the future what the probable consequences of each alternative are, and then selecting one alternative as the most desirable one because it maximizes what is desired within the limitations of what is attainable. In contrast, to be "emotional" means to act upon feelings, attitudes, and needs. The "emotional" person perceives and solves problems in terms of what he desires and wants rather than in terms of reality factors. This does not mean, however, that he is *necessarily* unrealistic in his courses of action, since his emotions may be consistent with reality. But it is not uncommon for the emotional person to be unrealistic, particularly in his choice of an occupation. (See Chapter 7 for a fuller discussion of unrealistic vocational choices.)

As with the problem of whether vocational choice is conscious or unconscious behavior, research evidence on the role of rationality and emotionality in choice is either nonexistent or inconclusive. There are no studies of rational problem solving in relation to the selection of an occupation, although some of the recent work on the higher mental processes is suggestive of several possible lines of investigation (Johnson, D. M., 1955; Kleinmuntz, 1966). The research of Bruner, Goodnow, and Austin (1956) on the development and use of categories in thinking, for example, provides a number of models for the analysis of how individuals may approach the problem of classifying occupations as "desirable" or "undesirable." Similarly, the economic and statistical theories of decisions, games, and all manner of choice have direct implications for the study of rationality in vocational choice (see Chapter 3). The application of these theories to choice phenomena, however, has not been extensive and has not dealt directly with the problem of whether choices are made in a rational fashion or not (see Chapter 6). Studies of emotional factors in relation to vocational choice are more plentiful than those on rational decision making, but they are not definitive, primarily because the instruments used to measure needs and motives are largely unvalidated (see Chapter 9). Until the pertinent research on the measurement of needs and motives is available, as well as on the role of the higher mental processes in choice, any conclusions about the relative significance of emotions and reason in the selection of occupations are necessarily speculative and tentative. It would seem justified to conclude, however, that both factors are most likely involved in choice, possibly with some complex interactions between them. Thus, it may be that: (1) individuals with the same motivation but different reasoning modes may choose different occupations and (2) individuals with different motivations but the same approach to problem solving may choose the same occupation.

Vocational Choice: Compromise or Synthesis?

Ginzberg and Super disagree on whether an individual's vocational choice represents a compromise between the factors involved in the selection of an occupation or whether it is based upon a synthesis of these factors. The former (Ginzberg et al., 1951, p. 27) concludes that:

> The decision concerning an occupational choice is, in the last analysis, a compromise whereby an individual hopes to gain the maximum degree of satisfaction out of his working life by pursuing a career in which he can make as much use as possible of his interests and capacities, in a situation which will satisfy as many of his values and goals as possible.

Super (1956, p. 250) has criticized this formulation on two counts:

> First, it does not describe how the compromise takes place. Secondly, it recognizes the action and interaction of each of these types of factors [interests, capacities, values, and realities] relatively late in the development of the individual, and leaves the impression that, once a late-developing factor comes into play those which have played a part earlier are no longer of much consequence.

On the basis of these considerations, Super (1956, p. 250) proceeds to formulate his own point of view, which is that "when wholesome development takes place the process is not so much one of *compromise* as one of *synthesis*."

This statement gives a clue concerning why Super and Ginzberg have arrived at different conclusions about the roles of compromise and synthesis in choice. These two theorists start from quite different assumptions about the nature of adjustment and development. From several of his writings it is apparent that Super (1951b; 1953; 1955; 1957) rejects the older, and psychoanalytically influenced, conception of adolescence as a period of *Sturm und Drang* (storm and stress) when the "return of the repressed" forces the individual to work out some kind of *rapprochement* or compromise between his biologically based impulses and the dictates of society. Instead, Super interprets development as a continuous process during which the individual's personality is formed in childhood and elaborated upon in adolescence through an integration or synthesis of his experiences of self, others, and the environment (Kuhlen, 1952). In contrast, Ginzberg follows orthodox psychoanalytic theory which "describes all behavior as a compromise or arbitration between the complete expression of primitive needs, on the one hand, and social demands and prohibitions, on the other" (Forer, 1953, p. 362). Ginzberg (1951, p. 202) observes that: "In ordering his life with respect to the future, the adolescent must be able to compromise in making his plans and pursuing them" (cf. Berg, 1953). He continues to note that: "Without this ability to compromise, he is certain to suffer serious frustration either because he has set himself impossible goals, or is unable to change basic approaches which are unsuited for the accomplishing of reasonable goals." In other words, Ginzberg sees compromise as a *sine qua non* of normal development, whereas Super assumes that compromise is indicative of arrested development.

The one study which is relevant to the problem of whether vocational choice is a compromise or a synthesis tends to support Ginzberg's interpretation, although the results are open to some criticism and question, as will be discussed later. Small (1953) studied 50 better-adjusted and 50 maladjusted boys who ranged in age from 15 to 19, there being 10 in each group at each age level, to determine the extent to which their vocational choices reflected a compromise between their needs and reality. He tested the hypothesis that: "Individuals with different ego strengths will show differences in the use they make of reality and wishful fantasy in making their vocational choices" (Small, 1953, pp. 1–2). Small assumed that the difference between the general adjustment levels of the normal and the disturbed boys in his two samples reflected differences in the strength of their egos. In other words, he defined ego strength in terms of adjustment status and expected that those with greater ego strength would have more realistic vocational choices.

What Small found, when he analyzed the first and second vocational choices of his Subjects, was that the better-adjusted boys, as predicted, were more realistic in their first choice than the maladjusted boys. In addition, however, he discovered that (1) the second choice of the normal boys was *less* realistic than their first choice and that (2) the second choice of the disturbed boys was *more* realistic than their first choice.[2] To explain these findings Small gathered additional data from interviews and projective tests which indicated that the

[2] It is important to note, however, that the second choice of the normal boys was *more* realistic than either of the choices of the maladjusted boys.

better-adjusted boys expressed "environment-involvement" fantasies about their first choices and "environment-avoidance" fantasies about their second choices. The former consisted of the expression of socially desirable needs, such as impulse restraint and acquisition, whereas the latter dealt with the satisfaction of more egocentric and asocial needs, such as impulse release and exhibition. Small interprets these results to indicate that realistic vocational choices are based upon compromise and that the ability to compromise varies with degree of ego strength. In general, he concluded that his study supported Ginzberg's (1951, p. 186; italics in original) proposition that: *"Compromise is an essential aspect of every choice."*

Two considerations should guide the interpretation of Small's study: First, he did not directly measure compromise but only inferred it from the realism of the first and second vocational choices of the two groups of boys; and, second, he did not demonstrate that *all* the boys compromised in making their vocational choices. With respect to the measurement of compromise, Small equated it with the making of a realistic choice, but this may be the result of synthesis as well as compromise, just as Super maintains. Probably our best hypothesis about compromise and synthesis in choice is that both may play a part, depending upon how restrictive reality conditions are for the individual. When freedom to choose is maximal, it is possible that choice might be based solely upon synthesis. As freedom to choose decreases, however, amount of compromise increases and choices are based upon some adjustment between the individual's needs and reality.

Vocational Choice: Event or Process?

For many years, from the pioneer writings of Frank Parsons through the work of MESRI to the research of the late 1940s (e.g., Dresden, 1948; Myers, W. E., 1947; Wilson, W. E., 1948), the accepted conception of vocational choice, with a few but notable exceptions (e.g., Carter, 1940; Super, 1942), was that an individual arrives at a particular point in his life, usually upon graduation from high school, when he selects his future career. Parsons (1909) writes that an individual's vocational choice is his "greatest decision" and that it occurs at that time in his life when he is about to enter the world of work. Much as Parsons emphasized the instantaneous nature of choice and enumerated the factors which affect the selection of an occupation at the "choice point," Paterson and Darley (1936), Williamson and Darley (1937), and others (e.g., Bell, H. M., 1938) also conceptualized choice as a decision which the individual makes at a given moment in time. According to this traditional viewpoint, the young person gives little thought to his vocational choice until he reaches the end of high school and is confronted with the problem of entering an occupation and establishing himself as a gainfully employed worker.

In marked contrast to this "crossroads" conception of vocational choice as a one-time event, Ginzberg et al. (1951) introduced the idea that choice is a process which transpires over a prolonged period of time. Influenced by the work of Lazarsfeld (1931) and Buehler, K. (1929), both of whom argued that *how* individuals make vocational choices may be more significant than *why* they make them, Ginzberg adopted a genetic approach to the study of choice and proceeded to identify and trace the series of vocationally relevant decisions through which an individual passes before he enters the world of work. His major finding was that "an individual never reaches the ultimate decision at a single moment in time, but through a series of decisions over a period of many years" (Ginzberg et al., 1951, p. 27). For most individuals the process of choosing an occupation takes approximately 10 years, from the age of 10 to the age of 21. Super (1956) has elaborated upon Ginzberg's conclusion that choice is a process by emphasizing that it is a *continuous* process. By "continuous" Super (1953, p. 187) means that "there is no sharp distinction between choice and adjustment. Instead, they blend in adolescence, with now the need to make a choice and now the need to make an adjustment predominating in the occupational or life situation."

In an excellent analysis of vocational choice as an event and as a process, however, Beilin (1955) presents a convincing argument for retaining both concepts. He reasons that there are basically two ways in which data on choice can be collected and organized: through "point-in-time" analyses or through "progressive-time-sample" comparisons. The concept of choice as an event is appropriate for the former, whereas the concept of choice as a process is relevant to the latter. Using this framework, Beilin distinguishes among four types of studies of choice, the first two of which analyze choice as an event ("point-in-time") and the last two as a process ("progressive-time-samples"): (1) studies conducted at typical "choice points," such as the beginning and end of high school; (2) studies focusing upon the "field" interactions between choice and other variables: (3) "historical" studies of the relationships of past experiences to present choices; and (4) "developmental" studies of trends in choices over time.

Although Beilin's distinctions between the various ways in which vocational choice can be studied are useful for classifying research findings, they do not resolve the issue of whether choice is an event or a process as far as theory construction is concerned. There does seem to be a solution to this problem, however, suggested by a principle from developmental psychology which states that there are individual differences in the *rates* at which people develop (Jersild, 1946). Each person progresses in his development at a slightly different rate: levels of maturity are reached at different times, and spurts and starts in growth vary from one individual to another. As a result, at any one point in time, when a number of individuals are compared, they may tend to differ because their rates of development are not exactly the same. In other words, the differences which exist between individuals when we view their vocational choices as events may be due to the differences in the rates of development which characterize them when we consider their choices as processes. Point-in-time differences may also be attributable to nondevelopmental factors, however, and consequently to test the hypothesized relationship between choice as an event and as a process it is important to keep in mind that these other variables should be adequately controlled.

DEFINITIONS OF VOCATIONAL CHOICE

Interestingly enough, no one has explicitly defined vocational choice as either an event or a process, although the general meaning of these terms is implicit in the writings of the trait-and-factor psychologists, on the one hand, and Ginzberg, Super, and others (e.g., Dysinger, 1950), on the other. As has been mentioned, *event* refers to a vocational decision at a given moment in time, such as the choice of medicine at the beginning of college, and *process* designates a series of such decisions over a period of time. These definitions of choice as an event and a process may be adequate for some purposes, but they are too general and ambiguous for theory construction and empirical research. There is little agreement, for example, upon whether choice is the same as vocational preference or vocational aspiration. To clarify some of these matters, this section reviews the various ways in which vocational choice has been defined and, from a critical analysis of these, develops an operational definition of choice which gives it a more explicit meaning.

Vocational Choice Defined as Preference

Vocational choice has often been defined as what the individual *prefers* to do. Given a number of vocational alternatives, he expresses his preference for one or another, and this constitutes his choice. More specifically, he indicates that he has ranked two or more occupations along some continuum of desirability or favorability, usually one of liking-disliking. There are several studies in the field of vocational psychology in which choice is defined as preference, where the latter refers to the individual's first-ranked (best-liked) occupation (Fryer, 1931; Gilger, 1942; Trow, 1941). Super (1953) states that Ginzberg defines choice in this way and criticizes him for it, but Ginzberg's discussion of preference in relation to both choice and interest would indicate otherwise. He writes as follows:

> Our contention is that when people say they "have no interests" they really mean that none of their interests is strong enough to be

> used as a basis for a vocational choice. If this premise is correct, then a still more generalized "preference" pattern would be of small aid in solving the choice problem. Interests imply more differentiation and complexity than "preferences," and in order to make them effective factors in the choice process we must look for those differentiating criteria which establish a hierarchy among an individual's interests [Ginzberg et al., 951, p. 245].

Although Ginzberg does not give a definition of choice in this passage, or elsewhere in his theory for that matter, he clearly implies that choice is not the same as either preference or interest.

Actually, Super's objection is to the use of the term "choice," which he says has different meanings at different age levels, if it is not defined as training for or entry into an occupation. He writes that:

> To the 14-year-old it [choice] means nothing more than preference, because at that age the need for realism is minimized by the fact that the preference does not need to be acted upon until the remote future. To the 21-year-old student of engineering, on the other hand, "choice" means a preference which has already been acted upon in entering engineering school, although the final action will come only with graduation and entry into a job [Super, 1953, p. 12].

In this example, Super reasons that decisions made at the younger age levels are not as highly related to reality as decisions reached at the older age levels, since the necessity to act upon them is not as great as it is later on. To reflect this distinction between earlier and later decisions, Super suggests that "preference" should designate *unimplemented* courses of action, such as preparation for or entry into a specific occupation. Roe (1956, p. 251) says much the same thing when she writes that:

> With small children, "choice" of an occupation means something quite different from what it means even in high school, and choice means something else again when one is actually faced with the necessity for taking a job. We might reserve the term preference for all stages up to the final one of actually entering upon an occupation.

To accept the distinction between choice and preference which Super and Roe propose, however, may or may not aid clarification. The problem is that their distinction is based upon an analysis of the differences in the content or substance of vocational decisions at different points in the individual's development, rather than an analysis of the behavior involved in making a choice or expressing a preference. Whether a course of action is implemented or unimplemented has little to do with the definition of choice and preference. It can be argued that any course of action which is undertaken by an individual indicates that he has made a choice, but the choice is *not* the same as the course of action, just as the selection of an occupation is not the same as entry into an occupation. Given two or more alternative courses of action, an individual must make a choice *before* he can act in one way or another. In other words, the "choice act" can be defined independently of the course of action an individual follows. Thus, it would seem that the implementation of a course of action is not a presumptive criterion of the difference between choice and preference.

To distingush between choice and preference it is necessary to understand (1) what behaviors each entails and (2) how these behaviors are related. As has been mentioned, when an individual expresses a preference he ranks two or more occupations along some continuum of desirability or liking. In contrast, when he makes a choice, he ranks two or more occupations along a continuum of his estimated chances of actually entering them. In expressing a preference, he indicates what he would *like* to do; in making a choice, he predicts what he *probably* will do. In other words, as Ginzberg suggests in the passage quoted, choice is more comprehensive than preference. All choices presume preferences, but all preferences do not necessarily imply choice. An individual makes a vocational choice on the basis of a number of factors, including an appraisal of his abilities, an assessment of his personal traits and values, a knowledge of occupational opportunities, etc., as well as a consideration of his preferences. He may *choose* selling as a vocation because it requires only a high school education and opportunities in it are good, but he may *prefer* engineering because it offers greater prestige and status.

Studies of the relationship between choice and preference support the distinctions which have just been made with respect to the two concepts. Open-ended questions designed to elicit choice and preference (see discussion to follow) yield responses which definitely differ. In a sample of 330 boys and girls in the eighth, tenth, and twelfth grades in three Detroit schools, Trow (1941) found that 59 percent had choices and preferences which were different. When compared with the actual census distribution of workers in the occupations mentioned, it was apparent that the difference between choice and preference was one of realism. Because choice is more comprehensive than preference and is based upon more factors, it tends to correspond more closely to the occupational distribution than does preference. This does not imply, however, as Super (1953) has contended, that choice means different things at different age levels. Regardless of age level, choice can be defined as what the individual predicts he *will* be doing in the future, and preference can be defined as what he would *like* to be doing. It is possible that the correlation between choice and preference is higher at the younger age levels than it is at the older ones, but this indicates only that choice is based upon more factors as age increases (see Chapter 5).[3]

Vocational Choice Defined as Aspiration

As well as being defined as preference, vocational choice is frequently equated with occupational aspiration, particularly by those who use a sociological frame of reference for the conceptualization and investigation of choice phenomena (e.g., Empey, 1956; Sewell, Haller, & Strauss, 1957). By "occupational aspiration" is usually meant what the individual considers to be the ideal vocation for him. Defined in this way, aspiration is quite similar to, if not identical with, a person's fantasy choice (Trow, 1941) as elicited by such interview and open-ended questions as "What would you do if you could do what you really wanted to do?"

Typically, the answers to questions about aspiration are quantified by assigning them scores on an occupational-prestige scale. For example, Lurie (1939) scored the aspirations of 954 adolescents on the Barr rating scale for occupations by assigning them corresponding scale values and found that the mean rating for his sample, which was 12.9 ("kindergarten teacher"), exceeded the national average occupation (in 1939) by 3.8 scale points. He concluded from this finding that he had measured aspiration rather than a more realistically oriented choice. In another study, Stubbins (1950) followed essentially the same procedure as Lurie, except that he used the interview to pose the question: "If you had every opportunity to follow any career you wished but still had to work for a living, what occupation would you choose?" Again, values for the responses were derived from a ranking of occupations according to their prestige, in this instance on a scale especially devised by Stubbins. A variation and elaboration of this method of measuring aspiration is to determine the discrepancy between a young person's ideal occupation and his father's occupation, as was done by Stefflre (1955), but this procedure is seldom used because discrepancy scores are less reliable, are difficult to treat statistically, and mean different things at different occupational levels because of "ceiling" and "floor" effects (Empey, 1956). Probably the most sophisticated and satisfactory measure of vocational aspiration has been devised by Miller, I. W., and Haller (1964), who have constructed an eight-item Occupational Aspiration Scale (OAS), based upon 80 of the occupations in the Hatt (1950) prestige scale (see Chapter 2), which has acceptably high reliability and correlates moderately positively with such variables as number of years of college

[3] An additional consideration, which has direct implications for research, is that if choice is defined operationally in different ways at different age levels, as Super and Roe suggest, it would not be possible to study developmental trends in choice from one point in time to another, since the measures of it would not be comparable.

planned, high school grade point average, intelligence, socioeconomic status, etc.

Whether occupational aspiration is defined by a single score on a scale or a discrepancy between scores, it almost always refers to the *level* at which an individual wishes to work. It seldom, if ever, refers to the field which one wants to enter. Viewed in this manner, it becomes more apparent why the sociologist interprets choice as aspiration. When he studies choice phenomena, his interest is not primarily in how and why people select the occupations they do, but rather it is in their strivings to be upwardly mobile socially. Since the occupation to which an individual aspires is one index of his desire to improve his social position, the sociologist usually investigates occupational aspiration, not vocational choice. Unfortunately, he sometimes gives the impression that he is studying the latter, or he is misinterpreted as doing so. Just as choice is distinct from preference, however, it is also distinct from aspiration. Not only does choice involve a specification of field as well as level of anticipated work, but, as in the case of its comparison with preference, choice is more comprehensive than aspiration. Whereas choice is based upon a consideration of the many factors which may affect future job satisfaction and success, aspiration is formulated solely in terms of the individual's wants and wishes, i.e., irrespective of the limitations imposed by reality.

This interpretation of the differences between choice and aspiration is supported by the findings of several studies. Trow (1941) investigated the relationship between choice and aspiration, as well as between choice and preference, and found that the agreement between the former two variables was even less than that for the latter two variables. Only a small percentage of his sample had choices which corresponded to their aspirations. Similarly, Gilger (1942) obtained results which indicated some overlap between choice and aspiration, but also considerable differences. Approximately the same proportion of his 579 male technical school Subjects chose occupations in the "manufacturing and mechanical" fields as aspired to them (29.9 versus 21.3 percent), but a much larger segment aspired to work on a "professional" level than chose it (20.3 versus 5.6 percent). These data are old, having been gathered in the early 1940s, but they are nevertheless accurate, as a more recent study by Stephenson, R. M. (1957) has shown. When this investigator compared the choices and aspirations of 1,000 ninth-grade males and females, he found a positive, but low, relationship between them. For example, 73 percent of his sample aspired to business and professional occupations, but only 40 percent expressed congruent choices.

This research on the relationship of vocational choice to preference and aspiration leads to two conclusions: (1) these concepts or variables are relatively distinct ones, but (2) they are also related to each other. They are distinct because they differ in the extent to which they represent reality-oriented selections of occupations, and they are the same because they all involve the selection of an occupation, regardless of the basis for the selection. We can represent these differences and similarities graphically as shown in Figure 4-1, where choice, preference, and aspiration are ordered along a continuum of reality orientation. In this scheme, choice is more realistic than either preference or aspiration, and preference is more realistic than aspiration. In making a choice, the individual considers as many factors as possible which may affect his employment and progress in an occupation and selects one which he thinks will provide him with the greatest degree of success and satisfaction. In expressing a preference, the individual indicates which occupation he likes the best and would enter, if certain contingencies, such as financial support for training, could be arranged. In stating an aspiration, the individual indulges in fantasy and conceives of the "merely possible"—what he wishes he could do *if* he could enter his ideal occupation.

Vocational Choice Defined Operationally

Thus far, a number of different ways in which vocational choice has been conceptualized and defined have been considered. Research supports some of the concepts and definitions of choice but is either inconclusive or nonconfirmatory with respect to others. Our task now is to use what has been substantiated about the nature of vocational choice and from this body of knowledge develop an operational definition of the concept which will give it an explicit, empirical referrent. By "operational" definition is meant one which specifies the meaning of a concept with reference to observable and measurable physical properties. Such physical properties include the positions and relationships of objects in space, their color, form, and substance, their movements, their changes with time, etc. These properties are observable if they can be sensed and discriminated, and they are measurable if they can be quantified. To define a concept operationally, we enumerate the physical properties which dis-

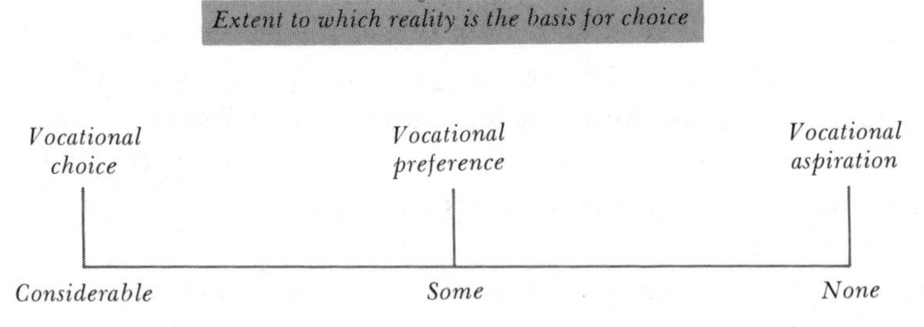

Figure 4-1. The relationship of vocational choice to vocational preference and aspiration on the reality continuum.

tinguish or "set it off" from other concepts. For example, we might say that an individual is *aggressive* (concept), if he reduces the *efficiency* (physical property) of another individual in attaining a common goal, where "efficiency" refers to expenditure of time, amount of effort, or monetary cost (Ackoff, 1953, p. 62). In the discussion which follows, we shall attempt to formulate, using essentially the same form as we did in this example, an operational definition of choice which enumerates what the distinguishing physical properties of a "choice" are.

1. As was concluded in the first section of this chapter, a vocational choice is a *response*. Furthermore, as the next section "Measures of Vocational Choice" will establish, it is always a *verbal* response. An individual always designates his selection of an occupation symbolically, since he cannot physically choose a vocation as he can other things, such as articles in a self-service department store or food in an automat. As a verbal response, an individual's vocational choice is an observable *change* in his behavior. When he states his choice verbally, he changes from a state of silence or rest to one of talking or writing, which we can observe because we can hear him speak or see him move. In other words, a vocational choice is a behavioral event, because certain properties (silence, rest) of the individual change to other properties (talking, writing) when he states his probable future occupation. Finally, to the extent that the individual makes a series of such statements over a period of time, each of which is slightly different from the others, but all of which are related to eventual occupational entry, then vocational choice is a process, since any process is no more than "a sequence of events which *together* yield a specified product or state" (Ackoff, 1953, p. 64). As a process, choice has certain characteristics, and we shall discuss these in detail in the next chapter.

2. We have narrowed the concept of vocational choice down considerably by specifying, first, that it is not just any kind of response, but rather a *verbal* response, which, for example, serves to distinguish it from occupational entry, and, second, that it is not primarily a process but that it is basically an *event,* which makes clear the distinction between a process and its elements. Further specifications are necessary, however, to define choice, because it is clear that both preference and aspiration are also verbal responses. To differentiate choice from these related concepts, we can draw upon the research cited earlier which shows that choice is more reality-oriented than preference and aspiration. When an individual makes a vocational choice, he considers what his *probable* occupation will be, not what his *possible* (preference) or *fantasy* (aspiration) occupations might be. His choice expresses his appraisal of his chances of entering an occupation and of being well adjusted in it. This means that his choice is more "realistic" than either his preference or aspiration, because he bases it upon his perception of reality and his estimate that he can

implement it successfully. Thus, when presented with a stimulus such as "What kind of job do you think you will probably be able to do when you are through school?" (Trow, 1941), he responds by indicating his vocational choice. In contrast, different stimulus questions, such as "If you could be sure to get the education and training that you would need, what kind of job would you choose?" and "If by some magic you could be anything you want, what would you like to be?", are asked to elicit his preference and aspiration, respectively.

3. On the basis of the foregoing comments and observations, we can now define vocational choice operationally as follows: *An individual, X, makes a vocational choice if he expresses an intention to enter a particular occupation.* Several assumptions underlie this definition, which is condensed to make it readable. First, to simplify the definition it is assumed that the verb "expresses" refers to observable behavior, such as declaring a choice in speech or writing. Second, by "intention" is meant the individual's best estimate of his future occupation based upon a consideration of reality factors as well as preferences and aspirations. Third, to make a vocational choice the individual may select more than one occupation, but he may *not* select all possible occupations. In other words, he must make a discrimination among occupations to accomplish a choice. Finally, if he cannot discriminate among occupations, either because he rejects them all or accepts them all, then he has "no choice" (see Chapter 7).

We have formulated an operational definition of vocational choice by enumerating the physical properties which differentiate this kind of behavior from others, but we have not considered as yet the conditions which must be present for the "choice act" to occur. And, without adequate empirical studies, it is difficult to specify what they are. In lieu of data, probably the best approach to take is to apply principles established in areas related to choice phenomena and draw inferences which can be tested in appropriate research. The area which is most relevant to the analysis of vocational choice is that which deals with the choice of commodities. Edwards, W. (1954) has made a comprehensive review of the theory of decision making as it applies to consumer behavior, and we can extrapolate from his summary several concepts which are applicable to the selection of an occupation. These concepts, in addition to some others based upon psychological principles, suggest three necessary conditions for the occurrence of a vocational choice:

1. *A "choice supply."* There must be two or more occupations from which to choose. The individual must have an option. If there is no option, a vocational choice is impossible.

2. *Incentive to make a choice.* The individual must be motivated to choose an occupation. In our society, the incentive is the social expectation that every man must work.

3. *Freedom to choose.* The individual must be free to exercise his option in the choice of an occupation. If he is restrained from doing so, he cannot make a vocational choice.

These conditions would seem to be necessary for an individual to choose an occupation. They may or may not be *sufficient.* Most theories of decision making would specify these factors as essential but would disagree on others. The traditional economic theory of riskless choices would add that an individual must be completely informed about the courses of action open to him, be infinitely sensitive to differences between the alternatives, and be rational in his decisions, in the sense that he can order them and maximize some utility by implementing them (Edwards, W., 1954, p. 381). Whether these or other conditions must be present for the making of vocational choices, however, is a matter for further investigation.

Tyler (1961a) has initiated a series of studies which may provide the needed data. In order to analyze individual differences in patterns of choice, she presents a Subject with a board on which there are the names of 100 occupations, each printed on a small card and arranged in a standard order. She gives the Subject the following instructions: "I would like you to place over here in the *Would Not Choose* column all of the occupations you see as out of the question for a person like you. If you can't make a decision, place the card under *No Opinion*" (Tyler, 1961a, p. 195). With this choice situation, Tyler has obtained results which indicate that the selections individuals make are fairly consistent with each other from one occasion to another and that these choice patterns reflect variations between individuals in their decision-making styles and their personalities. Tyler has not varied the conditions under which Subjects are required to make choices, but it would seem that her "choice board" is peculiarly suited to such experimentation and that research of this type might lead to a better understanding of the bases upon which choices are made and the conditions which affect them.

MEASURES OF VOCATIONAL CHOICE

The predominant techniques which vocational psychologists have used to measure vocational choice are the interview, the open-ended question, and the questionnaire. As we shall see, each of these techniques has special applications. The interview is generally used when the investigator is interested in collecting intensive personal-history data on a small sample of Subjects. The open-ended question is more structured than the interview, but it still allows some freedom in response comparable to that afforded by the interview, and it is a convenient way to elicit choices when the investigator wants to gather data on a large group of Subjects. The questionnaire is the most highly structured of the three techniques, although in its early stages of construction it is usually developed from the other two approaches. Consequently, it provides for a considerable range in responses, yet yields data which are readily amenable to statistical analysis. In the discussion which follows, we shall consider the characteristics of each of these techniques in greater detail and review their reliability and validity as measures of vocational choice.

The Interview, Open-ended Question, and Questionnaire

Because the *interview* is more adaptable and flexible than the other techniques, it is often preferred in research which is designed to survey an area with the purpose of identifying variables and developing hypotheses rather than testing formal theoretical propositions. In the work of Ginzberg et al. (1951), for example, a primary goal of the research was to discover *how* individuals make vocational choices. To accomplish this objective, these investigators decided to use the interview as a means for exploring a Subject's thinking about the problem of choice and his approach to solving it. They formulated a tentative outline for the interview, which covered discussions of the following topics:

1. *The self:* capacities, interests, values, and time perspective
2. *Reality:* family, environment, world of work, and life plan
3. *Key persons:* parents, siblings, relatives, peers, neighbors, and teachers

Although these topics are relatively comprehensive, in the sense that they deal with most of the known variables in choice, the interviews were not restricted to them, since the researchers were also interested in other factors which the Subjects might introduce in the course of an unstructured conversation.

Ginzberg's team held only one interview with each Subject, but sometimes it is necessary to conduct several interviews to ensure that the desired data on choice are secured. In the initial phase of the Career Pattern Study, for example, each Subject in the sample was interviewed four times in order to gather information on his (1) free time, (2) reactions to school, (3) familial relationships, and (4) vocational plans (Super, Crites, Hummel, Moser, Overstreet, & Warnath, 1957). Some questions from the last interview in the series, which illustrate some of the "leads" and "primers" that an interviewer may use to stimulate a Subject, are reproduced in Table 4-1.

Small (1953, p. 10) has developed a less structured approach which he calls the "job-concept" interview and which he describes as follows:

> The Job-Concept interview was designed to elicit the phantasy content of the individual's job thinking. His vocational aversions and

***Table 4-1. Schedule for an Interview on Vocational Choice** (From Super et al., 1957, pp. 122–123)*

LEAD 1: We've talked about school, your activities outside of school, and your family. This time let's talk about your plans for the future. What would you like to be by the time you're thirty?

PRIMERS:
a. What would you do as a ______ (occupation named)?
b. Why do you want to be a ______ (occupation named)?
c. Most boys have a general idea of the kind of people they want to be when they grow up. What sort of person do you want to be?
d. How do you expect to achieve that ambition?

BE SURE TO GET:
Work values and attitudes
Desire versus expectation (e.g., wishes versus perception of ability)
Alternatives
Reasonably planful versus haphazard
Optimistic versus pessimistic
Occupational goal, information, and reasons for choices

LEAD 2: How far do you intend to go with your education?

PRIMERS:
a. What sort of education do you want? Why?
b. Do you expect to be able to get it?
c. Do you think you can handle it? (If college or other beyond high school)

BE SURE TO GET:
Type and level of education
Clarity of plans

reasons for them are evoked. Identifications are explored. The individual's comprehension of the realities involved in his vocational choice is studied—his concept of what is done on the job and how. He is then led into an expression of deeper phantasy, by being asked to describe a future typical day of employment in his chosen work and to tell what he believes to be the attitude of family, friends, society, and self to those in the occupation. The "typical day" and "attitudes" become projections of himself. Finally, to reach a still deeper level, we ask for the subject's actual or made-up dreams about his vocational choices.

Armstrong (1957) has also devised an interview procedure which appears to have some promise, but it deals more with vocational interests than choices.

The *open-ended question* has features which resemble both the interview and the questionnaire: it stimulates responses which are made voluntarily by the Subject, rather than suggested to him in the form of a statement, but it limits responses to only those questions which are posed, although sometimes space is provided for additional comments. The form of this technique is, of course, the question, which asks a Subject to declare his vocational choice. Sometimes a statement such as "Occupation I am planning to enter" (SVIB booklet) will not be in an interrogative form, but it clearly implies a question, and it is also open-ended. The content of the open-ended question varies from one study to another, as is shown in Table 4-2, and this variation causes considerable confusion in making generalizations about the results of these studies, because the substance of the question directly affects the response which is obtained (Trow, 1941). There is definitely a need for research on what Underwood (1957) has referred to as "operational identification" and "stimulus variable elaboration." With respect to measures of vocational choice, these concepts mean that we must determine the extent to which (1) different stimuli elicit the same response (operational identification) and (2) similar stimuli evoke different responses (stimulus variable elaboration), if we are to reduce some of the confusion which has existed in the previous use of open-ended questions.

Until data on these problems are available, it would seem desirable to agree upon some standard open-ended question which would reduce differences between future studies of vocational choice. Trow's (1941) questions, which were mentioned earlier and which are reproduced in Table 4-3 as they might be used in research, appear to be the best available for several reasons.[4] First, their wording is straightforward and concise and has a relatively low level of reading difficulty. Second, although Trow named them differently, the ques-

Table 4-2. Examples of Open-ended Questions Used in Studies of Vocational Choice

Study	*Question*	*Measure of*
1. Carp, 1949	a. "My probable occupation will be. . . ."	Choice
	b. "My desired occupation is. . . ."	Aspiration
2. Gilger, 1942	a. "What kinds of work do you feel you are best prepared to do at present?"	Choice
	b. "What vocation, or life work, do you want most of all to undertake?"	Preference
	c. "If you were financially able, and free to choose without restriction, what kind of work would you like to prepare for?"	Aspiration
3. Hurlock & Jansing, 1934	a. "What vocation or profession are you most likely to follow?	Choice
	b. "What vocation or profession would you like most to follow?	Preference

[4] These questions might also be modified, in order to provide Subjects with the option of indicating that they are "undecided." For example, the instructions might be revised to include a last sentence which reads: "If you have no vocational choice as yet, print 'undecided' on the line for Probable Occupation."

Table 4-3. Trow's Open-ended Questions about Probable, Possible, and Fantasy Vocational Choice Which Correspond to Measures of Choice, Preference, and Aspiration

Vocational Choice Inventory

INSTRUCTIONS: Listed below are three questions about vocational choice. Read them and then answer them in the spaces provided. Use specific occupational titles, such as Life Insurance Salesman rather than Sales.

1. PROBABLE OCCUPATION (Choice). What kind of job do you think you will probably be able to do when you are through school?

2. POSSIBLE OCCUPATION (Preference). If you could be sure to get the education and training that you would need, what kind of job would you choose?

3. PHANTASY OCCUPATION (Aspiration). People sometimes think about what they would like to be although they don't really believe it could ever come true. If by some magic you could be anything you want, what would you like to be?

tions correspond nicely to the definitions we have formulated of choice, preference, and aspiration. And, third, as the remainder of this section will bring out, Trow's questions have acceptable reliability and validity for the measurement of choice, preference, and aspiration.

The *questionnaire* presents the Subject with a list of occupations, such as those in the Lehman Vocational Attitude Quiz (Lehman & Witty, 1929), from which he makes his choices. Or, a questionnaire may contain several statements about vocational plans, and the Subject is instructed to endorse those which are applicable to him. A variation on both of these approaches is to have the Subject rank-order the three most important statements in each of a number of areas relevant to his choice. Crowley (1959) used this format to construct a checklist which would inventory the vocational goals of high school seniors. Interested in what the Subject sets as his goals and what he sees as the obstacles and aids to their attainment, he proceeded to develop the checklist through three phases. In the preliminary phase, open-ended questions were used which permitted Subjects complete freedom in stating what they saw as their goals, obstacles, and aids in five "time-of-life" groupings: 1 year, 5 years, 10 years, 20 years, and lifetime. From the resulting responses, 470 items were written and classified in the appropriate time periods for administration to a new sample (see Table 4-4). In this second phase, three different scoring keys were tried out, from which one was accepted as the most promising. Interviews were then conducted to validate responses to the checklist. The final phase was devoted to further refinement of the checklist and an analysis of it in relation to other variables, such as intelligence and socioeconomic level.[5]

[5] For other studies in which questionnaires have been developed, although less extensively than Crowley's, see Culver (1935); Moser, W. E. (1949); and Nick (1942).

***Table 4-4. Sample Items from Crowley's Questionnaire** (1959, p. 490)*

GOALS:	
1 year:	Be accepted by the school I want.
5 year:	Graduate from college or technical school.
10 year:	Be settled in a job which will be the best for me.
20 year:	Have a job where I like the kind of work.
Lifetime:	To live a very happy life.
OBSTACLES:	
1 year:	I don't work as hard as I should.
5 year:	I might not be smart enough.
10 year:	My education might not be good enough.
20 year:	My job won't be a source of satisfaction to me.
Lifetime:	I will not have used my money, brains, and talent wisely.
HELPS:	
1 year:	I have some experience in the work I want.
5 year:	I try to organize my life plans and know what I want.
10 year:	I am able to do good work in my specialty.
20 year:	I'll be well established and settled down.
Lifetime:	I put myself completely into the work I like.

Reliability of the Interview, Open-ended Question, and Questionnaire

Evidence on the *reliability of the interview* as a measure of vocational choice is sometimes misleading, because it often consists only of data on interjudge agreement in rating transcripts for the content of choices, preferences, or aspirations (e.g., Small, 1953). Interjudge agreement indicates how consistent and objective interview ratings are, but it does not demonstrate reliability (Champney, 1941). To establish the interview as a reliable measure of choice, it is necessary to show that it elicits essentially the same choice on different occasions, spaced relatively close together. The only study of this type which has been found was conducted by Schmidt and Rothney (1955) on the consistency among the choices of 347 high school students who were interviewed in their sophomore, junior, and senior years as part of an intensive guidance program and were followed up six months after graduation. They found that only 34.9 percent were consistent, i.e., made no changes, in their choices during the last three years of high school, whereas 33.6 percent were inconsistent. When the post–high school occupations or training of the students were compared with their choices, to determine whether the latter were consistent with what they were doing, the percentages were somewhat higher, as shown in Table 4-5. It should be noted, however, that "consistency" in this analysis was defined as agreement between post–high school activity and *any* of the choices the student made before he graduated.[6]

[6] It might be argued that, since Schmidt and Rothney used *guidance* interviews to elicit choices, in which exploration and change rather than stability of choice were presumably

Table 4-5. Number of Percentage of Counseled Subjects Entering Post–High School Occupations or Training Which They Had Chosen during High School Year Indicated *(Schmidt & Rothney, 1955, p. 144)*

High school year	*Number*	*Percentage*
Sophomore	161	46.4
Junior	171	49.3
Senior	186	53.6
Total	518	50.0

Data on the *reliability of the open-ended question* as a measure of vocational choice comes primarily from two studies, one by Trow (1941) and the other by Strong (1952). In the former, Trow retested a group of 41 Subjects with his "choice" question after a period of 5 months and found that the reliability was quite high. He reports a contingency coefficient (C) of .935. This degree of reliability in choice, however, which is comparable to that of the most stable phenomena (e.g., aptitudes), seems improbably high. Furthermore, it is not clear from Trow's article how he computed such a contingency coefficient. The maximum C for a 3 by 3 chi-square table, which is what he would have had to use, is only .82 (Garrett, 1958, p. 395), thus making the one he obtained questionable. At best, the reliability of choices as assessed by the open-ended question in Trow's study would have to be less than his estimate.

Strong (1952) objects to the estimation of reliability by procedures like Trow's, because he says it measures change in choice on an "all-or-none" basis. He prefers to assess reliability on a continuous dimension and suggests the use of correlations between the scales of the SVIB as one approach. The method he proposes is to (1) classify the vocational choices made on test and retest according to the corresponding scale on the SVIB and then (2) express the amount of change in choices by the correlation between the scales. For example, if an individual changed his choice from engineer to chemist, it would be only a slight change, because the correlation between the engineer and chemist scales on the SVIB is .88, but if he shifted his choice from engineer to lawyer, it would be a considerable change, because the correlation between these two scales is only .44.

Using this system, Strong compared the choices of 306 Stanford males when they were freshmen with their choices when they were sophomores. He elicited choices with the statement, "Occupation I am planning to enter." For this sample, he obtained an average reliability coefficient of .80. We might question this estimate, however, for two reasons. First, the correlation between choice and vocational interests is far from perfect. In fact, as we shall note in Chapter

encouraged, it is not surprising they found such a low percentage of consistency. Kohout and Rothney (1964) compared a counseled with an uncounseled group, however, and obtained no significant differences in the consistency of their choices (see Chapter 5).

6, it averages approximately .50. Consequently, estimating the reliability of choice from the correlation of cognate interest scales is not the same as computing it between two choices. Second, because the correlations between SVIB scales are partially an artifact of the interrelationships of the weights used in the scoring system (Strong, 1955), they are somewhat spurious and yield estimates which are either higher or lower than they should be. How far Strong's coefficient deviates from the true reliability of choice is difficult to say. In general, it seems reasonable to conclude that it is probably somewhat lower than the .80 Strong reports, particularly for a period as long as a year at the beginning of college.

In contrast to the work which has been done on the reliability of the interview and open-ended question, no studies have been found which deal directly with the *reliability of the questionnaire.* Lehman and Witty (1929, 1931b, 1931c) used the Lehman Vocational Attitude Quiz in several studies to investigate the relationship of vocational choice to age, but they employed the cross-sectional rather than the longitudinal method of analysis. As a consequence, they obtained data on different samples at successive age levels instead of on the same sample on different occasions. Likewise, Crowley (1959) failed to gather evidence on the reliability of his life-planning questionnaire.

With respect to all the techniques for measuring vocational choice, it is too often the case that evidence on their reliability is not wholly adequate, but it is good enough to allow us to draw at least some conclusions. First, although data on the questionnaire are lacking, it is probably even more reliable than the interview and open-ended question by virtue of its greater structure and more extensive standardization. Second, the best estimate of the reliability of the various techniques is in the .70s and possibly in the .80s. And, third, all the techniques are sufficiently reliable to measure choice as a phenomenon, although they are probably better suited for the study of *group* changes in choice than they are for the analysis or prediction of individual variations in choice.

Validity of the Interview, Open-ended Question, and Questionnaire

Validity of the Interview. Evidence on the content validity of the interview as a measure of vocational choice comes primarily from interjudge agreement in rating verbatim protocols. In an analysis of the fantasy content of vocational choices given in job-concept interviews, Small (1953) found that he and a fellow research psychologist at the Vocational Advisory Service of New York agreed remarkably well in their ratings, but that neither of their ratings correlated with those of the staff counselors and that the latter tended to disagree among themselves. Small reports that he and his colleague made the same ratings "200 times in 200," but he does not report how many times they disagreed with the counselors. As a part of the Career Pattern Study

(Super & Overstreet, 1960), various kinds of vocational behaviors reported during interviews with ninth graders were rated on specially devised scales, including one called Concern with Choice and another named Consistency of Choice within Fields, Levels, and Families. The conclusion drawn from these ratings of choice was that judges could attain a fairly high degree of agreement in their ratings, the lowest *r* being .57, with the majority of *r*'s ranging between .78 and .96.

Although these studies support the general conclusion that the interview is a valid technique for measuring vocational choice, at least as far as its content is concerned, one qualification should be kept in mind. As Small's study illustrates, interjudge agreement depends to some extent upon the sophistication and common orientation of the raters: Small and his associate achieved much greater agreement between themselves than they did with the counselors who were seeing the clients in the study. Likewise, in the Career Pattern Study, the relatively high degree of interjudge agreement may have stemmed from the similarity of the judges rather than from the fact that they *independently* perceived the same behavior in the same way, since they constituted a highly homogeneous group which had worked together for many years. Until we know more about how bias in the sampling of judges affects their ratings, it is probably best to consider the interjudge agreement attained in these studies as an overestimate.

Studies on the concurrent validity of the interview as a measure of vocational choice are less plentiful, but more soundly designed, than those on its content validity. Small (1953) correlated his ratings of fantasy choices elicited in the job-concept interview with two other, independent measures of the same variables and found reasonably high relationships. Using the rank-order correlational method, he obtained a *rho* of .44 between the job-concept interview and the Thematic Apperception Test and a *rho* of .52 between the job-concept interview and a case-history summary prepared by counselors. Because *rho*'s are exact estimates of *r,* they indicate acceptable validity for the interview, coefficients for which should range in the .40s and .50s to compare favorably with standardized tests. We can conclude from Small's findings that the interview yields responses about choice which are similar to those obtained by other methods.

The main criterion for assessing the predictive validity of the interview in the measurement of vocational choice is eventual "occupation entered" or "occupation engaged in" over a period of years. As with vocational interest inventories, the reasoning is that the interview has predictive validity if choices elicited in it agree with the individual's future occupation. That the choices expressed in the interview situation relate to later employment is apparent from the results of three studies:

1. In the investigation by Schmidt and Rothney (1955), which was discussed earlier in connection with the reliability of the interview, the findings indicated that approximately 50 percent of the sample entered the occupation they declared as their choice in the interview. The relationship between choice and occupation varied, however, with the consistency or stability of the individual's choice: a greater percentage (66.9 versus 49.4 and 41.7) of students who expressed the same choice in their sophomore, junior, and senior years of high school entered the corresponding occupation than students who made a new choice in their senior year or who had a consistent choice for only the junior and senior years. Thus, in the case of the interview, as with tests, the reliability of the measuring instrument or technique places a ceiling upon its validity.

2. With college rather than high school students, Dyer, J. R. (1932) followed up a sample of 101 Subjects at Kansas University to determine whether the (*a*) occupation they entered upon graduation and (*b*) occupation they were in five years later agreed with the choices they expressed in interviews when they were still in college. He discovered that for both the initial and extended employment of his sample there was a high degree of agreement with earlier choices. Table 4-6 from his study shows that approximately 80 percent followed the occupation of their choice upon leaving college and at the end of five years. Moreover, about the same percentage reported that they would not change their occupation, even if they were offered a gift of $100,000 as an inducement!

3. A study by McArthur and Stevens (1955) confirms the findings of Schmidt and Rothney and of Dyer, but suggests that the predictive validity of interview-derived choices differs for individuals from different social classes. The interview choices of upper-class Harvard undergraduates correlated higher with their occupations 14 years later than did the choices of middle-class Harvard students, presumably because boys from the upper class more often follow their father's occupation or enter the family's business. Thus, social-class status as well as reliability influences the predictive validity of the interview, but

Table 4-6. The Permanence of First and Other Choices after College and Five Years Later *(From Dyer, J. R., 1932, p. 238)*

Vocation actually followed on leaving college	*N*	*Vocation followed at end of 5 years*	*N*
First college choice	82	First college choice	79
Second choice	9	Second choice	10
Third choice	3	Third choice	3
Fourth choice	1	Choice not previously mentioned	9
Choice not previously mentioned	6	Total	101
Total	101		

apparently not enough to make it invalid for estimating an individual's future occupation from the choice he expresses in an interview.

Validity of the Open-ended Question. Work on the validity of the open-ended question as a measure of vocational choice is not nearly as extensive as the research on the interview. There are only the studies by Trow (1941) and Strong (1953) on its content and predictive validity, and interrelated studies by Glick (1963; 1964; 1965a) on its concurrent validity, but these are comprehensive and thorough enough that they provide us with sufficient evidence for sound conclusions.

Trow reports three different kinds of data which support the content validity of the open-ended questions he designed to measure probable, possible, and fantasy choice.[7] First, only 17 percent of Trow's sample of 330 high school boys and girls answered the three questions in the same way. They tended to interpret the questions about probable and possible choice as more similar than the questions about possible and fantasy choice, but in each instance they responded differentially to a high degree: 53 percent expressed different probable and possible choices and 68 percent declared different possible and fantasy choices. Second, when asked to rate their choices on a scale of liking-disliking, students who had different probable and possible choices indicated a significantly greater liking for their possible choice. In other words, they discriminated between the desirability of the vocational choices elicited by the distinctive content of the probable and possible choice questions. And, third, they made responses to the three open-ended questions which, as we mentioned before, differed along a dimension of "realism." As compared with the actual distribution of workers across occupational levels, the greatest degree of agreement was with their probable choices, then their possible choices, and lastly their fantasy choices. In short, Trow's open-ended questions have demonstrated content validity, because they evoke different responses from the same individual.

In Strong's (1953) study of the validity of the open-ended question, he assessed the predictive usefulness of this approach by relating choices made in response to the SVIB statement "Occupation I am planning to enter" to "occupation engaged in" 19 years after college graduation. Although Strong's follow-up covered almost 20 years, he argues that the optimal interval should be between 5 and 15 years. He reasons that, after this length of time, an individual may move along the established lines of job advancement and progression to a position which by its title appears *as if* it is in another field of

[7] Trow's terminology is used here to summarize his study, but we can understand his three kinds of "choice" to refer to what has been defined as choice, preference, and aspiration, respectively.

endeavor, and this introduces error into "occupation engaged in" as a criterion variable. Strong adjusted his findings for misclassifications in occupational membership arising from promotion to manifestly different positions, but still found that they influenced his results. The percentage of agreement between responses to the open-ended question and "occupation engaged in" ranged from 38 to 61, depending upon the occupational classification procedure which was used. By classifying choices in cognate interest areas on the SVIB, Strong obtained an average *r* between choice and occupation of .69, which is encouragingly high, but which may be subject to the same criticisms made earlier of his reliability study of choice.

Taking a different approach, Glick (1963, p. 91) started with the hypothesis that "the college undergraduate is capable of differentiating between two types of occupational choice: (1) the occupation that he would most like to follow as a career (occupational aspiration); and (2) the occupation that he, realizing that there would be obstacles in his way, realistically believed he would follow as a career (occupational expectation)." To test this hypothesis he asked 339 college undergraduates to respond to two open-ended questions about their aspirations and expectations (probable choices) and then related the discrepancies between these to (1) their anticipated frustration at not being able to realize their aspirations and to (2) the factors contributing to their anticipated frustration. He found that the greater the discrepancy between aspirations and expectations, as determined by classifying them in a system similar to Super's (1957; see Chapter 2), the greater the anticipated frustration. The factor which the students said contributed most to the latter was "lack of money" to establish themselves in these aspired-to vocations and "lack of a graduate degree."

In a second study, Glick (1964) investigated several other correlates of the discrepancy between aspiration and expectations, including class in college, academic standing, and father's occupation, but found only that father's occupation was significantly related to anticipated frustration. He also followed up most of his original sample when they were college seniors and discovered that the percentage of them who anticipated frustration in fulfilling their aspirations had decreased (Glick, 1965a). In other words, their aspirations and expectations were more similar the last year in college than they were earlier, but Glick neglected to report what the direction of the convergence was, i.e., did aspirations become more like expectations or vice versa? In either case, his findings support the validity of open-ended questions in eliciting differential responses about aspiration and choice which are related to independently defined variables.

Validity of the Questionnaire. Empirical evidence on the validity of the questionnaire as a technique for measuring vocational choice is practically nonexistent. Despite some of the obvious advantages of the questionnaire for the large-scale collection of data and sophisticated statistical analyses, only one study has been found which deals with the construction and development of a choice questionnaire, and it leaves much to be desired as far as formal validation is concerned. The study is the aforementioned one by Crowley (1959), who devised a questionnaire which appears to have both some content and some concurrent validity. As examples of content validity, he cites such statements as "Graduate from college or technical school," "Be settled in a job which will be best for me," and "Have a job where I like the kind of work." From the wording of these items, it would seem that there would be little difficulty in obtaining a high degree of interjudge agreement on what they measure, but unfortunately Crowley does not report the relevant data. As a result, the content validity of his questionnaire remains a matter of speculation rather than fact.

The concurrent validity of Crowley's inventory is somewhat less conjectural, although it rests upon only minimal empirical findings. To check "the tendency to select expected, rather than true, items" in his questionnaire, Crowley conducted "validating interviews" with 14 Subjects, in which he asked about their vocational plans, the obstacles they saw to the fulfillment of them, and the aids they anticipated in overcoming the obstacles. From the interview responses of this very small sample, he concluded that the answers to his questionnaire were undistorted by test-taking biases and that, therefore, they were valid. It is difficult to accept this conclusion without some qualification for two reasons: First, it is quite possible that the same response bias operated in both the interview and questionnaire and produced invalid results from both; and, second, it is a less than desirable procedure to use the interview as a criterion when its validity as a measure of choice is still being established. Although it requires the passage of time, the most appropriate method for validating the questionnaire is to compare responses to it with occupation entered or occupation engaged in. In other words, we need data on its predictive validity before we can evaluate evidence on other aspects of its validity.

In general, research on the validity of the interview, open-ended question, and questionnaire as techniques for measuring vocational choice is far from adequate, but still it indicates that responses elicited by these approaches are related to other choice behaviors in both the present and the future. Decisions about which technique to use in a given situation depend in large part upon the purpose of the investigation. If the research objective is to study a relatively few cases very intensively, the interview offers the advantages of flexibility in questioning a Subject as well as personal contact with him. If the goal is to survey the vocational choices of a large group to establish base rates or collect data for descriptive statistics, the open-ended question is economical and straightforward. If the intent of the study is to test formal hypotheses and make statistical inferences, the questionnaire is most appropriate, because it usually yields scores on a higher level of measurement than either of the other two techniques. The validity of the various measures is substantially the same, although the research by Trow (1941) and Strong (1953) shows some advantage for the open-ended question. Furthermore, this technique is reliable enough to use with confidence in tracing trends in the stability of choices over extended periods of time. Of the several devices for measuring vocational choice, it seems to be the best for reasons of reliability and validity as well as economy and practicality.

INDIVIDUAL DIFFERENCES IN VOCATIONAL CHOICE

Now that we have an idea of the techniques which are available to measure vocational choice and have some impression of how reliable and valid they are, we can summarize the research in which they have been used and arrive at some conclusions about the individual differences which exist in the selection of an occupation. To do so, however, it is necessary first to classify the responses which have been elicited in the various studies according to some system, so that they can be analyzed and collated. The best system for this purpose appears to be Roe's two-dimensional classification scheme, which is both comprehensive and current. Not only does it provide a convenient framework for summarizing the choices which individuals make according to "field" and "level," but it is a system into which choices can be classified reliably (see Chapter 2). In the following discussion, it has been used to group and synthesize the results of studies on individual differences in vocational choice.

The Fields of Vocational Choice

Since the late 1920s, the three most popular fields of vocational choice have been engineering, medicine, and teaching. Variations from this overall trend occur, of course, particularly in rural areas where a plurality of young males decide upon agricultural occupations for careers (Sisson, 1941), but in the larger urban centers the base rates seem well established. In an analysis of the choices of entering freshmen (*N* not given) at the College of the City of Detroit in 1927, Cunliffe (1927) found that 20.7 percent selected medicine as their vocational goal. The next two most frequently chosen fields were teaching (16.9 percent) and business (12.9 percent). Data gathered by Beeson and Tope (1928) on 2,000 high school boys indicated that engineering was their most popular choice. Sparling (1933) writes that 53.9 percent of a sample of 888 male college students selected medicine as their first vocational objective, and Threlkeld (1935) reports that the professional occupations chosen most often by 1,883 male college seniors were law, teaching, and medicine. Hurlock and Jansing (1934) discovered some variations in the choices of native and foreign-born boys in technical and academic schools, but engineering stood out as the most preferred occupation for the entire group. For 34,472 high school senior boys, Byrns (1939) also found that the most attractive occupation was engineering as a vocational choice for samples of male college freshmen from cities ($N = 454$), towns ($N = 297$), and farms ($N = 200$), the respective percentages of choice being 41.85, 34.34, and 22.00.

The most comprehensive and up-to-date study of the fields of vocational choice was conducted by Davis in 1961 (Davis, J. A., & Bradburn, 1962; Davis, J. A., 1964; 1965), and it tends to substantiate these earlier findings. He sent a self-administered questionnaire to a sample of 33,982 graduating seniors from 135 colleges and universities. He asked them (1) to indicate what their "career preference" was at the beginning of college, (2) what their anticipated career field was, and (3) what their plans for graduate training were.[8] As in other studies, Davis (1965, p. 74) found that teaching (primary and secondary teaching, excluding college and junior college) was one of the most frequently chosen fields, approximately one-third (32.2 percent) of his sample selecting it. Engineering ranked third, being chosen by 8.3 percent, but business and administration took second place, ahead of medicine, with 18.2 percent. This "reversal" may have been due to the heterogeneity of the business category, which included secretaries along with higher-level occupations. More than three-quarters of the sample (77.2 percent) said that they were planning to pursue some kind of graduate training, but only about one-fifth (20.2 percent) had actually been accepted by June, 1961. Thus, Davis's study generally corroborates the results of previous research, which has shown that teaching and engineering (and possibly medicine) are the most frequently chosen occupational fields. It also highlights the fact that a large percentage of college seniors are considering continuing their education rather than entering the world of work.

The Levels of Vocational Choice

Several studies have shown that young people tend to select occupations which stand high in the prestige and skill hierarchy. The extensive investigation of

[8] Much of Davis's analysis of the undergraduate decisions of his sample dealt with the changes which took place in choice between the freshman and senior years, although, as he notes, the data on the earlier choices were retrospective. That they have been distorted by "looking backward" is suggested by his finding that only 8 percent had "no preference" as freshmen, whereas most other studies, which have elicited choices *at the time* Subjects were freshmen, set the figure closer to 20 percent (see Chapter 7). Since longitudinal data are available on the stability of choices during the college years (see Chapter 5), they are to be preferred to Davis's findings.

13,528 adolescent males and females in Maryland conducted by Bell, H. M. (1938) revealed that, although many of them had to take any job they could find as a result of depressed economic conditions, 38.3 percent of them wanted professional-technical jobs and an additional 18.5 percent desired office-sales positions. In a survey of 279 male freshmen at Wesleyan University, Sisson (1938a) found that 83 percent expressed a choice for an occupation at the professional level. Similarly, Myers, W. E. (1947) has reported that high percentages of both boys and girls choose occupations at the upper levels. In his sample of 444 high school graduates, 60 percent of the boys intended to enter one of the professions and 71 percent of the girls selected a clerical occupation. The findings of Wilson, A. B. (1948) on veterans of World War II are consistent with those already cited: 38.7 percent of them wanted to head for some kind of professional or semiprofessional occupation and 39.3 percent had one of the skilled trades as an objective. Similarly, Hutson (1962) found in two surveys, one conducted in 1930 and the other in 1961, that the tendency for a preponderance of junior and senior high school boys to choose occupations in the professions and skilled trades had not changed substantially during this 31-year period. Probably the major factor in the disposition of adolescents to choose professional and skilled occupations is the glamour and status associated with these levels of vocational endeavor. This does not mean, however, as some investigators have concluded (e.g., Bell, H. M., 1938; Myers, W. E., 1947), that the choices are *necessarily* unrealistic. As we shall see in Chapter 7, evaluations of choice realism involve a number of considerations and criteria.

The Fields and Levels of Vocational Choice

With one possible exception,[9] there have been no studies which have analyzed the vocational choices of young people by both "field" and "level." Current occupational classification systems take into consideration field as well as level, however, and vocational choices should be analyzed along both dimensions. Is there a tendency for individuals to choose professional and skilled occupations in only certain fields, or do they select them regardless of the primary focus of activity? Is there a greater percentage of vocational choices at certain levels within a field than others, or are the choices equally distributed over the various levels? These and related questions need to be answered, if our knowledge of the varieties of vocational choice is to be complete.

To provide current data on vocational choices classified by both field *and* level, the writer administered Trow's questions to 735 male and 581 female college freshmen at the University of Iowa in the fall of 1959. Their probable,

[9] The study by Osipow (1966) cited in Chapter 2 collected the appropriate data for an analysis of vocational choices classified by field and level, but only the findings on consistency of first and second choices were reported.

possible, and fantasy vocational choices[10] were classified according to Roe's (1956) system, and the percentages for each field-by-level combination were computed for males and females separately, as shown in Tables 4-7 and 4-8. In addition, the parts of Trow's study on (1) the number of Subjects who made probable, possible, and fantasy vocational choices and (2) the amount of agreement among these three kinds of choices were replicated. The results for the males led to two major conclusions: First, there tends to be an "interaction" between level and field when choices are classified along both of these dimensions. That is, the highest percentage of choices in a field changes from one level to another. More specifically, the concentration of all three kinds of choice in Field VI (Science) on Level 1 shifts to Fields IV (Technology) and VII (General Cultural) on Level 2. Similarly, the fields change again on Level 3, with II (Business Contact) and III (Organization) having the highest percentages, at least for probable and possible choices. From these trends, we can conclude that there is a relationship between the choice of level and field, largely irrespective of the kind of choice (probable, possible, or fantasy) which the individual makes. Stated somewhat differently, we can say that, given a certain level of choice, the chances are greater that it will be in one field than in another.

Second, there tends to be a relationship between level of choice and realism of choice. The percentages of probable, possible, and fantasy choices at Levels 1 and 2 are exactly reversed in order of magnitude. At Level 1, the percentage of fantasy choices is greater than the percentage of possible choices, and the latter is greater than the percentage of probable choices. In contrast, on Level 2 the percentages are greater for probable and possible choices than for fantasy choices. Evidently, individuals who make choices at Level 2 estimate that their chances of implementing their vocational objectives are better than those who select occupations at Level 1. In other words, Level 2 represents a more realistic level of vocational choice. Because level is related to field, the "realism" trend in probable, possible, and fantasy choices most likely differs from one field to another also, but this tendency is not as apparent as it is for levels, particularly Levels 1 and 2. The percentages for Level 3 are essentially the same for probable, possible, and fantasy choices and consequently show no systematic covariation between the level and realism variables. The data for females support essentially the same conclusions as those for males, the only difference being which fields have the highest percentages of choices.

The replicated analyses from Trow's study yielded results which agreed quite well with the original findings. First, for both sexes, there is a slight tendency for them to express their probable and possible choices more often

[10] Again, Trow's terminology, instead of choice, preference, and aspiration is used to facilitate comparisons with his findings.

Table 4-7. Percentages of College Freshman Males Who Made Probable, Possible, and Fantasy Vocational Choices in Certain Fields and Levels, $N = 735$

Level of responsibility and skill	Kind of vocational choice	Field of choice: I. Service	II. Business contact	III. Organ-ization	IV. Tech-nology	V. Outdoor	VI. Science	VII. General cultural	VIII. Arts and entertainment	Total
		%	%	%	%	%	%	%	%	%
1	Probable	7.6	0.0	0.0	1.0	1.0	77.1	2.9	10.5	15.8
	Possible	7.2	0.0	0.6	1.1	0.0	79.0	3.9	8.3	26.3
	Fantasy	3.9	0.0	18.5	3.9	0.0	54.6	3.4	15.6	36.4
2	Probable	2.2	2.7	8.2	30.3	0.5	17.2	35.2	3.6	55.2
	Possible	2.9	2.4	15.7	27.9	0.0	16.2	28.5	6.4	54.7
	Fantasy	1.3	0.4	35.1	13.8	2.7	5.8	11.1	29.8	40.0
3	Probable	4.2	27.1	35.9	10.4	5.7	2.6	7.8	6.3	29.0
	Possible	6.9	20.6	28.2	20.6	3.1	2.3	10.7	7.6	19.0
	Fantasy	10.5	3.0	10.5	29.3	9.8	2.3	11.3	23.3	23.6
Total	Probable	3.3	8.4	13.5	18.0	1.9	20.3	20.0	4.9	
	Possible	4.5	4.9	13.2	18.2	0.5	28.2	17.4	6.7	
	Fantasy	3.4	0.7	17.8	10.6	2.6	17.4	6.4	17.7	

NOTE: All choices were at the first three levels in Roe's classification scheme. Chi-square tests for probable, possible, and fantasy choices by field and level yielded values which were all significant beyond the 0.001 level.

Table 4-8. Percentages of College Freshman Females Who Made Probable, Possible, and Fantasy Vocational Choices in Certain Fields and Levels, *N* = 581

Level of responsibility and skill	*Kind of vocational choice*	*Field of choice*								
		I. Service	*II. Business contact*	*III. Organ-ization*	*IV. Tech-nology*	*V. Outdoor*	*VI. Science*	*VII. General cultural*	*VIII. Arts and entertainment*	*Total*
		%	%	%	%	%	%	%	%	%
1	Probable	29.4	0.0	0.0	0.0	0.0	47.1	11.8	11.8	6.2
	Possible	23.2	0.0	0.0	0.0	0.0	58.5	9.8	8.5	15.0
	Fantasy	9.1	0.0	1.8	0.0	0.0	55.2	4.2	29.7	33.3
2	Probable	8.0	1.0	0.8	0.0	0.0	31.8	57.6	0.8	70.6
	Possible	16.6	1.5	2.7	0.6	0.0	32.8	41.9	3.9	60.7
	Fantasy	10.9	0.6	6.3	1.1	0.0	24.0	36.6	20.6	35.4
3	Probable	0.8	9.4	32.3	0.0	0.0	36.2	7.1	14.2	23.2
	Possible	3.0	13.5	19.5	0.0	0.0	35.3	7.5	21.1	24.3
	Fantasy	3.9	18.1	9.0	3.9	4.5	5.8	7.1	47.7	31.3
Total	Probable	7.2	2.8	7.6	0.0	0.0	31.8	40.6	4.3	
	Possible	13.4	4.0	6.0	0.3	0.0	35.1	27.0	8.3	
	Fantasy	6.9	5.0	4.8	1.4	1.2	24.4	14.1	27.4	

NOTE: All choices were at the first three levels in Roe's classification scheme. Chi-square tests for probable, possible, and fantasy choices by field and level yielded values which were all significant beyond the 0.001 level.

than their fantasy choices, perhaps because most people base their vocational choices upon probabilities (estimated chances) and possibilities (preferences) rather than dreams and wishes (aspirations) and consequently have less idea of what their fantasy choice is. Second, there is marked differentiation between the responses to the three kinds of choices. Each of Trow's questions elicits different choices, although the extent of agreement is greater between probable and possible (males, 53.9 percent; females, 59.4 percent) than probable and fantasy (males, 21.0 percent; females, 21.2 percent). As these percentages reveal, the possible (preference) question elicits responses which are between the probable (choice) and fantasy (aspiration) extremes, but which are more similar to the former in content. In general, then, the more recent study by the writer substantiates Trow's earlier conclusions and adds the new fact that there is a relationship between level and field of choice.

5
THE DEVELOPMENT OF VOCATIONAL CHOICE

As was pointed out in the preceding chapter, the selection of an occupation can be conceptualized as a process made up of a series of events or "choice acts" which takes place over a considerable period of time, usually during the 10 years from the end of childhood to the beginning of youth, and which largely terminates when the individual enters an occupation. The purpose of this chapter is to describe this process and to review the research which has been conducted on it. The chapter is organized into three sections. The first deals with the characteristics of the vocational choice process as hypothesized in different theories and as established by empirical research. The second discusses the various schemata which have been proposed to represent the stages in the development of choice and presents what data there are on the nature of each stage. The final section summarizes several longitudinal, as well as a few cross-sectional, studies of vocational development which have been launched in recent years and which will most likely produce most of the research on choice and related phenomena in the years to come.

VOCATIONAL CHOICE AS A DEVELOPMENTAL PROCESS

The concept of vocational choice as a process implies more than just change, although this is certainly a necessary condition for the development and maturation of behavior. The changes which take place in choice behavior over time must be orderly and patterned; they cannot be random and unsystematic for development to occur. The changes must be interrelated and conducive to an end product or state, and they must proceed in certain sequences and according to established principles. As a developmental process, vocational choice has a definite form and content which distinguishes it from events which follow each other in time but which are otherwise unrelated. What the formal and substantive characteristics of the choice process are is our concern here.

We shall review all the aspects of the developmental nature of choice which have been hypothesized, as well as the empirical research which has accumulated on them. These aspects of the vocational choice process include: (1) its continuity (or discontinuity), (2) its irreversibility, (3) its exclusive nature, (4) its dimensions, and (5) its variations and deviations.

The Continuity of the Vocational Choice Process

Most of the developmental theories of vocational choice with which we are familiar either imply or state explicitly that the choice process is a continuous one. Although not formulated as a proposition in their theory, Ginzberg and his associates clearly view the process of occupational choice determination, as they call it, as one which has no "breaks" or disjunctions in it once it begins. They conclude that "occupational choice is a developmental process: it is not a single decision, but a series of decisions made over a period of years. Each step in the process has a meaningful relation to those which precede and follow it" (Ginzberg et al., 1951, p. 185). The individual proceeds uninterruptedly from his early fantasy-loaded choices, through choices based upon his interests, capacities, and values, to the crystallization and specification of one choice which he implements by entering an occupation. Only in special cases, which Ginzberg calls "pseudocrystallization," does the individual make a firm choice at an earlier age and then change it later on. The typical sequence is to progressively specify one's choice, with no discontinuities in the process.

Super (1953) also assumes that the process of vocational choice is continuous, but he is more explicit about it. He writes that "choice is a continuous process going on over a period of time, a process rather far removed from reality in early youth but involving reality in increasing degrees with increasing age" (Super, 1953, p. 187). He sees no discontinuities in the individual's vocational development or in his personal and social development. He writes that: "The evidence suggests that the exploratory experiences of adolescence in most cases merely clarify, elaborate upon, and confirm the concept of the self which has already begun to emerge and to crystallize. As a rule, adolescent exploration is an awakening to something that is already there rather than the discovery of something new and different" (Super, 1951b, p. 88). In other words, the basis for the individual's personality and for his vocational future is laid during the early, formative years of his life, and any modifications which occur subsequently are in the nature of refinements rather than comprehensive changes. Similar viewpoints which have emphasized the continuity of the choice process, although not necessarily its relationship to personal development, have been expressed by Dysinger (1950), Beilin (1955), and Nelson, R. C. (1962).

Research on the continuity of the vocational choice process is scarce, but that which is available presents a picture of what happens in the development of choices quite different from the one offered by theory. The most notable study on this problem is one conducted by Gesell, Ilg, and Ames (1956), who traced the choices of 115 boys and girls from the time they were 10 until they were 16. Unique because of its longitudinal nature, this investigation allows the extrapolation of trends in the choices of the same group of Subjects from "progressive-time-sample" comparisons over a 7-year period. The major trend which emerged from the analysis of the data was the tendency for the sample to crystallize choices at *two* points in time during adolescence: once at approximately age 13 and again at about age 16. In between these two ages, there was a period of "indiscriminateness" and one of "indecision." As Table 5-1 shows, at the age of 14, only 1 year after they had expressed definite choices, most of

Table 5-1. Characteristic Vocational Choice Behaviors at Different Age Levels between the Years of 10 and 16 *(Gesell, Ilg., & Ames, 1956, pp. 376–382)*

Age	*Vocational choice behaviors*
10 YEARS:	Plans for their future careers are rather indefinite among many of our Tens, and the careers chosen are much more varied than in the years which follow. Many Tens give several choices, often quite unrelated.
11 YEARS:	More Elevens than Tens have a definite choice of career, and only very few have no idea of what they want to do. More now can make a single choice, and, as choices become more realistic, the variety of occupations chosen becomes smaller.
12 YEARS:	The trend toward a single, definite choice of future career continues. Many fewer now make several choices or express indecision. Boys are now more definite in choice, and more likely to give only one choice than are girls.
13 YEARS:	Thirteen marks the peak for single, definite choices about future work. Earlier ages sometimes made multiple choices rather capriciously; later ages, with greater realism, recognize the difficulty of making a single certain choice. Thirteen tends to assert his choice without indecision.
14 YEARS:	Fourteens show less certainty in their choice of career. More individuals make multiple choices, and the group as a whole makes a greater variety of choices than at thirteen or fifteen.
15 YEARS:	Many Fifteens are quite indefinite about their choice of future career—more so than at any age since eleven. Though the group as a whole names many fewer possible careers than earlier, individuals find it difficult to decide on a single choice within this range.
16 YEARS:	Somewhat more decisiveness appears among Sixteens in their choice of careers than among Fifteens, though a few girls are undecided. A considerable variety of choices is mentioned. Boys most often choose engineering, law, architecture, politics, and medicine. Girls choose art, teaching, and child psychology. Journalism and science are often mentioned by both boys and girls.

the sample were uncertain about their vocational future and, presumably as a consequence, they became indiscriminate in their choices, making several rather than one or a few. At age 15, there are fewer choices, but still there is no firm or confident selection of an occupation: indecision seems to have replaced the indiscriminateness of the previous year. It is not until the age of 16 that progress is again made, as it was at age 13, toward a resolution of the choice problem.

To depict these trends in vocational choice graphically, Figure 5-1 was constructed. It shows both the findings of Gesell, Ilg, and Ames and the expected course of development in choice as proposed by Ginzberg, Super, and others. It is clear from a comparison of these two schemata that they do not "fit" each other. The empirically based curve reveals a discontinuity in the process of choice at about the midpoint of adolescence, whereas the theoretical curve indicates continuous narrowing down or "funneling" of a wide range of choices to one or a few throughout the period.

Much the same phenomenon as reported by Gesell has been found in another study, but one which is less definitive because its data come from cross-sectional rather than longitudinal analyses. Mackaye (1927) surveyed the choices of elementary and high school students, from both urban and rural

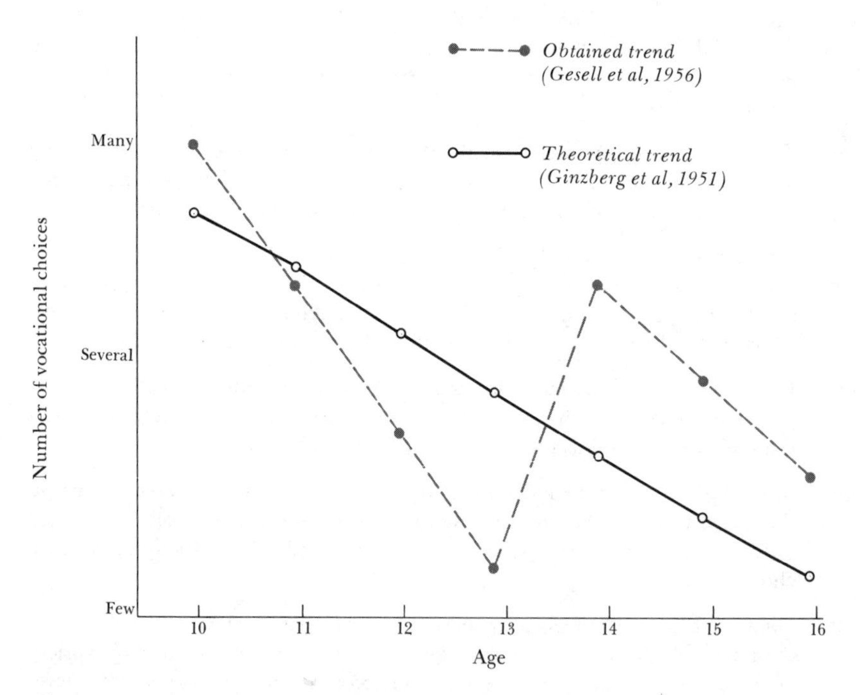

Figure 5-1. Comparison of Gesell et al. (1956) data with theoretical curve of continuous vocational development during adolescence.

areas, and compared the younger with the older Subjects to determine when "fixation," as he calls it, takes place in the formation of choices. The comparisons indicated that there is an early period of crystallization of choice, much as Gesell discovered, during which goals are definite and firmly established, but this certainty gives way to indecision and lack of goal-directedness at the beginning of high school, which would be at approximately age 15. Mackaye (1927, p. 366) observes that at this stage in his choice development the individual "opens a reevaluation of his experiences in the light of his personal necessities" and "his attention is turned again to the matter of making a vocational choice." In short, there is a "break" in the process of choosing an occupation which occurs in middle adolescence and which represents a shift from certainty to uncertainty in choice, as manifested in the greater number of occupations the young person considers at this time and his attitude of indecision about specifying one of them as his choice.

Why does this disjunction in the choice process occur? What precipitates it? Both Gesell and Mackaye offer the same answer: When the individual reaches midadolescence, he becomes more aware of the realities which affect his selection of an occupation. No longer can he rather simply and naïvely base his choice upon his fantasies or preferences. For the first time he realizes that there are other considerations he must make. Although he might dream of being a famous surgeon or a prominent engineer or a renowned scientist, he becomes disquieted by the fact, which he may try to suppress but which nevertheless remains a reality, that he is not doing as well as he had expected in high school chemistry and physics or as well as would be necessary to follow one of his fantasy-derived careers. He develops a cognizance of the reality which impinges upon him, and which imposes limitations upon his endeavors, that he did not have before, and he begins to reevaluate his vocational plans. As a result, he expresses uncertainty and indecision where previously he had seemed definite and resolved about what he wanted to do.

Comment. It might be argued from Ginzberg's point of view that the studies of Gesell et al. and Mackaye support his conceptualization of the choice process in adolescence. Both studies indicate that the adolescent takes increasing account of reality as a basis for his choice as he grows older, and this is the trend which Ginzberg noted when he asked his Subjects how they had gone about arriving at their choices. What Ginzberg does not conclude from his data, however, is that as a result of the impact of reality considerations the individual changes his choice or returns to a state of "no choice." Yet this is what appears to happen in the studies which we have available and which lead us to the conclusion that the vocational choice process is *not* necessarily a continuous one. There is at least one discontinuity in it, and there may be others, for example, at the time the individual is about ready to enter an occupation (Tiedeman & O'Hara, 1963).

The Irreversibility of the Vocational Choice Process

The concept of the continuity of the vocational choice process is closely related to the proposition that it is largely irreversible in its course. In other words, if it is assumed that the choice process proceeds with no discontinuities or interruptions, this means that there are no reversals in it. The process builds up an inertia which largely predetermines future actions and limits possible alternatives. For example, at the beginning of high school, typically in the ninth grade, the young person must make a "preoccupational" choice of academic curriculum, which requires a selection from among various courses of study, such as college preparatory, commercial, industrial arts, and general.[1] Usually, this decision about high school major presumes prior considerations of long-term goals, which direct immediate curricular choices and which circumscribe future courses of action as they relate to shifts in curriculum, selection of a school for advanced training, and placement on a job.

Ginzberg et al. (1951, pp. 193–196) identify five factors which they see as contributing to the irreversibility of the choice process:

1. *Familial support for training.* Because families assume the responsibility for the support and education of their children for only a set period of time, changes in vocational objectives are limited by the availability of their financial resources for training.

2. *Preparation for college and work.* Changes from one curriculum to another are restricted by the amount of time remaining after the shift to meet the requirements for further training or for employment.

3. *Imminence of marriage.* The prospect of marriage in the early years of adulthood tends to inhibit alterations in vocational decisions which would lengthen the period of preparation and necessitate a postponement of occupational entry and the establishment of a family.

4. *Reluctance to admit poor planning and failure.* A change in one's vocational goals may mean an admission of poor planning or of failure to implement plans. Such admissions may be repugnant to the individual, and this may impel him to continue in his original course of action.

5. *Advantages and disadvantages of changing goals.* The disadvantages of a change in goals may outweigh the advantages.

Furthermore, even if a person alters his plans, there is no guarantee that the

[1] Super (1960) has argued that, although most school systems are presently organized so as to require ninth graders to make "preoccupational" choices, they might better be established so that the adolescent at this stage of his vocational development might *explore* himself and the world of work instead of having to choose—perhaps prematurely.

new course of action will resolve the uncertainties about one's choice which prompted it. To these factors which tend to make the choice process irreversible we might add those of cost and expenditure of effort. Certainly, every time an individual reverses his plan he incurs at least some loss of money, because of the costs involved in buying new books, forfeiting college application deposits, moving from one school to another, or any number of other expenses. And, unless he changes to a closely related area of study or work, there is the possibility that skills and proficiencies acquired in past endeavors will have little applicability in future activities.

Comment. There is no research evidence on the irreversibility of the choice process, although the studies which we shall review later in this chapter on changes in choice over prolonged periods of time certainly imply that such a phenomenon exists. But, if this is the case, how can we reconcile it with our previous conclusion that the choice process is not wholly continuous? One answer to this dilemma, which is also suggested by the data on the stability of choices, is that choices become irreversible only *after* a particular point in the individual's development. In other words, they become increasingly irreversible as the individual grows older and after he reevaluates his choice in mid-adolescence. Early in the choice process he can change his goals rather drastically, because his commitment to and involvement in any one course of action is not great enough for him to lose very much. After he has entered an advanced training school or college, however, he finds that changes are more costly, and his choice becomes more stabilized during this period.

The Exclusive Nature of the Vocational Choice Process

Implicit in our discussion of the vocational choice process as continuous and irreversible, has been the notion that the process of making a choice involves a progressive narrowing down of the alternatives available to the individual—an exclusion of those occupations which for one reason or another are not desirable or feasible. (See the discussion of developmental trends in decision making in Chapter 3.) As depicted in Figure 5-2, when the individual enters early adolescence and faces the task of making a choice, the range of occupational pursuits open to him encompasses a large number of the 21,000 different jobs in the American economy. Even at a particular skill level, such as the semiprofessional or technical, the possible occupations from which he can choose are numerous and include such diverse ones as policeman and tool-and-die maker. His choice problem is to eliminate many of these alternatives, to narrow down the range to those occupations for which he is best fitted.

As Dysinger (1950, pp. 219–220) observes, the choice process involves a series of negative decisions:

> At each stage, there are negative decisions. These are of importance in vocational planning. When the child has grown to the point that he no longer plans to be a cowboy, he has developed. At later stages of development, the negative decision continues to be important. Entire fields may be eliminated, and the possible choices may in this way be narrowed. Positive choices often follow a series of negative decisions. One of the most difficult situations in vocational planning occurs when fairly mature youth have made few negative decisions.

Ginzberg et al. (1951, p. 119) also note that "in adolescence the range of potential choices must be narrowed, for only then will crystallization be possible." Likewise, as Super and Bachrach (1957, p. 109) point out, Tyler "stresses the exclusion process, which she describes as a rejection of certain vocational fields which clearly sets the limits of future possibilities."

Considerable indirect support for these inferences comes from several studies on vocational interest and self-concept development during the adolescent period:

1. In a number of investigations of vocational choice and interests in the high school years, Carter and his associates (Carter & Jones, 1938; Carter, Taylor, & Canning, 1941) found that interests remain more stable than choices during this stage of development. From this fact, Carter (1944, p. 17) concluded that interests, as measured by standard inventories, are more realistic than choices early in adolescence because "young persons who cannot make

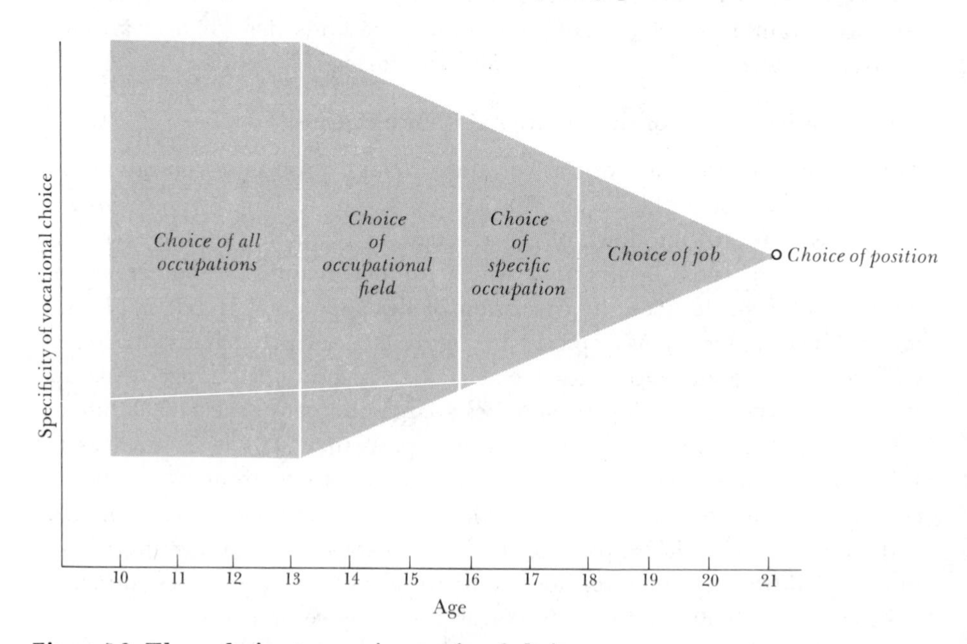

Figure 5-2. The exclusion process in vocational choice.

valid generalizations such as are required in vocational choice can nevertheless provide valid responses to items which are of limited scope."[2] Since the agreement between choice and interests increases with age (Super, 1947), the implication is that what develops during adolescence, partly as a function of increased self-knowledge and occupational information, is the individual's capacity to make inductions and deductions about his chances for vocational adjustment in different occupations.

2. O'Hara and Tiedeman (1959) have reported results on young people's estimates of their measured aptitudes, interests, and values which generally show that there is a clarification of the vocational self-concept during the adolescent years. Although there are some shortcomings in this study, which we shall discuss later, the data on the overall trend toward increased self-knowledge appear sound and reliable. Older adolescents (the study included only males) have a somewhat better idea of how capable they are, what their likes and dislikes are, and which values are the most important to them. In other words, they seem to be better able to appraise themselves objectively at the end of adolescence, defined as the period between the ninth and twelfth grades, than they are at the beginning.

3. In an analysis of the relationship between expressed and inventoried interests, Sinnett (1956) gathered data which indicated that individuals understand the nature of the less complex occupations in the world of work at an earlier age than they do the more complex ones. Clerical, sales, and technical occupations are the first ones the individual learns about, and social service and scientific occupations are the last ones. Furthermore, Sinnett found that the degree of agreement between rated and measured interests is higher for those occupational fields about which the individual gains an early knowledge. To extrapolate from these findings, we can say that as the individual grows older, he knows more about more occupations and, as a result, he has a better understanding of what his interests are.

Comment. The studies just reviewed do not deal directly with the exclusive nature of the vocational choice process, but they are relevant enough to lend some support to its postulation and to suggest a conceptual framework which may lead to the needed research. As Figure 5-3 indicates, we can conceive of the vocational choice process and related variables along two dimensions:

[2] In effect, an interest inventory "reasons" for an individual, whether he is able to or not. As Super and Crites (1962, pp. 407–408) have explained, "in answering the questions in an interest inventory an individual records a series of self-perceptions, which in turn are summated by the scoring scale in such a way as to reveal the similarity or dissimilarity of his self-concept to the self-concept which has been found to be characteristic of persons in the occupation being scored."

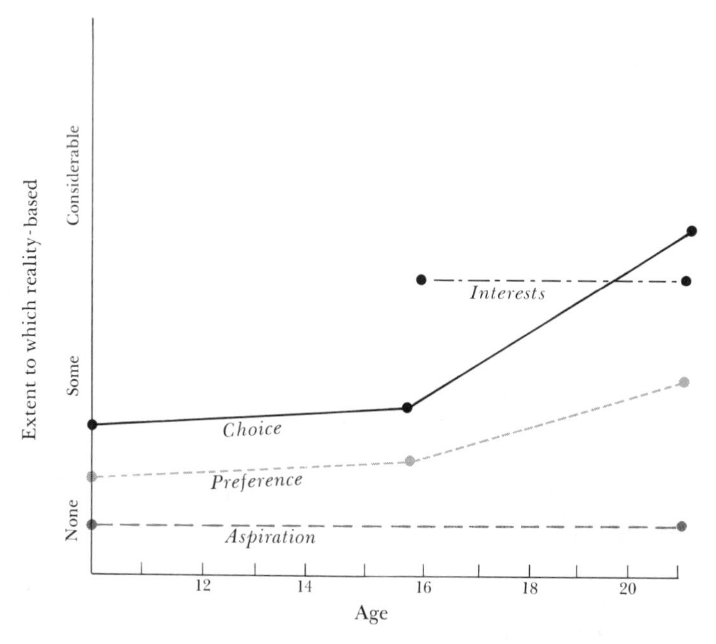

Figure 5-3. A conceptual scheme for the vocational choice process and related variables during adolescence.

(1) the extent to which choice, preference, aspiration, and interest are reality-based,[3] and (2) the age levels which are included in the choice stage of vocational development. At the lower age levels, choice can be differentiated from preference and aspiration along the reality continuum, but the differences among the three variables are not great. In fact, they all differ more from interest than they differ from each other, since at this point in his development the individual reacts in much the same way to all stimuli, with a generalized "positive" set. He has only begun to differentiate among occupations and to evaluate realistically his chances for success in them. The major part of the exclusion process is yet to come.

As the individual grows older, he becomes more cognizant of the realities which place limitations upon what he can do, and he develops dislikes as a consequence of adverse experiences with his environment. The result is that his choices and preferences are now more reality-based, and the occupational

[3] Note that this dimension and the positions of choice, preference, and aspiration on it at age 21 are the same as were used to define these concepts in Chap. 4. What we are doing here is looking at the continuum over the entire range of age in the adolescent period, and as we do so, it is apparent that the relationship of choice to the other variables changes. This does not mean, however, that the definition of choice also changes: it is still the individual's statement of the occupation he *intends* to enter. The choice is simply not as reality-based earlier as it is later in his development.

alternatives which appear feasible to him are fewer in number. The exclusion process is well under way, and the range of choices is being rapidly narrowed. Note that these changes occur primarily, however, after midadolescence, which seems to be the point of discontinuity in the choice process and which is indicated in Figure 5-3 by the precipitous positive slope in the choice and preference lines between ages 15 and 16. With the greater reality orientation which is characteristic of choice at this time, its agreement with interest increases and its agreement with aspiration decreases, since there are no significant changes in these latter two variables during adolescence.[4]

Finally, when the individual reaches his early twenties, the exclusion process terminates as he selects an occupation, or a small group of related occupations, as the one which he intends to enter. His choice is based to a considerable extent upon reality, but also involves his more fanciful and subjective interests, preferences, and aspirations. His choice is more realistic than any of these because it represents an appraisal of his limitations, both personal and environmental, as well as his assets and potentialities. Consequently, there is still some lack of agreement between choice and interest, but at this point in time it is in the direction of the former being more reality-based.[5] The gap between choice and preference has widened over the years, but it is still small enough that a change in contingencies might make it possible to implement a preference. And, the discrepancy between choice and aspiration should be about optimal for the individual to be sufficiently motivated to strive for advancement and status in his occupation (Lewin, 1936), since these are the tasks he must accomplish in order to progress normally in the next stage of his vocational development, which is the *establishment* stage of vocational adjustment (see Chapter 12).

The Dimensions of the Vocational Choice Process

We have just concluded that vocational choices are increasingly based upon considerations of reality factors as the individual develops. In other words, one dimension along which the choice process proceeds is the extent to which reality plays a part in the making of vocational decisions. In addition to this dimension, which pertains wholly to the basis for an individual's choice, there

[4] Some may argue that interests do change after midadolescence, but the bulk of the accumulated research evidence is against this interpretation (Super & Crites, 1962), unless it is contended that weaker patterns become stronger. This is true, but these do not represent "significant" changes in the sense that new *kinds* of interests replace old ones.

[5] One exception to this statement may be in the area of life insurance sales, where Strong (1943) has found a correlation of .48 between interest scores and amount of insurance sold. In other words, for this occupation the relationship between choice and interest should be somewhat higher than for others, because interest correlates with success, which is a reality factor.

are others which have been hypothesized which have to do primarily with an individual's attitudes toward the problem of choice and his ability to solve it. Most of the work which has been done on conceptualizing and defining these dimensions comes from the research of the Career Pattern Study (Super, 1955; Super & Overstreet, 1960), but Ginzberg et al. (1951) as well as others have also made contributions, and consequently we have a fairly comprehensive list of the continua which comprise the choice process in adolescence. Descriptions of these continua, which are largely hypothetical as a result of the lack of relevant research, are given in the following paragraphs:

1. *Orientation to choice.* To make a choice it is necessary first to be aware of the social expectation that one must choose an occupation as his life's work. The choice process begins when the individual develops this awareness and continues as he becomes increasingly oriented to the decisions about high school curriculum, part-time work, college, etc., which he must make in the present and in the future (Super, 1955).

2. *Clarification of vocational self-concept.* Super (1955, p. 155) calls this dimension "crystallization of traits and aptitudes" and defines it as "the degree to which abilities and traits have taken shape, providing consistent bases for action." He points out that it is a developmental continuum and that "the more highly developed and integrated the individual's ability and trait system, the greater his readiness to cope with the developmental tasks of vocational choice and adjustment."

3. *Occupational information.* Much as the individual learns more about himself as he grows older, he also gathers more information about occupations and how to enter them. The information he has increases in relevance, reliability, and specificity as he develops, and he uses it more often as a basis for his decisions (Super, 1955).

4. *Independence.* One of the primary dimensions along which emotional and social development take place is from dependence to independence. Super (1955) has hypothesized that the choice process proceeds in the same direction. In early adolescence, the individual relies rather heavily upon others for choice determination, but as he matures he becomes more and more self-sufficient in his decision making. He develops from what Ginzberg (1951, p. 210) has called the "passive" person to what he has termed the "active" person: "The 'active' person takes positive steps in his own behalf. The 'passive' type responds to external pressures; he reacts to major forces instead of seeking to control them." Ginzberg goes on to link active-passive involvement in choice, or independent-dependent choice behavior, to the orientations of the individual toward "work" and "pleasure." The "work-oriented" person pursues his goals with determination and persistence and is not easily deflected from them. Also, he foregoes current gratifications or postpones them. In contrast, the "pleasure-

oriented" individual has only vaguely defined objectives and is easily distracted in his endeavors by the desire for immediate satisfactions: "To him the returns from work and the concomitant satisfactions have an importance equal to or greater than the job itself" (Ginzberg et al., 1951, p. 209).

5. *Planful daydreaming and fantasy.* An essential component of effective decision making seems to be an optimum use of daydreaming and fantasy to conceptualize oneself in different kinds of work, as in Small's (1953) job-concept interview, and to eliminate unsuitable occupational alternatives through tryouts in thought rather than through the more expensive and time-consuming process of trial and error. Supposedly, the capacity to use daydreaming and fantasy constructively in making choices increases with age as the individual is better able to control his motor behavior and consequently has more moments of physical inactivity during which he can reflect upon his vocational future. Because control is characteristic of the work-oriented person, we would expect a relationship between this dimension and the preceding one.

6. *Means-end cognizance.* The younger person has difficulty in relating his goals to the steps he must take to reach them, because he has not developed the ability to conceive what the appropriate associations are and because his time perspective has not sharpened sufficiently for him to project accurately into the future (Ginzberg et al., 1951). As he matures, however, he can increasingly specify the means he must employ to reach his ends, and he can relate immediate and intermediate decisions to remote objectives through planning.

7. *Consistency of choices.* Super (1955; 1961a) has reasoned that the consistency or agreement among an individual's choices should increase as he matures. He summarizes his point of view as follows (Super, 1961a, p. 35): "It has been argued that *consistency of vocational preferences* ['choices' in our terminology] shows intensity and validity of interest, and that it is better to work consistently toward one clear-cut goal than wastefully to keep shifting objectives." Thus, one dimension of the choice process should be movement from the expression of choices which are inconsistent, or largely unrelated to each other, to the declaration of choices which are consistent because they are in the same "field" or at the same "level."

Super (1955) has delineated another dimension of the choice process, which he calls "wisdom of vocational preferences," but this is essentially the same continuum which we have referred to as the "reality basis" for choice. In this connection, a possible confusion in terminology and interpretation should be clarified. The "wisdom" and "reality basis" of vocational choice are sometimes called the "realism" of choice, and these terms should be considered synonymous. Some misunderstanding has arisen on this matter, because of the distinction which has been made between "reality as a basis" for choice and the "realism of choice." In an observation upon Small's (1953) study, Beilin (1955, p. 57) notes that: "Small reports not upon the increasing use of realism *as a basis* for choice as does Ginzberg but upon the realism *of* the choice, which is not the same." It is difficult to conceive, however, of choices which are based upon reality and which are *not* realistic. If an individual takes into consideration the fact that he has below-average scholastic ability and, as a result, decides to take a semiskilled job as a punch-press operator, he has based his choice upon reality, *and* his choice is realistic.

Research on the dimensions of the vocational choice process is limited to a point-in-time study of ninth-grade boys reported by Super and Overstreet (1960), in which they investigated the following variables: (1) concern with choice, (2) use of resources in orientation, (3) specificity of information, (4) specificity of planning, (5) extent of planning activity, (6) consistency of vocational preferences within fields, levels, and families, (7) degree of patterning of measured interests, (8) interest maturity, (9) liking for work, (10) degree of patterning of work values, (11) orientation toward rewards of work, (12) acceptance of responsibility for choice and planning, (13) independence of work experience, (14) agreement between ability and preference, (15) agreement between measured interests and preferences, (16) agreement between measured interests and fantasy preference, (17) agreement between occupational level of measured interests and level of preference, and (18) socioeconomic accessibility of preferences. Data on each of these variables, or "indices" of vocational maturity as they were called, was gathered from interviews, ratings, or standard tests. The primary analysis of the data, and the one which we shall summarize here, was a factor analysis of the intercorrelations of the various indices, but the relationships of the indices with such nonvocational variables as intelligence, socioeconomic status, personality adjustment, urban-rural residence, etc., were also determined.

In general, the results of the intercorrelational and factorial analyses were negative. Contrary to the expectation that the indices would be correlated positively because, even though they are distinct, they are part of the same process, the data revealed only a few *r*'s which were significant and only 38 percent of the total variance which could be accounted for by the factor analysis. The names of the factors and the indices which had the highest loadings on them are as follows:

Factor 1. Planning orientation: acceptance of responsibility for choice and planning, specificity of information, and extent of planning activity

Factor 2. Independence of work experience: defined by the index of the same name

Factor 3. The long view ahead: awareness of need for ultimate choices (included in the index for concern with choice), specificity of information, and specificity of planning

Factor 4. The short view ahead: specificity of high school plans

Factor 5. The intermediate view: awareness of factors in choice (included in the index for concern with choice)

From these findings, Super and Overstreet (1960) concluded that the primary dimension of the choice process in early adolescence is an orientation toward planning for the future and that secondary dimensions include the anticipation of immediate, intermediate, and remote vocational developmental tasks.

Variations and Deviations in the Vocational Choice Process

We have been focusing upon the general characteristics of the vocational choice process, the ones which seem to be evident in the development of all individuals, and several of these appear to be fairly well established by empirical research. But, there are also variations and deviations in the choice process which are equally notable, although not quite as well substantiated factually. The terms *variation* and *deviation* are the ones which Ginzberg et al. (1951) used to describe particular kinds of choice patterns which have special characteristics. Since Tiedeman (1952) has questioned the use of more than one of these terms, saying that deviation is the same as variation, it is important to present Ginzberg's definitions of these concepts, because the meanings which he gives to them are not just statistical, as Tiedeman assumes, but also psychological, and consequently the use of both appears to be justified. Ginzberg et al. (1951, p. 127) define variation and deviation as follows:

> The behavior of some individuals during the period of decision-making cannot be considered mere variations from the norm, but must be classified as deviations. If one finally succeeds in crystallizing a choice within a few years of the time of the average, it can be considered a variation. But if the individual is unable to crystallize a choice at all, or is able to do so only at a much later age than is typical of the group to which he belongs, his case must be considered a deviation.

The *variations* in the choice process are not usually apparent until the latter part of adolescence, when the differences between individuals are accentuated by the increasing pressure upon them to act in accordance with their plans as they approach the point of transition from high school to advanced training or occupational entry. The variations which become manifest at this time are in (1) the range or number of occupations the individual has considered and (2) the point in time when the individual crystallized his choice. Some individuals have made many choices in many fields and have had a "wide" range of choice. Because they are attracted to a variety of occupations, they often have difficulty in specifying one occupation as the one they intend to enter, and they remain undecided into their twenties. Most individuals decide upon a broad occupational area early in the choice process, and the changes which occur in their goals are directed toward the selection of one of the occupations within the larger field. These young people have an "average" range of choice. Finally, a few individuals specify their choice very early in their vocational development and do not seriously consider any other alternatives. These "single track" individuals, as Ginzberg calls them, have a very "narrow" range of choice, because they usually have a special talent or aptitude, such as mathematical or musical ability, which brings them intrinsic satisfaction through its use, as well as bringing them recognition by others, and which is easily translated into occupational terms.

A narrow range of choice may be related to early crystallization of choice, but Ginzberg says that there is no *necessary* connection between the two types of variation in the choice process. There are too many factors which counteract or overdetermine the relationship. An individual may have considered only a few occupations for himself but not have chosen one of them until late in adolescence, after he has had an opportunity to learn more about himself and work. Conversely, a person may have narrowed his choice down from a wide range of alternatives to a few during the early years of his vocational development because he matured personally more rapidly than his peers. Ginzberg points out that early crystallization of choice is related to the individual's general emotional and intellectual development and to his work-related experiences. Only when there is late crystallization do we generally find a relationship with range of choice. In this case, the late crystallization usually comes about as a result of the individual's inability to choose between a number of unrelated but equally attractive occupations. In other words, he has what has been termed an "approach-approach" conflict (Shaffer & Shoben, 1956).

The distinction between a variant choice pattern of late crystallization and a *deviant* pattern with many of the same characteristics is a fine one. Ginzberg et al. (1951) point out that the two types of patterns can be differentiated, however, by two criteria: First, the deviant choice is usually based upon a consideration of only one factor and a factor which is predominant at an earlier age than that of the individual. For example, by this criterion, a 20-year-old who chose an occupation exclusively in terms of his interests would have a deviant pattern. Second, a deviant pattern also involves late crystallization, but as a result of personality difficulties rather than a slower rate of vocational development, as is the case with a variant pattern. A deviant choice pattern often reflects an "avoidance-avoidance" conflict, which stems from a pervasive character trait of *indecisiveness* rather than a superficial and temporary *indecision,* as Tyler (1961b, pp. 201–202) as well as Ginzberg (1951, p. 127) has observed. Contributing to the individual's indecisiveness are three factors: (1) responsiveness to parental aspirations and pressures, (2) powerful fantasies about being admired and successful, and (3) the persistence of childhood interests, e.g., spending a great amount of time in building model airplanes or collecting stamps, into early adulthood.

According to Ginzberg (1951, p. 126), the overall effect of these factors is to produce a "pseudocrystallization" of choice, which he maintains is "the most important single factor in delayed crystallization." What happens is that the individual makes a choice at about the time he is expected to (between the ages of 17 and 18), but he bases it upon parental desires, his fantasies, or his hobbies. Then, as he grows older and tries to implement his choice, he finds that he is dissatisfied with it. He realizes that it does not represent his interests, capacities, and values, and he rejects it, so that in his early twenties, when he should be specifying his choice, he has none.

In a complementary analysis of variations and deviations in the choice process, Lo Cascio (1964) has introduced the concepts of (1) delayed and (2) impaired vocational development. He compares and contrasts these patterns of behavior in accomplishing vocational developmental tasks with those characteristic of continuous or normal vocational development. As Figure 5-4 indicates, the latter involves four steps or phases: (1) the individual becomes aware

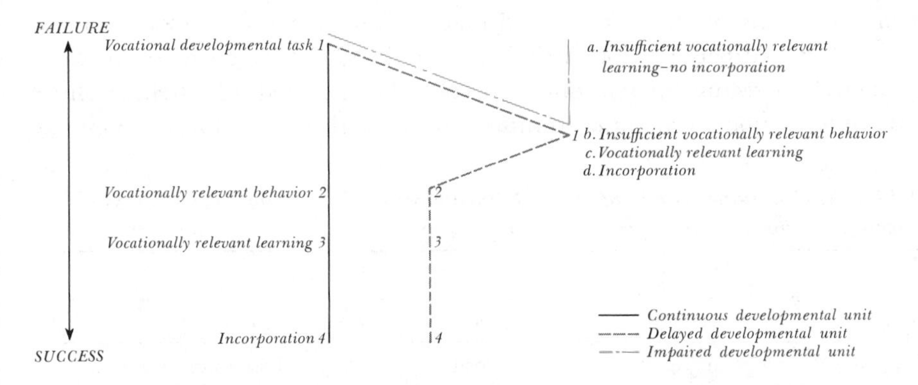

Figure 5-4. Continuous, delayed, and impaired vocational development. *(From Lo-Cascio, 1964, p. 886.)*

of a vocational developmental task which he must master, e.g., the choice of a college major; (2) he reacts appropriately in terms of previously learned responses; (3) he learns new responses in the process of dealing with the task; and (4) he incorporates these responses into his behavioral repertoire for the accomplishment of future tasks. In contrast, delayed vocational development does not proceed as smoothly, there being a greater lapse of time and less efficiency in coping with tasks. The delay is occasioned by the individual's not having sufficient relevant vocational behavior to bring to bear upon the tasks with which he is confronted. Once he eventually learns the appropriate responses for mastering a task, he then incorporates them into his repertoire, but his vocational development has nevertheless been delayed in the first instance. In impaired vocational development, there is not even the acquisition of task-relevant behavior, and there is no incorporation, because the individual lacks awareness of the task he is expected to accomplish, or, if he is aware of it, he is unable or unwilling to cope with it. Defined in these ways, Lo Cascio's concepts of delayed and impaired vocational development roughly correspond to Ginzberg's descriptions of variant and deviant choice patterns, respectively.

There are two studies which are relevant to our discussion of variations and deviations in the choice process, although one of them deals with interests rather than choice:

1. Case (1954) constructed a questionnaire consisting of a variety of items on an individual's vocational planning and attitudes which he administered to 403 male and female undergraduates at Washington State College (*N* for each sex was not reported). He used three of the items to constitute one group of Subjects which supposedly had "crystallized" choices and another group which had "pseudocrystallized" choices. Subjects were classified into two groups on the basis of their answers to the questions shown in Table 5-2. They were then compared on the remaining items to determine which ones differentiated them. From this analysis, Case found that individuals with pseudocrystallized choices "wanted better incomes than their fathers," cited "good job market" as their main reason for selection of a college major, and admitted to "little or no information on job opportunities." In short, they tended to be more like

Table 5-2. Questions Used in the Delineation of True- and Pseudo-crystallized Vocational Choice Groups *(From Case, 1954, p. 86)*

	Kind of crystallization	
Question	*True*	*Pseudo*
Certainty of college major	"Positive"	Less than "positive"
Satisfaction with present major	"Very satisfied"	Less than "very satisfied"
Information obtained on occupational field of interest	"A lot"	"Little" or "none"

the immature pleasure-oriented person than the mature work-oriented individual, whom Ginzberg et al. (1951, pp. 208–210) describe.

2. The writer (Crites, 1960) investigated the relationship of ego strength to vocational interest development to determine whether the individual's ability to integrate his experiences and organize them into consistent behavioral tendencies was related to his degree of interest patterning. The findings indicated a moderately high correlation ($r = .46$) between ego strength and interest patterning in male Subjects ($N = 31$) over 21 years old, but a low relationship ($r = .09$) in younger Subjects ($N = 19$). Since degree of interest patterning increases with age (Strong, 1943), it was concluded that if an individual's interests remain unpatterned or uncrystallized into early adulthood, this deviation may be related to inadequate ego functioning, which is usually associated with difficulties in parental relationships and identifications (Singer, J. O., 1955). In other words, the older adolescent with unpatterned interests appears to have personality and parental difficulties like those which Ginzberg saw in his Subjects who had delayed crystallization of their choices.

Comment. Case's study suggests what some of the factors are which play a part in the pseudocrystallization of choice, but we cannot have full confidence in the reliability of his findings, even though they are reasonable, because his methodology had a flaw in it. Instead of constituting his two groups on some criterion which was independent of the questionnaire on which he compared them, he used the same instrument to measure both pseudocrystallization of choice and attitudes toward occupations and work. As a result, the variables in his study are not experimentally independent, as sound research design requires. Consequently, we do not know whether the relationship between them is due to their intrinsic covariation or to a generalized response set to all the items in the questionnaire. Similarly, the writer's study of ego strength and interest patterning is suggestive but hardly conclusive. Not only was it based upon small numbers of Subjects, but it dealt with interests rather than choice. Only to the extent that the results are stable, and it is legitimate to generalize from findings on interest development to variation and deviation in the choice process, can we conclude that the study lends support to Ginzberg's hypotheses about why some individuals delay much longer than others in the crystallization of their choices.

STAGES IN THE DEVELOPMENT OF VOCATIONAL CHOICE

It has been hypothesized that the vocational choice process, like most processes which involve progressive changes in a product or organism, can be broken down into various phases or stages, which are usually further subdivided into smaller intervals called *periods*. The idea that the process of making a choice might proceed through a series of stages was originally introduced by Super (1942), who had been impressed by Buehler's, C. (1933) analyses of the life histories of 400 older people in Vienna, which revealed definite stages in their development. It was not until Dysinger (1950), Ginzberg et al. (1951), and Miller, D. C., and Form (1951) elaborated upon the stages in choice and work, however, that the concept assumed theoretical significance and prompted appropriate research. In this section, we shall discuss (1) what the various criteria for defining a stage are, (2) what stages in the choice process have been hypothesized, and (3) what research there is to support the existence of these presumed stages and their characteristics. We shall focus upon only those stages which characterize the choice process, leaving the discussion of the stages in vocational adjustment for Chapter 12.

The Definition of Stages in Vocational Choice

The criterion used by Buehler, C. (1933) to delineate life stages in development was a *behavioral* one. She identified stages in the histories of the old people in her study by plotting the incidence in their emotional, sexual, social, and vocational behavior against their chronological age. She found that, although there were individual differences in the age of onset of a particular stage, probably resulting from differences in developmental pace, there were certain ages at which given behaviors were predominant. For example, in the first stage, the individual's behavior was largely dependent, because of his position in the family and neighborhood, whereas in later stages it became more independent because of his increased economic self-sufficiency. At various ages throughout the total life span, other kinds of behaviors defined the beginnings and ends of distinctive stages in the individual's development. Figure 5-5, which is adapted from a condensation of Buehler's research by Frenkel-Brunswik (1952), illustrates how behaviors such as those listed in the left-hand column characterize different segments of a person's life. Note that some of the behaviors overlap each other considerably, whereas others are essentially independent.

Another approach to the definition of stages in the choice process comes from Havighurst's (1953) research on *developmental tasks.* He defines these as tasks "which arise at or about a certain period in the life of the individual, successful achievement of which leads to his happiness and to success with later tasks, while failure leads to unhappiness in the individual, disapproval by the society, and difficulty with later tasks." Super and his associates (1957, p. 132) have translated this general definition of a developmental task into vocational terms as follows:

> *Vocational developmental task:* A task encountered at or about a certain period in the life of an individual and deriving from the

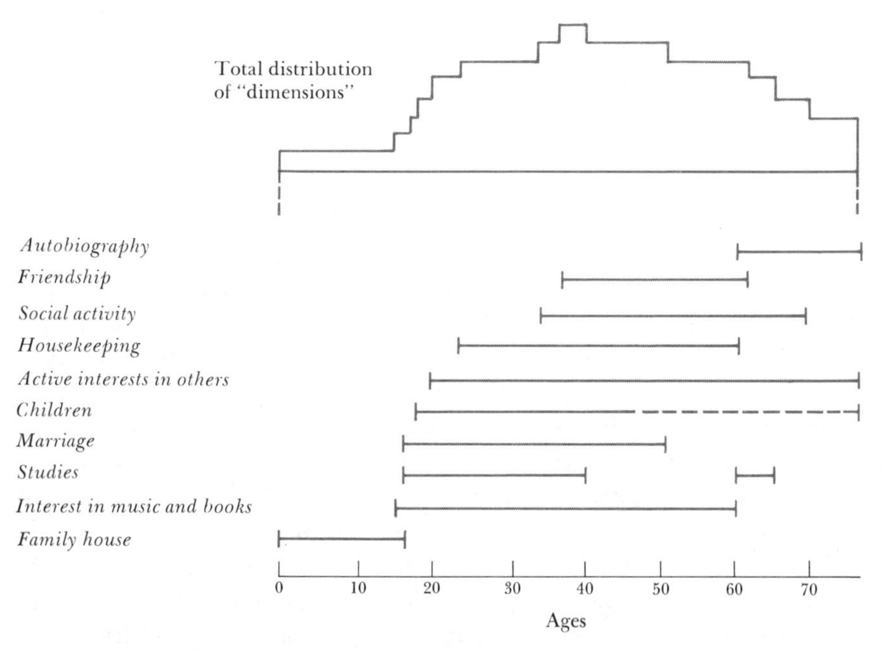

Figure 5-5. Buehler's definition of developmental stages as illustrated by the life history of one Subject. *(From Frenkel-Brunswick, 1952, p. 97.)*

> expectation that the members of a social group manifest a relatively orderly behavioral sequence in preparing for and participating in the activity of work.

Conceptualized in this way, vocational developmental tasks can be used to identify different stages in choice. Table 5-3 lists some of the tasks which the individual encounters as he develops vocationally and the stages which correspond to them.[6] Although the relationship is certainly not perfect, these stages

Table 5-3. Vocational Developmental Tasks in Adolescence *(From Super et al., 1957, p. 44)*

HIGH SCHOOL ADOLESCENT	1. Further development of abilities and talents
	2. Choice of high school or work
	3. Choice of high school curriculum
	4. Development of independence
YOUNG ADULT	1. Choice of college or work
	2. Choice of college curriculum
	3. Choice of suitable job
	4. Development of skills on the job

[6] See Rapoport and Rapoport (1965) for a delineation of parallel vocational and familial-marital developmental tasks.

are much the same as those which can be defined behaviorally, since behaviors which are appropriate for the mastery of a task usually develop at the same time that the task becomes paramount.

Still another way to define stages is the method used by Ginzberg et al. (1951), who were primarily interested in *how* vocational choices are made. Rather than either behavior or tasks, they used the individual's *basis for choice* and *crystallization of choice* as the criteria for delineating two "periods" and several "stages" in vocational development during adolescence.[7] By "basis for choice" they referred to what the individual considered the most important factor in his selection of an occupation. There were four of these factors—interests, capacities, values, and reality considerations—which Ginzberg's Subjects mentioned as bases for their choices and which followed each other in this sequence over time. Each of these factors defined a stage in what was termed the "tentative" period of vocational choice. By "crystallization of choice," Ginzberg meant the extent to which the individual had narrowed down the total possible number of occupations open to him to a few closely related ones which he intended to prepare for and seek employment in. Three stages in this process were identified, depending upon the specificity of the individual's choice: exploration, crystallization, and specification. These stages comprise the "realistic" period in choice determination, which follows the "tentative" period and which emerges from it through a "transition" stage of increasing awareness on the part of the individual of the limitations which reality imposes upon him.

Commenting upon the various criteria which have been suggested for delineating stages in the choice process, O'Hara and Tiedeman (1959, p. 294) have noted that further refinements are needed and propose what these might be:

> Although the concepts of "period" and "stage" are frequently used in regard to career development, they are difficult to define. However defined, though, both words ordinarily connote a time interval in which something is prevalent which is not prevalent at another time. Thus, "period" and "stage" suggest discreteness, dominance, and irreversibility.

They illustrate these concepts by depicting the stages in Ginzberg's tentative period as shown in Figure 5-6. In this diagram, *discreteness* is indicated by the vertical lines which set off the interest, capacity, and value stages. If extended, these lines would intersect the points on the age scale at which a given factor first becomes a basis for choice and then becomes a constructive force in choice.

[7] In Ginzberg's terminology, which is what is used here, "stage" refers to the shortest rather than the longest interval in vocational development.

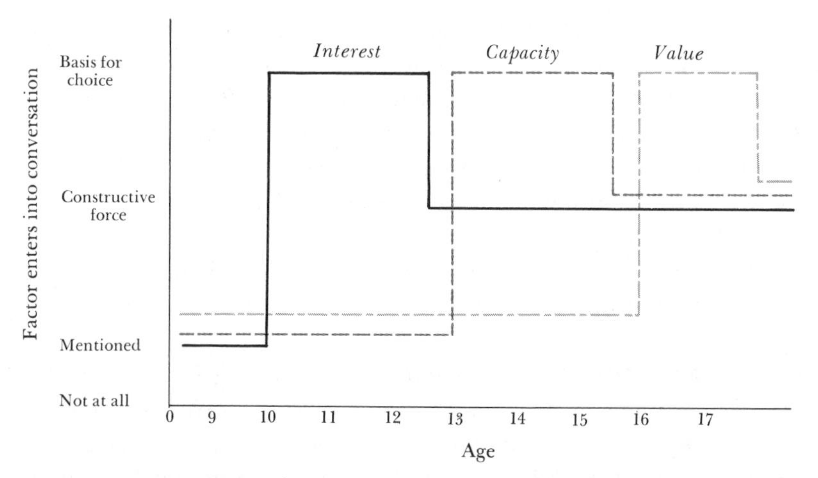

***Figure 5-6. Ginzberg's Tentative Period in vocational choice as diagrammed by O'Hara and Tiedeman** (1959, p. 293).*

Dominance is defined by the preeminence of one factor in relation to the others as a basis for choice. In other words, a factor is dominant when it is (1) discrete and (2) the sole basis for choice. *Irreversibility* is equated with the continual influence of a factor as a constructive force in choice after it is discrete and dominant as a basis for choice. Note that this definition of irreversibility is different from Ginzberg's and even implies some reversibility, since O'Hara and Teideman (1959, p. 294) reason that: "Adolescent imbalance causes an element to be the sole basis for choice, but, having been so, the element returns to the more mature position of being a constructive force operating simultaneously with others to effect differentiation of occupational choice."

Comment. Although O'Hara and Teideman's concepts of discreteness, dominance, and irreversibility contribute considerably to the definition of stages, whether identified in terms of behavior, tasks, or bases for choice, there are three aspects of their formulation which need discussion and possible modification:

1. It should be recognized that their criteria for defining stages are appropriate for a cross-sectional analysis of the choice process, as theirs was, but they are not necessarily the best for longitudinal studies. In the latter case, a more adequate definition of a stage is in terms of the relative growth which occurs in two different time intervals.

2. They imply that each of their criteria is sufficient to define a stage. In fact, they use the criteria in this way in their analysis of data on the clarification of the vocational self-concept in adolescence (see discussion to follow). It would seem, however, that, although each of the criteria is *necessary* for the definition of a stage, no one of them is sufficient. As Figure 5-6 makes clear, irreversibility without discreteness cannot define the limits (the beginning and end) of a stage, because it is a continuous function of age. Similarly, discreteness without irreversibility cannot distinguish between "stages" in developmental variables and "variations" in nondevelopmental variables. And, dominance without discreteness and irreversibility cannot establish a stage as preeminent for a given time span in development, since it is defined by the other two factors. In short, it takes all three criteria to define a stage in the choice process.

3. Their definition of irreversibility is somewhat confusing for two reasons: (1) They state, as has been mentioned, that irreversibility involves *some* reversibility, which seems to be a contradiction in terms, and (2) they represent it in Figure 5-6 as a line which is *parallel* to the base (or age) line, rather than as a line with positive slope. If irreversibility means that vocational behavior develops as a monotonic increasing function of age, however, which O'Hara and Tiedeman (1959, p. 299) *also* assert, then their diagram needs the revisions shown in Figure 5-7.

In this revised schema, the line with positive slope represents the irreversibility of a variable which has a continual effect upon the choice process as the

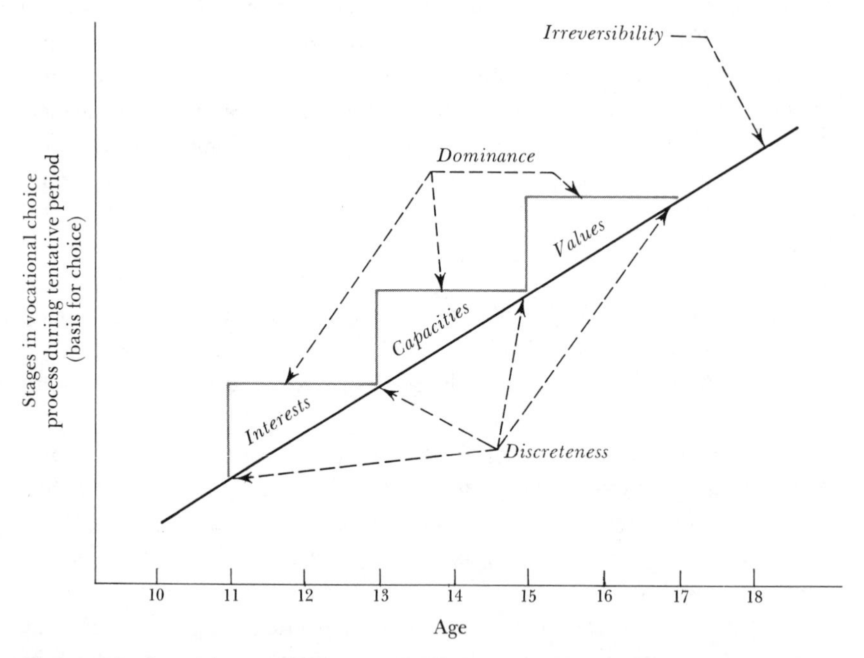

Figure 5-7. A revision of O'Hara and Tiedeman's diagram of Ginzberg's Tentative Period in vocational choice.

individual grows older, whether it was predominant during one period or not. The vertical lines which intersect the sloping line identify the points at which stages begin and, to this extent, define one aspect of their discreteness. The horizontal lines which connect the verticals with the sloping line complete the discreteness of the stages and indicate when a variable is dominant in the process of selecting an occupation. Thus, this conceptualization recognizes that in order to define a stage, it is necessary to demonstrate that it is discrete and dominant as well as irreversible.

Hypothesized Stages in the Development of Vocational Choice

Ginzberg's Fantasy, Tentative, and Realistic Periods. The first or *fantasy* period of the choice process, according to Ginzberg et al. (1951), begins as early as the age of 3 or 4, when the child first formulates a response to the question "What do you want to be when you grow up?" During the years from 4 to 6, the child selects occupations primarily on the basis of the intrinsic satisfactions which they offer—the "function pleasure" which they promise from performing their duties and tasks. By the age of 8 or 9, there is a shift in the basis for choice to a focus upon the results of work, the satisfactions which stem from the outcomes of an occupational endeavor. Characteristic of both the earlier and later choices of children is the wish to become an adult as well as a recognition of the inevitability of work in the future. The future is conceptualized in categorical terms by children when they express their vocational choices: it is seen as "not now—later." The vocational planning of the very young lacks continuity between the present and the future, and it reflects little or no cognizance of the relationship between means and ends.

In this period, there is only a dim awareness of how one goes about attaining an occupational goal, primarily because vocational choices in childhood are largely unrealistic. They are the product of fantasies, daydreams, and the desire to grow up, rather than experiences based upon considerations of reality. Near the end of the fantasy period, however, there is a discernible change in the vocational behavior of the 10- and 11-year-old toward greater realism. He gradually develops the realization that the problem of vocational choice is *his* responsibility. And, he begins to formulate tentative choices as best he can from his limited knowledge of self and reality. The first portion of Table 5-4 presents the approximate chronology of the "typical" child's vocational development and socialization as hypothesized by Ginzberg and his associates.

The next period, which Ginzberg calls the *tentative* period, starts at about the tenth year of life and generally lasts until graduation from high school in the seventeenth or eighteenth year. It is a period during which the adolescent searches for an appropriate basis for his vocational choice. Because he bases his

Table 5-4. Ginzberg's Descriptions of the Periods in the Vocational Choice Process (1951, p. 59 et passim)

Period	*Vocational orientation*	*General development*
FANTASY	Shift in basis for choice: Function pleasure (ages 4–6) Results of work (ages 8–9)	Increased capacity to accomplish specific tasks
	Behavioral characteristics: Recognition of having to work Wish to become an adult Distorted time perspective (future: "not now—later")	Increased objectivity about self
	No urgency to make a choice, unlimited fantasy No means-end cognizance	Increased concern with reality
	Development toward tentative period: Reliance upon parents for choice Dissatisfaction with parents' suggestions Acceptance of choice as personal responsibility	Increased pressure from parents to form good working habits
TENTATIVE	Sharpening of time perspective: Recognition of continuum between present and future; present and future linked Recognition that actions in present will condition those in the future	Increased awareness that self will change
	Greater awareness of reality barriers to choice More aware that adult work is same from day to day Desire to choose work which will be continually satisfying	Increased awareness that currently pleasurable activities may not be pleasurable in future
	Attempts to create image of future self, which tentative choice makes concrete Anticipated satisfactions from tentatively chosen occupations guide present actions rather than immediate satisfactions	Increased libidinal pressures which drive individual to immediate gratifications interfere with planning for the future

choices first upon his interests and then upon his capacities and finally upon his values, and because he has insufficient information about each of these factors to commit himself to a final choice, his actions and decisions have a definite tentative quality which characterizes them until he reaches the greater maturity of late adolescence and youth. Nevertheless, he makes gains and progresses in his vocational development toward greater awareness of his assets and liabilities and the limitations imposed by the environment.

Probably the most notable advance in his vocational thinking is in the sharpening of his time perspective. No longer does he think of time as a dis-

Period	*Vocational orientation*	*General development*
	Choices are tentative because: They are based upon a self image which is not firm They are often changed in the Realistic period The individual lacks information about training and work	Increased desire to gain emotional independence from impulses
	As conflicts and tensions are resolved, tentativeness gives way to considerations of reality in choice	Recognition of necessity to resolve early emotional conflicts, particularly with father ("return of the repressed")
REALISTIC	New approach to problem of choice is brought about by reality pressures, as well as resolution of conflicts Individual is forced by imminence of school graduation to recognize that he cannot remain undecided any longer	Differentiation of likes and dislikes
	Individual looks backward and forward in making a choice and realizes that major changes in self image are costly and unfeasible	Further development of ego functions
	Individual can no longer explore what he would like to do and how he would like to do it He must now deal with concrete demands, e.g., how to gain admission to a college or advanced training institution	Acceptance of adult responsibilities

crete variable: he recognizes it as a continuum which extends from the "right now" to the remote future. And, as a consequence, he realizes that his present behavior directly affects and restricts his future actions and alternatives. Accordingly, he strives to look ahead and to conceptualize his "future self" as a guide to his present decisions. Increasingly, he makes his vocational plans in anticipation of the satisfactions which the future will bring rather than the immediate gratifications of the present, which he deemed as the most important factors in choice during the fantasy period. As he postpones satisfactions and becomes more goal-directed, he appreciates more and more the influence which reality has upon the course of his vocational development, and, as a result, he assumes a more instrumental attitude toward choice. For the first time he approaches the problem of vocational choice with the realization that he must take action. He must deal directly with the realities of securing further training or finding a job. As indicated in the second portion of Table 5-4, the tentative period encompasses the individual's efforts to come to grips with the task of selecting an occupation and establishing it as a goal for future attainment.

Following the tentative period and extending through the later years of adolescence to the time of occupational entry, the *realistic* period corresponds less to a definite age range, as is characteristic of the earlier phases of vocational development, than to individual differences in personality and variations in environmental circumstances. Subdivided by Ginzberg (1951) into three stages, the realistic period represents the individual's efforts to reach a compromise between his needs and reality and to finally resolve the problem of vocational choice. Some individuals have little difficulty in arriving at a satisfactory solution to the selection of an occupation, whereas others experience considerable doubt and indecision, usually because their emotional development is retarded or their resources for occupational preparation are inadequate. Sooner or later, however, all individuals go through the three stages of the realistic period: exploration, crystallization, and specification. In the exploratory stage, they take stock of the past and review the decisions which they have made. At this time, (1) they eliminate many occupations as unsuitable possibilities, (2) they realize the importance of selecting an occupation which will bring real satisfaction, and (3) they recognize the difficulty of making a choice because of conflicts among various factors, e.g., interests and capacities. In the crystallization stage, they effect some compromise among the factors in choice and commit themselves to a general vocational goal. They stop exploring and start formulating definite plans for the future. And, finally, in the specification stage, they take the first steps toward attaining their objectives. They reveal a willingness to specialize and a resistance to any deflection from their chosen course of action. Thus, in the realistic period, they have achieved greater goal direction, independence, and realism in their vocational behavior, much as Super and Overstreet (1960, p. 32) have also pointed out.

Super's Exploratory Stage. Super (1953) follows Ginzberg's subdivision of adolescence into the tentative and realistic periods, but he places a greater emphasis upon the role of the family and the self-concept in vocational development than upon the part played by the ego functions and emotions. Elaborating upon Miller, D. C., and Form's (1951) original interpretation of the relationship between socialization and vocational behavior, Super (1957) interprets adolescence as a period of cultural adaptation during which the individual makes the transition from childhood to adulthood and engages in a process of exploration of the self and the world of work. The exploration takes place in the three primary areas of socialization—the home, the school, and the work setting.[8]

In the home, the adolescent learns about himself and occupations through continual contact with parents, siblings, and relatives who describe and discuss their jobs and through involvement in the activities of the family. As Super (1957, p. 84) observes, the home is "a hotel, a restaurant, a recreation center, a school, a laundry, a carpentry shop, an electrical shop, a farm, and a variety of other industrial, educational, and agricultural enterprises." In the school, the young person supplements the knowledge gained in the home with exploration of self and work through his performance in formal courses and extracurricular activities and in informal associations with peers and teachers. He tries out, evaluates, changes, and accepts or rejects the perceptions of himself and occupations which he acquired during the preceding phase of his development, which Super calls the *growth* stage. In the workplace, if he works, the teenager evaluates his interests, capacities, and values and develops a self-concept which he then translates into vocational terms.

According to Super (1957), the adolescent draws upon his experiences in the home, school, and world of work to clarify his impressions of self gained in childhood, to increase his information about occupations, and to achieve a synthesis of his conceptions of self and work in the expression of a vocational choice. Once he has a tentative idea of who he is and what he wants to be, the young person enters a transition period between school and work which is characterized by what Super refers to as *reality-testing*. This stage in the individual's vocational development involves his getting a job and adapting himself to the culture of the world of work, which is quite different from the one to which he is accustomed. No longer does the individual have the reassuring support or even the perceived stability of the school in making his way, and often he has severed his psychological as well as financial ties with home and family, so that in a very real sense he is "on his own." He must now meet and

[8] Hadley and Levy (1962) have analyzed Super's discussion of the exploratory stage, as well as later stages in the process of vocational adjustment, within the framework of "reference group" theory, their main point being that throughout the course of vocational development these groups, which include parents, peers, teachers, professional and fraternal associations, etc., serve both "normative" and "comparative" functions for the individual as he seeks standards for reality-testing his vocational behavior.

deal effectively with the realities of a competitive, impersonal, status-oriented work society, whereas before he could enjoy the protection and security of the school culture.

Miller and Form's Work Periods. Miller, D. C., and Form (1951) view the stages in the process of vocational choice from the assumptions and orientations of the industrial sociologist and consequently define what they call "work periods" rather than choice periods or phases in the development of the self-concept, such as Ginzberg and Super propose. The first period in Miller and Form's schema of the total work life is the *preparatory work period.* Defined as the time before an individual has any work experience, this period consists largely of his socialization in the home and school. The home provides the primary role models for him to learn about different types of work, the advantages and disadvantages which they offer, and the opportunities in them. Miller, D. C., and Form (1951, p. 521) explain the relationship between role models and choice as follows: "The workers whom the child observes become his models. He watches their behavior and then rehearses it in the world of fantasy or of play. This rehearsal involves a *taking of the role,* putting himself vicariously into the place of the worker, and imagining what the worker does and how he feels.... Vocational goals are formed and developed essentially by this role-taking device." The school supplements this basic learning about the nature of work with indoctrination in the proper habits of work. Miller, D. C., and Form (1951, p. 523) identify five prescriptions about good "work ways" which the school teaches: "(1) the pupil is trained to stay on the job and learn his lessons; (2) the pupil is trained to obey authority; (3) the pupil is encouraged to develop initiative and to rise socially; (4) the pupil is trained to develop character; (5) the pupil is trained to get along with his teachers and his schoolmates." Through such instruction, the young child is prepared for his initiation into the world of work.

In the second or *initial work period,* which is defined as "a period of job impermanence beginning when the worker seeks his first jobs during his span of school enrollment and continuing until he has terminated his education" (Miller, D. C., & Form, 1951, pp. 535–536), the individual experiences direct, personal contact with the world of work for the first time. He works only part-time during the regular school year, or possibly full-time in the summer and sees his job as only temporary, but he soon learns that work places many demands upon him and that he must meet certain expectations in order to hold his job, such as "accepting responsibility," "working hard," "getting along with people," "valuing money," and "building a reputation as a good worker." Slowly but surely, as he is exposed more and more to these expectations in the workplace, he internalizes them, and they become values which direct his behavior. He develops a wish for independence, a wish to demonstrate his ability to get along with people, a wish to have and to manage money, and a wish to make a good job record. Often the young person is thwarted and frustrated in realizing these values because of such conflicting realities as the impersonality of co-workers and employers and the disappearance of apprenticeship work experiences, but he generally finds a way to cope with them effectively and looks forward to the day when he will be a full-time worker.

That time comes when he makes the transition from school to work, when he is on the threshold of the *trial work period.* After finishing his training, the individual begins looking for his first permanent job, usually without realizing that if he is like most other young workers, he will change occupations at least once and probably more before he stabilizes in one. This "trying out" an occupation, and then rejecting it in favor of another, happens because of the influence of a variety of factors, including the individual's lack of occupational information, the differences in social mores and values between the school and work cultures, and such factors as the routine of repetitive work, the commands of an authoritarian supervisor, dishonest business procedures, deviant personal habits of fellow workers, and the insecurity of work (Miller, D. C., & Form, 1951, pp. 629–631). Despite the disillusionments and disappointments he experiences, however, the individual usually makes the transition from school to work and in so doing completes the last stage in the vocational choice process.

Comment. We can compare and contrast the three conceptualizations of the hypothesized stages in the choice process by reference to Figure 5-8. From this diagram, it is apparent that Ginzberg has made finer subdivisions than the others and has adopted a more strictly psychological terminology for the stages. Super seems to represent a middle position between a psychological and sociological interpretation of the stages and emphasizes the interaction of the developmental and socialization processes in his use of the terms "growth" and "exploration." Finally, Miller and Form highlight the impact of social institutions, particularly the home and school, upon the work life of the individual as he progresses through the "preparatory" and "initial" periods and tries to orient himself to the sociology of the marketplace. All three schemata picture the choice process in adolescence as one which involves the young person's progressive learning about himself and about the world of work.[9]

[9] See Harris (1961) for a discussion of the role of work experiences in facilitating the adolescent's transition to adult maturity.

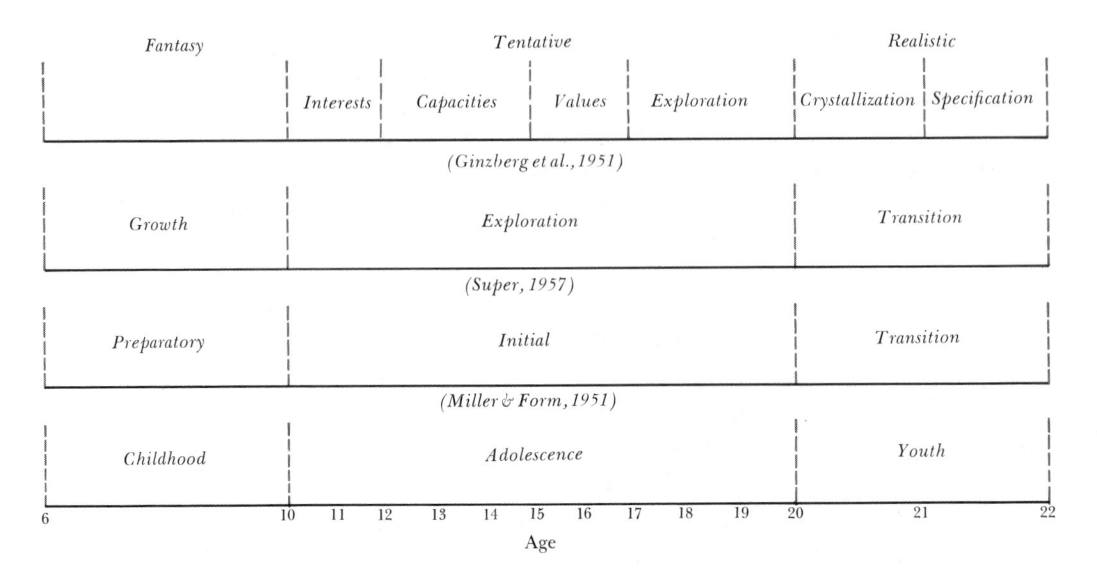

Figure 5-8. Stages in the vocational choice process as proposed by Ginzberg (1951), Super (1957), and Miller, D. C., and Form (1951).

Research on the Stages in the Vocational Choice Process

Research evidence on the stages in the formation of a vocational choice is mostly indirect and, in many instances, inconclusive because of shortcomings in sampling and experimental design. Ginzberg's study, which should be the most relevant one on stages, suffers the most from methodological flaws. Only eight Subjects were interviewed at each of eight grade levels for a total sample of 64. Analysis of the interview protocols was subjective, with no attempt to determine interjudge agreement on the statements which Subjects made. And, inferences were made about changes in the bases of choice with increasing age, but the samples were selected by grade level. Because of these limitations in Ginzberg's investigation, it is probably better to consider it a piece of survey research (see Chapter 13), which is a source of many provocative hypotheses, rather than a definitive analysis of choice behavior, and to turn our attention to other studies for findings on the stages in making a choice. We can use Ginzberg's designations for the stages, however, to organize and summarize the available research, since it seems to fit into his framework more readily than into the others.

The Fantasy Period. Interestingly enough, there is more research on this period in choice than there is on the succeeding ones, and at least two of the studies which have been conducted on it have been prompted by Ginzberg's theory. To determine how valid Ginzberg's inferences about fantasy choices were, O'Hara (1959) made an analysis of interviews with a group of 15 boys in the first, third, fifth, seventh, and ninth grades who were attending a summer school "enrichment" program in suburban Boston. From responses to such questions as "Who are You?", "What sort of boy are you?", "What kinds of things do you like to do?", and "What will you be when you grow up?", he concluded that the major basis for choice during this early period is "liking" for an activity or occupation. A factor of almost equal importance, however, appeared to be the influence of "key persons" as role models for these young boys. O'Hara emphasizes this finding and points out that his Subjects tested choices suggested by "significant others" against the reality of their capacities and values. On the basis of these observations, which are necessarily limited in their applicability because of the sample size, O'Hara suggests that the upper limit of the fantasy period may be at the age of 8 or 9 rather than at 10, as hypothesized by Ginzberg.

Two other studies tend to support O'Hara's conclusion, although they were not conducted to directly evaluate it. In a previously mentioned investigation, Mackaye (1927) surveyed the vocational choices of 765 boys in grades 1 through 6 (approximate age range of 6 to 12) and found that there was a sizable group which had crystallized their "interests," as he called them, at an early point in the elementary school years. (Parenthetically, it will be recalled that they then reopened the problem of choice at about halfway through adolescence.) In the other study, Norton (1953) gathered data on male and female teachers and male factory workers which indicated that the mean ages of their first vocational choices were 9.7, 8.8, and 12.9, respectively. Only the factory workers developed their career goals later than the age which O'Hara sets as the terminal point for the fantasy period or stage. Why there is this difference between teachers and laborers is not exactly clear, although we can speculate that it may reflect differences in social-class background which affect the emphasis placed upon setting goals and planning for the future.

In contrast to these findings, several additional studies have shown that Ginzberg's age boundary for the end of the fantasy period may be earlier than is actually the case. Davis, D. A., Hagan, and Strouf (1962, p. 628) asked 116 boys and girls who averaged 12 years of age (with a range of 11 to 16 years) "to write paragraphs telling what they would like to be when they grew up and why they had made that particular choice." The papers were then analyzed to determine whether their choices were "fantasy" or "tentative" according to the following definitions: "Fantasy occupational choices were defined as translations of simple needs and impulses into occupational goals. Tentative choices indicated those decisions based upon capacities, interests, and values of the individual" (Davis, D. A., et al., 1962, p. 628). The results showed that 60 percent of the total sample had tentative choices, but when boys and girls were compared, there was a marked difference between them. Whereas 74 percent of the girls had tentative choices, only 41 percent of the boys had similar choices. In other words, a majority of the boys were still in the fantasy period. This would mean that, rather than being too high, Ginzberg's age boundary for this stage may be too low.

In a series of three investigations which spanned the years of transition between the fantasy and tentative periods, Lehman and Witty (1929, 1931b, 1931c) collected extensive data on the choices and preferences of 26,878 boys and girls in the age range from 8½ to 18½ years. Using the Lehman Vocational Attitude Quiz, they asked their Subjects to rank occupations according to various instructions, including "the three occupations which they would like best to follow." Figure 5-9 summarizes their findings for one segment

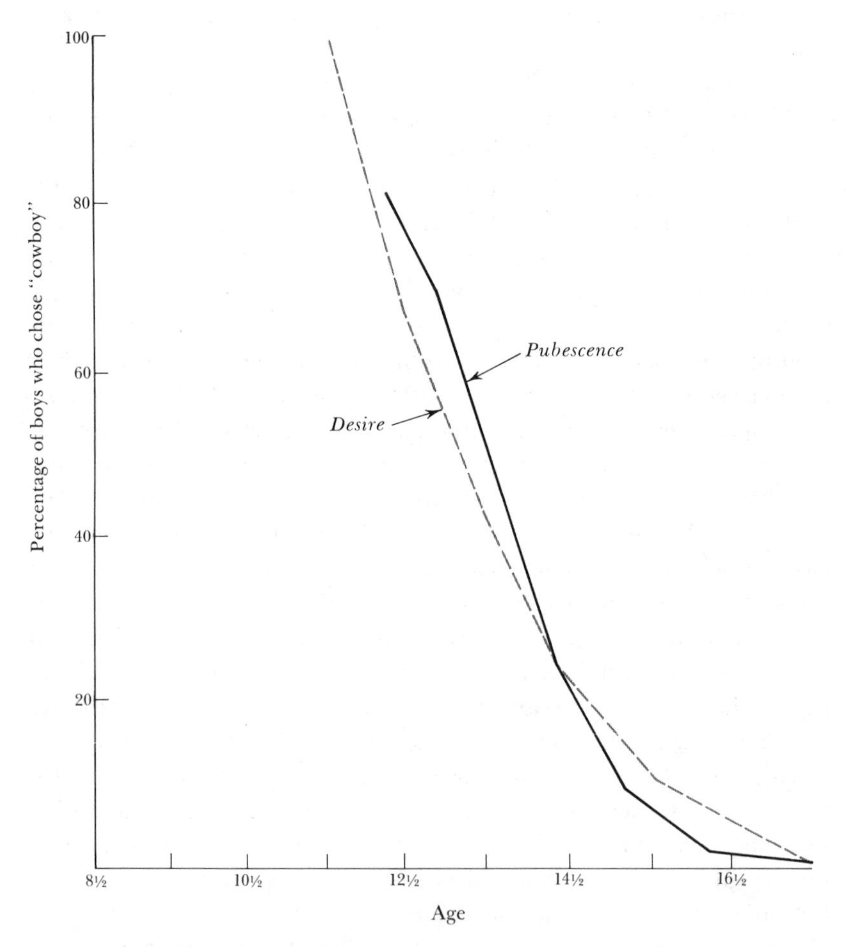

***Figure 5-9. The trend in the "desire" of boys to be a cowboy in pubescence as found by Lehman and Witty** (1931c, p. 98).*

($N = 7{,}000$) of the total sample on differences between age groups in response to this stimulus. It is obvious from the negative slope of the curve that the appeal of being a cowboy decreases dramatically as age increases. It is also apparent that liking for this largely "fantasy" occupation drops off markedly between 12½ and 13½, which is later than the time the fantasy stage is supposed to terminate. Thus, these data do not support Ginzberg's formulation.

The Tentative Period. The major study of this stage in choice making is the one by O'Hara and Tiedeman (1959), who investigated the clarification of the vocational self-concept during adolescence. These investigators tested 1,021 boys in the ninth, tenth, eleventh, and twelfth grades of a private Catholic day school in Boston with the following tests: (1) the Verbal Reasoning, Numerical Ability, Mechanical Reasoning, Space Relations, and Abstract Reasoning subtests of the Differential Aptitude Test (DAT) battery; (2) the Kuder Preference Record, Form C; (3) the Allport-Vernon-Lindzey Study of Values; (4) the Work Values Inventory of the Career Pattern Study; and (5) Gough's Home Index for social-class status. In addition, the Subjects were administered a questionnaire in which they were asked to estimate their test scores from definitions of the various variables given in the test manuals. The analysis involved a comparison of the correlations between actual and estimated scores for the several grade levels, the hypothesis being that the correlations would be higher for the upper grades if there is a progressive clarification of the vocational self-concept during the high school years. An additional hypothesis was that there would be stages in the increased awareness of aptitudes, interests, and values which would correspond to those proposed by Ginzberg for the tentative period.

To test these hypotheses, O'Hara and Tiedeman computed what are called "canonical correlation coefficients" to express the degree of relationship between tested and estimated scores on each variable for each grade level. The canonical correlation coefficient indicates the maximum correlation between two linear composites of two or more variables. In this case, the two linear composites were the combined test scores for a measure and the combined estimates for the same measure. Figure 5-10 presents the plots of the canonical coefficients by grade level for interests, work values, general values, and aptitudes. Although statistical tests of the differences between these coefficients were not made, O'Hara and Tiedeman assumed that the trends for interests, work values, and aptitudes were "significant" and that the trend for general values was nonsignificant but similar in form to the others. From these data, they concluded that interests and work values manifest stages, as indicated by the parabolic shape of their curves, and that general values and aptitudes are continuous functions without stages. Furthermore, they observe that all the

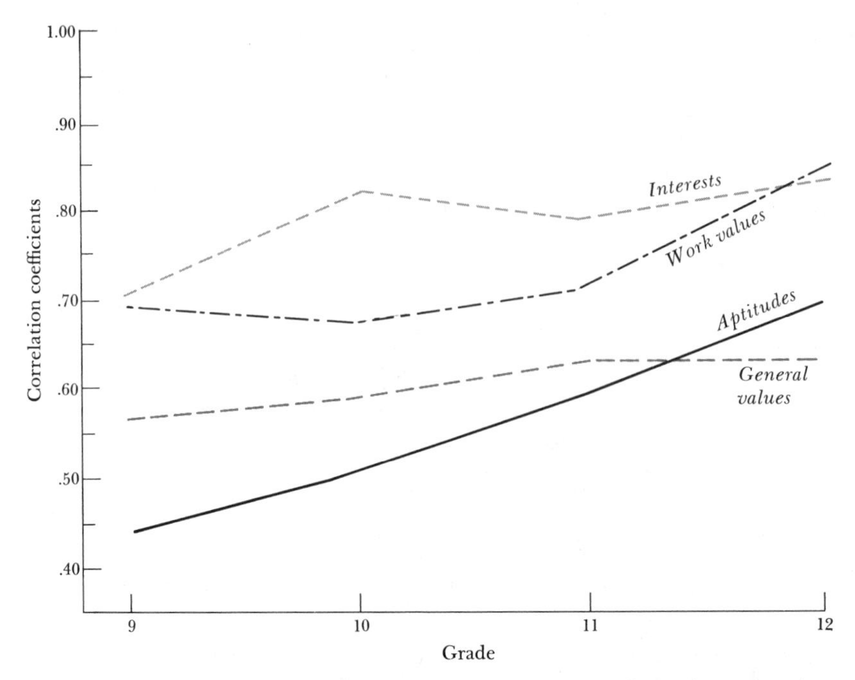

Figure 5-10. O'Hara and Tiedeman's** (1959, p. 295) **trends in the estimation of scores on measures of aptitudes, interests, values, and work values during adolescence.

trends are irreversible and that interests and work values tend to predominate over general values and aptitudes (between the ninth and twelfth grades). They note especially that estimates of aptitudes are particularly poor during this period. With reference to Ginzberg's interest, capacity, and value stages, they point out that their data do not contradict his formulation, but that they do imply that the stages in the clarification of the vocational self-concept, as measured by agreement between test and estimated scores, are different. Awareness of interests and work values characterizes the entire tentative period, rather than the preeminence of one and then the other.

There are three considerations, however, which should be made in interpreting the results of O'Hara and Tiedeman's study:

1. The differences they found in the canonical correlation coefficients between the ninth and twelfth grades may be due simply to sampling fluctuations rather than increases in the clarification of the vocational self-concept. They qualify the interpretation of their results with such statements as "Setting consideration of sampling variability aside" and "If sampling variations are completely ignored," but they do not take into account the possible effects of differences between the samples for the various grade levels. Since the samples were cross-sectional ones, and since there was no test of significance for the canonical correlation coefficient at the time the study was made, they have only a tenuous basis for inferring that there are systematic trends in their data.

2. Their use of the canonical correlation coefficient leads to conclusions different from those of the zero-order *r*'s, which they also report. Table 5-5 presents the latter for tested and estimated scores by variable and grade level. For example, there are no significant increases, as evaluated by *t* tests made by the writer, for the Verbal Reasoning, Symbolic Reasoning, and Abstract Reasoning subtests of the DAT between the ninth and twelfth grades. Similarly, for each of the other variables, only about one-half of the scales reflect nonchance increases. In short, the canonical correlations suggest that *all* aspects of the vocational self-concept are clarified in the tentative period, whereas the product-moment correlations indicate that this is true of only *certain* aspects.

3. In drawing the conclusion that interests and work values predominate over aptitudes and general values in the grade range studied, O'Hara and Tiedeman neglect the possibility that it might be easier to estimate scores on some variables than on others. If this is true for interests and work values, it would account for the higher canonical correlation coefficients for these variables, rather than their psychological predominance in the clarification of the vocational self-concept. There is also the problem of how applicable results obtained in a private parochial metropolitan school are to other high school populations. Thus, it would seem wise to accept O'Hara and Tiedeman's data and interpretations cautiously until they have been replicated with a different methodology on more representative samples. The most which we can conclude from their findings at present is that an overall trend toward clarification of the vocational self-concept in adolescence probably exists.

Two other studies of the tentative period have dealt with related problems, but in different ways. Montesano and Geist (1964) gave an open-ended form of the latter's (Geist, 1959) Picture Interest Inventory (PII) to 30 boys each in grades 9 and 12, in order to determine differences between the groups in the reasons they gave for their vocational choices. It was found that the various categories of reasons (or "bases," in Ginzberg's terminology) were highly related for the two grades, the *rho* being .82, but that there were differences in frequencies within categories. Three times as many twelfth graders cited "assessment of abilities" (capacities) as a reason for their choices, indicating that this factor becomes an increasingly salient one in the choice process as the adolescent matures. In the second study, Watley (1965) asked 534 male engineering freshmen to indicate when they decided to enter this field and then followed them up at the beginning of their second year to find out whether there were any relationships between time of decision and such variables as

***Table 5–5. Zero-order Correlations between Actual and Estimated Test Scores on the Variables Studied by O'Hara and Tiedeman** (1959, p. 297)*

Area	*Variable*	*Grade 9*	*Grade 10*	*Grade 11*	*Grade 12*
APTITUDE:	Verbal reasoning	.30	.26	.31	.26
	Numerical ability	.32	.40	.43	.51
	Mechanical reasoning	.26	.38	.41	.58
	Space relations	.24	.24	.26	.18
	Abstract reasoning	.19	.08	.03	.13
INTEREST:	Outdoor	.50	.48	.47	.50
	Mechanical	.49	.58	.57	.66
	Computational	.58	.60	.60	.69
	Scientific	.51	.54	.46	.68
	Persuasive	.24	.53	.48	.32
	Artistic	.59	.48	.43	.50
	Literary	.41	.43	.54	.57
	Musical	.59	.63	.61	.65
	Social service	.44	.45	.60	.60
	Clerical	.32	.32	.37	.50
SOCIAL CLASS:	Social class	.42	.29	.42	.35
VALUES, GENERAL:	Theoretical	.19	.16	.10	.18
	Economic	.22	.30	.25	.44
	Aesthetic	.32	.37	.43	.46
	Social	.19	.37	.46	.45
	Political	.28	.36	.27	.28
	Religious	.23	.31	.32	.46
VALUES, WORK:	Creative	.42	.50	.45	.57
	Aesthetic	.39	.36	.44	.39
	Planning	.19	.25	.25	.28
	Theoretical	.33	.27	.32	.40
	Variety	.44	.37	.52	.47
	Independence	.27	.34	.33	.30
	Supervision	.12	.10	.14	.09
	Work conditions	.15	.07	.22	.20
	Associations	.24	.18	.19	.35
	Way of life	.23	.33	.35	.40
	Social welfare	.46	.55	.57	.61
	Security	.28	.28	.35	.48
	Material	.38	.38	.52	.56
	Prestige	.23	.31	.19	.35
	Mastery	.08	.07	.07	.04

(1) ability, (2) academic achievement, (3) interest, (4) father's educational level, and (5) size of community. His major findings were that: as compared with students who chose engineering at an early age, those who waited until the last year of high school (1) scored significantly lower on the Minnesota Scholastic Aptitude Test, (2) had lower scores on the SVIB Engineer scale, (3) obtained lower GPA's in both high school and college, (4) dropped out of engineering more frequently, (5) came more often from small communities, and (6) had fathers with less education. In other words, cast into Ginzberg's conceptual scheme, it can be said that a late decision to pursue engineering as a career is a *variant* choice pattern for some adolescents, but a *deviant* one for others, the differentia being whether they are more or less successful later on.

The Realistic Period. We have discussed one of the studies on this stage, by Small (1953), at considerable length in other contexts, and a brief summary of it should be all that is necessary to present his results on whether the realism of choice increases with age. It will be recalled that Small investigated the choices of 10 normal and 10 maladjusted boys at each of the age levels between 15 and 19 to test the hypothesis that: "Individuals with different ego strengths will show differences in the use they make of reality and wishful fantasy in making their vocational choices." To measure realism of choice, he compared the personal characteristics of the boys, as rated by their counselors, with the job requirements of their chosen occupation, as listed in Part IV of the DOT, and devised what he called a "reality deviation" score. He reasoned that, if Ginzberg's suppositions about this period were correct, then the older, normal boys should have smaller reality deviation scores than the others. Contrary to expectation, however, Small (1953, p. 4) found that: "Instead of a linear relationship between age and reality, something different appears to take place in both groups (normal and maladjusted) at each age. The change is sometimes toward greater realism and at other times to less realism." In light of these findings, he concluded that there is "no evidence of a developmental progression towards greater realism of vocational choice, but much evidence that reality factors and fantasy drives operate simultaneously at all ages in the selection of a vocational goal" (Small, 1953, p. 17).

It is difficult to evaluate Small's study and to understand why he obtained the results he did, because he neglects to report mean "reality deviation" scores for the various age levels or statistical tests of the differences between them. About the only possible explanation, in lieu of the necessary data, is that the age range was not sufficiently wide to provide an adequate test of the hypothesized differences in realism of choice. In the previously cited study by the writer (Crites, 1960), the critical age in the crystallization of interest patterns was 21 years, and in the investigation by Culver (1935), which is reviewed below, 50 percent of his sample did not choose a specific occupation until the junior year of college, which is roughly equivalent to an age of 21 years. Consequently, it is possible that Small's age range, which had an upper limit of 19, was too restricted to reveal the trends in choice realism which have been hypothesized as the individual approaches the time of occupational entry.

Three studies on the *age* at which choices are made, however, support Ginzberg's theory. In the investigation by Culver (1935), 153 male juniors at Stanford University were asked to complete a 10-item questionnaire on their vocational field, specific vocational choice, reasons for the choice, the certainty of their choices, and the expected rewards of work. Analysis of the questionnaire responses indicated that there was 63 percent permanence in choice of occupational *field* between high school and the junior year of college but only 16.6 percent permanence in choice of *specific* occupation during the same period. In contrast, between the freshman and junior years of college there was 80.2 percent permanence in choice of field and 46.4 percent in choice of specific occupation. The overall percentages for the total period of years between high school and college, as depicted in Figures 5-11*a* and 5-11*b*, show a definite trend toward the specification of choice as the individual grows older. Thus, Culver's data clearly confirm Ginzberg's division of the realistic period into the exploratory, crystallization, and specification stages.

Kaplan (1946) asked 282 former clients (sex not specified) of the University of Idaho counseling center to report their full-time occupation and the age at which they first became interested in it. He found that the modal age was 18 years, with a range from approximately 15 to 20 years of age. If the age of first interest in an individual's eventual occupation corresponds to the beginning of the realistic period, then Kaplan's findings also agree with Ginzberg's delineation of the stages in the choice process. Similarly, Forrest (1961) has reported that, for a group of 292 male National Merit scholars, whose vocational choices were elicited when they were high school seniors and approximately three years later when they were college juniors, 50 percent chose the same field at the two points in time. These findings, based upon data secured from a high-ability sample, correspond rather closely to Culver's and provide additional support for Ginzberg's description of the realistic period.

Ginzberg states that this stage in the process of vocational choice determination comes to an end with the specification of the occupation the individual intends to enter, and Blau et al. (1956) enumerate the choice and selection factors which interact at the time occupational entry takes place, but these formulations have been largely analytical, and there has been no empirical research specifically designed to test them. There are several studies conducted over the past two or three decades, however, which are relevant to the con-

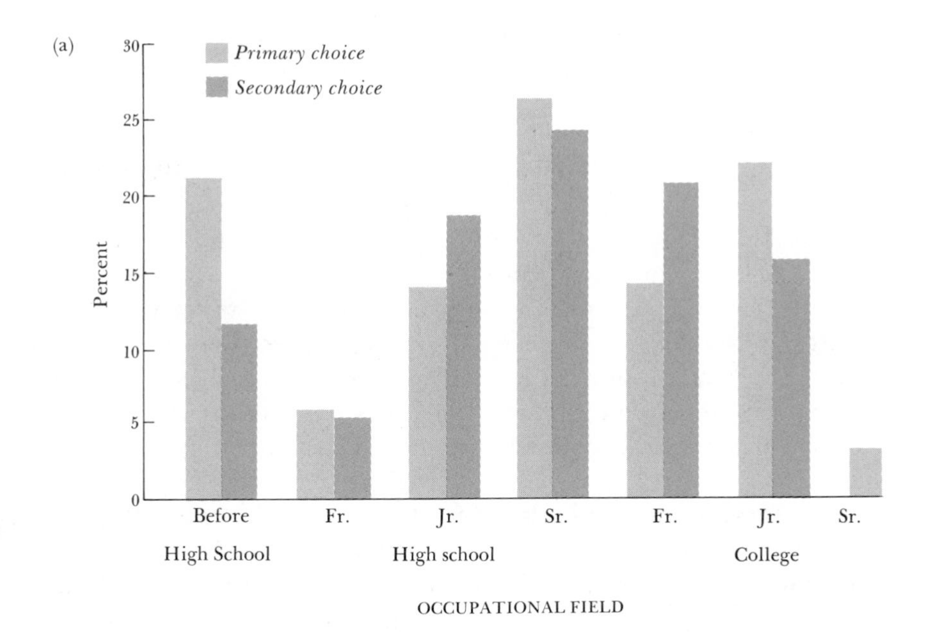

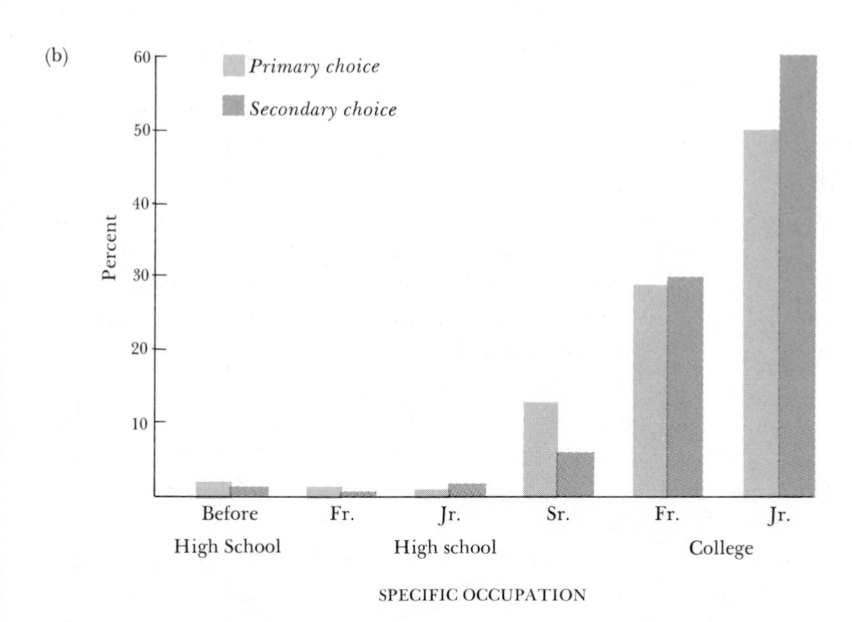

Figure 5-11. Graphs of Culver's (1935) data on the choice of occupational field and specific occupation during the high school and college years.

ceptual schemata of Ginzberg and Blau and which should be discussed in connection with them. These investigations can be broadly grouped into three categories: (1) what job applicants look for in a company; (2) what employers look for in job applicants; and (3) the relationship between applicant characteristics and employer recruiting decisions.

1. Over a period of several years, Jurgensen (1948) asked 3,345 male job applicants to rank 10 factors which they considered to be more or less important in the company for which they might work. These factors were: advancement, benefits, company (name or prestige), co-workers, hours, pay, security, superior, type of work, and working conditions. He found that the three factors which were most frequently ranked highest were security, advancement, and type of work, in that order. Jurgensen concluded that, contrary to popular opinion, which holds that pay is the most important consideration in seeking a job, applicants are more interested in the intangible outcomes of work.

Likewise, Dickinson (1954b) has reported that approximately 1,200 male college seniors, planning to enter various occupational fields, rank type of work, advancement, and human relations as the three most important factors in deciding upon a position. There were some differences in the ranking of these factors across the fields of accounting, administration, engineering, sales, and teaching, but they were among the top three in all fields, with the exception of sales and teaching, where the former ranked salary ahead of human relations and the latter valued security more than advancement.

An experimental study of this problem was conducted by Richardson, L. A. (1966), who devised 16 hypothetical "job offers," in which he systematically varied (1) location of the position, (2) starting salary, (3) type of work, and (4) company size. He then asked 113 male senior business administration majors to scale the job offers according to a paired-comparisons procedure. Contrary to the findings of Jurgensen and Dickinson, his results indicated that starting salary was the most significant factor, and location of the company was next in importance. It should be noted, however, that the salary differential between the high and low offers was $800, which may have been so large that it overdetermined what the usual effects of the other factors are in real-life employment situations. Until Richardson's findings can be replicated in a study of *actual* job offers, the best conclusion which can be drawn from this research on what job applicants look for in a company is that they are less concerned about the monetary return of work, at least within a range which includes neither very low nor very high salaries, than they are with such factors as security, advancement, and type of work.

2. One of the first studies on what employers look for in job applicants was conducted by Endicott (1944), who surveyed the hiring practices and policies

of 70 companies and found that most of them placed the greatest emphasis upon a prospective employee's ability to get along with others. Only about 20 percent of these firms stressed outstanding academic achievement—and then primarily for research and technical personnel. They preferred the candidate with some part-time work experience, but only when "other things were equal." In short, they stressed facility in human relations above all other factors. Similarly, in an interview study of 24 companies, using leads much like those in Endicott's questionnaire, Wilder and Riggs (1948) also found that employers are primarily concerned with how an applicant is going to get along with both his co-workers and the public and are only secondarily interested in background factors. In sharp contrast to these findings, Dickinson (1955) has reported that a sample of 1,233 employers ranked intelligence, judgment, and training as the most important factors in career success, with sociality (ability to get along with others) tied for fourth with conscientiousness out of seven factors. The difference in the results of this study and the others, however, may be due to the ranking instructions which were given to the employers. Dickinson did not ask them specifically what they look for in a job applicant, but what contributes to success. Also, he forced their rankings and restricted them to the factors he had selected. It is not surprising, therefore, that his findings differed from those of the other studies.

3. The one study which has attempted to determine empirically what the relationship is between applicant characteristics and employer recruiting decisions presents a picture of which factors are the salient ones in the employment process quite different from that gained from survey data. For 211 male college seniors, majoring in business administration at the University of Minnesota, Carroll (1966) correlated 19 personal characteristics with four criteria of job-seeking success (see Table 5-6). Only three of the characteristics were significantly related to the criteria: appearance rank correlated with number of visit offers (.26), with job-visit ratio (.30), and with combined criterion (.27); office experience correlated with number of job offers (.20), and with visit-

Table 5-6. Correlations between Personal Characteristics and Criteria of Job-seeking Success *(From Carroll, 1966, p. 422)*

Characteristic	*No. visits*	*No. job offers*	*Visit-interview ratio*	*Job-visit ratio*	*Combined criterion*
Appearance rank (handsome is +)	+.26			+.30	+.27
Marital status (married is +)		+.09			
Office experience (yes is +)		+.20	+.18		

interview ratio (.18); and marital status correlated with number of job offers (.09). From these results, Carroll (1966, p. 423) concluded that: "Thus, the variables studied accounted for only a small amount of the variance in the campus job-seeking success of Minnesota business school graduates in 1961 in spite of the fact that a fairly large number of obvious and often mentioned characteristics were studied." It should be noted, however, that "ability to get along with others" was not included, although the studies we have already reviewed indicated that it ranks high in the selection hierarchies of employers. Also noteworthy is the correspondence of Carroll's finding that appearance correlates with more criteria of job-seeking success than any other characteristic with Endicott's observation that this same factor was frequently mentioned as important by the employers in his study.

Comments. The most striking conclusion which emerges from this review of theory and research on the stages in the choice process is that theory has far outstripped research. We have a fairly comprehensive conceptual framework of the stages through which an individual supposedly passes in arriving at a choice, but only a few of the objective details are filled in. Among these are the age boundary for the end of the fantasy stage, which is approximately 13 years, and the crystallization and specification of choice in the realism period, which takes place between the ages of 18 and 21 in normal vocational development. There is some evidence that choices become more realistic as the individual matures, but exactly when and how are questions which remain to be answered. The study by O'Hara and Tiedeman represents an orientation which may produce the necessary data, but many more well-designed and properly executed investigations are needed before our knowledge and understanding of the stages in the choice process will be satisfactory. Similarly, direct tests of the framework proposed by Blau et al. for conceptualizing the process of occupational entry must be made. What indirect evidence is available from studies of job applicants and employers tends to support the hypothesized immediate determinants of induction into the world of work, which they have delineated, but little is known about the conditions which affect them and the nature of the interactions between them.

LONGITUDINAL STUDIES OF VOCATIONAL DEVELOPMENT

Most of the research which we have discussed thus far has been cross-sectional in design, including the study by Ginzberg et al. (1951). Since it appeared, however, and particularly since 1960, several longitudinal investigations of vocational development have been initiated, and preliminary results from them are now available. They are discussed here, with reference to their (1) design, (2) major findings, and (3) conclusions. Critical comments on data collection and methodology are made where appropriate. The projects which are reviewed are the following: (1) Super's Career Pattern Study, (2) Gribbons and Lohnes's study of Readiness for Vocational Planning, (3) the writer's Vocational Development Project, (4) Holland's studies of his theory of vocational choice, and (5) Project Talent. In addition, four other studies of lesser scope and duration are also summarized.

Super's Career Pattern Study (CPS)

A general description of the *design* of this 20-year study of approximately 140 boys, from the time they were in ninth grade to their establishment in the world of work at about age 35, was given in Chapter 1, and the first report of empirical results was discussed earlier in this chapter in the section entitled "The Dimensions of the Vocational Choice Process." A further word on the data-collection and statistical procedures of CPS is necessary, however, for an understanding of the results which are being obtained. Essentially two kinds of data were gathered when the sample was in the ninth grade: (1) traditional psychometric data from standardized tests, such as the Bennett Mechanical Comprehension Test, the Kuder Preference Record (Vocational), and the Guilford-Zimmerman Temperament Survey; and (2) interview data from four interviews with the Subjects and one interview with their parents. When CPS was originally conceived, back in 1950–1951, its central concepts and focus still stemmed largely from trait-and-factor theory, although new ideas were being rapidly developed, and it was not long afterward that the CPS staff started to construct the indices of vocational maturity for the ninth-grade level. Since most of the psychometric data were not appropriate for this purpose, however, heavy reliance was placed upon the interviews as a source of relevant data on vocational maturity. Likewise, when later theory building accorded a principal role to the self-concept in the work of CPS (Super, Matlin, Starishevsky, & Jordaan, 1963), interview data from the twelfth grade and 25-year-old follow-ups, as well as the ninth grade, were again turned to, this time for the measurement of the dimensions and metadimensions of the self-concept. Other instruments have been used to quantify the self-concept, viz., a modified version of Kelly's, G. A. (1955) Role Construct Repertory Test, and to obtain follow-up data on vocational adjustment, but most of the CPS research on the self and vocational maturity has been based upon judges' assessments of these variables from interview protocols.

The *major findings* of CPS since Super and Overstreet's (1960) monograph have not been published, but they were reported upon in a series of symposia at the 1966 convention of the American Personnel and Guidance Association.[10] The results can be classified into three general categories:

First, three studies of role models and self-concepts, and some of their correlates, have been conducted, in which only a few scattered significant relationships were found, but these appeared to be theoretically meaningful ones. Among them, the ones which stand out are: the "test-retest" correlations of certain metadimensions (Clarity, .26; Scope, .37; and Overall Regnancy, .46) between the ninth and twelfth grades; the correlations of these same metadimensions, plus a few others, with several criteria of vocational adjustment between the twelfth grade and age 25; and the correlations of the Modified Role Construct Repertory Test with some selected behavior-relevant variables, which indicate that it relates primarily to personal-adjustment status.

Second, three studies of vocational maturity and its correlates have yielded somewhat disappointing results. What significant correlations there were between vocational maturity and other variables in the ninth and twelfth grades were mostly in the .20s and .30s, but there was sufficient evidence to conclude that "Occupational Information—Training and Educational Requirements" is a dimension of vocational development which spans the period of the high school years. In general, however, a Subject's standing on the twelfth-grade measures of vocational maturity could not be predicted from his ninth-grade scores.

Finally, the most promising findings have been obtained from the 25-year-old follow-up, for which complete data were secured on a remarkably high 94 percent of the original sample. Not only have Super and his associates been able to define and measure various aspects of vocational adjustment at this point in the adult career which have not been studied previously, but they have found that 12 out of 25 variables at the ninth- and twelfth-grade levels correlate significantly with them. Most of these relationships are with socioeconomic level, intelligence, and academic achievement while in high school, however, rather than with adolescent vocational maturity.

Conclusions. It is still too early in the work of CPS to draw any definitive inferences from the findings which have thus far accumulated. Considerable progress has been made in conceptualizing and refining the definition of the self-concept, and a theoretically relevant methodology for measuring it has been formulated, but there have been some problems with data collection. The best measure of the self-concept, and the one which most closely fits the model for translating "psychtalk" into "occtalk" (see Chapter 3), is the Modi-

[10] These papers are available in mimeograph form from CPS, Teachers College, Columbia University, and will be published as monographs in the near future.

fied Role Construct Repertory Test, but it is too late now to use it in the CPS longitudinal studies. Consequently, interview data have been relied upon for devising measures of the self-concept, but whether they are "rich" enough remains to be seen, since the interviews (at least in the ninth and twelfth grades) were not specifically designed to elicit responses which might be analyzed according to the metadimensions of the self. Similarly, the research on vocational maturity has been circumscribed by the limitations of the interview data which have been pressed into service to measure this construct. What errors may enter into CPS's conclusions about vocational development as a result, however, will probably be less ones of commission than of omission, since the concept of vocational maturity and the procedures to assess it were not devised until after the ninth-grade interviews were conducted. In contrast, the data collection for the 25-year-old follow-up appears to have been carefully planned out beforehand, and, with the high percentage of Subjects participating in it, should yield sound results on many aspects of vocational development during the adult work years.

Gribbons and Lohnes's Study of Readiness for Vocational Planning (RVP)

Stimulated by CPS's research on vocational maturity, Gribbons and Lohnes launched a similar project in 1958, but of shorter duration and more restricted scope. The basic *design* of this study was to conduct interview-derived analyses of "readiness for vocational planning" over a period of 10 years, from the time the sample (total $N = 110$: 56 boys, 54 girls) was in the eighth grade until most of it was established in the world of work at approximately age 23. Thus far, data have been gathered in the eighth, tenth, and twelfth grades. The primary source of data for the study has been a 40-minute, semistructured interview, during which a Subject is asked 41 questions about his educational and vocational development, e.g., "What curricula are there that you can take?" and "What occupations have you thought about as your possible life work?" The interview responses are then scored according to eight presumed dimensions of RVP: (1) Factors in Curriculum Choice; (2) Factors in Occupational Choice; (2) Verbalized Strengths and Weaknesses; (4) Accuracy of Self-appraisal; (5) Evidence for Self-rating; (6) Interests; (7) Values, and (8) Independence of Choice. In addition, data on intelligence and socioeconomic level have been obtained, and the stratification of the sample on sex has allowed analyses of this factor. The so-called "criterion" variables of the study have been curricular choice, educational and occupational goals, and certain aspects of family background and status. Analyses of the data have been accomplished almost solely with multivariate statistical techniques, including canonical correlation, discriminant function analysis, principal components factor analysis, and analysis of variance.

The *major findings* of this project can be summarized with reference to the problems which have been investigated:

1. *The interrelationships of the RVP scales.* Analyses of the correlations among the RVP dimensions at both the eighth- and tenth-grade levels have shown that they are largely independent of each other, the highest r being .49 for Factors in Curriculum Choice versus Factors in Occupational Choice (eighth grade), with most of the coefficients in the .20s and .30s (Gribbons & Lohnes, 1964a).

2. *Relationships between eighth- and tenth-grade RVP scales.* The intercorrelations of the RVP dimensions between grades were lower than they were within grades, all of the r's being significant at only the .05 level and all but 4 out of 22 being in the .20s (Gribbons & Lohnes, 1964a). The total possible number of correlations was 64. Thus, approximately one-third were significant.

3. *Differences between RVP scale means at the eighth and tenth grades.* There were significant gains on all the RVP dimensions between the two grades, although most of the differences in the means were very small relative to the standard deviations of the score distributions. The greatest changes were on two dimensions—Factors in Curriculum Choice and Factors in Occupational Choice (Gribbons, 1964).

4. *Relationships of RVP scales to other variables.* No significant sex differences on the RVP dimensions at either the eighth- or tenth-grade levels were found. There was a significant multiple R of .57 between the scales and Otis intelligence in the eighth grade, however, but not in the tenth grade. A low positive correlation ($R = .24$) was obtained between RVP and socioeconomic status, indicating that these two variables are only slightly related, and high correlations ($R = .50$ in both grades) were found between RVP and level of vocational choice (Gribbons & Lohnes, 1964a).

5. *Predictive significance of the RVP scales.* The RVP scales discriminated the curricular groups of college preparatory, business, and industrial arts–general equally well in the eighth and tenth grades, but the discriminations were not clear-cut. The college-bound students could be efficiently classified from their RVP scores, primarily on the dimension of Evidence for Self-rating, but not the others, evidently because in the interviews Business and Industrial Arts–General students describe themselves in much the same ways as do College Preparatory students (Gribbons & Lohnes, 1964b). Using twelfth-grade data for criteria, it was found again that the usefulness of the eighth- and tenth-grade RVP scales was about the same. In general, these variables were significantly related to several indices of level of occupational choice, but to only a few aspects of educational aspirations and family status.

Conclusions. In contrast to the CPS research on the dimensions of vocational maturity (Super & Overstreet, 1960), Gribbons and Lohnes's RVP measures do not load on a general factor of vocational development at either the eighth or the tenth grade. Like CPS, however, they found only low-order relationships between vocational behavior and time (grade level), which suggests that neither project may be measuring variables which change systematically as the individual grows older and progresses educationally. Gribbons and Lohnes's findings on the low relationships between the eighth- and tenth-grade RVPs, and the lack of any additional efficacy of the latter in predicting twelfth-grade status on relevant criterion variables, gives pause to speculate concerning what is going on in the data or analyses, particularly since the RVP means increase between the eighth and tenth grades. How is it possible for the eighth- and tenth-grade RVPs to predict twelfth-grade criteria equally well when there is little or no relationship between the eighth- and tenth-grade RVPs? Gribbons and Lohnes do not address themselves to this problem, which would appear to be a critical one for the interpretation of their findings. What may be happening is that the shifts in the rank orderings of Subjects from the eighth to the tenth grades are such that they almost perfectly counterbalance each other and thus yield comparable predictions for the twelfth grade. If this explanation is correct, however, the implication is that, although their status on the twelfth-grade criteria remains the same, some students may actually become *less* vocationally mature, relative to their classmates, between the eighth and tenth grades.

Crites's Vocational Development Project (VDP)

This project was originally conceived, while the writer was associated with CPS, to contruct a standardized measure of vocational development, which, unlike interview-derived indices, would be objective, easily administered to large numbers of Subjects, and related to time (age and/or grade). The *design* for VDP was derived from a "model for the measurement of vocational maturity" (Crites, 1961b), in which a combined *rational-empirical* approach to test construction was formulated. In brief, this model stipulates that a useful measure of vocational development (or any variable, for that matter) must be theoretically relevant, in that the constructs it assesses can be dealt with as part of the linguistic and logical systems used to deduce hypotheses, and that it must enter into statistically significant relationships with other variables. Among the latter, a necessary relationship for any measure of development, whether vocational, intellectual, personal, or social, is with some index of time, usually chronological age or grade. In VDP, it was further specified that this relationship must be monotonic: it should not significantly reverse itself, although it need not be strictly linear. Accordingly, the Vocational Development Inventory (VDI), which consists of an Attitude Scale and Competence Test, was constructed so that the variables in it represent central concepts in vocational development theory, and its scores, at least in the first instance, relate monotonically to time (Crites, 1964). For example, the concepts used to write items for the Attitude Scale, which assesses dispositional response tendencies in the individual's vocational development, were these: (1) involvement in the choice process, (2) orientation toward work, (3) independence in decision making, (4) preference for vocational choice factors, and (5) conceptions of the choice process. In contrast, the variables measured by the Competence Test, which focuses more upon comprehension and problem-solving abilities, are: (1) problems in vocational choice, (2) planning, (3) occupational information, (4) knowledge of vocational self, and (5) goal selection.

The *major findings* of VDP pertain only to the Attitude Scale, since work has just begun on the Competence Test. To standardize the Attitude Scale, 100 items were selected from a pool of approximately 1,000, which had been gathered from statements made by clients in vocational counseling and studies of vocational choice, and were initially administered in two experimental forms to approximately 5,000 elementary and high school students in grades 5 through 12. Both males and females were included in the sample, in about equal proportions, to determine sex differences, but, by and large, there were none in their responses to the Attitude Scale. The purpose of this initial standardization was to select items for a final scale which were monotonically related to age and/or grade. One-way analyses of variance between groupings on these two variables, and subsequent *t* tests between adjacent means, indicated that grade yielded better differentiation and more items than age. Consequently, a new form of the Attitude Scale was constituted, which contained 50 grade-related items, the scoring key being derived from the majority responses of the twelfth-grade sample.

Supplementary analyses of these items uncovered several unexpected results which not only have implications for vocational development theory, but also have opened up new lines of inquiry. One finding was that there was a pronounced tendency for younger Subjects to answer "True" to most of the items in the Attitude Scale, whereas older Subjects were more discriminating, making both "True" and "False" responses. Another finding was that there are "stages" in item trends between the fifth and twelfth grades which closely correspond to the transitional points in the educational structure, i.e., between elementary and junior high school and between junior and senior high school. There were some other unanticipated findings, such as a phenomenon which has been tentatively called "regression in vocational development at a choice point," but the principal outcome of this first study of VDP was the standardization of an Attitude Scale comprised of theoretically relevant items with a "built-in" relationship to grade as an index of time (Crites, 1965).

Conclusions. It was tentatively concluded from these findings that the dispositional response tendencies measured by the Attitude Scale *probably* change systematically as the adolescent matures vocationally, but it should be pointed out that, although VDP is a longitudinal study, these initial data were wholly cross-sectional. The time span for VDP is eight years, and when the last follow-up has been completed, the standardization of the Attitude Scale, as well as other analyses, will be replicated on longitudinal data. In the interim, the Competence Test will be completed and tried out, and further studies of the Attitude Scale will be made. A program of research with these instruments has been outlined and summarized in Table 5-7. It distinguishes among four kinds of interrelated research activities: survey, technique, theoretical, and applied (see Chapter 13 for definitions and discussions of these). Each aspect of this research program is conceived of as contributing to the others. Thus, survey research suggests variables to be measured in technique research and hypotheses to be tested in theoretical research. Technique research provides the instrumentation that is essential for the conduct of both theoretical and applied research. And, theoretical research, which will be conducted primarily in the laboratory, isolates stimulus variables and treatment conditions which can be studied in applied research. The overall plan of VDP, then, is to integrate field and experimental research in order to investigate both theoretical and practical problems. Whether this can be done successfully or not remains to be seen.

Holland's Studies of His Theory of Vocational Choice

The *design* for Holland's tests of his theory of vocational choice (see Chapter 3) has stemmed almost directly from the theory itself. It will be recalled that it involves a "matching" of personality types with environmental models. Holland has given operational definitions to each of these classes of variables and has studied them, both longitudinally and cross-sectionally, by differentiating the personality types on various aspects of the environment, as well as on a host of other demographic and questionnaire factors. Thus, the design for Holland's studies is primarily of the group-difference type, with chi square, *t* tests, and analysis of variance being the major statistical techniques, although he occasionally supplements these with correlation when investigating tangential problems. The Subjects for the studies which will be reviewed here were all National Merit finalists, which means that they were a highly select group of college-age men and women as far as their general aptitude was concerned.

Table 5-7. Summary of Problems and Hypotheses of the Vocational Development Project

Problems	*Hypotheses*
SURVEY RESEARCH To determine the dimensions and parameters of vocational development phenomena: What vocational behaviors develop as the individual matures? Which is the more significant variable in the development of vocational behaviors—age or grade?	There are several vocational behaviors, e.g., consistency, indecision, and realism in vocational choice, which might be monotonically related to time (age or grade) and hence might be considered to be dimensions of vocational development. Other vocational behaviors which may also develop are: certainty, range, and specificity of vocational choice, and satisfaction with vocational choice.
Are there group differences in the development of vocational behavior, or are group trends similar?	Vocational development phenomena are general in nature, i.e., they are not specific to any particular group, such as males or females.
TECHNIQUE RESEARCH To construct a standardized measure of vocational maturity in late childhood, adolescence, and early adulthood: Further development and study of the Attitude Scale of the Vocational Development Inventory. Construction and standardization of the Competence Test of the Vocational Development Inventory. Interrelationships of the Attitude and Competence Tests, and other vocational behaviors.	The general hypothesis which underlies the construction of the subtests of the Vocational Development Inventory is that this instrument will measure vocational behaviors which mature as the individual grows older or progresses in school. Other hypotheses which will also be tested pertain to the psychometric characteristics of the VDI. Studies will be made of its factorial structure, item content and format, internal consistency, stability, susceptibility to test-taking sets, and validity. Finally, it will be related to the other hypothesized dimensions of vocational development to determine whether vocational maturity is a construct comprised of several related variables or not.
THEORETICAL RESEARCH To test hypotheses about the nature and course of vocational development which have been deduced from theories or inferred from empirical findings: Evaluation of the assumption made by Ginzberg et al. (1951) and Super (1953) that the process of vocational development is a continuous one.	The most reasonable hypothesis about the continuity of vocational development, in light of Gesell's findings, may be that the overall trend in the maturation of vocational behaviors is continuous, but that there may be significant reversals at certain points in time when external factors, such as the transition from elementary to junior high school, may momentarily produce a regression to earlier behaviors.
Analysis and classification of the stages in vocational development which Ginzberg et al. (1951) and others have delineated.	The general hypothesis is that there are stages in vocational development which have clearly defined beginnings and endings and which are char-

Problems	*Hypotheses*
Investigation of the relationship between earlier and later vocational development (Super et al., 1957).	acterized by the preeminence of certain behaviors. And, there is the further hypothesis that "success with the tasks of one stage (such as occupational choice) is related to success with tasks in later stages (such as job adjustment)."
Correlation of vocational development with emotional, intellectual, physical, and social development (Super, 1955). Relationship of various psychosocial variables, such as family attitudes, personality adjustment, and socioeconomic status to vocational maturity (Super et al., 1957).	One hypothesis about the correlates of vocational development stems from the proposition that "vocational development is a special aspect of general development." The prediction which follows from this generalization is that vocational development should be related to emotional, intellectual, physical, and social development. Another hypothesis specifies that vocational development should also be related to certain nondevelopmental status variables, particularly such antecedent conditions as family interpersonal atmosphere (Roe, 1957).
APPLIED RESEARCH To identify the best methods and procedures for facilitating vocational development in adolescence: What is the utility of the Attitude Scale in "check-pointing" the vocational development of elementary, secondary, and college students who are progressing normally in the maturation of their vocational behavior? How useful is the Attitude Scale in screening elementary, secondary, and college students with delayed or impaired vocational development for guidance and counseling services?	The hypothesis to be tested in research on "check-pointing" and screening the vocational development of students is the practical one of whether an instrument like the Attitude Scale can improve upon the identification of students wich vocational problems over the base rates for these problems. In other words, the expectation is that the test has a higher hit-miss ratio in classifying students as vocationally mature and immature, at a given point in time, than does classifying them all as one or the other according to the base rates, assuming that the latter do not involve markedly divergent proportions in the mature and immature categories.
Which are the best guidance and counseling procedures to follow in order to enhance the vocational development of students at all educational levels, in both a preventative and curative sense? How effective are occupational orientation courses in facilitating the vocational development of students throughout the educational system?	The major hypothesis to be tested is that vocational guidance and counseling are effective in facilitating the vocational development of students. A corollary hypothesis is that certain methods and techniques of guidance and counseling are more effective than others. Also, there is the hypothesis that occupational courses, either separately or in combination with guidance and counseling, contribute to optimal vocational development.

Holland has since used Subjects from the American College Test program, which has provided him with more representative samples on aptitude as well as other variables.

There are two series of studies which Holland has conducted on his theory, one based upon longitudinal data and the other upon cross-sectional data.[11] There are three studies in the longitudinal series: (1) 1- and 2-year follow-ups of choice and related variables (Holland, 1962), (2) a 4-year prediction of stability in choice (Holland, 1963a), and (3) a 1-year analysis of change in major field of study (Holland & Nichols, 1964b). In the cross-sectional series, there are four studies, identified by the variables which were related to the personality types: 1) vocational images (Holland, 1963b), (2) self-descriptions (Holland, 1963c), (3) coping behaviors and competencies (Holland, 1963d), and (4) vocational daydreams (Holland, 1963e). One study cuts across the two series, being longitudinal in design, but dealing primarily with the cross-sectional variables. Since Holland (1964a) includes it with the cross-sectional studies, it will be discussed as part of that series.

It would be virtually impossible to review here even the *major findings* of Holland's series of studies, because they are so extensive and cover such a wide range of variables, but some summary statements based upon his results can be made. First, data from both the longitudinal and cross-sectional studies indicate that the personality types (Realistic, Intellectual, Social, Conventional, Enterprising, and Artistic) can be systematically differentiated with respect to a variety of attributes, some of which are: identification with famous people, self-ratings of traits and skills, inventoried personality characteristics, extracurricular activities and hobbies, family background, achievement, educational aspirations, and vocational choice. Second, findings on Holland's hypothesis (see Chapter 3) that *level* of vocational choice is a function of intelligence plus self-evaluations were more equivocal, since not only were the choice levels of the high-aptitude National Merit scholars restricted to the upper extreme of the occupational hierarchy, but, for the purposes of the analyses, college major field had to be substituted as an intermediate "measure" of vocational choice.[12] Third, convincing evidence has been accumulated that congruency and consistency in personality type–environmental model interactions are related to both stability in choice of college major field and vocational goal. Finally, Holland has established that there is considerable "operational identification" (Underwood, 1957, p. 205) in his definitions of

[11] Holland's cross-sectional studies are such an integral part of his overall research program that they are discussed here with his longitudinal investigations.

[12] See Chap. 6 for summaries of studies by Schutz and Blocher (1961) and Stockin (1964) on this same hypothesis and by Osipow, Ashby, and Wall (1966) on the relationship between personality types and choice.

personality types. Whether he used his Vocational Preference Inventory (VPI) or selected scales from the Strong Vocational Interest Blank (SVIB), he obtained essentially the same results.

Conclusions. The weight of the evidence which Holland has gathered in support of his theory of vocational choice is indeed impressive. There is little doubt that systematic (statistically significant) relationships exist between the personality types and choice phenomena, whether these are educational or vocational, and between the stability of these behaviors over time and personality-environmental agreement. Some limitations in Holland's studies, however, most of which he has noted, should be mentioned. First, the question of whether or not his findings, which have come almost exclusively from high-aptitude Subjects, can be generalized to other populations remains to be determined. He is currently engaged in doing this with data from the ACT program. Second, although most of the differences among the personality types were as expected, i.e., they made "psychological" sense, there were some which were contradictory. They did not "fit" the stereotyped orientations, and consequently some explanation for them must be formulated. Holland has not dealt theoretically with this problem as yet. Finally, many of the differences among personality types, despite the fact that they were statistically significant, were small. Holland (1962, p. 43) cautions: "The reader is reminded that many of these attributes belong to several types or differ only slightly from type to type." Thus, as with any typology, care must be taken not to think of Holland's personality types and environmental models as mutually exclusive and independent classes.

Project Talent

One of the most extensive studies ever to be conducted in vocational psychology, Project Talent was begun in 1960 under the direction of John C. Flanagan at the American Institutes for Research. Its *design* called for the drawing of a 5-percent probability sample of American high schools or approximately 400,000 students (male and female) in grades 9 through 12. These Subjects were tested with an extensive battery of instruments (Flanagan et al., 1962), which took two days to administer and which included measures of general ability, special aptitudes, interests and temperament, biographical information, home background, and future plans. A number of follow-ups have been scheduled and will be conducted at intervals of 1 year, 5 years, 10 years, and 20 years from the graduation dates of the original high school classes. The first follow-ups have now been completed, and the results have been reported by Flanagan and Cooley (1966). The data analyses in these studies have been derived from an updated trait-and-factor model, the essence of which is the discrimination of criterion groups on test variables by means of various methods of multivariate analysis. The groups which were constituted from the data gathered in the follow-ups included: (1) post–high school educational placements (4-year college, junior college, technical or vocational school, no further schooling); (2) 4-year colleges (each specific college constituting a group); (3) post–high school work (job categories); and (4) career plans. Using analysis of variance, multiple discriminant function analysis, Mahalanobis D^2 analysis, and classification probabilities analysis, the Project Talent investigators have compared these criterion groups on a variety of variables scored from the 1960 test battery.

Only the *major findings* on post–high school work and career plans will be summarized here. With respect to the former, noncollege high school graduates from all classes (i.e., grades 9 through 12) were employed most often in the following kinds of jobs: clerical and sales, protective, skilled, service, and unskilled. High school dropouts were in essentially the same types of work, but a larger percentage of them were unskilled laborers. When a comparison was made between Subjects in occupations who planned to remain in them as careers and a total group which also included Subjects who did not intend to stay in their present jobs, it was found that the differentiation between occupations was sharper for those who were career-oriented. Flanagan and Cooley (1966, p. 101) state that: "Since occupational-group differentiation is improved when future career plans are considered, it clearly indicates that those planning to leave tend not to resemble the typical members of that group." In other words, birds with *different* feathers *don't* flock together, to put it in traditional Matching Men and Jobs phraseology.

As far as career plans were concerned, 27 and 23 percent of the non-college-bound males from the ninth and twelfth grades, respectively, had vocational choices at the business and skilled levels, whereas the percentages were 76 and 79 for those going to college from the same classes. Analyses of the stability of career plans from the time of the 1960 initial testing to the follow-up revealed that there was considerable change in vocational choice through the high school years. The percentages of overall stability for the various grades were as follows: ninth, 16.8 percent; tenth, 18.9 percent; eleventh, 25.0 percent; and twelfth, 31.4 percent. As is apparent from the trend in these figures, choice stability increases as occupational entry is approached, but even in the twelfth grade it is quite low. The explanation most likely lies in the fact that *specific* occupational titles were asked for, rather than broad occupational fields, which fact would definitely affect stability percentages (see Chapter 4).[13]

[13] Flanagan and Cooley 1966, p. 182) also point out that: "Obviously, the extent to which plans are considered stable depends upon how one classified plans in the first place. For example, plans will appear to be more stable if broader categories are used." Cf. Remstad and Rothney (1958).

From an analysis of the efficacy of the Project Talent battery in predicting changes in career plans, it was found that the measures of motives (interests and temperament) were slightly better predictors than tests of abilities, but that, "Neither ability nor motive measures were better predictors than simply asking the ninth grade boy what he wanted to become" (Flanagan & Cooley, 1966, p. 204).

Conclusions. Flanagan and Cooley draw two general conclusions from the Project Talent follow-up studies: (1) that career plans made in high school are unstable and *therefore* unrealistic, and (2) that, since they are unstable, measures of more stable characteristics, viz., the 1960 test battery, should be used to predict career plans. The first conclusion appears to the writer to be a *non sequitur.* It does not necessarily follow that, *if* career plans are unstable in adolescence, *then* they are unrealistic. In fact, given the increased stability of choice from the ninth to the twelfth grade, exactly the opposite conclusion would seem to be more reasonable. As the adolescent grows older and presumably matures vocationally, he changes his earlier, less realistic choices to ones which better jibe with reality, much as the research reviewed in the first part of this chapter indicates. With regard to the second conclusion, it is not supported by the finding that ninth-grade plans predicted follow-up plans as well as the standardized tests of abilities and motives in the Project Talent battery. Despite whatever instability there may be in early choices, evidently their common variance with later choices is great enough that it counterbalances the higher reliability, but lower predictive validity, of the standardized tests. The question arises, then, whether it would not be considerably more economical, in terms of testing time, simply to elicit a vocational choice in early adolescence, rather than to administer an extensive battery of tests, if the only purpose is to predict later choice. Obviously, Project Talent has other purposes than this one, but the implication for studies of lesser scope is clear.

Other Studies

Cooley (1963a; 1963b; 1964b) has reported a study of potential scientists, in which he used much the same theoretical approach as that used by Project Talent. Upon the basis of multivariate analyses of his Subjects' educational decisions and career plans, he classified them into the following four groups: (1) Potential Scientist Pool (PSP); (2) College-Nonscience (CNS); (3) Noncollege-Technical (NCT); and (4) Noncollege-Nontechnical (NCNT). A major difference between this study and Project Talent, however, was the use of the 5-year overlapping longitudinal sampling design shown in Table 5-8. The advantage of this method of sampling is that within the span of 5 calendar years 16 years of vocational development can be encompassed. Thus, Cooley was able to gather data on the careers of both science- and nonscience-oriented

Table 5-8. Overlapping Sampling Design for the Longitudinal Study of Scientific Careers *(From Cooley, 1964b, p. 91)*

Sample group	*Number of students*	*Elementary*	*Junior high school*	*High school*	*College*	*Graduate school*
Grade 5	143	5 6	7 8 9			
Grade 8	167		8 9	10 11 12		
Grade 11	192			11 12	13 14 15	
Grade 14	105				14 15 16	17 18
Grade 16	93				16	17 18 19 20
Total	700					

students from the fifth grade through the end of graduate school (award of the doctorate).

Using a large battery of tests and ratings, as well as interviews, his major findings were that: (1) ability measures are primarily related to the choice of science as a career during the period of transition from high school to college, but not prior to junior high school nor after college; (2) as in Project Talent, asking an adolescent whether he wants to be a scientist or not is just as predictive of later vocational development as are inventories of interests, although there is some evidence that patterns of the latter have significant long-term validity; and (3) measures of personality, whether they are objective (Guilford-Zimmerman Temperament Survey) or projective (Rorschach), contribute negligibly, if at all, to the discrimination of prospective scientists and nonscientists.[14] It should be remembered, however, that, in both Cooley's research and Project Talent, early choice was an even better predictor of later choice than were measured interests.

In Chapter 4, a study by Schmidt and Rothney (1955) on the consistency of interview-elicited vocational choices in grades 10 through 12 was discussed, in which they found about 50 percent stability. To determine whether the nature of these interviews, which were conducted as part of a guidance program, had an effect upon choice consistency, Kohout and Rothney (1964) compared the choices, occupations, and future plans of an intensively counseled group of

[14] Relevant to these findings is a comparative analysis conducted by Mierzwa (1963, p. 31) on the relative usefulness of these "systems of data," i.e., ability, interest, personality, and also environmental, in which he found that:

> The ability, environmental, and temperament systems did not differ significantly in their capacity to classify subjects. The interest system contained information that produced 22 more hits than the temperament system, and this difference exceeds the 0.01 level. This further confirms the earlier conclusion that the interest system has substantial relevance for the choice of a science or non-science career by adolescent boys.

students with those of a nonintensively counseled group. Their general finding was that there were no significant differences between the two groups in the percentages of each which had the same choice over long periods of time. In contrast to the earlier study, however, Kohout and Rothney found much lower stability percentages, possibly because they used a different stimulus question to evoke vocational choice. One last study which should be mentioned in this context, although it was not longitudinal, has been reported by Mathewson and Orton (1963) on the relationship of vocational imagery to vocational maturity. They developed a semiprojective, self-appraisal instrument called What I Think about Myself, in which they asked a Subject to write about (1) an imagined career or occupation, (2) any recent idea he had about a career or work interest, (3) the image which stands out from all others, and (4) the ideas and feelings he most often has about himself. Scores based upon these productions were combined into a vocational maturity score, which was related to several other variables, including age, GPA, Otis IQ, achievement tests, and extracurricular activities. The only correlation which was significant ($r = .46$), however, was between vocational maturity and number of extracurricular activities.

6

THE CORRELATES OF VOCATIONAL CHOICE

In this chapter, we turn our attention to the correlates of vocational choice, to the variables which are systematically related to an individual's selection of an occupation. Once these variables are identified we shall then have some empirical basis for understanding and explaining individual differences in vocational choice and in patterns of vocational development. Probably the most convenient and meaningful conceptual framework for organizing and discussing the research which has been done on the correlates of vocational choice is the S-O-R paradigm used so extensively in psychology for the analysis of relationships among variables (Underwood, 1957). In this schema, S, O, and R stand for stimulus, organismic, and response variables, respectively. Since our primary interest is in the correlates of vocational choice, which is itself a response variable, the empirical evidence which we shall review is mostly on S-R, O-R, and R-R relationships (Brown, J. S., 1961; Spence, 1944). We shall also be concerned, however, with research on the so-called "hypothetical constructs" and "intervening variables" which are sometimes postulated to conceptualize the correlates of vocational choice. Thus, this chapter is divided into four parts, one for each of the variables in the S-O-R framework and one for theoretical variables.

STIMULUS VARIABLES

In Chapter 4, a stimulus was defined as a physical incident or event which is related to a response, and in Chapter 3 several stimuli were discussed which are supposedly associated with vocational choices. These stimuli were (1) the *culture* in which an individual lives, (2) the *subculture* of which he is a member, (3) the *community* where he resides, and (4) the *immediate environment* which impinges upon him, each of which influences vocational decision making in a different way—at least according to most sociological, and some psychological, theories of choice. Which of these stimuli, in fact, influences the individual's choice of an occupation, and what the contribution of each is, will be our main interest in this section as we review the research which has accumulated on the stimulus variables which are related to differential vocational choices.

Culture

Studies of the impact of the individual's culture upon his vocational choice are scarce, but those which are available show that culture subtly affects the selection of an occupation independently of other stimulus variables, such as social class, school, and family. A culture consists of all the folkways, habit patterns, and various *modus operandi* which a human society develops to cope with the environment and to interact with others. White (1952, p. 15) writes that:

> [A culture includes] routine matters such as eating with the fingers or with chopsticks or with knife and fork. It includes belief about the nature of the world and the means of propitiating hostile forces: ceremonial dances, or employment of medicine men, or support of scientific research. It includes ideal patterns of conduct, such as gentle cooperativeness or warlike assertiveness or individual enterprise and self-reliance. In this sense no societies, however simple, are without a culture, and no individuals are uncultured. The concept of culture refers to the total way of life of a society, the heritage of accumulated social learnings that is shared and transmitted by the members of that society.

In the discussion which follows, the influences of two very distinct and contrasting cultures upon vocational choice are examined: the culture of the Mescalero Apache Indian and the culture of the twentieth-century American.

The Apache Culture. Ross, W. F., and Ross (1957) have reported an unusual study which they conducted on the vocational behavior of a tribe of Mescalero Apache Indians. Their report dramatically reveals the indirect, but nonetheless real, influences of a culture upon the vocational choices of its members. At the time of the study, the tribe numbered approximately 1,200 persons who lived on a reservation in the high country of the White Mountains of south central New Mexico. The reservation was relatively small, consisting of only 719 square miles, but it included an area which offered the basis for a fairly diversified economy. There were 4,000 acres of tillable land, about 200,000 acres of open grazing land, and nearly 250,000 acres of forest land. Most of the economy of the Mescalero (approximately one-half) is devoted to the raising of livestock; the remainder is divided among farming (about one-fourth), the operation of a sawmill, and a tourist enterprise. Some of the income of the tribe comes from wages earned in the nearby towns of Ruidoso, Tularosa, and Alamogardo, but most of it comes from work on the reservation, either for the tribe or for the local government agency. Some members of the tribe have sought their fortunes elsewhere and have been quite successful, but most of the Mescalero have remained on the reservation or returned to it after completing their education at an American technical school or university.

A number of objective and projective tests, which included measures of aptitude, interest, and personality, were administered to a large sample of the Mescalero, and fairly extensive psychometric data were secured on 143 individuals. This group averaged 29 years in age, with a range from 11 to 59 years, and had a mean educational level of 8.9 grades. On a measure of general intelligence (SRA Nonverbal Form), they had an average IQ of 98.12, with a range from 66 to 138. Their special aptitudes, as assessed by the Flanagan Aptitude Classification Tests (FACT), were most highly developed in tasks which required attention to detail (Scales), new learning (Coding), and immediate recall (Memory). Their lowest aptitudes were on the spatial visualization (Assembly), perception of forms (Components), and numerical operations (Arithmetic) problems. Combinations of their special aptitudes into the patterns necessary for different occupations revealed that they had most aptitude for clerical and secretarial work and least for artistic jobs. On the Kuder Preference Record (Vocational) their pronounced clerical aptitude was supplemented by high clerical interest scores. They also had high artistic interest, however, which did not correspond with their artistic aptitude. Their lowest scores on the Kuder were on the Social Service, Literary, and Scientific scales, with the Mechanical, Musical, and Persuasive scales in the middle range. The most notable aspect of their Rorschach protocols was their tendency to respond to the inkblots as wholes rather than to parts of the stimuli.

These psychological characteristics of the Mescalero, and their relationship to vocational choice, are interpreted by Ross and Ross in terms of the patterns of acculturation which are predominant in this Apache tribe. These people can verbalize their need for service and business-contact occupations in their economy, and they realize that some of them should become beauticians, barbers, waitresses, teachers, nurses, and public-relations personnel. But, nevertheless, they choose and enter quite different occupations, most of them being employed as office workers, road crewmen, cooks, woodcutters, fire fighters, machine operators, and store cashiers. One explanation for this apparent contradiction between professed goals and actual behavior is found in the cultural background and general personality development of the Mescalero. Ross, W. F., and Ross (1957, p. 274) write as follows: "Our observations of infant care, interview data, and the test data all point to the probability that the affectionally frustrated personality patterns go back to early patterns of family relationships and patterns of enculturation." In other words, it is possible that the culturally approved and accepted practices of child rearing, which tend to thwart the satisfaction of the young Mescalero's needs for affection, produce an adult personality which seeks emotional security in working with things and nature rather than in working with people, where the chances for further rejection by others are much greater. Thus, the Mescalero develops interests in the more highly structured and routinized clerical activities of the bank or business establishment and in the largely isolative duties and tasks of mechanical and manual occupations.

Ross and Ross consider the Mescaleros' pronounced artistic interests and proclivity for whole responses on the Rorschach to be consistent with the foregoing interpretation of their vocational choices. They reason as follows (Ross, W. F., & Ross, 1957, p. 274): "Our theory here is again based on the personality findings: having cut themselves off from other means of self-expression, particularly with regard to people, they need some emotional outlet, hopefully to be found in creating things with their hands." This conclusion would appear to be sound only if the form level of the whole responses given by the Mescalero to the Rorschach was of a high quality. If it was, then the usual interpretation is that the individual has considerable organizational interest and capability (Klopfer, Ainsworth, Klopfer, & Holt, 1954), much like that which has been found to be typical of successful artists (Prados, 1944; Roe, 1946c). If the form level was mediocre or vague, however, the whole responses of the Mescalero would have a quite different meaning. Indefinite form perception usually indicates a lack of perceptual discrimination, an inability to go beyond a global impression of a situation, and is often a sign of maladjustment. Ross and Ross do not report the complete results they obtained with the Rorschach, and, consequently, it is difficult to draw any firm conclusions. It can at least be said, however, that there is some evidence from their study that early cultural training is associated with later vocational preference and choice, irrespective of the exact personality dynamics which link the two together.

The American Culture. In contrast to cultures like that of the Apache and other more primitive societies, the core values of the American culture reflect a greater degree of optimism and faith in the future (Kluckhohn, 1953). In America the dominant value orientation is that of the "tradition of opportunity"—the belief that each man has the chance to be successful, to "get ahead," to "reach the top." Chinoy's (1952) study of automobile workers indicates that the "tradition of opportunity" is as strong today as it was when

Horatio Alger first wrote his "rags to riches" stories during the latter part of the nineteenth century. Despite frustrations of lofty aspirations based upon a faith in the "tradition of opportunity," he notes that his group of working-class Subjects nevertheless clings to the promise of advancement and "better things to come" which is implicit in the American credo. Contrary to some interpretations of the data on freedom in vocational choice, Chinoy concludes that the men in his sample have *not* "limited their horizons to the class horizon" (Hollingshead, 1949, p. 285) and have not abandoned the "tradition of opportunity." What they have done is to "scale down" their aspirations, in the face of undesirable realities, so that they agree more with the opportunities which are actually open to them. Thus, they have equated "getting ahead" with wage increases, rather than promotions, with "conspicuous consumption," rather than recognition for achievement, and with the success of their children, rather than themselves, in obtaining a higher level of educational and occupational status.

Chinoy's research implies that *all* members of the working class still endorse the "tradition of opportunity" and, in one way or another, believe that a person has the freedom to choose what he wants to do and to be successful at it, by dint of hard work and perseverence. An intensive study of the educational and occupational aspirations of so-called "common man" boys by Kahl (1953) suggests, however, that such a generalization is not justified. Rather, it would appear that only a particular segment of the working class endorses and follows the "getting ahead" value. Kahl found, in a comparison of two groups ($N = 12$ each) of senior high school boys from "common man" class backgrounds, one of which had higher career goals than the other, that the attitudes of their families directly influenced their aspirations. Although the boys in the two groups had comparable intelligence and all were capable of going to college, only 1 out of the 12 from families in which the value orientation was "getting by" wanted to attend college, whereas 8 out of 12 from families with a "getting ahead" orientation planned to get a higher education. Similarly, with respect to their vocational choices, the social-class value of getting by led to lower aspirations than the cultural value of getting ahead. In other words, as Kluckhohn (1953) has observed, there are both dominant and variant values within a given culture, and the variant values, which are often associated with a social class, may affect behavior every bit as strongly as the dominant values. This seems to be what is happening in the formulation of vocational choices at the lower social levels: some individuals select their occupations in terms of the dominant cultural values of getting ahead, whereas others choose their careers in terms of the variant social class emphasis upon getting by.

Taking a different approach to the same problem, Empey (1956) has investigated the effects of American cultural ideals upon vocational choice by comparing the *absolute* and *relative* aspirations of high school male seniors (*N* not reported) from different social classes. He measured absolute occupational aspirations by assigning to an individual's choice a rank from 10 (high) to 1 (low) on a revision of the Hatt (1950) and Smith (1943) prestige scales, and he assessed relative occupational aspiration by computing the differences between the ranks of the father's occupation and the son's choice on the same scales. Also, he compared the ranks of each Subject's preferred and anticipated occupations to determine the amount of congruence between them. With these measures of occupational aspiration, he then proceeded to test the following three hypotheses (Empey, 1956, pp. 704–705; italics in original):

1. The *absolute* occupational status aspirations of male high school seniors from the middle and upper classes are significantly higher than those of seniors from the lower classes.
2. The *relative* occupational status aspirations of lower class seniors indicate that they *prefer* and *anticipate* having significantly higher occupational statuses than their fathers.
3. Seniors from lower strata are more inclined than those from middle and upper strata to reduce their occupational aspirations significantly when faced with the necessity of choosing between their *preferred* and *anticipated* occupations.

Empey's findings supported hypotheses 1 and 2 but not 3. Boys from the upper social classes, as determined by their father's occupational level, had preferred *and* anticipated vocational choices which were significantly higher than those of boys from the lower social classes, as shown in Table 6-1. Also,

Table 6-1. Average Preferred and Anticipated Vocational Aspiration Levels of Seniors from Different Social Strata *(From Empey, 1956, p. 706)*

		Preferred		*Anticipated*	
	Father's status	*N*	*Level of aspiration*	*N*	*Level of aspiration*
(High)	10	6	7.83	6	7.83
	9	12	7.92	8	8.36
	8	52	7.63	42	7.26
	7	57	7.26	41	7.32
	6	174	6.61	132	6.45
	5	97	6.87	69	6.46
	4	184	6.47	129	5.99
	3	115	6.25	87	5.70
	2	56	6.07	45	5.69
(Low)	1	11	5.36	6	4.50
All strata		764	6.65	565	6.32

boys from the lower social strata aspired more often to an occupation at a higher prestige level than their father's as compared with boys from the higher social levels. However, boys from the lower classes did not adjust their aspirations downward more than upper-strata boys when asked to indicate their anticipated occupation. In fact, as the data in Table 6-2 reveal, there was a tendency for the middle social levels to make a greater adjustment to reality than either the upper or lower extremes on the class continuum. In light of these results, Empey (1956, pp. 708–709) draws the following conclusions:

> Thus, these findings do not support two important schools of thought on the occupational aspirations of lower-class youths: (1) that lower-class youth have limited their occupational aspirations to the class horizon; or (2) that lower-class youth have the same lofty occupational aspirations as those from upper strata. Instead, they show that, while the lower-class youngsters aspired to get ahead, they aspired to occupations at different status levels than those from higher strata.

Stated somewhat differently and more generally, in order to summarize the other studies as well as Empey's, we can say that the American culture definitely affects the making of vocational choices, but that the effects are not uniform either between or within social classes.

Subculture

Next to the overall culture in the experience of the individual is the more specific subculture in which he lives. This level of his environment, on a proximity-remoteness dimension, is closer to his everyday life than the more

Table 6-2. Reality Estimates of Seniors as Measured by the Distance between Their Average Preferred and Anticipated Occupational Levels *(From Empey, 1956, p. 708)*

	Father's status	*N*	*Average reality score*	*d.f.*	*Needed χ^2 value for significance at 1 per-cent level*	*Obtained χ^2 value*
(High)	10	6	−0.001	3	11.341	2.112
	9	12	+0.46			
	8	52	−0.37	4	13.277	5.048
	7	57	+0.06	5	15.086	1.082
	6	174	−0.16	6	16.812	4.516
	5	97	−0.41	5	15.086	15.035
	4	184	−0.48	7	18.475	2.300
	3	115	−0.55	6	16.812	9.128
	2	56	−0.38	5	15.086	6.383
(Low)	1	11	−0.85			
All strata		764	−0.35	9	21.666	3.3361

abstract culture, with its general credos and principles and values, but more distant than the concrete realities of the community. The subculture of the individual consists primarily of his social class, his racial background, and his place of residence. We consider now the extent to which the subculture, and its various aspects, affects an individual's vocational choice.

Social Class. White (1952, p. 18) observes that: "A child grows up not merely in the American culture but in the sub-culture of his social class: we cannot hope to understand him without taking account of these direct pressures and traditions." The concept of "social class" has been defined in many ways, all of which emphasize that a class is a state of mind—a consciousness of the differentiating characteristics of people. In one of the classic definitions of social class, Centers (1949, p. 78) writes that "a class is no more nor less than what people collectively think it is." Similarly, Warner, Meeker, and Eells (1949, p. 23) note that:

> To belong to a particular level in the social-class system of America means that a family or individual has gained acceptance as an equal by those who belong in the class. The behavior in this class and the participation of those in it must be rated by the rest of the community as being at a particular place in the social scale.

Several criteria are used by people to determine an individual's social standing, but the best single indicator of class is an individual's occupation. Warner et al. (1949) report that occupation correlates .91 with a composite of several subjective and objective ratings of social class placement and standing. Some of the studies to be reviewed here use several criteria to define social class, but most of them use only occupational level.

The most comprehensive study of social class and vocational choice which has been done is the one conducted by Hollingshead (1949) of Elmtown's youth. This investigator asked raters in the community of Elmtown to evaluate the social standing of its 535 families according to four criteria: (1) the way a family lived, (2) its income (occupation) and possessions, (3) participation in community affairs, and (4) prestige in the community. From the ratings which were obtained, it became apparent that Elmtown had five discernible and reliably identifiable social classes, each with distinctive characteristics, and that they differentially affected vocational choice, as indicated in Table 6-3. Perhaps a better understanding of this relationship can be grasped from Figure 6-1, which shows graphically the percentages of choices at different occupational levels by the several classes. It is apparent that a preponderance of upper-class youth have selected occupations at the higher levels as compared with their lower-class peers. The latter tend more often to choose voca-

***Table 6-3. Vocational Choice in Relation to Social Class** (From Hollingshead, 1949, p. 469)*

	Class			
Vocational choice	*I and II*	*III*	*IV*	*V*
Professional or businessman	27	57	72	16
Clerical worker	2	32	64	25
Craftsman	1	19	54	32
Farmer	4	16	20	6
Miscellaneous	0	13	40	57
Undecided	1	21	62	94
Total	35	158	312	230

tions at the clerical, craftsman, and service levels. Thus, on the basis of these data, we can concur with Hollingshead's (1949, p. 285) conclusion that:

> The pattern of vocational choices corresponds roughly with the job patterns associated with each class in the adult work world. Therefore, we believe that the adolescent's ideas of desirable jobs are a reflection of their experiences in the class and family culture complexes. These adolescents are not only aware of the differential prestige attached to vocations, but they also know the position of themselves and their families in the prestige system, and they understand the connection which exists between the father's occupation and the family's economic and prestige positions.

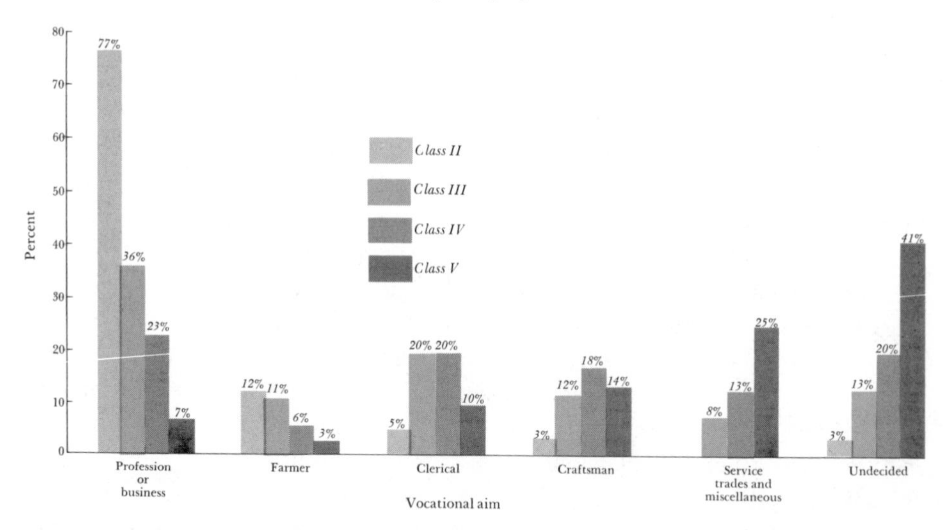

***Figure 6-1. Vocational choice in relation to social class.** (Based upon data from Hollingshead, 1949.)*

One question concerning the validity of this generalization which legitimately can be raised is whether the influence of social class upon vocational choice is independent of the relationships of class standing to other variables. It is well known, for example, that social class is related to degree of intelligence: individuals from the higher strata are generally brighter than those from the lower strata. Does it follow that class differences in choice are simply a reflection of class differences in intelligence, rather than differences in social attitudes and orientations? Sewell, Haller, and Straus (1957) posed this as a problem for investigation in a study they did of the educational and occupational aspirations of 4,167 male and female high school seniors in Wisconsin (1947–1948). They asked their Subjects whether they planned to go to college and what occupation they planned to enter. The responses to these questions were classified according to the Subjects' (1) level of intelligence, as measured by the Henmon-Nelson Test of Mental Ability and (2) level of father's occupation, as ranked on the Hatt (1950) Scale. Tables 6-4 and 6-5 present the results for males and reveal definite trends from the social class level to another *within* intelligence quintiles: the higher the class standing, the greater

Table 6-4. Percentages of High School Males at Various Intelligence Quintiles with Vocational Aspirations at Different Social Class Levels *(From Sewell et al., 1957, p. 72)*

	Parental occupational prestige status quintiles					
Intelligence quintiles	*V (Hatt: 93–72)*	*IV (Hatt: 72–67)*	*III (Hatt: 67–60)*	*II (Hatt: 60–55)*	*I (Hatt: 55–39)*	*Total percent (N)*
V (IQ: 139–119)	90	79	79	71	66	79 (384)
IV (IQ: 119–113)	71	70	53	57	61	63 (384)
III (IQ: 113–109)	58	62	51	55	43	54 (383)
II (IQ: 109–102)	66	45	32	41	24	40 (383)
I (IQ: 102–59)	34	35	23	26	32	30 (383)
Total percent (*N*)	68 (384)	59 (384)	47 (383)	48 (383)	43 (383)	53 (1917)

Table 6-5. Percentages of High School Males at Various Intelligence Quintiles with Educational Aspirations at Different Social Class Levels *(From Sewell et al., 1957, p. 72)*

	Parental occupational prestige status quintiles					
Intelligence quintiles	*V (Hatt: 93–72)*	*IV (Hatt: 72–67)*	*III (Hatt: 67–60)*	*II (Hatt: 60–55)*	*I (Hatt: 55–39)*	*Total percent (N)*
V (IQ: 139–119)	84	48	55	64	45	63 (278)
IV (IQ: 119–113)	54	51	51	37	35	45 (278)
III (IQ: 113–109)	41	42	43	29	32	37 (278)
II (IQ: 109–103)	45	36	21	27	22	29 (278)
I (IQ: 103–59)	25	19	16	18	17	18 (277)
Total percent (*N*)	57 (278)	38 (278)	36 (278)	33 (278)	27 (277)	39 (1389)

the tendency to have higher-level aspirations. As the authors of the study point out, this relationship "does not deny the importance of intelligence to educational and occupational aspirations, but suggests that status makes an independent contribution to these aspirations" (Sewell, Haller, & Strauss, 1957, p. 73).[1]

Racial Background. The color of an individual's skin defines an aspect of his subculture, not so much because of the manifest physical difference which singles him out, but because of the social reactions to it. In the Deep South, for example, where the Negro stands at the bottom of the class system and sometimes also the caste system (Davis, A., Gardner, & Gardner, 1941), he finds that he is not allowed to choose or train for certain "white" occupations, even though they may be well within the scope of his capabilities. In the North as well, he learns that some occupations are not open to him, and consequently

[1] For additional evidence on the influence of social class upon vocational choice, see Galler (1951) and Werts (1966).

he tends to exclude them from his deliberations about his vocational future. As a result, he chooses an occupation not only in terms of the factors which also affect the decisions of whites, but, in addition, he makes his selection in terms of his racial background.

Almost without exception, studies of the vocational choices of Negro youth show a consistent tendency for them to select three occupations more often than any others: (1) physician, (2) teacher, and (3) musician. Also popular are the occupations of lawyer, engineer, and farmer. Most of these occupations tend to be at the upper occupational levels and hence somewhat unrealistic for a majority of Negro children who usually come from the lower socio-economic levels. Hyte (1936) reports that 75.2 percent of his sample of 870 Negro high school boys chose occupations at the professional level, but that only 11.6 percent of their fathers were actually engaged in professional work. Likewise, Gray (1944) found that 38 percent of her sample of Negro boys and girls in Tennessee selected occupations which fell in the two upper groups on Taussig's scale, whereas only 17 percent planned to enter occupations in the lower two groups. More recently, with a sample gathered in California, Lawrence (1950) obtained comparable results: 39.1 percent of his Subjects had vocational choices at the professional and semiprofessional levels and 14.7 percent at the skilled and semiskilled levels.

Some insight into the vocational choice process for Negro young people has been provided by Brazziel (1961), who studied the reasons why 72 sophomores and 98 seniors at Virginia State College (Norfolk Division) chose teaching as a career. More than half of the total group reported that they had entered teaching as a second choice, and slightly less than half indicated that they intended to use it as a stepping-stone to another occupation. When asked their reasons for selecting a less preferred vocation, more than 90 percent of them responded: "I need a sure job when I graduate." Other frequently cited reasons were: "I did not know of specific jobs I could be sure of in other fields"; "I am married to or plan to marry a person in my community"; and, "The curriculum in my preferred field is too difficult for my background." Brazziel also investigated the time when a decision was made to pursue teaching as a vocation and the "significant others" who had the greatest influence upon this decision. Elementary school majors made their choice when they were still in grade school, and secondary school majors, during high school and the first year of college. "The most influential persons in the decision of the students to become teachers were parents and public school teachers.... The most effective combinations of influences seem to have been that of the homeroom teacher and parents for secondary majors, and elementary teachers and parents for elementary majors" (Brazziel, 1961, p. 740). Thus, cognizance of race and the limitations it imposes upon occupational opportunities by both young and old apparently leads to choices which are considered to be "second best" but realizable.

Comparisons of the vocational choices of Negro and white young people highlight the differences which are attributable, at least in part, to racial background. The available studies are somewhat inconclusive because no attempt was made in the comparisons to control other factors which are also related to choice, such as intelligence, but usually the differences between racial groups on these variables are small enough that their effect upon choice would be negligible (Anastasi, 1958; Tyler, 1965). An indirect comparison was made by Gray (1944) who compared her results with those reported by Boynton (1936). She summarized the similarities and differences as follows (Gray, 1944, p. 244):

> With white boys the four most favored occupations were: farmer with 18 per cent, and pilot, mill or plant worker, and doctor, each of the last three being mentioned by 8 per cent of the group. The first four among the Negro boys include two of these, doctor with 16 per cent and farmer with 14 per cent. Pilot is mentioned by less than 1 per cent of the Negro children and mill worker by only 12 per cent. This last difference is probably explicable in terms of specific environmental influences, since a larger number of Boynton's children came from industrial towns. Teacher, which 8 per cent of the Negro boys selected, was mentioned by only 2 per cent of the white cases.

Witty, Garfield, and Brink (1941) gathered data on both Negroes and whites for a direct comparison of their choices, which, from the findings presented in Table 6-6, are quite different. The occupations which rank the highest for Negroes are postal work, musician, physician, and lawyer, whereas for whites they are engineer, aviator, mechanic-machinist, and forester. The contrast in these choices of the two groups appears to be between the extremes of the Things versus People dimension of interests: Whites prefer occupations which are largely "thing-oriented," and Negroes select occupations which are mostly "people-oriented." Although further research is needed, we might speculate that this difference reflects their racial backgrounds and the subcultural values associated with them.

Geographic Region. It has been well established by cultural anthropologists (e.g., Kluckhohn, 1953) and ecologists (e.g., Faris, 1944) that there are systematic subcultural differences between various regions of a country, between rural and urban areas, and even between sections of the larger cities. As a result of the interaction between the heritage which people bring to an area

Table 6-6. A Comparison of the Vocational Choices of Negro and White Boys *(From Witty et al., 1941, p. 127)*

Occupations	*Percentage*	
	White (N = 334)	*Negro (N = 405)*
Engineering	25.4	10.8
Aviation	21.2	9.8
Mechanic-machinist	11.0	6.9
Forestry	7.7	.2
Office work-bookkeeping	7.1	1.4
Accounting	6.2	1.4
Agriculture	5.9	.4
Law	5.9	12.0
Printing	5.6	3.9
Architect	5.0	.7
Medicine-surgery	4.7	13.3
Journalism	4.7	.9
Salesman	4.7	.9
Draftsman	4.4	1.2
Chemist	4.4	1.4
Carpentry-woodwork-cabinet making	4.4	.2
Teaching	4.4	9.1
Photography	4.1	.2
Business	2.6	7.1
Art–commercial art	2.4	5.4
Navy–naval officer	2.0	.0
Musician	2.0	15.0
Electrician	1.7	3.4
Postal work	1.1	21.9
Civil-government service	1.1	8.3
Pharmacy	.5	5.1

and its physical and climatic features, there typically develops a subculture with customs, mores, and values which distinguish it from other subcultures in different geographical regions. The East, South, Middle West, and Far West represent distinctive subcultures, each with its own style and pattern of living, as do the rural and urban areas of the country and cities. As several studies have shown, these differences between subcultures demarcated along geographical and residential lines are often reflected in the vocational choices of adolescents.

Anderson, W. A. (1932) analyzed the vocational choices of 619 college males from the open country (places of less than 500 population and farm regions), towns (population 500 to 2,500), and cities (over 2,500 population) and found relationships between place of residence and (1) the desire to change residence from place of birth and rearing, (2) certainty of vocational choice, and (3) kind of occupation chosen. Those students who grew up in the open country and towns wanted to move to a city much more often than not, and they also expressed considerable uncertainty about their vocational choices. Only about 20 percent of the 276 boys in the sample who were from a rural area stated farming as their vocational choice; 80 percent named occupations which necessitated residence in a town or city. City boys selected engineer and manufacturer more frequently than boys from the towns and open country, who chose farmer more than any other occupation. Engineer was a close second, however, and this probably reflects the rural boy's desire to leave the country and pursue a career in an urban area. Also, it should be remembered that all these Subjects were college students who presumably had a higher level of ability than that required by most of the occupations which are found in a farm region. Consequently, the factor of ability was confounded with place of residence in this study and makes it difficult to interpret the results. It would seem, however, from the data on the number of country Subjects who chose farmer, that place of residence is related to vocational choice independently of other variables.

Two other studies of choice and geographical background tend to support this conclusion. In his study of Maryland youth, who were largely representative of 16- to 24-year-olds throughout the nation in marital status, race, farm-nonfarm residence, native-foreign parentage, and school status, Bell, H. M. (1938) obtained the results reported in Table 6-7. The general trend is for boys and girls from urban areas to desire further vocational training at all levels of choice. In particular, those from the farms less frequently want to train themselves for jobs in the trades and crafts. In another study, Sisson (1941) asked 951 male and female freshmen to indicate their choices and places of residence on a personnel form used at Louisiana State University. He neglected to report the criteria for place of residence, however, which he classified as city, town, and farm; consequently, it is not possible to compare his findings *directly* with those of Anderson. We can only conclude that, if

Table 6-7. Types of Vocational Training Desired by Out-of-school Youth *(From Bell, H. M., 1938, p. 71)*

Place of residence	*Profes-sional*	*Business and secretarial*	*Trades and crafts*	*Domestic or personal*	*Agricul-ture and related*	*Other types; uncertain*
Farm	25.4%	19.6%	26.8%	9.5%	7.5%	11.2%
Village	36.1	26.7	22.6	8.1	0.7	5.8
Town	41.9	28.1	15.7	6.8	0.9	6.6
City	39.2	25.0	24.7	8.1	0.3	2.7

the sizes of the places of residence in Sisson's study are comparable to those in Anderson's investigation, then Sisson found essentially the same relationships. City boys choose engineering approximately one-half of the time, whereas farm children select an agricultural occupation almost as often (41.85 percent versus 36.50 percent, respectively). Thus, it would seem on the basis of available evidence, that geographical location, as a stimulus variable, is related to vocational choice.

Community

Despite the theoretical significance of the community as a factor in vocational choice, very little work has been done on its actual relationship to an individual's selection of an occupation. To the knowledge of the writer, there are no studies of how the neighborhood in which one lives affects his choice, although there is evidence that it is related to a variety of other behaviors (e.g., Reckless, Dinitz, & Murray, 1957). Also, what research there is on the part which a young person's peer group plays in his choice and the influence which his ethnic group has upon his vocational thinking and decision making is more suggestive than definitive. But there is some research, and a review of it may point to further lines of investigation and more systematic consideration of the problem.

McGuire and Blocksma (1953) drew conclusions from data which they collected on *peer-group* associations and vocational choice, but they did not report the actual data; consequently, it seems advisable to only quote their summary of what they found, rather than to evaluate their analysis and inferences. They write as follows (McGuire & Blocksma, 1953, p. 15):

> There is considerable evidence that adolescents in most need of vocational counsel from outside the home circle are the ones who vary from their family level and type of occupation. Among the approximately forty per cent of youth who differ from their family level, nearly half are *climbers.* They aspire above the family pattern, usually are accepted by high status age-mates, respond to education, and profit by guidance when moving from school or college to the first job. A smaller proportion can be termed *strainers.* Pushed by their parents or by their own personal aspirations, they have responded positively to the school but they have had less success with their peers. Some lack the abilities to cope with the kind of work demanded of them. Others have never learned to work with people. Guidance people encounter some of the same characteristics in middle-class *clingers* who are "trying to hang on" to the way of life of their parents. Only one in twenty youth, it would seem from our data, turn out to be *decliners* or downward mobile in their occupational choice and career pattern compared with their families.

McGuire and Blocksma (1953) attributed most of the variation from family level to the influence of peers, particularly in the cases of climbers and strainers. Boys and girls who follow these patterns of choice supposedly do so because their age-mates encourage them to or because they think they will stand a better chance of being accepted by their age-mates. There is still some question, however, about the extent to which peer pressures, independently of family ambitions, contribute to vocational choice. Further research is needed to determine the differential effects of these two variables upon choice.

The evidence on the relationship of *ethnic group* to vocational choice is scarce and far from conclusive. It comes from two studies designed to investigate other problems and is indirect at best. Hurlock and Jansing (1934) found that the most popular vocational choice of foreign-born adolescents, regardless of whether they were undertaking a course of study in an academic or in a technical school, was aviator. Other occupations were largely passed over: about 27 percent of the foreign students in technical schools chose engineering, and approximately 18 percent of the academic students preferred physician and musician, but only a low percentage selected one of the other 10 occupations named by one or more of the Subjects in the sample. In the other study, Jones, E. S. (1940, p. 224) mentions incidentally, in discussing the relationship of intelligence to choice, that: "The poorest relationships were from high schools where there was a large recent Italian population. Apparently, many Italian youngsters anticipate medical or legal training, regardless of their ability." Here the implication is that Italian youth choose to be doctors and lawyers more than other groups. More evidence is necessary, however, before we can come to any firm conclusions about ethnic-group membership and choice. The best that can be said at present is that there is some indication of a relationship, but that it needs to be substantiated by further research.

Immediate Environment

According to theory, the immediate environment of the individual, which includes his family, school, and church, has the most direct and significant impact upon his vocational choice of all the stimulus variables. As the basic social and psychological unit in the transmission of the culture and the development of personality, the family conditions almost all the responses the individual makes early in life and continues to exert control over his behavior into adolescence and sometimes adulthood. Similarly, the school acts as a socialization agent which rewards and punishes the individual for his actions and thereby teaches him to respond in certain ways and not in others and to develop certain attitudes and values about such vocationally relevant matters as achievement and satisfaction. The church augments this training with attention to the individual's moral and spiritual life by delineating for him what is right and wrong and what constitutes the "good life." Each of these institutions, in its own way as well as collectively, presumably influences the individual in his selection of an occupation. How and to what extent this influence is exerted is discussed in the following review of research on the relationships of the family, school, and church to vocational choice.

The Family. Studies of the family and vocational choice are of three different kinds: (1) those which have investigated the extent to which sons follow the occupations of their fathers; (2) those which have analyzed the part which identification with the parents plays in choice; and (3) those which have tested hypotheses about the effects of interpersonal relationships with the parents upon the selection of an occupation.

The first type of study, on *father's occupation,* has been by far the most popular and numerous, although not necessarily the most definitive.[2] There have been at least 15 investigations of "occupational inheritance," but none of them has demonstrated a *strong* relationship between the occupations of fathers and sons, other interpretations notwithstanding (e.g., Jenson & Kirchner, 1955; Samson & Stefflre, 1952). As Table 6-8 shows, a summary of the various studies indicates that the percentage of sons who choose or enter the *same* occupation as their fathers is only about 12 or 13 percent. When the percentage of sons on a given level who have fathers at the same level is considered, the figures are somewhat higher. Only when adjacent levels are combined does a significant relationship between the son's and the father's occupation emerge (Table 6-9). Most of the conclusions which are drawn about occupational transmission from father to son are based upon data analyzed in this fashion, but such conclusions are not valid, because the method of analysis is inappropriate and hence the results are inaccurate. By combining adjacent levels to compute percentages for sons of fathers at a *given* level, the same sons are counted at more than one level. Furthermore, the levels which are generally used are so broad that a combination of those which are adjacent to each other covers from one-fourth to two-thirds of the entire range in occupational level. The most reliable data on the relationship between the occupations of fathers and sons comes, therefore, not from an analysis of combined levels but from single levels. And, although, the classification schema

[2] There is a related literature on what has been termed "occupational origin," but it deals only indirectly with the phenomenon of "occupational inheritance." The former is defined by rating the father's occupation on a prestige scale, such as the Hatt, and then relating the score to variables like geographical region of son's residence and decade of birth. For studies of this type, see Adams, S. (1953; 1954) and More (1960). See also a survey by Dyer, W. G. (1958), in which he found that both white-collar and manual families do *not* encourage their children to follow the father's occupation, which may explain why occupational inheritance or transmission is not greater than it is.

Table 6-8. Summary of Studies on the Relationship of Father's Occupation to Son's Vocational Choice

Investigators	*Percent (or correlation) who chose same* kind *of occupation as father*	*Percent (or correlation) with occupation on same* level *as father*
Anderson, 1932	12.0%	
Beckman, 1929		49.3%
Jenson & Kirchner, 1955		Manual: 71.0%
		Nonmanual: 63.0%
Jones, 1940		$r = .40$
Krippner, 1963		$r = .22$
Kroger & Louttit, 1935		19.1%
Mowsesian, Heath, & Rothney, 1966		1–26.0%
Nelson, 1939	$C = .23$	
Pinney, 1932	(No statistics, but this conclusion: "The father's occupation seemed to play a very small part, although there was some evidence of its influence," p. 287.)	
Proctor, 1937	13.0%	57.0%
Samson & Stefflre, 1952		$C = .29$*
Sears, 1915	(No statistics, but this conclusion: "The boys tend very largely to select some occupation other than that of their own fathers," p. 756.)	
Sisson, 1938a	$r = .003$	

* This contingency coefficient was computed by the writer from the χ^2 value reported by Samson and Stefflre (1952, p. 36).

***Table 6-9. Relationship of Father's Occupational Level to Son's Vocational Choice** (From Davidson & Anderson, 1937, p. 24)*

Occupational level of fathers	*Percentage of sons on same level or adjacent levels*
Professional	61.1
Proprietors, etc.	60.1
Clerks, etc.	61.5
Skilled	73.5
Semiskilled	68.1
Unskilled	71.9

used to determine levels may affect the results obtained (Remstad & Rothney, 1958), the estimates presented in Table 6-8 would appear to be fairly representative and stable.

That there is *some* association between father's occupation and son's vocational choice suggests that the long-proposed hypothesis that *parental identification* is a significant variable in the selection of an occupation may be true (Carter, 1940; Bordin, 1943; Super, 1953).[3] To test the hypothesis more directly, Crites (1962b) investigated the relationship of degree, kind, and pattern of identification with the father and mother, on the one hand, to vocational interest patterning and masculinity-femininity of interests, on the other. The Semantic Differential and the Strong Vocational Interest Blank, as measures of parental identification and interest patterning, were administered to three groups of male Subjects: (1) an original sample of vocational-educational clients ($N = 100$); (2) a replication sample of vocational-educational clients ($N = 100$); and (3) a generalization sample of nonclients ($N = 150$). The results which were obtained were the same in all three groups and indicated that *"identification with both parents influences the formation of vocational interest patterns, but identification with the father is more important than with the mother"* (Crites, 1962b, p. 269; italics in original). As Figure 6-2 shows, sons who have close identifications with their fathers develop interests in business-detail occupations, whereas those who identify only slightly with their fathers form interests in the verbal-linguistic field. Figure 6-3 reveals that sons who have like-sex identifications are interested in the organizational aspects of business, whereas those with cross-sex identifications acquire preferences for occupations which involve working with ideas, language, and people. These findings on parental identification pertain to the development of interest patterns and not necessarily to the making of a vocational choice. It seems likely, however, in light of the fairly substantial correlation between interests and choice (see discussion to follow), that similar results would be obtained if a measure of choice was used rather than an interest inventory.

A study by Segal and Szabo (1964) of accounting and creative-writing students bears out this supposition. These investigators were interested in replicating a part of a previous study by Segal (1961, p. 208; see discussion to follow) in which he hypothesized that: "Signs of a more rigid fearful identification are seen in accounting students as compared to a seeking for the completion of multiple identifications in creative writing students." To test this hypothesis two groups of 15 students each from accounting and writing at the University of Michigan, who also had appropriate high and low scores on the cognate scales of the SVIB, were compared on 16 items in a sentence-completion

[3] For a study of the teacher as a model for or influencer of vocational choice, see Day (1966).

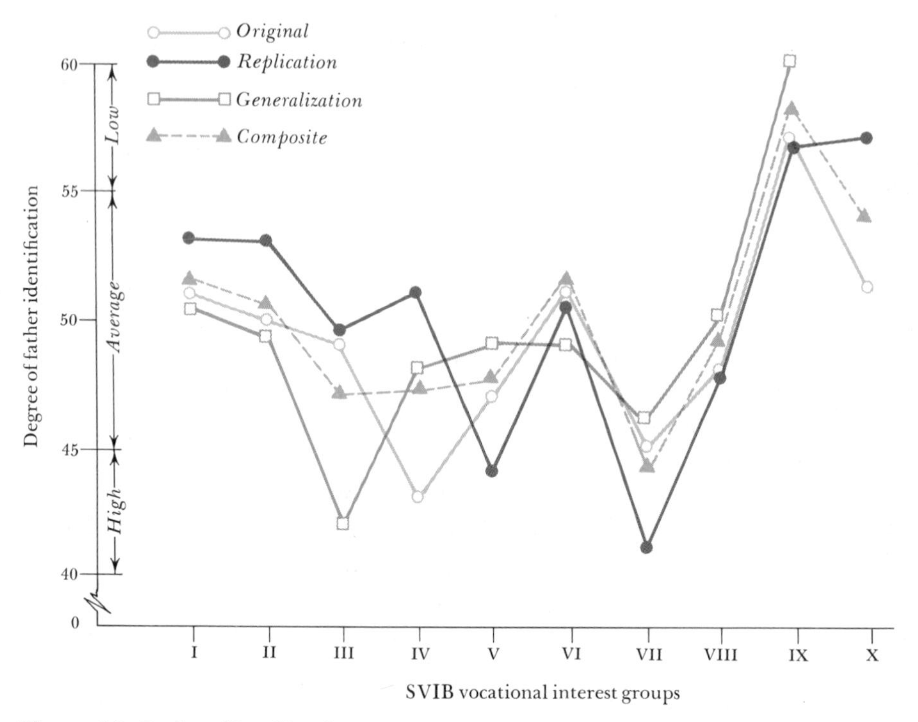

Figure 6-2. Father identification means for SVIB primary and secondary interest patterns. *(From Crites, 1962, p. 267.)*

test. In all but four statistical tests, the predicted differences between the accountants and writers were significant. The former had generally (1) more positive attitudes toward their parents, (2) more favorable attitudes toward other people, and (3) more accepting attitudes toward authority and rules. Segal and Szabo (1964, p. 254) interpret the more positive attitudes of the accountants towards others as a generalization of their attitudes toward their parents, and they draw the overall conclusion that "the results were in line with the hypotheses, and show a primarily significant difference in attitude between these groups. . . ." This inference appears to be justified, although more confidence could be had in it if more was known about the psychometric characteristics (reliability, validity) of the sentence-completion test which was used to measure identification.

The last family variable which we shall consider as a possible determinant of vocational choice is the individual's *interpersonal relationships* with his parents and their attitudes toward him. Studies of these variables have been formulated from two rather distinct theoretical orientations, despite the fact that they all deal with essentially the same problem. One orientation is that proposed by Roe (1957) and discussed in Chapter 3. Briefly restated, she

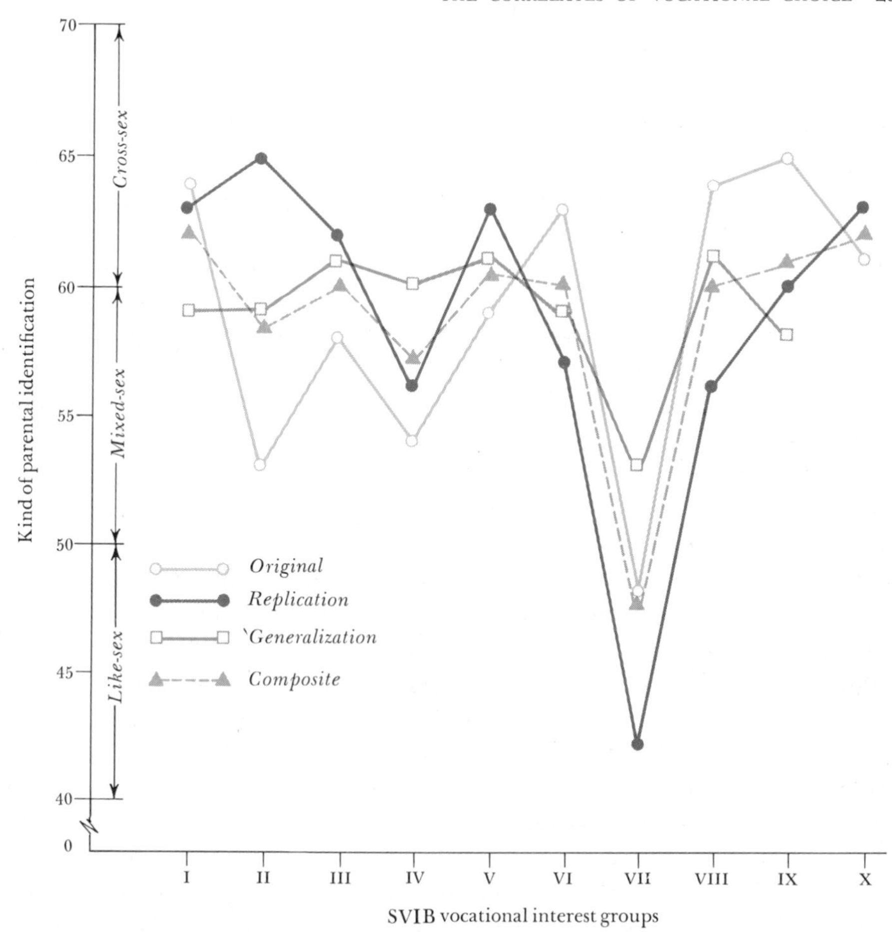

Figure 6-3. Kind of parental identification means for SVIB primary and secondary interest patterns. *(From Crites, 1962, p. 268.)*

hypothesizes that parental attitudes of (1) acceptance, (2) avoidance, and (3) concentration are differentially associated with the vocational choices of children reared in these three family interpersonal atmospheres. One of the first studies conducted to test Roe's hypotheses was reported by Grigg (1959) who found only one difference between 24 graduate nurses and 20 female chemistry, physics, and mathematics majors on a short 15-item questionnaire about early experiences in the family. The two groups differed significantly in their responses to a statement about childhood interest in "gadgets and things" but not in their retrospections about how their parents reacted to them. In a comment on this study, Roe (1959) criticized Grigg (1) for using an unvalidated measure of parental attitudes and (2) for selecting two groups for comparison which might be expected to be more similar than different, since both are in the general field of science. Also, she questioned using female rather than male Subjects to test propositions which were formulated primarily from research on the latter (Roe, 1953a).

Subsequent studies by other investigators, however, as well as by Roe, have yielded only minimal support for her hypotheses. Hagen (1960, p. 255) found negligible differences between the occupations of Harvard graduates from different family psychological atmospheres and concluded that: "Roe's theoretical scheme in its literal translation and specific application lacks validity." Similarly, Switzer, Grigg, Miller, and Young (1962), in a study of male ministerial students and chemistry majors (N's = 40 each), were unable to differentiate the two groups in ways predicted by Roe's theory, but they did find differences between the attitudes of fathers and mothers as they related to choice. They note that: "When referring to 'parental attitude' as a variable, the question may be *which parent* is being considered and perhaps how that attitude is perceived by the child within the context of the attitude of the other parent" (Switzer et al., 1962, p. 47; italics in original). In another study, Utton (1962, p. 51) obtained a few significant differences, most of them contrary to Roe's hypotheses, among female social workers ($N = 33$), occupational therapists ($N = 23$), dietitians ($N = 41$), and laboratory technicians ($N = 28$), and he concluded that his results made "it necessary to question Roe's theory so far as these particular occupations are concerned." Using the Brunkan-Crites (1964) Family Relations Inventory (FRI), which is scored for mother and father Acceptance, Avoidance, and Concentration, Brunkan (1965) was unable to differentiate college undergraduates classified according to the fields of vocational choice in Roe's system. Much the same findings have been reported by Roe and Siegelman (1964) and Green and Parker (1965) with Roe's Parent-Child Relations Questionnaire (PCR), but in both of these studies relationships between parental attitudes and person-nonperson orientation have been established, although they were of a low order.

None of these studies of Roe's theory is without its defects and shortcomings, and it may be that these are producing the largely negative results on her hypotheses. For example, most of the investigations have used instruments or methods to measure parental attitudes which are unvalidated or unstandardized (Brunkan & Crites, 1964). Furthermore, the samples in most cases have been questionable because of their highly select nature. Hagen (1960) used a sample in which 57 percent of the Subjects came from an "overdemanding" atmosphere, and Grigg (1959) and Utton (1962) both used female Subjects despite the fact that Roe's hypotheses were intended to apply only to males. As Switzer et al. (1962) point out, another consideration may be that the significant family variable in choice is differences between the attitudes of the father and mother and that studies of overall parental attitudes are unproductive for this reason. Additional research is definitely needed to assess the effects of these various factors upon tests of Roe's hypotheses, as well as such demographic and status variables as intelligence and socioeconomic level. It may be found, for example, that the latter "moderate" the relationships of parental attitudes to vocational choice, so that they obtain for some levels of intelligence and social position but not for others (see Chapter 14).

A second orientation which has served as a theoretical frame of reference for studying the relationship of parental attitudes to vocational choice is largely psychoanalytic, but also partly sociological, in origin and precept. There are three studies which have stemmed from it, two on kind of vocational choice and the other on level of vocational aspiration. In one of the studies of choice, Nachmann (1960) formulated several hypotheses about the childhood experiences of lawyers, social workers, and dentists, whom she predicted would differ along three dimensions: (1) their degree of verbal aggression, (2) their concern with human justice, and (3) their exercise of a privileged curiosity into the lives of others. All but two of Nachmann's hypotheses were substantiated by data gathered on 20 male students in each of the fields under investigation. Her conclusion that these results support her predictions is open to question, however, because of a methodological flaw in her study. To obtain background information on her Subjects she had "experienced clinicians" interview each student, but she reports that the interviewers were aware of the hypotheses to be tested. She argues that this knowledge *probably* did not affect her findings, because most of the questions asked were of a factual nature, such as "What was your father's occupation?" Many questions must have been susceptible to bias and interpretation by the interviewers, however, since data on certain hypotheses[4] could not have been gathered through purely factual interviewing. Consequently, there is the possibility of lack of experimental independence between the variables in Nachmann's study, and, as a result, there is no way of knowing whether the relationships which were found between them are attributable to the procedures used to collect the data or to their intrinsic covariation. The fact that so many of the hypotheses were supported probably indicates that the latter is the case, but we can have only qualified confidence in this conclusion.

Similarly, in the other study of choice, which stemmed from the same theoretical framework as Nachmann's (Bordin et al., 1963), Galinsky (1962) also confounded his hypotheses with his data by personally conducting all the interviews with his Subjects. The latter were 40 graduate students in clinical

[4] For example: "Social workers will tend to have experienced severe and traumatic deprivation in the first two years of life; for lawyers traumatic experience will be mentioned as later and less severe; and dentists will tend not to have experienced any sudden or severe traumatic event" (Nachmann, 1960, p. 245).

psychology ($N = 20$) and physics ($N = 20$), who were compared on a number of coded responses taken from the interview protocols by three judges (agreement about 90 percent). The main focus of the study was upon differences between these two preoccupational groups in the extent to which their parents had encouraged or redirected their curiosity about interpersonal relationships. The general hypothesis was that the clinical psychologists had experiences in their families which nurtured their curiosity about relationships with others, whereas the physicists had their interest rebuffed and displaced to nonpersonal (intellectual) pursuits (cf. Roe, 1957). Subsidiary hypotheses predicted that the clinicians and physicists would also differ in the discipline they received, their ability to tolerate the emotional expressions of others, their capacity for nurturance, and their need to work alone or with someone. Galinsky reports statistical results on only one of the hypotheses; he summarizes the findings on the others in narrative form. Consequently, it is somewhat difficult to draw unambiguous conclusions about what he found. Some hypotheses were confirmed; others were supported by some coded responses but not others; and still others were not confirmed. Galinsky (1962, p. 305) states that "seven of the eleven hypotheses tested were in the main confirmed," but what this means exactly cannot be determined from the data he reports. In lieu of more explicit statistical analyses and more rigorous separation of theory and method, few defensible inferences can be made from Galinsky's study. His hypotheses are provocative ones, however, which should be tested again in further research.

In the investigation of level of vocational aspiration, Dynes, Clarke, and Dinitz (1956 p. 212) deduced from the personality theories of Adler and Horney the proposition that "individuals with high aspirations are characterized by greater difficulty in their interpersonal relations within the family of orientation than those with lower aspirations." The assumption was that "unsatisfactory interpersonal relations in early childhood produce insecurity which is translated into neurotic striving for power, recognition, and success" (Dynes et al., 1956, p. 212). Data gathered by questionnaire from 153 male and 197 female college Subjects indicated that level of vocational aspiration is significantly related to several aspects of interactions with the parents in the formative years of life. College students who aspired to high occupational levels more often (1) felt that their parents did not want them (cf. Roe's "avoidance" attitude), (2) felt that their parents showed favoritism to siblings, (3) felt less attachment to their parents, and (4) were generally less happy in childhood. Furthermore, they confided less frequently in their fathers and were more fearful of punishment from them. They did not differ from "low aspirers," however, in (1) degree of conflict with their fathers and siblings, (2) in the extent to which they confided in their mothers, (3) in their feelings that their parents compared them unfavorably with their siblings or peer groups concerning accomplishments in school and athletics, and (4) in their estimations of the degree of disappointment their parents might have in them if they did not live up to expectations. On the basis of this negative evidence, in conjunction with the positive findings, Dynes et al. (1956, p. 214) concluded that "differences in aspiration are more closely related to subtle interpersonal factors than to overt parental pressures."

This conclusion is probably the best that can be drawn from the evidence we have reviewed on the family and vocational choice. It is certainly obvious from the research on Roe's hypotheses that the relationships between parental attitudes and choice are not gross, easily detectable ones. In reflecting upon this problem, Nachmann (1960, p. 250) observes of her study that:

> This experience has left us with the conviction that the most fruitful method to follow is neither the wholesale comparison of occupations and tabulation of whatever differences appear, nor the selection of dimensions on the basis of the special interests of the researcher and a hastily erected theoretical structure, but that of expending a major effort in isolating meaningful dimensions and pursuing them to a factorial purity.

The search for such dimensions will be a difficult one, however, since so many variables intervene between childhood experiences in the family and adolescent or adult behavior that the relationships are often obscured, if not completely overdetermined (Orlansky, 1949). We can agree with Roe (1962) that whatever relationships are found will probably be low to moderate ones rather than moderate to high ones.

The School. Three studies on the relationship of the school to vocational choice have been located, but none of them provides us with very reliable knowledge of the role of this institution in the decision-making process. In a largely informal, survey type of study which included no statistical tests of differences or relationships, Carlin (1960) investigated the associations between college major, as an index of vocational choice, and (1) favorite high school teacher, (2) favorite high school extracurricular activities, and (3) effectiveness of occupational information courses in high school. Results based upon 500 Subjects indicated, first, that approximately one-third (35 percent) chose college majors in the same subject as was taught by their favorite high school teacher. Whether this relationship was independent of other factors which might lead to interest in these subjects, such as previous successful performance in them, was not determined. Second, about 30 percent of the sample selected a college major which was closely related to their favorite high school extracurricular activity, but again the relationship is not a clear-cut one, since most of the activities and majors involved a common special talent, such as physicial ability for high school athletes who decided to major in physical education in college. Finally, 41 percent of the Subjects reported that a high school course in occupations helped them in their vocational decision making. This finding appears to be the most significant of those obtained by Carlin and indicates that the school may have some differential effect upon the process of vocational choice, since it is about the only social institution which disseminates occupational information in a formal and systematic manner.

In the second study of the school as a stimulus to vocational choice, Wilson, A. B. (1959) analyzed the educational and vocational aspirations of students from 13 high schools which were classified into three groups: upper white-collar, lower white-collar, and industrial. The plans of the students for further education and careers after the completion of school were compared between groups of schools within levels of parental occupation or education, as shown in Table 6-10. The purpose of the comparisons was to show that the school exerted an influence upon the vocational behavior of the students independent of that attributable to social class, as measured by parental occupation and/or education. Wilson, A. B. (1959, p. 844) interpreted his data as in support of the conclusion that "the dominant climate of opinion within a school makes a significant impact upon students' occupational goals. . . ." This inference does not follow from his method of analysis, however, at least as he describes it. As the names which he gave to the groups of schools imply, and as the data which he reports make clear, the differences between schools are little more than differences between social classes. Table 6-11, which is

Table 6-10. Percentages of Students Aspiring to Go to College by School Groups and Father's Occupation *(From Wilson, A. B., 1959, p. 839)*

	School group		
Father's occupation	*Upper white-collar*	*Lower white-collar*	*Industrial*
Professional	93%	77%	64%
	(92)	(39)	(11)
White-collar	79	59	46
	(174)	(138)	(111)
Self-employed	79	66	35
	(68)	(90)	(37)
Manual	59	44	33
	(39)	(140)	(221)
Weighted mean of percentages	80	57	38
Total	(373)	(407)	(380)

Table 6-11. Distributions of Selected Background and Status Variables by School Groups *(From Wilson, A. B., 1959, p. 838)*

	School group		
Variable	*Upper white-collar*	*Lower white-collar*	*Industrial*
FATHER'S OCCUPATION			
Professional	22%	8%	2%
White-collar	42	29	25
Self-employed	17	20	8
Manual	10	30	49
Not available	9	12	15
FATHER'S EDUCATION			
Some college or more	65	35	14
High school graduate	20	29	26
Some high school or less	14	32	54
Not available	2	3	6
MOTHER'S EDUCATION			
Some college or more	56	31	12
High school graduate	34	41	39
Some high school or less	9	25	45
Not available	1	3	4
RESIDENCE IN CALIFORNIA			
Over 25 years	58	48	32
RACE			
White	98	78	66
RELIGION			
Catholic	21	27	38
N	(418)	(480)	(457)

reproduced from Wilson's study, shows that each of the "class" variables is highly related to school group. Since the relationships are not perfect, however, it is possible that the school has some independent effects upon choice, but if there are any, they are inextricably confounded with those of social class in Wilson's analysis. Thus, we cannot say, on the basis of his study, whether the school has an impact upon vocational choice or not.

Finally, Astin (1965) has investigated the effects of the college environment upon the vocational choices of high-aptitude students (National Merit finalists and recipients of Letters of Commendation) between the time they were freshmen and seniors. The hypothesis he tested was that "during college the *student's vocational choice comes to conform more and more to the dominant or modal choice in his college environment*" (Astin, 1965, p. 28; italics in original). In order to test this hypothesis, it was necessary first to control for those characteristics of students which might have influenced their selection of a particular college; otherwise, the characteristics would be confounded with the effects of the college upon choice. To do this, Astin adjusted the *actual* choices of the sample ($N = 1{,}010$ males) at the time of graduation by subtracting from them the *expected* choices, as predicted from freshmen input data. The residual was then related to several measures of the college environment. Because the N was so large, all but two of the partial correlations between college "effects" and vocational choice, with initial student characteristics controlled, were significant at the .05 or .01 levels, but the highest of these was only .13. Astin (1965, p. 33) concluded, therefore, that "the student's career choice at graduation from college is affected far more by his characteristics as an entering freshman than by the characteristics of his college environment," but he went on to observe that "since a sizeable proportion of variance in the students' career choices is still unaccounted for, the possibility remains that the students' choices were markedly affected by environmental factors which we were not able to assess." It might be added that, if these factors are going to be identified, a different experimental design should be used, so that there is a matched control group from a noncollege environment. Without such a control, it can be legitimately argued that changes in vocational choice may be a function of any number of other variables in addition to or in combination with college environment.

The Church. Incidental to his main study, Wilson, A. B. (1959) gathered some of the few data which are available on the role of religious affiliation in vocational choice. He summarizes them as follows (Wilson, A. B., 1959, pp. 837–838):

> Altogether, 58 per cent of the Protestants and only 47 per cent of the Catholics in the sample aspire to go to college. But within educational and occupational strata the difference between Protestants and Catholics is small and unsystematic, while within each religious group the differences between occupational and educational strata are large. For example, among the children of professionals with at least some college education, 87 per cent of both Protestants and Catholics wish to go to college; among the children of manual workers who are high school graduates, 44 per cent of the Protestants and 46 per cent of the Catholics so wish; 34 per cent of the Protestants and 28 per cent of the Catholics whose fathers are manual workers who have not finished high school, want to go to college.

From this survey, then, there is little evidence which indicates a relationship between the church with which an individual is affiliated and his educational and/or vocational aspirations and plans.

Essentially the same conclusion can be drawn from a study by Mack, Murphy, and Yellin (1956), although these investigators used occupational membership rather than vocational choice as the criterion variable. They predicted that, despite the differences in values represented by the Protestant "activist directive" orientation of salvation through works and the Catholic "quietist directive" emphasis upon otherworldly salvation, the upward-mobility ethic of the American credo would overdetermine the influence of the individual's religious affiliation upon his vocational aspirations. In other words, their hypothesis was the null hypothesis that there would be no differences between Protestants and Catholics in their desire to be successful in their occupations, where the latter was assessed by their income goals and plans for the future. Tests of the hypothesis within each of three occupational groups (salesmen, bankers, and engineers), which were subdivided into two age categories (less than 35 and more than 35 years old), yielded chi-square values which were all nonsignificant and which led the authors of the study to conclude that "there is no evidence in these data that the Protestant ethic (American dream of upward mobility and success) is participated in any less by Catholics than by Protestants in contemporary United States" (Mack, Murphy, & Yellin, 1956, p. 300).

ORGANISMIC VARIABLES

Organismic variables have been defined in several different ways, the definitions usually varying with the central interest of the investigator or theorist, and consequently it is important for purposes of discussion to clarify which definition is being used. Sometimes the term *organismic* is used to designate a particular kind of personality theory, such as those of Goldstein, Angyal, Maslow, and Lecky (Hall & Lindzey, 1957), in which the unity and coherence of the individual as an integrated whole are emphasized. More typically, however, organismic refers to "some measurable organic characteristics, property, or state of an organism" (Brown, J. S., 1961, p. 17). Here, the distinction which is usually made is between the constitution of the individual and his external conditions of living, both physical and psychological. For example, Sheldon (1940, p. 2) writes that "constitution refers to those aspects of the individual which are relatively more fixed and unchanging—morphology, physiology, endocrine function, etc.—and may be contrasted with those aspects which are relatively more labile and susceptible to modification by environmental pressures, i.e., habits, social attitudes, education, etc." Of the great number of O variables which have been defined and investigated in other fields, however, only three have been studied in relation to vocational choice. These are the following: the endocrine glands, physique or body-build, and heredity.

The Endocrine Glands

Only one study has been found on the relationship of the endocrine system to vocational choice, and it deals exclusively with the influence of the gonads upon the preferences of adolescent boys. Sollenberger (1940) conducted an intensive investigation of the behavior and male hormone excretion of two groups of boys over periods up to 6 months, in order to identify the correlates of sexual maturation during adolescence. The boys were inmates in a "cottage-type" reform school, where the investigator was a "house parent." The age range of the groups was from 12 years 9 months to 16 years 10 months. Sollenberger reports that none of the boys was neurotic or psychotic, but it must be assumed that they were not psychologically healthy, since they were by definition "delinquent." One group of 10 boys was studied initially to determine which of a battery of paper-and-pencil tests might differentiate the sexually mature and immature. Included in the test battery were: Furfey's Test of Developmental Age, Lehman's Play Quiz, and the Pressey Interest-Attitude Test. Sexually mature boys were defined as those who had a high degree of androgenic hormone activity as established by analyses of 24-hour urine samples. Correlations between this index of sexual maturity and the tests revealed that only the Furfey developmental scale was highly enough related for further study. It correlated .65 with hormone activity and .57 with rankings of the boys by two raters (interjudge agreement = .86) according to how much they were like adults in their overall behavior.

The second group of boys, numbering 23, was analyzed for quantity of hormone excretion as before but was administered only the Furfey test. This time the correlations were not as high as in the first group, but the Furfey still was related to sexual maturity, the r being .51. An item analysis of the statements in the Furfey, which cover such topics as "Things to Do," "Things to Be When You Grow up," "Things to Have," "Things to See," and "Things to Think about," indicated that some items were more discriminating than others. In the section headed "Things to Be When You Grow up," for example, the more sexually mature boys preferred to be stock brokers, authors, jewelers, and builders rather than blacksmiths, postmen, scientists, and chauffeurs. Inconsistent differences occurred in preferences for two occupations, however, where the more mature group selected "king" and "circus performer" more often than the immature group. Despite these reversals on this one subtest, the two groups differed markedly on total score, the critical ratio between their respective means of 133 and 115 being 3.00, which is significant at the .01 level. As a result, Sollenberger (1940, pp. 183–184) drew the following conclusion:

> It appears, therefore, that there is a positive relationship between the gonadal hormone content of boys and their maturity of interests and attitudes and that these interests and attitudes are more affected, within the particular age range studied, by the maturational status of the organism than they are by chronological age.

Although this study is unique as far as the problem of endocrine factors in vocational choice or interests is concerned, it should not be interpreted as more definitive than it is, which has sometimes been the case (Super & Crites, 1962). There are several limitations and shortcomings to Sollenberger's investigation. First, the numbers of Subjects in his two groups of boys were very small and hardly appropriate for the computation of product-moment correlation coefficients, which he reports. Similarly, the small *N*'s should have dictated the use of *t* tests rather than critical ratios in the item analyses. Second, the samples of Subjects on which the data were gathered were very unusual ones, consisting of boys in a reformatory; therefore, it would be extremely hazardous and probably erroneous to generalize the results to normal adolescent males. Third, the Furfey as a measure of either choice or preference leaves a considerable amount to be desired. We might well wonder whether the same findings could be obtained with one of our better standardized questionnaires or interest inventories. Fourth, Sollenberger does not make clear the part which age plays in the interpretation of his results. He found that hormone activity correlated with both age and the Furfey, but that the latter two variables were unrelated. This seems strange, since the Furfey was standardized on age groups, and Sollenberger interprets it as an age scale in his item analysis. Certainly, further research is needed to clarify this matter as well as the others already noted. Until it is available, probably our best conclusion about Sollenberger's study is that it *suggests* the existence of a relationship between gonadal hormone secretion and vocational choice (loosely defined) but that it should be considered as survey research only and not as conclusive.

Physique

There is very little empirical research on the relationship of physique to vocational choice, but what there is lends some support to the idea that individuals with different body types select different occupations for their future careers:

1. Fagin (1950) determined the somatotypes of 473 male college students and compared them on their SVIB scores. He also rated them on degree of gynandromorphy, which indicates the extent to which an individual has the physical characteristics ordinarily associated with the opposite sex. For males a high "g" index would mean such feminine attributes as a soft body, broad pelvis, and wide hips. Fagin predicted that the somatotype groupings would differ in their vocational interests and that there would be a relationship between gynandromorphy and masculinity-femininity of interests. His findings only partially confirmed his hypotheses, but there was some evidence that physique and interests are associated. Analysis of variance between somatotypes yielded significant differences on nine SVIB scales as well as differences in

masculinity-femininity of interests between Subjects who had high and low "g" ratings. On the basis of his results, Fagin (1950, p. 219) commented as follows:

> The relationships found are of some value in contributing to a theory of vocational interests. Although most of the variability in interests is apparently due to social learning, there is a small body of evidence that constitutional factors contribute something to differences in interests. The conclusions of this study can reasonably be interpreted as additional evidence in support of this viewpoint.

2. Whereas Fagin used interests as his "choice" variable, Begelman (1951) selected college major as an index of vocational objective. The Subjects in his study were 727 male undergraduates who were taking courses in eight different areas or schools: agriculture, business, engineering, forestry, pharmacy, lower division (general education), education, and physical education. The Subjects were not actually classified into distinct somatotype groupings, but they were rated or measured on the pertinent components, which included height, weight, fat, and muscle. Begelman (1951, pp. 151–152) conducted numerous analyses of the physique data which are too extensive to present here but which he summarizes as follows:

> Very little relationship was found between body build and occupational choice.
>
> *Height:* Physical Education students and Education students were taller than the other groups. Business and Forestry students were shorter than all other groups with the exception of Pharmacy.
>
> *Weight:* Physical Education students were significantly heavier than all other persons.
>
> *Fat:* No significant difference was found at the 5 percent level in the areas of adipose tissue.
>
> *Muscle:* No significant difference was found at the 5 percent level in the area of muscle tissue.

Thus, again the evidence for a relationship between physique and choice is scant, but nevertheless it exists and must be accounted for theoretically.

3. Finally, as part of a larger study, French, W. L. (1959) has reported on the somatotypes of 232 Harvard graduates who were followed up in their occupations 12 years after they were initially rated on Sheldon's scales. For some reason, only endomorphy and mesomorphy differentiated the occupational groups and in ways which were not readily explicable, as French, W. L. (1959, p. 97) points out in the following observations:

> Endomorphy, essentially a measure of fatness, differentiated the occupational groups, but there seemed to be no commonsense rationalization to this phenomenon. The various engineering occupations

> were distributed at several points along this continuum and teaching occupations did not cluster at any one spot. However, the legal groups were all above the mean on this scale.
>
> Mesomorphy, which is a measure of hardness, toughness, and muscularity, significantly differentiated the group, but it was difficult to make any generalizations. Production supervision, security, brokerage, general business management, and technical sales were highest, in that order. The lowest was foreign service followed by psychiatry, teachers of college English, and editing.

These findings per se, although suggestive, are not particularly outstanding, but in conjunction with others which French obtained they gain in significance. Using a variety of scores from ability and personality measures, as well as the somatotypes, French performed a multiple discriminant function analysis of the differences between the occupational groups and found that the most differentiating variable was a combination of Sheldon's physique and personality types. Unfortunately, in discussing these results French does not graphically present the discriminants, and consequently we do not know which occupations clustered on the different somatotypes, although presumably they were similar to those quoted above.

Heredity

A study conducted by Carter (1932) on twin similarities in vocational interests is the only one which has been found on the role of hereditary factors in choice phenomena. The approach he took was to compare three groups of twins: (1) 43 pairs of identical (monozygotic) twins; (2) 43 pairs of like-sex fraternal (dyzygotic) twins; and (3) 34 pairs of opposite-sex fraternal twins. The SVIB was administered to all pairs of twins, and correlation coefficients for 23 scales in each of the samples were computed. Carter's (1932, p. 652) hypothesis was that:

> The identical twins are expected to show greater similarity than the fraternal pairs, because of more similar heredity, and perhaps also because of more similar environments. It is likely that both heredity and environment has an effect upon family resemblances in interests of the type here considered.

The results upheld the hypothesis, in that the average correlation for all scales for the identical twins was .50 and for the fraternal twins was .28. There was little or no difference between the like- and unlike-sex fraternal twins, the *r*'s being .26 and .30, respectively. From these findings Carter (1932, p. 653) concluded that:

> Since it is certain that the interests of the monozygotic twins are more similar than those of the fraternal twins, and since the data suggest that there is no greater similarity of like-sex fraternal twins

> than of unlike-sex twins, it seems probable that hereditary factors are more important in determining interests than are environmental factors. This conclusion can only be made tentatively, however, since a part of the greater similarity of identical twins must be attributed to greater similarity of environment. The present writer believes that such greater similarity of environment is a fact which must be taken into consideration, but it is a far less important fact than the greater similarity of heredity.

Super and Crites (1962) have questioned Carter's conclusion because objective evidence to substantiate the assumption that the environments of identical twins are more similar than fraternal twins is lacking. Actually, there is some reason to believe that the assumption may be erroneous, since one of its implications does not follow factually. If the assumption were valid, we would expect fraternal twins to be more similar in their interests than fathers and sons, but several studies (e.g., Strong, 1943; 1957) have shown that there are no differences, the *r*'s for both fraternal twins and father-son pairs being about .28. The reasoning here is indirect, however, and highlights the need for additional research more than it proves the case for the relatively greater influence of heredity on interest development, as Super and Crites (1962, p. 401) propose when they write that "the greater similarity of the interests of identical twins, as contrasted with those of fraternal twins, is not due to the *potentially* greater similarity of their environments, but rather to the *demonstrably* greater similarity of their heredities." Before this or comparable conclusions can be drawn, carefully controlled studies, which include comparisons of identical and fraternal twins with randomly formed pairs of unrelated individuals as well as with each other, must be performed. And, needless to say, they must deal with vocational choice in addition to interests, if our knowledge on this problem is to be complete.

RESPONSE VARIABLES

Just as vocational choice is a response variable (see Chapter 4), so are a host of other behaviors in which there are definable and reliable individual differences. In this section, our concern is with which of these other response variables are systematically related to vocational choice. Of the numerous behaviors which have been correlated with choice, three stand out as entering into more significant relationships than any others. These are (1) aptitudes, (2) interests, and (3) personality.

Aptitudes

Studies on the relationship of an individual's aptitudes to his vocational decision making have dealt almost exclusively with general, rather than special, aptitudes. And, they have related general aptitude not only to choice, but also to preference and aspiration. Consequently, in the review of the studies which follow, they have been classified and summarized in accordance with which aspect of occupational selection (choice, preference, or aspiration) they investigated, so that explicit and specific conclusions can be drawn. Only those studies which seemed most adequate in sample size and methodology have been selected for discussion. There are a number of other studies on aptitude as a correlate of vocational choice (Bradley, 1943; Byrns, 1939; Feingold, 1923; Gribbons & Lohnes, 1966b; Moser, W. E., 1949; Sisson, 1938b), but they are not reviewed here because one or another of several defects in their designs and/or procedures make their findings questionable.

Vocational Choice. There are three studies of general aptitude, or intelligence, in relation to choice which have yielded results in which we can have some confidence. The studies are less replications of each other than they are investigations of slightly different aspects of the same general problem, but taken together they support the conclusion that aptitude and choice are related:

1. In one of their many studies with the Vocational Attitude Quiz, which consists of a list of 200 representative occupations, Witty and Lehman (1931) analyzed the relationship of scores on the National Intelligence Tests, Forms 1 and 2, to the occupations which 900 boys in grades 5, 6, and 7 selected as the ones they would "most likely follow" (choice). To compute correlation coefficients between intelligence and choice, the investigators determined the amount of mental ability required for each occupation from the Barr Scale of Occupational Intelligence. The correlations which they obtained for each grade were as follows: (*a*) fifth grade, .41; (*b*) sixth grade, .52; and (*c*) seventh grade, .58. They also found that, regardless of grade, the less intelligent boys in their sample, as compared with the brighter ones, (*a*) expressed a "willingness to enter" more occupations, the mean number of occupations being 24 and 14 respectively, and (*b*) selected occupations which were more frequently chosen by younger boys. From their various analyses, Witty and Lehman (1931, pp. 744–745) concluded that:

> Collectively, the data presented in this article reveal immature attitudes on the part of the dull boys and relatively mature attitudes on the part of the bright boys. The dull group expressed willingness to enter a conspicuously larger number of occupations than did the bright group. The dull boys appeared to choose occupations somewhat indiscriminately. This attitude also characterizes boys of younger chronological ages. Maturity of response was associated positively with mental age in all sections of this quiz.

In short, this study revealed a relationship of aptitude to both number and maturity of vocational choices.

2. Wrenn (1935) has reported on several comparisons of high and low intelligence groups which indicate marked differences in their vocational choices. Out of a total sample of 10,000 junior college students who had taken the American Council on Education Psychological Examination, he selected a "high" group which consisted of 195 males who scored at (or higher than) the 95th percentile and a "low" group which was made up of 157 males who were at (or below) the 15th percentile. The estimated mean IQs of the two groups were about 140 and 95, respectively. He obtained three sets of results from comparing these groups which are relevant to the relationship of aptitude to choice. First, as shown in Figure 6-4a, the high-IQ group more often chose an occupation at the professional level, but it is significant that over one-half of the low-IQ group also chose at the same level, despite their more limited ability. Second, in Figure 6-4b, it is apparent that more students with high IQs tend to make the same vocational choice over a period of two years

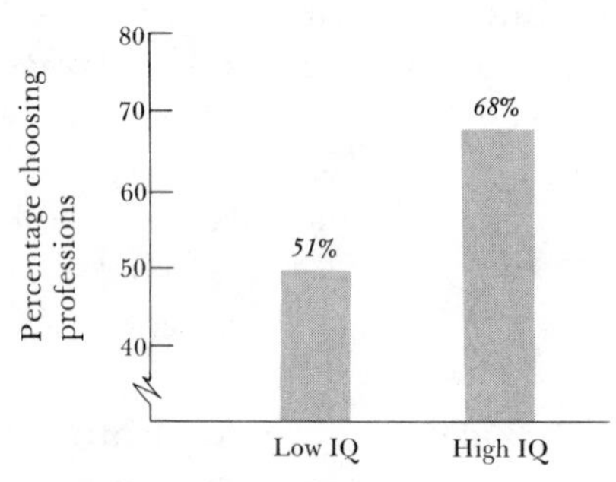

(a) Percentages of low- and high-IQ groups which selected a profession as their vocational choice.

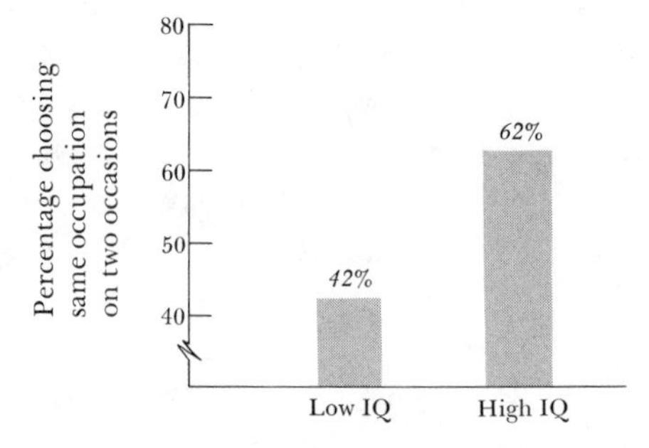

(b) Percentages of low- and high-IQ groups which selected the same occupation as their choice in 1929 and in 1931.

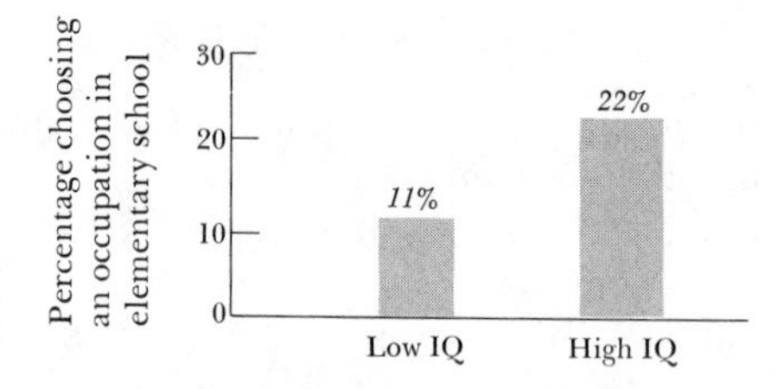

(c) Percentages of low- and high-IQ groups which made an occupational choice in elementary school.

Figure 6-4. Summary of results on relationship between intelligence and vocational choice. *(After Wrenn, 1935.)*

than students with low IQs. In other words, the brighter students are more persistent in their choices, and, as Wrenn also notes, they are usually more decisive in their selection of an occupation, i.e., more of them have made a choice of some sort. Finally, as Figure 6-4c indicates, a greater percentage of those with high IQs make a vocational choice during the elementary school years. It should be noted that this percentage is not very high, being only about one-fifth of the group, and that it is not necessarily *good,* in the sense of being more vocationally mature, since early choices may reflect pseudo-crystallization (see Chapter 5). We can agree with Wrenn's (1935, p. 219) conclusion from these data, however, that they "point to the greater consistency, permanence, and suitability of the vocational choices of students high in academic intelligence as measured by the *Psychological Examination* than of students low in such intelligence."

3. One of the most recent studies of aptitude as a factor in choice was conducted by Holden (1961, p. 37) to test two hypotheses: (1) "Students at the lower range of the IQ continuum are more likely to change the level of occupational choice between grades 8 and 11 than students in the upper range of the IQ continuum," and (2) "As they progress through the grades from 8 to 11, students at the lower levels of scholastic ability would, as a group, tend toward vocational choices that are more suitable to their scholastic abilities." To gather the appropriate data to evaluate these hypotheses Holden interviewed a group of 109 Subjects about their post-high school educational and vocational plans when they were in the eighth grade, and then he followed them up when they were in the eleventh grade with a second interview. Thus, he obtained rather rare longitudinal data on a sample which was large enough for proper statistical analyses, and he found support for both of his hypotheses. Not only did lower-ability Subjects change the level of their vocational choices more than high-ability Subjects from eighth to eleventh grade, but they definitely tended to "lower their sights." For example, whereas 78 percent of them chose occupations in the eighth grade which required four or more years of college, the percentage choosing at the same level in the eleventh grade dropped to 11 percent. Similarly, none of the lower-ability group chose occupations while in eighth grade which could be entered with no post-high school education, but 67 percent made such choices in the eleventh grade. The evidence of Holden's study, then, corroborates the cross-sectional findings of Lehman and Witty and agrees with the results of Wrenn's analyses that general aptitude is related to several aspects of vocational choice, but particularly to the *level* and *stability* of choice.

Vocational Preference. Investigations of aptitude in relation to preference are less numerous and less conclusive than those on choice, but they nevertheless demonstrate that an individual's general intelligence is correlated with the occupation he would "like" to enter if he could:

1. A study which analyzed the relationship of aptitude to both choice and preference provides a transition between studies which have dealt exclusively with one or the other of the two variables and also allows a comparison of the relative magnitudes of their correlations with aptitude. Jones, E. S. (1940) has reported the findings shown in Table 6-12, which generally indicate a slightly higher association of aptitude with choice (probable occupation) than with preference (preferred occupation). It is evident from these data, however, that the correlations vary considerably, depending upon whether the Subjects are from a predominantly rural or predominantly urban area. The relationships are uniformly higher for the boys who attended schools in the agricultural area surrounding Buffalo than for the boys who went to schools in the city. In commenting upon this difference, Jones, E. S. (1940, p. 223–224) offers the following explanation:

> We believe this indicates that the rural high school is more efficient than other schools in orienting its male students occupationally according to ability levels. This may be due to smaller classes and a closer relation between teacher and student; it may be the result of economic selection and residence, since most sons of farmers feel that they cannot afford to leave home for college, whereas the city boy can frequently attend some college even if he is poor intellectually and economically.

Whatever the reasons are for the differential rural-urban relationships among aptitude, choice, and preference, Jones's study establishes that they do exist and must be considered in interpreting the role which aptitude plays in vocational decision making.

2. To determine the relationship of aptitude to the individual's vocational preferences, rather than choices, Porter, J. K. (1954) constructed a questionnaire which asked respondents to state the kind of work they would "prefer

Table 6-12. Correlations of General Aptitude with the Preferred and Probable Occupations of Boys from Different Residential Areas *(After Jones, E. S., 1940, p. 226)*

High school	*Preferred occupation*	*Probable occupation*
Buffalo	.30	.28
Suburban (industrial)	.25	.30
Suburban (residence)	.10	.36
Rural	.51	.63

to be doing" when they were 25 years old, which he told them was the age when "most people have completed their education and have begun to work in their chosen occupation." He administered the questionnaire, which also asked for a statement of their vocational "plan," to a sample of 100 high school senior boys and assigned prestige values to the level of their preferences from the Smith, M. (1943) and Hatt (1950) occupational scales. The preferences were then correlated with plans (scored in the same fashion) and intelligence, as measured by the Adaptability Test. Preferences and plans were highly interrelated, the *r* being .88, despite Porter's efforts to define the latter as a more realistic and total course of action, instead of only an expression of liking-disliking. Preferences and intelligence were moderately correlated, the coefficient being .36, which was significant at the .01 level and which supports the conclusion, based upon both this study and the one by Jones, that preferences as well as choices are related to general aptitude.

3. Perrone (1964) compared 192 senior high school boys, classified into Roe's system by the field of their vocational preference, on measures of (1) goal orientation, (2) dogmatism, (3) creativity, (4) verbal IQ, and (5) nonverbal IQ. He found differences between the preference groups only on the last three, but these were largely according to expectation. In general, the nonperson occupational groups, e.g., Science and Organization, scored higher on all three variables, being more creative and intelligent than the person-centered groups, e.g., Service and Business Contact. Perrone (1964, p. 978) concluded that "the most significant finding of this study is that boys with similar scores on cognitive measures tend to indicate a preference for similar occupational groups."

Vocational Aspiration. Only one study of aptitude in relation to aspiration has been found, but because of its comprehensiveness and relatively large sample it appears to afford fairly reliable evidence for sound conclusions. In this investigation, Stubbins (1950) correlated scores on the Wonderlic Personnel Test, Form B, with vocational aspirations assigned values on a specially constructed occupational prestige scale. Aspirations were elicited by the following question in interviews with 219 male veterans undergoing vocational advisement after World War II (Stubbins, 1950, p. 350):

> In order to choose a suitable occupation, you and your counselor should know your fundamental interests. One way of expressing these interests is to tell what occupation you would follow if you had complete freedom to choose. Or, as this question puts it: If you had every opportunity to follow any career you *wished* but *still* had to *work for a living,* what occupation would you choose?

Using product-moment correlational procedures, Stubbins obtained an *r* of .43 between intelligence and aspiration. This relationship was higher than any of the others which he studied, e.g., aspiration versus education, work experience, father's occupation, age, etc., but he concluded that it was nonetheless rather low, an opinion that is somewhat difficult to accept since an r of .43 is almost as high as the correlation of intelligence with grades. It would seem that a coefficient of this magnitude, which approaches some of the highest we know, provides substantial evidence for a relationship between aptitude and aspiration.

Interests

There is a considerable amount of research on the relationship of vocational choice to interests, but it has been prompted by problems different from our concern with *why* the two variables are related, and, consequently, many of the studies which have been done are only indirectly relevant to our discussion. In particular, most of the studies have dealt with the relationship of *expressed* interests (Super, 1947; Super & Crites, 1962, p. 378), rather than choice, to *inventoried* interests and have used as measures of the former various kinds of ranking, estimating, and rating procedures. The purposes of these studies were generally either (1) to determine whether an interest inventory was "valid" by correlating it with expressions of interest or (2) to establish whether the two kinds of interests are interchangeable and one (usually expressed interest) could be used in vocational counseling in place of the other. As data accumulated on these two problems, it became increasingly apparent that expressed interests, because of their unreliability, were not adequate criteria for an interest inventory and also that expressed and inventoried interests are not highly enough interrelated to be considered interchangeable. Because the relationship of expressed interests to choice may also be only moderately high, indicating that the two variables are relatively distinct and unique, we are faced with the problem of deciding whether to review and summarize the findings on the agreement between expressed and inventoried interests as well as between the latter and choice.

If for no other reason than for comprehensiveness, it would seem advisable to discuss both kinds of research, but there are additional, and more compelling, reasons than this one. First, such a survey will allow a comparison of the respective relationships of choice and expressed interests to inventoried interests, and, second, it may suggest further research, not only on these relationships, but also on those which may obtain between choice and expressed interests. Consequently, in this section, which covers the relationship of choice to interests and the factors associated with this relationship, research on expressed interests is included.

Relationship between Choice and Interests. As the results of the research which will be reviewed here will bring out, the relationships of choice *and* expressed interests to inventoried interests are essentially the same, the correlations ranging in the .40s and .50s depending upon which interest inventory is used (see next section). To provide an overview of the studies which have been done on choice and interests and to have an organizational schema for their discussion, Table 6-13 was prepared. The studies are summarized as they have been classified according to the rows of the table:

1. *Choice.* The most conclusive data on agreement between choice and interests comes from two investigations, one being a follow-up of the other, conducted as part of the California Adolescent Growth Project. In the first study, Carter and Jones (1938) administered the SVIB to a group of 208 high school students, including 78 boys and 130 girls. This total group was subdivided into two smaller samples for purposes of analysis in the following way: (1) the SVIBs for 83 Subjects were scored for at least seven scales which were correlated with several other variables, whereas (2) the SVIBs for 125 Subjects were scored only for the single occupations chosen by them for a comparison of choice and interest. The results of the analyses for these two groups revealed three trends: First, about two-thirds (64.9 percent) of the total sample had SVIB letter ratings above "C" on the occupational scale which corresponded to their choice; second, only about one-third (34.8 percent) of the Subjects had C's or higher on scales which did not correspond with their choices; and, third, of those Subjects who had no choice, only a small percentage (25.5 percent) obtained scores above C on the SVIB. In other words, there was a definite tendency for choice to agree with interest when the

Table 6-13. Studies Which Have Investigated the Relationship of Vocational Choice and Expressed Interests to Inventoried Interests

	Strong Vocational Interest Blank	*Kuder Preference Record, Form C*	*Cleeton Vocational Interest Inventory*	*Lee-Thorpe Occupational Interest Inventory*
Vocational choice	Carter & Jones, 1938; Carter, Taylor, & Canning, 1941; Darley, 1941			
Ranked interests		Kopp & Tussing, 1947; Rose, W., 1948	Kopp & Tussing, 1947	Brown, M. N., 1951
Estimated interests	Arsenian, 1942	Crosby & Winsor, 1941		
Rated interests	Moffie, 1942; Berdie, 1950	Berdie, 1950		

selected occupation and SVIB scale were the same, as compared with when they were different or there was no choice.

In the second study, 73 boys and 73 girls out of the original group of 208 were followed up every year for three years between the tenth and twelfth grades (Carter, Taylor, & Canning, 1941). Table 6-14 summarizes the findings for each grade level by sex. The analyses were made in the same way as in the previous study: First, the percentage of the sample which had a vocational choice and which scored higher than a C on the cognate SVIB scale was computed; and, second, the percentage which had ratings greater than C on scales different from the chosen occupation ("Arbitrary Scales") was determined. As the data in Table 6-14 show, and as Carter et al. (1941, p. 305) concluded, "High school boys and girls, when tested with the Strong *Vocational Interest Blanks,* receive significantly higher percentages of *A* and *B* ratings on scales appropriate to vocational choice than when scored on arbitrarily-selected scales." Although not shown in Table 6-14, there was a definite tendency for the boys in the sample to obtain more A's and C's and fewer B's in the twelfth grade as compared with the others, indicating a crystallization of interest patterns as they grew older. This trend in their interest development accounts for the fact that the percentage of SVIB scores greater than C for the boys' chosen occupations decreased as they progressed through high school. The obvious sex differences in Table 6-14, with the girls having a considerably higher percentage of agreement between choice and interest than the boys, is discussed in the next section.

The only other study on choice in relation to interests is one reported by Darley (1941), in which he analyzed data on 1,000 clients who applied for counseling while in college. Using a two-way chi-square table, he classified choices according to their corresponding SVIB interest pattern, where the

Table 6-14. Summary of Results from a Longitudinal Study of Agreement between Vocational Choice and Interests *(Carter, Taylor, & Canning, 1941, pp. 298ff)*

		Chosen scales		*Arbitrary scales*	
Grade	*Sex*	*N*	$\% > C$	*N*	$\% < C$
Tenth	Boys	39	76.5	189	36.9
	Girls	38	73.1	224	33.3
Eleventh	Boys	45	81.8	154	30.6
	Girls	59	90.7	388	48.2
Twelfth	Boys	39	68.4	147	32.8
	Girls	43	91.5	316	46.3

NOTE: The *N*'s for "Chosen Scales" are less than the total sample sizes because some boys and girls had no vocational choice. The *N*'s for "Arbitrary Scales" are greater than total sample sizes because they include comparisons of choice with several SVIB scales.

latter was defined by the number of A's, B+'s, and B's in an occupational group, or according to the judgments of five out of six counselors, where there was no similar SVIB pattern. Contingency coefficients were then computed for various combinations of choices and no choices with primary, secondary, and tertiary patterns on the SVIB. The highest *C* value was .57 for the relationship between choices (excluding "no choice" cases) and primary interest patterns (excluding "no pattern" cases). This coefficient dropped considerably when other classifications of choices and interests were included, such as "choice–no choice" versus secondary SVIB patterns. For the less "pure" categorizations, the *C*'s ranged from .35 to .44. Darley correctly interprets these contingency coefficients to be "good" approximations to product-moment *r*'s, since they were based upon a large number of rows and columns in the chi-square table, but he nevertheless considers them to be indicative of rather low relationships between choice and interests. His conclusion stems, however, not from a concern with the theoretical significance of the association between the two variables, but with the problem (noted previously) of whether choices can be substituted for interests in counseling. If we view his results from the standpoint of their relevance for a theory of vocational choice, we must conclude that they support interest as a correlate of choice.

2. *Rankings of interest areas.* Kopp and Tussing (1947) asked three groups of high school students to rank the interest areas on the Kuder Preference Record, Form C, according to their preference for them and then determined the relationship of the rankings to those obtained by ordering their Kuder scores from high to low. A similar analysis was also performed on data gathered with the Cleeton Vocational Interest Inventory. The numbers of Subjects in the three groups were as follows: (1) 115 boys, 117 girls; (2) 45 boys, 46 girls; and (3) 120 boys, 163 girls. For the Kuder the overall correlations (*rho*'s) for the various groups were .59 (boys) and .53 (girls). In a similarly designed study, but with 60 veterans as the Subjects, Rose, W. (1948) obtained a median *rho* of .64 between rankings of occupations on 3- by 5-inch index cards and the corresponding interest areas on the Kuder. He found that about two-fifths of the *rho*'s for the Subjects in his sample fell between .50 and .74, and about one-fourth between .75 and .99. Approximately one-third were less than .50, and only three correlations were negative. Brown, M. N. (1951) also used a sample of veterans, but tested them with the Lee-Thorpe Occupational Interest Inventory rather than the Kuder or Cleeton. For 65 Subjects who were patients in a general VA hospital, he found a range of *rho*'s for the sample from −.35 to .99, with a median of .62. Thus, his results agree quite closely with those of Rose and are generally comparable to those reported by Kopp and Tussing, all of which indicate a moderately high relationship between ranked and inventoried interests.

3. *Estimates of interests.* Two studies have investigated the relationship between estimated and inventoried interests, one with the Kuder and the other with the SVIB. Crosby and Winsor (1941) had 222 male and female college students estimate their interests by marking a line on the Kuder profile sheet at the percentile rank at which they thought they would score. At the time of the study, the Kuder was scorable for seven interest areas, so that there were seven estimates and seven interest scores for each Subject which were correlated by the rank-difference method. The average *rho*'s obtained for the various Kuder scales were as follows: scientific, .48; computational, .56; musical, .58; artistic, .41; literary, .57; social service, .39; and persuasive, .62. For the entire sample, the mean *rho* across all scales was .54. Arsensian (1942) obtained results with the SVIB which indicated somewhat less agreement between estimated and measured interests, when the former were assessed by asking 360 college freshmen to predict how similar their likes and dislikes were to those of men in 27 different occupations. The corrected contingency coefficient (*C*) for a 5 by 5 table, in which one criterion of classification was "estimates" and the other was "scores," was .33. This value was based upon a 41 percent agreement of estimates with scores on the Subjects' five highest SVIB scales. Arsenian (1942, pp. 296–298) notes, however, that: "The chances of the students' stated occupational preferences falling among the five highest scores on the Strong Blank is considerably higher for the students' first choice than for any others." Thus, although the two investigations of estimated interests yielded coefficients of relationship which were not exactly the same, it seems reasonable to conclude that they are within the same range and indicate a moderate positive correlation between estimated and inventoried interests.

4. *Ratings of interests.* Rated and estimated interests are much the same, except that in the former some kind of graphic rating scale is used rather than a profile sheet with percentiles on it. Moffie (1942) designed rating scales for each of six SVIB groups which required the Subject to make a vertical mark on a horizontal line at the point most descriptive of his interest in the particular occupational field, the continuum ranging from "no interest" to "extreme interest." The rating was then quantified by scoring the response with a millimeter ruler which was placed along the horizontal line. The analysis consisted of the correlations between these rated interest scores and the scores on the cognate group scales for the SVIB. Moffie found that the coefficients, which were as follows, varied considerably from one group to another: I. Biological Sciences, .20; II. Physical Sciences, .36; V. Social Welfare, .23; VIII. Business Detail, .47; IX. Business Contact, .21; and X. Verbal, −.07. The average of these *r*'s, when computed from z transformations, was .33. Berdie (1950) obtained higher mean *rho*'s for both the SVIB and Kuder than this

value, probably because his rating scale was more appropriate, at least for the SVIB. He had 500 male clients, who applied for counseling at the University of Minnesota Student Counseling Bureau, rate the *similarity* of their interests to those of men in each of the SVIB groups, which he also keyed to the Kuder scales, rather than the *strength* of their interests, as Moffie had done. Since the SVIB measures similarity and not strength of interest, Berdie's procedure would seem to be the better one for this inventory. With this method, he found that the median contingency coefficient for the SVIB was .43 and for the Kuder was .52, but like Moffie he discovered that the *C*'s were higher in some groups and areas than in others. The highs and lows were different, however, in the two studies, with Berdie's highest correlations being in the Computational for the SVIB and in Verbal for the Kuder. Why these differences occur and what the factors are which affect the relationship of choice to interests are the topics of the next section.

Factors Associated with Relationships between Choice and Interests

Because the obtained relationships between choice and interests were not as high as originally expected, the *r*'s, *rho*'s, and *C*'s being in the .40s and .50s rather than the anticipated .70s and .80s, several investigators tried to identify other factors which might have been attenuating the correlations or which might account for their variation in magnitude between individuals, groups, and interest areas. Our concern here is with what these factors are and an evaluation of their effects:

1. *Type of interest inventory*. Berdie (1950) tested the hypothesis that the interest measure which is used in assessing agreement between rated and inventoried interests affects their intercorrelation. From an observation made by Paterson (1946) that the Kuder is more "transparent" and hence easier to fake than the SVIB, he reasoned that rated interests would agree more closely with the former than with the latter. And this is exactly what he found: as reported previously, the median *C*'s for the Kuder were about 9 correlation points higher. Berdie (1950, p. 48) concluded from his study that:

> In agreement with Paterson's hypothesis concerning the relative subtlety of the two tests, scores on the Kuder tend to have a closer relationship to self ratings of interests than do the scores on the Strong. This may be a function not only of the items in the tests but also of the categories used in grouping the scales and defining the self ratings, although these categories were achieved through careful study of both tests.

We can agree with the contingency proposed in this last statement of Berdie's, but not with his conclusion about it. It seems quite possible that, if he had used rating scales which assessed *strength* rather than *similarity* of interests, the correlations with the Kuder, which measures the former (Super & Crites, 1962), would have been even higher than they were. In any case, however, it seems justifiable to conclude that type of interest measure influences agreement between rated and inventoried interests, with the relationship being greater when the inventory is less subtle.

2. *Interest area.* Using Berdie's data, Sinnett (1956) attempted to find out why the degree of agreement between rated and inventoried interests varied from one interest area to another. His hypothesis was that the variation is a function of two factors: (1) the *temporal order of understanding jobs,* which he defined as the time in life when an individual acquires a realistic perception of a job; and (2) the *complexity of jobs,* by which he meant how simple and concrete their duties and tasks are. Sinnett had four judges rank the various interest areas, such as Social Service, Musical, and Sales, along these two dimensions and then correlated the rankings with Berdie's contingency coefficients for each interest area. The *tau*'s for the SVIB, which were computed separately for the Computational and Clerical areas, were (1) .50 and .61, respectively, for temporal order of understanding jobs and (2) .58 and .69, respectively, for complexity of jobs. For the Kuder, the *tau*'s were .16 for both temporal order of understanding and complexity of jobs. The relationship between these two variables, incidentally, was .87 (*tau*), which indicates that they define essentially the same dimension and that, in the opinion of judges, the first jobs about which individuals gain an understanding are the less complex ones. Sinnett (1956, p. 116) explained his differential findings for the SVIB and Kuder as follows: "The fact that higher relationships were found between the predictors and the data for the *Strong* may be due to the *Strong's* tapping identifications with a particular vocation, whereas the *Kuder* may be closer to the self-percept." This explanation would be valid, however, only if the variation between interest areas was the same for the two interest inventories, and it was not. The rank-order (*rho*) correlation between the magnitudes of the contingency coefficients across interest areas for the SVIB and Kuder, as computed by the writer from Berdie's data, is only .13. It is apparent, therefore, that it is not just differences in what these inventories measure which account for Sinnett's findings but rather other factors, which at present are unknown. Thus, the most that we can infer from his study is that the temporal order of understanding and complexity of jobs are related to differences between interest areas in agreement of rated and inventoried interests on the SVIB but not on the Kuder.

3. *Age and sex.* Several studies have investigated the effects of age upon the relationship of expressed interests (not choice) to measured interests and have established that there are none. Arsenian (1942) compared a group of Subjects

which overestimated their interests with a group which underestimated them and found "no reliable age difference between the groups." Similarly, Rose, W. (1948) concluded that "age appears to have little weight in determining the correlation" between ranked and inventoried interests. His 30 cases with the highest correlations were exactly the same in the number who were 24 years or older as his 30 cases with the lowest correlations. Likewise, in the study by Brown, M. N. (1951) of ranked interests there was no correlation with age, the r being .02 between age and interest agreement. In contrast to these findings on age, which are negative, the accumulated research on sex differences is more positive. As Table 6-14 shows, Carter, Taylor, and Canning (1941) found a definite tendency for the girls in their sample, when tested in the eleventh and twelfth grades, to have a higher percentage of agreement between their choices and interest scores than the boys. Just the opposite tendency has been reported by Kopp and Tussing (1947), however, who found slightly higher correlations for boys in three out of four comparisons on the Kuder and Cleeton. We are left, therefore, with the *fact* of sex differences in agreement between choice and interests but without a *conclusion* about their direction or magnitude.

4. *Intelligence*. The data on intelligence as a factor in the relationship between choice and interests is equivocal: some studies report positive correlations, whereas others report only negligible associations. Carter and Jones (1938), in the earlier investigation of their longitudinal sample, do not present any statistical results, but they conclude that the Subjects who had a choice, and thus tended to have letter ratings above "C" on the cognate SVIB scale, were "reliably brighter" than those with no choice. Wrenn (1935) also found that Subjects who were brighter had a higher degree of agreement between their choices and SVIB scores, the percentages being 45 percent for his high-IQ group and 22 percent for his low-IQ group. Crosby and Winsor (1941) obtained a *rho* of .42 between estimated and measured interests on the Kuder and intelligence, which is the highest relationship discovered in any of the studies. Arsenian (1942) interprets his data to indicate a difference between his over- and underestimators, but actually the value of t (1.20) which he reports is not significant. Finally, Brown (1951) correlated Otis IQs with an index of a Subject's ability to estimate his interests, but the *rho* was only −.11. The findings on intelligence, then, are far from conclusive: we need a carefully designed and executed study to clarify the extent to which an individual's general ability plays a part in the relationship of choice to interests.

5. *Personality*. Arsenian (1942) also compared his over- and underestimators on three of the four scales of the Bell Adjustment Inventory, but, as with intelligence, the differences were nonsignificant, although he concluded that they were systematic and meaningful. In a more recent study, Norell and

Grater (1960) analyzed differences between what they called high and low "interest awareness" groups on the Edwards Personal Preference Schedule (EPPS). They asked judges to decide which of the EPPS scales individuals with high "self-awareness" would score high and low on and then predicted that Subjects whose estimated interests agreed with their SVIB scores would be high in self-awareness as defined by the EPPS. Table 6-15 summarizes their predictions and their results, which show that there are significant differences at the .05 and .01 levels between the high and low "interest awareness" groups on only the EPPS Order and Succorance scales. Norrell and Grater (1960, p. 291) conclude, however, that:

> The differences between the measured needs of the two groups were in the direction predicted by the judges for each of the 12 scales. Expanding the binomial shows that making 12 accurate predictions out of 12 chances would occur only 1 time out of 4096 trials on the basis of chance alone. Thus, it was conclusively shown that needs which judges felt would limit self-awareness also limit the accuracy with which individuals are able to estimate their interests.

This interpretation of their results is questionable, because in 10 out of the 12 predictions the differences between the groups could be attributed to chance. A prediction is usually considered "accurate" in a study of this type only if the group differences are statistically reliable and in the hypothesized direction. Since only two predictions meet these criteria, and since the groups

Table 6-15. Predicted Differences between High- and Low-awareness Groups on the EPPS and Their Actual Mean Scores *(From Norrell & Grater, 1960, p. 291)*

Need	*Predicted direction for high-awareness group*	*Mean score for high-awareness group (N = 11)*	*Mean score for low-awareness group (N = 32)*	*t*
Achievement	High	13.82	13.59	.19
Deference	Low	10.73	11.92	.94
Order	Low	7.91	11.22	1.96†
Autonomy	High	16.00	15.03	.70
Affiliation	High	13.73	12.81	.84
Intraception	High	17.45	16.38	.65
Succorance	Low	7.54	11.50	2.50*
Dominance	High	17.64	17.25	.23
Abasement	Low	12.54	14.56	1.29
Nurturance	High	13.73	12.81	.92
Change	High	18.45	15.81	1.66‡
Heterosexuality	High	19.82	17.16	1.53‡

* Significant at 1 percent level.
† Significant at 5 percent level.
‡ Significant at 10 percent level.

were very small (*N*'s = 11 and 32), it is possible that even these predictions are due to chance (Type I error). Our best conclusion is, therefore, that personality variables have not been demonstrated to be factors in the relationship of choice to interests.

In addition to the factors which we have considered as possibly affecting the agreement of choice and interests, there have been several others which have been investigated, but not with any notable results. Bateman (1949) expected to find that high school students who had had work experience of one type or another would have a higher relationship between choice and interests than those with no work experience, but he found exactly the opposite tendency in two of the three secondary schools he studied. Mehenti (1954) related a number of presumed indices of vocational maturity to discrepancies between choice and interests, but was able to identify only a few differences between Subjects with high and low agreement. Finally, Wallace (1949) has studied such variables as (1) simulation of interest scores on scales appropriate to the chosen occupation, (2) extent of opportunity to gather information about occupations, (3) self-conflict, and (4) specific aspects of background and self-appraisal and has been successful in demonstrating relationships between some of them and expressed-inventoried interest congruency. All in all, however, most of the research on the factors which affect choice in relation to interests is either negative or inconclusive. About the only variables which seem to be significant are (1) the type of inventory used to measure interests and (2) sex.

Personality

Since Dodge's (1938; 1940; 1943) early studies of clerks, sales persons, and teachers, and even before (Fryer, 1931), there has been a lively interest in the relationship of personality to vocational behavior. Most of the pertinent research, however, has been on occupational differences in personality characteristics or vocational interests in relation to personality traits. Only recently, since approximately 1950, has attention been given to the hypothesis that personality plays a part in the determination of vocational choices. As a consequence, the literature on this problem has burgeoned during the past decade and a half. One of the most productive lines of investigation has been stimulated by the "self-concept" theory of Super (1951b; 1957; 1963), which has provided the conceptual frame of reference for at least 10 published studies, as well as several others which are currently in progress (see Chapter 5). As we shall point out in Chapter 14, one of the distinguishing characteristics of a "good" theory is its heuristic value, and Super's seems to be producing as much, or more, research than any other theoretical point of view. There has been a considerable amount of significant other work on personality as a correlate of vocational choice, however, and it is reviewed here as well. Thus, the discussion which follows has been organized according to the various aspects of personality which have been studied in relation to choice: (1) the self-concept; (2) ego processes; and (3) other variables, such as self-evaluation, utility for risk, values, and life goals.

The Self-concept. In one form or another, several studies have tested Super's (1951b, p. 92) hypothesis that: "In choosing an occupation one is, in effect, choosing a means of implementing a self-concept." Englander (1960; 1961) had female majors in elementary education ($N = 62$), another area of education ($N = 31$), and another field ($N = 33$) complete Q sorts of (1) items about "self" and (2) statements about elementary teachers. He found that the elementary majors had the greatest degree of congruency between the sorts and concluded that: "Individuals select or reject teaching in accordance to their respective perception of it as being compatible or incompatible with the self concept" (Englander, 1960, p. 263). Using a somewhat different approach, Morrison (1962) obtained corroborative results. For two groups of nursing ($N = 44$) and education ($N = 43$) majors, his findings indicated that Q sorts of self and "own occupation" were more congruent than for self and "other occupation." Similarly, Blocher and Schutz (1961) have reported that both "actual" and "ideal" self descriptions are more closely related to the occupations which twelfth-grade boys consider "most interesting" than to those they rank as "least interesting." They interpret these results to indicate that "claimed vocational interests are an outgrowth of attempts to develop and implement satisfying concepts of self in relation to the world of work" (Blocher & Schutz, 1961, p. 316). Oppenheimer (1966) has pointed out, however, that, although these findings generally support Super's hypothesis, they are based upon data gathered with standardized measures of the self-concept, rather than ones developed from the Subject's phenomenological field. With a modified version of Kelly's (1955) Role Construct Repertory Test to assess the latter, based upon the model proposed by Super et al. (1963; see Chapter 3), he, nevertheless, found that the two measurement procedures yielded essentially the same results: "People prefer occupations perceived as congruent with their self concepts" (Oppenheimer, 1966, p. 194). Thus, the evidence from a number of investigations, with different Subjects and different measuring instruments, generally supports the proposition that the self-concept is related to vocational choice.

Two further studies of the self-concept have related it to (1) choice with self-esteem as a moderator variable and (2) choice realism. In complementary analyses, Korman (1966) tested the general hypothesis that the relationship between the self-concept and choice holds for Subjects with high self-esteem but not for those with low self-esteem. His results supported this expectation, and he concluded that they provided "negative evidence for a simple 'match self to occupational stereotype' process in vocational choice" (Korman, 1966, p. 485). It should be noted, however, that he used *t* tests rather than analysis of variance for his group comparisons, and consequently he did not properly test for the interaction he hypothesized between self-esteem and the implementation of self in choice. In other words, it is possible that he obtained more significant differences between groups than he would have in the appropriate factorial design (Lindquist, 1953). In the other study, Anderson, T. B., and Olsen (1965) related the congruency between self and ideal self to realism of choice, on the expectation that Subjects who were more congruent would be more realistic. Their sample consisted of 96 male and female high school seniors who were classified as "realistic" or "unrealistic" in their choices, depending upon whether they had the aptitudes, as measured by the Flanagan Aptitude Classification Tests (FACT), requisite for the field and/or level of their chosen occupations. No significant difference was found between the realistic and unrealistic Subjects on the congruency of their self and ideal-self concepts. It can be concluded, therefore, that, although the self-concept appears to be related to vocational choice, this relationship may be a rather complex one, and it may not extend to the realism of choice.

Finally, four studies on changes in the self-concept and related choice or occupational variables have been reported, all of which have yielded generally positive findings:

1. Warren (1961, p. 164; italics in original) predicted that *"changes in college field of specialization, or college major, are likely to occur when a discrepancy exists between self concept and expected occupational role,"* but he found only that Subjects who made two changes of major field had *less* self-role discrepancy than those who changed just once, presumably because the former moved into a more appropriate field of study.

2. This interpretation is consistent with the findings of James (1965, p. 311) on two hypotheses he tested: (1) "each time an individual thinks of himself as a member of his chosen occupation, any incongruity he perceives between his self-expectations and his concept of persons in his chosen occupation will create pressure for attitudes toward both to change until congruity between them is attained"; and (2) "the more frequently these changes toward congruity occur, the more likely it will be that the changed attitudes will become permanent." His data, which were cross-sectional, supported both hypotheses, but, as he points out, the study should be replicated on longitudinal data before the results can be considered conclusive.

3. Stephenson (1961b) obtained follow-up, but not longitudinal, data on a large group ($N = 343$) of medical school applicants to determine whether their vocational self-concepts as physicians had crystallized before or after their

application for graduate training. Since approximately 80 percent of his Subjects eventually entered either medicine or medically related fields, despite being initially rejected by medical schools or failing in them, he concluded that "the self concept of the premedical student has crystallized prior to making application to a school of medicine" (Stephenson, 1961b, p. 216). This seems to be an overinterpretation of his data, however, since he did not actually measure the self-concept. It would be more accurate to say simply that medical school applicants tend to persist in medicine or related occupations.

4. Whether there are unequivocal relationships between self- and vocational concepts after occupational entry has not as yet been demonstrated, although there is some confirmatory evidence from a study by Schuh (1966). He found that "myself" and "my job" concepts were correlated on the Semantic Differential on two dimensions, evaluative and hastiness, but not on a third, aggressiveness, for two groups of college seniors followed up on the job.

Ego Processes. Since Ginzberg's (1951) study, there has been an increasing emphasis upon the role of the ego processes or functions in vocational choice. Developed from the id through identification with the parents, the ego encompasses the various adjustment mechanisms or habit patterns which the individual has acquired to mediate between the gratification of impulses and the fulfillment of social obligations and responsibilities. These modes of adjustment vary from one individual to another and supposedly have differential relationships to the selection of an occupation. Two studies have explored the part played by the ego processes in choice, each of them dealing with different aspects of how the individual goes about accomplishing the task of establishing an occupational goal which allows for the satisfaction of needs in a socially acceptable way:

1. A well-conceived and theoretically meaningful analysis of accounting and creative-writing students by Segal (1961) illustrates some of the relationships which must be delineated in order to make predictions about choice and ego processes from complex developmental antecedents. To simplify and summarize Segal's reasoning, Table 6-16 was prepared. It shows the associations which he deduced from psychoanalytic and ego psychology between the experiential and personality factors which seem to be involved in the choice of accounting and creative writing. Consistent with the generally accepted stereotypes of these occupations, Segal notes the conforming tendencies of accounting students, which appear to stem from their almost complete identifications with their parents, and the rebelling attitudes of the creative-writing students, which seem to arise from their inadequate identifications with their parents. As a result of these kinds of early parental identifications and related emotional learnings, different ego defenses are developed by the two groups and

***Table 6-16. A Summary of Segal's Descriptions of Accountants and Creative Writers** (1961, pp. 203–205)*

Vocational choice	*Occupational stereotype*	*Dominant personality characteristics*	*Early childhood development*	*Ego defenses*
ACCOUNTANT	"Financial detective"; alert, accurate, methodical, honest, persevering, dependent, economical, routine work, respected, "organization man"	Conforming: accepts social values, does not deviate from society's demands for accuracy, preciseness, and correctness	Willingness to sacrifice individuality for guarantees of parental love and affection, fearful of instinctual gratification with parents, severe supergo	Isolation, reaction formation, intellectualization
CREATIVE WRITER	"Free spirit," expression of feelings and emotions, talented, independent, "odd," "Bohemian"	Rebelling: indifference to and rebellion against social norms, concern with unrestricted creativity	Inconsistencies in parental behavior arouse frustrations, hypersensitivity to environment, search for people who can be trusted, fluid identifications, ill-defined self-concept, inability	Projection, repression, denial

are used by them to choose a compatible occupation. According to Segal, accounting students select their field as a vocation because it offers them an opportunity to conform to social expectations, as these are institutionalized in business practices and procedures, and to employ their main adjustment mechanisms in work, these being isolation, reaction formation, and intellectualization. Similarly, creative-writing students pursue their particular type of work because it allows them to be nonconforming and independent and to deal with reality as they will—through projection, repression, and denial. From these general hypotheses about the two groups, Segal made the specific predictions which are listed in Table 6-17 and tested them by comparing 15 accounting students with 15 creative-writing students.

To measure the variables specified in the hypotheses, such as "general adjustment level," "acceptance of social norms," "emotional control," and "hostility," Segal used seven cards of the Rorschach (cards V, IX, and X were omitted), the Bender-Gestalt, and a vocational autobiography, which asked the Subjects to trace the stages they went through in arriving at their choices. The tests of the hypotheses involved 30 variables assessed by these instruments, on which differences between the accounting and creative-writing students were found at the .05 level or beyond in 17 comparisons. As Table 6-17 shows, most of the hypotheses were supported or partially supported, and only one was

***Table 6-17. Segal's Hypotheses and Results** (1961, pp. 206–210)*

	Hypotheses	*Results*
1.	Accounting students and creative writing students show no differences in their general adjustment level.	*Supported*
2.	Accounting students show a greater acceptance of social norms than creative writing students.	*Partially supported.* On the Rorschach, accounting students reacted in a more practical and formal way, whereas creative writing students manifested more integrating and theorizing tendencies. There were no differences on the Bender-Gestalt.
3.	Accounting students show greater attempts at emotional control than creative writing students, while creative writing students show greater awareness of feelings and emotions.	*Partially supported.* Creative writing students expressed a greater number of emotions in response to the Rorschach, but not in a different way than the accounting students.
4.	Compulsive defenses are seen with greater frequency in the accounting students as compared to the creative writing students.	*Unsupported.* There were no differences between the two groups on the Rorschach and Bender-Gestalt indices.
5.	Creative writing students show greater expressions of hostility than accounting students.	*Supported.* The creative writing students were higher on Rorschach scales of both latent and overt hostility.
6.	Creative writing students show greater tolerance for ambiguity and greater ability to deal with complex, emotional situations.	*Supported.* Creative writing students used a greater variety of responses in reacting to the Rorschach and adjusted to the test initially more integratively.
7.	Signs of a more rigid, fearful identification are seen in accounting students as compared to a seeking for the completion of multiple identifications in creative writing students.	*Supported.* Creative writing students saw more human movement in the Rorschach inkblots and, in the Vocational Autobiography, referred less frequently to significant adults as influential in their career choice.

not supported at all. In those instances where there was partial or no support, the measuring instrument was the Bender-Gestalt, which Segal says may not be as appropriate for the study of normal Subjects as other devices. We might also question the use of the Rorschach and the way in which it was interpreted before we accept Segal's positive findings unequivocally, since the validities of this technique, and the signs derived from it, are not well established (Cronbach, 1949; Zubin et al., 1965). We could have greater confidence in the supported hypotheses if Segal had presented evidence on the validity of such indices as Davidson's (1950) adjustment score, Schneider's, S. F. (1953) hostility scales, and Wheeler's (1949) identification signs. Also, he accepts the interpretation of *M* as a "struggle for a self" (Hertzman & Pearce, 1947) rather than as a measure of "creativity" (Singer, 1955), without presenting an argument or relevant empirical proof. Thus, as with the studies of self-concept and choice, we must conclude that Segal's findings are provocative but far from definitive.

2. The other study of vocational choice and the ego processes is one with which we are already familiar from its discussion in Chapter 4. It is the investigation of compromise which was conducted by Small (1953), who compared the job-concept fantasies of better and poorer adjusted boys and found that they differed in the extent to which their first and second choices reflected "environment-involvement" or "environment-avoidance." In most of their fantasies about their first choices, which were the more realistic ones, the better-adjusted boys expressed needs, such as Order, Achievement, Recognition, and Affiliation, which would be integrative with respect to social expectations and mores if they sought to satisfy them. In contrast, the poorer-adjusted boys had significantly stronger needs, such as Inward Pain and Tension Discharge, which reflected their inadequate relationships to social realities and inability to compromise. In addition to these findings, however, which were consistent with theoretical expectations, Small also found certain "reversals" between the two groups. For the better-adjusted Subjects, these occurred in the needs for Acquisition, Impulse Restraint, and Asking, in which categories they scored higher in their first choice but not in their second. Similarly, the poorer-adjusted sample scored higher on Emulation, Impulse Release, Exhibition, Justification, Outward Pain, and Dependence in their first choice but not in their second.

Small says these reversals shed light upon the differential realism of the first and second choices of the two groups, but this is simply using one unexplained phenomenon to rationalize another. We still do not know why it is that on a *few* of the needs the score differences are not in the same direction for both choices. Also, it must be remembered that, although the second choice of the better-adjusted group was less realistic than their first, it was nevertheless *more* realistic than the first choice of the poorer-adjusted group (Chapter 4). Considering all these differences and the inconsistencies among them, it appears that there may be an artifact in Small's data which is not readily apparent. Otherwise, how can we account for the seeming contradictions in his findings? His *post hoc* explanations are not very satisfying, and there is no other evidence on the issues involved. Consequently, it would seem prudent not to put very much stock in the "reversals" which Small found in either choices or needs and to conclude simply that the better-adjusted Subjects expressed more "environment-involvement" needs in their first choices than did the poorer-adjusted Subjects.

Other Aspects of Personality. There are several other studies on personality in relation to vocational choice which deal with variables different from those already mentioned, although some conceptual connections with them can be discerned. These variables are the following: (1) self-evaluation and personality types from Holland's (1959; 1966b) theory of vocational choice (see Chapters 3 and 5); (2) "utility for risk" and decision-making abilities; and (3) values and life goals.

1. Three studies conducted by investigators other than Holland on his theory of choice have been reported, two on his "self-evaluation" hypothesis and one on his hypothesis relating personality types to occupational models. Schutz and Blocher (1961) tested Holland's prediction that there is a relationship between choice and self-evaluation, which encompasses "one's status needs, perception of level of competence and potential competence, and the self-estimate of one's worth with respect to others."[5] In a sample of 135 male high school seniors, they obtained an r of .34, significant at the .01 level, between (*a*) self and ideal-self congruency and (*b*) SVIB Occupational Level scores. They neglected to control for intelligence, however, and consequently the effects of this variable upon the correlation were not determined. That intelligence does influence self-evaluation and level of choice has been established in a further investigation of Holland's hypothesis by Stockin (1964), but he also found that intelligence does not account for all the variance in level of choice. He summarizes his results as follows: "When IQ ranks only are used to predict occupational level, only 57 'hits' are obtained; using intelligence plus self-evaluation, 82 correct predictions occur or an increase of 25 hits (15 percent greater accuracy)" (Stockin, 1964, p. 602). Thus, both of these studies lend support to the proposition in Holland's theory that level of vocational choice is a function of self-evaluation, as well as intelligence. Similarly, a study by Osipow, Ashby, and Wall (1966) provides evidence for the other major part of Holland's theory, viz., the relationship between personality types and field of vocational choice. These investigators found that, although some types were more highly related to choice than others, college students choose occupations consistent with their personalities. They also discovered that the relationship was stronger for students who were more certain about their choices.

2. Research on decision-making variables, such as "utility for risk," has increasingly interested vocational psychologists, but it has been largely disparate and unintegrated in its focus:

[5] For a study by these same investigators on Bordin's (1943) theory of vocational interests, see Schutz and Blocher (1960).

a. In one of the first studies of risk-taking propensities and vocational choice, Ziller (1957) obtained significant differences between Subjects who chose sales work (the "risk-takers") and those who were undecided, but Stone (1962) was unable to replicate these findings, although there were notable differences between the two investigations.

b. Dilley (1965) has reported the construction of a measure of decision-making ability and its relationships to intelligence, achievement, and participation in high school extracurricular activities. Since these variables have been shown to be correlates of vocational maturity (Super & Overstreet, 1960), he infers that decision-making ability, which was also related to them, is likewise a correlate of vocational maturity. This conclusion does not necessarily follow, however, because it is possible that decision-making ability and the other variables are correlated with different components of vocational maturity, which is presumably factorially complex (see Chapter 5).

c. A more direct study of the theoretical significance of decision making has been conducted by Harren (1966), who developed a *Q* sort from Tiedeman and O'Hara's (1963) delineation of the stages in the decisional process, in order to determine whether they actually exist and whether they are related to choice of college major and occupation. He found not only that the four stages enumerated by Tiedeman and O'Hara are present in the decision making of college students, but that there are probably several other stages as well.

d. Two other studies, in a different theoretical framework, viz., the achievement motivation model of Atkinson (1957; 1958; Atkinson & Litwin, 1960; McClelland, Atkinson, Clark, & Lowell, 1953), have established that risk-taking tendencies are related to both vocational aspiration and choice. Using the concepts of achievement motivation (approach tendency) and fear of failure (avoidance tendency), Burnstein (1963) and Morris (1966) have found that Subjects who are high on these variables, or on the difference between them (resultant motivation), aspire to or choose vocations of intermediate risk, as far as their probability of success in them is concerned.[6]

e. Finally, one other study should be mentioned in this context, although it did not deal directly with a decision-making variable. Blum (1961) devised a measure of the "desire for security," which not only correlated with high and low scores, respectively, on the Order and Change scales of the Edwards Personal Preference Schedule, but it also differentiated among groups of Subjects classified by the job setting they preferred, with the mean security scores for "Work for Self" and "Work for a Small Company" being lower than those for "Work in Civil Service" and "Work for a Large Company."

[6] See also Mahone's (1960) study of fear of failure in relation to choice unrealism, which is discussed in Chapter 7.

3. Although there have been several studies of occupational values reported in recent years,[7] only a few of these have provided data on the relationship of this aspect of personality to vocational choice. The most comprehensive analysis of the problem has been made by Rosenberg (1957), who collected questionnaire data on three large samples of college students, one of them selected to be representative of eleven universities throughout the country. The general design of the survey was to determine whether there were differences between vocational choice groups in their average value hierarchies and what the relationships of certain personality orientations were to choice. The principal findings indicated that students choose vocations which are generally compatible with their values. Thus, those who planned to enter architecture, journalism-drama, and art ranked highest in "self-expression–oriented" values; those who were headed for social work, medicine, and teaching ranked highest in "people-oriented" values; and those who selected real estate–finance, hotel-food administration, and sales-promotion ranked highest in "extrinsic-reward–oriented" values. Likewise, Rosenberg found that there were similar differences among choice groups on such variables as "faith in people," "self-confidence," and "self-other" attitudes. These findings are generally consistent with those of Astin and Nichols (1964) who found marked differences between 36 career fields of 1965 National Merit Subjects in five factored areas of life goals: Personal Comfort, Scientific Contribution, Prestige, Altruism, and median expected income after 10 years in the world of work. The question which arises in the interpretation of such studies as these is: How different are their results from those on the relationship of choice to interests? It may well be that values and interests are essentially the same variable (Super & Crites, 1962) and consequently would be similarly related to choice.

THEORETICAL VARIABLES

In addition to stimulus, organismic, and response variables, psychologists often write about and use, in both their research and theory building, what have been referred to as "hypothetical constructs" and "intervening variables." What is meant by these concepts, however, despite their currency in psychology, is difficult to specify, since they have been given several different definitions (Tolman, 1936; 1950; Mac Corquodale & Meehl, 1948; Bergmann, 1953; Ginsberg, 1954; Bechtoldt, 1959; Spence, 1960). Because there are divergent opinions about the nature and value of theoretical variables, it might seem to be unduly hazardous to proceed with a discussion of their relevance for the conceptualization of vocational choice phenomena, particularly when knowl-

[7] See: Dipboye and Anderson (1959); Glick (1964); Gribbons and Lohnes (1965b); Miller, C. H. (1956); Singer and Stefflre (1954a; 1954b); Sprinthall (1966); Thompson, O. E. (1966); and Wagman (1965).

edge of the empirical laws which govern the latter are often fragmentary or unreliable rather than well established, as they should be for theory construction (Bergmann & Spence, 1941). If we are cautious to define what we mean by these concepts and select appropriate studies to illustrate how they can be utilized in vocational psychology, however, such a review might not only clarify existing constructs, but it might also stimulate the accumulation of the raw data which are needed as a basis for further theoretical formulations.

Hypothetical Constructs

Let us start with hypothetical constructs and define them generally as *concepts which summarize the relationships between two or more response variables.* An hypothetical construct need not refer to anything more than the empirical relationships between behaviors, which are sufficient for the definition of this type of concept. It does not necessarily represent some nonobservable entity or state or condition within the organism, although such interpretations are often made of such hypothetical constructs as the "mental" factors extracted from the intercorrelations of ability tests and the "ego" processes inferred from adjustive behavioral syndromes (Cronbach & Meehl, 1955). Rather, an hypothetical construct is a convenient conceptual tool for integrating and summarizing behaviors which are independently definable but which bear some systematic relationship to each other. For example, Bernardin and Jessor (1957) subsumed such related behaviors as (1) reliance upon others for approval, (2) reliance upon others for help or assistance, and (3) conformity to the opinions and demands of others, each of which was assessed by a different experimental procedure, under one hypothetical construct which they called *dependence.*

To illustrate the use of an *hypothetical construct as a correlate of vocational choice,* we can cite a study by Minor and Neel (1958, p. 40) who tested the following three hypotheses about achievement motivation in relation to level of preference ("choice" in our terminology):[8]

1. There is a significant relationship between a person's *n* Achievement score and the prestige rank of his occupational preference.
2. There is a difference as to the ranking of occupations between those subjects with very high, those with moderate, and those with very low *n* Achievement scores.
3. There is no difference as to the suitability of the preferred occupation for each subject between those in the very high, moderate, and very low *n* Achievement groups.

[8] Hammond (1654; 1956; 1959), Bendig and Stillman (1958), Astin (1958), and Crites (1961a) have reported studies of other motives which may be related to choice, but these investigations seem to be more pertinent to a discussion of vocational motivation in relation to job adjustment, which is presented in Chapter 9.

Achievement motivation was defined as "competition with a standard of excellence" and was conceived to encompass many phases of an individual's "activities, interests, social contacts, physical endeavors, [and] accumulation of goods" as well as his vocational goals and objectives. It was measured in accordance with procedures developed by McClelland, et al. (1953), which assess achievement motivation through analysis of an individual's fantasies as elicited by TAT-like pictures. These investigators have reported that *n* Achievement scores derived from ratings of a Subject's imagery are related to a variety of relatively distinct efficiency types of behavior, such as college grades (with aptitude held constant), rate of performance, and rate of learning. Thus, achievement motivation defined in this way qualifies, at least provisionally, as an hypothetical construct. The only limitation is that the behaviors which it subsumes, such as grades and rate of learning, might be more highly correlated than they are.

The results on the relationship of achievement motivation to vocational preference (choice) supported two of the three hypotheses proposed by Minor and Neel. With respect to the first hypothesis, a *rho* of .74 was found between *n* Achievement scores and the prestige level of preferences in a group of 50 male veterans. In other words, the higher the achievement score, the higher the prestige level of the Subject's chosen occupation. The second hypothesis was not supported by the data: there was no evidence of differential prestige rankings of occupations from one level of achievement motivation to another. Finally, the third hypothesis was confirmed. There was a statistically significant tendency for Subjects who had moderate or low levels of achievement motivation to choose occupations which were more consistent with their age, education, intelligence, and financial resources. Stated somewhat differently, Subjects with high achievement motivation had less realistic vocational choices.[9]

Although this study serves our purpose of illustrating how an hypothetical construct can be related to vocational choice, its findings should be interpreted conservatively for two reasons. First, as Minor and Neel themselves point out, they failed to control for the effects of intelligence upon the correlation between achievement motivation and prestige level of choice. Since intelligence is related to both variables (McClelland et al., 1953; Stubbins, 1950), it is quite possible that it produced the correlation between them. Second, because the term achievement *motivation* is used to label this particular hypothetical construct, there is the danger of concluding that it is, therefore, a motivational variable and that, as such, its relationship to choice affords some evidence in support of the need theories of vocational choice. As Farber (1955) has noted, however, it has not been demonstrated that McClelland's *n* Achievement scores measure a variable with motivational or drive properties. The studies which

[9] Cf. Mahone (1960).

were available at the time of Farber's review could be interpreted as showing only that the imagery-derived achievement scores were related to other associative tendencies and did not necessarily either energize behavior or produce learning (Brown, J. S., 1961). This is not to say that an hypothetical construct cannot have motivational qualities, which it can if it fulfills the appropriate criteria, but only to make clear that the construct of achievement motivation in Minor and Neel's study is not necessarily a motivational one.

Intervening Variables

In contrast to hypothetical constructs, intervening variables can be defined as *concepts which summarize the relationships between two or more stimulus and response variables.* These kinds of concepts are introduced because of some observed disproportionality between stimulus conditions and the responses which organisms make to them. By "disproportionality" is meant a condition in which a change (or a constancy) in one variable is not reflected directly in the other. For example, we may vary the value of a stimulus and obtain either no concomitant variation in response or only a partial variation. Or, we may record a variation in response when there is either none in the stimulus or only a partial one. To establish the existence of a disproportional relationship between stimulus and response variables, it is necessary to demonstrate first that the form and/or magnitude of the relationship changes under different conditions, e.g., variations from occasion to occasion, from task to task, or from situation to situation. As Spence (1960, p. 86) has noted with respect to the use of intervening variables in the explanation of learning phenomena, "the objective is to introduce a set of concepts which, in combination with the experimental variables and the particular initial and boundary conditions of the environment and the organism, will provide for the deduction of the many different, specific empirical relations that are found in the several kinds of learning situations."

Studies which exemplify the use of an *intervening variable as a correlate of vocational choice* are difficult to find. Only one investigation would seem to approximate the conditions necessary to introduce an intervening variable as an explanatory concept. Merwin and DiVesta (1959) designed an experiment in which they analyzed the choice of teaching as a vocation under conditions of positive and negative reinforcement. From a total sample of 67 Subjects who had chosen teaching as a career and 151 Subjects who had not, Subjects were randomly assigned, within the two choice classifications, to three experimental situations, each of which involved listening to a 14-minute tape-recorded communication. Group 1 heard a *positive* communication on "teaching is a good career because it satisfies the achievement need"; Group 2 listened to a *negative* communication on "teaching is a good career because it does not involve satisfaction of the achievement need"; and Group 3 was exposed to a *control* communication on "going to college." Before and after the experiment, all Subjects completed a rating scale on the extent to which they perceived teaching as an occupation which would satisfy their needs for achievement. In addition, in a pretest they rated the strength of their needs for Achievement, Affiliation, Dominance, and Exhibition on two different Likert-type scales, the results of which indicated that the teaching group had greater Affiliation needs, whereas the nonteaching group had stronger Achievement, Dominance, and Exhibition needs. The purpose of the study was to determine whether positive and negative communications about teaching as a source of achievement-need satisfaction would produce changes in the perceptions of this occupation as an achievement-need satisfier.

The results showed that the positive communication, i.e., "teaching satisfies achievement needs," produced a change in the perceptions of both the teaching and nonteaching groups in the direction of viewing teaching as a means for satisfying achievement needs. In contrast, the negative communication, i.e., "teaching does *not* satisfy achievement needs," brought about a change in perceptions of teaching as an achievement-need satisfier only in the group with nonteaching choices. There were no changes in the control group. Thus, the Subjects with teaching as a choice responded in the same way as Subjects with nonteaching choices to the positive communication but not to the negative communication. In other words, there was a disproportionality in their response to the positive and negative stimuli as compared with the responses of the nonteaching group. In short, we have here a situation in which the postulation of an intervening variable to account for the disproportionality would make sense. Merwin and DiVesta (1959, p. 407) do not interpret their findings in this manner, although they come close when they conclude that "subjects accept information more readily when the information coincides with their existing, or initial, convictions."

The connection which these investigators do not make is between the differences in the needs of the two groups and their differential reactions to the positive and negative communications. It seems likely that the teaching group, which had stronger Affiliation than Achievement needs, would *not* change its perception of teaching as a satisfier of the latter under conditions of negative communication, because their achievement needs were less prepotent in their need hierarchy (Roe, 1956) than their affiliation needs. In other words, the important consideration to them was that teaching would satisfy their affiliation needs, *not* that it would *not* satisfy their achievement needs. If they learned that teaching would fulfill their achievement *as well as* affiliation needs, however, as they did under the positive communication, then it seems equally probable that they would change their perception of teaching in the direction of seeing it as a satisfier of achievement needs. Thus, we can posit as an intervening variable the differences between the two groups in the strengths of their affiliation and achievement needs.

We should hasten to point out, however, that this interpretation is not complete as it is now formulated. At this stage of the analysis, it is only a *post hoc* explanation of the results from Merwin and DiVesta's study: the intervening variable which supposedly accounts for the data is also defined by the data. As Spence (1960, p. 62) has noted, to establish the generality of an intervening variable concept, the concept must be employed to make predictions to new data and be supported by them. It might be hypothesized, for example, that if the differences in the affiliation and achievement needs of the teaching and nonteaching groups constitute an intervening variable, then we might expect that the Subjects who chose teaching would remain in education only as long as their affiliation needs were being satisfied or until their achievement needs became prepotent over their affiliation needs. Admittedly, it would be difficult to test such an hypothesis because of the measurement and design problems involved, but it will only be to the extent that they can be solved that research and theory on the correlates of vocational choice will progress from a largely descriptive exploratory stage to a more deductive explanatory stage.

7

PROBLEMS IN VOCATIONAL CHOICE

We have discussed the process of what might be termed *normal* vocational choice, but, with the exception of Ginzberg's (1951) and Lo Cascio's (1964) analyses of certain variations and deviations in vocational development (see Chapter 5), we have not given systematic consideration to the problems which may arise in making career decisions. This chapter, which is divided into four sections, deals with what these problems are and how we might better understand their nature and etiology. The first section reviews and evaluates the various classification or diagnostic systems which have been devised for the definition of vocational problems. The second proposes a new schema for identifying problems in choice, which has been designed to be more comprehensive, objective, and generally usable than the older ones. The third presents an analysis of the problem of indecision in vocational choice and covers theory and research on the factors which seem to contribute to the inability of some individuals to select an occupation. And the fourth summarizes what we know about the problem of unrealism in vocational choice, focusing upon its origins and extent and interpretation. Thus, this chapter can be seen as the concluding one on the process of vocational choice and as a transitional one to the next part on the dynamics of vocational adjustment, since the problems which arise during adolescence in the choice of an occupation are often directly related to the difficulties an individual experiences in adjusting to the world of work (see Ginzberg et al., 1951, Chapter 15).

SYSTEMS FOR DEFINING VOCATIONAL PROBLEMS

Most of what we know about the problems which arise in the vocational choice process comes from observations and inferences made in counseling young people who are attempting to decide upon which course of study to follow or which occupation to enter. It is not surprising, therefore, that the systems for defining vocational problems which we shall discuss in this section often refer to the counseling situation and its content, rather than to everyday decision-making activities and dilemmas, and frequently cite case studies of clients to illustrate and delineate a particular type of problem. Furthermore, the systems generally encompass more than the diagnosis of vocational problems, dealing with difficulties in other areas of life functioning as well, i.e., the educational, financial, personal, and social. Consequently, in order to describe and explain the diagnostic systems clearly and understandably it will be necessary to present most of them in their entirety. The main emphasis, however, will be upon how they conceptualize and define vocational problems. For purposes of discussion, the systems have been grouped into three categories: (1) sociological, (2) psychological, and (3) general. All the major systems which have been proposed for the identification of vocational problems are included in these classifications.

Sociological Definitions of Vocational Problems

The term "sociological" is not a particularly apt one for these diagnostic systems, because they focus upon the psychological problems of the individual as well as his relationships to social institutions, but they have been referred to previously in this way, and it would seem to be less confusing to retain the designation than to change it here. It was originally used by Bordin (1946, pp. 173–174), who wrote as follows:

> Examination of this diagnostic system indicates that primarily it represents an attempt to describe the individual in terms of his adjustment to the demands of his environment. . . . This type of description might be termed a sociological description of the individual which starts at the individual describing the organization of his behavioral characteristics and predicting what his reactions will be to his social environment.

As applied to vocational choice behavior, this means that an individual's problem is analyzed with respect to the difficulties he is experiencing in coping with the social expectation, as translated into a developmental task during adolescence, that he select an occupation for his life's work.

Sociological definitions of vocational and other types of problems were first formulated by Williamson and Darley (1937) who enumerated the following kinds of difficulties which are typically encountered by college-level students: financial, educational, social-emotional-personal, family, physical or health, and vocational. Williamson (1939b) later revised this list, elaborating upon the nature of vocational problems as follows:

1. *No choice.* Williamson (1939b, p. 428) writes about this problem:

> When given opportunity to record or to declare their vocational choice, students may state that they have none or that they are unable to make a choice. Many students will not have any clear idea as to possible choices of interest to them. Other students will have one or more preferences but will be unable to choose from those preferences.

This definition of "no choice" closely parallels the one which we formulated earlier (Chapter 4) and highlights the fact that some individuals cannot discriminate sufficiently among occupations, for whatever reason, in order to select one as their choice.

2. *Uncertain choice.* Williamson (1939b, pp. 428; 406) distinguishes between this problem and "no choice" by the criterion that a choice has been made but the individual has doubts about it. He cites as an example the student who seeks confirmation of his decision making from an authority figure, such as an instructor or counselor. Uncertainty may also be resolved through tryout experiences, however, as in the case described by Ginzberg (1951, p. 123) of the student who ignored the problem of making a vocational choice and concentrated upon obtaining an education until rather late in his vocational development, at which time he decided to major in economics after having taken a course in this field which he liked very much.

3. *Unwise choice.* Williamson (1939b, pp. 458–459) identifies several subtypes of unwise choices, all of which, he notes, involve a disagreement between the individual's abilities and interests, on the one hand, and the requirements of the occupation which he selects, on the other. Illustrative of this type of problem are the following:

> Students with insufficient or no evidence of specialized aptitudes often choose goals requiring primarily the specific ability which they lack. Included in this category are students who begin engineering training despite a record of persistent difficulty, and sometimes failure, in mathematics courses.
>
> Students with no appropriate claimed or measured interests often choose occupational goals entirely foreign to their real ambitions because of family pressures or because of the supposed financial advantages of an occupation. . . .
>
> Occasionally students, especially boys, choose, or find it necessary to accept occupational goals which require less scholastic aptitude then they possess. These include many of the large number of "good college risks" who never go beyond high school or even drop out of high school.

In each of these problems, the individual's vocational choice is ill-advised or unrealistic because either or both his aptitudes and interests do not support it.

4. *Discrepancy between interests and aptitudes.* At first glance, this problem category may appear to be only a special case of the preceding one, but it is actually different. In unwise choice, it is assumed that the individual's interests and aptitudes are consonant with each other and that his choice is what deviates from expectation, whereas in discrepancy between interest and aptitudes there is some disagreement in the type and/or amount of these two variables. Williamson (1939b, pp. 442–443) delineates three kinds of discrepancies: (1) interest in an occupation for which the individual has insufficient ability; (2) interest in an occupation below the individual's ability level; and (3) interests and abilities at the same level but in different fields. The rationale for this problem category is that discrepancies between interests and aptitudes may eventually result in poor vocational adjustment: too much or too little aptitude for a job at a given interest level, or aptitude in a field different from the field of interest, may lead to job dissatisfaction, job failure, or both (Latham, 1951; Lipsett & Wilson, 1954).

Using the concepts of field and level of vocational choice, Hahn and McLean (1955, p. 51) have suggested that Williamson's problem categories can be translated into five possible patterns of choice:

1. No choice.
2. Appropriate field–appropriate level.
3. Appropriate field–inappropriate level.
4. Inappropriate field–appropriate level.
5. Inappropriate field–inappropriate level.

These combinations of field and level make clearer what the possible problems in choice may be, and they bring out the fact that the anchor point for defining any problem in choice should be "appropriate field–appropriate level," which Williamson does not include in his system. It should be recognized, however, that Hahn and McLean's schema is very general and does not include some of the problems which are in Williamson's system, such as uncertain choice and some of the subtypes of unwise choice.

Psychological Definitions of Vocational Problems

Bordin (1946) has evaluated and criticized Williamson's problem definitions by applying three criteria which he argues an adequate set of diagnostic constructs should meet. First, the definitions of behavioral problems should lead to a greater understanding of what the difficulty is which an individual is experiencing and why it has occurred—in other words, what the "causes" are which produced it. To give an example, if we can classify a person according to a diagnostic category with respect to *some* of his symptoms and expressed concerns, then the category is a good one to the extent that it affords both a fuller description of the problem and a basis for prediction of other behaviors. Second, the categories in a diagnostic system should be independent of each other. That is, information about individuals who have been classified into one category should not provide a better-than-chance probability of making inferences about the characteristics of persons who have been classified into a different category. This does not mean, however, that the problem categories should necessarily be mutually exclusive. As Bordin (1946, p. 172) points out: "We could no more expect this than we should expect that there will be no individuals who have measles and whooping cough or any other combination of diseases at the same time." Finally, as far as counseling practice is concerned, the diagnostic categories should be related to differential treatment processes. If a client is diagnosed as having an educational problem, then this problem categorization should suggest a different type of counseling process than that which would be followed if he had a vocational problem.

From an analysis and appraisal of Williamson's diagnostic system with these three criteria, Bordin concluded that definitions of problems based upon the sociological locus of an individual's difficulties are inadequate. First, the categories do not give a fuller understanding of a person's problem because they have little predictive value. In an unpublished study which Williamson and Bordin conducted at the Student Counseling Bureau of the University of Minnesota, they found that "various characteristics of the individuals were not predicted so much by the single classifications, except for vocational, as by various combinations. In other words, again it looked as though there was some more basic classification which might be somewhat reflected by the present ones" (Bordin, 1946, p. 175). Second, as a result of the same study, Bordin concluded that the Williamson categories are not independent. The possible exception was the "vocational" category, into which 23 percent of the client sample with no other problems was classified, but even it combined with the "educational" category in 27.7 percent of the cases. In all, there appeared to be a fairly high frequency of occurrence of two or more problem categories together. Bordin (1946, p. 175) observed that: "These results would appear to suggest strongly that there is a deeper level of analysis than is represented by these categories. It suggests that these categories would appear in the relation of surface symptoms to a set of categories representing a deeper level of analysis." Finally, according to Bordin (1946, p. 174), the sociological categories do not point to unique ways of assisting clients who have different problems:

> Some individuals who present vocational problems or education problems or financial or personality problems might be helped by giving them information. Yet others who present difficulties in the same area must be dealt with in terms of their feelings. Thus, the

> assignment of the individual's difficulties to one of this set of classes of difficulties does not provide a basis for prediction of the relative success of different treatments.

Convinced that there were more basic psychological categories into which the problems of relatively normal individuals could be analyzed, Bordin proceeded to develop a system of diagnostic constructs which was based upon the observation of clients over extended periods of time and upon answers to the following questions: "Why cannot this individual work this thing out himself? What is stopping him from being able to find a satisfactory solution? How is he different from his fellow students who appear to be facing the same problems and working them out successfully for themselves?" (Bordin, 1946, p. 176). Answers to these questions, in conjunction with concepts drawn from developmental and social-role theories of personality, led to the formulation of five problem categories:

1. *Dependence.* Some individuals encounter difficulties in "growing up" and becoming "psychologically weaned," and as a consequence they rely heavily upon others for direction and guidance. Rather than making decisions for themselves, whether they be vocational, educational, financial, or whatever, dependent individuals ask others what they should do.

2. *Lack of information.* Unlike individuals who are overly dependent, usually because of arrested or retarded psychological development, persons who lack information, either about themselves or the world of work, can make decisions, but they have not had the necessary environmental experiences to do so.

3. *Self-conflict.* Into this category are classified individuals who have a "conflict between the response functions associated with two or more self-concepts or between a self-concept and some other stimulus function" (Bordin, 1946, p. 178). One illustrative case would be the adolescent boy who is a superior student and who also excels at football. Whichever way he sees himself or whichever role he plays, he must attempt to reconcile the conflict stemming from special stereotypes which exist between the concepts of the "intelligent weakling" and the "dumb athlete."

4. *Choice anxiety.* Individuals who are confronted with two or more alternative solutions to a problem which are equally unattractive or punishing are classified into this problem category. Whatever course of action the individual elects to follow, he is "in for it." Bordin cites as an example the returning veteran who wants to go to college, but whose wife would have to work and sacrifice her education if he did. To take a job, however, even with the opportunity for some on-the-job training, would mean settling for an ultimately lower socioeconomic position in life and possibly the persistent dissatisfaction which stems from unfulfilled aspirations.

5. *No problem.* The last category in Bordin's system is comparable to Hahn and McLean's "appropriate field–appropriate level," which was mentioned earlier. The individual has made a realistic choice but needs reassurance that it is the best one for him.

In an empirical study of the incidence and correlates of Bordin's diagnostic constructs (see discussion to follow), Pepinsky (1948) renamed one of the original problem categories, further analyzed and elaborated upon another, and added a new one to increase the system from five to eight categories. He changed the name of Bordin's No Problem category to Lack of Assurance, which more adequately connotes the meaning of this type of problem and which serves to distinguish between individuals who seek counseling in order to verify their decisions and plans and those who accomplish this either on their own or with nonprofessional assistance. He subdivided the Self-conflict category into three different types of conflict problems, the definitions depending upon the elements or factors which are incompatible with each other. These include: Cultural Self-conflict, which involves limitations and restrictions placed upon the individual by his environment or culture group; Interpersonal Self-conflict, which is precipitated by the criticisms of others, notably the parents, concerning an individual's goals and objectives; and Intrapersonal Self-conflict, which arises within the individual as a result of competing response tendencies to play desired and imposed roles. Finally, upon the suggestion of another psychologist (Dr. W. W. Cook), he added a category to Bordin's system—Lack of Skill. This type of problem encompasses any deficiency or difficulty in the proficiencies which are necessary to reach a goal, assuming that the individual otherwise has sufficient aptitude and has decided what he wants to do. Included in this category are problems in reading, mathematics, study habits, study procedures, speech, social manners, and personal appearance.

Additional changes in Bordin's constructs have more recently been proposed by Byrne (1958) who has pointed out that neither the original system nor Pepinsky's revision of it, both of which were developed on college samples, is applicable to the problems which are characteristic of high school students. Bryne (1958, p. 184) further observes that "the constructs proposed in the late forties describe a counselee's problem still too much at the psychological periphery as far as cause of the problem is concerned." Consequently, he has proposed the following modifications and additions to the Bordin-Pepinsky problem definitions:

1. *Immaturity in situation.* This category corresponds to Dependence in the earlier systems but is seen by Byrne as a broader problem construct which includes reliance upon others along with a general fixation on behavior appropriate for an earlier age but not for present situations.

2. *Lack of problem-solving skill.* This category is restricted to only skill deficiencies in the solution of problems and excludes the so-called "teachable" skills, e.g., reading, study technique, etc.

3. *Lack of insight.* This category, in combination with the following one, replaces the Self-conflict constructs. Byrne defines lack of insight as a problem in self-understanding (with no further elaboration).

4. *Lack of information.* This category is the same as before, except that its comprehensiveness has been increased as has been indicated.

5. *Lack of assurance.* No change in this category.

6. *Domination by authority person or situation.* This is a new category suggested by Byrne (1958, p. 186) which he describes as follows:

> A major source of difficulty in a pupil's making a choice, plan, or adaption is the existence of a situation, usually including one or more persons, which prohibits him from making the choice, plan, or adaptation. The persons in these situations are able to force the pupil to unwanted action, or to deny him action he wishes to take, because of their authority position, and this means their potential or actual use of force.

Here the emphasis is upon interpersonal conflict, much as in the Interpersonal Self-conflict category of Pepinsky's system. Byrne excludes Choice Anxiety from his schema, because he rightly interprets anxiety as a symptom, rather than a cause, of a problem and concludes that a category based upon such a condition has little diagnostic utility.[1]

General Definitions of Vocational Problems

The problem diagnostic systems which we have just discussed are essentially unidimensional as far as the bases for defining categories are concerned. They use either the sociological locus of a problem or the psychological factors which appear to have been the causal ones in the development of a problem, usually as inferred from the life histories of a sample of clients who have undergone counseling, as the definitional criteria. By combining or adding to these criteria, however, it is possible to devise a more comprehensive and general system for the definition of vocational and other types of problems and to relate the system more readily to other variables, particularly those which are involved in the counseling and choice processes. There are two diagnostic systems which have been formulated which illustrate this approach.

As a result of his research on communication and relationship in counseling, Robinson, F. P. (1950, p. 167) found that there was a definite need to devise a set of diagnostic constructs which would not only provide informa-

[1] For a critical comment upon Byrne's proposals, see Gilbert (1958).

tion about the content and causes of an individual's problem but which would also reflect differences in "the dynamic interaction of client and counselor." The differences in interaction in which he was interested have reference to such aspects of the counseling process as amount of client talk, degree of client insight, division of responsibility between client and counselor, working relationship between client and counselor, and degree of acceptance of client by counselor. In a first attempt to develop appropriate problem categories which might be differentially related to these process variables, Robinson classified the problems presented by clients during their interview sessions into a fourfold discussion unit system which included the following: study-skill, vocational-guidance, therapy, and scholastic-question topics. A study of the correlations of these categories to "average responsibility" and "average talk ratio" revealed, however, that they all involved "thinking things through." Consequently, using the client-counselor interaction as the criterion, they were lumped together to define one type of problem, despite their manifest differences in content and possible causes.

Eventually, from empirical analyses such as this one, Robinson evolved a set of three broad problem categories which could be related to different kinds of counseling techniques and goals:

1. *Adjustment problems.* This category was subdivided into nonemotional and emotional difficulties in order to distinguish between problems which had to be treated by providing needed information and aiding recall, on the one hand, and by accepting and interpreting suppressions and repressions of painful feelings and experiences, on the other. Problems in vocational decision making were classified as primarily nonemotional, whereas various kinds of intra- and interpersonal maladjustments were considered emotional.

2. *Problems of skill.* Included in this category were not only the traditional deficiencies in reading and similar skills, but also inefficiencies in problem solving and higher-level adjustment techniques. By the latter, Robinson means those modes of adjusting to life which allow the individual more adequately and enjoyably to fulfill his potentialities and contribute to society. Thus, he might further develop his "readiness to adjust" by learning how to relax more effectively, how to engage in truly "re-creative" avocational activities, how to establish lasting and rewarding friendships, how to gain fuller insights into his own and the world's characteristics, and how to increase his social and emotional maturity.

3. *Immaturity.* This category includes the dependence problems mentioned by Bordin and Pepinsky, but it also encompasses other aspects of development. Robinson (1950, p. 172) writes that "the end goal of mature attitudes should be larger than mere independence. Thus the mature individual is characterized by independence, self-acceptance, a consistent philosophy of life, social

responsibility, etc. An adolescent progressing along the pathway to such maturity may display problems of dependence, overconscientiousness as to the opinion of others, religious or moral worries, egocentrism, etc." This definition of "immaturity" is similar to the one proposed by Byrne, but is probably even more comprehensive in the sense that Robinson conceives of maturity as more than the absence of fixations and regressions—it has the positive connotation of attaining a higher-level adjustment to adult life.

In an effort to further conceptualize and elaborate upon these diagnostic constructs, Robinson, F. P. (1963) has synthesized them with various categories proposed by others and has added new ones of his own. In this classification system, he distinguishes between "remedial" problems, which arise because of deficiencies and/or disabilities in the individual, and "developing strengths," which involve the constructive use of the individual's potentialities. With respect to the latter, Robinson (1963, p. 329) makes these comments:

> Personality integration, self insight and acceptance, educational and vocational planning, and philosophy of life are illustrative of several aspects of developing strengths in personal adjustment. Cooperation and loving are two positive aspects of relating to others that are different from reducing conflict with significant others. In the area of knowledge emphasis is given to competence rather than broad achievement primarily to emphasize an aspect which is more apt to come from individual rather than from class work.... Independence, civic and family responsibility and an idiosyncratic but extensive range of interests are examples of growing maturity.... In a skill deficiency the student has a notion of what are better levels of performance and he is motivated not to appear too deficient. On the other hand, few even among superior adults will have picked up any higher-level skills through self-instruction so the student has little idea of what is possible....

Other than his mention of vocational planning, as an aspect of developing strengths for personal adjustment, Robinson does not explicitly link his schema with the process of vocational development, but two areas of it, maturity and knowledge, would seem to be particularly relevant. Moreover, the general concept of developing strengths corresponds to Super's idea of "synthesis" and explicates the processes which may be involved in normal, as contrasted with delayed or impaired, vocational development.

Much as Robinson used several variables to design a system of diagnostic constructs, Berezin (1957) has combined the sociological categories of Williamson with the psychological concepts of Bordin to derive a two-dimensional classification of problems which covers both content and causes. The content categories are the usual ones of (1) emotional, (2) educational, and (3) vocational, but the causal categories, although based upon the older diagnostic schemata, are more comprehensive:

1. *Intrapersonal conflict* (INTRA): conflict between self-motives
2. *Interpersonal conflict* (INTER): conflict in motivations between self and significant others
3. *Environmental conflict* (EC): conflict between the self and the culture, society, or situation
4. *Developmental* (D): lack of experience
5. *Lack of skill* (S)
6. *Lack of understanding of self* (LUS)
7. *Lack of information* (LI)
8. *Self-actualization* (S-A)

Taken together, these content and causal categories make up a 24-cell schema for the classification of almost any problem which might be defined. Apostal and Miller (1959) have developed a manual from Berezin's schema for use in counseling, with some changes in the number and names of the categories, but otherwise it is essentially the same system, simplified for everyday applications.[2]

Research on Definitions of Vocational Problems

Despite the importance that has been attached to the diagnosis of vocational and other types of problems in the individual's adjustment and development, there is only a small body of empirical evidence available for the evaluation of the systems which have been proposed. Some of the research which has been done has already been discussed in presenting the various problem schemata, e.g., Williamson and Bordin's unpublished study of the former's sociological constructs and Robinson's findings on the relationships of the traditional categories to counseling process variables. The studies which remain to be reviewed were designed, at least in part, to follow the recommendations of Bordin and Pepinsky for what might constitute an "ideal" set of problem categories. We have mentioned the three desiderata suggested by Bordin: (1) A diagnostic system should identify the "causes" of problem behavior; (2) it should include only categories which are largely independent of each other; and (3) it should indicate which treatment process is the best one for a given type of difficulty. In addition to these criteria, Pepinsky (1948, pp. 11–12) has proposed two others: (1) Diagnostic categories should be as inclusive as possi-

[2] For a further discussion of the use of this diagnostic system in counseling activities and research, see the papers by Callis (1965), Shepherd (1965), Johnson, R. W. (1965), and Borresen (1965).

ble—they should cover a wide variety of problems; and (2) diagnostic categories must lead to consistent and accurate classification of problems—one person should be able to categorize a sample of cases in essentially the same way on two different occasions, separated in time long enough to preclude the effects of memory, and two or more persons should agree to a fairly high degree in their independent diagnoses of the same cases. The research which is summarized in the following paragraphs, however, deals only in a limited way with these various aspects of the incidence, reliability, and validity of diagnostic constructs and does not deal at all with their relationships to differential treatment or counseling processes.

Sociological Definitions. In addition to the informal study by Williamson and Bordin of the frequency of occurrence and overlap of the original content categories, there is one other investigation of these problem definitions which has been reported. Darley and Williams (1950) read the case folders of 490 men and 341 women clients seen for counseling during 1 year and classified them in accordance with Williamson's categories, a distinction being made between major and minor problems. The results of this analysis are presented in Table 7-1, where it is seen that for both men and women the most frequently diagnosed problem was "educational," with "vocational" next highest in occurrence for men and "personal-social-emotional" for women. For both sexes family problems ranked fourth in order of incidence. Only a few cases had "no problem areas of major significance." The predominance of "educational" problems in this list is striking, but Darley and Williams offer no explanation of why they were the source of major concern to the clients in the

Table 7-1. Percentages of Clients with the Various Types of Problems in Williamson's Diagnostic System *(Darley & Williams, 1950, p. 99)*

Diagnosed problem area	*Percentage of men*	*Percentage of women*
Major financial problems	15.5	9.7
Minor financial problems	26.5	13.5
Major educational problems	63.3	42.8
Minor educational problems	29.8	41.4
Major vocational problems	28.4	8.2
Minor vocational problems	52.2	57.8
Major personal-social-emotional problems	18.4	26.1
Minor personal-social-emotional problems	31.8	30.8
Major family problems	14.5	19.4
Minor family problems	25.3	23.2
Major physical-health problems	4.3	7.3
Minor physical-health problems	9.0	17.0
No problem areas of major or minor significance	5.3	17.6

study. One reason may be, however, that the sample was not a representative one. All the Subjects were enrolled in the General College, which offered a 2-year curriculum on a somewhat lower prestige level than the regular university, and 54.7 percent of the men and 21.9 percent of the women applied for counseling because they wanted to transfer out of the General College. Consequently, the picture which we get of the problems of college students from Darley and Williams's data may be distorted by the atypical nature of their sample, which was evidently concerned or dissatisfied with their educational status.

Psychological Definitions. The major study on diagnostic constructs as interpreted from a psychological point of view is the one which was conducted by Pepinsky (1948) on Bordin's system. This investigation was based upon 115 clients with nondebilitating problems of simple maladjustment, and it yielded results on three aspects of the diagnostic constructs described previously: (1) the extent to which judges were able to agree upon their classification of clients according to the problem categories; (2) the degree of uniqueness or distinctiveness of the problem categories; and (3) the aptitude, interest, and personality correlates of the problem categories:

1. Pepinsky reports two kinds of data on interjudge agreement in the use of the diagnostic constructs: the agreement for each category and the agreement for all categories. With respect to the former, he found that the highest degree of agreement among three judges was only 31 percent for the Lack of Assurance category and dropped to as low as 13 and 15 percent for Cultural Self-conflict and Dependence, respectively. The percentages were somewhat higher for two judges, but they still tended to cluster in the 40s and 50s. As far as agreement on all categories is concerned, three judges concurred in only 15 to 20 percent of the cases, and two judges made the same classifications 22 to 37 percent of the time. Although there is no way by which to translate these percentages of agreement into reliability coefficients, it is clear that they are quite low and fall considerably below the standards for accuracy of measurement that we set for tests.

2. The uniqueness of the problem definitions is also indicated by two types of evidence. First, there is the average number of categories used per case by the judges, which was 2.3 when Self-conflict was considered as a single category and 2.7 when it was subdivided, Choice Anxiety being omitted in both instances because of too few cases. Second, there are the data on the extent to which any one category was used in conjunction with one or more others in making a diagnosis, which showed that Lack of Assurance, Lack of Information, and Lack of Skill were relatively independent, but that the other categories were rather highly interrelated. Thus, it would appear that a set of

eight problem definitions is not very parsimonious and should be reduced for theoretical as well as practical purposes.

3. To determine the correlates of the diagnostic constructs Pepinsky compared, by means of chi-square and t tests, the clients in a given category with all others, regardless of their problem, on a variety of tests including the American Council on Education Psychological Examination, the Cooperative Achievement Tests, the Minnesota Personality Scale, and the Strong Vocational Interest Blank. Of the 784 comparisons which were made, only 227 or 29 percent were significant at the .05 or .01 levels. Pepinsky discusses the differences which he found with respect to each category, but they did not follow any discernible pattern and were often difficult to rationalize. The one variable which appeared to consistently differentiate the categories was what might be termed a *general maladjustment factor*. Cases diagnosed as Lack of Assurance were definitely better adjusted than those classified as Intrapersonal Self-conflict, 76 percent of whom manifested some evidence of maladjustment. The remaining categories tended to fall between these extremes. That there were no other dimensions along which the categories might be aligned may be a result of the fact that the low interjudge reliabilities placed an upper limit upon the magnitude of their possible relationships to other variables.

The only other study which has been done on the Bordin constructs has yielded essentially the same disappointing findings as Pepinsky's, despite its more sophisticated design and measuring instruments. Sloan and Pierce-Jones (1958) had four judges independently rate, on a 5-point scale, the extent to which each of 64 clients exhibited the characteristics of the Bordin-Pepinsky problem types. From the data thus obtained, they determined degree of interjudge agreement for the four raters, which ranged from a high of 40.3 percent for Intrapersonal Self-conflict to a low of 25.0 percent for Lack of Information. The overall percentage of agreement for the categories was 26.5. The interrelationships of the categories were fairly high, with Intrapersonal Self-conflict occurring in conjunction with other kinds of problems 38 out of 119 times (32 percent). The most independent category, other than Choice Anxiety which had very few cases in it, was Dependence which occurred in conjunction with other constructs only 5 out of 119 times (4 percent). A comparison of each category with an unselected college norm group on the Minnesota Multiphasic Personality Inventory (MMPI) revealed several differences, but as in Pepinsky's study there was no meaningful pattern of personality traits which seemed to characterize clients in the different problem categories. There was evidence again, however, of differentiation along a general maladjustment dimension. Cases with Lack of Information as their problem deviated from the norm group on only the *Mf* scale of the MMPI, their score indicating greater interest in ideas, language, and people than in material things, whereas cases with Intrapersonal Self-conflict or Interpersonal Self-conflict differed from the norms on seven MMPI scales, including *D, Hy, Pd, Mf, Pa, Pt,* and *Sc* (all scores were greater than $T = 58$). Thus, it would appear that individuals with problems which are more vocational in nature (e.g., Lack of Information) tend to be better adjusted than those with personal problems, a conclusion which has been independently corroborated by other studies (Gaudet & Kulick, 1954; Goodstein, Crites, Heilbrun, & Rempel, 1961).

General Definitions. Robinson (1950) gives little indication of the reliability and validity of his diagnostic categories, aside from the fact that they correlate with certain process variables in counseling, but Berezin (1957) reports fairly comprehensive data on her two-dimensional problem-classification schema. She had judges in both a research and a service setting apply her system to cases with which they typically worked and obtained results which were fairly consistent from one setting to the other. With the "content" categories (vocational, etc.) there was a high degree of agreement in classification: the three research judges agreed on 75.8 percent of their diagnoses, and the service judges concurred 72.5 percent of the time. The findings on the "causal" categories (INTRA, etc.), however, were not as encouraging: perfect agreement within the two groups of judges was reached in only 27.6 (research) and 37.3 (service) percent of the cases. The percentages of multiple categorizations, which indicate the degree of intercorrelation among categories, were essentially the same as those obtained in the study by Sloan and Pierce-Jones (1958). INTRA and INTER occurred together in 28.81 and 36.0 percent of the cases classified by the research and service judges, respectively, and LUS in conjunction with all others was used 22.1 and 31.4 percent of the time by the two groups of judges, respectively. Analyses of the interrelationships of the content and causal categories showed that the most frequent "causes" of vocational problems were Lack of Understanding of Self, Lack of Information, and Interpersonal Conflict. To the extent that these results are stable, which is largely a function of the reliability of Berezin's diagnostic system, they appear to be congruent with current theory on the relationship of vocational adjustment to other areas of life functioning (Super, 1957, Chapter 22; see also Chapter 8) and with observations made in counseling practice on the etiology of vocational problems.

A NEW SYSTEM FOR DEFINING VOCATIONAL PROBLEMS

With the possible exception of Williamson's definitions of problems in occupational orientation, most of the systems of diagnostic constructs deal with the difficulties which arise in vocational decision making more or less indirectly and superficially. No attempt has been made to develop a comprehensive classification system for defining vocational problems. Even Williamson (1939b, p. 404) writes, in commenting upon his categories of No Choice, Uncertain Choice, Unwise Choice, and Discrepancy between Interests and Aptitudes, "Undoubtedly there are many additional problems which beset students who seek to choose appropriate vocational goals." He goes on to point out the need for consideration and analysis of such problems as those faced by young people who have multiple-patterned interests and who, as a result, are undecided about their vocational choices. We might add to Williamson's observations that the available research on vocational choice problems, being as negative as it is, also suggests the desirability of further conceptualization and investigation of the how and why of deviant decision-making processes. Consequently, in this section we shall summarize some of the difficulties which have arisen in defining vocational and other types of problems and, using what conclusions can be drawn as a basis for revisions of existing schemata, propose a new system of vocational-problem constructs which promises to be more reliable, internally consistent, and comprehensive.

Critique of Existing Systems for Defining Vocational Problems

One of the major shortcomings of the diagnostic systems which we have reviewed has been their *unreliability*. Almost without exception, the outstanding finding on the constructs proposed by Williamson, Bordin, Pepinsky, and Berezin has been that judges cannot independently classify clients according to the constructs and attain an acceptable degree of agreement on their categorizations. One of the reasons for such low interjudge agreement may be that none of the systems provides very explicit rules for the definition and identification of problems. A question about even using judges can be raised, however, if it is possible to specify what all the definitional criteria for a particular type of problem are and to enumerate what their various combinations in degree and kind are. For example, Stephenson (1961a) has introduced a pattern-analysis method for the SVIB which lists all the possible combinations of scores for interest groups with varying numbers of occupational scales. To pattern-analyze a SVIB one simply compares the obtained pattern in each group with the possible ones for primary, secondary, and reject interests. The procedure is wholly objective, with no margin for error, and, consequently, it is perfectly reliable. If a similar approach could be taken to the definition of vocational problems, unreliability would no longer be a variable which would affect diagnoses.

A second drawback of existing systems is that their categories are not *independent* and *mutually exclusive*. An individual may be classified into two or more categories simultaneously, and, consequently, a correlation between problem types is built into the diagnostic systems. An example from Williamson's (1939b) categories is the student who chooses an occupation above his aptitude level (Unwise Choice) and who also has interests at a higher level than his aptitude (Discrepancy between Interests and Aptitudes). Similarly, in the other systems an individual may be diagnosed as having more than one problem, the average number of problems per person ranging between two and three (Berezin, 1957; Pepinsky, 1948; Sloan & Pierce-Jones, 1958). To eliminate multiple classification from these systems it is necessary to use a different combination of defining criteria for each type of problem. Thus, to pursue the example from Williamson's categories, if both a person's choice *and* his interests disagree with his aptitude, then he would be classified as having a problem different from either Unwise Choice or Discrepancy between Interests and Aptitudes. In other words, for the categories in a diagnostic system to be independent and mutually exclusive, the criteria of classification must be unique for each problem.

A third problem with the available diagnostic systems is that they are not necessarily *exhaustive*. By this characteristic of a classification system is meant whether all observed cases can be categorized. If they cannot, then the system is restrictive and less than adequate for several reasons. First, its applicability is obviously limited, as Byrne (1958) has pointed out with respect to the Bordin-Pepinsky constructs which were developed on a college population and which are not wholly appropriate for use in diagnosing the problems of high school students. Second, its reliability may be adversely affected, particularly if diagnoses are made by judges. If all possible categories for the classification of a case are not available to the judges, then they may be forced to classify a case with a problem not included in the system into an inappropriate category. To the extent that they do this, in a presumably random fashion, their percentage of agreement will be lowered. Finally, if a system is not exhausative, its empirical meaningfulness or significance may be reduced. The usefulness of a system of problem categories is ultimately a matter of its statistical relationships to other variables. If the constructs do not correlate with other behaviors, conditions, or treatment processes, then there is no reason to use them. And, they will not correlate extensively with other variables, if they cover only a limited range of problems.

Criteria for Defining Vocational Problems

The primary reason that the diagnostic systems of Williamson, Bordin, Pepinsky, and the others are less than adequate with respect to the characteristics of categories which we have just discussed is that they are not based upon *explicit definitional criteria*. None of the systems identifies in operational terms the dimensions along which the problems of individuals are to be diagnosed. They give only general descriptions of the diagnostic constructs, rather than specific statements about the kinds and degrees of variables which are the relevant ones for the definition of a particular problem. If we were to base a diagnostic system on certain selected variables, however, we could then make an exhaustive enumeration of their possible combinations and arrive at a set of problem categories which would have the objective attributes we are seeking. First, assuming that the variables we use can be measured in some standard way, i.e., by tests, inventories, questionnaires, etc., the categories they would form would be highly reliable, since a case could be classified solely in terms of his test scores—judges would not be necessary. The only source of unreliability would be the error variance of the measuring devices. Second, the categories would necessarily be mutually exclusive and hence independent, because, given an individual's scores on the defining variables, he could be assigned to one and only one category in the system. For example, if he had high scores on variables x and y, he would be classified differently than if he had low scores on both x and y, a high score on x and a low score on y, a low score on x and a high score on y, or any other possible score pattern. And, third, the categories would be exhaustive, again because they are constituted by all possible combinations of the criterion variables.

The task now is to select some appropriate variables for the definition of vocational problems. Two of the most likely and reasonable variables for this purpose would seem to be *aptitudes* and *interests*. Not only are they measurable with standard instruments, but they are (1) largely independent of each other, (2) relevant to vocational choice, and (3) valid predictors of future vocational behavior. Any classification schema which is multidimensional is more efficient to the extent that the variables which constitute its dimensions are unrelated. Since aptitudes and interests are essentially orthogonal (see Chapter 2), they would form a categorical system which would be truly two-dimensional. Also, a system based upon the aptitude and interest dimensions would be relevant to the vocational decision-making process. As we saw in the last chapter, there is considerable evidence which indicates that both aptitude and interest are related to choice. Furthermore, there is a wealth of research which shows that both aptitude and interests predict eventual level of attainment in the occupational hierarchy as well as persistence in an occupation over a long period of time (e.g., Clark & Gist, 1938; Strong, 1943; Super & Crites, 1962). These findings, in conjunction with others on agreement among aptitudes, interests, and occupation in relation to job satisfaction and success (Latham, 1951; Lipsett & Wilson, 1954), provide us with an empirical base for defining vocational problems in terms of the agreement of choice with aptitude and interest.

To define agreement operationally, the classification schema shown in Figure 7-1 was adapted from Roe (1956) and modified in accordance with the

Roe levels	Measured aptitudes general population percentiles	I. Service	II. Business contact	III. Organization	IV. Technology	V. Outdoor	VI. Science	VII. General cultural	VIII. Arts and entertainment	Roe groups
		V.	IX.	VII. VIII, XI	III, IV	IV.	I, II	X	I, VI	SVIB
		Social service	Persuasive	Clerical, computational	Mechanical	Outdoor	Scientific	Literary	Artistic, musical	KPR
1	99									
2	91									
3	90 / 76								Stage scenery designer	"Adjusted" choice
4	75 / 50									
5	49 / 26									
6	25 / 1									

Figure 7-1. Worksheet for defining vocational problems. *(After Roe, 1956.)*

Minnesota Occupational Rating Scales (Paterson, Gerken, & Hahn, 1953) and research on aptitude and interest tests (Science Research Associates, 1960; Kuder, 1960; Strong, 1943). The interest groups on the SVIB and the interest scales on the Kuder Preference Record (Form C) have been classified according to the field category in Roe's schema which seems to be most appropriate. In some instances, the same SVIB groups were assigned to more than one Roe category, because they included occupations from different fields, such as Artist and Architect in the SVIB Biological Science group. For the Kuder, it was not necessary to use a scale more than once, but it should be noted that both the Artistic and Musical scales are keyed to Roe's Field VIII—Arts and Entertainment. Along the aptitude dimension, Roe's levels have been equated with percentile ranges which may be obtained from any measure of general aptitude. These percentiles were derived from the Minnesota Occupational Rating Scales and seem to be satisfactory, with one exception. They must be adjusted to the intelligence and/or educational level of the sample which is being diagnosed. For an unselected high school sample, they would not introduce any distortions, but in a college group, which is more select as far as ability is concerned, the percentile ranks obtained from the aptitude measure would have to be revised upward. Thus, a college freshman who stood at the 25th percentile on college norms would be at approximately the 50th percentile on general population norms. Consequently, in Figure 7-1 his "actual" aptitude level would be in the 3 and 4 range rather than the 5 and 6 range. Note that "interest level," as might be measured by the Occupational Level scale of the SVIB, has not been incorporated into the system as a criterion variable, because it applies to only this interest inventory and also because it was found to place too many restrictions upon the classification of choices.

Use of the New System

To use the new system for defining vocational problems it is necessary to have (1) a measure of an individual's general aptitude, as yielded by tests like the American College Test battery composite or the Ohio State Psychological Examination total score, (2) his interest pattern as assessed by either the SVIB or the Kuder, and (3) his vocational choice, as elicited by a questionnaire such as Trow's (see Chapter 4). With Figure 7-1 as a worksheet, the first step is to locate the individual's aptitude level according to the percentile rank of his test score, making any adjustments which are necessary to equate it to general population norms (most test manuals have conversion tables which can be used for this purpose). The second step is to determine whether he has an interest pattern and what it is if he has one. For the SVIB, Stephenson's (1961a) pattern-analysis procedures can be used as can Callis's (1954) coding technique for the Kuder. If there is no interest pattern, a notation indicating this should be made in the cell which cites the name of the interest inventory used (SVIB or KPR). If there is a single or multiple interest pattern, the appropriate interest group should be marked in some way, e.g., with a check. For the Kuder, only significantly high scores are considered. The final step is to "plot" the individual's vocational choice in the appropriate aptitude-interest cell, using Roe's (1956) occupational classification system. If the choice is not included in her system, then a judgment must be made about where to classify it. Given an accurate description of the occupation, however, as can be found in the *Dictionary of Occupational Titles,* such judgments can be made with a high degree of accuracy (Moser, Dubin, & Shelsky, 1956).

Once the individual's aptitude level, interest pattern, and vocational choice have been plotted on Figure 7-1, the extent of agreement among these three variables can be determined. With respect to aptitude, the choice is at the level required by the occupation, or it is above or below it. Similarly, the choice is in the appropriate interest field, or it is not.[3] Depending upon the extent to which the individual's choice agrees with his aptitudes and interests, we can identify what his vocational problem is. The possible problems which can arise in making a choice will be listed here under the three major divisions of adjustment, indecision, and unrealism.

Problems of Adjustment

1. The *adjusted* individual's choice is in the field of his interest and is on the appropriate aptitude level. He may have a multiple interest pattern, but his choice agrees with at least one of the patterns. In effect, he has "no problem" (Bordin, 1946), although he may come for counseling because he "lacks assurance" (Pepinsky, 1948).

2. The *maladjusted* individual's choice neither agrees with his field of interest nor with his level of aptitude. The problem here is one of complete disagreement among the variables involved in the decision-making process.

Problems of Indecision

1. The *multipotential* individual has two or more choices, each of which agrees with his field of interest and is on the appropriate aptitude level. He may have a multiple interest pattern, but his choices must be consistent with one of the patterns. His problem is that he cannot decide among these alternatives.

2. The *undecided* individual has "no choice." He may also have no interest pattern, a single or multiple pattern, and aptitude at a high, average, or low

[3] On the SVIB, an individual may sometimes have an A or B+ on the occupation of his choice, but no primary or secondary in the same interest group. When this happens, his interests and choice are considered to be consistent, regardless of interest patterns in other groups. (See discussion to follow for an example.)

level, but regardless of his status on these variables, the fact that he cannot state which occupation he intends to enter in the future is what defines his problem.

3. The *uninterested* individual has at least one choice (he may have more than one) which is on the appropriate aptitude level, but he has no patterned interests.

Problems of Unrealism

1. The *unrealistic* individual's choice agrees with his field of interest, or there is no interest pattern, but it requires a level of aptitude that is higher than his tested level.

2. The *unfulfilled* individual's choice agrees with his field of interest, but it is on an aptitude level which is below his measured capability.

3. The *coerced* individual's choice is on the appropriate aptitude level, but is not congruent with his field of interest. Although his problem may appear to be one of adjustment or indecision, it is listed here because a choice has been made. What makes it "unrealistic" is its being in the wrong interest area. Strong (1955) has found, for example, that if an individual enters an occupation for which he does not have appropriate interests ("C" on the SVIB), the chances are about 5 to 1 that he will eventually change to another occupation.

Figure 7-2 has been designed to show the various vocational problem categories and how they are defined.[4] For a given category, the shaded areas indicate which variables agree or disagree with each other and what the combinations are. For example, in the "coerced" category the chart shows that the measured aptitude of the individual agrees with the aptitude required by the occupation of his choice, but his measured field of interest disagrees with that of his choice. Similarly, for the other categories, the pattern of agreement-disagreement among the defining variables can be determined from an individual's test and questionnaire data, and his vocational problem can be identified accordingly.

To illustrate the use of the system, suppose we have the following data on a male college freshman and want to determine his vocational problem:

1. *Aptitude:* 75th percentile on Ohio State Psychological Examination total score, manual norms for college freshmen
2. *Interests:* primaries in the SVIB Technical and Business-contact groups, with "A's" on Artist and Architect in the Biological Science group
3. *Choice:* stage-scenery designer

[4] The writer is indebted to Dr. Richard J. Brunkan for conceptualizing this diagram.

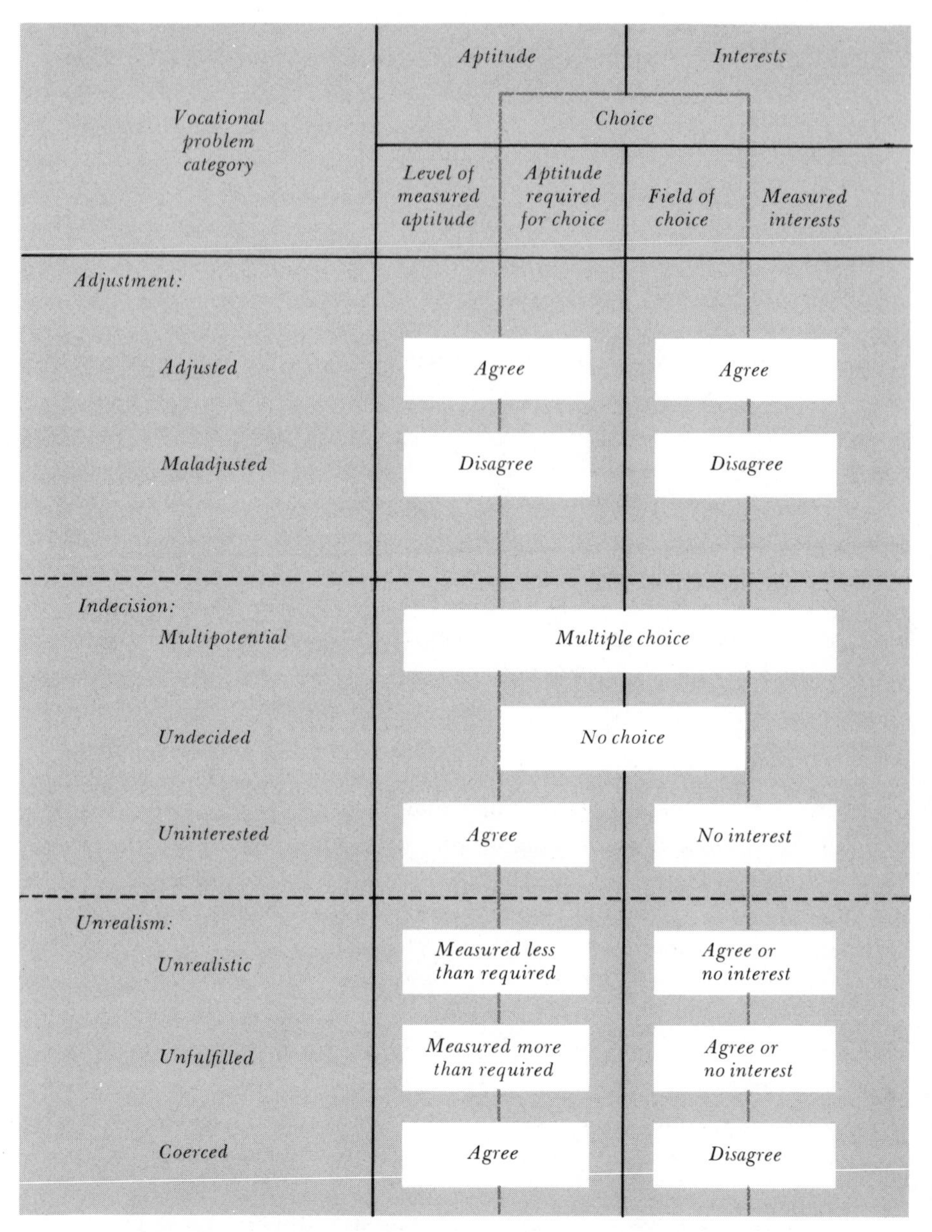

Figure 7-2. Definitions of the vocational problem categories.

The first step would be to locate his aptitude level, which in terms of general population norms would be at approximately the 90th percentile and which would put him at Roe's Level "3" in Figure 7-1. The second step would be to identify his field of interest. He has a multiple primary pattern, but the A's in Artist and Architect are most congruent with his choice, although certainly the Technical and Business-contact patterns are complementary, the latter being relevant if he eventually becomes a producer. Thus, his interest field would be Group VIII—Arts and Entertainment. We would also classify his choice in this field at Level "3" where "designers" are listed, probably checking the categorization with the job description in the *Dictionary of Occupational Titles* (Volume I) for "stage-scenery designer." Once we have made these decisions, his vocational problem can be determined. In this case, since the individual's choice agrees with both his aptitude and interest, he would be classified in the *adjusted* category.

Limitations of the New System

The foregoing example highlights some of the limitations of the proposed system for defining vocational problems, because it is evident in this case that not all the significant factors in the choice of stage-scenery designer as a vocation have been taken into consideration. In particular, the individual's special artistic ability, which is rated at a required A level in the MORS for this occupation, was not included as a variable in appraising the adequacy of his choice. Also, the individual's personality, financial resources for training, and military service commitments were not assessed in deciding whether he had a vocational problem. Likewise, no evaluation of employment opportunities was made. In other words, it should be clear that the system has limitations, that, in particular, it utilizes only two criteria, aptitude and interest, for the definition of vocational problems. These factors are critical in making a satisfactory choice, however, and their use as the primary dimensions for the system provides a baseline for the identification of difficulties in the individual's vocational decision making.

Research on the New System

Although we know that the proposed system has mutually exclusive and independent categories, which permit an exhaustive classification of cases, a considerable amount of research must be done before we can have confidence in the empirical utility and worthwhileness of this approach to the definition of problems in vocational choice. The base rates for the problem categories in samples of clients and nonclients should be computed, so that *norms* can be compiled and infrequently used categories can either be combined with others or possibly eliminated. Also, studies of the *validity* of the system should be conducted. The content validity of the categories is well supported by the defining procedures, and the concurrent validity of the categories could only be established by relating them to judges' ratings, which they are designed to replace, but their construct and predictive validities need to be investigated. As far as the construct validity of the categories is concerned, it would be interesting to relate them to certain laboratory tasks which involve conflicts comparable to those which we might hypothesize as underlying the different types of vocational problems. For example, we might predict that "undecided" individuals would have longer reaction times in responding to an "avoidance-avoidance" conflict pattern on a light board than unselected Subjects (Sarbin & Jones, 1955) or that "unrealistic" persons would consistently overestimate the standard line in the Müller-Lyer illusion (Underwood, 1966). With respect to the predictive validity of the system, we would expect that "undecided" individuals would flounder or change jobs more often than others and that "unrealistic" persons would be less successful in their jobs than those with different problems. Eventually, after the categories have been extensively validated, it would be possible—and desirable—to relate them to differential treatment processes to determine whether some kinds of counseling are more effective with one type of vocational problem than another.

At present, only one study can be reported in which the new system has been used, but it yielded a few positive findings which support its theoretical significance. Brunkan (1966) classified 289 male college students according to the procedures for defining vocational problems and then analyzed differences between the categories on two variables: (1) parental identification and (2) perceived parental attitudes, the Semantic Differential being used to measure the former and the Brunkan-Crites (1964) Family Relations Inventory (FRI) the latter. Parental identification scores were derived for both the father and mother, as seen in reality and ideally. Perceived parental attitudes were assessed by six scales of the FRI: Father Acceptance, Father Avoidance, Father Concentration, Mother Acceptance, Mother Avoidance, and Mother Concentration. The results of the analyses were largely negative, except that a rather complex relationship was found between parental identification and types of vocational problems. Brunkan (1966, pp. 399–400) summarizes this finding as follows:

> The significant *t*'s [following an overall *F* test] indicated that when there was a greater discrepancy between degree of identification with the father as compared to the mother, with stronger father identification and weaker mother identification, there was a greater probability of (*a*) adjusted and (*b*) unfulfilled problems. A moderate but significant discrepancy was associated with (*a*) maladjusted, (*b*) undecided, and (*c*) unrealistic problems. And no significant difference was found for (*a*) multipotential, (*b*) uninterested, and (*c*) coerced problem categories.

In short, Brunkan found that the strength of father identification *relative* to mother identification is related to the kinds of vocational problems which male college students have. Why relatively greater father identification was associated with the particular problem categories mentioned, i.e., "adjusted" and "unfulfilled," is not wholly clear, but it seems psychologically reasonable, given the patterns of sex typing in our society, that sons who closely identify with their fathers should be fairly well adjusted in their vocational decision making. Brunkan (1966, p. 400) suggests, however, that they might also be unfulfilled "due either to strong dependency because of which they feel no need to exert themselves to achieve, or to a fear of failing their fathers if they should compete at the expected level." Obviously, further research is needed to investigate these alternatives and to establish the utility of the diagnostic system.

INDECISION IN VOCATIONAL CHOICE

Indecision in vocational choice refers to the inability of the individual to select, or commit himself to, a particular course of action which will eventuate in his preparing for and entering a specific occupation. Note that this definition of indecision is a general one which encompasses the three "problems of indecision" which were defined in the previous section. The problem of the *multipotential* individual is not that he is unable to make a choice but rather that he makes too many choices (two or more) and cannot designate one as his goal. His difficulty arises because he cannot choose from among his choices. In contrast, the *undecided* individual's problem is that he cannot make any choice from among the alternatives which are available to him. More specifically, the necessary conditions for making a choice obtain, i.e., a choice supply, incentive to make a choice, and the freedom to choose (see Chapter 4), but the individual nevertheless cannot complete the choice act. Finally, the *uninterested* individual has made a choice, and he has made only one, but he is uncertain about it, because it is not supported by an appropriate interest pattern. He is attracted to his chosen occupation, but at the same time is repelled by it. Thus, all three problems involve indecision, but for clearly different reasons.

Theories of Indecision in Vocational Choice

The term "theories" is used advisedly to describe the explanations of indecision in vocational choice which have been proposed because, despite the unquestioned importance of indecision as a concept and behavioral phenomenon, it has not been systematically explicated by those who have written about it. There are some hypotheses which are provocative, however, and which can serve as a basis for further analysis of the nature of indecision and for its empirical investigation.

Developmental Aspects of Indecision. Several theorists have noted the tendency for indecision in vocational choice to decrease as age increases: more older individuals seem to have made a vocational choice as compared with younger individuals. In his extensive review of vocational interests and choice, Carter (1944, p. 54) concluded: "Inability to make a choice is not a matter of chance; growth toward vocational choice is apparently integrated with other aspects of development, rather than an independent phenomenon." Similarly, Tyler (1961b) has observed that the difficulty which some individuals experience when they are confronted with the necessity of declaring an occupational goal or making subordinate decisions which will lead to a goal often stems from their vocational immaturity. She writes: "Choices come in sequences, and a person may find it impossible to make a later one if he has not settled the earlier ones" (Tyler, 1961b, pp. 201–202). As Havighurst (1953) has pointed out (see Chapter 5, p. 33), success with earlier developmental tasks is related to success with later ones. Dysinger (1950, p. 200) has also commented upon indecision in vocational choice and has emphasized that: "There are periods of indecision, even indifference, which run through the whole developmental process. Long periods of time may intervene between steps toward vocational maturity."

Empirical support for these propositions about vocational indecision is practically nonexistent. About the only studies which are available are those by Gesell et al. (1956) and Mackaye (1927) which were discussed in Chapter 5. The results of these investigations indicated that there is some trend toward greater decisiveness as the individual grows older, but it is not a continuous one, as has been generally assumed. Rather, there is a period between the ages of 14 and 15 when many young people evidently reconsider their earlier choices in light of new reality considerations and again become undecided, as they had been around ages 9 and 10. By the age of 16, however, they have reoriented themselves vocationally and can state much more certainly what they plan to do. More data are needed before much confidence can be had in these conclusions, but at least what we have can serve to guide further research toward answering such questions as: What are the actual percentages of individuals who are undecided at different age levels in adolescence? What factors are related to the trends which occur in indecision, e.g., the impact of reality? And, what are the characteristics of individuals who deviate from the trends?

Factors in Indecision. Even though it is assumed on the basis of present evidence that indecision increases during midadolescence before final vocational choices are made, it is still not known *why* some individuals have reached a decision about their occupation and others have not *at a given age level.* As Carter (1944, p. 54) makes clear: "The tendency to have a vocational preference is associated with age, but of course not merely as a product of maturation, and certainly not entirely as a result of efforts in deliberate teaching."

In other words, how can we account for the fact that there are individual differences in indecision which are not a function of age? Tyler (1961b) has proposed that there are at least four factors which may produce a state of vocational indecision in the individual:

1. *Influences emanating from family and friends.* Tyler cites as an example a boy whose mother wants him to be a minister but who has become weakened in his faith. He does not want to disappoint his mother, but he also does not want to enter the ministry. As a result, he remains undecided.

2. *Aspects of the occupational role one plays.* An occupation may have both desirable and undesirable features, such as army chaplain which combines authoritarian and altruistic role expectations (Burchard, 1954). An individual considering such an occupation may be in a quandary because he is both attracted to it and repelled by it.

3. *Equipotentiality.* An individual may be fitted for several different occupations and find it difficult to choose from among them. Tyler (1958) has identified the problem involved in this case as one of the individual's inability or unwillingness to make negative decisions and thus limit the development of his potentialities to one area. She notes that "for most adolescents or young adults, self-actualization involves a real problem of renunciation of parts of the self that can never come to fruition" (Tyler, 1958, p. 7).

4. *Limitations imposed by circumstances.* Sometimes indecision will arise because reality prevents the implementation of a plan and no other alternative course of action can be formulated.

Indecision versus Indecisiveness. Vocational indecision has been defined as the individual's inability to express his choice of an occupation when he is asked to do so. Such a state of inaction, or no response, can be further analyzed, however, in terms of how long it takes a person to make a choice and what the making of a choice means to him. Dysinger (1950, p. 200) makes the following distinctions between what he sees as two types of indecision:

> In the first, the youth is postponing the issue or is considering the attraction of several fields. This is a wholesome experience, particularly when it stimulates the youth to explore the vocational world more thoroughly. The second type of indecision represents the avoidance of the pain of decision. Decision challenges to sustained effort and opens possibilities of failure. Many youth are frightened by the finality of a specific plan and take refuge in indecision.

Tyler (1961b, p. 201) has elaborated upon this latter kind of indecision, saying that it "represents a general *indecisiveness* growing out of personal problems rather than doubts related to this specific issue [of choosing an occupation]." She is referring here to those individuals who seem to have difficulty in making all sorts of life decisions, whether they are of great or little significance. Forer (1953, p. 366) concurs with these observations when he concludes that: "The individual who can not [sic] make a vocational decision or has no preferences . . . is likely to be an emotionally maladjusted person. Often the deciding process is a threat; and wanting things, expressing needs, and obtaining some kind of gratification are emotionally unacceptable."[5]

To distinguish between indecision and indecisiveness makes sense psychologically, and the differences between the two concepts appear to be clear-cut, but it is nevertheless rather difficult to translate them into operational definitions which are practicable for research. One approach which might be taken would be to define the "indecisive" individual as the one who cannot make a vocational choice even after all the conditions for doing so, such as a choice supply, incentive to make a choice, and the freedom to choose, are provided. The main problem with this procedure, however, is that it assumes we know what the necessary and sufficient conditions are, and these have not as yet been determined. Also, assuming that the conditions are known, there is the additional problem of deciding how much time should elapse after the individual is exposed to them before he is considered to be "indecisive." Must he make a choice immediately, or can he wait for a while? Clearly, further work must be done before indecision and indecisiveness can be differentiated empirically as they have been conceptually.[6]

Extent of Indecision in Vocational Choice

Although there has been only limited research on the incidence of indecision in vocational choice over extended periods of time, as has been pointed out, there have been several studies of indecision at given points in time, usually the end of high school or the beginning of college. Most of these studies are quite old now, a large percentage of them having been done in the 1930s, but they at least give a picture of what the extent of indecision was during those years, and, with appropriate qualifications, they have implications for the present. In addition to the research on indecision in choice, there is the closely related research on the extent to which young people have patterned or unpatterned vocational interests. Together, the investigations of choice indecision and interest patterning give some idea of how extensive the inability to decide upon an occupational goal is during the adolescent years.

[5] For a "clinical" and case-study analysis of vocational indecision as a problem in the search for identity, see Galinsky and Fast (1966). Cf. Erikson's (1959, p. 92) observation that: "In general it is primarily the inability to settle on an occupational identity which disturbs young people."

[6] As a first step in this direction, see the experimental design proposed in Chap. 13, in which an attempt is made to operationally define indecisiveness and to distinguish it from indecision.

Vocational Choice. Table 7-2 summarizes a considerable amount of the data which have accumulated on indecision in vocational choice and would seem to support the following conclusions:

1. The range in percentages across studies is considerable, extending from 5.0 percent to 61.1 percent, but the central tendency of the distribution is in the high 20s, or low 30s. The median percentage is approximately 30 percent, with 16 out of the 26 percentages (the three for the total groups were not counted) in the range between 20 percent and 40 percent.

Table 7-2. Extent of Indecision in Vocational Choice

Study	*Sex*	*N*	*Educational level*	*Percent undecided*
Anderson, W. H., 1932	Male	673	College	33.3
			Freshmen	38.3
			Sophomores	35.1
			Juniors	34.3
			Seniors	21.2
Beeson & Tope, 1928	Male	2,000	High school seniors	19.0
	Female	2,000		12.3
Byrns, 1939	Male	34,472	High school seniors	24.2
Coxe, 1930	Male	4,564	High school	11.5
	Female	4,993		6.0
Cunliffe, 1927	Male & Female	(Not reported)	College freshmen	9.0
Kilzer, 1935	Male & Female	2,274	High school seniors	52.8
Kohn, 1947	Male	approximately 400	College	20.0
Mitchell, 1933	Male	750	High school freshmen	16.0
	Female			5.0
Tucci, 1963	Male	163	College	18.0
Webb, 1949	Male	171	College	52.6
	Female	70	College	61.1
Williamson & Darley, 1935	Male	32,063	High school seniors	35.0
	Female	36.272		30.8
	Male	4,091	1929	37.1
	Female	4,636		36.8
	Male	4,701	1930	28.3
	Female	5,551		20.7
	Male	6,963	1931	32.4
	Female	8,034		27.4
	Male	7,923	1932	35.3
	Female	8,866		32.2
	Male	8,385	1933	39.9
	Female	9,185		35.8

2. There is a slight tendency for males to be somewhat more undecided than females, but statistical tests of differences between the percentages for the sexes, where they could legitimately be made, revealed that the differences were not significant. Evidently, girls experience about as much indecision about their vocational choices as do boys.

3. Finally, although there are no consistent differences in the percentages of indecision at the high school and college levels, there is a very definite trend in the data reported by Anderson, W. A. (1932) for the higher college classes to be more decided than the lower, as would be expected from vocational development theory.

Further research on vocational indecision, which is badly needed to bring most of the findings in Table 7-2 up to date, should be designed to avoid some of the shortcomings of the older studies and also to gather data which they did not attempt to collect. In particular, the stimulus questions used to elicit vocational choice should be worded in such a way that the respondent can indicate that he is undecided. (See the suggested modification of Trow's open-ended questions in Chapter 4.) In addition, it would be informative to find out how undecided individuals approach the problem of vocational choice. What has been their thinking about choosing an occupation? What are their attitudes toward making a choice? And why are they having difficulty in resolving the problem of vocational choice? A recent doctoral dissertation by Hall, D. W. (1963) at the University of Iowa has suggested that one factor in indecision may be the level of an individual's general anxiety.[7] It would seem reasonable to hypothesize that other motivational and personality factors might also affect the decision-making process.

Vocational Interests. Darley and Hagenah (1955) have reported data from an extensive normative study of the SVIB at the University of Minnesota which provide us with a fairly adequate basis for estimating the extent to which college freshmen have patterned vocational interests. The sample from which the data were gathered consisted of 1,000 male students who enrolled in the College of Science, Literature, and the Arts, the Institute of Technology, or the General College during the 3-year period from 1939 to 1941. For each student there was a SVIB which was pattern-analyzed according to a revision of Darley's (1941) earlier method. The number of times each pattern occurred in the sample, both separately and in combination with certain other patterns, was then determined, and the resulting frequencies constituted the normative data. In the total sample of 1,000 cases, there were 193, or 19.3 percent, who had no primary pattern. In other words, approximately one-fifth of these

[7] See also Goodstein's (1965) theoretical analysis of the role of anxiety in indecision, and the experimental paradigm based upon it which is presented in Chapter 13.

college freshmen had interest scores on the SVIB which did not cluster sufficiently to give them a primary pattern, defined by Darley and Hagenah as a plurality or majority of A and B+ scores in an interest group. Similarly, 260 cases, or 26.0 percent, of the sample had no secondary pattern, which meant that there was no interest group on their SVIB with a preponderance of B+ and B scores. Finally, a very small percentage, 2.2, had no primary with no secondary, indicating there were only a few students who had completely unpatterned profiles.

In an effort to understand the nature of unpatterned vocational interests more fully, Bernstein (1953) studied the relationship of several personal background and family variables to the presence and absence of primary patterns on the SVIBs of a sample of 142 ninth-grade boys in the Career Pattern Study. He hypothesized that boys with no primary interests would (1) come more often from broken homes, particularly those in which the father was absent, (2) have fathers with lower occupational levels, (3) manifest a greater incidence of scholastic underachievement, and (4) have a greater number of adjustment problems. Despite the cogency of these hypotheses, most of which are implied by Carter's (1940) theory that interests develop from the adjustment and identification processes, there was no support for them in Bernstein's study. Why this was the case is not clear. It may have been that the effects of interest immaturity were confounded with those of the hypothesized correlate variables, since the sample was relatively young. The writer (Crites, 1960) found in a study discussed earlier (see Chapter 5) that ego strength correlated with degree of interest patterning only after the age of 21, presumably because most of the change in interests due to development does not take place until that time. In other words, the effects of other factors which affect interest patterning (including the lack of it) may not be identifiable until interest development has run its course.

In another study of unpatterned interests, but with the Kuder Preference Record (KPR) instead of the SVIB, Shoemaker (1959) determined which interest areas were rejected and accepted by a sample of 1,928 (913 boys, 1,015 girls) high school students in grades 9 through 12. He defined "rejection" as a significant difference between the percentage of his Subjects who obtained low scores on a KPR scale and the 25 percent who were expected to get low scores as established by national norms. In other words, if 40 percent of Shoemaker's sample scored below the 25th percentile on a KPR scale, and the difference between these percentages was significant, then this was considered to be a "rejection" area of interest. Similarly, if a percentage significantly greater than 75 scored above this percentile, then this was defined as an "acceptance" area of interest. What Shoemaker found was that the total sample of boys, i.e., irrespective of grade level, rejected the Musical, Persuasive, and Social Service areas of interest. And, they did not accept any areas. When further analyses were made across grades, the data indicated that the boys increased their *rejection* of the Artistic, Outdoor, and Scientific areas and increased their *acceptance* of the Musical and Persuasive areas. Because Shoemaker does not report any actual percentages, it is difficult to interpret these findings. Evidently, musical and persuasive interests are rejected by boys in the high school years, but to a lesser extent as they grow older.[8]

Correlates of Indecision in Vocational Choice

Research on the factors which are related to choice indecision can be broadly divided in two types: (1) studies in which data on indecision were gathered as part of an investigation of another problem and (2) studies which were specifically designed to analyze the nature of indecision. The studies of the first type are considerably older than those of the second type, which suggests that there is a recent (and welcome) recognition of indecision as a phenomenon for study in its own right. The *older studies* will be briefly summarized, and then the newer ones will be reviewed in greater detail:

1. In an early study of student attitudes and vocational choice, Nelson, E., & Nelson, N. (1940) found that the Subjects in their sample who were undecided were also somewhat below the median of their total group on two scales of the Thurstone type designed to measure conservative-liberal and religious attitudes.

2. Sisson (1941) has reported that in a sample of 951 male and female college freshmen there was a slight tendency for those from urban backgrounds to be more undecided, the percentages being as follows: city, 11.23 percent; town, 13.80 percent; and farm, 8.50 percent.

3. Kilzer (1935) found that high school senior boys who were college-bound tended to be slightly more decided (56.9 percent) than those who were not going to college (47.8 percent).

4. In his survey of veterans, Kohn (1947) discovered that about four out of five who had no vocational choice said in counseling interviews that family or friends had suggested to them what they ought to do vocationally.

5. Achilles (1935) compared the self-reported scholastic standing of decided and undecided groups of college students and found that 41 percent of the former, but only 26 percent of the latter, rated themselves as above the average of their class. Similarly, Sanborn (1965) has reported that high- and low-

[8] With data from another study (O'Hara & Tiedeman, 1959), however, O'Hara (1962) was unable to replicate Shoemaker's findings. The former found considerably more "acceptance" patterns and greater stability of interests across grades. As O'Hara notes, the reason for these divergent results may well be the marked differences between the two samples in the studies, his coming from a private parochial school in Boston and Shoemaker's from a public high school in Missouri.

achieving superior-aptitude college students (males and females combined) differ significantly in the specificity of their vocational choices, the latter being disproportionately undecided. In contrast, Williamson (1937) found that there was no systematic relationship between actual grade point average and whether a student had or had not decided upon an occupation. Why his study differs from the others is not clear, unless the difference is due to different methodology and sampling.

One of the first of the more *recent studies* of the correlates of indecision to appear in the literature was conducted by Holland and Nichols (1964a). Although these investigators viewed their study as the development and validation of an indecision scale, what they did, in effect, was to find the *item* correlates of membership in a decided and an undecided group. By inspection, not factor analysis, they identified three clusters of items in their scale: "(1) a socially oriented cluster of school offices, baby sitting, belonging to clubs, dating, etc.; (2) an artistic-creative cluster; and (3) an aggressive, narcissistic, perhaps psychopathic cluster including participation in weight lifting, wrestling, etc." (Holland & Nichols, 1964a, p. 29). Findings on the relationship of the scale to other variables, however, were spotty: it correlated with several self-ratings of ability and measures of personality for boys, notably Barron's Independence of Judgment Scale (.26), but not for girls; and it did not relate significantly (at the .05 or .01 levels) to change in either major field of study or vocational choice in the original standardization sample, but did with major field for boys (.02 level) in a cross-validation sample. In short, the scale's usefulness is largely descriptive: it provides a psychological "picture" of the vocationally undecided individual, but it does not predict his choice behavior with much accuracy.

Using a "shotgun" approach to identify some of the possible correlates of indecision, Ashby, Wall, and Osipow (1966) classified 228 college freshmen (186 males, 46 females) into three groups, varying in the certainty of their vocational choices, and compared them on 23 different variables, plus seven scores from the SVIB. The groups were defined as follows: Decided (81 males, 27 females); Tentative (79 males, 12 females); and Undecided (26 males, 3 females). The variables included measures of personality, academic aspiration, scholastic aptitude, high school GPA, and family-background factors, e.g., parents' income, birth order, etc., as well as seven "group" scores from the SVIB. Analyses of variance were used to compare the Decided (D), Tentative (T), and Undecided (U) Subjects on each variable and indicated that these groups differed significantly (at the .01 level) on a self-rating of intellectual orientation, academic ability, English achievement, SAT-V, high school GPA, and first semester college GPA. In each instance, the D group ranked highest; U, intermediate; and T, lowest (with the exception of the intellectual rating, on which U and T had identical means). There were no systematic differences among the groups on the SVIB. One finding which was significant at the .05 level, however, was the higher mean of the U group on the Dependence scale of the Bernreuter, which corresponds to an observation made by Holland and Nichols that the undecided individual may be of the oral dependent type. Ashby et al. (1966, p. 1041) comment that "the USs are capable enough, but for some reason need extra support and encouragement in working out their plans."

In contrast to the approach taken by Ashby et al., Kahoe (1966) selected an explicit theoretical framework to deduce hypotheses about the correlates of indecision. The theory he chose was developed by Herzberg, Mausner, and Snyderman (1959; see Chapter 9 for a detailed discussion) to account for differential sources of vocational motivation and satisfaction. In brief, it proposes that satisfaction with work stems from the so-called "motivator" factors which are found in the work itself, e.g., achievement, recognition, and responsibility, whereas dissatisfaction arises from the absence of certain "hygiene" factors, e.g., job security, working conditions, company policies, etc. Applying these concepts to indecision, Kahoe (1966, p. 1031) reasoned that:

> Motivation-oriented youth are assumed to have tendencies to approach a variety of "interesting" situations and to seek satisfaction from activity. They are thus likely to place themselves in a position to encounter some occupational activities that they identify as personally gratifying or at least potentially satisfying. Hygiene seekers, on the other hand, with tendencies to avoid novel situations and to seek gratification from extrinsic or hygiene rewards, tend to preclude the kinds of experience that lead to occupational identifications.

It would follow, therefore, that undecided Subjects should be more "hygiene-oriented" than those who have decided upon a vocation. In general, Kahoe's findings supported this hypothesis, but they were of borderline significance (.05 level) in most instances and should be replicated before any firm conclusions are drawn. In particular, it would appear from his description of the procedures he used to measure the "motivation-hygienic" orientations that further work needs to be done on them. Not only were they complex and involved, which makes interpretation difficult, but their relationships to other behavior-relevant variables are unknown.

UNREALISM IN VOCATIONAL CHOICE

Unrealism in vocational choice means that the occupation which the individual has selected as the one he intends to enter is not consistent, in some way, with either his aptitude or his interests. In the diagnostic system which was proposed earlier in this chapter, three problems of unrealism were identified and defined. The first, and most common, of these is the problem of the *unrealistic* individual who chooses an occupation which requires a greater degree of aptitude, whether general or special, for its successful performance than he possesses, despite the fact that his interests agree with his choice. A typical example is the person who has mechanical-scientific interests and who wants to become an engineer, but who has ability only sufficient to succeed as a draftsman. The second type of unrealism problem is that of the *unfulfilled* individual, who, in contrast to the unrealistic person, selects an occupation on a level below that on which he could successfully perform in terms of his aptitude. He is unrealistic because he distorts reality by underestimating what he can actually do. Finally, there is a third kind of unrealism problem which characterizes the *coerced* individual, whose choice is consistent with his aptitude level, but not with his field of interest. Usually, in this case, the choice reflects the aspirations or wishes of the parents or, less frequently, it results from the individual's lack of awareness of his interests.

Theories of Unrealism in Vocational Choice

As with indecision, using the term "theories" to refer to hypotheses about the development and causes of unrealism in vocational choice may be a misnomer, but for lack of a more appropriate term it has been used to describe the various explanations which have been proposed concerning how and why unrealistic choices are made. Perhaps as some of these explanations are tested and evaluated in research on the new system for defining vocational problems they will more closely approximate what we usually think of as "theories."

Developmental Aspects of Unrealism. Probably the fullest statement of the relationship of unrealism to vocational development has been made by Ginzberg and his associates (1951). As was discussed in Chapter 5, they divided the total span of the choice process between ages 10 and 21 into three periods, the Fantasy, Tentative, and Realistic, each of which supposedly involved somewhat more realistic decision making by the individual. In other words, there was an overall tendency for the individual's choices to become more realistic as he matured. At first, he based his selection of an occupation almost entirely upon his "wish to be an adult"; then, he formulated it in terms of his personal characteristics—his interests, capacities, and values; and, finally, he worked it out as a compromise between his needs, on the one hand, and reality factors, on the other. Ginzberg saw a definite progression in the realism of the individual's choices from the fantasy-laden aspirations of late childhood to the reality-tested goals of early adulthood.

The obvious implication of this formulation for research is that degree of realism in vocational choice is linearly related to age, and, as mentioned in

Chapter 5, Small (1953) tested this proposition for age levels 15 through 19, but was unable to find empirical support for it. He accounted for this finding by reasoning as follows (Small, 1952, pp. 30–31):

> In the study of development from fantasy to reality emphasis [in vocational choice], it is actually the development of the ego that is being observed. Yet the ego probably does not develop in the simple linear way that Ginzberg implies, especially during adolescence. Reality perception may be weakened temporarily by the need of the ego to defend itself against the strong tide of impulses accompanying puberty. To assume linear progression is to oversimplify a complicated developmental process. What may prove to be irreversible is not the choice itself, but the *mode* of choice-making. That is, once reality becomes the chief consideration in choice-making, it probably remains the major determinant.

Actually, Ginzberg et al. (1951, p. 96) would appear to be in agreement with Small's last observation when they note that the choice process and age are not perfectly correlated during the stages of the realistic period: "the amount of time which he [the adolescent] requires to pass through the three stages of the period of realistic choices depends more on specific elements of his personality and on external reality than on age."

Unfortunately, at the present time, we do not have data available to evaluate which of the many interpretations of choice realism in relation to age is correct. It was pointed out in Chapter 5 that the age range covered by Small's study may have been too restricted to reveal the expected relationship, and Ginzberg's data were gathered on such small *N*'s that it is not advisable to place much confidence in the reliability of his results. What is needed is research based upon a wide range of age levels from early to late adolescence before any definitive conclusions can be drawn.

Factors in Unrealism. When we look at choice realism cross-sectionally, rather than longitudinally, and ask what its correlates are we again find much more opinion than fact. Many of the hypotheses which have been advanced to explain unrealistic choices are provocative ones, however, and a review of them may stimulate appropriate research on the problem.

1. From experiences with clients in vocational counseling, Korner (1946) has suggested that there are several different origins of unrealistic choices, which can be classified into the following three categories: (*a*) influence of teachers or other members of the school staff; (*b*) influence of the family; and (*c*) influence of individual psychological factors. She points out, however, that most unrealistic choices are the result of not one but several influences which have a combined effect upon the individual's decision making.

2. Levin (1949) has emphasized that a factor which is often overlooked as a possible source of unrealism in choice is what he calls "status anxiety." This is the feeling of apprehension and uncertainty which an individual experiences about his socioeconomic status and which motivates him to improve his position in society, to be "upward mobile." Because of an individual's status anxiety, Levin (1949, p. 33) points out that: "Occupational goals may be selected which are uncongenial to basic interests, fundamental aptitudes, and even the essential personality structure."

3. The glamour and prestige of occupations have often been cited as factors which contribute to unrealism in vocational decision making, and now Cautela (1959) has added to these the symbolic value of occupations as another variable which may have a similar, but possibly more pervasive, effect upon the quality of an individual's choice. By the "symbolic value of occupations" he means their subjective appeal to the individual as means for fulfilling his needs. Thus, Cautela cites as an example the college student who chose to be a surgeon in order to sublimate the aggressive feelings he had towards his parents, despite the fact that his aptitudes and interests did not indicate probable success and satisfaction in medicine.

4. A closely related factor in choice unrealism is the individual's ego involvement in the career goal he has announced for himself and, because of this commitment, his reluctance to change his objective even though it may not be the one for which he is best fitted. Bell, H. M. (1960) has summarized several cases which illustrate how difficult it is sometimes for a person to give up an unrealistic course of action because it is threatening to the ego to admit errors in judgment, particularly when others know the decision which has been made. A high school senior, for example, found that he did excellent work in mathematics and science courses and consequently told his parents and friends that he had decided to become a nuclear physicist. In college, however, he did much better in his nonscience courses than in physics. When he was advised to change his major, he found it difficult to give up his original plan: "He could hear himself say: 'I am going to be a nuclear physicist.' His mother's voice spoke with pride: 'John is going to be a great scientist.' Father's voice at Rotary Club said: 'John is going to the university to work on the atom smasher' " (Bell, H. M., 1960, p. 734). Not until he had to leave college as a result of low grades in his science courses was he able to face the unrealistic nature of his vocational choice and change it to a more appropriate field.

Extent of Unrealism in Vocational Choice

Research on unrealism in vocational choice is somewhat uneven in quality, some studies being considerably better than others in both conceptualization and methodology. It is also largely inconclusive in the results it has yielded. Some studies, almost all of which have been the less well-designed ones, have shown that there is a high incidence of choice unrealism in the decision making of young people. In contrast, others have produced findings which have been interpreted as establishing the general realism of the choices of adolescents and young adults. In the review of research which follows, the data on both sides of the question are summarized and evaluated as a basis for drawing some conclusions about the extent to which unrealism in choice exists.

Studies Indicating Unrealism in Choice. The typical design of studies which have indicated unrealism in choice has been to compare the distribution of choices of high school and college students with the distribution of workers in occupations. The rationale for this procedure has been that, if the choices are realistic, they should have the same frequency or percentage distribution as is found in the world of work. In other words, identical or similar distributions would indicate that individuals could enter the occupations they chose. They could act upon or implement their choices and thus make them "realities."

Without exception, the studies which have used this criterion of realism have shown that there are marked discrepancies between distributions of choices, on the one hand, and distributions of workers in occupations, on the other. In one of his early surveys of vocational choice, Sisson (1937) compared the career goals of college freshmen with the percentages of alumni engaged in the corresponding occupations. He found that there was little agreement among the percentages, primarily because the college students "over-chose" the professional occupations, i.e., a disproportionate number of them selected occupations at the professional level as compared with alumni in these occupations. With large samples of high school students (34,472 boys and 42,479 girls) as her Subjects, Byrns (1939) obtained similar results when she compared their choices with the number of workers actually employed in the occupations they selected. Again, there was a notable overselection of high-level occupations. Myers, W. E. (1947) has reported much the same findings from two surveys of choices and workers in the Washington, D.C., area, one having been made in 1940 and the other in 1946. He found that both studies indicated that high school students are unrealistic in their choices. Other investigations by Coxe (1930) and Wilson, W. E. (1948) have generally corroborated the finding that there is not a high degree of agreement between choices and occupations.

In evaluating the results of these studies, a number of considerations should be made. First, it is probably true that, at least to some extent, the choices of the Subjects were unrealistic. Undoubtedly, some individuals chose occupations on a level higher than the level of their ability, because they were attracted by the obvious advantages of these more prestigeful and remunerative occupations. Second, it should be recognized, however, that most of the Subjects in these studies, being high school seniors and college freshmen, constitute relatively select samples in ability as compared with the general population. They have survived longer in school, and, on the average, they are more intelligent. Consequently, to the extent that ability is related to occupational level, and there is good evidence that it is (Clark & Gist, 1938; Stewart, 1947), we would not expect brighter students to have choices which correspond exactly with the occupational distribution of workers. Rather, they *should* choose a higher proportion of occupations on the professional and managerial levels, and they would be realistic to the extent that the proportions agreed with those of workers on *these* levels, not across the entire range of the occupational hierarchy. But, third, even if this procedure were followed, it should be pointed out that it yields only an estimate of how realistic the choices of a *group* are. It does not provide information on the realism of a particular individual's choice. As Lockwood (1958; p. 98) has observed: "it fails to emphasize that a given youth, for example, among the approximately '50 per cent' who aspire to 'professional' jobs, where approximately '6 per cent' are gainfully employed, could well be one of the successful ones in whatever percentage of opportunity that occurs." Fourth, another consideration which should be made in assessing the adequacy of "distribution" studies of choice realism is whether choice, preference, or aspiration has been measured (see Chapter 4). Stephenson (1957) has reported data which indicate that, according to expectation (e.g., Trow, 1941), aspirations are considerably less realistic than choices when both are compared with the occupational distribution of workers.

Studies Indicating Realism in Choice. When criteria other than the percentage of workers in different occupations are employed to assess the adequacy of vocational choices, the results uniformly reveal that individuals usually make realistic choices. Father's occupational level was used by Carp (1949) to determine whether the son's choice was realistic or not, and he found that most of the choices, 44.7 percent, were at or below the father's level, with only 24.9 percent above it (28 percent were undecided). Latham (1951) devised a Planned-Job–Aptitude index, which expressed the degree of agreement between an individual's choice and his ability, and obtained data for it on approximately 1,600 high school seniors. In general, the results showed that choices were appropriate to aptitudes: individuals chose occupations which were more consistent with their ability than were the occupations they did not choose. Finally, Lockwood (1958) constructed a Realism Index Scale which can be used by judges to rate the wisdom of an individual's choice from the cumulative record and applied it to a stratified random sample of 508 high school graduates on whom complete data were available. The latter included: vocational preference, sex, height, weight, health defects, age, IQ, scholastic average, hobbies and interests, school adjustment, and work experience. The average realism score for the total sample, as determined by two judges, who agreed very highly with each other in their ratings ($r = .95$), was 5.5, which, in terms of the calibrations on the scale, indicated a considerable degree of choice realism. Lockwood (1958, p. 101) concluded that: "If we assume that ratings 1 through 3 represent unrealistic preferences, then we find that 27 students, 5 per cent, were unrealistic. By subtraction, 95 per cent of these students were judged to be realistic in varying degrees."[9]

Whether we can take these findings on the extent of realism in choice at face value or not is difficult to say. The studies appear to be reasonably well designed, and the *N*'s are quite large, but the base rates which result seem almost too good to be true. This is particularly the case with Lockwood's study, in which only 5 percent of his sample was judged to be unrealistic in their choices. Some individuals are going to be unrealistic, not because they aspire to an occupation beyond their capabilities, but because they choose one below their possible level of performance. If unrealism is defined in this way, as "undershooting" as well as "overshooting" one's expected or probable level of success, then it should occur at all levels of ability and amount to more than 5 percent. What our best estimate of choice unrealism in the population is, however, is practically impossible to specify without additional data. Informal experience based upon counseling with clients who have made unrealistic choices would suggest that the incidence of this type of problem is probably between 20 and 30 percent during the later years of adolescence (ages 17 to 21).

Correlates of Unrealism in Vocational Choice

In one of the few studies which have been found on the correlates of unrealism in choice, Stubbins (1948) compared two groups of veterans, one judged to be unrealistic and the other realistic in their vocational objectives, on several different background factors. These included such variables as voluntary versus involuntary application for counseling, age, father's occupational level, number of older brothers, pension, education, marital status, and work experience. A veteran was considered to be unrealistic in his choice if his counselor decided that, upon the basis of his intelligence, aptitudes, and

[9] For other measures of realism in vocational choice, see Sparling 1933), Chernow (1956), and Hewer (1966).

previous education, he could not be approved for further training under Public Law 16. Of the total group of 224 veterans, 25.9 percent were classified as unrealistic. The remainder included veterans who were undecided and who were "undershooting" their potentialities, but for the purposes of the study they were grouped together as having "realistic" choices. Comparisons of the two groups yielded differences between them on only a few of the factors, possibly because the "realistic" veterans were heterogeneous in their choice problems. The unrealistic clients volunteered more often for counseling, had fewer years of education, and were less likely to be receiving a pension.

In another study, which has already been briefly mentioned, Lockwood (1958) analyzed the relationship of choice realism to rental districts of residence, race, sex, school attended, and intelligence. Even when the relationship of each factor to realism was determined with variation in other variables controlled, however, only one significant result was obtained, and its interpretation is equivocal. Intelligence was found to be related to realism, but the reason most likely is that the judges knew the IQ of the Subjects when they rated their choices on the Realism Index Scale. Consequently, there was what amounts to "criterion contamination," or lack of experimental independence of the variables, and it is not possible to determine whether the relationship between intelligence and realism was an intrinsic one or not.

In a study based upon data collected as part of the Career Pattern Study, Super (1961a) related what he refers to as "Wisdom of Vocational Preferences" to indices of "Consistency of Vocational Preferences" and selected psychological and social variables. With 105 ninth-grade boys as Subjects, he tested the predictions that (1) Wisdom and Consistency of Vocational Preferences would be moderately correlated with each other (.20 to .35) and that (2) each would be similarly correlated with other variables according to certain theoretical expectations. Of the *r*'s which were computed between the various indices of Wisdom and Consistency, none was statistically significant which could not be considered an artifact of the operations used to define the indices. In other words, the indices which were related were not experimentally independent. Likewise, the results on Wisdom and Consistency in relation to such "correlate" variables as age, socioeconomic level, intelligence, scholastic achievement, etc., were all negative or artifacts. Consequently, it would appear that Wisdom and Consistency are not related to each other or to certain other variables. To draw such a conclusion, however, might be unjustified for at least two reasons. First, there were so many artifacts in the measurement procedures that *any* interpretation of the data is hazardous. And, second, it is not at all clear (explicit) why some of the predicted relationships were expected theoretically. For example, why should the Socioeconomic Accessibility of Vocational Preference be correlated with Peer Acceptance. Super fails to provide a rationale for hypothesizing relationships between variables such as these when the null hypothesis would seem to be the more reasonable one.

Drawing upon Atkinson's (1957; 1958) theory of achievement motivation, Mahone (1960) has reported a unique approach to the problem of establishing the correlates of unrealism in vocational choice. In general, he hypothesized that fear of failure, which is a negative form of achievement motivation, would be related to unrealistic decision making. Fear of failure was defined as the "relatively stronger disposition to avoid failure than to approach success" (Mahone, 1960, p. 254). To measure it, both positive and negative achievement motivation must be assessed. Thus, Mahone used scores from McClelland's (1953) *n* Achievement test and Alpert's (1957) Debilitating Anxiety Scale to classify Subjects on these two variables, respectively, into four groups: High *n* Achievement–High Anxiety ($N = 31$); High *n* Achievement–Low Anxiety ($N = 36$); Low *n* Achievement–High Anxiety ($N = 28$); Low *n* Achievement–Low Anxiety ($N = 40$). These groups were then compared on the following variables: (1) realism of vocational choice with ability as the criterion, (2) realism of vocational choice with interest as the criterion, (3) subjective goal discrepancy (the difference between a Subject's estimate of his own ability and his estimate of the ability required for his chosen vocation), and (4) accuracy of estimated ability (the difference between a Subject's estimated and measured ability). The expectation was that the Low *n* Achievement–High Anxiety (fear of failure) group would be more unrealistic in their choices with both ability and interest as the criteria, would have greater subjective goal discrepancies, and would be less accurate in estimating their ability. Chi-square tests were used to test these predictions, and from them Mahone (1960, p. 260) concluded that "the major hypothesis was clearly supported." Given Mahone's definition of "fear of failure," this conclusion would be true, however, *only* if there were no main effects of either or both of the variables used to define it. In three of the four analyses, either *n* Achievement or Anxiety was related to the dependent variable. Consequently, it is not known in these instances which variable is the one that is contributing to the significant variance and in what magnitude.

A study of more limited scope was conducted by Pool (1965) on the commonly held hypothesis that emotionally disturbed individuals are unrealistic in their vocational choices. He compared a group of 20 Subjects with physical handicaps and a group of 20 Subjects with psychiatric problems on ratings of the realism of their choices made by three experienced vocational counselors (interjudge agreement, r's = .76, .77, and .77). The mean scores of the two groups were 14.05 and 15.80, respectively, and they were not significantly different. Pool (1965, pp. 207–208) concluded, therefore, that:

> The findings leave little doubt that the psychiatric group was as realistic in its vocational choices as the physically handicapped group.... At the very least, the results suggest that the emotionally disturbed group may have vocational aspirations [choices, in our terminology] as realistic as those of the physically disabled.

We can agree with this inference from his data, however, only to the extent that his physically handicapped group was actually better adjusted than his emotionally disturbed group. That it possibly was not, on the hypothesis that poor adjustment status *is* related to realism of choice, is suggested by his comment that the physically handicapped group had the larger reality-deviation mean rating. To test this alternative interpretation of Pool's findings, his study needs to be replicated with an independent measure of adjustment on which the groups can be differentiated.

III
THE DYNAMICS OF VOCATIONAL ADJUSTMENT

8
THE MEANING OF VOCATIONAL ADJUSTMENT

In making a vocational choice an individual is, in effect, making a prediction of his future vocational adjustment. When he expresses his intention of entering a particular occupation, he is estimating that, of the occupations which are known to him, this is the one he thinks will bring him the greatest happiness, wealth, recognition, or whatever it is he is seeking. As we saw in the last chapter, he may have difficulty in making a choice or prediction, or, if he does make one, it may be less than adequate by certain criteria: he may choose an occupation for which his aptitudes are insufficient. Which criteria are used to evaluate choice as well as on-the-job performance and progress after entry into the world of work depends upon what is meant by "vocational adjustment." It is the purpose of this chapter to survey some of the different ways in which this concept has been defined and to review the research which is relevant to them. Accordingly, the chapter has been divided into the following three parts: (1) concepts of vocational adjustment, (2) vocational adjustment in relation to general adjustment, and (3) a Model of Vocational Adjustment.

CONCEPTS OF VOCATIONAL ADJUSTMENT

There are many different concepts and definitions of vocational adjustment, but common to all of them is the idea that vocational adjustment refers to the state or condition of the individual in relation to the world of work at any given moment after he has entered an occupation. What the nature of the individual's state or condition is, however, and why he relates to work as he does are not matters upon which general agreement can be found. In order to have some basis for comparing and contrasting the various concepts of vocational adjustment which have been proposed, we can ask the following question about each of them: Which aspect of the relationship between the worker and his work is considered to be the most important? Both nonpsychological and psychological answers to this question will be reviewed in this section, as well as a recently formulated general theory of vocational adjustment.

Nonpsychological Concepts of Vocational Adjustment

The nonpsychological meanings of vocational adjustment are those which focus primarily upon the work component of the relationship between the individual and what he does for a livelihood. They emphasize the factors and systems which are involved in work as an activity and minimize the role of the worker as an agent in this process. Each of the nonpsychological concepts of vocational adjustment which will be summarized here—the historical, economic, and sociological—views the behavior of the individual as a relatively unimportant aspect of his relationship to work.

Historical Meanings of Vocation and Work. During antiquity, being vocationally adjusted meant, by and large, being fortunate enough to be a member of the leisure or ruling class, since work was considered to be onerous at best. In tracing the history of work through the ages, Tilgher (1962, p. 11) notes that:

> To the Greeks work was a curse and nothing else. Their name for it—*ponos*—has the same root as the Latin *poena,* sorrow. For them *ponos* was colored with that sense of a heavy burdensome task which we feel in the words fatigue, travail, burden. The turn of phrase which in English is restricted to downright drudgery, the Greeks applied to physical work of every sort.

The ideal occupation for the Greeks, in the literal meaning of the term as the *occupying* of one's time, was to search for truth and seek spiritual freedom. In commenting upon what constitutes an ideal education, Aristotle (1943, p. 321) argues in his treatise *Politics* that:

> There can be no doubt that children should be taught those useful things which are really necessary, but not all useful things; for occupations are divided into liberal and illiberal; and to young children should be imparted only such kinds of knowledge as will be useful to them without vulgarizing them. And any occupation, art, or science, which makes the body or soul or mind of the freeman less fit for the practice or exercise of virtue, is vulgar; wherefore we call those arts vulgar which tend to deform the body, and likewise all paid employments, for they absorb and degrade the mind.

Similarly, Cicero concluded that "there are but two occupations worthy of a free man: first, agriculture [because it brings independence]; next, big business, especially if it leads to an honorable retirement into rural peace as a country gentleman" (Tilgher, 1962, p. 12). As Wrenn (1964, p. 25) has pointed out: "In both Greece and Rome the heavy work was done by slaves; in fact slavery was instituted to relieve the citizen of the curse of work."

If cultivation of the mind and freedom from the burden of physical toil were the hallmarks of the Greco-Roman civilization, then interest in the after-life and man's preparation for it were equally distinguishing of the period which followed. The Middle Ages brought with it a preoccupation with man's destiny and fate which was unmatched in the history of the world, but, until Luther introduced a new departure, the meaning of work remained essentially unchanged. In the theology of the Catholic Church, as set down in the writings of St. Augustine, St. Benedict, St. Thomas, and others, work was seen primarily as a means to the most important end in life—expiation from sin and eventual salvation. "Furthermore, work which St. Augustine and St. Benedict dignify by their notice is that done in a religious order. The work done by outsiders in the great world is regarded with indulgent charity but is in no way honored. And high above even intellectual monastery work, the Fathers placed pure contemplation, passive meditation on divine matters" (Tilgher, 1962, p. 15). Luther radically changed this concept of work by proclaiming that work has intrinsic value; that it should be at the center of each person's life, not just the monk's; that all work is worthwhile and all men should work. But most importantly, he maintained that through his work man serves God: "There is just one best way to serve God—to do most perfectly the work of one's profession.... So long as work is done in a spirit of obedience to God and of love for one's neighbor, every variety of labor has equal spiritual dignity, each is the servant of God on earth" (Tilgher, 1962, p. 18).

Out of the Reformation there developed a new meaning of vocation which was to become the central theme in conceptualizing man's relation to work in the centuries to follow. In the older Hebraic-Christian tradition, the concept of vocation had many roots, some with very special connotations, but in general it conveyed the meaning of a "calling." Early medieval religious practice restricted the scope of *vocation,* however, so that the term applied only to the clergy, who were considered to have been "called" by God to their life and work. It was this meaning of vocation which Luther's notion of the "priesthood of the believer" challenged and Calvin's doctrine of predestination transformed into a dialectic of work divested of its religious significance and infused with values which have emerged in the twentieth century as achievement, competition, and materialism. Today, the concept of vocation has become almost completely secularized:

> Obviously—and by a process much investigated in recent decades by historians, economists, and sociologists—this Reformation rediscovery

> of the vocation of every man was the basis of our whole modern approach to daily work, in America or any other society deeply steeped in Protestant presuppositions. Long after the Deity has been ushered out of everyday commerce and professional life, people push on here with a vocational intensity unknown in any other culture. . . . With all its glory and tragedy, its mighty works and its ulcers and ruthless competition, this motive for work is in our history a Protestant affair, deeply grounded in past theological claims which have been largely forgotten today [Nelson, J. O., 1963, p. 165].

Economic Definitions of Vocational Adjustment. Economists have not given much direct attention to the problem of conceptualizing or defining vocational adjustment, although they have traditionally been concerned with phenomena which are intimately involved in man's relation to work. Ginzberg and Berman (1963, p. 16) characterize the scope of the economist's interest in the behavioral aspect of vocational adjustment as follows:

> The economists have focused their attention on various institutions characteristic of the contemporary economy and political structure that help to determine the demand and supply of labor, the conditions under which people work, and the wages and fringe benefits which they receive. But they seldom, if ever, directed their attention to the individual men and women who work.

In general, this evaluation is substantially correct, although in fairness to the economist it should be pointed out that only recently has theory and research on work behavior reached a stage of development and sophistication which has suggested implications for economic activity. Furthermore, the economist has studied several variables which are, if not explicitly then implicitly, involved in a comprehensive definition of vocational adjustment. Among these, which include the occupational distribution of workers (Thomas, L. G., 1956), the conservation of human resources (Ginzberg, Ginsburg, Axelrad, & Herma, 1951), labor mobility (Palmer, G. L., 1954; Parnes, 1954), and the relationship between economic and sociooccupational institutions (Moore, W. E., 1955), the most important and relevant is unemployment, and the factors which contribute to it.

As an economic criterion of vocational adjustment, unemployment is a poignant and pervasive one. The primordial meanings not only of work, but also of life in general, are affected and often changed when a man has no regular job, whether the reason is (1) retirement, (2) intermittent employment, or (3) chronic unemployment (Wilensky, 1964). In Table 8-1 are listed some of the work functions and associated meanings, as identified by Friedmann and Havighurst (1954), which unemployment may preclude or place at

Table 8-1. The Relation between the Functions and Meanings of Work *(From Friedman & Havighurst, 1954, p. 7)*

Work function	*Work meaning*
1. Income	*a.* Maintaining a minimum sustenance level of existence *b.* Achieving some higher level or group standard
2. Expenditure of time and energy	*a.* Something to do *b.* A way of filling the day or passing time
3. Identification and status	*a.* Source of self-respect *b.* Way of achieving recognition or respect from others *c.* Definition of role
4. Association	*a.* Friendship relations *b.* Peer-group relations *c.* Subordinate-superordinate relations
5. Source of meaningful life experience	*a.* Gives purpose to life *b.* Creativity; self-expression *c.* New experience *d.* Service to others

the periphery of a person's life. For the unemployed individual, "The central fact of his work experience is job chaos—the lack of any stable work milieu, organizational context, or career to which he could respond in a cheerful or alienated way. Such is the condition of a large minority of the American labor force, and perhaps of marginal workers in every advanced country" (Wilensky, 1964, p. 131). Approximately 5 percent of the labor force in the United States in 1964, which numbered 73 million individuals over 14 years of age, were unemployed and consequently, by this criterion, *not* vocationally adjusted.

Several factors have been proposed as contributory to such a large segment of the work-eligible population being unemployed, but opinion is divided concerning their relative significance. Some labor experts, such as Wolfbein (1964, p. 170), contend that: "The common denominator which ties the jobless together is their lack of skill; this is what makes it so difficult for them to find a place in the growing employment totals." Others, such as Froomkin (1964, p. 32), argue that the critical factor in unemployment is not skill but "the result of change in the style of conducting business and of the displacement of job openings from manufacturing to service enterprises." Similarly, economists disagree about the effects of automation upon unemployment, some maintaining that job opportunities are lost through the greater mechanization of industrial processes and others concluding that whatever labor dislocations result are only temporary ones and will be rectified in the near future (Mann & Hoffman, 1960). The causes of unemployment are debated, then, but the effects are clear-cut: Life without work has little meaning (Ginzberg, 1942).

Probably the most articulate statement of this proposition has been made by Karl U. Smith (1962, pp. 21–22) in a paper entitled "Work Theory and Economic Behavior," the main thesis of which is that "man at every stage of his development, as a distinctive species and as an integrated individual, is a product of behavior organized through the sustained use of tools to control the environment." Smith takes as the point of departure for his analysis of vocational adjustment two shortcomings which he sees in neoclassical economic theory: first, this theory's reliance upon outdated and unsubstantiated mentalistic concepts of behavior, which emphasize purely rational judgments in producing, buying, selling, etc., to account for the motivation of economic man in the marketplace; and, second, its nonevolutionary character which has obscured the important role played by human development in the changing economic patterns of modern industrial society. In place of these orthodox economic doctrines, Smith proposes a biosocial interpretation of work which is based upon the assumptions that (1) human evolution and economic evolution are equivalent and (2) work is the primary activity which integrates man with his environment. The common factor which joins these two principles together, and which is the most distinctive feature of Smith's theory of work, is the emphasis he places upon man's use of tools to control the environment. His concept of the reciprocal interaction between the use of tools and the physiological mechanisms of behavior in mastering the environment is depicted in Figure 8-1. To Smith, then, man's vocational adjustment is largely a function of his design and utilization of tools and, more importantly, is the central reality of his existence.

Sociological Concepts of Vocational Adjustment.[1] Much as the economist concentrates upon the analysis of labor-market phenomena such as unemployment, rather than the individual who may be unemployed, the industrial and occupational sociologist focuses his study primarily upon the work group and its organization and functioning, instead of the worker who is a member of it. As a consequence, sociological concepts of vocational adjustment deal more with the relationship of the individual to the work group, and his role in it, than with either the economic or psychological aspects of his behavior on the job. Miller, D. C. (1964, p. 115; italics in original) states explicitly the emphasis of sociological definitions of vocational adjustment when he writes:

[1] What anthropological literature there is on vocational adjustment deals almost exclusively with incentives to work in primitive societies. See Hsu (1943), Firth (1948), and Curle (1949).

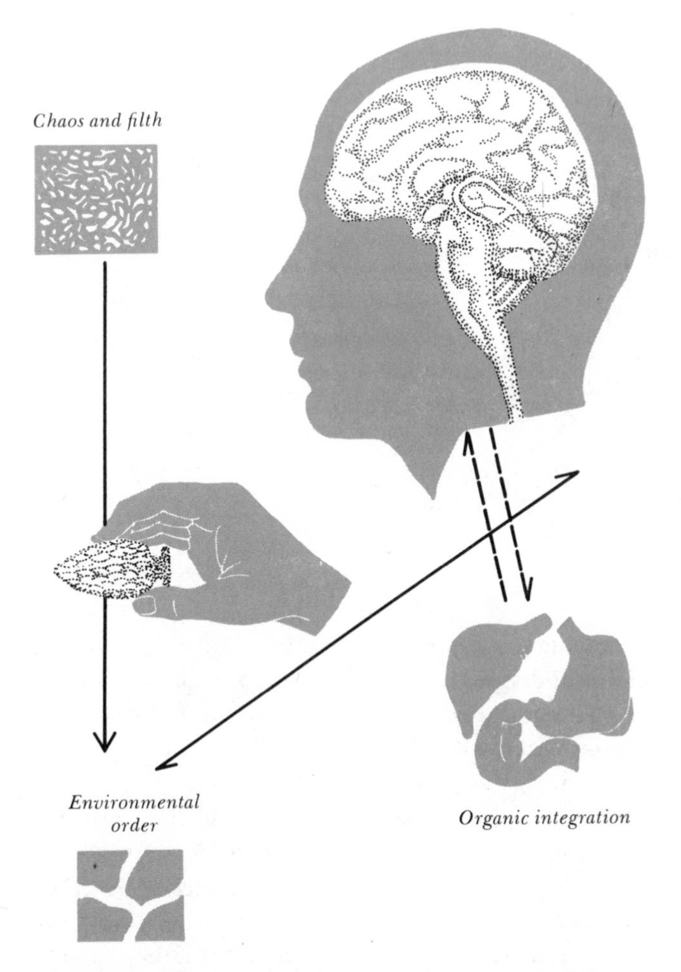

Figure 8-1. The use of tools to create an organized human environment out of the chaos and filth of the animal level of survival. *(From Smith, K. U., 1962, p. 23.)*

> *The requirements and social demands made upon the work position and work group by the social structure of the work organization may be more important in determining the behavior of a worker than is the personality of the worker himself.*

He goes on to add that conflicts in human relations in the industrial setting can usually be traced to role strains built into the organizational structure and not so much to the personality characteristics of work-group members.

Several sociologists have conceived of vocational adjustment as an interaction between the worker and the role he plays in the work group (Miller,

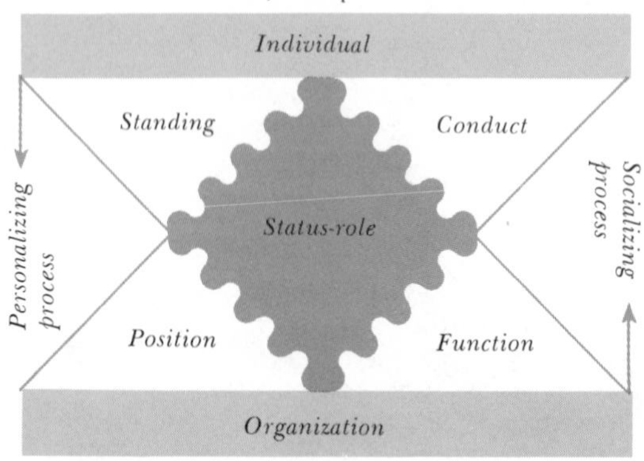

Figure 8-2. The vocational adjustment of the individual to the industrial organization through the "fusion process." *(From Bakke, 1953, p. 20.)*

D. C., & Form, 1964; Schneider, E. V., 1957; Solby, 1944), but probably the most comprehensive and articulate formulation has been made by Bakke (1953). The adjustment of the individual to his work takes place, according to Bakke, through what he calls the *fusion process.* As depicted in Figure 8-2, the fusion process involves an interaction between the individual and the organization which has the effect of changing each, to a certain degree, so that they become "adjusted." Through a formal *socializing process,* the organization selects and inducts its members by means of test batteries, interviews, orientation meetings, and training programs. It also indoctrinates the worker in the folkways of his work group, which consist of the traditional and expected ways of behaving on the job, e.g., amount and content of talking, mode and style of dress, social conventions and habits, etc. By a *personalizing process,* the individual imprints his image upon his work position by emphasizing certain aspects of it and minimizing others.[2] He fits the work role to his personality, as best he can, by bargaining with the organization for special considerations, altered conditions on the job, and other restructurings of his duties and tasks which stamp them as peculiarly his own. Out of the interaction of these two processes, the one which specifies the positions and functions of the organization and the other which brings to bear the conduct and standing of the individual, there develops a particular work role and status which define the individual's vocational adjustment. The fusion process is an ongoing phenomenon, but at any given point in time, after entry into a work position, the worker's relationship to his work can be delineated with

[2] Cf. Darley and Hagenah (1955, pp. 17–18) and Kelley (1940).

respect to what he is expected to do within the organization and how well he manages to do it.

Hughes (1958) has extended this analysis of what he refers to as "work and the self" to deal with some of the less obvious aspects of vocational adjustment, which he considers to be the essence of man's relation to work. His primary interest is in understanding "the social and social-psychological arrangements and devices by which men make their work tolerable, or even glorious to themselves and others" (Hughes, 1958, p. 48). To study this problem he takes as a point of departure the assumption that: "Insofar as an occupation carries with it a self-conception, a notion of personal dignity, it is likely that at some point one will feel that he is having to do something that is *infra dignitate*" (Hughes, 1958, p. 50). Consequently, among other similar facets of work, Hughes has analyzed how men in a variety of occupations, but especially in lower-level ones, handle the necessity of doing "dirty work," by which he means some job duty or task, such as disposing of garbage for the apartment house janitor, that is physically disgusting, symbolically degrading, or morally questionable. He found that dirty work can either be considered an odious and undesirable component of a person's work, as it was for the janitor, or be "knit into some satisfying and prestige-giving definition of role," as it most likely is for the physician. Dirty work may also be dealt with by willfully delegating it to others of lesser status.

In addition to "dirty work," Hughes has also investigated another infrequently recognized dimension of vocational adjustment: the maintenance of a certain freedom and social distance from those people most crucially and intimately concerned with one's work. This is a problem particularly for workers in any kind of service occupation, when they are forced to have their competence judged by those they serve, despite their feeling that they are better qualified to evaluate their performance than anybody else. Also, in occupations which administer to emergencies there is the problem that the consumer often feels he is being treated routinely rather than with special attention and consideration commensurate with his aggravated condition. Hughes (1958, p. 54) points out that the tension which exists between the producer and consumer may be less a matter of superficial ill will and misunderstanding on the part of the consumer than one of "ego-wound and possibly antagonism" on the part of the producer, because he feels that his dignity has been offended. Work and the self are inextricably confounded and interrelated in Hughes's concept of vocational adjustment.

Assuming that this proposition is true, it would follow that, if an individual cannot be himself in his work, then he would be less than optimally adjusted vocationally. He would be what the sociologist would term "alienated from his work." Fromm (1947, p. 72) speaks of "work alienation" when he discusses the "marketing orientation" as one of the nonproductive personality types in our society: "In the marketing orientation man encounters his own powers as commodities alienated from him. He is not one with them but they are masked from him because what matters is not his self-realization in the process of using them but his success in the process of selling them." The individual who develops the marketing orientation meets the demands of the labor market by adapting himself to the expectations and specifications of potential and actual employers. In Riesman's (1950) terminology, he becomes the "other-directed" person, who patterns his behavior in accordance with what he thinks people want him to be and to do. "Instead of the locus for self-evaluation being an internal one, it now rests primarily upon others. The use of the individual's abilities is devalued unless those abilities pay off in the form of occupational success" (Brigante, 1958, p. 85). The implication for the individual's vocational adjustment is straightforward—and devastating. In a word, he transforms himself into a commodity, which is sold to the highest bidder on the labor market.

Using these and similar observations (e.g., Arendt, 1958; Marx, K., 1960; Seeman, M., 1959) as a frame of reference, Wilensky (1964) has attempted to elaborate upon the definition of work alienation and give it operational meaning. He states his verbal definition of the concept as follows: "We may speak of the man whose work role poorly fits his prized self-image as work alienated" (Wilensky, 1964, p. 140). Wilensky measured work alienation operationally by asking Subjects in interview questions about the attributes of their "prized self-image" and the attributes of the work situation which correspond to them, as shown in Table 8-2. He then derived a "work alienation score" through matching the two lists of attributes: the less they agreed with each other, the more work-alienated the individual was considered to be. Contrary to the expectations of Fromm, Riesman, and others, however, Wilensky found that only a handful (approximately 15 percent) of 1,156 employed men on whom he obtained work-alienation scores had as much as one discrepancy between their prized self-image and work-situation attributes, and less than 1 percent had three or more discrepancies. Wilensky (1964, p. 146) comments upon these results as follows:

> Obviously, work alienation may be more widespread than this strict measure indicates. Many aspects of male identity were not tapped (e.g., masculinity), although it is possible that work situations can confirm or deny them. Direct questions, as we have seen, discourage admission of discontent.

He fails to consider the possibility, however, that, despite the *apparent* validity of informed opinion, it may not jibe with what is actually the case.

Table 8-2. Attributes of the Work Situation Which Correspond to Attributes of the "Prized Self-Image" *(From Wilensky, 1964)*

Attribute of prized self-image (both perceived and valued)	*Attribute of work situation (both perceived and valued)*
Sociable	Can talk sociably on the job (shoot the breeze) at least four or five times a day
Intelligent	Plenty of chance to use own judgment
Conscientious (competent, efficient)—person who believes that if a thing is worth doing, it is worth doing right	Chance to do work well—do a good, careful job Chance to do the things you're best at—use the kinds of skills that you have
Independent—a man who won't hesitate to go it alone when he thinks he should	(For those with a boss) boss not always breathing down your neck—not watched too closely
Ambitious—person who tries hard to get ahead	Good chance for promotion where you work

He reports data which suggest an alternative hypothesis to the work-alienation interpretation which may have promise for further study. From the work-alienation index, a measure of work "indifference" was also derived, and Wilensky (1964, p. 146) found that "more than one in five of the young white-collar men and one in three of the older blue-collar men score indifferent on *all* attributes." In other words, it may be that a sizable segment of the labor force can better be characterized as indifferent to their work rather than alienated from it. As Dubin (1958, p. 257) has noted, the indifferent individual may be peculiarly suited to routine and repetitive work because of his "shallow emotional response to anything." In an industrial society which is becoming increasingly automated and bureaucratized, it may not be surprising to find that more and more workers can best be described as indifferent to their work.[3]

Psychological Concepts of Vocational Adjustment

In contrast to the nonpsychological ways of viewing vocational adjustment, the psychological place the greatest emphasis upon the individual in relation to his work. They attempt to analyze and conceptualize the part which his

[3] See Pearlin (1962) and Zurcher, Meadow, and Zurcher (1965) for additional studies of work alienation. For investigations of the meaning of work in contemporary society, see: Dubin (1955); Neff and Helfand (1963); and Thompson, A. S., and Davis (1956). See also the collection of papers on work and leisure edited by Smigel (1963) and the article by Cohen, J. (1953) on work and play.

personal characteristics and learning experiences play in how and why he adjusts to his vocation as he does. We shall consider three major psychological interpretations of vocational adjustment—the trait-and-factor, psychodynamic, and developmental—as well as several related, but somewhat distinct, concepts.[4]

Trait-and-factor Concepts of Vocational Adjustment. There are three assumptions or principles which constitute the essence of the trait-and-factor concept of vocational adjustment:

1. By virtue of his unique psychological characteristics, each worker is best fitted for a particular type of work.
2. Groups of workers in different occupations have different psychological characteristics.
3. Vocational adjustment varies directly with the extent of agreement between worker characteristics and work demands.

In the early days of vocational psychology, these propositions, which were more or less grounded in factual evidence, were interpreted literally. Under the impact of the scientific-management movement in the first decades of the twentieth century, as expounded by Taylor and Gilbreth and others, personnel selection procedures were designed in order to put "square pegs in square holes and round pegs in round holes." In other words, it was rather rigidly assumed that for each individual there was one, and only one, occupation for which he was best suited and that when he was placed in it he would be ideally adjusted vocationally. Similarly, in vocational advisory work the prevailing philosophy was much the same, although it was tempered somewhat by a greater awareness of the latitude which exists in matching men with more than one job (Parsons, 1909, p. 3).

The square-peg concept of vocational adjustment was the predominant one through the period of World War I, but soon thereafter its underlying assumptions were exposed to considerable criticism. Among the objections which were raised against it, there were three which subsequently led directly to major modifications or revisions of the original square-peg notion:

1. Scott and Clothier (1925, p. 14) pointed out that in this concept of vocational adjustment:

> There is no recognition . . . of the fact that men and jobs are changing in themselves, and plastic, yielding here and giving there to out-

[4] General discussions of mental health and work can be found in Menninger, W. C. (1952), French, J. R. P., Kahn, and Mann (1962), and Kornhauser (1962; 1965).

> side pressure. There is no acknowledgement of the common fact that with exposure to a square hole, a round peg (we are speaking of human pegs now) tends to become squarish; there is no appreciation that the square hole takes on a certain round appearance.

They went on to propose what they called the "worker-in-his-work-unit" concept of vocational adjustment, which emphasizes that the individual and his job cannot be considered separately, as pegs and holes; that one affects the other, in an interactional sense; and that the individual's vocational adjustment is a function of the degree of balance which he achieves among his capacities, interests, and opportunities within the work situation (Scott, Clothier, & Spriegel, 1954). Similarly, Kitson (1925), Crawford and Clement (1932), Paterson and Darley (1936), and Super (1942) objected to the square-peg definition of vocational adjustment because, in the words of Paterson and Darley (1936, p. 124), "Men and jobs grow through mutual interaction; human behavior is not static or fixed.... Adjustment implies mutual give and take, or becoming rather than just existing."[5] From this line of reasoning there developed the more refined and sophisticated concept of vocational fitness, or what is better known as the Matching Men with Jobs approach, which is discussed at greater length below.

2. Anderson, V. V. (1929, p. 2) also criticized "that static and fixed conception of man's nature that conceives of measurable and rigid pigeonholes into which each individual may be neatly placed" for the same reasons, but he added a consideration which had not been made previously. He argued that "work failure [poor vocational adjustment] in the majority of instances does not so much seem to be due to the lack of ability—that is, as far as measurable aptitudes for the performance of a task are concerned—as to the presence of other factors of a more dynamic nature that influence the total personality and the general health of the worker, that handicap or interfere with the use of such abilities as he actually possesses" (Anderson, V. V., 1929, p. 2). This focus upon the nonintellective and personality factors which influence a person's vocational adjustment has been reflected to some extent in trait-and-factor theory, but it has found its most complete explication in the psychodynamic concepts of vocational adjustment (reviewed in the next section).

3. Finally, there has been a growing recognition of the fact that vocational adjustment is not a point-in-time phenomenon, as implied by the square-peg concept, but a developmental process which begins with entry into the world of work and which ends with the advent of retirement—and sometimes even extends into this period of life. The so-called "new look" in trait-and-factor theory, for example, focuses upon the career pattern or work history as the dependent variable in studying vocational adjustment, rather than occupa-

[5] Cf. Bakke's (1953) concept of the "fusion process" discussed earlier.

tional differences in aptitudes, interests, and personality characteristics (see Chapter 3).

There evolved from these criticisms of the square-peg definition of vocational adjustment what has become known as the concept of "vocational fitness," which differs from the earlier point of view in one critical respect: it neither limits the number of different occupations for which an individual may be fitted nor the number of different individuals who may be suited for an occupation. In other words, it recognizes that a person may be qualified to be successful and satisfied in more than one occupation and that an occupation may be broad enough, in its duties and tasks, that workers with different attributes may nevertheless be adjusted in it. Thus, Super (1953) writes of the multipotentiality of the individual for different occupations and the heterogeneity within occupations for different individuals.

Psychodynamic Concepts of Vocational Adjustment. The term *psychodynamic* is used here in the same way as it was in Chapter 3 to mean "any psychological system that strives for explanation of behavior in terms of *motives* or *drives*" or that posits "a psychological process that is changing or is causing change" (English & English, 1958, p. 418). And, again, there are the same three points of view which can be classified as psychodynamic: the psychoanalytic, need, and self theoretical orientations. The purpose of the following discussion is to summarize the conceptualizations of vocational adjustment of each of these positions.

In orthodox *psychoanalytic* theory, work is considered to be a means to the end of achieving a satisfactory general adjustment to society rather than as an end in itself. Freud (1962, p. 27) explicates this viewpoint in discussing libido theory:

> No other technique for the conduct of life attaches the individual so firmly to reality as laying emphasis on work; for his work at least gives him a secure place in a portion of reality, in the human community. The possibility it offers of displacing a large amount of libidinal components, whether narcissistic, aggressive or even erotic, on to professional work and on to human relations connected with it lends it a value by no means second to what it enjoys as something indispensable to the preservation and justification of existence in society.

According to Freud, the transformation of "constitutionally reinforced instinctual impulses" through work is by means of sublimation: work provides a means for expressing destructive and sexual drives in socially acceptable forms. Menninger, K. A. (1942) has elaborated upon this theme in arguing that work represents a sublimation of aggressive instincts through their fusion with erotic impulses. He assumes that "all work represents a fight against something, an attack upon the environment," but that "in work, as contrasted with purposeless destruction, the aggressive impulses are molded and guided in a constructive direction by the influence of the creative (erotic) instinct" (Menninger, K. A., 1942, pp. 171; 173). Hart (1947) calls this the "integrative" function of work and attributes man's creative and humanitarian efforts to it.

Underlying these orthodox psychoanalytic concepts of vocational adjustment is the common assumption that work is *not* intrinsically satisfying. Freud (1962, p. 27) observes that "work is not highly prized by men" and that "people only work under the stress of necessity." Similarly, Menninger, K. A. (1942, p. 173) reasons that "work tends to be regarded as a necessary evil," because it is invested with resentment of the societal expectation (authority) that all men *must* work. Hendrick (1943a; 1943b) has questioned this assumption, however, and has proposed in its place what he calls the "work principle," which posits that work has some intrinsic value and is more than just a mechanism for adjusting. It provides the individual with an opportunity to use his mental abilities and motor skills and hence constitutes a primary source of satisfaction. Hendrick admits that work also satisfies some of the basic instincts of man, but hastens to point out that these gratifications are only the by-products of work. The basic instinct which work fulfills is the desire to exercise and to apply one's intellectual and muscular resources, to master the environment through the executant functions and processes of the ego. In Hendrick's opinion, then, work serves not merely as a means to an end: it is an end in itself.

The rejoinder of Menninger, K. A., (1942) to this viewpoint is that mastery involves the purposive and expedient direction of energies to overcome resistances and consequently satisfies the destructive instinct rather than the work instinct. Similarly, Oberndorf (1951) has asked whether work satisfactions arise from the sensations associated with bodily pleasures or from the sense of well-being produced by achievement. The conclusion he reaches, on the basis of analysis of case studies, is as follows:

> Persons who constantly regard work as something difficult and unpleasant are those who have not emerged from the necessity of immediate reward and who are reluctant to assume responsibility (self-support) inherent in maturity. The protraction of infantile pleasure or the necessity for its denial as one matures determines the overinvestment or underinvestment of libido in work. This interrelationship is a close and continuous one and it seems futile to attempt to distinguish whether such libido is preponderantly sexual or ego (Oberndorf, 1951, p. 84).

In other words, the issue raised by the orthodox psychoanalysts and ego psychologists may be a "straw man." According to Oberndorf, the most important consideration in vocational adjustment is not whether work satisfies the destructive or mastery instincts, but whether the individual over- or under-invests either kind of libido in work.

In her concepts of normal and neurotic adjustment to work, Horney (1950) has deviated even more than Hendrick from traditional Freudian formulations of libido theory and its implications for the meaning of man's relation to his vocation. Horney's basic assumption is that there are two qualitatively different types of motivation which find expression in work: one of these is the normal, healthy striving to maximize one's potentialities, to progress toward the fulfillment of the "real" self; and the other is the neurotic, debilitating compulsion to actualize an "idealized image" of the self, to search for the glory of a self conceived in fantasy, but with little or no basis in reality. The urge to self-realization and the search for glory motivate both normals and neurotics, the difference being a quantitative one, and consequently aspects of each are discernible in the work habits and attitudes of most people. The manifestations of these motivations, however, vary from one worker to another, depending upon his predominant way of adjusting to life. The *expansive, aggressive* individual overrates his abilities, underrates the difficulty of tasks, and generally perceives the work situation as a foil to enhance his "effortless superiority." The *self-effacing, compliant* person works well when in contact with people, but grows anxious when by himself, feels overwhelmed by feelings of "I can't," and experiences intense guilt over personal achievements and praise. The *resigned, detached* individual resents deadlines as a form of coercion, fails to work up to his capacity, and finds little satisfaction in work. Each in his own way labors under the inhibitions that neurotic ambition and the needs for perfection and vindicative triumph place upon the fulfillment of his potentialities in work. To Horney, in contrast to other psychoanalysts, the will to work is thus a subtle blending of the normal desire for self-realization and the neurotic search for glory.

The theory of *needs* which has been most often used in conceptualizing vocational adjustment is the one proposed by Maslow (1954; see Chapter 3). To recapitulate it briefly here, Maslow proposes that there are eight needs, arranged in a hierarchy of prepotency, which motivate man's behavior. The lower-order, physiological needs, such as hunger, thirst, sex, and safety, are usually routinely satisfied in our society, and consequently it is the higher-order, psychological needs, such as esteem, understanding, and self-actualization, which are more frequently the effective motivators. How these needs are satisfied, or frustrated, in the work situation has not been explicitly formulated, however, in the sense that specific needs have not been related to specific aspects of work, e.g., the need for belongingness versus role played in the work group. Only some rather general statements of these relationships have been made, such as the following one by Roe (1956, p. 33): "Occupations as a source of need satisfaction are of extreme importance in our culture. It may be that occupations have become so important in our culture just because so many needs are so well satisfied by them." Miller, D. C., and Form (1964) are somewhat more specific, when they point out that needs like belongingness and love have traditionally been frustrated by management policies, and as a result informal work groups and unions have been organized to satisfy these needs. They go on to draw the general conclusion that "increasing numbers of workers at all levels of the labor force are achieving high satisfaction of their physiological and safety needs" but that "deprivation is occurring in the social, esteem, and self-actualization needs" (Miller, D. C., & Form, 1964, p. 618).

Much as with need theory, the application of *self* theory has been primarily in the analysis of vocational choice rather than the conceptualization of vocational adjustment. The most notable exception has been Super's (1951b; 1957) interpretation of vocational adjustment as the implementation of one's self-concept in an occupational role. He describes the dynamics of the individual's relationship to his work as follows:

> Holding and adjusting to a job is for the typical beginning worker a process of finding out, first, whether that job permits him to play the kind of role he wants to play; secondly, whether the role the job makes him play is compatible with his self-concept (whether the unforeseen elements in it can be assimilated into the self or modified to suit the self); and, finally, it is a process of testing his self-concept against reality, of finding out whether he can actually live up to his cherished picture of himself [Super, 1951b, pp. 88–89].

According to Super (1957), each person aspires to play a role in his work which he has learned to value in the home, school, and community. To the extent that the role expectations of the occupation the individual chooses and enters allow him to realize his role aspirations he is vocationally adjusted. If he is expected to conform to work-group decisions about regulating productivity in an assembly job, but he resents authority over which he has no control and wants to set his own work pace, he would be less well adjusted vocationally than if he had greater freedom in controlling his behavior.

Developmental Concepts of Vocational Adjustment. Some attention has been given to the analysis of vocational adjustment within a developmental frame of reference, as was indicated in Chapter 5, but most of it has been incidental to the formulation of other concepts, such as vocational maturity. The most articulate schema is Super's (1961b; 1963) recent theoretical work on career prediction and vocational life stages in adolescence and adulthood. He makes a distinction between the heuristic models which have been used in the traditional Matching Men and Jobs approach to vocational adjustment and the problem which is involved in studying careers. He argues that the familiar "regression" and "discriminant" models are appropriate for making occupational predictions, but not for career predictions. Their inappropriateness arises from the fact that they disregard intermediate and subsequent statuses of the individual in his career between the time he enters it and the time he is followed up. In other words, in the occupational prediction model, the individual's behavior is sampled and assessed at only two points in time rather than throughout his career. Furthermore, Super (1961b, p. 11) notes that this approach "matches youth and jobs and assumes that, once the match is made, the lucky pair lives happily ever after." Actually, there are many attitudes and behaviors which are part of the process of adjusting to work as the individual progresses in his career which have never been formally defined and enumerated. Super (1963) makes a start in filling this gap by specifying some of the tasks which the individual must accomplish after he enters an occupation. These tasks and the stages in which they occur are shown in Table 8-3.

One of the major variables in vocational adjustment which must be measured, if career progression is to be viewed developmentally, is the work history. Tiedeman and O'Hara (1963) have listed the defining characteristics

Table 8-3. The Tasks and Related Coping Behaviors of the Establishment Stage of Vocational Development *(After Super, 1963, p. 81)*

Tasks	*Attitudes and behaviors*
Implementation of a vocational preference (ages 21–25)	Recognizing the need to implement a preference
	Planning to implement a preference
	Executing plans to qualify for entry
	Obtaining an entry job
	Recognizing the need to stabilize
	Planning for stabilization
Stabilization in a vocation (ages 25–35)	Becoming qualified for a stable regular job or accepting the inevitability of instability
	Obtaining a stable regular job or acting on resignation to instability
Consolidation of status and advancement in a vocation (ages 35–40)	Recognizing the need to consolidate and advance
	Obtaining information as to how to consolidate and advance
	Planning for consolidation and advancement
	Executing consolidation and advancement plans

of the work history as: (1) the kinds of positions, e.g., clerk typist I, which the individual holds in the course of his work life; (2) the sequence in which he holds these positions, i.e., with reference to some "levels" factor such as ability, responsibility, or socioeconomic status; and (3) the amount of time he spends in each position. As a criterion or dependent variable, the work history might reflect vocational adjustment in several ways, depending upon whether the worker has many positions of short duration at the same level, progresses from positions at lower levels to positions at higher levels, moves from higher to lower positions, holds no position for a period of time, etc. The analogue which Tiedeman and O'Hara (1963, p. 68) suggest for the work history is that of the "holding relay" in an accounting machine:

> Suppose we imagine that a relay, one to a row, is either open or closed as the bank of relays is controlled in time. If a relay is open, a person is occupying the position corresponding to the relay; if closed, the person does not occupy the position. Each relay operates independently of all others. Each relay may be wired so that, once open, a subsidiary impulse continuously reactivates the control of the relay so as to keep the relay open. Such wiring is referred to as a holding relay. By means of the concept of holding relay we may encompass all that we need to consider in the problem of choosing positions; namely, a system where any set of relays may be activated at a particular instant, but, when once activated, remains activated continuously until de-activated.

The probabilities associated with whether a person will "hold open" a particular position, by staying in it, or close it and open another, by changing positions, are considered by Tiedeman and O'Hara along two dimensions: (1) whether the person is employed or unemployed, and (2) whether he sought or was tendered a new position. For example, if an individual is employed and seeks an offer for another position, he will have a predisposition to accept the offer if it is made.

Havighurst (1964) has collected case-study materials on the careers of four young men which illustrate some of the vocational adjustment patterns that are followed during the early stages of establishment in an occupation and which have suggested certain new conclusions about what the nature of vocational adjustment throughout the life span may be in the future. Two of the young men, Ray and Phil, had careers which were the mode before the Great Depression of the 1930s. Ray disliked high school, was the leader of a "tough" gang, and finally dropped out of school just before his sixteenth birthday to take a job in a laundry. He soon changed to a construction job, learned it quickly, progressed to the position of assistant foreman, and was being considered for the next foreman's vacancy at the age of 25. Similarly, Phil had no great interest in school, although he received average or above-average grades, and went right to work in a shoe store upon graduation. He also was promoted rapidly and was looking forward to a partnership in the business by the time he was 25. In contrast to Ray and Phil, the other two cases appear to typify career patterns on the contemporary scene: more and more young people are following one or the other of them. Joseph was an intensely work-oriented boy who began thinking seriously about his future vocation while only 12 years old. He pursued his educational goals assiduously and was awarded a fellowship to study physics in college, which, according to his plan, would lead to a career as a space scientist. Kenny was exactly the opposite of Joseph. Not only did he early lose interest in school, but he was a constant source of difficulty for his teachers. Moreover, he began to develop a criminal record and was continually in trouble with the authorities. At 25 he was a marginal worker with little or no prospect of steady employment.

Analysis of these, and other, case materials on the vocational adjustment and development of a large sample of youth have led Havighurst (1964) to conclude that there are three groups of workers which can be distinguished: (1) the maintainers of society, (2) the ego-involved entrepreneurs of society, and (3) the alienated. Havighurst estimates that approximately 50 percent of the labor force is in the first group, which is largely indifferent to their work; about 35 percent are in the second group, which is highly work-oriented; and roughly 15 percent are in the fast-growing third group, which openly rejects work either because they are unwilling to conform to ordinary social expectations (upper–middle-class beatniks) or because they have never learned the basic habits of industry as a result of parental neglect and deprivation (lower-class delinquents).

A General Theory of Vocational Adjustment

Dawis, England, and Lofquist (1964, p. 3) have proposed a "theory of work adjustment" which can be considered general in nature not only because it encompasses concepts and principles from many of the points of view we have just reviewed, but also because it "builds on the basic psychological concepts of stimulus, response, and reinforcement, and provides a research paradigm for the generation of testable hypotheses. "Furthermore, the theory is cast within a developmental context and takes cognizance of the fact that vocational adjustment is a process which evolves over time. The individual is seen as being born with certain "response potentials" which, in interaction with "potential reinforcers" in the environment, produce behaviors which constitute a primitive set of cognitive, perceptual, and motor "abilities."[6]

[6] For a discussion of the role of ability in formulating theories of behavior, see Baldwin (1958).

Similarly, a primitive set of "needs," e.g., achievement, attention, affection, etc., is developed from those reinforcers in the environment which occur most frequently in the reinforcement of the individual's responses. " 'Abilities' then are broad, but recognizable, classes of responses generally utilized by the individual, while 'needs' refer to the reinforcing properties of broad but recognizable categories of environmental conditions" (Dawis et al., 1964, p. 5). As the individual grows older, his abilities and needs become more highly differentiated, so that by preschool age the "inception of the work personality" is well under way.

The experiences which follow, from the beginning of school until entry into the world of work, serve to selectively reinforce the traits which have begun to emerge during the early years of life:

> The individual experiences differential utilization of his abilities because of differing social-educational requirements. This results in a set of more specific abilities operating at different strengths. A set of more specific needs, with different needs at different strengths, also develops as a result of the individual's experiences with different social-educational reinforcer systems [Dawis et al., 1964, p. 7].

The strength of the individual's abilities and needs depends primarily upon the extent to which they have been reinforced in the past. If they have been frequently reinforced over a long period of time, they develop into relatively fixed ability and need sets which complement each other and which constitute what Dawis, England, and Lofquist call the "stable work personality." They further define abilities and needs operationally by the tests which are available to measure them. Thus, at the time of occupational entry, the individual's "work personality" is seen as the product of social and educational experiences which have differentially reinforced certain abilities and aroused certain needs: together, these characteristics of the individual will determine how he will respond to the work environment. "The process by which the individual (with his unique set of abilities and needs) acts, reacts, and comes to terms with his work environment is called work adjustment" (Dawis et al., 1964, p. 8).

The major criterion of work adjustment in this theory is whether or not a worker remains in a given work environment once he has entered it. The longer he persists in it, the better is his vocational adjustment. If he leaves the work environment, and hence is vocationally maladjusted, it may be for either one or a combination of two reasons:

> "Leaving the work environment" may occur because the individual is no longer "satisfactory," i.e., he no longer exhibits the "appropriate" behavior and is forced to leave. On the other hand, "leaving

> the work environment" may be an action initiated by the individual because he is no longer "satisfied," i.e., some other work [sic] work environment is "more attractive" or his former work environment makes him "dissatisfied," or both. These conditions, under which the individual's relationship with a given work environment is terminated, imply two important indicators of the work adjustment process: satisfactoriness and satisfaction [Dawis et al., 1964, p. 8].

These two terms, *satisfactoriness* and *satisfaction,* will be defined more completely in a later section ("The Components of Vocational Adjustment"), but suffice it to say here that the first refers to the quality of the worker's performance on the job, as judged primarily by others, but also by himself, and the second refers to the worker's positive-negative feelings about his job. Given various levels of satisfactoriness and satisfaction, Dawis, England, and Lofquist deduce a series of propositions and research hypotheses about work adjustment which can be tested and evaluated empirically, in both cross-sectional and longitudinal studies. The hypotheses are too numerous to reproduce here, but the propositions of their theory are presented in Table 8-4. The authors of this theory also demonstrate its comprehensiveness in embracing other concepts of vocational adjustment and indicate its implications for vocational counseling, education, and certain special problem areas.

VOCATIONAL ADJUSTMENT IN RELATION TO GENERAL ADJUSTMENT

To define a concept like vocational adjustment, it is necessary to demonstrate how it differs from closely related concepts. As we shall see in the discussion which follows, some vocational psychologists think that there is very little difference between vocational and general adjustment, whereas others argue that the two are distinct phenomena. After reviewing these variant points of view, we shall summarize the available research on the issue and attempt to arrive at a resolution of it.

Contrary Viewpoints on the Relationship of Vocational Adjustment to General Adjustment

That an individual's vocational adjustment is largely a reflection of his general adjustment is a hypothesis which has found widespread acceptance in the field of vocational psychology, particularly among vocational counselors, for many years.[7] Pruette and Fryer (1923) early pointed to the influence of affective factors upon vocational adjustment and documented their observations

[7] General discussions of this topic in related fields, especially industrial psychology, can be found in Bender (1944), Cantoni (1955), Smith, M. (1936), and West (1951).

***Table 8-4. Propositions from a Theory of Work Adjustment** (Dawis, England, & Lofquist, 1964)*

PROPOSITION I. An individual's work adjustment at any point in time is defined by his concurrent levels of satisfactoriness and satisfaction.

PROPOSITION II. Satisfactoriness is a function of the correspondence between an individual's set of abilities and the ability requirements of the work environment, provided that the individual's needs correspond with the reinforcer system of the work environment.

Given Proposition II, these corollaries follow:

COROLLARY II*a*. Knowledge of an individual's ability set and his measured satisfactoriness permits the determination of the effective ability requirements of the work environment.

COROLLARY II*b*. Knowledge of the ability requirements of the work environment and an individual's measured satisfactoriness permits the inference of an individual's ability set.

PROPOSITION III. Satisfaction is a function of the correspondence between the reinforcer system of the work environment and the individual's set of needs, provided that the individual's abilities correspond with the ability requirements of the work environment.

Given Proposition III, these corollaries follow:

COROLLARY III*a*. Knowledge of an individual's need set and his measured satisfaction permits the determination of the effective reinforcer system of the work environment for the individual.

COROLLARY III*b*. Knowledge of the effective reinforcer system of the work environment and an individual's measured satisfaction permits the inference of an individual's set of needs.

PROPOSITION IV. Satisfaction moderates the functional relationship between satisfactoriness and the correspondence of the individual's ability set with the ability requirements of the work environment.

PROPOSITION V. Satisfactoriness moderates the functional relationship between satisfaction and the correspondence of the reinforcer system of the work environment with the individual's set of needs.

PROPOSITION VI. The probability of an individual's being forced out of the work environment is inversely related to his measured satisfactoriness.

PROPOSITION VII. The probability of an individual's voluntarily leaving the work environment is inversely related to his measured satisfaction.

Combining Propositions VI and VII, we have:

PROPOSITION VIII. Tenure is a function of satisfactoriness and satisfaction.

Given Propositions II, III, and VIII, this corollary follows:

COROLLARY VIII*a*. Tenure is a function of ability-requirement and need-reinforcer correspondence.

PROPOSITION IX. The correspondence between the individual (abilities and needs) and the environment (ability requirements and reinforcer system) increases as a function of tenure.

with case studies of workers who could not adjust to their jobs, despite being qualified for them intellectually, because of emotional disturbances. Similarly, Fisher and Hanna (1931) and Paterson and Darley (1936) have reported cases in which the personal maladjustment of the worker was directly related to his vocational maladjustment. More recently, Super (1951b, p. 89; italics in original) has concluded that "the nature of *vocational* adjustment is clearly very similar to the nature of *personal* adjustment, for the former is a specific aspect of the latter." He has also hypothesized that changes in one aspect of adjustment, whether vocational or general, will have salutary effects upon the other (Super, 1954), as has Forer (1953, p. 362) who observes that:

> Occupational adjustment can probably further personal adjustment in two ways: (*a*) by gratifying needs which are not completely gratified in non-occupational behavior (without frustrating other needs), and (*b*) by permitting an outlet for neurotic needs whose expression in other situations would lead to disaster or by providing sufficient neurotic gratification to prevent dissolution of the personality.

Menninger, K. A. (1942) and other psychoanalysts, adjustment psychologists (e.g., Shaffer & Shoben, 1956), and occupational sociologists (Clark, R. E., 1953) have also noted that vocational adjustment is a function of general adjustment.

There are others who maintain, however, that vocational and general adjustment are not necessarily related. Ginzberg (1962, pp. 23–24) states emphatically that:

> There is no direct link possible between the categories of mental illness and work adjustment.... There are, of course, seriously disturbed people who cannot fit into any normal work group. But most people are only a little disturbed and only at times, and they can fit into most work groups.

Much the same line of reasoning, although somewhat more qualified, has been expressed by Hoppock (1963, p. 105; italics in original):

> Instead of assuming that all vocational maladjustment is caused by emotional maladjustment, we might get nearer the truth if we explored the hypothesis that *in some cases* emotional maladjustment causes vocational maladjustment while *in some cases* vocational maladjustment causes emotional maladjustment.

In other words, Hoppock would allow for some correlation between vocational and general adjustment, but he does not consider it to be a high one. Likewise, Gellman (1953) is of the opinion that vocational adjustment is not a direct function of general adjustment, but he says that there may be a relationship between the two under certain conditions. What these are he does not specify in detail, although he mentions that "personality dynamics" may be involved.

Research on the Relationship of Vocational Adjustment to General Adjustment

The research which has been conducted on this problem, considering its conceptual and definitional importance, is surprisingly less than might be expected and often only tangentially relevant. Of the few studies which are available, however, one is a classic which is usually cited in any discussion of the issues involved in whether vocational and general adjustment are related. It is presented in considerable detail here, not only because of its recognized significance, but also because it is not generally available. The other studies are then summarized more briefly, and all the results are interpreted with respect to the question: Is vocational adjustment a special aspect of general adjustment?

The *classic study* referred to was conducted by Friend and Haggard (1948) as part of the research program of the Family Society of Greater Boston, a community psychological service which provided vocational counseling to a large number of workers, both employed and unemployed, during the period from 1934 to 1943. Unlike the research of MESRI, this study was concerned primarily with matching jobs to the personality of the worker rather than to his ability. The conceptual definition of vocational adjustment which Friend and Haggard (1948, p. 13) formulated as a guideline for the study and which reflects this emphasis was "the degree of balance between the satisfactions which the individual is seeking from his work and the satisfactions which the job provides." In other words, their basic criterion of vocational adjustment was satisfaction rather than success, although they also investigated what they called "vocational achievement." Other variables, of secondary interest, which were included in the investigation were improvement of clients after counseling and job values.

The data for the study were obtained from existing case records compiled on each client or Subject while he was in counseling by his vocational counselor and a social worker. The records contained not only the usual notes on the counseling process, but also the results of an extensive battery of tests and a complete personal-background history. To collate and quantify these data for the statistical analyses of the study, a "rating schedule" was devised which organized the information on a client into seven areas: (1) early life; (2) mature or current family life; (3) early or beginning jobs; (4) response to counseling; (5) personality and general work reactions; (6) reactions to specific working conditions; and (7) general work capacities, adjustment, and improvement. In all, there were 173 items in the rating schedule, which was applied to 80 case records, each one taking an average of 130 hours to rate! There were 67 men and 13 women in the study sample, all of whom were from the lower socioeconomic levels and unemployed at the time of their counseling. With only one exception, they were in the age range of 16 to 36 years, were usually the oldest child in the family, were predominantly "Yankee" in ethnic background, were mostly educated through some high school, were about equally married and unmarried, and were diagnosed in 60 out of the 80 cases as neurotic or as "having some neurotic tendencies."

The basic design of the study for the statistical analyses was to compare "extreme groups" of Subjects on the various items of the rating schedule, using a two-way chi-square table. In other words, groups of Highs and Lows selected from the total sample were cross-classified into the categories of each item in the rating schedule, such as "practically none," "some," and "considerable." The rating schedule was also used to constitute the comparison groups. For example, the groups of primary interest in the study, the Adjustment Highs and Lows, were formed according to whether Subjects had consistently "good" or "poor" ratings on the following items: general ability to use job qualifications, amount of specific use of client's abilities in jobs, general ability to feel satisfied, overall judgment of job satisfaction, overall stability or continuity of employment, prediction of adjustment in possible future depression period, contribution of current jobs to long-time employment outlook, and overall judgment of work adjustment. Each criterion group consisted of approximately 25 percent of the sample, the *N*'s ranging from 19 Highs and 20 Lows in the Improvement-after-Counseling comparison to larger *N*'s in the other group-difference analyses.

Because there were multiple comparisons on 173 items or "dependent" variables, it is practically impossible to present the results of the study here or even to summarize them in detail. An impression of what Friend and Haggard (1948) found can be gained, however, from a sampling of the conclusions which they drew:

1. On the relationship of family background to vocational adjustment: "Early homes are clearly the breeding ground for attitudes which make for a good or poor adjustment, and of the needs which individuals strive to fulfill in their work" (p. 50).

2. On the relationship of current family life to vocational adjustment: "The individual's capacity to stand on his own feet, evaluated in this later chapter of life when the achievement of independence takes the measure of emotional maturity, splits the two groups [adjustment Highs and Lows] more sharply than it did in childhood, portending the link between personal and job adjustment" (p. 51).

3. On personal versus vocational adjustment: *"One of the tightest links in* *our findings draws together the person's work and his personal adjustment"* (p. 137; italics in original).

4. On the dynamics which relate general and vocational adjustment: *"The worker appears to compromise with life by going after the identical and specific satisfaction in work denied him years before"* (p. 138; italics in original). And, "A specific manifestation of this tie between family and job attitudes is found in the frequency with which the worker endows his superior with the selfsame qualities of the parent, and currently feels toward the boss as he formerly did toward the parent" (p. 105). And, "We can view these current work attitudes . . . as *reaction formation* to the piling-up of earlier events at home, at school, and at previous work" (p. 63; italics added).

5. On the dynamics of vocational adjustment: The maladjusted worker's self-defeating behaviors "seem to be ways of settling early parental scores; or of handling the guilt which demands constant failure; or of protecting himself against fears of being unable to cope with work" (p. 59). And, "Ambivalence and self-attack, then, would seem to serve as a delaying action in protecting the individual from his fear of failing on the job. By overreaching toward too-difficult goals and by rigidity he may compulsively try to prove his adequacy in order to banish doubts of its existence. By job failure, he appears to launch a counteroffensive against his parent and simultaneously penalizes himself" (pp. 91–92).

Whether or not these conclusions should be accepted depends primarily upon whether they can legitimately be drawn from Friend and Haggard's data. Certain methodological flaws in the study suggest that they probably cannot, except with considerable caution and qualification. First, the rating schedule was used both to constitute the criterion groups *and* to measure the "dependent" variables. In other words, the two sets of variables were *not* experimentally independent, and consequently it is unknown whether any relationships between them are due to this factor or to intrinsic covariation or both. The number of items which differentiated between the criterion groups may be spuriously high because of a "built-in" correlation among the variables. Also, second, it may be high because the items tended to be positively correlated with each other, which had two effects: Subjects who scored high (or low) on correlated items which were used to form criterion groups were classified as extreme on more than one variable. Thus, the groups had overlapping membership, as Friend and Haggard note, and consequently the chances were increased that, if an item differentiated between one set of Highs and Lows, it would probably differentiate between a related set. Moreover, since the items on which the groups were compared were intercorrelated, the chances were that, if one item discriminated between Highs and Lows, related items would too. In short: it is possible that more significant findings were obtained than should have been the case, because neither the "criterion" nor the "dependent" variables were experimentally or statistically independent.

This effect may have been counteracted, however, by two additional shortcomings of the study. First, only the Highs and Lows were used in the group comparisons. The Middles were omitted. Consequently, any nonlinear relationship between the "criterion" and "dependent" variables, which might have been significant, were not investigated. And, second, as Friend and Haggard (1948, p. 50) note, the Highs in their criterion groups were not as "high" as the Lows were "low." In other words, the Highs were only in the "fair" range of the continuum on adjustment, whereas the Lows were at the lower end. Under the null hypothesis that there was no difference between the Highs and Lows on the "dependent" variables, then, the fact that both groups were not at the extremes of the adjustment continuum would make it more difficult to differentiate them. In light of these considerations, what *can* be concluded from the study? About the most that can be said is that the results *tend* to support the relationship of family background and general adjustment to vocational adjustment. The criterion groups did *not* completely overlap; the "criterion" and "dependent" items did *not* correlate perfectly; and, the Highs and Lows were *not* as disparate in adjustment as they should have been. Consequently, it would seem that *some* of the significant findings of the study are not due to the influence of these factors.

Other studies of this problem, however, have generally yielded less equivocal findings.[8] Super (1949) and Super and Crites (1962) have reviewed the accumulated research on the relationship of both paper-and-pencil and projective tests to job success, job satisfaction, and job stability, and have concluded that, although the correlations are often low, such tests as the Bernreuter Personality Inventory and the Rorschach do relate to various criteria of vocational adjustment (see, for example: Kates, 1950a, 1950b; Seagoe, 1946; Williams & Kellman, 1956).

Probably the most definitive evidence comes from two studies by Heron (1952a; 1955) on the relationship of various objective personality measures to two criteria of vocational adjustment: satisfactoriness and satisfaction. In the first study, he found that an "emotional instability" factor (many Worries + much Static Ataxia + many Annoyances + many Interests) correlated .45 with satisfactoriness, defined as "the extent to which a man is a source of concern to his supervisors." In other words, workers who were less emotionally stable

[8] For a related literature on the incidence of psychological disorders among industrial workers and the effects of emotional maladjustments upon productivity, see Brodman (1945); Fraser, Bunbury, Daniell, Barling, Waldron, Kemp, and Lee (1947); Marlowe and Barber (1952; 1953); Schachter, Willerman, Festinger, and Hyman (1961); and Weider and Mittelman (1946).

were a greater source of concern to their supervisors. Their instability did not affect their productivity, however, the correlation between these two factors being nonsignificant. In the second study, which was designed as a "cross-validation" of the first, although there were notable differences between them, Heron obtained a multiple correlation of .38 between a set of four personality measures and job satisfaction, as assessed by a 15-item inventory, but he was unable to replicate the correlation between the personality tests and "source of concern" to employer, which in this study also included indices of productivity or job performance. In short, he found a relationship between adjustment and satisfactoriness in one study, and between adjustment and satisfaction in the other.

Finally, it should be mentioned that, in a case-study analysis of the vocational adjustment of emotionally unstable soldiers in the Canadian army, Jaques and Crook (1946, p. 230) concluded that: "The poor adaptability of neurotic soldiers requires that conditions of work satisfy personal needs if good occupational adjustment is to be obtained."[9] This conclusion agrees with Super and Crites's (1962, p. 516) observation that: "It has been shown by surveys of employment records . . . that personality problems are the most common cause of discharge from employment."[10]

Interpretation of Findings. Despite the fact that the weight of the research evidence seems to support the relationship of vocational adjustment to general adjustment, it is equally apparent that the relationship is not a clear-cut one. In other words, it is not high enough to conclude that the two variables are identical, and it is not low enough to assume that they are independent. The pertinent question, then, is why do they tend to be moderately related? One explanation, based upon the differential development of mechanisms for adjusting in various life areas, has been proposed by Super (1957, p. 298), who reasons as follows:

> The basic modes of adjustment, both personal and social, learned in the primary family situation set the pattern for adjustment in other later situations. But since the individual continues to learn, new modes of behavior are acquired, new adjustment patterns develop, and personal and social adjustment in the home may differ in important ways from adjustment at school or at work. It is thus to be

[9] Cf. Ginzberg (1943) and Miner and Anderson (1958).

[10] See the following references for the literature upon which this statement is based, as well as studies of related topics: reasons for discharge—Brewer (1927a; 1927b), Gaudet and Carli (1957), and Hunt (1936); exit interviews—Melcher (1955), and Smith, F. J., and Kerr (1953); and why workers quit—Baruch (1944), McNaughton (1956), Palmer, D. L., Purpas, and Stockford (1944), Taft and Mullins (1946), and Walton (1960).

> expected that the intercorrelations of scales measuring personal, social, family, peer-group, school, and work adjustment would be positive and significant, but substantially short of unity.

Super also points out that "general" adjustment is definable only in terms of the several kinds of adjustment which the individual makes. Assuming that these are only partially interrelated, as he does, it would follow that no one type of adjustment, including vocational, would correlate either very high or very low with the composite.

In addition to the effects of differential experiences upon the development of adjustment modes, there is another variable which may also play a part in the relationship between vocational and general adjustment. This is the occupation itself. Depending upon its nature and the use the individual makes of it, it may attenuate or accentuate the relationship between vocational and general adjustment. For example, Danskin (1955, p. 134) has described the typically chaotic and often marginal living and working conditions of the professional dance musician, who moves continually, eats out frequently, drinks heavily, is plagued by domestic troubles, and experiences chronic job insecurity. It is not surprising, therefore, that: "By the time he becomes professionally adjusted, the musician typically has become culturally and socially maladjusted." In other words, in an occupation like this the better-adjusted worker would be the poorly adjusted person, and the correlation between vocational and general adjustment would be negative in such occupations or at least attenuated if considered over all occupations. In commenting upon the general adjustment of the eminent scientists whom she studied, Roe (1953a, p. 52) discusses the dynamics of this phenomenon at length:

> It should . . . be pointed out that for many of these subjects, the career itself has served as a technique for handling the personal problems. In some instances the basic problem has been, in a sense, extrapolated into a more general one, and the subject has then settled down to working on the general problem. This is a very neat and effective method. In other instances, absorption in the career has made possible the encapsulation of the difficulty in such a manner that it can be almost ignored by the subject.

In answer to the question "Are vocational and general adjustment related?", then, we can answer with a qualified "Yes," but hasten to add that further research is needed on *why* the relationship exists and *what* variables affect it.

A MODEL OF VOCATIONAL ADJUSTMENT

Each of the concepts of vocational adjustment which we have discussed thus far has made a contribution to our understanding of man's relation to work,

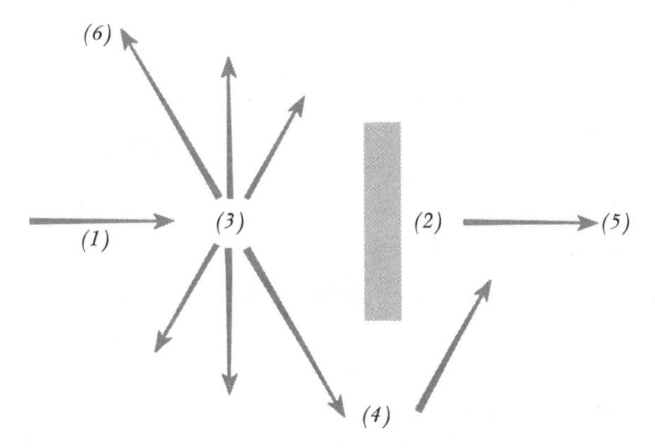

Figure 8-3. A model for the process of vocational adjustment. *(After Shaffer & Shoben, 1956.)*

but, although some of the concepts are quite comprehensive and some are actually theories which encompass several variables (e.g., Dawis, England, & Lofquist, 1964), none is sufficient as a frame of reference for the large body of research which has accumulated on vocational adjustment phenomena. To provide a conceptual schema for organizing and comprehending this research a Model of Vocational Adjustment is proposed in the following section which will be used as a general outline for the material covered in the next four chapters.

The model which has been adopted to conceptualize vocational adjustment comes from the area of adjustment psychology (Shaffer & Shoben, 1956), but has also been used in general (Dashiell, 1949) and experimental (Underwood, 1949) psychology with some modifications and variations. It is presented in schematic form in Figure 8-3. The first aspect of the model which should be noted is that it depicts vocational adjustment as a process, much as Bakke (1953), Super (1951b), and others have suggested with several interacting components. Paraphrasing Shaffer and Shoben (1956, p. 9), the dynamics of the vocational adjustment process, as shown in Figure 8-3, might be somewhat like this:

A worker is motivated, either by external or internal stimuli, to behave in certain ways on the job (1), such as to seek acceptance from co-workers, strive for prestige and recognition, achieve greater job freedom, etc. When he is thwarted in his behavior (2), either by some external circumstance (frustration) or by competing response tendencies (conflict), he attempts to adjust by making some response (3) which will eliminate the thwarting conditions or reduce the tension or anxiety they arouse in him. If he makes a response which is effective (4), he is readjusted vocationally and experiences either job satisfaction or job success or both (5). However, if he fails to respond in a way which either temporarily solves or permanently resolves his problem, he will persist in a state of frustration or conflict and be vocationally maladjusted (6).

In this model the degree or quality of an individual's vocational adjustment is evaluated primarily along two dimensions, job satisfaction and job success, as has been proposed by Lurie (1942), Lurie and Weiss (1942), Heron (1952a; 1954), Gellman (1953), and Scott, Dawis, England, and Lofquist (1960). It is recognized, however, that there are other criteria of vocational adjustment, such as occupational persistence (Strong, 1943; 1955) and vocational fitness (Scott et al., 1960), and that these might also be included in the model.

Furthermore, it should be noted that vocational adjustment is a *developmental* process which takes place over a long period of time (Scott et al., 1960; Super, 1957), with discernible stages in it (Miller, D. C., & Form, 1951; 1964; Super, 1957; 1963), and accordingly the model should be thought of as projected over the total span of the work years. That is, at any given point in time between occupational entry and retirement the dynamics of the individual's vocational adjustment should be as represented by the model. The content or nature of the components in the process will change as the individual grows older, so that an early motivation for material security may give way to a later motivation for social service, but the dynamics of the process, the sequence in which the components appear and interact, should remain the same. Because the substantive aspects of the components change, however, developmental trends in them should be taken into consideration, particularly with respect to the criteria of vocational adjustment. In other words, the model should be interpreted as a comprehensive one which encompasses not only cross-sectional definitions of satisfaction and success, but also the cycles which are known to occur in them throughout the work life of the individual.

9
VOCATIONAL MOTIVATION

The first component in the Model of Vocational Adjustment which we shall discuss is vocational motivation. We shall attend to the age-old question of "Why do men work?" and consider some of the answers which have been given. In the first part of the chapter, some of the conceptual schemata which have been formulated to explain vocational motivation are presented. Then, some of the methods which have been developed to measure vocational motivation are described, and conclusions about their reliability, validity, and general usefulness are drawn. In a third section, a classic and a recent study of vocational motivation are summarized, and their findings are related to the accumulated research on motivational factors in work. Finally, this chapter also deals with the second component in the process of vocational adjustment, reviewing theory and research on the thwarting conditions which the worker encounters in his attempts to satisfy his vocational motives and the adjustment mechanisms he uses to overcome these obstacles. Thus, the following topics are covered: (1) theories of vocational motivation, (2) measures of vocational motivation, (3) studies of vocational motivation, and (4) problems in vocational adjustment.

THEORIES OF VOCATIONAL MOTIVATION

There are several theories of vocational motivation which might be reviewed in a discussion of why men work. Most of the theories of vocational choice summarized in Chapter 3, for example, have implications for this topic (Zytowski, 1965). The majority of them do not deal directly with vocational motivation, however, and consequently do not provide comprehensive conceptualizations of this aspect of the vocational adjustment process. In contrast, the theories of vocational motivation which will be presented here were formulated specifically to deal with the problem of explaining what motivates the individual to work. One is a rudimentary "stimulus-response" theory; a second is an "adaptation level" theory; and the third is a "cognitive" theory of vocational motivation.[1]

A Stimulus-response Theory of Vocational Motivation

As implied by the definitions of stimulus and response given in Chapter 6, a stimulus-response theory of behavior is one which is constructed to explain variations in the responses of organisms by demonstrating or postulating corresponding variations in stimuli. In other words, in its most general form, a stimulus-response theory is based upon the assumption that responses (R) are functionally related to stimuli (S), as expressed in the formula $R = f(S)$ (Spence, 1944). Thus, it has been established that, despite their unpopularity among workers, wage-incentive programs (stimulus) do increase productivity (response) under certain conditions (Viteles, 1953, p. 29). Assuming that variations in a response are proportional to those in a stimulus, and that other stimuli have been properly controlled, it is sufficient to explain the response variations by reference to the stimulus variations. There are special cases, however, as mentioned in Chapter 6, when an intervening variable must be postulated to account for disproportionalities in the relationship between stimulus and response, e.g., when vigorous responses are evoked by a weak stimulus (Brown, J. S., 1961, p. 29). The use of intervening variables as theoretical constructs is particularly widespread, if not logically necessary (Brown, J. S., 1961), in the general field of motivational research and conceptualization, and it would be expected that they would be similarly utilized in work on vocational motivation.

Such has not been the case, however, except in a very general sense. The one statement of the possible relationships which may obtain between certain stimulus dimensions and job-performance behaviors has conceptualized the intervening motivational variables as *directly* related to the stimuli and responses. In other words, they "intervene" only in the sense of providing a conceptual link between the stimuli and responses; they do not account for disproportionalities in the relationships between these variables. The theory being referred to is one which Viteles (1953) adapted from earlier work by Charron (1951). It is summarized in Table 9-1, where it will be noted that the stimulus variables are called *incentives* by Viteles. These include the various job-related factors which may influence the individual's motivation to work and, in turn, affect his job performance. Viteles (1953, p. 76) notes that: "Incentives may be *positive* in character, in the sense of facilitating or promoting a particular form of behavior, or *negative* in the sense of inhibiting or ham-

[1] For other theoretical statements on vocational motivation, see Ginzberg (1954) and Moore, H. (1949).

Table 9-1. The Variables in Viteles's (1953) "Stimulus-Response" Theory of Vocational Motivation

Incentives	*Motives*	*Performance*
Fair wages	Economic security	Higher production
Pension plan	Emotional or personal security	Fewer absences
Compensation for sickness and disability	Self-expression	Decreased lateness
Death benefits	Self-respect	Improved quality of work
Bonuses	Recognition status	Active participation in company programs
Profit sharing		
Good working conditions		
Pleasant relations with associates		
Participation		
Knowledge of results		
Development of skills		
Recognition of efforts, etc.		

pering response of one kind or another." Thus, he conceives of an incentive as either reinforcing (strengthening) responses or extinguishing (weakening) them—but they do this only indirectly. "Whether positive, such as material rewards, praise, anticipated success, etc., or negative, such as reproof, penalties, removal of privileges, etc., 'incentives do not cause or initiate the behavior to which they are directed. . . . The immediate function of the incentive is to tap motives and to change attitudes which in turn redirect effort' and modify behavior." In short, Viteles sees incentives as the positive and negative reinforcing conditions which arouse the worker's job motives and which, through them, effect changes in job performance.

According to Viteles, the *motives* which incentives activate in the worker are states of tension which "cannot be observed directly." He concludes that "it is possible only to infer the existence of drives, needs, and wants, in part, from observed changes in behavior, especially in controlled experimental situations; in part, from *measurements of attitudes* which express the way in which and the extent to which given objects or situations are felt to satisfy wants, needs, desires, etc." (Viteles, 1953; p. 73; italics in original). Of these two approaches, he emphasizes the latter, defining an *attitude* as a "*state of readiness* for motive arousal or a reaction in a characteristic way to certain stimuli or stimulus situations" (Viteles, 1953, p. 74; italics in original). An attitude also implies an affective reaction or personal value on the part of the individual: he evaluates stimuli as being *positive* (attractive) or *negative* (aversive). And he *may* respond accordingly by either moving toward the stimulus (adient reaction) or away from it (avoidance reaction). If a worker considers his wages to be fair (positive attitude), the expectation would be that his production would be higher (job performance) than if he thought his wages were unfair. Given relationships between job attitudes and performance like this one, Viteles (1953, p. 74) proposes that attitudes can be "conceived as integrations mediating between the fundamental psychological processes and reactions." By this he means that attitudes are "intervening" or linking variables from which the worker's motives can be inferred and his performance can be predicted.

The dependent variable in Viteles's conceptual schema is, of course, job performance, which he defines primarily as the *efficiency* behaviors of the worker—how well he accomplishes the duties and tasks of his job. He does not include job satisfaction as part of job performance, but he does state that "workers with higher intrinsic job satisfaction are the more productive workers, at least in some job situations" (Viteles, 1953, p. 11). In other words, job satisfaction is not *directly* related to the worker's motives and attitudes; it is seen only as a possible outcome of job performance. Thus, Viteles's "theory of vocational motivation" is a stimulus-response theory which rests largely upon reinforcement concepts and which proposes that vocational adjustment (job performance and, to some extent, job satisfaction) is a function of goal-related job incentives as mediated by the worker's motives and attitudes.

An Adaptation-level Theory of Vocational Motivation

One of the major criticisms which has been levelled against stimulus-response theories of behavior, and which might also be made of Viteles's theory of vocational motivation, is that organisms frequently strive *not* to satisfy their needs or reduce their drives but rather to increase or intensify them, at least within certain limits (Shaffer & Shoben, 1956). Vroom (1964, p. 12) summarizes this criticism as follows: "There is considerable evidence that organisms, under many conditions, do not seek to avoid stimulation but to attain it. The optimal state does not appear to be the absence of stimulation as drive reduction theory would imply." The issue is far from closed, as the rejoinders of drive theorists make apparent (Brown, J. S., 1961), but it has provoked some new departures in explaining why organisms often engage in highly stimulating activities. One of these is adaptation-level theory, which proposes that the individual's frame of reference must be taken into consideration in order to determine the value of a stimulus to him. Helson (1948), Hebb (1949), and McClelland et al. (1953), among others, have suggested that:

> The satisfying and dissatisfying properties of any stimulus are dependent on the size of the discrepancy between the stimulus and a

> hypothetical neural organization or adaptation level, which has been acquired as a result of past stimulation. If the stimulus is mildly different from the adaptation level, it is pleasant; if it is highly different from the adaptation level or very similar to the adaptation level, it is unpleasant [Vroom, 1964, p. 12].

Operationally, an individual's adaptation level is defined as that value or magnitude of a stimulus which elicits a neutral or indifferent response. Adaptation-level theory consists of propositions which relate this concept primarily to perceptual phenomena (Helson, 1959), but recently it has also been utilized in vocational psychology.

Katzell (1964) has formulated a theory of vocational motivation in which the concept of adaptation level is central. He begins by translating the adaptation-level model into vocational terms by equating the worker's job values to magnitudes of stimuli which evoke higher levels of job satisfaction than other magnitudes of the stimuli. That is, a job value is operationally defined as that magnitude of a stimulus which produces the most pleasing response (hedonic tone) in the individual. For example: material reward would be a job value, if large amounts of it are more satisfying to the worker than lesser amounts of it. For each job value, defined in this way, there is an adaptation level for the individual which has resulted from past exposure to the stimulus, so that: "The extent to which a stimulus evokes an effective response that is less than maximally pleasurable is postulated to be directly proportional to the absolute discrepancy between the magnitude of the stimulus and its corresponding value, and inversely proportional to the value" (Katzell, 1964, p. 343). Expressed symbolically in equation form, this proposition states the following functional relationship:

$$d_x = f\left(\frac{X_i - V_x}{V_x}\right)$$

where d_x represents the departure from maximum pleasantness, or the relative amount of displeasure or, in vocational terms, job dissatisfaction; X_i represents the magnitude of a stimulus, e.g., a wage-incentive plan; and V_x represents the magnitude of a stimulus of Type X, e.g., material reward, which evokes the most pleasurable effect, i.e., the job value. Note that $X_i - V_x$ is the numerator of the right-hand term because it is *directly* proportional to job dissatisfaction and V_x (actually, $1/V_x$) is the denominator, because it is *inversely* proportional to job dissatisfaction. Finally, it should also be noted that job satisfaction is defined by Katzell as the complement of job dissatisfaction, or $s_x = 1 - d_x$.

It is apparent from this application of adaptation-level theory to the interrelationships of job characteristics (X_i) and job values (V_x) that Katzell (1964, p. 341) conceives of job satisfaction as the outcome of "interactions between job incumbents and their job environments: incumbents possess values or needs, and jobs are more or less instrumental in providing fulfillments or reinforcements." Stated somewhat differently, job satisfaction is a function of the extent to which "job features match the values of the incumbent." Katzell (1964, pp. 349–352) cites illustrative research in support of this assumption and summarizes it in the following five propositions:

1. Job satisfaction is positively associated with the degree of congruence between job conditions and personal values.
2. The more important or intense the values involved, the greater is the effect on job satisfaction of their attainment or negation.
3. Satisfaction with a given job or occupation will vary with the values of the incumbents.
4. Differences in job satisfaction among people having similar values will be associated with differences in their jobs or occupations.
5. The presence of certain job characteristics serves usually to evoke satisfaction, whereas their absence results only in neutral feelings; other characteristics serve usually to evoke dissatisfaction, whereas their absence likewise results only in neutral feelings; still others tend to evoke satisfaction when present in moderate amounts, but dissatisfaction results when they exist in amounts that are either too large or too small.

In a later section of this chapter ("Studies of Vocational Motivation") and in Chapter 11, we shall have occasion to review many of the studies referred to by Katzell in drawing these conclusions and evaluate the extent to which they support his theory.

In addition to the relationship of job satisfaction to job value, Katzell analyzes two other problems in constructing his adaptation-level theory of vocational motivation: the relationship of job satisfaction to job behavior (i.e., job performance or job success) and job-related changes in job values. With respect to the latter, he notes that:

> The value magnitude and intensity (importance) of a particular kind of stimulus may be changed through (1) satiation with the stimulus, (2) deprivation of the stimulus, (3) habituation to the stimulus, (4) association of the stimulus with another stimulus of high or low value, or (5) inducing a person to make a decision or commitment that is inconsistent with one of his values [Katzell, 1964, p. 357].

Katzell relates these assumptions about stimulus satiation and deprivation to Maslow's concept of the prepotency of motives, pointing out that as initially potent job values are satisfied, the less potent ones in the hierarchy become the determiners of job behavior, until they too are satisfied. Among these higher-order job values, self-actualization is the most important one. In this connection, then, Katzell's theory of vocational motivation is quite similar to some of the "need" concepts of vocational adjustment which were discussed in the last chapter.

A Cognitive Theory of Vocational Motivation

Vroom's (1964) cognitive theory of vocational motivation is a new one, but its antecedents in industrial and vocational psychology date back several decades. It owes its emphasis upon the work group and work role to the research of Elton Mayo and his associates in the 1930s, which culminated in the now-classical Hawthorne studies, but it also has roots in the "field" theory and research of Kurt Lewin, which was prominent during the same era. Reflecting the ninteenth-century work on electromagnetic fields in physics, Lewin proposed that the behavior of organisms is a function of the field in which they exist at the time the behavior occurs. He assumed that within the field there are objects or events which are positively or negatively valent and which constitute the goals of the organism. Behavior in the field is motivated by the forces which these goals exert upon the organism. In other words, Lewin conceived of behavior as being instigated primarily by the existing field, rather than antecedent conditions as in stimulus-response theories, and as being goal-directed or purposeful. He also attributed to the organism "internalized representation of [the] environment" or what Tolman (1948) has called "cognitive maps." There are other aspects of Lewin's field theory which might be mentioned, such as his use of topological concepts to represent the forces operating upon the organism, but these are not central to the theory of vocational motivation which we shall discuss.

In constructing a cognitive model to account for the motivation of work behavior, Vroom has drawn upon three concepts from Lewin's field theory:

1. The *concept of valence* is defined in terms of the individual's attraction toward the outcomes of two alternative courses of action or states of nature, x and y. If the outcomes are particular or specific ones, his affective orientation toward them is referred to as a *preference*; if the outcomes are part of a larger class of outcomes, however, his desire for them is termed a *motive, value* or *interest*. In either case,

> An outcome is positively valent when the person prefers attaining it to not attaining it (i.e., he prefers x to not x). An outcome has a valence of zero when the person is indifferent to attaining or not

> attaining it (i.e., he is indifferent to x or not x), and it is negatively valent when he prefers not attaining it to attaining it (i.e., he prefers not x to x [Vroom, 1964, p. 15].

2. The *concept of expectancy* refers not to the individual's attraction or aversions with respect to outcomes but to his subjective estimate that a particular act will be followed by a particular outcome (or class of outcomes). Since many choices between alternatives involve uncertainities or risks, the individual's behavior is determined not only by his preferences or motives, but also by his expectancies of attaining certain goals or objectives.

3. Together, the concepts of valence and expectancy lead to the *concept of force,* which is defined as follows: "*The force on a person to perform an act is a monotonically increasing function of the algebraic sum of the products of the valences of all outcomes and the strength of his expectancies that the act will be followed by the attainment of these outcomes*" (Vroom, 1964, p. 18; italics in original). In short, the combination of valences and expectancies results in a "dynamic" called *force* which has both direction and magnitude and which is the instigator of the individual's behavior.

Vroom (1964, p. 6) relates the concepts of valence, expectancy, and force to vocational behavior through what he calls the *work role,* which he defines as "a set of functions to be performed by a role occupant, the performance of which contributes to the production of goods and services." Assuming that the economy provides the opportunity for an individual to enter a work role, whether he will or not depends upon whether "the valence of outcomes which he expects to attain from working are more positive than the valence of outcomes which he expects to attain from not working" (Vroom, 1964, p. 29). Work roles have positive valence for the individual to the extent that:

1. They provide *wages* to the role occupant in return for his services.
2. They require from the role occupant the *expenditure of mental or physical energy.*
3. They permit the role occupant to contribute to the *production of goods or services.*
4. They permit or require of the role occupant *social interaction* with other persons.
5. They define, at least in part, the *social status* of the role occupant.

Each of these properties of the work role, with the possible exception of the second, has demonstrated motivational significance for the individual, in the sense that they attract him to, rather than repel him from, work as a means of attaining other outcomes, i.e., material well-being, affiliation with others, prestige, etc. Expenditure of mental or physical energy may or may not have positive valence for the realization of other outcomes, as was implicit in the conflicting psychoanalytic concepts of vocational adjustment discussed in the last chapter. Some argue that "work is drudgery," and hence it would have negative valence, whereas others maintain that it is intrinsically satisfying, and thus it would have positive valance. Vroom (1964, p. 34) resolves this dilemma by reasoning that:

> Conceivably there is some optimal level of activity [expenditure of energy]. Lower amounts are unpleasant and tend to result in an increase in activity level; and higher amounts, as in fatigue, are also unpleasant and tend to result in a decrease in activity level. In terms of our model, the valence of energy expenditure could be positive after prolonged inactivity but negative after prolonged activity.

In other words, a work role would be attractive to an individual only to the extent that it promised to satisfy his particular desire for the expenditure of mental and physical energy.

If the individual chooses to work, as most individuals in our society do, the theoretical problem of explaining vocational motivation becomes the threefold one of predicting (1) which occupation he will enter, (2) how much he will like it, and (3) how well he will do in it. That is, what will be the individual's occupational choice, job satisfaction, and job performance? Vroom's (1964, pp. 278–284) hypotheses concerning the latter two, based upon the foregoing definitions of valence, expectancy, and force, are as follows:

1. Job satisfaction
   a. The valence of a job to a person performing it is a monotonically increasing function of the algebraic sum of the products of the valences of all other outcomes and his conceptions of the instrumentality of the job for the attainment of these other outcomes.
   b. The force on a person to remain in a job in which he is presently working is a monotonically increasing function of the product of the valence of that job and the strength of his expectancy that he will be able to remain in it.
2. Job performance
   a. The valence of effective performance on a task or job is a monotonically increasing function of the algebraic sum of the products of the valences of all other outcomes and the worker's conceptions of the instrumentality of effective performance for the attainment of these outcomes.
   b. The force on a person to exert a given amount of effort in performance of his job is a monotonically increasing function of the alge-

braic sum of the products of the valences of different levels of performance and his expectancies that this amount of effort will be followed by their attainment.

THE MEASUREMENT OF VOCATIONAL MOTIVATION

Not until recently has there been much attention given to the measurement of vocational motivation, partly because theoretical interest in this phenomenon has heightened only within the past decade, but mostly because of the formidable definitional and psychometric problems which are involved. Brown, J. S. (1961, p. 24) notes that, despite the currency and vitality of the concept of motivation, "its meaning is often scandalously vague." Some say that motivation is essentially unconscious, and should be measured by "indirect" methods, such as projective techniques, whereas others argue that it is surely conscious, and should be assessed by "direct" methods, such as paper-and-pencil inventories (Allport, 1953). Freudians maintain that motivation is biologically based and consists of one or possibly two classes of instincts (Eros and Thanatos—life and death), whereas their critics propose that it is learned and encompasses many instigators to action, e.g., Maslow's (1954) hierarchy of eight needs. Many experimentalists subscribe to Melton's (1941) analysis of motivation into the three functions of (1) energizing the organism, (2) directing behavior, and (3) selecting responses, but a few (e.g., Brown, J. S., 1961) attribute only the energizing role to motivational variables. About the only point upon which there is general agreement in the field of motivation is that a considerable amount of further conceptualization and research remains to be done. Because vocational motivation has been subjected to even less systematic study than other aspects of motivation, this conclusion will be particularly apparent in the following discussion of (1) measures of vocational motivation, (2) factor analyses of vocational motivation, and (3) vocational motivation versus vocational interests.

Measures of Vocational Motivation

Although several different measures of motivation have been used to study occupational differences and vocational adjustment, they have been either too general or too specific in their content and purpose to be considered measures of *vocational* motivation. Such instruments as the Edwards Personal Preference Schedule and the Thematic Apperception Test are examples of motivational measures which are largely *non*vocational in nature and which consequently have several limitations for research on vocational motivation.[2] The

[2] See Tomkins (1947, Chap. 9), however, for the interpretation of TAT protocols for vocational variables.

most important of these is that they necessitate *assuming* one of the major hypotheses to be tested in research on vocational motivation, namely, that work not only is a means to the end of satisfying the individual's basic drives or needs but that it is also an end in itself which yields certain intrinsic satisfactions. Conversely, the questionnaires and rating scales which have been used in the many studies of job attitudes and preferences (Herzberg, Mausner, Peterson, & Capwell, 1957) are so restricted in their scope that they fail to measure dimensions of vocational motivation which are transsituational and which cut across all types of occupations. Thus, questions which elicit the worker's attitude toward the specific duties and tasks he performs on his job provide data which have few implications for the analysis of vocational motivation in other work settings. Finally, both types of measures—general and specific—are difficult to incorporate, as the empirical referents of concepts, into a meaningful theory of vocational motivation. These considerations suggest, then, that we might most profitably concentrate upon a review of measures of vocational motivation which are *vocational* in two respects: (1) in their content and (2) in their frame of reference.

The Work Values Inventory (WVI). Constructed as one of the basic instruments of the Career Pattern Study (Super & Overstreet, 1960), the WVI consists of 210 diads which are scored for 15 work values: Altruism, Creativity, Independence, Intellectual Stimulation, Esthetics, Achievement, Management, Way of Life, Security, Prestige, Economic Returns, Surroundings, Associates, Supervisory Relations, and Variety. The two statements in a diad, examples of which are "Create something new" and "Manage people and activities," are keyed to different work values, and the examinee is instructed to choose the one which is more important to him, thus making the scales of the WVI ipsative and subject to all the limitations of such scales (Baurnfeind, 1962), one of which is that they should not be intercorrelated and factor-analyzed (Guilford, 1952). Nevertheless, Super (1962) has reported the relationships among the WVI scales in order to test the hypothesis that they cluster into groups of intrinsic, concomitant, and extrinsic work values (Ginzberg et al., 1951). Contrary to his prediction, however, he found that 71 out of a possible 105 *r*'s were negative, and he concluded that: "Apparently the value structure of individuals cuts across Ginzberg's trichotomy, so that people are best characterized as seeking some intrinsic values, certain rewards, and particular concomitant satisfactions" (Super, 1962, pp. 233–234).

A more parsimonious interpretation of his findings is that they are an artifact of the ipsative nature of the WVI scales, since the central tendency of the expected distribution of *r*'s among them would be a negative coefficient which would approach .00 in the limiting case of an infinite number of scales (Radcliffe, 1963). In other words, his results do not *necessarily* indicate that work values cannot be grouped into Ginzberg's intrinsic, concomitant, and extrinsic categories. Less equivocal evidence on the WVI has been gathered by several other investigators who have shown not only that a modified, *free-response* version of the inventory has a demonstrable factorial structure (O'Connor & Kinnane, 1961), but also that it is related to vocational interests (Kinnane & Suziedelis, 1962), family background (Kinnane & Pable, 1962), certain life values (Kinnane & Gaubinger, 1963), and parental influence (Kinnane & Bannon, 1964). Research remains to be reported, however, on the relationship of the WVI to vocational success and satisfaction, although studies are currently in process in both the Career Pattern Study and the Specialty Oriented Student project (Hoyt, 1963; 1965).

The Initiative Scale (IS). Ghiselli (1955; 1956a) has developed the IS to quantify what he calls "initiative," which he defines as follows:

> There seem to be two aspects to initiative. One is motivational and involves the beginning of actions. The other is cognitive and concerns the capacity to note or discover new means of goal achievement. The first aspect implies a certain forceableness and self-assurance. The second implies an ability to see courses of action or implementations that are not readily apparent to others. Both aspects have the common characteristic of being self-generative.

Thus, Ghiselli aligns himself with those who would ascribe both the energizing and directing functions to a motivational variable, and his construction of the IS reflects this orientation.

Items for the IS were selected empirically from a pool of 64 pairs of adjectives (e.g., industrious-practical), administered under forced-choice instructions, by differentiating the responses of two groups of advanced undergraduates, one of which ($N = 118$) ranked "chance to show initiative" as either first or second out of eight occupational objectives and the other ($N = 71$) which placed it sixth, seventh, or eighth in order. From this comparison, 17 items were identified which significantly discriminated between the groups. In another sample of 300 male and female workers, which was representative of the adult employed population classified by occupational group, Ghiselli (1956a) found that the Kuder-Richardson Formula 20 internal consistency coefficient for this set of items was .85, indicating that they constitute a relatively homogeneous scale. He also found that the IS correlated .57 (r_{bis}) with ratings of initiative, .24 with proficiency in supervisory activities, .35 with management success, and .55 with a measure of self-assurance. Men and women do not differ significantly on the IS, but age and occupational groups do. In fact, there is an interaction between age and occupation, so that IS scores increase with age at the higher occupational levels and decrease at the lower levels. Evidence on the reliability and validity of the IS is, therefore, generally favorable.

There are two shortcomings of Ghiselli's work with the scale, however, which should be mentioned. First, he sometimes makes statements about differences between groups without running the appropriate statistical tests. For example, he states that the difference between mean IS scores obtained under standard and "fake-good" instructions was "slight and hence, the indication is that scores on the scale are not greatly influenced by faking" (Ghiselli, 1955, p. 162), but he does not report a t test for the significance of the difference. Similarly, he does not conduct an analysis of variance test for differences between occupational groups on IS, although he concludes that "mean scores show a progressive increase from the lower to the higher occupations" (Ghiselli, 1956a, pp. 316–317). Second, his reasoning and results on the relationship of the IS to intelligence are inconsistent. In his first study, Ghiselli (1955, p. 164) argued that the IS should measure something other than intelligence and, on the basis of a .09 correlation with ratings of practical judgment, he concluded that "whatever the initiative scale measures, it clearly is not intellectual ability." In his second study, however, he maintains that: "Since initiative is conceived as having certain cognitive aspects, it can be postulated that it should be related to measures of general intellectual ability" (Ghiselli, 1956a, p. 312). And, he reports an r of .26 (significant at the .01 level) between the IS and an intellectual scale, *but* he then states, with reference to this correlation coefficient, that "it is rather low and can be taken to indicate that initiative and intelligence have relatively little in common" (Ghiselli, 1956a, p. 316). Needless to say, further conceptualization and study of the IS in relation to intelligence is needed.

The Minnesota "Need" Questionnaires. Some of the most comprehensive research which has been accomplished on the measurement of vocational motivation has stemmed from the Minnesota Studies in Vocational Rehabilitation under the general direction of Dawis, England, and Lofquist. In order to test their theory of work adjustment, summarized in Chapter 8, these investigators found it necessary to devise their own measure of "needs," which, along with "abilities," is one of the major variables in their theory. The model they followed in constructing the Minnesota "need" questionnaires was taken from the theory, which "implies a measurement procedure in an experimental setting, where various classes of stimulus conditions can be presented experimentally to an individual and the reinforcement values of these stimulus conditions measured as an index of need strength" (Weiss, Dawis, England, & Lofquist, 1964, p. 6). Accordingly, items were written for the "need" questionnaires which symbolically (verbally) represented stimulus conditions in the work setting and which respondents could rate according to their reinforcement values. The first of the two "need" questionnaires developed by the Minnesota group was called the N-Factors Questionnaire (NFQ) and consisted of 48 items, allocated equally to each of the following 12 dimensions, which were adapted from the earlier work of Schaffer (1953): Achievement, Authority, Co-workers, Creativity and Challenge, Dependence, Independence, Moral Values, Recognition, Security, Self-expression, Social Service, and Social Status. Data from a sample of 521 disabled and 493 nondisabled workers indicated that the NFQ had certain desirable psychometric characteristics, such as relatively independent scales, but that it also had certain defects, such as several scales with unacceptable reliabilities. As a result, it was decided to develop a new questionnaire, which would be based upon the NFQ but which would not have its shortcomings.

The second "need" questionnaire has been named the Minnesota Importance Questionnaire (MIQ) in keeping with its instructions which require the respondent to rate on a 5-point scale the extent to which each of 100 statements about his "ideal job" are important to him. There are five items, such as "I could do something [on my ideal job] that makes use of my abilities," keyed to each of the following 20 scales: Ability Utilization, Achievement, Activity, Advancement, Authority, Company Policies and Practices, Compensation, Co-workers, Creativity, Independence, Moral Values, Recognition, Responsibility, Security, Social Service, Social Status, Supervision—Human Relations, Supervision—Technical, Variety, and Working Conditions. Results obtained from samples of 507 disabled and 453 nondisabled workers indicate that the MIQ has satisfactory reliability and some validity. The Hoyt internal-consistency estimates for the MIQ were found to be quite high for an instrument of this type, the median reliability for the 20 scales being .87. A factor analysis of the scale intercorrelations yielded two factors which accounted for approximately 57 percent of the total variance. One of these factors had loadings on all but three scales and was interpreted as a "general vocational need" dimension; the other was comprised primarily of the Authority, Responsibility, and Social Status scales and was identified as a "status need" dimension.

Several group-difference analyses have established that the MIQ differentiates significantly between disabled and nondisabled workers, occupational groups at different skill levels, and preemployment and employed groups. Moreover, many of these differences were consistent with the investigators' theory of work adjustment and lent support to it. For example, the theory states that "the development of a need set depends upon experiences of the individual with the reinforcers appropriate to the needs represented in the set" (Weiss et al., 1964, p. 51), the implication being that MIQ "need" scores would be lower for groups of individuals who have relatively little or no employment experience, and this was found to be true in the comparison of college undergraduates with employed workers. The former had significantly lower scores on 17 of the 20 MIQ scales.

In their interpretation of results of this kind, however, the Minnesota investigators may have made what may prove to be the major conceptual error in their research. They started with a theory which they wished to test. In order to do this they had to operationally define the concepts in the theory. One of these was the concept of "needs," which, for reasons of convenience and practicality, they chose to measure with questionnaires, although they recognized, as has been mentioned, that it might be directly assessed in a laboratory situation where "various classes of stimulus conditions" could be presented experimentally to a Subject and their relative reinforcement values determined by some standard procedure. They proceeded to study the psychometric characteristics of the "need" questionnaires and tested hypotheses with them which were deduced from their theory of work adjustment, such as the predicted lower mean scores of inexperienced individuals on the MIQ. It is at this point that some question can be raised about their logic, for they go on to reason that: "If these hypotheses concerning occupational [and employment] differences are not refuted by the data, it would seem that some validity can be ascribed to both the MIQ and the *Theory of Work Adjustment*" (Weiss et al., 1964, p. 40).

In other words, they are proposing that the *same* set of data can be used to establish that (1) the MIQ is a valid measure of needs *and* that (2) the theory is supported by fact. The logical fallacy in this argument is one of circular reasoning: if the theory is valid, then the MIQ should differentiate between occupational and employment groups; and if the MIQ differentiates between occupational and employment groups, then the theory is valid. The validity of a theory must be demonstrated *independently* of the evidence which is gathered for the definition of the concepts or terms in it (Bergmann, 1957). The Minnesota investigators follow this principle with respect to the concept of "abilities" in their theory: nowhere do they maintain that the validity data on standardized ability tests also supports their theory. They might also have followed it in validating the MIQ against the only relevant criterion for it: the reinforcement values of actual stimulus conditions in the work setting or, as a less preferred alternative, reproductions of them in the laboratory. Until the MIQ is validated in this manner, its validity must be *assumed* in any tests which are made of the theory of work adjustment.

Other Approaches. Thus far, we have discussed only paper-and-pencil measures of vocational motivation, but some other types should be mentioned, although they have not been as extensively studied. One of these is a projective technique called the Vocational Apperception Test (VAT), constructed by Ammons, Butler, and Herzig (1949; 1950) and patterned after the Thematic Apperception Test. The rationale for this instrument is based upon the assumptions that vocational behavior is closely related to personality functioning and that in responding to a series of unstructured pictures of work situations an individual will reveal his motivations for working and his mechanisms for adjusting to a vocation. Examples of motives which are scored on the VAT are: Security, Altruism, Seclusion, Independence, and Idealism. The reliability and validity of the scores, however, are largely unknown. Reviews of the VAT in Buros (1953) consider it to be an intriguing and potentially useful approach to the assessment of the "vocational personality" but are critical of its psychometric development. In short, the VAT represents "a good idea, poorly executed."

Of greater promise as measures of vocational motivation, primarily because of their more extensive empirical study, are two scales for the assessment of "unconscious motivations for teaching" developed by Stern, Masling, Denton, Henderson, and Levin (1960). Called the Attitude (A) and Gratification (G) scales, they were constructed from comments made by 29 teachers who were intensively interviewed about their primary sources of gratification from teaching. As Table 9-2 shows, it was found that teachers seek many different kinds of gratifications from the roles they play in the classroom and form attitudes which reflect their motivations and satisfactions. The A and G scales were designed to assess these respective dimensions, and preliminary data on them indicate that they are potentially useful for this purpose. The test-retest reliabilities for the various scoring keys of both scales are in the .70s and .80s, with only a few exceptions which are in the upper .60s. The items of the scales discriminate reasonably well between high and low scorers, and appropriate group differences were found between student teachers characterized as

Table 9-2. Gratifications and Attitudes Sought in Different Teaching Roles *(From Stern, Masling, Denton, Henderson, & Levin, 1960, p. 15)*

	Role	*Gratifications*	*Attitudes*
1.	Practical	Instrumental rewards	Detachment
2.	Status-striving	Prestige	Professional dignity
3.	Nurturant	Children's affection	Providing love
4.	Nondirective	Children's autonomy	Encouraging self-actualization
5.	Critical	Promoting teachers' rights	Reforming schools
6.	Preadult-fixated	Vicarious participation	Identification with children
7.	Orderly	Obsessive compulsions	Developing good pupil habits
8.	Dependent	Support from superiors	Cooperation with authority
9.	Exhibitionistic	Children's admiration	Showmanship
10.	Dominant	Children's obedience	Maintaining discipline

"teacher-centered" and "student-centered." Although restricted to one occupation, these scales are provocative and might well be taken as models for similar measures of vocational motivation in other occupations. Finally, the interview as a technique for assessing vocational motivation should be noted. Stern and his co-workers employed it in their pilot work on the A and G scales, and, as will be discussed below, Herzberg, Mausner, and Snyderman (1959) used it as their basic method for collecting data.

Factor Analyses of Vocational Motivation

Factor analysis has been applied in two ways in the measurement of vocational motivation: (1) in the development of scoring keys for scales and (2) in the study of interrelationships among scales. We shall deal with the construction of factorial measures of vocational motivation first and then review a factor analysis of their correlations with each other. The three inventories described that will be described here are no less measures of vocational motivation than those considered in the last section. In fact, one of them, the Occupational Attitude Rating Scales, is considerably better in several respects. They are included here only because factorial methods were used in their development and in some of the subsequent research on them.

The Occupational Attitude Rating Scales (OARS). The OARS consists of four 10-item scales—Materialistic, Competitive, Technical, and Humanitarian —which Hammond (1954; 1956; 1959) has derived from a series of factor-analytic and related studies. The examinee is instructed to rate each item, examples of which are "earn big money" and "help others help themselves," on a 5-point scale ranging from *much liked to much disliked.* The 40 items in the current version of the OARS were culled from earlier 70- and 90-item editions by having judges sort the items into 12 "cluster piles" and then factoring the intercorrelations of these categories for samples of 200 male and 400 female college freshmen. The original 12 "cluster piles" were reduced to 6 and finally to 4 by means of the Wherry-Winer (1952) method for factoring large numbers of items. Consequently, the resulting scales are relatively independent, the highest intercorrelation being an r of .28 between Materialistic and Competitive, and they are also fairly unidimensional, the internal consistency coefficients ranging from .66 for Materialistic to .80 for Humanitarian. There are no test-retest reliability data on the OARS, but the split-half estimate for the total test, corrected by the Spearman-Brown formula, is .75.

Evidence for the validity or usefulness of the OARS comes from two studies. In the first, Hammond (1956) found that there appeared to be marked differences in the OARS mean scores of college students with different vocational choices. She failed to test the differences for statistical significance, however, which means that they may or may not have been greater than what would have been expected on the basis of chance sampling fluctuations. In the second study, the data are somewhat more definitive, since Hammond (1959) conducted *t* tests of the differences between the means of college engineering students administered the OARS in 1953 and again in 1958 and found that those who had successfully completed the curriculum had OARS scores which agreed more closely with the faculty's perception of the "ideal" student at the end of the training period than at the beginning. As the writer has pointed out elsewhere (Crites, 1963a), these findings suggest that the OARS is related to persistence in an activity and acquisition of responses appropriate to the attainment of a desired goal, both of which are criteria of a motivational variable, and consequently they support the validity of the inventory as a measure of vocational motivation.

The Job Incentive Rankings (JIR). Interested in developing a taxonomy of job incentives, Bendig and Stillman (1958) designed a study in which they could determine whether the incentives most preferred by college students could be located on a hypothesized "need achievement versus fear of failure" dimension, derived from the work of McClelland, Atkinson, Clark, and Lowell (1953) on achievement motivation. The incentives which these investigators asked their Subjects to rank from high to low along a continuum of how important they are in selecting a job were the following: opportunity to learn new skills, friendly fellow workers, freedom to assume responsibility, good job security, good prospects for advancement, full insurance and retirement benefits, recognition from supervisors for initiative, and good salary. A sample of 267 Subjects provided the rankings of the job incentives, as well as additional information on their vocational choices and any other incentives they considered important in deciding upon a career.

For a factor analysis of the rankings, a random sample of 100 Subjects was drawn, and scores of 1 and 0 were assigned to each incentive by dichotomizing them into those ranked 1 to 4 (scored as 1) and 5 to 8 (scored as 0). Three factors were identified in the analysis of the incentive intercorrelations: the first was the hypothesized "need achievement versus fear of failure" dimension; the second was tentatively named "interest in the job itself versus the job as an opportunity for acquiring status"; and the third was interpreted as "job autonomy versus supervisor dependent." Incentive factors which were suggested by the Subjects, in addition to those yielded by the factor analysis, included these: opportunity to help others, job satisfaction, and job interest and variety. No analysis was made of the relationship between the factored incentives and the vocational choices of the sample, nor were data reported on the reliabilities of the rankings. The confidence which can be had in the JIR as a measure of vocational motivation must be tempered, therefore, by this lack of evidence on its psychometric characteristics.

The Work Satisfaction Questionnaire (WSQ). Adopting a different conceptual scheme as a frame of reference, Astin (1958) has constructed the WSQ to measure the vocational motivations associated with Ginzberg's classification of the sources of work satisfaction as intrinsic, concomitant, and extrinsic. This instrument consists of 21 statements about the general characteristics of jobs, such as "directing, controlling, and planning the activities of other employees," which the respondent rates on a 7-point Likert-type scale of "desirability." For a sample of 200 male college freshmen, Astin computed the product-moment correlations among the items and then performed a "B-coefficient" cluster analysis on them. He was able to identify four fairly distinct clusters: managerial-aggressive, status-need, organization-need, and one which he refrained from naming. None of the clusters corresponded to Ginzberg's categories, however, with the possible exception of the status-need cluster which included several items, such as "A job where the work itself is uninteresting to me but which pays a very high salary," that appeared to define an extrinsic motivation to work. Additional analyses of the item clusters showed that they were essentially independent of each other and that some of them were related to vocational choice. For example, college students who plan careers in sales and persuasive occupations have higher scores on the managerial-aggressive cluster, and those who choose science have higher scores on the organization-need cluster. Astin does not report reliability estimates for the cluster scores, and there are no other published data on them. Consequently, the WSQ should be considered only a potentially useful measure of vocational motivation, about which little is known.

Factor Analysis of OARS, JIR, and WSQ. Several of the scales of these three instruments, although bearing different names, appeared to the writer (Crites, 1961a) to be related, either because their empirical validity was similar or because their items were similar. For example, the Materialistic (OARS) and Managerial-Aggressive (WSQ) scales both discriminate students who choose business from those who choose other fields, and the Managerial-Aggressive (WSQ) and Achievement-Need (JIR) scales both contain items which state a preference for job autonomy ("A job where I do *not* work under instructions" and "Freedom to assume responsibility"). It seemed reasonable, therefore, to intercorrelate the scales of the three inventories and factor-analyze them in an attempt to clarify the nature and structure of vocational motivation. The results of this analysis, for a sample of 300 male and female (150 each) college students, are depicted graphically in Figure 9-1, where the larger circles represent the five factors which were extracted and the smaller circles indicate the scales which loaded on more than one factor.

Since the factors were originally labelled, it has seemed appropriate to change the name of Factor C from "Social Approval" to "Behavior Control" (Caplow, 1954), in order to make more explicit its emphasis upon a motivation for *power* over others, however altruistic or benevolent this desire might be. Otherwise, subsequent research on the factors, some of which will be summarized here, has tended to support the designations and interpretations given to them. More generally, it can be concluded that they constitute a relatively good sampling of fairly distinct (independent) dimensions in the domain of vocational motivation, representing the needs for autonomy (Job Freedom),

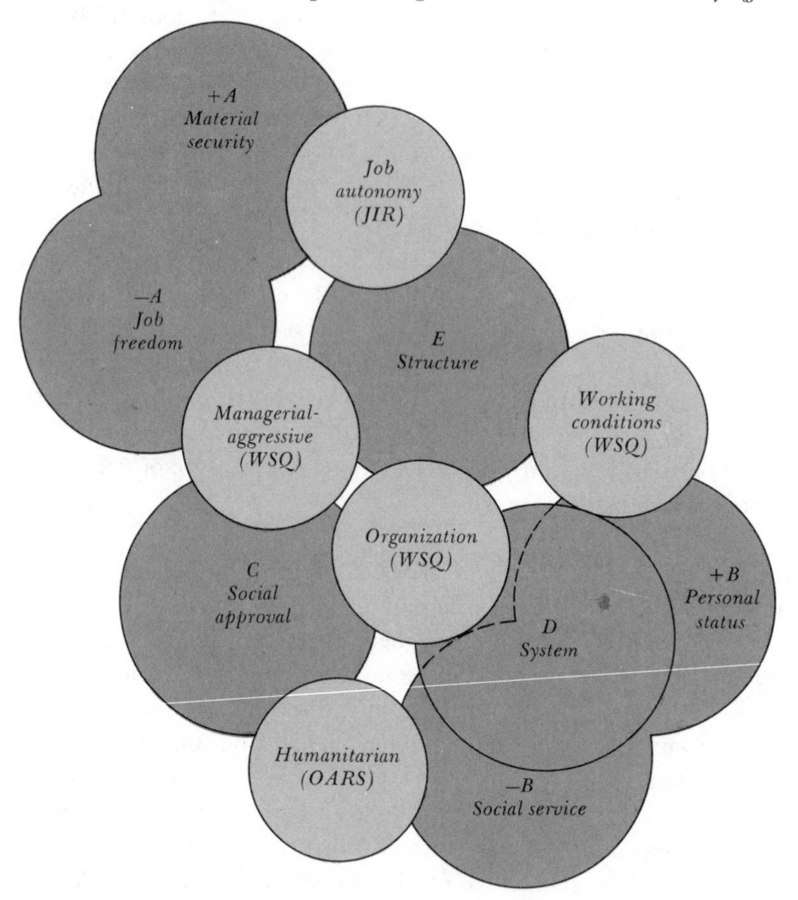

Figure 9-1. Factorial structure of scales designed to measure vocational motivation. *(From Crites, 1961a, p. 332.)*

order (System), security (Material Security, Structure), service (Social Service), and status (Personal Status, Behavior Control), and that they correspond rather closely to Ginzberg's concepts of intrinsic (Job Freedom, System, Social Service), concomitant (Structure), and extrinsic (Material Security, Personal Status, and possibly Behavior Control) sources of work satisfaction. To measure these factors, the writer (Crites, 1963a) has developed a 78-item inventory called the Vocational Reaction Survey (VRS) which simply recasts the best (highest factorial loadings) items from the OARS, JIR, and WSQ into the same grammatical form and uses standard instructions for responding to them. A five-position IBM answer sheet can then be utilized to obtain scores for the various types of vocational motivation.

Other Studies. Brief mention should be made of three other factor analyses which have obtained somewhat similar results, although the measuring instruments and statistical methods were different.

1. Gordon, O. J. (1955) found four factors in an analysis of "needs and morale" for 179 accounting and clerical workers grouped into 21 work units within an organizational division and a comparable number (exact N not given) in 15 work units in another division. The first factor was identified as "Morale" or general satisfaction of all needs, which was not included in Crites's (1961a) study. The second factor, "Recognition of Status," corresponds to Personal Status, and the third factor, "Self-respect," is similar to Job Freedom. The fourth factor was not named by Gordon, since it appeared in only one of the organizational divisions.

2. Schutz and Mazer (1964) administered a 60-item questionnaire on reasons for choosing counseling as a career to a sample of 153 graduate students and then factor-analyzed the inter-item correlations with the principal components method. They extracted a large number of factors, 18 in all, but two of these stood out as more significant than the others, together accounting for about 28 percent of the total variance. The first of these was named "Status-Prestige" and appears to be quite similar to the Personal Status factor. The second was called "Altruism-Social Service" and corresponds closely to the Social Service factor in the writer's study (Crites, 1961a). The remaining factors in Schutz and Mazer's investigation were more specific than these two, although some of them could be related to the previous findings on the OAR, JIR, and WSQ.

3. Finally, O'Connor and Kinnane (1961) obtained findings with their modification of the WVI which most closely corroborate those of the writer. These investigators identified the following six factors in the WVI, which are listed along with their counterparts from the factor analysis of the OARS, JIR, and WSQ:

O'Connor & Kinnane (1961)	*Crites (1961a)*
Security-Economic-Material	Material Security
Social-Artistic	Social Service, Behavior Control
Work Conditions and Associates	Structure
Heuristic-Creative	System
Achievement-Prestige	Personal Status
Independence-Variety	Job Freedom

There is some consistency, then, in the findings on the number and kind of vocational motivation factors which can be defined, and, even more encouraging, the fact that these results have been established with different measuring instruments indicates that a certain degree of what Underwood (1957, p. 205) has termed *operational identification* has been achieved.

Vocational Motivation and Vocational Interests

There has been a considerable amount of speculation about the relationship between vocational motivation and vocational interests which asserts that vocational interests *are* vocational motives. Darley and Hagenah (1955, p. 191) have observed that "occupational interests reflect, in the vocabulary of the world of work, the value systems, the needs, and the motivations of individuals." Similarly, Strong (1955, p. 142) has reasoned that: "Interest scores measure a complex of liked and disliked activities ... equivalent to a 'condition which supplies stimulation for a particular type of behavior'.... Interest scores are consequently measures of drive." The empirical evidence in support of these statements, however, is not nearly as conclusive as the statements appear, as will be brought out in the following summary of research on (1) the Occupational Level scale of the SVIB as a measure of "drive" and (2) the relationship of vocational motivation factors to vocational interests.

The Occupational Level (OL) Scale as a Measure of "Drive." In his first monograph on the clinical interpretation of the SVIB, Darley (1941) suggested that the OL scale assessed the individual's eventual adult "level of aspiration," and in Strong's (1943, p. 465) classic book on the SVIB Darley wrote: "I am becoming clinically more convinced ... that the occupational level score is an excellent quantitative statement of a form of motivation ... that is referred to in the literature as 'drive.'" Research findings on this hypothesis have been equivocal enough, however, that whether the OL scale is a measure of vocational motivation or not is still an open issue.[3] The OL scale has been related

[3] See Carkhuff and Drasgow (1963) for the most recent review of the literature on the OL scale. These reviewers concluded, as did Barnett et al. (1952), that "the OL scale measures just what it was intended to measure: the occupational level to which an individual's interests correspond" (Carkhuff & Drasgow, 1963, p. 283). They cite 38 references on the OL scale and related research.

to several types of variables, including (1) self-rated level of aspiration (Barnett, Handelsman, Stewart, & Super, 1952), (2) teachers' and peers' ratings of "drive" (Ostrom, 1949b; Barnett et al., 1952), (3) interview ratings of "drive" (Ostrom, 1949b), (4) satisfaction with college curriculum (Berdie, 1944b), (5) satisfaction with being unemployed (Barnett et al., 1952), (6) vocational and educational plans (Barnett et al., 1952), and (7) academic achievement in high school and college, with scholastic aptitude held constant (Kendall, 1947; Ostrom, 1949a).

From this welter of studies, only the findings on OL in relation to ratings of "drive" are unequivocal. Ostrom (1949b) obtained r's which ranged between .39 and .61 for OL with interview, peer, and teacher ratings, and an r of .53 with a total score on the ratings combined. Likewise, Barnett et al. (1952, p. 16) report r's of .23 and .25 (.05 level) for two schools in which teachers' ratings of "level of aspiration" were correlated with OL. In the other investigations, either OL did not correlate with the variables or it did sometimes but not others (Barnett, Stewart, & Super, 1953). As a consequence, conflicting conclusions have been drawn about what OL measures. Barnett et al. (1952, p. 29) state flatly that: *"The evidence does not warrant interpreting the OL score as a measure of drive"* (italics in original). In contrast, Darley and Hagenah (1955, pp. 117–118) continue to take the position that the OL scale is "a meaningful index of the students' [sic] occupational aspirations and the attendant status correlates of occupations."

Whether these differences of opinion will ever be resolved is in itself a moot point, and proffering still another opinion may simply confuse matters further. Nevertheless, it seems worthwhile to suggest a new way of looking at the data on the OL scale, which, if it is not considered an opinion, may be viewed as a recentering of our thinking on the problem. If we asked which of the variables OL has been related to constitutes the most *relevant* criterion for validating it as a measure of "drive," we would be hard pressed not to answer that the interview, peer, and teacher ratings of drive, as obtained primarily by Ostrom (1949b) but also by Barnett et al. (1952), are probably the most pertinent. And, it is exactly with these variables that the correlations with the OL scale have been found. Logically, the correlations with all the other variables, and particularly with grades, which have been studied most often, are basically irrelevant to the validity of the OL scale as an index of drive. In order to correlate OL with these variables, the assumption must be made *first,* either implicitly or explicitly, that the scale measures drive. The reasoning would be as follows: *If* OL is a measure of drive, and if drive is related to variable x, then OL should be related to variable x. Suppose it is argued, however, that the major premise of this syllogism need *not* be assumed to study the relationship of OL to variable x. But, then, why study the relationship at all? The minor premise clearly states that "drive is related to variable x." Therefore, if it is not assumed that OL measures drive, there is no reason to expect it to be related to variable *x*.

Actually, we do not have to *assume* the truth of the major premise at all, if we accept the findings on the relationship of OL to the ratings of drive. If OL is considered to be a valid measure of drive, however, how can its nonsignificant and contradictory relationships to the other variables be explained? To answer this question, the truth of the minor premise in the syllogism must be evaluated: it may well be that the *x* variables are the ones which are unrelated or inconsistently related to drive rather than OL. To illustrate, consider grades, which are assigned on almost as many bases as there are students. In some schools, it may be that teachers take drive into consideration in giving grades and hence OL correlates with them, but in other schools, it may be that grades reflect a student's personal attractiveness, neatness, punctuality, obedience, or father's position on the board of education, and consequently OL is not related to them. Before we conclude that OL is not a measure of drive, therefore, it may be worthwhile to establish that the variables we expect it to correlate with should be related to drive.

The Relationship of Vocational Motivation Factors to Vocational Interests. The factors which O'Connor and Kinnane (1961) extracted from their analysis of a free-choice version of Super's Work Values Inventory were related by Kinnane and Suziedelis (1962) to interest patterns on the SVIB for 191 college freshmen and sophomore males. For each vocational motivation factor, the analysis compared the proportion of Highs and Lows which had A's and B+'s in a SVIB interest group with the theoretically expected proportion. The results showed that each factor was related to at least one SVIB group, and some were related to several. Security-Economic-Material, the cognate of Material Security in Crites's (1961a) study, was positively correlated with primary and secondary interest patterns in the Physical Science, Technical, and Business Detail groups and negatively related to the Biological Science, Social Service, and Literary groups. In contrast, Social-Artistic, best represented by Crites's Social Service and Behavior Control factors, was positively associated with primaries and secondaries in the Social Welfare, Business Contact, and Literary groups and negatively correlated with the Physical Science, Technical, and Business Detail groups. Heuristic-Creative, the writer's System factor, was positively related to Physical Science and Technical but negatively correlated with Business Contact. Finally, Independence-Variety (Job Freedom) had negative relationships to Technical and Business Detail, as did Achievement-Prestige (Personal Status) with Technical, but neither factor had positive correlations with any of the SVIB groups.

From these findings Kinnane and Suziedelis (1962, p. 146) drew the following conclusion: "The results indicate a very high degree of relationship between work-values and inventoried interests. They support the notion that the individual's patterning of inventoried interests closely reflects his ways of valuing work." We can agree that their data established a significant relationship between work values and vocational interests, but the type of analysis they used does not allow them to infer that the magnitude of the relationship was "very high." To make this kind of statement a correlational, rather than an extreme-groups, analysis is necessary.[4]

Such a study was conducted by Crites (1963c), and, with certain qualifications, the *r*'s supported the inference that there is at least a moderately high relationship between vocational motivation factors and vocational interests. Product-moment correlations were computed between each of the vocational motivation factors mentioned earlier (Crites, 1961a) and each of the occupational and nonoccupational scales of the SVIB for a sample of 130 male undergraduates. Lindquist (1953) Type I analyses of variance were also run to compare Subjects with primaries and secondaries in each interest group to those with no patterns on the various vocational motivation factors. To summarize the correlational data for ease of interpretation, average *r*'s for each factor in each interest group were computed. These revealed several notable patterns of relationships, which Crites (1963c, p. 283) summarized as follows:

> The motivation factors which accounted for the largest amount of variation in interests across the 11 SVIB groups were the System, Social Service, and Behavior Control variables. In combination, these motives seem to correspond rather closely to the "Things versus People" bipolar factor identified by Thurstone (1931) and Strong (1943) in factor analyses of SVIB, which suggests that this interest-motivation dimension may be the basic one along which occupations are differentiated.

Although both of these studies demonstrated that there is a relationship between vocational motivation factors and vocational interests, the nature of the relationship was not exactly the same in the two sets of findings. Whereas Kinnane and Suziedelis found that Security-Economic-Material was related to several SVIB groups, Crites obtained only nonsignificant correlations between Material Security and interests. In contrast, Crites found that Job Freedom was positively related to both Biological Science and Physical Science, but Kinnane and Suziedelis reported only negative correlations between Independence-

[4] Although not a study of vocational motivation *factors* in relation to vocational interests, Ivey (1963) did intercorrelate the scales of the WVI and the KPR, but with few positive findings. He comments that: "The results of this study do not seem to support fully the findings of Kinnane and Suziedelis. The findings here suggest a smaller degree of relationship between interests and work values than has previously been indicated" (Ivey, 1963, p. 122). It should be noted, however, that Ivey used the forced-choice version of the WVI, as well as the KPR as his measure of interests.

Variety and the Technical and Business Detail groups. Any number of factors may have contributed to these differences, but probably the most parsimonious explanation is the twofold one that (1) the measures of the vocational motivation factors were not the same and (2) the statistical analyses were different. It should be noted, however, that in both investigations the greatest amount of differentiation among interest groups and scales was along the Things versus People vocational motivation dimensions, i.e., Social-Artistic and Heuristic-Creative in Kinnane and Suziedelis's study, and Social Service, Behavior Control, and System in Crites's study.

STUDIES OF VOCATIONAL MOTIVATION

In addition to the studies which have been cited on the measurement of vocational motivation, and on its relationship to vocational interests, there are several others which are worthy of note. Among these, there is the classic series of experiments conducted at the Hawthorne Plant of the Western Electric Company during the late 1920s and early 1930s which set the stage for much of the later research in industry on vocational motivation, job satisfaction, and morale. More recently, there is the study by Herzberg, Mausner, and Snyderman (1959) of the attitudinal and motivational factors in career satisfaction, which has suggested a new departure in conceptualizing and investigating the problem of why men work and experience the satisfactions and dissatisfactions they do. Finally, there are Centers's (1948; Centers & Bugental, 1966) surveys of the vocational motivations which are predominant for workers at different levels of the occupational hierarchy.

A Classic Study

There probably has never been a program of research in applied psychology which has had as pervasive and persistent an impact upon policy and practice, theory and experimentation, as the one launched by the Western Electric Company at its Hawthorne Plant on the outskirts of Chicago in 1924. Usually associated with the names of Elton Mayo, F. J. Roethlisberger, and T. N. Whitehead of the Harvard Graduate School of Business Administration, this long line of studies was actually initiated by a group of Western Electric engineers, under the direction of George A. Pennock and C. E. Snow, who were interested in the "relation of quality and quantity of illumination to efficiency in industry" (Roethlisberger & Dickson, 1939, p. 14). This group of investigators conducted three experiments on the effects of illumination upon productivity which eventually led to what is known as the Hawthorne studies and which dramatically shifted the focus of industrial research from the physical factors that affect work to the psychosocial factors that affect work.

Under more and more rigorous conditions of control of extraneous variables, from one experiment to the next, it was found that the efficiency of the experimental groups increased as illumination of their work area was intensified. But, it was also discovered that the productivity of the control group, which worked in a room with *constant* illumination, went up almost apace with that of the experimental group! In commenting upon this wholly unexpected finding, Snow (1927, p. 132) said that: "We were . . . unable to determine what definite part of the improvement in performance should be ascribed to improved illumination." The consensus of the engineers was that, although they had utilized a control group, they evidently had not been successful in equating it with the experimental group on all relevant variables, i.e., those which might influence productivity (Pennock, 1930). Consequently, they decided that the next step in their research should be to design and carry out a study in which the controls were complete and unquestionable.

It was at this juncture that Mayo and his co-workers became involved in the Hawthorne studies and conducted the first relay assembly room experiment. In this investigation, five female workers were selected to assemble telephone relays, which consist of about 35 small parts joined together in a fixture with machine screws, in a room partitioned off from the main shop. There was a long bench in the room at which the operators assembled the relays, a work area for the layout operator who arranged the component parts for them, and desks for the "supernumeraries," which included the observer for the experiment, a clerk, and a typist. To measure productivity or output a recording device was wired to a gate on a chute into which the operators dropped the completed relays, and holes were perforated on a paper tape to indicate how many relays each operator assembled in a given period of time. The independent variables or treatment conditions in the experiment primarily involved manipulations in the *hours of work:* rest periods, stopping time, and length of workweek. In other words, at the beginning of this experiment it was still thought that the critical factors in productivity were the physical conditions of work.

Not until the results showed that output generally went up as the experiment progressed from one period to another, including those in which the original hours were reinstated, was the hypothesis formulated that it was the social psychological nature of the *work group* which was the basic factor in the productivity of the relay assembly operators. More specifically, there appeared to be two variables operating: First, as compared with the general shop workers, the test-room operators evidently were more highly motivated to produce more because they had been singled out for the experiment and had been given special attention and consideration. This differential or preferential treatment is what is commonly referred to as the "Hawthorne effect." And, second, the test-room operators soon became a closely knit work group, in which each member did her best to up output and hence increase the earnings of all, since the wages of each operator were set by the special-group rate.

To explore further the role of work-group attitudes and interpersonal relationships in productivity, the Hawthorne investigators first tested out and rejected alternative hypotheses to the social psychological interpretation of their findings, including the influence of fatigue, monotony, and wage incentives upon output, and then proceeded with one of the most innovative approaches to the study of vocational motivation and satisfaction which had ever been undertaken in industry. Upon the suggestion of one of the test-room observers, they decided to ask the workers "to express frankly their likes and dislikes about their working environment" (Roethlisberger & Dickson, 1939, p. 191). Thus, they began a program of interviewing which would not only be vast in scope, with over 21,000 employees participating in it over a period of 3 years, but which more importantly would make a far-reaching contribution to the theory of personnel counseling (Dickson, 1945; Wright, 1940).

The complaints and grievances which employees expressed in their interviews appeared to make sense only if they were interpreted within the context of the social organization of the working environment, as depicted in Figure 9-2. In discussing this conceptual schema, Roethlisberger and Dickson (1939, pp. 375–376) state that:

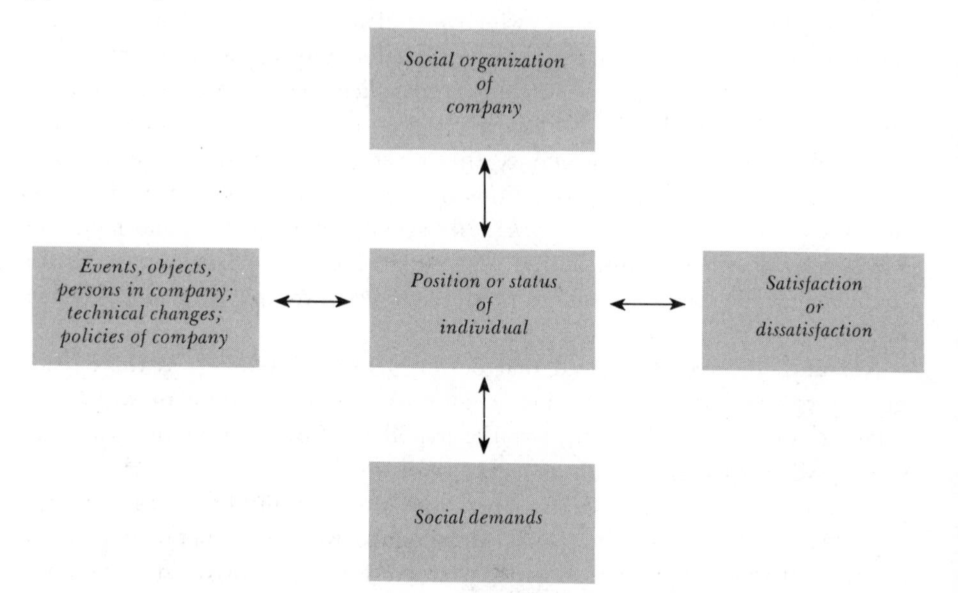

Figure 9-2. Factors related to employee complaints and grievances within the social organization of the work environment. *(From Rothlisberger & Dickson, 1939, p. 375.)*

> The meaning a person assigns to his position depends on whether or not that position is allowing him to fulfill the social demands he is making of his work. The ultimate significance of his work is not defined so much by his relation to the company as by his relation to the wider social reality. Only in terms of this latter relation can the different attitudes of satisfaction or dissatisfaction of individuals who are presumably enjoying the same working environment and occupational status be understood.

In other words, to explain the disproportionality between constant working conditions and differential responses to them by workers, the Hawthorne researchers postulated what amounts to a motivational intervening variable which they conceived of as the satisfaction of the worker's social needs through his work position. In the last study which they conducted, the bank wiring room experiment, before the Depression of the 1930s forced an end to their research, the Hawthorne group tested this "theory" of vocational motivation and concluded that their data supported it: the satisfactions which the worker gains from his work are largely determined by his work group, with its customs, duties, routines, and demands for conformity.

Comment. It is difficult to evaluate the Hawthorne studies for many reasons. On the one hand, their impact upon the industrial *Zeitgeist* in the 1930s and since cannot be denied. Impetus was given to research on the worker as a member of a group, the roles he plays in his work, the status he achieves through his work, and related problems. On the other hand, the Hawthorne studies fell far short of contemporary standards for scientific research in both design and methodology. Ironically enough, they were less well controlled than the illumination experiments upon which they were supposed to improve. The latter at least included a control group, whereas none of the Hawthorne studies was so designed. In the relay assembly and bank wiring room experiments, as well as all the others reported by Roethlisberger and Dickson (1939), the designs involved only manipulations of the independent variable in one group. There was no comparison with a group in which no stimulus variations were made. Hence, it is impossible to know whether the manipulated variable had an effect or not. The Hawthorne investigators concluded that it did not and, on the basis of other evidence, assumed that the social relations of the worker were the effective factors in his vocational motivation and satisfaction. But, even if there had been a control group, the number of Subjects in the experiments was too small for the purposes of statistical analyses of the data. Thus, it may be well to consider the Hawthorne studies more as survey research (see Chapter 13) than as scientific experiments. For, if they are placed in this perspective, their shortcomings in methodology are far overshadowed by their contributions to our ways of thinking about vocational motivation.[5]

A Recent Study

In 1957, Herzberg, Mausner, Peterson, and Capwell (1957, p. 7) reviewed the literature on a variety of variables, which they subsumed under the rubric of "job attitudes," and arrived at this conclusion:

> The one dramatic finding that emerged in our review of this literature was the fact that there was a difference in the primacy of factors, depending upon whether the investigator was looking for things the worker liked about his job or things he disliked. The concept that there were some factors that were "satisfiers" and others that were "dissatisfiers" was suggested by this finding.

They had found no study, however, in which both satisfiers and dissatisfiers had been investigated in relation to the same variables. Accordingly, they designed an investigation in which their basic hypothesis to be tested was that, given a worker at a neutral point on a bipolar continuum of job satisfaction-dissatisfaction, there would be some factors which, if present, would make him satisfied and others which would make him dissatisfied, but, if absent, these factors would not produce the opposite effect, e.g., if a "satisfier" is absent, it will not lead to dissatisfaction.

The approach which they formulated to test this hypothesis was conceived to avoid what they considered to be the fragmentary nature of previous studies:

> Studies in which factors affecting a worker's attitude toward his job were intensively investigated rarely included any information as to the effects of these attitudes. Studies of effects, similarly, rarely included any data as to the origin of the attitudes. In most cases in which either factors or effects were studied there was inadequate information about the individuals concerned, their perceptions, their needs, their patterns of learning. The primary need that emerged was one for an investigation of job attitudes *in toto,* a study in which factors, attitudes, and effects would be investigated simultaneously. The basic concept was that the factors-attitudes-effects (F-A-E) complex needs study as a unit [Herzberg et al., 1959, p. 11].

The similarity between this conceptual schema and others which we have discussed (cf. Viteles, 1953) is noteworthy, as is the use of "attitudes" as the motivational variable which intervenes between "factors" (stimuli) and "effects" (responses).

[5] For other commentaries on the Hawthorne studies, see Argyle (1953), Homans (1951), and Miller, D. C., and Form (1951).

The measurement of the F-A-E variables presented some problems to Herzberg and his associates, since they felt that the procedures which had been used in previous research were subject to many flaws, not the least of which was what they considered to be the restricted scope of objective measuring instruments. Consequently, they decided to use the "semistructured" interview to gather their data. In this approach, the Subject was asked the following question at the beginning of the interview:

> Think of a time in the past when you felt especially good or bad about your job. It may have been on this job or any other. Can you think of such a high or low point in your feelings about your job? Please tell me about it [Herzberg et al., 1959, p. 20].

Probe questions were then asked by the interviewer to gain further information, check the accuracy of the stories, and fill in missing details. After two pilot studies, in which this procedure was tried out and revised to make it more effective, interviews were held with over 200 accountants and engineers employed by Pittsburgh industrial concerns.

The sequence of events which a Subject related about a period in his work history when he felt exceptionally positive or negative toward his job was analyzed by judges into categories corresponding to the F-A-E variables (Herzberg et al., 1959, p. 28):

1. *First-level factors* (F): a description of the objective occurrences during the sequence of events, with especial emphasis on those identified by the respondent as being related to his attitudes. Example: a promotion.
2. *Second-level factors* (A): these categorize the reasons given by respondents for their feelings; they may be used as a basis for inferences about the drives or needs which are met or which fail to be met during the sequence of events. Example: a respondent's answer, "I felt good because the promotion meant I was being recognized."
3. *Effects* (E): the relationship of the first- and second-level factors to the respondent's productivity, turnover, interpersonal relations, attitude toward the company, satisfaction, and mental health.

The sequences of events were also analyzed along three other dimensions: (1) the *direction* of the feeling expressed by a respondent, i.e., whether it was positive (high) or negative (low); (2) the *range* of the sequence, i.e., over a considerable period of time (long) or not (short); and (3) the *duration* of the feelings mentioned by the Subject, i.e., long or short in time.

It is not possible to summarize here all the results which were obtained from analyses of these classifications and their interrelationships. Only those findings which are relevant to the major hypothesis of the study will be recounted. These can best be described by reference to Figure 9-3, in which the percentages of occurrence of each factor in the high (satisfied) sequences and low (dissatisfied) sequences are shown for short and long durations. In other words, this graph depicts the relationship between the F variables (achievement, recognition, etc.) and the A variables (high versus low, satisfied versus

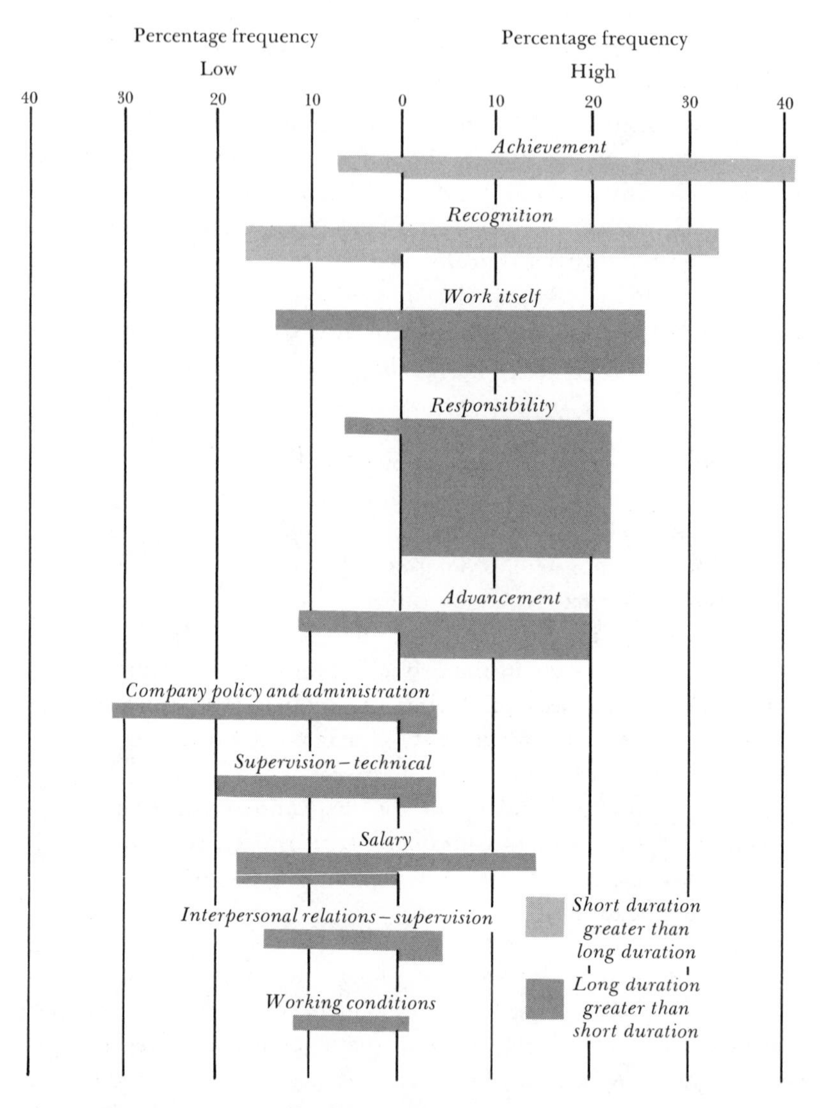

Figure 9-3. Factors contributing to dissatisfaction and satisfaction with work. *(From Herzberg, Mausner, & Snyderman, 1959, p. 81.)*

dissatisfied) but *not* the relationships of each of these with the E variables, which will be considered next. The width of the boxes in this figure indicate how frequently a factor led to a long-duration high or low attitude toward the job, and the shaded boxes for achievement and recognition signify that for these factors the high and low attitudes were more often of short than of long duration. From these findings, it can be seen that the factors which are relatively more to the *right* of the "0" percentage line (achievement, recognition, work itself, responsibility, and advancement) primarily stimulated feelings of satisfaction in the worker with his job, whereas those to the *left* of the "0" percentage line (company policy and administration, supervision-technical, interpersonal relations-supervision, and working conditions) usually evoked feelings of job dissatisfaction. Salary as a factor appears to contribute to both satisfaction and dissatisfaction, but Herzberg et al. (1959, p. 82) point out that it probably has more potency as a job dissatisfier than as a job satisfier.

In light of these data Herzberg and his co-workers (1959, p. 80) concluded that their original hypothesis should be revised to state that:

> The satisfier factors are much more likely to increase job satisfaction than they would be to decrease job satisfaction but that the factors that relate to job dissatisfaction very infrequently act to increase job satisfaction.

Furthermore, although the F and A variables were related to each other, only the latter were associated with the E variables. The *factors* which produce attitudes of job satisfaction or dissatisfaction evidently do not influence the worker's performance on the job, change of jobs, feelings about the company, interpersonal relationships, and mental health. The worker's *attitudes* about his job, however, *do* affect these variables, with the exception of interpersonal relationships which appear to be unrelated to both factors and attitudes. In this sense, then, attitudes can be thought of as "intervening" variables between factors and effects, although Herzberg did not cross-classify effects by combinations of factors and attitudes to determine whether there was a possible interaction between those two variables in their relationships to effects. If such an interaction exists, the conclusions they drew from their findings may need to be revised accordingly.[6]

Comment. More than any other theory of vocational motivation which has appeared in vocational psychology or related fields since the Western Electric studies, the one by Herzberg and his associates has aroused the greatest controversy and stimulated the most research. There have been more than 20 published and unpublished studies (mostly theses and dissertations) of Herzberg's

[6] For a general, nontechnical exposition of the findings of this and related studies, and their implications for work activities, see Herzberg (1966).

hypotheses, as well as several critiques of his theory. These cannot be reviewed in detail here, but Burke (1966, pp. 318–319) has prepared a convenient summary of most of the work which has been done on Herzberg's theory, and it is reproduced in Table 9-3, along with some of the more recent studies. The most readily apparent conclusion which can be drawn from this research is that it is equivocal: some of it supports Herzberg's theory; some of it confirms certain parts but not others; and some of it is clearly contradictory.

Other Studies[7]

In addition to the studies of Herzberg's theory, there are two others, both by Centers, on differences between occupational levels in vocational motivation which are important to summarize. In the first, which is almost a "classic" now, he (Centers, 1948) dealt with three problems, only the first being of interest here: (1) Do workers on different occupational strata have different vocational motives? (2) What are the sources of worker frustration? And, (3) are there differences between occupational levels in vocational satisfaction? Centers asked a nationally representative sample of 1,100 white male workers, classified occupationally as Large Business, Professional, Small Business, White Collar, Skilled Manual, Semi-skilled, Unskilled, Farm Owners and Managers, and Farm Tenants and Laborers, to indicate which of the jobs, described and listed in Table 9-4, they would choose if they had a choice. The jobs which the total sample selected most often were those which corresponded, according to Centers's definitions, to the following vocational motives: (1) independence, (2) self-expression, (3) security, (4) social service, and (5) interesting experience. When the job choices were classified by occupational strata, it was found that workers at the higher levels (business, professional, and white collar) preferred vocations which offered opportunities for self-expression, independence, and interesting experience, whereas workers at the lower levels (skilled manual and below) wanted jobs which promised security first, with independence and self-expression of secondary importance.

In an extension of this first study, conducted 18 years later, Centers and Bugental (1966) replicated these findings on the differences between occupational strata in vocational motivation and also collected new data on the rela-

[7] There is a growing body of research on the relationship of vocational motivation to organizational variables, e.g., staff versus line positions, middle versus upper management, which is tangentially relevant to vocational psychology, but which is the main subject matter of organizational psychology. It will not be reviewed here, for lack of space, but an overview of this work can be found in Porter, L. W. (1964) and Porter, L.W., and Lawler (1965). For key studies, see: Porter, L. W. (1958; 1961a; 1961b; 1962; 1963a; 1963b; 1963c); Porter, L W., and Henry (1964a; 1964b); Rosen, H., and Weaver (1960); Eran (1966); Friedlander (1965; 1966); Paine, Carroll, and Lette (1966).

Table 9-3. Summary of Studies on Herzberg's Theory of Vocational Motivation *(From Burke, 1966, pp. 318–319)*

Investigator	*Subjects*	*Procedure*	*Findings*
Friedlander (1963)	Engineers, supervisors, and salaried employees of a large manufacturing firm (200 of each)	Factor analysis of a 17-item questionnaire measuring the importance of various job characteristics to employee satisfaction	Three meaningful factors emerged. Two corresponded, in part, with motivators and hygienes, while the third seemed to draw from both motivators and hygienes.
Rosen (1963)	94 research and development personnel of varying specialities, educational levels, and organizational levels	Respondents rated the importance of the absence of 118 items to their desiring to leave their present position	Many of the most important items which if not present would cause the individual to seek other employment were similar to Herzberg's motivators.
Schwartz, Jenusaitis, & Stark (1963)	111 male supervisors employed by 21 public utility companies	Content analysis of written stories describing pleasant and unpleasant job experiences	Motivators were generally associated with pleasant experiences and hygienes with unpleasant experiences. One Herzberg motivator acted like a hygiene in this sample.
Ewen (1964)	1,021 full-time life insurance agents divided into an experimental sample (541) and a cross-validation sample (480)	Factor analysis of a 58-item attitude scale completed by the experimental sample	Six interpretable factors emerged, of which three were hygienes and two motivators. Two of the three hygienes acted like motivators in both samples; the other hygiene acted like a motivator in the cross-validation sample and like both a motivator and a hygiene in the experimental sample. One motivator acted both as a motivator and a hygiene.
Friedlander (1964)	80 students in an evening course in industrial or child psychology (part were full-time employees in various occupations and part were mem-	Respondents rated the importance of 18 variables to job satisfaction and job dissatisfaction	The results indicated that motivators and hygienes are not opposite ends of a common set of dimensions. The majority of these job characteristics seemed to be

Table 9-3. Summary of Studies on Herzberg's Theory of Vocational Motivation *(From Burke, 1966, pp. 318–319) (Continued)*

Investigator	*Subjects*	*Procedure*	*Findings*
	bers of a cooperative work-study program)		significant contributors to both satisfaction and dissatisfaction on the job.
Friedlander & Walton (1964)	82 scientists and engineers in various specialities	Semistructured interviews in which respondents were asked for the most important factors keeping them in the organization and factors that might cause them to leave the organization	Reasons for remaining in an organization (primarily motivators) were different from, and not merely opposite to, the reasons for which one might leave an organization (primarily hygienes).
Lodahl (1964)	50 male auto-assembly workers and 29 female electronics-assembly workers	Factor analysis of data obtained from a content analysis of interviews	Two technological and three attitude factors emerged. The technological factors were different for the two samples, but the attitude factors corresponded rather well. Two of the three attitude factors resembled motivators and hygienes.
Myers (1964)	282 male scientists, engineers, manufacturing supervisors, and hourly technicians and 52 female hourly assemblers	Content analysis of Herzberg-like interviews	Job characteristics grouped naturally into motivator-hygiene dichotomies. However, one Herzberg motivator acted like a hygiene and other Herzberg motivators acted both as motivators and hygienes. Different job levels had different job characteristic configurations. The female configuration was different from the four male configurations, suggesting a sex factor. Common Herzberg motivators were absent from the hourly tech-

			nician and hourly female assembler configurations suggesting a job-level factor.
Saleh (1964)	85 male employees at managerial levels in 12 companies	Herzberg-like interview, and a 16-item job-attitude scale (6 motivators and 10 hygienes) presented in a paired-comparison format	Preretirees looking backward in their careers indicated motivators as sources of satisfaction and hygienes as sources of dissatisfaction; preretirees looking at the time left before retirement indicated hygienes as sources of satisfaction.
Dunnette (1965)	114 store executives, 74 sales clerks, 43 secretaries, 128 engineers and research scientists, 46 salesmen, 91 army reserve personnel and employed adults enrolled in a supervision course	Factor analysis of *Q* sorts of two sets of 36 statements (equated for social desirability) for highly satisfying and highly dissatisfying job situations	Some Herzberg motivators were related to satisfying job situations but Hertzberg hygienes were not related to dissatisfying job situations. One Herzberg motivator acted like a hygiene. There was also a positive relationship between the importance of a factor as both a motivator and a hygiene contrary to the negative relationship expected under Herzberg's theory. Thus the same factors were contributors to both satisfaction and dissatisfaction.
Friedlander (1965)	1,468 civil service workers from three status levels (low, middle, and high GS rankings) and two occupational levels (blue-collar and white-collar)	Factor analysis of a 14-item questionnaire measuring the importance of various job characteristics to satisfaction and dissatisfaction	White-collar workers derived greatest satisfaction from motivators while blue-collar workers derived greatest satisfaction from hygienes suggesting that subgroups may have different work-value systems.

Table 9-3. Summary of Studies on Herzberg's Theory of Vocational Motivation *(From Burke, 1966, pp. 318–319) (Continued)*

Investigator	*Subjects*	*Procedure*	*Findings*
Gordon (1965)	683 full-time agents of a large, national life insurance company	Respondents rated their degree of satisfaction and dissatisfaction with 54 items comprising 4 scales (motivators, hygienes, both, hygienes minus both). A measure of overall job satisfaction, self-reported production figures, and survival data were also available	Contrary to expectations, individuals highly satisfied with motivators did not have greater overall job satisfaction than individuals highly satisfied with hygienes; and individuals highly dissatisfied with hygienes were not less satisfied than individuals dissatisfied with motivators. A positive relationship was found between satisfaction with motivators and self-reported production, but no relationship between hygienes and production. This study offered no support to the theory that specific job factors effect attitudes in only the direction. Support is offered that primarily the motivators bring about superior performance.
Halpern (1965)	93 male college graduates working in various occupations	Rating of satisfaction with four motivators, four hygienes, and overall job satisfaction on respondent's best-liked job	Although the respondents were equally satisfied with both the motivator and hygiene aspects of their jobs, the motivators contributed significantly more to overall job satisfaction than did the hygienes.
Wernimont (1966)	50 accountants and 82 engineers	Self-description of past satisfying and dissatisfying job situations using both forced-choice and free-choice items	More motivators than hygienes were used to describe both job situations. Concludes that both motivators and hygienes can be sources of job satisfaction and job dissatisfaction.

Ewen, Smith, Hulin, & Locke (1966)	793 male employees from several companies and organizational levels	IDI was used to test differential predictions from traditional and Herzberg's theory of vocational motivation	Test of eight hypotheses of the two theories were inconclusive: neither traditional nor Herzberg's theory was clearly confirmed or disconfirmed.
Graen (1966a)*	Same as above	Reanalyzed data collected by Ewen et al. (1966) but in a two-factor design rather than pairwise comparisons of group means	Linear relationships between both motivator and hygiene factors, on the one hand, and job satisfaction, on the other, tended to support traditional as opposed to Herzberg's theory.

* See also Graen (1966b) for research on a questionnaire developed to provide a standardized measure of Herzberg's constructs.

Table 9-4. List of Jobs and Corresponding Vocational Motives Studied by Centers (1948, p. 205)

Jobs	Vocational motives
A. A job where you could be a leader	Leadership
B. A very interesting job	Interesting experience
C. A job where you would be looked upon very highly by your fellow men	Esteem
D. A job where you could be boss	Power
E. A job which you were absolutely sure of keeping	Security
F. A job where you could express your feelings, ideas, talent, or skill	Self-expression
G. A very highly paid job	Profit
H. A job where you could make a name for yourself—become famous	Fame
I. A job where you could help other people	Social service
J. A job where you could work more or less on your own	Independence

tionship of occupational level to intrinsic-extrinsic sources of satisfaction. The list of job factors in Table 9-4 was revised, so that there were three intrinsic and three extrinsic statements about work which could be ranked by a respondent. A representative sample of 692 employed adults was interviewed to elicit their rankings of the vocational motives, and then these were compared across occupational levels and also between the sexes. Centers and Bugental (1966, pp. 194–195) summarize their results as follows:

> Job motivations were found to have the expected relationship to occupational level.... It can be seen [from differences in percentages] that all three intrinsic job components were more valued among white-collar groups than among blue-collar groups. Correspondingly, all three extrinsic job components were more valued in blue-collar groups than in white-collar groups.

That these findings might not have been unexpected was suggested by Centers's (1948) original study, in which the higher occupational strata differed from the lower on such motives as self-expression and independence, which are intrinsic by definition. The second study confirmed this expectation and also revealed that there were no consistent differences between the sexes in their rankings of the vocational motivation factors, although they did differ slightly on self-expression and co-workers. Interpreting their results in terms of Maslow's (1954) need hierarchy (see Chapter 3), Centers and Bugental (1966, p. 197) conclude that "it could be said that individuals in lower-level occupations are more likely to be motivated by lower-order needs (pay, security, etc.) because these are not sufficiently gratified to allow higher-order needs (the self-fulfillment in the job itself) to become prepotent."

PROBLEMS IN VOCATIONAL ADJUSTMENT

The second component in the Model of Vocational Adjustment outlined in the last chapter consists of the (1) thwarting conditions experienced by the individual in his work, either as conflict or frustration, and (2) the work-adjustment mechanisms he acquires in order to cope with the conflict and frustration. Relatively little conceptualization and investigation have been done on these phenomena, but that which is available is provocative of hypotheses which might be tested in future research. We shall discuss the thwarting conditions which have been identified in work first, and then consider the work-adjustment mechanisms which are typically used in reaction to them.

Thwarting Conditions in Work

By a "thwarting condition" is meant some obstacle, either internal or external, which the individual encounters in attempting to reach a goal. In the process of vocational adjustment, the goals are usually vocational success and satisfaction, although other objectives, such as securing employment or persisting in an occupation after entry, may also be sought. Thus, a salesman may desire the material security (motivation-goal) which comes from earning big bonuses (response) but is thwarted in his attainment of this goal, possibly by lack of self-confidence or competition from other salesmen or both. The thwarting condition may be a function of the salesman's personality (lack of self-confidence) or it may be an environmental factor (competition from other salesmen) which interferes with his goal attainment. If the thwarting condition is *internal,* it is usually referred to as *conflict,* whereas if it is *external,* it is generally called *frustration.* These two kinds of thwarting conditions are not mutually exclusive, since at any given moment a worker may be both conflicted and frustrated. What the empirical correlation between conflict and frustration is, however, has not been determined. And, there is no formal theory which would predict the magnitude of the relationship, although observation of workers who are thwarted by both conditions would suggest a low positive correlation between them.

Conflict in Work. What are the conflicts—the internal antagonistic feelings, motives, and response tendencies—which the individual experiences in his work? Ichheiser (1940) has distinguished four kinds of conflicts which may beset a worker. First, there are what he calls "conflicts of function," which arise from the nature of the job duties and tasks performed by the worker as part of his occupation. These would include, for example, conflicts occasioned by having to do something which the worker considers *infra dignitate* (Hughes, 1958), such as a janitor disposing of garbage. Second, there are "conflicts of conviction." An illustration might be the salesman who has to sell what he thinks is an inferior product: On the one hand, he wants to earn the money which will come from selling it, but on the other he feels he cannot do so ethically and honestly. Third, there are the so-called "conflicts of ambition." Ichheiser (1940, p. 109) says that this type of conflict occurs "whenever there is discord between the presumed or actual level of the individual's personality and the place which he occupies in the social hierarchy because of his occupational standing." The most common instance of this conflict is "when an exceptionally gifted individual cannot find sufficient scope for the display of his abilities." Finally, there are the "conflicts of response," which bear a close resemblance to conflicts of ambition but are distinguishable from them. Ichheiser (1940, p. 110) defines them as follows:

> In order to understand them we must realize that our occupational activity and position determine, in no small degree, the circle of people with whom we have every day to deal, both within and outside our occupation. When, therefore, there is a marked discrepancy between a person's desire for a certain social *milieu* and the kind of people whom he is obliged to meet and live with because of his occupation, conflicts of response arise.

Another classification of the conflicts found in work has been made by Robbins (1939) who has broadly grouped them into (1) disturbances of aim and (2) disturbances of function. He points out that the former may be manifested in two ways: First, a worker may formulate and express *grandiose* aims which belie a compulsion to be not just good but the very best in whatever activity is undertaken. Thus, he must be original in all that he does, which often necessitates denying the previous work of others; he must accomplish his aims immediately and without much effort; and he must turn out perfect work, which needs no modification or revision. In short, as Robbins (1939, p. 335) notes, the worker with grandiose aims has the attitude that " 'not only must I be God' but there should 'be no Gods besides me.' " Second, a worker may be beset by a pervasive *ambitionlessness* which makes it almost impossible to work. His attitude is one of defeat because of his "profound embarrassment in the ability to work" (Robbins, 1939, p. 336). He presents a work mien of disinterestedness and resignation, and renounces any ambition, although unconsciously he usually harbors grandiose aims.

In contrast to these disturbances of aim, which have to do with what the individual does or does not want out of his work, disturbances of function pertain to what the worker can or cannot do on the job. According to Robbins (1939, p. 337), dysfunctions in work "divide themselves into two gross areas: energy is misdirected or is partially or completely inhibited." If it is misdirected, the worker's efforts are dissipated and scattered, so that he seldom accomplishes any task. He becomes, in effect, a dilettante, whose work is superficial and devoid of general meaning. If the energy is inhibited, however, he does not even make an effort to work. He makes no wholehearted attempt to achieve any goal; he lets opportunities for advancement pass him by; and he generally assumes the attitude of "Why try?" In both cases, "Work is something foreign and alien to the neurotic, a task externally imposed, a duty to which they must submit and about which they have no choice. They can do nothing but comply. For the most part, states of inertia as well as lesser obstructions in the exercise of labor are associated with—and, in fact, spring out of deep hatred against working" (Robbins, 1939, p. 339). It is this hatred of work, on the one hand, and the necessity to work, on the other, which Robbins sees as the central conflict in work.

Horney (1947) has elaborated upon some of these ideas about conflict in work and has added others so as to formulate the most articulate and comprehensive analysis of the problem which has as yet been made. She begins by enumerating four factors which are necessary for "creative," as contrasted with routine, work and then proceeds to indicate how the inhibitions of a worker can interfere with each of them. First, with respect to the *gifts* (abilities) which are prerequisite for the performance of work, the inhibited individual may emphatically deny that he is capable of any productive effort, because of his constant self-berating and strong fear of ridicule. Or, in contrast, the expansive worker may aggrandize and exaggerate his potentialities, and, as a consequence, flounder in possibilities with little hope of realizing any of them. Second, the conflicted worker often has problems in being *consistent* in what he does. He may scatter his energies and interests in many directions, because he refuses to recognize his limitations, or he may begin a project but give it up prematurely because "it really was not worth doing any way." Third, another factor essential for creative work which is counteracted by conflicts is the individual's *self-confidence*. On the one hand, he may idealize and glorify his capabilities in his imagination to the extent that he could never live up to his concept of himself, and thus he loses whatever confidence he may have had in his ability to attain his goals. On the other hand, he may undermine his self-confidence by focusing upon his liabilities and become convinced that he could never succeed in any endeavor. Finally, few workers who are crippled by conflicts and inhibitions can develop a *genuine interest* in their work. They chafe under what they consider "unreasonable" authority; they resent having to be "on time" and having to meet deadlines, which they see as unduly coercive; they object to the routine aspects of their jobs as being "uncreative"; and so on. In short, they hate work, because it offends their neurotic pride.

Frustration in Work. Eaton (1952) has proposed seven hypotheses on why individuals experience frustration in their work; these hypotheses cover most of the external thwarting conditions which can be identified:

Hypothesis 1. "The worker is frustrated by the insignificance of his work." The rationale here is that the worker no longer can gain the sense of personal significance he seeks in his work because the task he performs on the assembly line is so far removed from the finished product.

Hypothesis 2. "The worker is frustrated by absentee ownership of the products of his work." To counteract this source of frustration some companies have instituted profit-sharing plans, designed to give the worker an opportunity to own a part, however small it might be, of the enterprise to which he contributes.

Hypothesis 3. "The worker is frustrated by the expectations of upward mobility which attend his labor." Our society fosters aspirations to higher-level occupations, but there is only a limited number of them; consequently, many workers will be frustrated in their desire to "reach the top."

Hypothesis 4. "The worker is frustrated by his lack of a defined role, and by the many alternatives available in his work." This proposition refers to the increasing number of occupations from which the worker must choose, and the frustration he feels from not knowing enough about them to make a satisfying choice.

Hypothesis 5. "The worker is frustrated by the changing techniques and conditions of his work." Workers are frustrated by technological advances which change their jobs for two reasons: (1) they do not initiate them or have control over them, and (2) they are deprived of the traditional routines and customs of their work which give it personal meaning and significance.

Hypothesis 6. "The worker is frustrated by the isolation of his work within the community." Because his job has become more and more complex, fewer people can comprehend what the worker does and accord him appropriate approbation for his accomplishments.

Hypothesis 7. "The worker is frustrated by the economic insecurity of his work." Eaton (1952, pp. 66–67) comments that: "Surely it would be difficult to argue that the worker finds satisfaction in the vagaries of a business cycle which determines, in large part, both the value of his remuneration and whether he will be employed at all."

Other than these hypotheses formulated by Eaton, there has been little or no conceptualization of the problem of frustration in work. Maier (1955) has discussed frustration generally as a psychological phenomenon but has not related it specifically to vocational behavior. Meltzer (1945) alludes to the significance of frustration in work adjustment but assigns it a peripheral role in relation to the importance of the worker's expectations about his job and associates as determinants of his success and satisfaction. And, finally, Brinker (1955) has emphasized that one of the most significant factors in frustration, at both the foreman and intermediate supervisory levels of the industrial organization, may be the failure of top management to delegate sufficient authority downward.

Studies of Conflict and Frustration in Work. Conflict as a problem in vocational adjustment has been investigated in three studies by occupational sociologists:

1. Burchard (1954, p. 528) selected *military chaplains* as Subjects, because, as he points out, "the ends specified by the two major institutions which define their social roles are in some respects mutually exclusive.... Chaplains not only share the dilemma of the Christian in war time; they also function as officers in both ecclesiastical and military organizations." On the basis of data gathered on 71 chaplains, through semistructured interviews, Burchard concluded that each of the following hypotheses was supported: (1) the position of the chaplain does lead to role conflict; (2) he resolves this conflict through rationalization and compartmentalization of role behaviors; (3) he strengthens, as a consequence, his role as an officer at the expense of his role as a minister; and (4) he serves as interpreter of the values of the military organization, helps resolve value dilemmas of individual service men, and helps promote smooth operation of the military organization.

2. Getzels and Guba (1954) also studied a military occupation, but the Subjects in this instance were 266 *officer-instructors* at the Air University, who were administered two inventories designed to assess role conflict, the general hypothesis being that the behavior expected of the "authoritarian" officer and the "democratic" teacher are basically incompatible. The results from several analyses of differences between officers at the Air University and between officers with varying backgrounds and status indicated that military instructors experience more or less role conflict as a function of "the congruency of personality needs and role expectations *and* the choice of a major role that is the more legitimate one" (Getzels & Guba, 1954, p. 175). In other words, those instructors who saw themselves primarily as officers, rather than as teachers, and who were committed to a military career, reported less role conflict.

3. McCormack (1956) conducted the third study, in which she found that *pharmacy students* attempt to avoid the conflict between being a businessman and a professional by idealizing both occupations. Thus, they conceive of themselves in the following way:

> Most expect to become proprietors, with the status of independent professionals, thus fusing the two systems and avoiding a final choice. In this process the entrepreneurial drive is modified by criticism of big business and by retreat from highly competitive circumstances; the professional drive is blunted by subordinating a service goal to individual achievement for its own sake [McCormack, 1956, p. 315].

In the study by Centers (1948) discussed previously, data were also collected on the frustrations and grievances of workers, by asking the following questions: (1) "What is it that you don't like about your job?"; (2) "Do you think your pay or salary is as high as it should be, or do you think you deserve more?"; (3) "Do you think you have as good a chance to enjoy life as you should have?" For the total sample, the most frequently mentioned source of frustration was "low pay" or "poor profits," but there were notable differences between occupational levels, as depicted graphically in Figure 9-4. The overall trends definitely indicate less frustration at the upper occupational levels; however, it should be noted that there are some "reversals" in the curves, e.g., "white-collar" workers are less satisfied with both their pay and opportunities for advancement than skilled workers. Centers (1948, p. 199) considers these exceptions to be indicative of the increasing alignment of certain professional groups, such as teachers, with the more distinctly laboring groups, and attributes this phenomenon to the former's mounting frustration with their work.

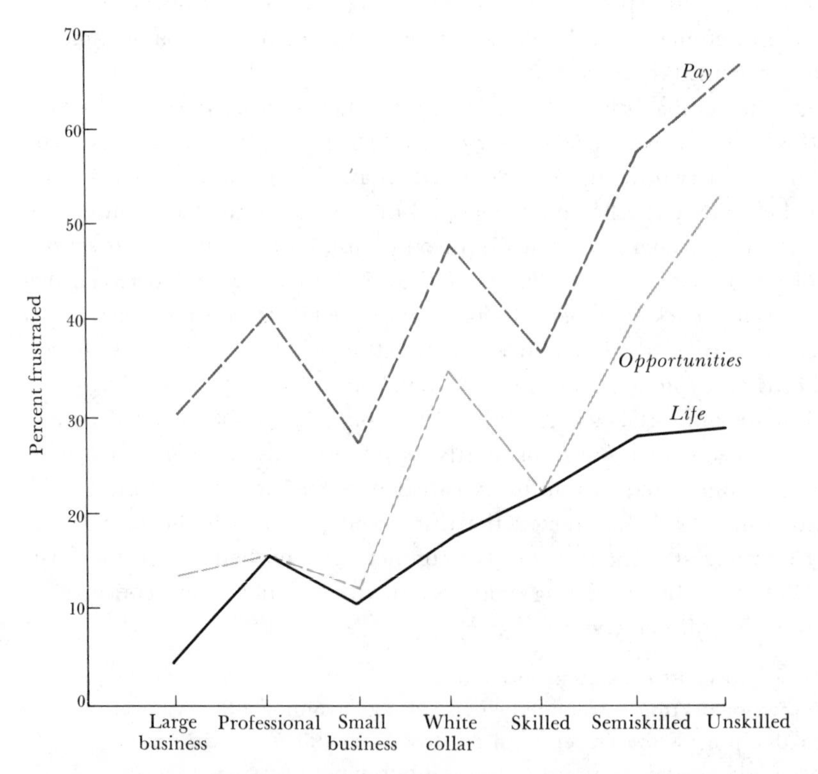

Figure 9-4. Differences between occupational levels in percentages of workers frustrated by their pay, opportunities to get ahead, and chances to enjoy life. *(After Centers, 1948, p. 198.)*

One more study should be mentioned in which Neel (1955) asked 5,700 hourly workers the following questions about their vocational adjustment: (1) "Does your work make you feel 'jumpy' or 'nervous'?" and (2) "Are you ever bothered or worried about any of the following things (lack of skill needed for job, money problems, health, failure to get ahead, etc.)?" In response to the first question, 30 percent of the sample indicated "occasionally," 30 percent "very seldom," and 30 percent "never." Only 5 percent said "most of the time" and 4 percent "fairly frequently." In other words, most workers do *not* consider themselves "jumpy" or "nervous" as a consequence of their work. The answers to the second question revealed that relatively small percentages of workers admit to "often worrying about" the problems which were listed, the most frequently mentioned one being "money problems" (27 percent). With respect to the relationship between the two questions, an average intercorrelation of .36 was found, with a range from .09 to .75. In addition, the questions were correlated with several other variables: (1) perceptions of and attitudes toward foremen; (2) attitude toward work group; (3) attitude toward working conditions; (4) attitude toward pay and promotion policies; (5) attitude toward the productivity system; (6) intrinsic job satisfaction; (7) attitude toward company generally; and (8) background factors. Most of the *r*'s were in the .20s, with only an occasional one in the low .30s. The highest correlation was .36 between "employees who are dissatisfied with their pay" and employees who "worry about money problems." Thus, there would appear to be some statistically significant but quite low relationships between the problems workers experience in their vocational adjustment and their attitudes toward various aspects of the job situation.

Work-adjustment Mechanisms

It is generally recognized in adjustment psychology that conflict and frustration produce anxiety and tension (Shaffer & Shoben, 1956). Since these emotional states are uncomfortable and distressful ones for the individual, he attempts to allay them by making some response which will reduce their intensity. In other words, the anxiety and tension aroused by conflict and frustration act as drive stimuli for the behavior of the individual. If he makes a response which has the effect of reducing his anxiety and tension, then the probability is that when he again experiences these feelings he will react in the same or a similar way. In short, as a result of drive reduction, he *learns* how to respond effectively to the anxiety and tension which beset him. What kind of response he learns depends upon a host of factors: his biological and constitutional makeup, his previous learning experiences, his present environmental circumstances, etc. It is conceivable that any number of responses might be learned, but actually it has been found that most of the individual's adjustment mechanisms can be classified into a relatively few categories or types. In the discussion which follows, we shall survey some of these, particularly as they apply to the work situation, and review what little research there has been on their measurement and relationships to other variables.

Varieties of Work-adjustment Mechanisms. Shaffer and Shoben (1956, p. 568) have taken the position that the ways in which an individual adjusts to his work are much the same as those which he uses to adjust to other life situations:

> The patterns of maladjustment shown by industrial workers are the same as those found among other people.... Bullying attitudes on the part of executives and foremen are readily recognized as compensations. Personal peculiarities may serve as attention-getting mechanisms. Rationalization is evident in chronic fault finding and in the blaming of others.... Daydreamers who escape from frustration into fantasy present special problems for industrial safety and efficiency. The more severe mechanisms of hysteria and the non-adjustive anxiety states account for much illness and absenteeism.... Somewhat less common, but sure to be met in any large organization, are delusional beliefs of being spied upon or discriminated against. In short, the entire gamut of maladjustments may be found in a store or factory, just as in a school or community. The whole person comes to work, and it is impossible to separate his purely economic self from the other aspects of his personality.

Meltzer (1945, p. 341) also contends that: "The mechanisms of personality adjustment found in industry cover almost the whole array of styles of behavior found in large clinics and in individual therapeutic work." In another paper, Meltzer (1946, p. 432) summarizes the possible solutions to vocational adjustment problems as follows: "A conflict can be resolved by sheer domination, it can be compromised with, it can be appeased or neglected, or it can be integrated."

This delineation of problem-solving strategies suggests a more comprehensive and inclusive analysis of work-adjustment mechanisms which may have not only clarificatory but also heuristic value. First, there are the work-adjustment mechanisms which are best characterized by *acquiescence* or *compliance*. If the worker's problem is one of conflict among competing aspirations or motivations, he makes little or no effort to solve his problem directly on his own, but rather he "gives up" and either endures his plight, in which case he will often consider himself a martyr, or seeks out someone else, upon whom he becomes dependent, to help him. If he is frustrated, he will usually follow much the same pattern, giving up or complying to environmental pressures rather than taking constructive action which would alleviate them. Second, there are the work-adjustment mechanisms which involve *control* or *manipulation*. If the worker's motives are conflicted, he consciously suppresses one or another of them, so that the problem is at least temporarily solved. Similarly, if he is frustrated, he typically manipulates the environment, i.e., changes it, so that it no longer is an obstacle to what he wants. Third, there are the work-adjustment mechanisms which are based upon *compromise*. The worker attempts to solve conflicts and remove frustrations by changing both sides of the equation which are creating his difficulties. In conflict, this means altering the various competing motives; in frustration, it means changing both the self and the environment. Finally, there are the work-adjustment mechanisms which can be called *integrative,* since they achieve a synthesis among the factors in conflict and frustration without the necessity of change. In other words, a solution (or, more accurately, a resolution) is found, so that all the antagonistic motives in a conflict are realized or frustrating circumstances are somehow circumvented. Obviously, solutions of this quality are extremely difficult to conceive, but they are possible and represent the best vocational adjustment which can be attained.

Measures of Work-adjustment Mechanisms. Although to the knowledge of the writer there are no standardized, or even research, tests to inventory or survey the ways in which workers adjust to their jobs, some idea of what they might be, and how they might be classified into the foregoing conceptual schema for work-adjustment mechanisms, can be gained from a sample of responses made to the Forer Vocational Survey (FVS). The FVS is an 80-item incomplete-sentences blank, which, according to its author (Forer, 1957, p. 2), was designed to "provide meaningful information about a variety of facts of work adjustment, attitudes, interests, and conflicts." Illustrative of the items in it are the following from the men's form: "Having to follow instructions makes me feel. . . ," "At work I feel tense whenever. . . ," "If I can't get what I want at work, I. . . ," and "When they said he had not enough skill, he. . . ." Responses can be classified and summarized in several different ways, e.g., "Reactions to Authorities," "Causes of Anxiety," and "Vocational Goals," but our interest here is in the work-adjustment mechanisms they reveal.

The FVS was given to a group of 20 employment counselors one summer as a part of a training institute, and these are some of the sentences they wrote which suggest possible ways of adjusting to various aspects of the job:

1. *When my suggestions were turned down, I:* "told them to go jump"; "let the subject drop"; "felt disappointed"; "attempted to find out why"; thought up some more."

2. *If I feel my co-workers don't like me, I:* "feel rather badly"; "seek my friendships elsewhere"; "try to analyze why they don't and attempt to change their opinion of me"; "try to understand myself better."
3. *When they blame him, he:* "gets mad"; "feels bad"; "tries to explain the situation to them"; "takes it out on his wife"; "really gets with it"; "tries to avoid the issue"; "accepts the blame if it was his fault; otherwise he explains why it wasn't his fault."

This is only a small sample of possible responses to a few incomplete-sentence stems, but it indicates that there are fairly marked individual differences in the ways workers would handle vocational adjustment problems and that these different modes usually range across a continuum of adjustment from less to more integrative solutions. With responses such as these elicited by the FVS, it is conceivable that a more standardized measure of work-adjustment mechanisms could be constructed which might increase our understanding of how workers cope with the conflicts and frustrations they encounter on their jobs.

Super's Studies of Compensatory Avocations. One work-adjustment mechanism which we have not mentioned is the compensation some workers seek through their *avocations* for dissatisfaction or failure in their vocations. In two pioneer studies of this mode of adjusting to work, Super (1940; 1941) obtained results on 273 employed adult men who were actively engaged in hobby groups devoted to (1) model engineering, (2) music, (3) photography, and (4) stamp collecting which supported a theory of "compensatory avocations," as opposed to a theory of "balance" between avocation and vocation. His most relevant findings can be summarized as follows (Super, 1941, pp. 60–61):

1. Men whose major avocations resembled their vocations tend to be satisfied with their jobs, whereas those whose major avocations do not resemble their vocations tend to be dissatisfied with the latter.
2. Men who have not changed occupations are likely to derive more satisfaction from their work than from their hobbies, whereas those who have changed occupations tend to derive more satisfaction from their avocations.
3. Occupational changes which result in greater similarity of vocation to avocation are more likely to result in job satisfaction than changes which lessen the similarity of vocation to avocation, those whose vocations resemble their avocations without occupational change being more likely to be satisfied with their jobs.

There was also a tendency for workers at the higher occupational levels to prefer their vocations more than their avocations, presumably because their work provided them a greater opportunity for expression of their dominant interests. On the basis of these results, Super (1941, p. 61) rejected the "balance" theory of avocations, which states that "better adjustment results when one's major avocation contrasts with, rather than resembles, one's vocation," and concluded that avocations may serve as compensatory mechanisms for vocations which conflict with or frustrate the worker's satisfaction of his motives and realization of his goals.

10
VOCATIONAL SUCCESS

This chapter deals with three aspects of vocational success. First, there is the problem of defining and measuring vocational success. What do we mean by "success," and how has the vocational psychologist quantified the concept? Second, there have been some outstanding series of studies on vocational success, and these are summarized along with the findings which have accumulated on the correlates of establishing oneself and "getting ahead" in an occupation. Finally, there is the question of whether vocational success can be predicted, a matter not only of practical concern in personnel selection, but also of theoretical interest in the explanation of vocational behavior. A classic study and a recent study on the prediction of vocational success are presented and discussed, as well as some of the current research which is being conducted on differential predictability. The topics of the chapter are, then, the following: (1) the definition of vocational success, (2) studies of vocational success, and (3) the prediction of vocational success.

THE DEFINITION OF VOCATIONAL SUCCESS

The definition of a psychological concept is always difficult to formulate, because of the sundry and subtle shades of meanings it usually has accrued in common parlance, and vocational success is no exception. When we survey the definitions which have been made of this concept, we find that they range from the relatively unrefined, but colorful, pulp magazine stories of overnight success, which abounded in the late nineteenth century, to the highly sophisticated, but sometimes sterile, operational criteria of contemporary psychological and sociological research. And, because of these multifarious meanings, it has been extremely difficult to establish methodologically sound criteria of vocational success, although many approaches have been proposed. Also, we discover that the work which has been done on the interrelationships and structure of vocational success criteria has been largely discrete and disparate in nature, most likely because of the unresolved measurement problems, but it is nevertheless suggestive of a model for conceptualizing success phenomena. In this section, we shall deal with this body of research and theory on vocational success under the following headings: (1) concepts of vocational success, (2) criteria of vocational success, and (3) dimensions of vocational success.

Concepts of Vocational Success

The concept of vocational success is paradoxically both general and specific in its meanings. Workers from all walks of life know what you mean when you ask them what "success" is. The concept has been institutionalized in the familiar stories of Horatio Alger's rise to fame and fortune and in the promise of the American credo that every man has an equal opportunity "to get ahead." There is an "ideology of success" (Gross, 1964) which cuts across the occupational hierarchy and acts as a powerful source of vocational motivation for professional, craftsman, and laborer alike. Yet, each man defines success in his own way—"Success for one man can never be success for another" (Hersey, 1936, p. 925). To the aspiring junior executive success means something different from what it means to the beginning college instructor. Chinoy (1952, p. 458) found, for example, that automobile workers equated success with security —"If you're secure, then you're getting ahead." Super (1951a, p. 7) eloquently puts it this way:

> "Success," as the world judges it, is fruitless and empty unless it is also seen as success by the individual. What would wealth have been to Ghandi, or the love and respect of humble men and women to Bismarck? What use had Thoreau for prestige and status, or Theodore Roosevelt for opportunities to be alone with himself and the universe? In the eyes of each of these persons, and of some others, each of them was successful; but in the judgment of many, each of them was a failure. Individual values and hence individual judgments, differ in such matters.

The dilemma of whether vocational success is a purely personal phenomenon, which cannot be defined nomothetically, or whether it has some generality of meaning has not been resolved, as will be apparent in the following discussion. Not only are there differences between the various nonpsychological and psychological concepts of vocational success which we shall review, but within these classifications there are varying emphases. Nevertheless, there has been at least one attempt to synthesize these different points of view in an effort to formulate a general concept of vocational success, and we shall discuss this concept after considering the others.

Nonpsychological Concepts of Vocational Success. In folk concepts of vocational success, at least in America, the mark of attainment has been almost exclusively a monetary one. "You are as successful as the size of your salary"—or what it allows you to buy. Economists point out, however, that success is not simply a matter of how much a person is earning at a particular point in time. Clark, H. F. (1936, p. 931) states that *life* earnings are "the best measure we have of the value to society of the work of any individual," because income may vary from one season to another or from one period of life to another. Sociologists admit that life earnings define one aspect of success, but they also include other factors which contribute to an individual's position and status in society, such as family connections and social origins (Olshansky, 1953). Furthermore, they have found that success has different meanings in different occupations. As noted previously, to automobile workers it means security (Chinoy, 1952). To custom furriers, who operate relatively small retail shops, success is equated with the size of their business and the income which it brings; in contrast, to business furriers, who sell mostly ready-made coats to an unselected clientele, success is defined more in terms of a good reputation among customers and colleagues (Kriesberg, 1952). Business executives have been characterized as successful to the extent that they "wholeheartedly adopt the role" which society expects them to play. According to Henry (1949, p. 291), this role represents a crystallization of middle-class attitudes and values, including achievement and mobility drives, decisiveness and self-directedness, and active and aggressive behavior. On a cultural level, success also has several connotations (Bingham & Freyd, 1926, p. 33), since, as Dressel (1953, p. 286) has observed, it "involves a value judgment which must of neccessity be different for different people and for different cultural patterns."

Psychological Concepts of Vocational Success. The predominant psychological concept of vocational success is one which was the cornerstone of personnel selection and evaluation procedures in industrial psychology from World War I to approximately 1950. It is that the success of a worker depends upon how well he performs his job. In the early days of industrial psychology, Bingham and Freyd (1926, pp. 30–31) wrote that:

> From the management's point of view, the successful employee, in contrast to the unsuccessful, does more work, does it better, with less supervision, with less interruption through absence from the job. He makes fewer mistakes and has fewer accidents. He offers a larger number of good original suggestions looking toward improvement of conditions or of processes. He ordinarily learns more quickly, is promoted more rapidly, and stays with the company.

Much the same emphasis is made by Pond (1936, pp. 941–942) who bases her concept of success upon the assumption that the key person in the industrial enterprise is the factory foreman. He is responsible for the training, supervision, and selection of personnel, and consequently,

> The successful workers in any department are those who consistently advance the goals of the foreman, and minimize his difficulties, namely, those who require the least supervision or training, who produce the quantity and quality of work desired, who show initiative and alertness in checking faulty conditions, and who cause the least friction of a personal nature, or obstruction of the work process.

These concepts of vocational success which focus upon the performance and efficiency of the worker are still current in contemporary industrial psychology, but they have been incorporated into more comprehensive concepts of vocational adjustment which encompass morale and satisfaction and personality-role factors as well as success criteria. Thus, recent texts in industrial psychology (e.g., Bass, 1965; Haire, 1964; Harrell, 1958; Siegel, 1962) index such topics as adjustment, motivation, and satisfaction but seldom vocational success.

In contrast, the field of vocational guidance early conceptualized vocational success as a more comprehensive phenomenon than job performance alone, possibly because of its greater concern with the happiness than the productivity of the worker. Included as an essential element of success was the contentment or satisfaction of the individual. Link (1936, p. 933) expresses this orientation as follows: "No matter whether a man earns much or little, is promoted rapidly or not at all, is a fast worker or a slow worker, is using his best capacities or not, so long as he is reasonably content, and his employer is content to keep him, he may be regarded as a vocational success." Similarly, Hersey (1936, p. 924) asks the question: "What is success from the vocational guidance standpoint?" and answers that: "In general, one can say that it means adjustment to all the varied phases of one's life, in line with one's abilities."

This concept of success was voiced not only by practitioners, but it was also translated into operational terms by researchers who were interested in evaluating the effects of vocational guidance. In particular, the work of the National Institute of Industrial Psychology and the Birmingham Education Department in England represents an attempt to evaluate more than the efficiency or performance facet of success (Allen, E.P., & Smith, P., 1940; Earle, 1931, 1933; Hunt, E. G., & Smith, G., 1945; Hunt, E. P., & Smith, P., 1938; Jennings & Stott, 1936; Macrae, Jennings, & Stott, 1937; Stott, 1936, 1939, 1950, 1956). These investigators have long argued that success cannot be adequately conceived of solely as earnings or output. Stott (1950, p. 112) has summarized this point of view as follows: "I would limit its [the concept of success] use to the attainment of the self-chosen goal. It follows, therefore, that, if this sense of the word is accepted, no man can be called successful unless something is known of his personal ideals and ambitions."[1] The English group developed measures of "attainment of the self-chosen goal" as part of their extensive follow-ups of vocationally advised young people, but they did not formulate any theoretical rationale for this definition of success.

In a paper entitled the "Psychology of Success and Failure," however, Lewin (1936) has provided such a rationale based upon concepts and principles drawn from his "field" theory of personality (Lewin, 1935). He begins with the observation that objective achievement, as defined by scholastic or vocational performance is *not* highly correlated with an individual's feelings of success or failure. On one occasion, an accomplishment may promote a strong sense of success, but on another occasion the same attainment may be experienced indifferently or even as failure. Lewin (1936, pp. 926–927) interprets such phenomena to indicate that:

> The experience of success and failure does not depend upon the achievement as such, but rather upon the relation between the achievement and the person's expectation. One can speak, in this respect, about the person's "level of aspiration," and can say that the experience and the degree of success and failure depend upon whether the achievement is above or below the momentary level of aspiration.

An individual's "level of aspiration" is defined as the goal he sets for himself in the accomplishment of a task, but he may also establish a broader objective which Lewin calls the "ideal" goal. Thus, a worker may set as his immediate goal promotion to supervisor of his section and as his ideal goal production manager of the plant in which he is employed. He may be more or less realistic in both his immediate and ideal goals, depending upon the factors which affect the setting and realizing of his level of aspiration. These contingencies include his experiences of success and failure with tasks, his ability to master tasks of a given difficulty, and his responsiveness to the expectations of others.

A General Concept of Vocational Success. Several discussions of vocational success have noted that the concept can be defined in different ways, depending upon the point of reference which is assumed (e.g., Strong, 1943, p. 14; Super, 1951a). Super (1951a, p. 7) writes that: "One tends to forget that success is not only a *social* or *objective* matter, but also a *personal* or *subjective* matter." Nevertheless, there has been only one attempt to formulate a general concept of vocational success which takes into account the various ways of

[1]Cf. Reeves, 1950.

evaluating a worker's performance on the job. Davies (1950, p. 8) has proposed a conceptual schema for vocational success which is based upon both objective and subjective criteria, since he argues that neither alone is sufficient to define success. What he suggests is to use as many criteria as possible to determine the individual's vocational success within the physical and psychological work environment, as depicted in Figure 10-1. Here it will be seen that most of the relevant individuals and groups, including the worker himself, which are in a position to evaluate vocational success are represented. In addition, however, Davies (1950, p. 12) introduces the "synoptic bystander," whom he describes as

> ... someone who is concerned not only with the adjustment of individuals and the well-being of working organizations, but with the benefit accruing to the community from the optimum use of talent and the attraction of the best men to the most important and useful occupations.

In other words, the "synoptic bystander" may be an interested layman, a government official, a manpower expert, a social planner—or, a vocational psychologist who is concerned with conceptualizing vocational success as comprehensively as possible.

Comment. It is apparent that vocational success means many things to many people. It should be noted that in each of these concepts, however, the worker

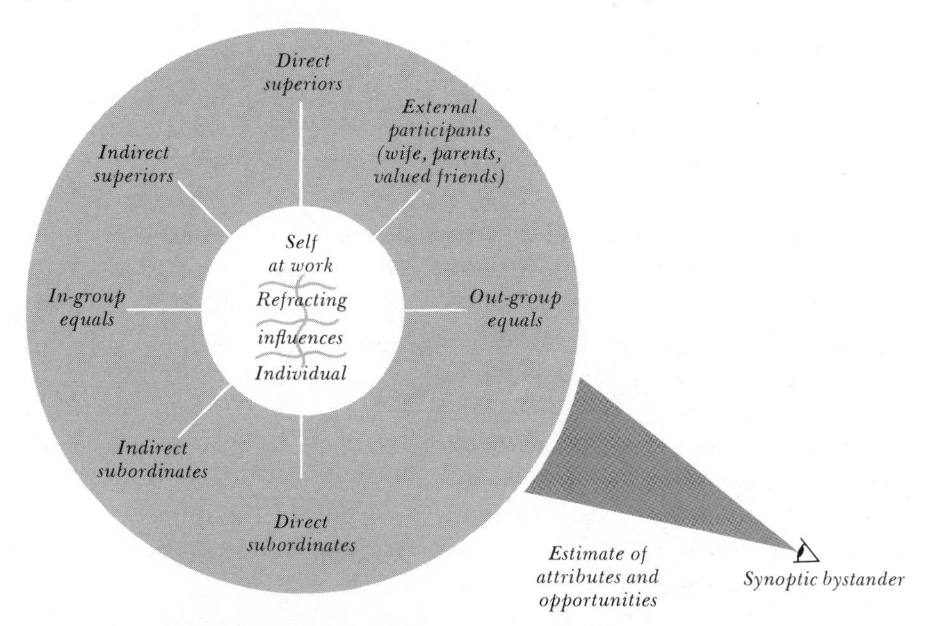

Figure 10-1. Davies's (1950, p. 16) schema for representing the various points of reference for evaluating vocational success.

behaves in such a way that a valued goal is achieved. In other words, although the behaviors and goals were substantively different, they were nevertheless "behaviors" and "goals." The implication is that we may be able to arrive at a general definition of vocational success if we think in terms of the *relationship* between behaviors and goals per se. The prototype of such a definition has been formulated by Ackoff (1953, p. 29) as follows: "The efficiency of a course of action for an objective in a specified environment is the probability that the action will result in the attainment of the objective." In other words, we can define *vocational success as the probability that a worker's behavior will achieve a particular goal in a given work environment.* By conceptualizing vocational success in this way, we can use methods of evaluating a worker's efficiency which are appropriate to his job, yet we can express his performance in terms of probabilities which can be compared with those of other workers in different jobs. Thus, we can achieve a concept of vocational success which is both specific *and* general in nature.

Criteria of Vocational Success

Many different definitions of the term *criterion* have been proposed, none of which has won universal acceptance, but most of which can be classified into two categories. First, there are those definitions which emphasize the meaning of a criterion as a *standard for measurement* (Cureton, 1951), such as the following:

> A criterion is a standard against which a measurement is made in estimating the validity of the measurement [A.E.R.A., 1952, p. 242].

> The term criterion is applied to a performance measure which is used as a standard in evaluating other measures [Bechtoldt, 1947, p. 357].

> Generally speaking, a criterion is a standard or rule used to provide a frame of reference for judging or testing something [Ryans, 1957, p. 357].

Implicit in these definitions is the value judgment that "something else is of greater importance than the standards themselves" (Ghiselli, 1956c, p. 1). Usually, the "something else" is a test, but it may also be a treatment condition in an experimental situation where the dependent variable is considered to be the "criterion."

Second, there are other definitions which emphasize exactly the opposite nature of a criterion as a *measuring stick for evaluating success and failure* (Bechtoldt, 1947). For example:

> A criterion of accomplishment is something which may be used as a measuring stick for gaging [sic] a worker's relative success or failure [Bingham & Freyd, 1926, p. 30].

> A criterion may be defined as a standard which can be used as a yardstick for measuring employees' success or failure [Stone & Kendall, 1956, p. 271].

> A criterion is a test by which a judgment can be formed of an individual's success in the work at which he is employed [Rasche, 1936, pp. 936–937].

Again, a value judgment is implicit in these definitions, as Fiske (1951, p. 93) has pointed out:

> A "criterion" is simply a label which we attach to something, such as the amount of work done or the ratings of a supervisor. Once the label is fastened on, we overlook the more or less subjective or arbitrary basis for its choice; we ignore the value-judgment required in selecting the criterion. We begin to treat the criterion behavior as the ultimate goal. . . .

The interpretation of a criterion as a "goal or ideal behavior" not only recognizes the value judgments involved in establishing standards for measurement or yardsticks for evaluation but, more importantly, it adds the connotation that a criterion is *dynamic* in nature (Ghiselli, 1956c). Particularly with respect to vocational success, a criterion involves a "defined action series" (Cureton, 1951) which takes place over time. Thus, English and English (1958, p. 130), in their dictionary of psychological terms, define a criterion as a "behavior goal by which progress is judged." Similarly, Lorge (1936, p. 958) writes that: "Success is a verbal ideal. . . . Success implies striving to a desired or purposed end." Other definitions which also highlight the dynamic character of a criterion include the following:

> The ultimate criterion is the complete final goal of a patricular type of selection or training [Thorndike, R. L., 1949, p. 121].

> For individuals on any given job there is, theoretically, some "ultimate" or "true" job standard by which individuals might be evaluated [Tiffin & McCormick, 1958, p. 35].

> A criterion is defined as a behavior or condition which is or can be described in terms of an ideal and which is a goal. That is, a criterion is the kind of behavior which is considered desirable and toward which one works [Jensen, Coles, & Nestor, 1955, p. 58].

These definitions suggest that, whether a criterion is to be used primarily for the construction of a measuring instrument or for the assessment of performance, it represents behaviors or goals which are valued as the outcomes of a course of action pursued over an extended period of time.

The Theory of Criterion Construction. There are several desiderata which are generally accepted as essential in order to construct adequate criteria of vocational success. Foremost among these is the *relevance* or validity of the criterion (A.E.R.A., 1952; Bechtoldt, 1947, 1951; Bellows, 1941; Jensen et al., 1955; Nagle, 1953; Ryans, 1957; Weitz, 1961). Thorndike, R. L. (1947; 1949, p. 125) has defined relevance as follows: "A criterion is relevant as far as the knowledges, skills, and basic aptitudes required for success on it are the same as those required for performance of the ultimate task." Logically, this means that a criterion must be both "pertinent" and "comprehensive"; it is pertinent if it excludes "all extraneous variables not strictly bearing on job performance," and it is comprehensive if it includes "all of the important components of the areas of performance delimited by the definition of success" (Bechtoldt, 1947, p. 359). Empirically, relevance has usually been demonstrated by the correlations of the criterion measure with the "ultimate" criterion or with other criterion measures. If these correlations are moderately positive, it is concluded that the criterion is relevant (Bellows, 1941; Nagle, 1955).

The problem in this approach, however, is that there is no "ultimate" criterion for the "ultimate" criterion. In the last analysis, then, the relevance of a criterion is based upon logical considerations rather than empirical evidence (Bechtoldt, 1947; Jensen et al., 1955; Thorndike, R. L., 1949). Astin (1964, pp. 809–810) has recently elaborated upon this point by distinguishing between a *conceptual criterion,* which is a "verbal statement of important or socially relevant outcomes," and a *criterion performance,* which is "any observable event which is judged to be relevant to the conceptual criterion." He goes on to conclude that:

> Since conceptual criteria are rational rather than empirical, the relevance of a criterion performance can be judged only on rational grounds. To illustrate: changes in a student's achievement test score (criterion performance) constitute a measure of "effective teaching" (conceptual criterion) only if one is willing to *assume* that the student's score is an important or socially relevant variable to be manipulated by the teacher. To establish this isomorphism empirically would require an independent measure of the teacher's effectiveness, and the relevance of that measure to the conceptual criterion would first have to be established in the same rational manner [Astin, 1964, pp. 810–811; italics in original].

In other words, Astin substitutes the "conceptual" criterion for the "ultimate" criterion and thus resolves the dilemma inherent in evaluating the latter empirically.

A second desirable characteristic of criteria is *reliability* (Bechtoldt, 1947, 1951; Bellows, 1941; Jensen et al., 1955; Nagle, 1953; Ryans, 1957). Thorndike, R. L. (1949, p. 127) comments upon this requirement of a criterion as follows: "A necessary but not sufficient condition for correlation between a criterion measure and the theoretically perfect ultimate criterion of success on a job is that the criterion measure have *some* reliability." What Thorndike means here is that a criterion need not have *high* reliability in order to be predicted. As long as its reliability is high enough so that it can be concluded that systematic (nonchance) differences in behavior have been measured (Underwood, 1957), and thus that the relationships of the criterion to other variables can be reproduced, the reliability of the criterion is considered to be acceptable.

But, of what magnitude must the reliability be for it to be "high enough"? At least two considerations are pertinent in attempting to answer this question, for which there is no really acceptable answer (Thorndike, R. L., & Hagen, 1961, p. 189). First, because criteria of vocational success are not static (Ghiselli, 1956c; Prien, 1966), it follows that those criteria which change with vocational development will *not* have very high reliability. Second, criteria with low reliability, however, cannot be expected to correlate with much of anything, since the theoretical ceiling for the correlation of one variable with another is the square of its reliability coefficient.

One way out of this dilemma, which is an omnipresent problem in the measurement of developmental variables, is to evaluate the reliability of criteria by using both internal consistency *and* stability estimates. If the internal consistency coefficients for a criterion are statistically significant on both test and retest, and if the stability coefficient between test and retest is also significant, there is presumptive evidence that the reliability of the criterion is "high enough." The significantly high internal consistency coefficients on the two occasions indicate that "variations in the measurement procedure itself" are not so great that individual differences in response to it are due solely to chance, and the significantly high stability coefficient indicates that they are not attributable only to "changes in the individual from day to day" (Thorndike, R. L., & Hagen, 1961, p. 182). In other words, together the two kinds of reliabilities reveal whether a criterion of vocational success discriminates systematically among individuals *within* different points in time as well as *between* different points in time.

Finally, although other desiderata of criteria have been proposed, such as "acceptability to the job analyst" (Bellows, 1941), "feasibility" (Ryans, 1957), and "precedence" (Weitz, 1961), the most frequently mentioned "criterion" for criteria, in addition to relevance and reliability, is *freedom from bias* (Bechtoldt, 1947; Bellows, 1941; Jensen et al., 1955; Ryans, 1957; Thorndike, R. L., 1947, 1949). In their paper, "The Theory and Classification of Criterion Bias," which is probably the most authoritative and comprehensive analysis which has yet been made of the problem, Brogden and Taylor (1950b, p. 161) define a *biasing factor* as "any variable, except errors of measurement and sampling error, producing a deviation of obtained criterion scores from a hypothetical 'true' criterion score." They then classify the sources of bias in criteria as follows:

1. *Criterion deficiency:* omission of pertinent elements from the criterion
2. *Criterion contamination:* introducing extraneous elements into the criterion
3. *Criterion scale unit bias:* inequality of scale units in the criterion
4. *Criterion distortion:* improper weighting in combining criterion elements

Criterion deficiency and criterion contamination directly affect the relevance of a criterion, since, as can be inferred from the previous discussion, the former is the opposite of what Bechtoldt (1947) has called the "comprehensiveness" of a criterion and the latter is the opposite of what he has termed the "pertinence" of a criterion. There is not space here for a discussion of the various sources of criterion contamination which have been identified, but some of the principal ones can be mentioned: (1) contamination by illicit use of predictor information (Bellows, 1941); (2) opportunity bias (Brogden & Taylor, 1950b); (3) experience bias (Bellows, 1941; Brogden & Taylor, 1950b; Ryans, 1957); and (4) rating bias, such as "halo effects" and "errors of illation" (Brogden & Taylor, 1950b). Criterion scale unit bias arises primarily when ratings are used to assess vocational success and there is a "piling up" of judgments at a particular point on the scale, e.g., the upper end. And, criterion distortion results from the improper assignment of weights in combining the elements of a criterion and, consequently, includes all the other types of bias: Criterion deficiency contributes zero weights to components which should have nonzero weights; criterion contamination involves the converse, i.e., use of nonzero weights for components which have zero weights; and, criterion scale unit bias applies different weights to different segments of the criterion which should have equal weights.

The Methodology of Criterion Construction. The history and present status of criterion methodology has been characterized by Wherry (1957, p. 2) as "unintelligent diligence" and by Guion (1961, p. 142) as a haphazard process which typically involves a series of expedient steps eventuating in the use of "the best available criterion." Studies of criteria of vocational success have often deserved such critical evaluations of their methodology, but less because appropriate methodology has been lacking than because it has not been employed. There are several methodological approaches which have been proposed for the construction of criteria (Brogden & Taylor, 1950b; Nagle, 1953; Guion, 1961), but none of them has satisfactorily resolved the recurrent problem of whether to predict each element in a criterion separately or to combine them into a composite—and, if the latter, by what procedure.

The pros and cons of combining and not combining criterion measures have been discussed at some length by Sluckin (1956a; 1956b) and have been summarized in Table 10-1. The advisability of combining criteria depends, in the first instance, upon the direction and magnitude of their intercorrelations. If the criteria are substantially negatively related to each other, then a composite of them will yield poorer discrimination among individuals than each criterion used separately. Similarly, if the intercorrelations are near zero, a composite criterion will be unstable, in the sense that an individual's standing (score) on it will change considerably with the addition or deletion of other criterion measures. Only when there are substantial positive correlations among the criteria should combination be considered, and then only when some *internal* weighting procedure is followed. To combine them with reference to some *external* variable, such as a set of predictors or the "ultimate" criterion, leads to logical difficulties: if a composite is formed on the basis of its relationship to predictors, there is criterion contamination; and if it is constructed in terms of its correlation with an "ultimate" criterion, the latter must be known—and probably should be used instead. To combine criteria according to an internal weighting system, however, is not without its problems. Sluckin (1956b, p. 66) reviews the six methods of internal weighting shown in Table 10-1, and concludes that: "Some form of weighting by reference to judgments of experts should preferably be considered whenever criterion measures are to be combined." For this purpose he recommends a procedure originated by T. L. Kelley during World War I and advocated by Toops (1944), in which judges allot "bids" to each criterion measure according to their presumed importance, the weights being the proportion of bids assigned to the various measures.

To accept Sluckin's (1956b) conclusion that the "bid" system of weighting is the best for combining criteria of vocational success, however, would fail to recognize the value of an approach which has been proposed by Brogden and Taylor (1950a). Sluckin criticizes this method as not comprehensive enough, because it does not provide for the combination of morale and satisfaction indexes into a composite criterion of vocational success. If success is defined as an *efficiency* variable, as is usually the case, then Brogden and Taylor's method certainly deserves consideration, particularly since it promises to solve two of the major problems in the combination of criteria: how to derive optimal weights and how to achieve a common scale metric.

What they suggest is to apply cost-accounting concepts and procedures to the analysis and development of success criteria. In other words, criteria are

Table 10-1. Summary of Procedures for Combining and Not Combining Variables in Constructing Criteria of Vocational Success

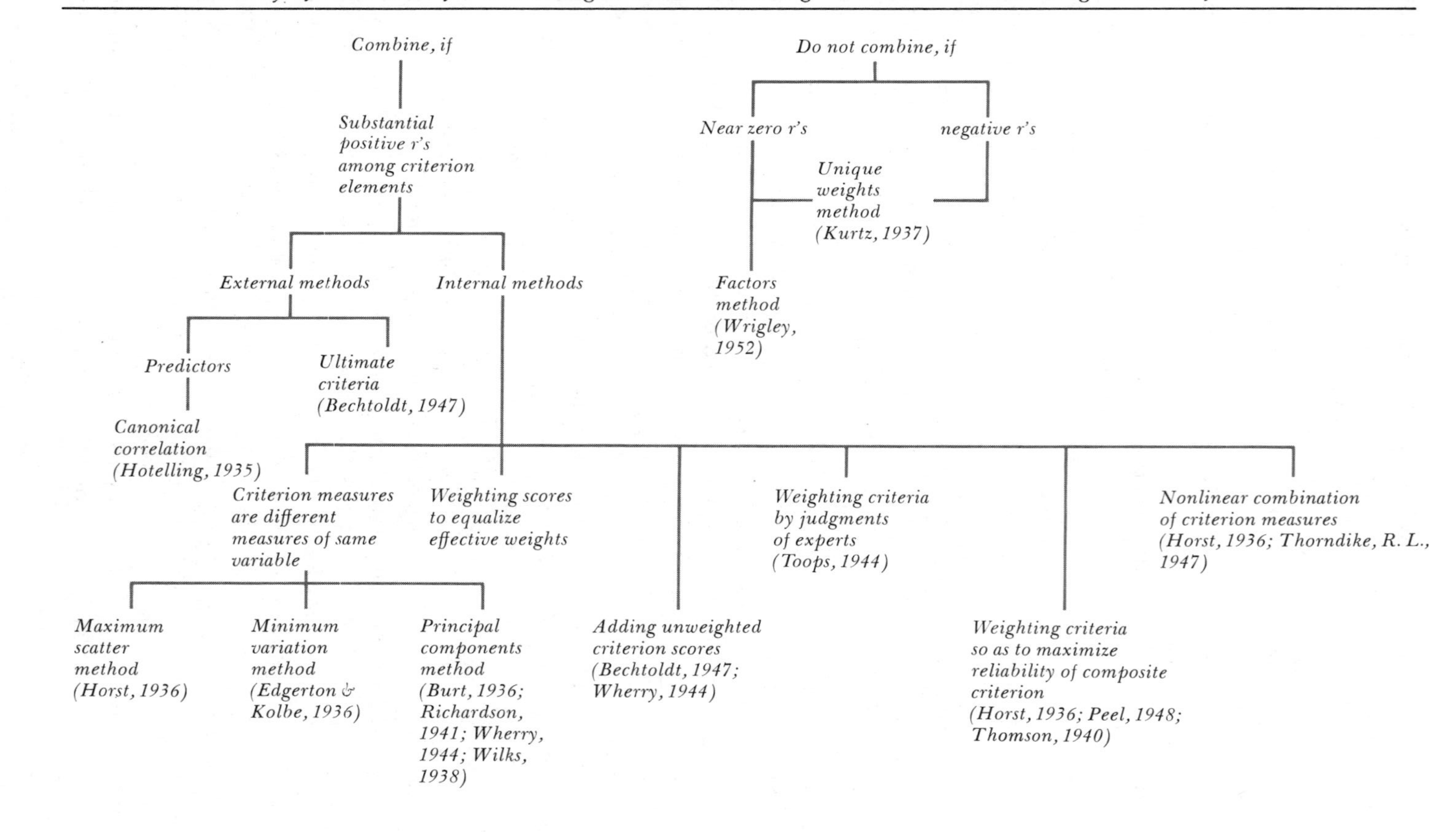

scaled in terms of their "dollar value." This evaluation is accomplished through a process of "tracing out" the exact nature and importance of the effect of each subcriterion variable on the overall efficiency of the organization, which, in this sense, constitutes the "ultimate" criterion. The advantages of this approach are that all criteria are scaled in the same unit of measurement (dollars), and hence they can be added to form a composite, and that each criterion variable is optimally weighted in proportion to its standard deviation when it is added in a composite. The limitations are that the "tracing out" process may be extremely difficult for variables which are more intangible in nature, such as the outcomes of a public relations program, and that ratings may have to be used when variables cannot be expressed in dollar units. As compared with other systems for scaling and weighting criteria, however, Brogden and Taylor's is preferable if for no other reason than it forces the criterion constructor to reduce vocational success variables to what have been called "primitive predicates" (Spiker & McCandless, 1954), i.e., the physical properties of phenomena (color, location, weight), which can then be translated into meaningful units of measurement.

The Classification of Criteria. There are several dimensions which have been proposed that might be used for the classification of criteria of vocational success. Most of these can be subsumed, however, under the more general rubrics of the "time," "type," and "level" dimensions suggested by Weitz (1961). The importance of *time* as a dimension for criteria was first noted by Thorndike, R. L. (1947; 1949) who distinguished among (1) immediate, (2) intermediate, and (3) ultimate criteria, depending upon when job performance was sampled and evaluated. Immediate criteria of vocational success can be applied at the moment the individual attempts to enter the world of work, the most obvious one being whether he can secure employment. Intermediate criteria might include such considerations as whether a worker can successfully complete an on-the-job training program or whether he is rated as satisfactory by his supervisors. Ratings would be classified as intermediate criteria, incidentally, because, as Thorndike, R. L. (1949, p. 122) points out: "We are not ultimately concerned with how a man is *rated* by his superiors but rather how well he actually *performs* in the crucial situations for which he has been trained." Ultimate criteria, or what might better be termed "remote" criteria because of the previously mentioned logical difficulties involved in defining "ultimate" criteria, are evaluations of performance on the job following entry and/or training. They would include such indices of success as number of errors in punching IBM cards or volume of insurance sales during a given period or merit pay increases.

The *type* dimension for the classification of criteria encompasses several different enumerations which have been made of criteria of vocational success, some of which are as follows:

BINGHAM AND FREYD (1926, pp. 34–42)	Time required to train worker; standing in corporation schools; quality and quantity of output; performance on standardized tests; accidents and loss due to breakage or claims; salary; commissions and bonuses; length of service or stability on job: advancement in the firm; degree of responsibility; membership in professional societies; trade status; ratings.
VITELES (1932, p. 205)	Quantity of output; quality of output; amount of spoiled work; number of accidents; cost of accidents; number of breakages; length of service or stability on the job; commissions; earned bonus; rate of advancement; standardized tests; number of operating mistakes.
OTIS (1940, pp. 79–88)	Quantity of production; quality of production; work samples; job tenure; length of training period.
TOOPS (1944, pp. 276–289)	Wages; production; quality of work; the rate (or, alternatively, the amount) of acquisition of new skills; supervisor's judgments; knowledge; job tenure; supervisory and leadership abilities; incidental factors.
SUPER (1951a, pp. 5–8)	Earnings and output; advancement; job stability; efficiency ratings; self-ratings.
SUPER AND CRITES (1962, pp. 36–40)	Proficiency measures; output records; ratings; self-ratings; administrative acts.

It will be noted that some of these different types of criteria, such as "time required to train worker" or "advancement," may also be cross-classified along the time dimension, thus suggesting a two-dimensional "time-type" classification system for some criteria of vocational success. Another basis for classification, which pertains only to type, is the "objective-subjective" distinction suggested by Viteles (1932), who considers rating scales and other indirect methods of assessing success to be subjective as compared with such objective indices as quantity of output or number of accidents. Finally, Thorndike, R. L. (1947; 1949) has differentiated between criteria which (1) evaluate performance in a specific task, such as a work sample, and criteria which (2) represent general summary evaluations of a total phase or large unit of training or on-the-job performance, such as piecework records over a period of time.

The dimension of *level* in the classification of criteria of vocational success has received relatively little attention in comparison with the time and type dimensions, but it is nonetheless salient for identifying the differences which exist among criteria. Weitz (1961) has observed that the level of performance which is taken as the criterion, such as number of ledger entries per hour made by a bookkeeper, may directly affect the conclusions which can be drawn about the relationships of the criterion to other variables. For example, suppose a vocational psychologist is interested in the factors which are related to success as a bookkeeper, and he chooses to study number of ledger entries per hour as a criterion of job performance. Suppose further that he wants to determine the relationship of a measure of clerical speed and accuracy, such as the Minnesota Clerical Test, to the criterion. He may find that bookkeepers who rank high on the criterion obtain high scores on clerical speed but only average scores on clerical accuracy, whereas those who rank in the middle range on the criterion have exactly the opposite pattern of speed and accuracy scores. Thus, he must conclude that different levels of the criterion have different relationships to other variables, the reason in this example being that the greater the speed of the clerical response, which is what "number of ledger entries per hour" defines, the less the accuracy of the response. In other words, as Weitz (1961) notes, the relationships between independent or predictor variables and the criterion may be curvilinear because of the differential significance of levels of the criterion. The implication is that we need to take level into consideration when we classify criteria and when we formulate hypotheses about them.

A Survey and Summary of Criteria. The number and variety of criteria which have been used in studies of vocational success are great, and a comprehensive review of them would require a separate monograph. Consequently, only a brief survey and summary are presented here, more as an introduction to and illustration of criteria that have been utilized than as an analysis and critique of them. What was done was to use Dorcus and Jones's (1950) *Handbook of Employee Selection,* which abstracts over 500 studies in which a criterion of vocational success was one of the variables, as a reference source to identify and enumerate as many criteria as possible. The definition and reliability of each criterion given by Dorcus and Jones were typed on 3- by 5-inch index cards, which were then sorted and classified by the writer into the categories shown in Table 10-2.

Table 10-2. Classification of Criteria of Vocational Success *(Compiled from Dorcus & Jones, 1950)*

Criteria	*Number*	*Reliability*		*Rater*		*Number of raters*	
SCALES							
General ratings							
Not given	100	Not given	167	Not given	23	Not given	115
Likert-type scale	65	.00–.20	4	Supervisor	136	One	55
"Good, Average, Poor"	40	.21–.30	0	Foreman	14	Two	18
Graphic rating scale	2	.31–.40	1	Superintendent	9	Three	16
Graphic rating scale and rank-order	2	.41–.50	3	Instructor	9	Four	4
Graphic rating scale and pair-comparisons	1	.51–.60	3	Principal	9	Five	2
Rank-order and pair-comparisons	1	.61–.70	10	Supervisor and colleagues	6	Six	2
Ratings converted to ranks	1	.71–.80	12	Owner	3	Seven or more	1
Checklist	1	.81–.90	8	Manager	3		
	1	.91–.100	5	Inspector	1		
Total	213		213		213		213
Efficiency ratings							
Ratings and rankings	5	Not given	7	Not given	2	Not given	5
Efficiency index	3			Not applicable	4	Not applicable	4
Percent efficiency (earned hours versus clock hours, errors)	2	.00–.30	1	Supervisor	3	One	0
		.31–.50	0	Foreman	1	Two	1
		.51–.70	2			Three or more	0
		.71–1.00	0				
Total	10		10		10		10
Rankings							
Rank-order	45	Not given	41	Not given	3	Not given	32
Pair-comparisons	3	.00–.70	0	Supervisor	39	One	7
		.71–.80	1	Instructor	3	Two	6
		.81–.90	2	Investigator	2	Three	1
		.91–1.00	4	Manager	1	Four	1

	N		N		N		N
						Five	1
						Six, seven, or more	0
Total	48		48		48		48
CLASSIFICATIONS							
"Good" versus "poor" workers	13	Not given	29	Not given	20	Not given	28
Satisfactory versus unsatisfactory	13	.00–.50	0	Not applicable	1	Not applicable	1
Classified as "outstanding" or not "outstanding"	2	.51–.60	1	Supervisor	9	One	1
Job classification	2	.61–.80	0	Foreman	1	Two or more	1
Successful supervisors versus those not promoted because of lack of ability	1	.81–1.00	1				
Total	31		31		31		31
ESTIMATES							
Estimates of job success	5	Not given	6	Not given	1	Not given	6
Estimate of ability	1	.00–.80	0	Supervisor	5	One, two, or three	0
Estimates of speed of learning based upon percentage of "bogey"	1	.81–1.00	1	Employer	1	Four	1
Total	7		7		7		7
GRADES							
Instructor's grades (on the job)	1	Not given	3	Superintendent	2	Not given	3
Grading by superintendent or foreman	1			Instructor	1		0
Grading for efficiency	1						
Total	3		3		3		3
JUDGMENTS							
Superior's judgment of success	10	Not given	11	Not given	4		
Judgments transformed into scores	1			Superior	5		
				Foreman	2		
Total	11		11		11		

Table 10-2 Classification of Criteria of Vocational Success *(Compiled from Dorcus & Jones, 1950) (Continued)*

Criteria	*Number*	*Reliability*	*Rater*	*Number of raters*
OUTPUT				
Production (no further description)	36	Not given	40	
Average paid-for production	9	.71–.80	6	
Bedeaux points	2	.81–.90		
Speed of posting for bookkeepers	2			
Number of transactions handled by sales clerks	2			
Service records	2			
Number of slips for ditto-machine operators	1			
Average number of sheets typed per day for typists	1			
Net dollars per sale	1	.91–1.00	1	
Selling cost for sales clerks	1			
"Cramp" and "pressure" exerted by telegraphers	1			
Total	58		58	
SALES				
Sales records (no further description)	5	Not given	13	
Average daily or weekly sales	5	.61–.70	1	
Total sales during first year	2	.71–.80	1	
Composite (gross sales, returns quota)	1	.81–1.00	1	
Other (new business, etc.)	3			
Total	16		16	
EARNINGS				
Average hourly earnings	6	Not given	16	
Earnings after learning period	5			
Piece-rate pay and annual salary	2			
Credit rating and Civil Service grade	2			
"Ability to make a comfortable living"	1			
Total	16		16	

ACCIDENTS			
Number of accidents	5	Not given	11
Accident rate per month	5	.00–.30	1
Accident responsibility	1	.31–.70	0
Ratio of number of accidents to number expected	1	.71–.80	1
Turnover and discharge due to accidents	1	.81–1.00	0
Total	13		13
JOB LEVEL			
Job level attained after a given number of years service	13	Not given	13
JOB SURVIVAL			
Length of service	7	Not given	10
Termination	3		
Total	10		10
WORK SAMPLE			
Work samples (no further description)	4	Not given	8
Graded job production on Likert-type scale	3	.00–.60	1
Speed of operation	2	.61–.70	0
Inspection of work	1	.71–1.00	1
Total	10		10
PROMOTION			
Promotion at the end of a given number of years	2	Not given	4
Upgrading	1		
Transfer from training gang to regular sales force	1		
Total	4		4

Here it can readily be seen that by far the most commonly used criterion of vocational success, at least to 1950, was some kind of psychological scale. Almost two-thirds (66.18 percent) of the criteria were operationally defined by scaling techniques. And, in most instances, it was the worker's supervisor who was asked to evaluate his success by these methods. Typically, only one rater or judge has been employed in using the scales, so that little is known about how much agreement can be attained in their application. Next to scales, the most popular criterion of vocational success has been output. As indicated in Table 10-2, this criterion has been defined in several different ways, most of which are specific to a given job function. In other words, output is a far less comprehensive or global criterion than is usually provided by scales. Criteria other than scales and output have been used only infrequently and with largely unknown success. In a handful of studies, composite criteria have been developed, but, despite their apparent advantages, their actual empirical merits have not been firmly established. For all but a few of the criteria which were reviewed no reliability data were reported. The exceptions were scales and output, for which gross estimates of their test-retest reliabilities would be .75 and .85, respectively.

Research on vocational success since 1950 has largely followed the trends of the past in using scales and output as criteria, but some new departures have been made, at least a few of which should be mentioned. Lamourea and Harrell (1963) have demonstrated that "operations-research" techniques can be used to evaluate vocational success, in this case the performance of research managers, and that, in their opinion, they are superior to "clinical" rating procedures. Bell, F. O., Hoff, and Hoyt (1963) compared three types of ratings —job-oriented, behavior-oriented, and trait-oriented—and concluded that each has its own merit. Hulin (1962) has suggested, on the basis of a study he conducted of executive success, that, because of the complexity of job performance and the extraneous variables which affect evaluations and indices of it, a linear combination of several "corrected" criteria is preferable to the use of any one criterion alone. Schultz and Siegel (1961; 1964) have taken much the same position, but they have developed it further (1) by applying multidimensional scaling techniques to job performance criteria and (2) by utilizing Thurstone and Guttman scaling techniques in conjunction with each other. Finally, note should be made of a recent trend in the construction of vocational success criteria which appears to be an outgrowth of the national emphasis upon the development of the sciences since Sputnik: the evaluation of scientific creativity and research productivity (Buel, 1960; 1965; Buel, Albright & Glennon, 1966; Buel & Bachner, 1961; Cotton & Stolz, 1960; Morrison, R. F., Owens, Glennon, & Albright, 1962; Smith, W. J., Albright, Glennon, & Owens, 1961; Sprecher, 1959; and Stolz, 1958).

Dimensions of Vocational Success

Is vocational success a unitary variable, or is it comprised of several dimensions? A number of studies have attempted to find an answer to this question, a few of them using multidimensional scaling techniques, as in the investigation by Schultz and Siegel (1964) already discussed, but most of them have employed one variant or another of factor-analytic methodologies.[2] Much of this research has been primarily exploratory in nature, with little or no theory to guide the investigators in their search for and interpretation of the factors in vocational success. Typically, the design of these studies has been to measure vocational success with either rating scales, checklists, or objective indices (such as absences, accidents, disciplinary actions, etc.); to intercorrelate scores from the various measures; and to factor-analyze the resulting matrix of correlation coefficients with any one of several procedures. To the knowledge of the writer, there have been no investigations in which the same data have been factor-analyzed by different methods and the findings compared to determine the possible effects of variations in the methods. Nor, have there been any studies in which factorial data for different occupations have been gathered. There is at least one study, however, in which different measures of vocational success have been compared (Wrigley, Cherry, Lee, & McQuitty, 1957), and three others in which the contribution of "halo" effects to the factorial structure of vocational success has been analyzed. The discussion which follows summarizes the findings of these studies under three topical headings: (1) factor analyses of vocational success; (2) a model of vocational success; and (3) occupational differences in the dimensions of vocational success.

Factor Analyses of Vocational Success. Table 10-3 presents an outline summary of 14 factor-analytic studies which have been done on vocational success. It will be noted, as indicated in the previous section, "A Survey and Summary of Criteria," that the most frequently used measuring device is the rating scale, usually of the Likert-type. Also popular in these studies, however, is the checklist of telegraphically phrased statements about work performance which utilizes the "True-False" response format. Whether these two kinds of measures yield different results has not been determined, but there is some evidence that different types of checklists produce unique findings. Wrigley et al. (1957, p. 25) found that different variables were measured by checklists comprised of (1) statements made by supervisors in describing the "best" and "poorest"

[2] A notable exception is a study by Seashore, Indik, and Georgopoulos (1960), in which they tested the hypothesis that there is no overall dimension of vocational success but did not use factor analysis. Instead, they made an "inspectional" analysis of the sign and size of the intercorrelations among five criteria of job performance, concluding that they were not unidimensional.

Table 10-3. Summary of Factor Analyses of Vocational Success

Investigator	*Measure of vocational success*	*Method of factor analysis*	*Occupation of subjects*	*Factors*
Bolanovich (1946)	Likert-type rating scale	Centroid—oblique solution	Field engineers (N = 143)	1. Attendance to detail 2. Ability to do present job 3. Sales ability 4. Conscientiousness 5. Organizing or systematic tendency 6. Social intelligence
Ewart, Seashore, & Tiffin (1941)	Graphic-type rating scale	Centroid—oblique solution	Production workers (N = 120)	1. Ability to do present job 2. Knowledge of job, versatility, and accuracy 3. Health
Grant (1955)	Graphic-type rating scale	Centroid—oblique solution	Division managers (N = 97)	1. Skill in dealing with others 2. Judgment 3. Effectiveness in supervising the work 4. Effectiveness in planning the work 5. Effectiveness in improving operating efficiency 6. Halo effect
Ryans (1952)	Likert-type rating scale	Centroid—oblique solution	Elementary school teachers, female (N = 275)	1. Originality, adaptability, and tolerance 2. Class control 3. Understanding and composed 4. Sociability 5. Personal appearance

Rush (1953)	Likert-type rating scale Sales records Grades in technical sales school	Centroid (type of solution not indicated)	Salesmen ($N = 100$)	1. Objective achievement 2. Learning aptitude 3. General reputation 4. Sales techniques and achievement
Turner (1960)	Rankings based upon ratings Objective measures: grievances, turnover, absences, suggestions, hospital passes, disciplines, absentee flexibility, scrap, expense tools, expense processing supplies, efficiency	Principal components orthogonal solution	Production foremen ($N = 102$ in Plant X, $N = 104$ in Plant Y)	1. Job performance 2. Employee relations 3. Scrap versus organization of production operations 4. Unnamed—different loadings for Plants X and Y
Creager & Harding (1958)	Checklist—81 statements rated on Likert-type scales	Hierarchical—orthogonal solution	Foremen ($N = 141$)	1. Social relations 2. Technical job knowledge 3. Administrative skills 4. Halo effect
McQuitty, Wrigley, & Gaier (1954)	Checklist—200 phrases checked as "True" or "False"	Square root—orthogonal solution	Supervisors of aircraft mechanics ($N = 428$)	1. Drive and initiative 2. Practical efficiency 3. Knowledge and intellectual powers 4. Social manner 5. Interest and morale 6. Character 7. Other (e.g., inexperience, tendency to mediocrity)

Table 10-3. Summary of Factor Analyses of Vocational Success *(Continued)*

Investigator	*Measure of vocational success*	*Method of factor analysis*	*Occupation of subjects*	*Factors*
Roach (1956)	Checklist—390 statements rated on Likert-type scales	Wherry-Winer—orthogonal solution	First-line supervisors ($N = 245$)	1. Personal compliance 2. Job knowledge 3. Direction of group performance 4. Rewarding performance and thoroughness of employee evaluation 5. Company loyalty 6. Acceptance of responsibility 7. Group spirit 8. Personal drive 9. Impartiality 10. Poise and bearing 11. Consideration 12. Open-mindedness 13. Cheerfulness 14. Approachability 15. Halo effect
Stoltz (1959)	Checklist—250 statements rated on Likert-type scales	Wherry-Winer—orthogonal solution	Physical science research workers ($N = 80$)	1. General productive behavior 2. Affability 3. Motivation 4. Ability to communicate 5. Creative ability
Wrigley, Cherry, Lee, & McQuitty (1957)	Checklist—200 phrases checked as "True" or "False"	Square root—orthogonal solution	Supervisors of aircraft mechanics ($N = 464$)	1. General job efficiency 2. Social maladjustment 3. Executive ability 4. Leadership

				5. Personal charm 6. Resourcefulness 7. Willingness and adaptability 8. Orderliness 9. Ability to motivate others 10. Mechanical proficiency
Ronan (1963)	Shop rating, school rating, math grades, absence index, injury index, lost-time accidents, grievances, disciplinary actions, promotions, supervisory ratings, personality disorder	Centroid—orthogonal solution	Skilled-trades apprentices (N = 137)	1. Safe worker 2. Successful school work 3. Supervisory evaluations 4. Adjustment
Richards, J. M., Taylor, Price, & Jacobsen (1965)	80 scores based upon interviews, colleagues' opinions, compendiums, records, transcripts, judges, and questionnaires	Principal components—orthogonal solution	Physicians (N = 190)	A total of 29 factors was extracted, covering aspects of the physician's practice (e.g., diagnostic thoroughness), self-evaluation of success, keeping abreast of the field, participation in civic organizations and professional societies, leisure planning, and achievement in undergraduate and medical education
Taylor, C. W., Price, Richards, J. M., & Jacobsen (1964)	80 scores based upon interviews, colleagues' opinions, compendiums, records, transcripts judges, and questionnaires	Principal components—orthogonal solution	Medical school faculty (N = 102)	A total of 25 factors was extracted, covering academic security, professional recognition for achievements, self-estimated research success, consulting, excellence as a clinician, academic orientation, administrative contributions, status seeking,

Table 10-3. Summary of Factor Analyses of Vocational Success (*Continued*)

Investigator	*Measure of vocational success*	*Method of factor analysis*	*Occupation of subjects*	*Factors*
				participation in civic organizations and professional societies, and achievements in education
Taylor, C. W., Price, Richards, J. M., & Jacobsen (1965)	80 scores based upon interviews, colleagues' opinions, compendiums, records, transcripts, judges, and questionnaires	Principal components —orthogonal solution	Medical general practitioners ($N = 217$)	A total of 30 factors was extracted, covering level of medical specialization, medical consulting, satisfaction from interpersonal relationships, diagnostic thoroughness, civic participation, and professional stability

mechanics they had known (Descriptive Inventory), (2) statements derived from previous factor-analytic studies (Factorial Inventory), and (3) statements gleaned from the literature on the assessment of vocational success (Survey Inventory): "The Descriptive Inventory stresses a mechanic's willingness for work and his dependability, the Factorial Inventory his social and emotional adjustment, and the Survey Inventory, his practical ability." Thus, one reason for the large number of factors which have been extracted in the studies summarized in Table 10-3 may be that each measure of vocational success, as a result of differences in content and format, leads to a somewhat different constellation of factors. As a perusal of the factors listed in the last column of the table reveals, both their number and nature vary from one study to another.

A Model of Vocational Success. In addition to the type of measure which is used to assess vocational success, another reason for the heterogeneity among the factors in Table 10-3 is that different methods of factor analysis were followed in extracting them. These included Thurstone's (1947) centroid method, with both oblique and orthogonal solutions, the hierarchical method of Schmid and Leiman (1957), Harmon's (1960) principal-components analysis, with Kaiser's (1960) varimax rotational procedure, the modified square-root method developed by Wrigley and McQuitty (in press), and the Wherry-Winer (1953) method for factoring a large number of variables. The method used determines whether a solution to a factor analysis will be oblique or orthogonal. With the hierarchical, square-root, and Wherry-Winer methods, it is not possible to get an oblique solution; an orthogonal solution is "forced" upon the data by these factor-analytic procedures. Another effect of choice of method is the number of factors which are extracted from a matrix. When unity is used as the communality estimate in a factor analysis, as it was by Richards, J. M., Taylor, Price, and Jacobsen (1965) and Taylor, C. W., Price, Richards, J. M., and Jacobsen (1964) in the principal-components method and by Wrigley et al. (1957) in the square-root method, more factors are usually found than when some other estimate, such as the multiple correlation between each variable and all other variables combined, is calculated. Consequently, it is not surprising that the various factor analyses reported in Table 10-3 do not agree better with each other than they do.

Further difficulty arises in interpreting the results of these studies, because in some of them, which measured vocational success with rating scales, the composition of the factors is inextricably confounded with "halo" effects. In other words, it cannot be determined whether the factors represent dimensions of vocational success or the systematic tendencies of supervisors to rate workers either high or low. Wherry (1952) has pointed out that "halo" effects usually emerge in a factor analysis as a principal general factor which "accounts for" a large percentage of the total variance. Both Grant (1955) and Roach (1956) found such a factor, the former reporting that it contributed 31 percent of the total variance as compared with 17 percent for the next highest factor. By using the hierarchical method of factor analysis, Creager and Harding (1958) were able to separate halo variance from that attributable to other sources and found that it amounted to 62.17 percent of the total common variance. The remaining "non-halo" variance was distributed across three orthogonal group factors which the authors named Social Relations, Technical Knowledge, and Administrative Skills. The implication of this study is twofold: First, halo effects can be separately identified in factor analyses of ratings of vocational success; and, second, after the halo variance has been isolated, there is still a considerable amount of residual variance which can be meaningfully analyzed and interpreted.

Whether the latter can also be concluded about the halo variance is a moot point. Roach (1956, p. 496) contends that it does *not* represent a dimension of vocational success, but that it is rather "a characteristic of raters" and "an artifact of measurement." On the other hand, Ronan (1963) points out that "halo" effects should not be summarily classified as error variance in ratings, since they may correlate significantly with other, independently defined indices of vocational success. He found that a factor he termed "supervisory evaluation," which might otherwise have been interpreted as a halo effect, related negatively to absences and disciplinary actions and positively to promotions, leading him to conclude that the so-called "halo" in supervisors' ratings may be more reality-based than is often thought.

Needless to say, it is difficult, if not impossible in certain respects, to draw any conclusions, much less definitive ones, from the results of these factor analyses of vocational success. There are simply too many uncontrolled conditions and variables in the designs of the studies to hazard interpretations of them. About the best that can be done is to present some speculations about the factorial structure of vocational success and hope that they may serve as hypotheses to be tested in future research. First, it seems reasonable to expect that at least one general factor will be identified which will represent Overall Vocational Success. This factor may be loaded with halo variance from rating scales, but it will, nevertheless, correlate with certain "objective" measures of vocational success, such as productivity and promotions. Second, there will most likely be several group factors which will define relatively distinct, yet related, dimensions of vocational success. That is, these factors will be oblique rather than orthogonal, assuming that a method of factor analysis is employed which allows such a solution. What the substantive nature of these factors will be depends upon the content of the scales and indices used to measure them. Similarly, how many of them will eventually be established depends upon the scope of the sampling of the vocational success behavioral domain which can be attained. Finally, it is conceivable that there will be some specific factors, such as hospital passes and scrap (Turner, 1960), which will not be related to any of the other dimensions of vocational success, but which will correlate with other variables, such as psychosomatic complaints or physical working conditions. As depicted in Figure 10-2, then, this model of the factorial composition of vocational success can be seen as having three levels: general, group, and specific.

Occupational Differences in the Dimensions of Vocational Success. Although similar constraints must be exercised in making statements about occupational differences in the dimensions of vocational success as were followed in interpreting the nature of the dimensions, there are some differences between the occupations listed in Table 10-3 which seem to be intrinsic ones. In other words, they appear to be related to the content of the occupations, i.e., job duties and tasks, rather than to type of factor-analytic methodology or measuring instrument. For example, Rush (1953) found a Sales Techniques and Achievement factor, with loadings on "percent of quota achieved," "sales approaches," "closing ability," etc., which was unique to his sample of salesmen. Likewise, the following factors, all of which might be seen as defining a Supervisory Relationship dimension, emerged in the studies of foremen (Creager & Harding, 1958; Turner, 1960), managers (Grant, 1955), and supervisors (McQuitty et al., 1954; Roach, 1956; Wrigley et al., 1957) but not in the others: Effectiveness in Supervising the Work, Employee Relations, Social Relations, Social Manner, Direction of Group Performance, and Ability to Motivate Others.

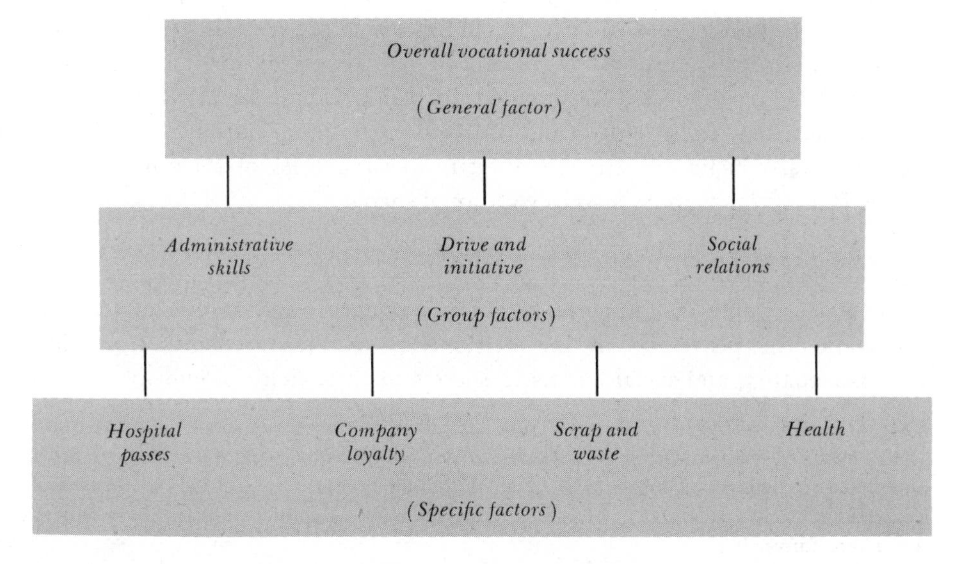

Figure 10-2. A hierarchical model of vocational success.

There are other differences which might be cited, as is evident in the last column of Table 10-3, but it may be more important to note a similarity among the occupations which characterizes all but two of them. This dimension was called Overall Vocational Success in the preceding section and seems to be defined by the following factors: Ability to Do Present Job (in both the studies by Bolanovich, 1946, and by Ewart, Seashore, & Tiffin, 1941), General Reputation, Job Performance Reputation, Technical Job Knowledge, Knowledge and Intellectual Powers, Job Knowledge, General Productive Behavior, General Job Efficiency, Supervisory Evaluation (quantity and quality of work), and Professional Recognition for Achievements (in both the studies by Richards, J. M., et al., 1965; and Taylor, C. W., et al., 1964). Thus, it can be concluded that there most likely *are* occupational differences in the dimensions of vocational success and that these probably cut across the group factor level in the model presented in Figure 10-2, but they do *not* obscure or overdetermine the general factor of Overall Vocational Success, which can be identified in most occupations.

STUDIES OF VOCATIONAL SUCCESS

Not only would it be practically impossible to review and summarize the voluminous literature on vocational success, but it would probably be unprofitable, partly because this has been done elsewhere (e.g., Dorcus & Jones, 1950; Super & Crites, 1962) but mostly because the studies are not good enough to warrant such consideration. Too often they have suffered from such shortcomings as small samples, faulty methodology, and inadequate criteria. Consequently, in this section two series of studies which are notable for the significance of their problems and their comprehensiveness, if not also for their findings, have been selected for detailed discussion. These are (1) Roe's studies of eminent artists and scientists and (2) Rothe's studies of output. In addition, some general conclusions are presented from summaries of (3) other studies on the factors which are related to vocational success.

Roe's Studies of Eminent Artists and Scientists[3]

Anne Roe's studies of eminence in art and science stand as one of the few systematic attempts to explore the relationships of a host of familial, intellectual, personality, and social factors to success in these fields of endeavor. As is

[3] For a general reference to the literature on scientific careers, see Super and Bachrach (1957). Also, of special interest are: Raskin (1936), on a comparison of eminent scientists and "men of letters"; Terman (1954), on the differences between gifted scientists and nonscientists; and Crane (1965), on the productivity and recognition of scientists at major and minor universities.

often true of research which proves to have widespread theoretical and heuristic value, as hers has over the years, Roe (1946a) began her studies by investigating a different problem—the relationship of alcohol to the creative work of painters. From this study, however, she found that she was able to approach the analysis of personality, which was one of her basic interests, from an entirely new direction—the work which men perform and the eminence which they attain through it (Roe, 1947). Consequently, she analyzed the data on artists from this viewpoint (Roe, 1946b; 1946c; and 1946d) and extended the initial research to include a group of paleontologists (Roe, 1946e). There followed within a few years her major studies of eminent biologists (1949a; 1951a), physicists (1951b), and psychologists and anthropologists (1953a). Also during this period, she collected data on somewhat less successful scientists for purposes of comparison (Roe, 1949b; 1950; 1952a). Three further reports dealt with special aspects of the data: the interrelationships of the tests which were used with the eminent scientists (Roe, 1951c), an analysis of the group Rorschach results which had been obtained from the other scientists (Roe, 1952b), and the role of imagery in scientific thinking (Roe, 1951d). Finally, Roe (1953b) summarized her various findings on scientists in a book entitled *The Making of a Scientist.*

The primary purpose of her research, as it eventually evolved from the original investigation of alcohol and creativity, has been stated by Roe (1951a, p. 2) as follows:

> The aim of the whole study is to determine whether there are any patterns in personality or life history which differentiate between the different groups of scientists to be studied or which differentiate them from the population at large.

We shall now summarize and discuss (1) the methodology which Roe used to identify differences between the occupational groups she studied, (2) the results she obtained, and (3) the conclusions which can be drawn from her findings.

Methodology. The concept of eminence, or vocational success, which Roe used in her studies was operationally defined somewhat differently for the artists and the scientists. The former were selected by her from a list of 45 painters, whose professional standing was determined by invitations to the large art shows, membership on art juries, awards and prizes, membership in the National Academy of Design, and/or listing in *Who's Who* (Roe, 1946a). The latter, with the exception of the paleontologists, were chosen on the basis of ratings made of their research excellence by a small group of colleagues, which was presumably made up of individuals who were themselves prominent and knowledgeable in the given field, although Roe never explicitly states what their qualifications as raters were. In contrast to the other scientists, the paleontologists were not necessarily eminent; they were simply available as a group for testing at an annual meeting of the Society of Vertebrate Paleontology (Roe, 1946e). Included in this group, however, were both scientists and technicians, the distinction in occupational level between them being a rough index of differential vocational success. Roe (1946e, pp. 317–318) remarks that: "Both samples [scientists and technicians] are excellent representations of the total groups," but the same could not necessarily be said about the eminent scientists, particularly the physicists whose cooperation was difficult to secure. These groups were small, the *N*'s ranging from 9 to 20, and consequently statistics based upon them may be unstable, but, as Roe (1953a, p. 46) points out, they nevertheless represent a high percentage of the best scientists in each field. The groups were also restricted to native-born men under 60 years of age who were primarily engaged in research, and not administrative, activities.

Data on artists and scientists alike were gathered by two methods: interviews and tests. The interviews were relatively unstructured, with no predetermined schedule of questions being followed. "The subject was asked to cover certain broad areas; beyond that, he was left to himself to include whatever occurred to him as of importance" (Roe, 1951a, p. 3). The areas upon which the Subject was requested to focus primarily were (1) his early vocational interests and decision making, (2) psychosocial development, including childhood illnesses, family background, heterosexual relationships, interpersonal problems, etc., (3) college and graduate school records, (4) professional history, (5) religion, and (6) recreation. The tests included both measures of intelligence and personality. The former was assessed by a specially constructed Verbal-Spatial-Mathematical (VSM) test, which was prepared for the studies by the Educational Testing Service. It was designed to provide sufficient "ceiling" in order to identify possible individual differences among the scientists at higher levels of these abilities. (It was not used in the research on artists.) Personality was appraised by two projective techniques: the Thematic Apperception Test (TAT) and the Rorschach. Wyatt's (1947) scoring system was used to summarize and analyze responses to the TAT; Klopfer and Kelley's (1942) scoring procedures and Munroe's (1944) Inspection Technique Score (ITS) were employed with the Rorschach. Interpretations of the results from these tests were augmented by data from the interviews and the comparison groups of other scientists.

Analyses of the interview and test data involved many different statistical procedures, among which were chi square, product-moment correlation, and analysis of variance. Because of the small *N*'s in the samples of eminent scientists, however, these techniques were not always appropriately applied. For the interrelationships of the VSM subtests, for example, the correct statistic was rank-order correlation, not product-moment, since the magnitude of the latter is extremely sensitive to sample size with *N*'s less than 100, as these were. But, in general, some confidence can be had in the statistical analyses and even more in the clinical validity of the data, which is probably more important in studies of this type. As Roe (1951a, p. 1) observes: "All that one can hope for in such work is to get some idea of the nature of the relationships, the points at which a direct attack can be made, and the sort of tools to use. In the beginning, the major approach has to be observational, and even this must be diffuse." In other words, Roe's studies were what we shall term later "survey research" (see Chapter 13) and should be evaluated as such, rather than as highly controlled experimental investigations.

Results. Roe's statistical findings are much too extensive to present in their entirety. Instead, they have been summarized in table and figure form. Table 10-4 presents abstracts of statements which Roe made on the basis of her interview observations and test results. No attempt will be made to discuss the table in any detail, since it should be largely self-explanatory, but a few general comments might be appropriate. First, when Roe initiated her studies, she followed the generally accepted interpretation of human-movement responses on the Rorschach as indicative of creativity. As a result of comparing the groups of scientists, however, she decided that these responses simply indicate more or less interest in people, with the social scientists providing a greater number of *M* than the biologists and physical scientists. Second, there are no established norms for the Munroe Inspection Technique Score (ITS), but Munroe (1944) has suggested that scores greater than 10 fall in the maladjusted range. By this criterion, then, all the occupational groups were "maladjusted," except the biologists, who were the best adjusted, and the paleontologists. As will be discussed later on, however, other criteria are also important and must be taken into consideration. Finally, Roe's (1946d, p. 4; 1953a, pp. 37, 45) conclusions about the use of the TAT and Rorschach to identify personality factors related to vocational success should be underscored: With respect to both artists and scientists, it was her opinion that these projective techniques were largely useless in appraising or diagnosing their career achievements.

To represent the relationships among the factors which Roe found to be significant in the eminence of the scientists (the artists are not included here) Figure 10-3 was prepared. It is modeled, at least in part, after a wiring diagram, in order to depict the great complexity of the patterns of background and personality variables which "feed into" vocational success as a scientist. Reading from left to right, what might be called the "lineage lines" of the scientists roughly correspond to a developmental continuum which extends

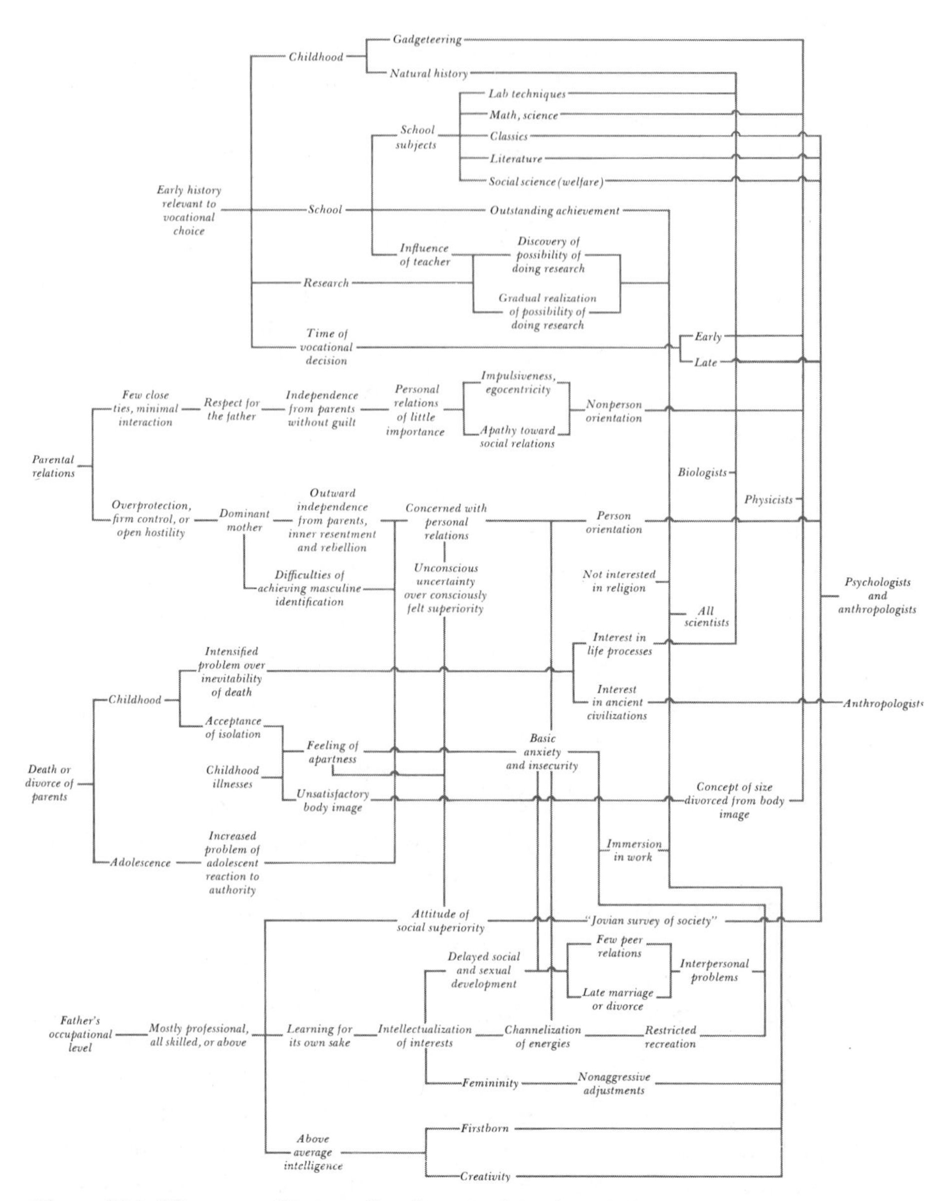

Figure 10-3. The career "lineage lines" of Roe's eminent scientists.

from birth to occupational entry (excluding that part of the figure which falls to the right of the "All Scientists" line). The "breaks" indicate that the lines do *not* intersect, and the "branches" indicate that two or more variables are equally related to a third. Where a horizontal line intersects with two or more vertical lines, it should be interpreted as "flowing" into both. For example: by tracing the top line from "Parental Relations" it can be seen that it intersects both the "Biologists" and "Physicists" verticals, showing that these occupational groups have a "Non-Person Orientation" in common. With the exception of the use of visual versus verbal imagery in scientific thinking, which had no clear developmental antecedents (see discussion to follow), an attempt was made in Figure 10-3 to represent all the findings enumerated in Table 10-4. Among these, the most important from Roe's standpoint are (1) the discovery (or realization) on the part of the scientists when they were still in high school or college that they could do *research* and (2) their almost total *immersion in work* following their entry into their chosen specialty. Other factors played a part in the particular field of science they selected as a vocation, but for all of them their success appeared to be primarily attributable to their intense involvement in what they were doing.[4]

Table 10-4. Summary of Roe's Studies of Vocational Success

Data	*Findings from interview and test data for biologists, physical scientists, psychologists, and anthropologists*
Early history relevant to occupational choice	Almost all the physical scientists "displayed early interest in mathematics, chemistry, physics, or gadgeteering, and very few . . . were ever interested in literature or the humanities. . . . Literature and the classics, and less frequently social-welfare interests, were common among both anthropologists and psychologists. . . . The biologists included men whose early interests had been in natural history, in literature, and in chemistry or physics. . . . In the histories of the social scientists and of the biologists the importance of the discovery of the possibility of doing research is highlighted, and this was often the factor that gave the final determination to their choice of vocation, or that fixed them in it once it was chosen. This particular aspect did not appear among the physical scientists" (Roe, 1953a, p. 22). "For the total group of scientists the median point of decision on a vocation is in the later undergraduate years, but it can be as early as high school and as late as postgraduate years . . . very few in the total group did any long range vocational planning" (Roe, 1953a, p. 22). The effects of losing a parent through death or divorce were different: "In the case of the biologists and physicists where the losses occurred very early, it seemed possibly to be a factor in the acceptance of isolation by the subjects, but among the psychologists and at least one of the physicists whose losses were later, the effect seems to have been more one of increasing the problems of adolescent reaction to authority, and this effect seems to have been greater in the case of the psychologists who have been more concerned with personal relations from the

[4] See Lodahl and Kejner (1965) for a report on the construction and initial validation of a scale to measure "job involvement," which might be used in research on the relationship of this variable to vocational success.

***Table 10-4. Summary of Roe's Studies of Vocational Success** (Continued)*

Data	*Findings from interview and test data for biologists, physical scientists, psychologists, and anthropologists*
	start. . . . A special factor, occurring generally only in the theoretical physicists, was the apparent effect of severe childhood illnesses which contributed to personal isolation" (Roe, 1953a, p. 22).
Psychosocial development	"Both the physicists and the biologists early developed ways of life which involved very much less of personal interaction, and neither group shows anything like the extent of rebelliousness and family difficulty that the psychologists and anthropologists show" (Roe, 1953a, p. 25). "Among the biologists and physicists it is rare for there to have been any extensive dating in high school or early college. Half of the social scientists began dating in high school and dated happily and extensively from then on" (Roe, 1953a, pp. 25–26).
Religion	"Of the 64 scientists studied altogether, whose religious backgrounds were not known when they were selected, none came from Catholic families. Five came from Jewish homes, and all of the rest had Protestant backgrounds. These include two Mormons and two Quakers. Among all of them the picture is much the same. Most went to Sunday school; very few now have any church connections" (Roe, 1953a, p. 27).
Recreation	All scientists have varied recreational interests, when they engage in recreation, which is seldom. The social scientists have a somewhat greater interest in social life than the others.
Verbal-spatial-mathematical test	"The mathematical test was not difficult enough for the physicists. Differences between the means of the different groups are small and not significant" (Roe, 1953a, p. 28).
Thematic Apperception Test	"The average length of the responses to each card differ considerably, with the social scientists giving significantly longer stories ($p < .05$) than the other two groups, who do not differ materially from each other" (Roe, 1953a, p. 35). "The full time range, which is significantly commoner among the social scientists . . . , may also be related to the social science group's willingness to verbalize at greater length" (Roe, 1953a, pp. 36–37). "There are no differences among the groups with regard to outcome—the proportions are remarkably similar. But there is a marked difference with regard to the certainty with which any outcome is predicted, the biologists being significantly more restricted in this regard than the others" (Roe, 1953a, p. 37). "In all groups the major levels are concrete-factual and endopsychic, with the biologists giving more stories characterized by the former" (Roe, 1953a, p. 37). "There are no marked differences in tone, in personal relations, or in assignment of presses among groups" (Roe, 1953a, p. 37).

***Table 10-4. Summary of Roe's Studies of Vocational Success** (Continued)*

Data	*Findings from interview and test data for biologists, physical scientists, psychologists, and anthropologists*
	"Both biologists and physicists are much less interested in interpersonal relations generally, and more inclined to handle them in distance-getting ways than are the social scientists, although many of these are uneasy about them" (Roe, 1953a, p. 37). "Both biologists and physicists show a considerable independence of parental relations, and without guilt, particularly in the case of the physicists, whereas the social scientists show many dependent attitudes, and much rebelliousness, accompanied frequently by guilt feelings" (Roe, 1953a, p. 37). "What is most striking about these results, however, is the fact that the TAT rarely gives any indication that the subject is a man of considerable attainments" (Roe, 1953a, p. 37).
Rorschach	". . . the social scientists are significantly more productive on the Rorschach; . . . the biologists use relatively fewer responses not dominated by form than the others; and . . . the biologists . . . are definitely better adjusted" (Roe, 1953a, p. 44). "The biologists are the least freely aggressive; the social scientists, particularly the anthropologists, the most so, and with greater likelihood of oral elements" (Roe, 1953a, p. 44).
Summary	Most of the scientists (53 percent) were from professional-level (father's occupation) homes, and none of them came from the unskilled level. "What seems to be the operative factor here is that in practically all of these homes, whatever the occupation of the father, learning was valued for its own sake. . . . This was certainly a major factor in the facilitation of intellectualization of interests" (Roe, 1953a, p. 47). "The biologists and physicists show a considerable present independence of parental relations, and without guilt for the most part. . . . The social scientists, on the other hand, are much less free of parental ties, in the sense that a number of them still harbor resentment and rebellion, even though they have achieved an outward independence. It is more than possible that this difference is a major factor in the choice of a vocation" (Roe, 1953a, p. 48). "Once it was fully understood that *personal* research was possible, once some research had actually been accomplished, there was never any question. This was it. . . . From then on, absorption in the vocation was so complete as seriously to limit all other activity" (Roe, 1953a, p. 49). "The social scientists stand apart as having been more concerned at an earlier age, about personal relations (or as being willing to tolerate this concern as such, without translation). . . . The other groups seem to have been able, fairly early, to work out an adaptation not nearly so dependent upon personal relations, but rather strikingly independent of them" (Roe, 1953a, p. 50).

As mentioned previously, in addition to her major studies of eminent artists and scientists, Roe conducted three other investigations. One of these was an analysis of the relationships of the VSM, TAT, and Rorschach with each other and with age for the total group of eminent scientists. The results showed that: (1) age was related only to the Spatial Test, with the younger Subjects obtaining higher scores; (2) only the Verbal and Spatial subtests of the VSM were significantly correlated with each other, the *r* being .332; (3) the Verbal score was positively related to the number of items tried on the Spatial (.317) and Mathematical (.369) subtests and to total *R* on the Rorschach (.264), and the latter was correlated with length of TAT stories (.499); (4) the Verbal subtest was positively associated with Rorschach human-movement responses and negatively with color responses, giving the picture of "the verbally skilled person, productive on the Rorschach, and rather introversive" (Roe, 1951c, p. 494); (5) "shading shock" on the Rorschach was not significantly related to VSM performance, thus indicating that anxiety did not result in a decrement in the latter; (6) number of whole responses on the Rorschach was positively correlated with length of TAT stories .339, age partialled out; and (7) number of human-movement responses on the Rorschach was related to having a future time orientation on the TAT (.297). A similar study was made of the group Rorschachs of the 382 scientists in the comparison samples, with the only notable finding being that age was essentially uncorrelated with the Rorschach determinants. Finally, in a study of the imagery of the eminent scientists, Roe (1951d) found that biologists and experimental physicists use primarily visual imagery in their thinking, whereas theoretical physicists and psychologists and anthropologists rely upon verbal imagery.

Conclusions and Interpretations. Three major conclusions were drawn by Roe from her studies of eminent artists and scientists:

1. *There was no clear-cut relationship between personality and vocational success.* Roe (1953a, p. 45) points out that: "In the overall picture the similarities are greater than the differences. This is to be expected from the fact that there is considerable heterogeneity within the separate groups, and from the fact that these men are all functioning adequately." What few differences could be established between the scientists are summarized in Figure 10-3 for each occupational group.

2. *Clinical maladjustment does not necessarily imply social maladjustment.* Roe (1951a, p. 58) observes that: It is necessary to distinguish between 'clinical maladjustment,' which means the presence of stresses in the personality structure, and 'social maladjustment,' or the expression of these stresses in behavioral terms." She goes on to add that:

> Practically all current psychological theory of development stresses strongly the central importance in any life of the richness of personal

> relations as a basis for "adjustment." But the data of this study demonstrate, and it seems to me conclusively, that a more than adequate personal and social adjustment in the larger sense of an adjustment which permits a socially extremely useful life and one which is personally deeply satisfying, is not only possible, but probably quite common, with little of the sort of personal relations which psychologists consider essential [Roe, 1953a, pp. 50–51].

The nature of these personal and social adjustments is basically feminine in both artists and scientists, i.e., intellectual and nonaggressive, and the mechanism for them is work. Roe (1953a, p. 52) explains that:

> The career itself has served as a technique for handling the personal problems. In some instances the basic problem has been, in a sense, extrapolated into a more general one, and the subject has then settled down to working on the general problem. This is a very neat and effective method. In other instances, absorption in the career has made possible the encapsulation of the difficulty in such a manner that it can be almost ignored by the subject. The price he must pay for this is another matter.

3. *Artistic and scientific occupations serve to satisfy both the need for autonomy and the need for homonomy.* To interpret the findings of her studies, particularly those which revealed great heterogeneity of personality within an occupational group, Roe (1946c; 1947; 1951b) drew upon Angyal's (1941) theory of personality, the basic proposition of which is that man seeks to fulfill two needs, one for autonomy and the other for homonomy. By the former is meant the tendency to master the environment, to gain control over it, and to turn it to one's own ends; by the latter is meant the tendency to fit oneself into larger social bodies, to identify with "superindividual categories," and to conform to external expectations and injunctions. According to Roe, higher-level occupations, such as those engaged in by artists and scientists, not only satisfy the homonymous drives, but also the autonomous ones, the latter finding expression primarily in creative activity. Thus, within these occupations, rather diverse personalities can satisfy the basic needs which motivate not only work behaviors, but also other behaviors. It is for this reason, then, that the vocation can be so remarkably salient as a *modus operandi* in adjustment.[5]

Comment. Roe (1953a) cites five limitations of her studies which place qualifications upon the conclusions drawn from them: (1) the small *N*'s in the samples; (2) the possible lack of comparability of the individual and group administrations of the Rorschach; (3) no comparisons with nonscientific occupations, other than the artists; (4) no relatively unsuccessful control groups;

[5] Cf. Fromm, 1962, p. 17, the function of creative activity in work in alleviating the feeling of apartness.

and (5) possible bias due to the high frequency of middle-class membership samples. To these some other shortcomings should be added. First, in this type of research there is always the danger that the data will be contaminated with the predilections and presuppositions of the investigator. Roe both conducted the interviews and interpreted the data from them, and she also did this in some instances with the tests. In other words, the data collection was *not* independent of its interpretation, and, consequently, it is difficult to determine what is fact and what is hypothesis. Second, although Roe uses personality theory to some extent to interpret her findings, her approach is basically atheoretical. Her clinical "hunches" are often fascinating and suggestive of hypotheses for further research, but she never pulls her research together within one conceptual framework. Even in her 1957 paper, "Early Determinants of Vocational Choice" (see Chapter 3), she builds upon her earlier studies but fails to make the linkages explicit. As a consequence, her theory appears to be oversimplified, and it may be for this reason that the tests of it have yielded mostly negative results. It does not take father's occupational level into consideration, for example, yet as Figure 10-3 indicates, this variable is a critical one in many aspects of the vocational development of scientists. Finally, she does not make any systematic effort to relate and integrate her studies with the mainstream of research in vocational psychology. In her three major studies, only 14 out of 68 references are to works which are even remotely vocational in nature.

Rothe's Studies of Output

As has been pointed out, one of the most obvious and relevant, but also one of the least frequently used, measures of vocational success has been the quantity and quality of a worker's output. Considerable speculation has accumulated concerning the nature of output and its relationship to other variables (e.g., Bedford, 1922; Ford, 1931; Yoder, 1942), but relatively few empirical investigations have been made of it (e.g., Bliss, 1931; Tiffin, 1942), particularly in recent years. The most notable exception is a series of studies initiated by Rothe in his doctoral dissertation which he has pursued now for a period of 15 years. His first two reports on the output of butter wrappers appeared in 1946 (Rothe, 1946a, 1946b); these were followed by three studies of machine operators (Rothe, 1947; Rothe & Nye, 1959; Rothe & Nye, 1961); one of chocolate dippers (Rothe, 1951b); and one of coil winders (Rothe & Nye, 1958). In these studies Rothe has not only gathered important data on output, but he has attempted, and has been successful, in "getting above" the data, in formulating and testing and modifying hypotheses about them. His approach to the investigation of output phenomena exemplifies the construction of a *functional* theory of vocational behavior, in which there is a continual interaction between data and hypothesis (see Chapter 14). In summarizing and discussing Rothe's studies, we shall deal with the following topics: (1) how he defined and analyzed output; (2) the results he obtained on several occupational groups; and (3) the conclusions he drew from his findings. A final section is devoted to some critical comments on his studies and some implications for further research.

Methodology. The definitions of output which Rothe has used are somewhat difficult to conceptualize without some type of graphical representation of them; consequently, the hypothetical curve shown in Figure 10-4 has been prepared. In this diagram, the units on the ordinate are "number of pounds of butter wrapped each fifteen minute period" during the workday. For machine operators, they might stand for "percentage of standard produced in an hour" and so on, depending upon the occupation. The abscissa represents the time dimension, scaled either in hours or days. With these coordinates, the following definitions of output for individuals and groups can be made:

1. *Individual output curve:* a plot of the quantity of production (number of pounds of butter wrapped, etc.) of one worker for successive increments of time (hours or days).
2. *Individual output trends:* a plot of the medians of a worker's quantity of production for several days.

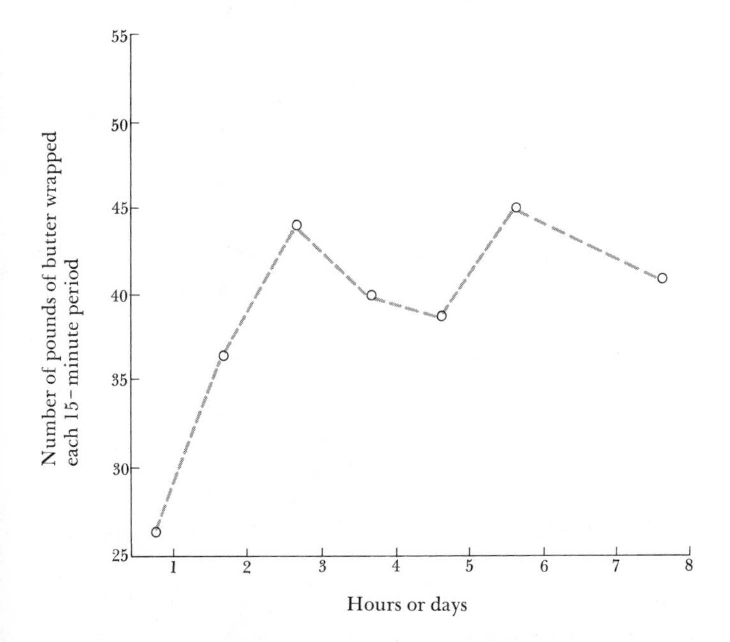

Figure 10-4. Hypothetical output curve. *(Based upon Rothe, 1946a.)*

3. *Group output curves:* a plot of the medians of several workers' quantity of production for hourly or daily periods.
4. *Group output trends:* either (*a*) a plot of the medians of group curves for several days, or (*b*) a plot of the medians of individual trends.

Rothe studied two aspects of output phenomena defined in these ways. First, he was interested in the *patterning* of output data, by which he meant the frequency distributions they formed when plotted against such dimensions as those shown in Figure 10-4. What is the shape of these distributions? Are they normal or skewed? And what are the implications of different patterns of output? Second, he investigated the *stability* of output curves, which he originally conceived as the "test-retest" reliability of a curve. That is, what is the correlation between workers' curves on different days? As will be brought out later, he revised his interpretation of stability in his later studies, but still defined it operationally by the correlation between two curves.

Rothe used several different occupational groups in his studies which varied not only in their demographic characteristics, but also in the conditions under which they worked:

1. *Butter wrappers.* There were eight Subjects in this group, all of whom were females ranging in age from 18 to 39 years. The operation they performed, in brief, was to wrap ¼-pound blocks of butter and place them on a conveyor belt. They were paid a straight wage, plus overtime, with no additional incentive.

2. *Machine operators.* These Subjects were all males employed in three different plants: Plant A—130 Subjects who worked on standards without any incentives; Plant B—42 Subjects who were paid according to an incentive system; Plant C—55 Subjects who had to perform to a certain level of standard production or face disciplinary action, including dismissal.

3. *Chocolate dippers.* Data were collected on an *N* which ranged from 15 to 18, depending upon absences. All Subjects were females who worked on incentives. Their job was to hand-dip chocolates.

4. *Coil winders.* The *N*'s in this group ranged from 21 to 27, and the Subjects were "mainly women." They worked in a plant with no incentive system.

As is apparent from the descriptions of these groups, they were diverse in many respects: size of *N*, sex, duties and tasks performed, and type of remuneration (wage or incentive). Despite these differences, however, Rothe was able to obtain results which displayed considerable consistency from group to group.

The patterning of the output data was evaluated by testing the frequency distributions for normality, using chi-square and beta-coefficient methods, and the stability of the curves was assessed by computing correlations between them for different points in time, as has been mentioned. In addition, what were called "intraindividual ratios" and "interindividual ratios" were calculated. The former is the ratio of a worker's fastest rate of production for a given period of time, such as number of pounds of butter wrapped in an hour, to his slowest rate; and the latter is the ratio of the mean rate of the fastest worker in a group to the mean rate of the slowest, where the mean rate is the average of a worker's rates for several units of time, i.e., hours or days. Finally, some supplementary analyses, such as the correlations among different workers' output curves, were made in order to answer questions which arose in the course of the studies.

Results. In his two studies of butter wrappers, Rothe found that there were at least four types of *output curves* for individual workers: (1) fatigue, (2) monotony, (3) straight-line, and (4) mixed. For groups of workers, the *output trends,*

> ... began low and rose steadily in the first morning work-spell, levelled off in the second morning work-spell, began at a lower level after lunch but rose quickly until they reached a peak for the day just before the afternoon rest period, and then showed a "dip" resembling a "monotony" curve, in the late afternoon spell while remaining at a generally lower level in this last period [Rothe, 1946a, p. 204].

The *patterning* of these output data was essentially normal, although it was noted that there were some workers whose curves indicated a generally higher level of production than those of others. In fact, throughout the series of studies the distributions of output data closely conformed to the normal curve, the only exception being the machine operators in Plant C, in which the distribution was negatively skewed. As will be discussed later, this lack of normality was apparently related to "restriction of output" in this group.

For the butter wrappers, the *stability* of output curves for individuals from day to day was quite low, the median r being .05. The group curves were somewhat more consistent, the median r being .30, indicating that "the group tended to show the same work pattern from day to day, although the correspondence was not very high" (Rothe, 1946a, p. 207). The group trends, which included interday as well as intraday variations in output, yielded even higher correlations, the median r being .51. And, the two methods of defining group trends were highly related (r = .87), as was expected, since they were quite similar. For the three groups of machine operators, the stability coefficients for output curves obtained over periods of 1 week or more varied considerably from plant to plant: in Plant A they were .57, .68, and .78 for three biweekly periods; in Plant B the median r for 2-week periods was .78; and, in Plant C, which was studied twice, once in 1958 and again in 1960, the median r's were .48 and .53, respectively. It will be remembered that only Plant B had an incentive system. For the chocolate dippers, who were also on an incentive plan, the median interweekly r was .85. And, for the coil winders who worked on a straight-wage basis, the median r for a 2-week interval was .64. In each of the groups, there was a wide range of stability coefficients, thus suggesting that it is extremely important which period of output curves is selected for study. Rothe and Nye (1958, p. 186) caution that "a researcher could be entirely misled by tests of statistical significance if he just happened to select a period of unusually high or low consistency."

The *intra- and interindividual ratios* of output were initially investigated by Rothe (1946b) to test a hypothesis proposed by Bedford (1922) that "restriction of output" is related to the shape and dispersion of workers' output curves. More specifically, Bedford predicted that, if output is being restricted, slow workers will exhibit curves which are negatively skewed and have large ranges in performance. As noted previously, Rothe obtained evidence of negatively skewed output curves in only one occupational group, the others being essentially bell-shaped distributions, but he did find some indication of a relationship between ranges of output within and between individuals and "restriction of output," or what he preferred to call "ineffectiveness of incentives."

In the study of butter wrappers, who were not given incentives, most of the intraindividual ratios were larger than the interindividual ratio. In other words, the output of these workers varied more from one unit of time to another, i.e., hourly or daily period, than it did from worker to worker. Thus, some support was demonstrated for Bedford's hypothesis. Rothe (1946b, p. 322) points out, however, that this phenomenon may be less one of "restriction of output" than one of the "ineffectiveness of incentives." He reasons as follows:

> From a psychological point of view, when workers restrict their output they feel that they have more to gain by producing below their optimum than they have from producing at their optimum. The problem is basically one of *incentives*. If the incentive is great enough, the workers will work at an optimum rate, that is, producing as much as they can, steadily, over a long period of time, without endangering their health or decreasing their away-from-the-plant activities. If the incentive is not great enough they will work below this optimum, that is, they will "restrict" their output.

From this rationale and from the findings he obtained on the patterning and stability of output curves under different conditions of incentivation, Rothe developed two hypotheses about "restriction of output" or "ineffectiveness of incentives" which he tested and revised in light of the data he collected throughout the series of studies. The statements of these hypotheses as they evolved follow:

> *Hypothesis 1.* The incentives to work may be considered ineffective when the ratio of the range of intra-individual differences is greater than the ratio of the range of inter-individual differences [Rothe, 1946b, p. 326].
>
> *Hypothesis 2.* If the intercorrelation of group output rates for two periods closely related in time is less than .80 the incentivation is not highly effective, while intercorrelation higher than .90 indicates effective incentivation [Rothe, 1947, p. 488].
>
> If the intercorrelation of output rates for two periods closely related in time is less than .50 the incentivation is not highly effective, while intercorrelation higher than .80 indicates very effective incentivation [Rothe, 1951b, p. 96].
>
> An intercorrelation of .80 or above indicates effective incentivation and an intercorrelation of .70 or less indicates ineffective incentivation. This leaves a twilight zone between .80 and .70 that needs clarification from further research [Rothe & Nye, 1958, pp. 185–186].

The second hypothesis was continually revised because the stability coefficients for output curves varied considerably from one occupational group to another.

All but one of Rothe's studies supported his hypotheses, the exception being the last study of machine operators, in which he found that, under conditions of no incentivation, the range of the interindividual ratios was greater than the range of intraindividual ratios, whereas the opposite should have been true. He concluded from this finding that the hypothesis relating incentives to intra- and interindividual ratios "clearly needs more evidence or more refining since it is strongly suspected that the incentivation in this situation was not very effective" [Rothe & Nye, 1961, p. 52].

Conclusions. From his investigations of output, Rothe reached several conclusions, the most important of which are the following: First, he concluded that: "In this entire series of studies of industrial output the most striking single result is the lack of consistency from time to time, especially when there is no financial incentive system in operation" (Rothe & Nye, 1958, p. 186). Because of this inconsistency, or instability, of output data, particularly for individual curves, Rothe (1946a, p. 210) recommends that "group trend lines should be used when work curves are used as criteria against which some variable is to be measured or validated since they form stable criteria."

Second, in light of the data he gathered on the hypotheses regarding the role of incentivation in output, he reformulated the concept of stability with which he had begun his research:

> It is apparent that the writer is attempting to demonstrate something other than "reliability" by proposing these hypotheses. That is, it appears that the consistency of output, from time to time, may reflect a real phenomenon and permit some prediction (such as an estimate of the effectiveness of the incentives in a situation) and not merely reflect the "reliability" or "unrealibility" of the criterion. The concept of "reliability" has been taken over from the realm of testing where it is related primarily to errors of measurement. Such errors undoubtedly exist in work such as is described in this article. But it is also very likely that there is a "consistency" or "inconsistency" of industrial output data that is a real phenomenon and not merely an error of measurement [Rothe, 1951b, pp. 96–97].

In other words, there may be systematic changes in output curves and trends which are attributable to some other factor than errors in the method used to record output data.

Finally, Rothe concluded that this "other factor" might well be the incentivation which is present to motivate workers to produce at optimum rates. He found evidence in his studies that, when effective incentives are present, not only are individual differences among workers' capabilities to perform tasks maximized, but also the stability of their output is at a higher level.

Comment. Rothe's research on output phenomena represents a commendable systematic approach to the investigation of a major criterion of vocational success, and as such it is difficult to criticize, other than on minor points. Some limitations of the studies should be noted, however, in order to exercise appropriate caution in their interpretation. For example: The *N*'s in the occupational groups were small, and the variations in stability coefficients from group to group may reflect this factor rather than the effectiveness of incentives. Also, the sex of the workers in the groups varied: Some were all females, and some were all males. A more serious shortcoming, however, was the lack of comparability of output data from one study to another. No attempt was made to reduce these data to a common dimension, such as the "dollar criterion" proposed by Brogden and Taylor (1950b), and consequently it is hazardous to draw conclusions which are applicable to all the studies. Finally, a conceptual or theoretical problem can be raised with which Rothe did not deal: are his two hypotheses on the effectiveness of incentivation independent of each other, or are they related? He treats them *as if* they are independent, but it may be that when the range of interindividual ratios is greater than the range of intraindividual ratios, the stability coefficients of output curves will *necessarily* be higher than an average of .80. In any case, the relationship between the two hypotheses needs further clarification.

Other Studies of Vocational Success

Over the years, a rather extensive literature on variables related to vocational success has accumulated, primarily because of the interest of industrial psychologists in identifying the correlates of job performance, and consequently we can deal only with the general findings here, rather than making a detailed analysis of specific studies. To provide an overview of the relevant research on what might be called the "correlates of vocational success," studies were classified along two dimensions: First, a broad distinction could be made between studies in which the correlates were nontest variables, such as age, education, or sex, and those in which they were test variables, which constituted the bulk of the research on personnel selection, the latter by far outnumbering the former. Second, studies were classified according to whether the factors investigated were concurrent or predictive. In other words, were they related to criteria of vocational success obtained in the present or in the future. In this case, the concurrent studies tended to be more numerous than the predictive. Two examples of the latter type of investigation will be presented at length in the next section, as well as a summary of some of the recent research on the problems involved in predicting vocational success. In this section, our concern is wholly with the concurrent correlates of vocational success, as measured by tests of intelligence, interests, and personality and as assessed by certain nontest methods.

Intelligence has been studied in relation to three different criteria of vocational success: (1) securing or retaining employment, (2) attainment on the occupational scale, and (3) status within an occupation. The most definitive studies of the first criterion were made as part of the MESRI research program (see Chapter 2), in which it was found that workers who were released from their jobs earlier in the Depression were less able than those who were retained for a longer period. In contrast, however, studies by Dearborn and Rothney (1938) and Lazarsfeld and Gaudet (1941) have shown that there is apparently no systematic relationship between intelligence and getting a job. With respect to the second criterion, the extensive data from both world wars well document the relationship of intelligence to the place reached on the "occupational ladder" (Yerkes, 1921; Stewart, 1947). On the average, the more intelligent are in the higher-level occupations, but there is considerable overlap among occupations in intelligence. Some relatively unskilled workers, e.g., riggers, are as bright as some professional workers, e.g., pharmacists. In contrast to the other two, the third criterion, status within an occupation, has not been found to be related consistently to intelligence. There are some studies (e.g., Bingham & Davis, 1924; Anderson, V. V., 1929) in which no relationship has been established and others (e.g., Pond & Bills, 1933; Hay, E. N., 1943) in which the opposite has been true.

Vocational interests have been correlated with vocational success in several studies, the most comprehensive work having been done by Strong (1943), who found that, in general, the two variables tend to be related to each other in a variety of occupations with different criteria of performance. The most impressive results, however, have been on the relationship of Strong's life insurance interest scale to various indices of success in this occupation. Strong (1943, p. 500) has summarized these findings as follows:

> We may conclude that the men who are employed in selling life insurance are not a random selection but are drawn for the most part from a relatively small subsample of the general population; in other words, successful life insurance agents score higher on the life-insurance-interest test than men in general. Second, the successful agent scores higher than the unsuccessful. Third, men with low insurance-interest ratings do not earn a living thereby and, fourth, do not stay in the business, in contrast to the men with higher ratings.

Studies by Bills (1938) and Knauft (1951) of life insurance salesmen are confirmatory of Strong's conclusions, as is a more recent investigation of clerical interest and proficiency by Stone (1960). Results with the other major measure of vocational interests, the Kuder Preference Record (Vocational), are less clear-cut, but they also indicate that interests and success are related in some occupations (Super & Crites, 1962, p. 487).

Personality as a factor in vocational success has been repeatedly investigated with different assessment devices and in different occupations, but the findings are still equivocal. The hypothesis that personality plays a part in successful job performance has been a powerful and venerable one, and there has been enough evidence, albeit of a fragmentary nature, to lend some support to it, but by in large the results have been negative. As has been noted, one of Roe's major conclusions from her studies of eminent artists and scientists was that personality, as assessed by the Rorschach and Thematic Apperception Test, is not systematically related to vocational success. Similarly, in the series of studies by Dodge (1938; 1940; 1943; 1948) of salespersons, clerical workers, and teachers, the differences between those who were successful and unsuccessful in these occupations on personality items of the Bernreuter type were small, seldom exceeding 20 percent, and only a few items differentiated between the high and low groups.

There has been a handful of studies, however, which have yielded contrary results and which have forced the question to remain open (see Super & Crites, 1962, Chapter 19). Among these, one of the most provocative was a Rorschach investigation of machinists conducted by Anderson, R. G. (1949), in which she found that some workers with low mechanical aptitude received high efficiency ratings from their supervisors, whereas others with high aptitude were given low ratings. Further analysis of the Rorschachs of these "deviant" workers indicated that it was apparently their personalities which determined their relative success. Thus, a cooperative or dependent worker might compensate for his lack of mechanical aptitude by being conscientious and hence be considered more efficient by his supervisor, if the latter valued such behavior, whereas the opposite might be true of a more talented but aggressive worker. Considerations such as these have led Super and Crites (1962, pp. 569–570) to propose that personality may act as a "suppressor"[6] variable—a compensating or handicapping factor in the attainment of vocational success—and that this may be why research which has viewed personality as being directly related to success has not demonstrated the expected relationships.

Other factors which have been related to vocational success include: childhood backgrounds (Allen, P. J., 1955); cognitive dissonance about wage inequities (Adams, J. S., & Rosenbaum, 1962); company rank (Bass & Wurster, 1953) and seniority (Jay & Copes, 1957); ethnicity and religion (Dalton, 1951); originality and associational fluency (Hills, 1958); maturity of self-perceptions (Ghiselli, 1964; Ghiselli & Barthol, 1956); oral communication (Pace, 1962); and religion (Brewer, 1930). Needless to say, this is not an exhaustive enumeration of the nontest correlates of success, but it gives a fair idea of the types of variables which have been related to job performance. And, it is apparent that no one study has been of sufficient scope to provide data on the interrelationships of the factors or their possible differential contributions to vocational success. One exception may be a study conducted by the Industrial Relations Center at the University of Minnesota (Schletzer, Dawis, England, & Lofquist, 1959), in which such factors as age, sex, education, economic pressures (number of dependents, marital status), and nature and origin of disability were related to the success of handicapped workers in gaining employment. But even in this investigation, which is more comprehensive than most of the others, no analysis was made of the intercorrelations of factors or their relative importance in employment success. In short, little is known about the demographic and stimulus variables which affect vocational success.

THE PREDICTION OF VOCATIONAL SUCCESS

The possibility of being able to predict an individual's vocational success has captured the imagination of layman and psychologist alike and has led to

[6] More accurately, personality may function as a "moderator" variable, as defined and discussed later in this chapter. A "suppressor" variable minimizes the relationships among two or more predictors in a multiple regression problem, whereas a "moderator" variable enters into relationships among manifestly uncorrelated variables.

innumerable attempts to find the "magic formula," whether an astrologer's signs or a statistician's regression equations, which will forecast a worker's future accomplishments (Kitson, 1948). As we shall learn in reviewing (1) a classic and (2) a recent study of the prediction of vocational success, no formula, much less a "magic" one, has as yet been found. Large-scale studies by E. L. Thorndike and his son, R. L. Thorndike, have produced predominantly negative results on predicting success by means of aptitude tests, as well as some nonintellective variables. The search for a formula continues, however, in a number of (3) other studies, and there is some prospect that it may be discovered, after all, in the research which is being done on differential predictability by Ghiselli and others.

A Classic Study

One of the first and one of the most frequently cited studies on the prediction of vocational success was an investigation conducted by E. L. Thorndike (1934) and his associates during the 1920s and early 1930s under the sponsorship of the Commonwealth Fund. Although antedated by the British National Institute of Industrial Psychology (Earle, 1931) and Birmingham (Allen, E. P., & Smith, P., 1932) studies on the use of tests in vocational guidance, and Woolley's (1926) study of the work of high school students in Cincinnati, the research by Thorndike and his group stands as the classic study in this area, not because it was better designed or more comprehensive but paradoxically because it yielded largely *negative* results.

Design of the Study. The problem of the study was to determine how well certain criteria of vocational success could be predicted from the cumulative records and test scores of elementary and secondary school students followed up after their entry into the world of work. Thorndike gathered data on his sample at approximately age 14.0 (grade 8B) and in two subsequent interviews, at ages 18 to 20 and 20 to 22. All the Subjects were from schools in New York City in 1921–1922 and were selected to be representative of a wide range of general intelligence and of eighth graders in the system at that time. The tests which they took at the beginning of the study included the following: arithmetic (solving problems), reading (comprehension of paragraphs), abstract intelligence (arithmetic score plus reading score), clerical intelligence (perceptual speed and accuracy, vocabulary, copying, etc.), clerical activities (underscoring key letters and numbers in context), and mechanical "adroitness" (for boys, the Stenquist Test in assembling a cupboard catch, a clothes pin, a chain, etc.; for girls, a specially constructed test in assembling beads on a string, inserting tape, making a rosette, etc.). The main type of analysis which was employed was correlational, with the predictors being related either singly (zero-order r) or in combination (multiple R) to the various criteria of vocational success on the two follow-ups.

Results. Although there were some notable findings on the prediction of *educational* success, such as the r of .53 between intelligence test scores obtained at age 14 and grade reached at leaving school, those on the prediction of *vocational* success were disappointing. The highest correlation of the school record and test predictors with the criteria of success was .26 between clerical intelligence and earnings for the clerical groups at age 20 to 22. In fact, the only significant correlations were found in this group. None of the r's in the mechanical and other groups was greater than $\pm.14$.

About the only other finding worthy of note was that, on the average, the correlations between the predictors and criteria at age 20 to 22 were 40 percent higher than those at age 18 to 20. Thus, it may be that the largely "academic" type of predictors obtained during the school years become efficacious only after workers have had time to advance to jobs in which success depends upon earlier educational experiences. It may also be, however, that they develop the requisite abilities and skills while they are progressing in their work. Since Thorndike's study did not include follow-ups at ages beyond 20 to 22, it provides no basis for favoring one or the other of these alternative interpretations.

Some related problems with which it did deal and the results on them are as follows: There was very little job change in any of the groups of workers, and it was not related to the criteria of vocational success. Subjects with higher test scores at age 14 tended more often to be successful at clerical as compared with mechanical work; parental influence did not appear to be a factor related to vocational success; and, interestingly enough, it was found that, regardless of intellectual abilities, the worker who was physically larger at age 14 was paid considerably more, especially in clerical work, than the average.

Conclusions. From these findings, Thorndike and his associates (1934, pp. 72; 60) drew a rather pessimistic conclusion about the value of vocational guidance:

> On the whole, the vocational histories of these boys and girls are not in accord with the opinions of those enthusiasts for vocational guidance who assume than an examination of a boy or girl of fourteen and a study of his school record will enable a counselor to estimate his fitness to succeed in this, that, and the other sort of work.... No combination of the facts gathered by us at age 14.0 would have enabled a vocational counselor to foretell how well a boy or girl would do in mechanical work six to eight years later, or how happy he would be at it. Estimating (somewhat optimistically) the prophecies for salary, level, and interest from the best possible mul-

> tiple regression equation as .14, .16, and .12, the judgments of the counselor would have had about 98 per cent as much error as if he had made them by pure guess.

In addition, it was concluded that the results of this study were generally in accord with those reported by the National Institute of Industrial Psychology and by Woolley, although at variance with those obtained by the Birmingham investigators. Others were to strenuously disagree with all these conclusions, however, as a storm of controversy broke upon the publication of Thorndike's study.

Comment. In one of the 1934 issues of *Occupations,* the editor, Fred C. Smith, observed that: "Surprise at the methods followed and vigorous dissent from the conclusions reached are greeting the publication of the Thorndike study of the possibility of predicting vocational success." The major criticism levelled at the study by Paterson (1934), Macrae (1934), Viteles (1936), and others was that the criteria of vocational success used by Thorndike were both conceptually and operationally deficient. Viteles (1936) expressed the concern that such criteria as earnings, job level, and interest in work are static if not combined clinically into a dynamic composite which recognizes their interrelationships and the changes which take place in them over time. Paterson (1934) attacked the validity of the criteria, which he said was largely unknown, and cited the variability in the determination of earnings from one employer to another as an example. Macrae (1934) pointed out that a worker might be considered "successful" in an occupation for which he was fitted but not earn high wages. Other criticisms were that: (1) Thorndike did not provide "guidance" to his Subjects and consequently he had no basis for drawing conclusions about this activity from his findings; (2) he misclassified Subjects according to the work they were doing by using such overly inclusive occupational groupings as "mechanical" to include anyone who exerted bodily strength or skill, e.g., prizefighters as well as tool-and-die makers; (3) he could not expect his tests, which measured only a few of the skills involved in these occupations, to predict success in such grossly grouped occupations; (4) he misinterpreted the British studies; and so forth and so on.

Thorndike, E. L. (1935) attempted to answer some of these criticisms, but, in general, his rebuttals were not convincing. In most of them he simply stated that his critics were wrong, without indicating why. In particular, he argued that the use of a more refined occupational classification schema "would not raise the value of any items of the school record or tests for prediction of earnings, interest, or level of job at 'mechanical' work to .40 or even .30" (Thorndike, E. L., 1935, p. 330), but he evidently failed to recognize that his tests might have had higher correlations with success in occupations grouped according to the abilities measured by the tests than by some other trait, such as bodily strength. It seems apparent that Thorndike's predictions would have been better had he eliminated the various sources of error variance in his criteria of vocational success which were noted by his critics.

A Recent Study

Much as his father had attempted to predict vocational success in the era of the Great Depression, Robert L. Thorndike, with the collaboration of Elizabeth Hagen, tried to accomplish a similar goal in the period following World War II. The two studies have many features in common: Both were prediction rather than developmental studies; both used only aptitude tests, as compared with other kinds, e.g., interest or personality, as the psychometric predictors; both involved no intervention or "treatment" of the Subjects, such as educational or vocational guidance; and, both utilized earnings or income as the primary criterion of vocational success. The main difference between the studies was in the samples on which data were collected. Whereas the elder Thorndike studied school children, the younger investigated the occupational membership and success of adult men who had been tested initially as part of the selection program for aviation cadet training in 1943. Another notable difference was in the quality of the tests available for the more recent investigation: they were considerably more refined and thoroughly studied than those used in 1921–1922. Furthermore, more advanced statistical methods, such as multiple discriminant function analysis, were developed during the intervening years, as well as high-speed data-processing machines and procedures. Whether these advantages enjoyed by the more recent study made any difference in the prediction of vocational success, however, is doubtful, as the following summary of Thorndike, R. L., and Hagen's (1959) study of "10,000 careers" brings out.

Design of the Study. Predictor data were available from the 1943 version of the Aviation Cadet Classification Test battery which included the following tests: reading comprehension, general information—navigator, mathematics, arithmetic reasoning, numerical operations (speed and accuracy), dial and table reading, speed of identification, spatial orientation, mechanical principles, two-hand coordination, mechanical experience, complex coordination, rotary pursuit with divided attention, finger dexterity, aiming stress, general information, discrimination reaction time, and mathematical background. Factor analyses of these tests indicated that they could be grouped according to five factors: general intellectual, numerical, perceptual spatial, mechanical, and psychomotor. In addition to the aptitude tests, responses to a 100-plus–item Biographical Data Blank, which covered such topics as "General Family and Personal Background," "Major Subject in College," "Activities Done a Number of Times," and "Work Experience," were also available for analysis. Criterion data were collected by a questionnaire mailed to approximately 17,000 former Air Cadets in 1955–1956, with about a 70 percent return. From the items on the questionnaire, seven criteria of vocational success were defined or derived: (1) monthly reported earned income; (2) number supervised; (3) self-rated success; (4) self-rated job satisfaction; (5) vertical mobility, as determined by progress in job level; (6) lateral mobility, as determined by job changes at the same level; and (7) length of time in occupation. Thus, the predictors were aptitude tests and biographical information, the criteria were answers to an educational and vocational questionnaire, and the intervening period of time was approximately 12 to 13 years.

Results. One analysis yielded the means and standard deviation on each test and the factors for the Subjects classified by the occupation in which they were engaged at the time of the follow-up. Some characteristic differences between occupations were found, e.g., the higher perceptual spatial aptitude of architects, the greater numerical fluency of treasurers, the superior general intelligence of college professors, the greater mechanical ability of airplane pilots, and the higher psychomotor skill of machinists, but probably one of the most important findings was that there was considerable overlap in the aptitudes between occupations, much as had been reported in both world wars with respect to intelligence (Yerkes, 1921; Stewart, 1947). A multiple discriminant function analysis of 22 selected higher-level occupations indicated that the differences which did exist among them could be accounted for primarily by a "quantitative" and a "mechanical versus verbal" dimension. For example, mechanical engineers are high on quantitative and average on verbal, whereas lawyers are high on verbal and average on quantitative. Again, however, the differences were not clear-cut, some occupations (e.g., industrial manager) being characterized strongly by neither discriminant. Two analyses were made of the Biographical Data Blank, one in which the items differentiating an occupation from all others combined were identified and one in which items were related to high and low income within an occupation. The most differentiating item *between* occupations was one which asked whether a Subject had had a college major before joining the Air Force; *within* occupations the items were essentially unrelated to income. Similarly, in the other major analysis which was made, there were only a few rather low correlations between the aptitude tests and the various criteria of vocational success.

Conclusions. On the basis of these findings Thorndike, R. L., and Hagen (1959, pp. 49–50) drew two conclusions:

1. When it comes to differences between groups, our results show that these were real, sometimes substantial and, in most cases, sensible. . . . While recognizing the real, sizable, and in most cases, sensible differences between groups we must also recognize that the variability within any group with respect to any given aptitude dimension was quite marked. It is easy to overemphasize the between-group differences.
2. With respect to prediction of success within an occupation, our conclusions must be quite different. As far as we are able to determine from our data, there is no convincing evidence that aptitude tests or biographical information of the type that was available to us can predict degree of success within an occupation insofar as this is represented in the criterion measures that we were able to obtain. This would suggest that we should view the long-range prediction of occupational success by aptitude tests with a good deal of skepticism and take a very restrained view as to how much can be accomplished in this direction.

It is difficult to argue with these conclusions, given the study which Thorndike and Hagen conducted. A question remains, however, whether the problem of predicting vocational success was adequately investigated in this research considering its inadequacies and shortcomings.

Comment. In the original report of their study, Thorndike, R. L., and Hagen (1959, p. 114) are cognizant that their methodology was not without limitations: "The factors tending to camouflage and suppress significant results in our data were many. In particular, our criterion measures were fallible, in many respects." In a subsequent paper, Thorndike, R. L. (1963) reviews in detail what some of these factors were, including the criteria used to assess vocational success, and comes to a rather startling conclusion. He proposes that: "Beyond survival in an occupation, 'success' is a meaningless concept, which we might as well abandon" (Thorndike, R. L., 1963, p. 186). He reasons that the concept of success has been obviated by what he calls the "institutionalization of rewards" in occupations. By this he means the fixing or codifying of earnings through union contracts or civil service regulations, so that success is less a matter of individual competence than it is of institutional policy.

This explanation is a compelling one, however, only if we make the assumption, as Thorndike apparently does, that the primary criterion of vocational success is how much a worker earns. Since, as was noted earlier in the chapter, success can be conceptualized in other ways, and since many extraneous factors, including "institutionalization of rewards" as well as others, introduce considerable bias into earnings or income as a criterion, it is difficult to accept Thorndike's assumption and discard the concept of success. Rather, it would appear to be profitable to analyze further what some of the problems are which are involved in predicting vocational success.

Other Studies

It is not possible here to review and summarize all the other studies which have been conducted on the prediction of vocational success.[7] Suffice it to say that most of them have yielded results which are largely negative (e.g., Carruthers, 1950; Ghiselli & Barthol, 1953). Instead, it would seem more informative to describe a recent trend in research on prediction which appears to have some promise for improving the accuracy with which vocational success might be forecasted. This line of inquiry has developed from the observation that the correlations between predictors and criteria are often higher in groups which are more homogeneous on some third variable than in those which are unselected. Thus, Abelson (1952) found that scholastic aptitude tests predicted college grade point average more accurately for females than males; Hoyt, D. P., and Norman (1954) discovered that the grades of college students with "normal" MMPIs are more predictable than those with "abnormal" profiles; and others (Drake, 1962; Fredericksen & Melville, 1954; Fredericksen & Gilbert, 1960; Stagner, 1933) have reported similar findings with different Subjects and variables. Also, the accumulating body of research on intraindividual response variability (Berdie, 1961; Fiske, 1957a, 1957b; Fiske & Rice, 1955) has led to much the same conclusion: predictions can be improved by introducing additional variables which reduce heterogeneity within the correlational groups.

In contrast to suppressor variables (McNemar, 1955, pp. 188–189), which minimize the correlations among predictors in multiple regression, these so-called "moderator" variables (Saunders, 1956) provide for the additive, interactive effects which sometimes are involved in predictions (Kahneman & Ghiselli, 1962; Lee, 1961). To illustrate how these variables function and to review some of the work which has been done on them, a series of studies by Ghiselli (1956b; 1960a; 1960b), which are the most relevant ones for the problem of predicting vocational success, are discussed at length.

In the first study (Ghiselli, 1956b), the problem was to establish empirically that individuals could be differentiated in terms of their predictability. In other words, the task was to develop a measure of individual differences in predictability which could be used in conjunction with a predictor to increase

[7] For example, there is an extensive literature on the relationship of academic achievement to vocational success, but, not only has it produced almost no positive findings, it has been ably and recently reviewed by Hoyt, D. P. (1965, "Summary"), who has concluded that: "Although this area of research is plagued by many theoretical, experimental, measurement, and statistical difficulties, present evidence strongly suggests that college grades bear little or no relationship to any measures of adult accomplishment."

the correlation with the criterion. For a sample of taxicab-driver candidates ($N = 193$), the predictor was a "tapping and dotting" test of manual dexterity, the criterion was "production during the first 12 weeks of employment" (not further specified), and the instruments to be tried out as measures of predictability were two inventories, one on "appropriateness of occupational level" and the other on "interest in jobs involving personal relationships," each of which consisted of 24 pairs of forced-choice items. The total sample was subdivided into an experimental group ($N = 100$) and a cross-validation group ($N = 93$), and correlations among the several variables were computed for the experimentals, all of which were less than .28. Differences were then determined for this same group between their standard scores on the predictor (tapping and dotting test) and the criterion (production), and these were correlated with the scores from the two inventories.

The *r*'s were .318 for "occupational interest" and .126 for "personal relationships," which meant that Subjects who had low scores on occupational interest also had small differences between their scores on the predictor and criterion. In other words, presumably the correlation between the latter variables would be higher for them than it would for Subjects with higher occupational-interest scores or Subjects selected on the personal-relationships inventory, which was essentially unrelated to the difference scores. To test this hypothesis further Ghiselli used the cross-validation group, in which it was found that for the most predictable Subjects (low occupational-interest scores) the correlation between predictor and criterion went up to .664 and for Subjects high and low on personal relationships the correlations were about the same, .100 and .130. From these data, Ghiselli (1956b, p. 376) concluded that:

> The results of this study point to the possibility of distinguishing applicants whose job performance can be predicted by ordinary selective procedures from those whose performance is poorly predicted. Selective procedures, therefore, can be improved not only by the addition of highly valid predictors to present procedures, but also by the addition of devices to screen out individuals whose levels of aptitude and job proficiency show little correspondence.

The second study (Ghiselli, 1960b) extended the work begun in the first by posing the problem of whether an inventory used as a predictor test could also serve as its own predictability measure. Two samples ($N = 232$ and $N = 251$) of college students were used, and again they were subdivided into experimental (N's $= 108$ and 119) and cross-validation (N's $= 124$ and 132) groups for the analyses. In the first sample, a sociability questionnaire and an intelligence scale scored from a self-description inventory were administered, and the correlation between them, with the former designated as the criterion and the latter as the predictor, was calculated. Then, within the experimental group "highs" and "lows" were segregated on the basis of their difference scores between the predictor and the criterion. Next, an item analysis was performed of responses to all the items in the self-description inventory, including those in the intelligence scale, to identify items which the "highs" and "lows" answered differently and hence which could be used to construct a predictability scale. Finally, in the cross-validation group, *r*'s between the predictor (intelligence scale) and the criterion (sociability questionnaire) were computed for increasing class intervals of approximately 7 percent, beginning at the lowest and culminating with the highest, on the predictability measure. In the second sample, exactly the same procedures were followed, with the exception that the predictor was an "initiative" scale (see Chapter 9), which is also scored from the self-description inventory.

The results from the two samples are shown in Figure 10-5, where it can be seen that the "validity coefficients" (*r*'s for predictor versus criterion) are considerably higher for cases with the best predictability scores, the "cutting" point being at a selection ratio of approximately 50 percent. Consequently, Ghiselli (1960b, pp. 7–8) drew the following conclusions:

> 1. The results of this investigation provide further confirmation of the fact that the exactness with which an individual's criterion score can be predicted from a test can itself be predicted.
> 2. The predictor tests used in the present investigation were scales of an inventory. From this same inventory, items could be assembled which provided adequate predictability scores. Hence one and the same inventory can provide predictor scores and in addition predictability scores which indicate the value of the predictor score of each individual.

The third study (Ghiselli, 1960a) dealt with still another aspect of the predictability problem, namely whether a measure could be developed which would indicate which of two tests would predict a criterion better for an individual. Given that D_1 symbolizes the difference between an individual's standard score on one predictor and the criterion, and D_2 represents the difference between his scores on a second predictor and the criterion, then $D_2 - D_1$ would indicate which predictor estimated the individual's criterion performance more accurately. And, a predictability scale which correlated with $D_2 - D_1$ would also provide a basis for stating which predictor was better. In three independent investigations, Ghiselli found that such a scale could be constructed. Each of the samples in these studies was divided at random into an experimental and cross-validation group. For each Subject in the experimental group, $D_2 - D_1$ was computed from two predictors and a criterion, and two

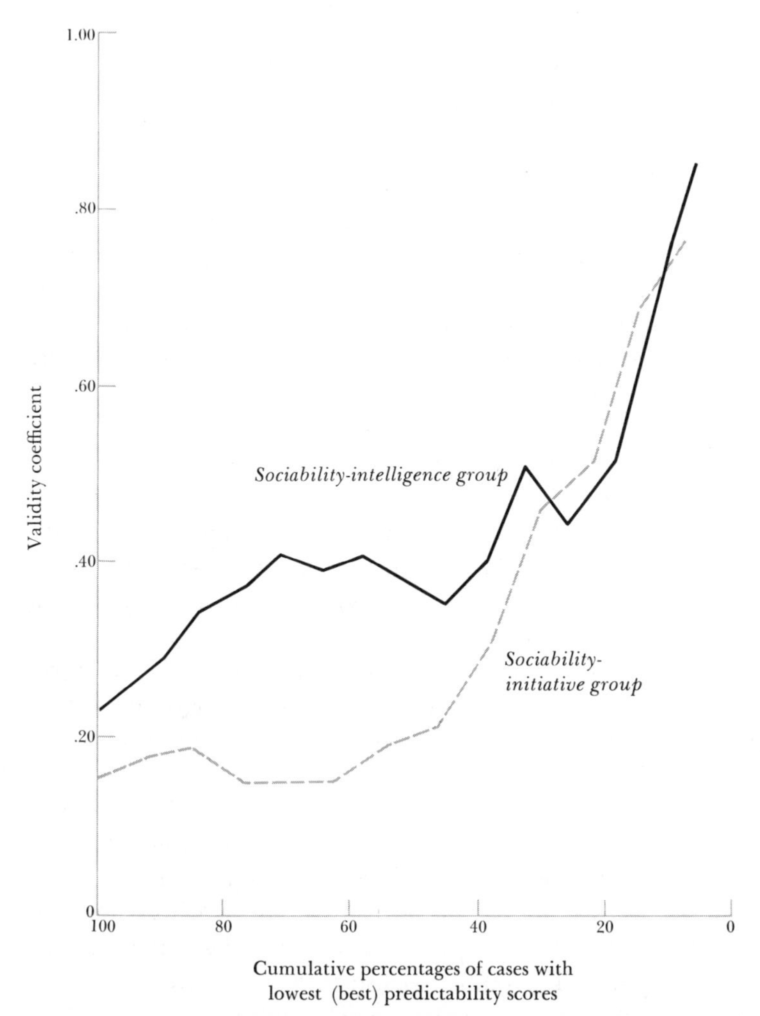

Figure 10-5. Relationship between "validity" coefficients and predictability scores in the sociability-intelligence and sociability-initiative groups. *(From Ghiselli, 1960a, p. 7.)*

further groups were formed, one with positive and one with negative $D_2 - D_1$ values. A predictability scale which differentiated between these groups was then applied to the cross-validation group in the following way: cut-off scores were established on the scale at regular intervals, and then "validity" coefficients between the indicated predictors and the criterion were computed, with the expectation that in the middle range of predictability scores the r's would be the highest. In all the samples this trend was found: the modal r's were almost exactly at the midpoints of the predictability scales. These results led

Ghiselli (1960a, p. 683) to conclude that: "The investigations reported here indicate that it is possible to develop an objective way of indicating for an individual which of two tests gives the better prediction of a criterion."

In a later paper Ghiselli (1963) cites some further evidence which substantiates the phenomenon of differential predictability, as it pertains to the reliability of tests as well as to the validity of predictors, and he also speculates about the implications which can be drawn from it for the general problem of predicting criteria of vocational success, as well as other variables. He points out that classical measurement and prediction theory does not provide for individual differences in predictability, because it assumes that errors of measurement and estimate are the same for all individuals or that, more accurately, they approach the same value as the number of parallel tests and/or criteria increase without limit. This does not mean that classical theory cannot accommodate the phenomenon of differential predictability. It can, if it is realized that the effect of moderator variables is to reduce error variance by increasing the homogeneity of the groups within which predictions are made. Ghiselli appears to prefer an alternative interpretation, however, which states that the common variance between a predictor and a criterion varies from one *individual* to another, rather than among *groups,* the implication being that cognizance should be taken of the interactions which exist among criteria, moderators, and predictors instead of "explaining them away" in terms of greater group homogeneity.

Comment. It is still too early in the development of this line of research on differential predictability to evaluate it adequately. The concept appears to be reasonable, and a beginning has been made in providing it with a rationale (Lee, 1961; Saunders, 1956). If it continues to be supported by sound empirical evidence, it may become the theoretical touchstone which has been so badly needed to account for the low correlations which studies like those of the Thorndikes have found between predictors and criteria of vocational success. Some nagging questions remain, however, which must be answered before we can accept the concept without reservations. First, it is not clear what the logical relationship between moderator and suppressor variables is and when, if at all, they have equivalent or highly similar effects. Second, it is not clear why moderator variables are not more general in nature than they have been found to be. With only a few exceptions, they are specific to the samples and/or the measures which are used to assess them. Finally, as Ghiselli (1960a, p. 684) has pointed out, it is not clear under what circumstances or conditions traditional multiple regression procedures will yield a higher relationship between predictors and criteria than predictability measures, and vice versa.

11
VOCATIONAL SATISFACTION

The Model of Vocational Adjustment outlined in Chapter 8 specified two outcomes of the process which the individual goes through in responding to the problems created by his work. One of these is vocational success, which we have just discussed; the other is vocational satisfaction, which is the subject of this chapter. We shall focus upon three general questions: What is meant by "vocational satisfaction"? How is it measured? And what are its sources? Also, we shall attempt to summarize the voluminous literature on satisfaction, which is the largest on any topic in vocational psychology, and present the findings of classic and recent studies on the incidence and correlates of dissatisfaction with work. Finally, we shall consider what the relationship of vocational satisfaction to vocational success is. If these phenomena are both outcomes of the process of vocational adjustment, would we expect them to be related or not? What is the empirical evidence on this question? There are, then, three major sections in the chapter: (1) the definition of vocational satisfaction; (2) studies of vocational satisfaction; and (3) vocational satisfaction in relation to vocational success.

THE DEFINITION OF VOCATIONAL SATISFACTION

Vocational satisfaction has been defined in many ways by many people. Some of the definitions are largely verbal in nature, what Underwood (1957) calls "literary" definitions, and others are rigorously operational, but most are somewhere in between—relatively general and unrefined attempts to give meaning to the experiences which workers report as satisfying and dissatisfying. The measures of vocational satisfaction which have followed from these conceptualizations have been equally numerous, but also frequently expedient and superficial. One of our objectives in this section is to review and evaluate these instruments and to draw some conclusions about their usefulness for research on vocational satisfaction. Another objective is to summarize the factor analyses which have been conducted on vocational satisfaction and to suggest possible interpretations of them. Thus, in the discussion which follows, three topics are dealt with: (1) concepts of vocational satisfaction; (2) the measurement of vocational satisfaction; and (3) the dimensions of vocational satisfaction.

Concepts of Vocational Satisfaction

In contrast to vocational motivation and success, vocational satisfaction has been conceptualized primarily within psychological frames of reference. It has not been as extensively studied in labor economics or occupational sociology, although some notable work has been done in these fields, such as that of the Survey Research Center at the University of Michigan. This is not to say, however, that, as a result, vocational satisfaction is a refined and well-understood concept in vocational and industrial psychology. Quite the contrary is more likely the case. Herzberg, Mausner, Peterson, and Capwell (1957, p. 1) begin their comprehensive review of job attitudes and satisfaction with the pessimistic observation that: "The very term 'job satisfaction' lacks adequate definition." Similarly, Katzell (1964, p. 342) notes that: "It has often been remarked that the term 'job satisfaction' is employed in a variety of ways." In this section, then, our task will be to present some of the sundry definitions of vocational satisfaction which have been formulated; to discuss their merits and shortcomings; and to attempt to arrive at a concept of vocational satisfaction which appears to have some heuristic value. Accordingly, the following topics are taken up in succession: (1) early concepts of vocational satisfaction; (2) contemporary concepts of vocational satisfaction; (3) concepts related to vocational satisfaction; (4) theories of vocational satisfaction; and (5) unresolved issues and problems in conceptualizing vocational satisfaction.

Early Concepts of Vocational Satisfaction. In one of the first psychological analyses ever made of the factors which contribute to an individual's dissatisfaction with his work, Fisher and Hanna (1931) proposed that dissatisfaction stems largely from emotional maladjustment. They noted that:

> The reason why this fact has not been adequately recognized by those interested in vocational adjustment is simple; just because he does not know, the individual seldom assigns the true cause as the factor underlying his vocational maladjustment. He is dissatisfied, and simply because his work fails to give him the satisfaction he is seeking, he thinks his work is to blame [Fisher & Hanna, 1931, p. 21].

The most notable other early conceptualization of vocational satisfaction was that of Hoppock (1935b, pp. 47–48), who defined satisfaction as "any combination of psychological, physiological, and environmental circumstances that causes a person truthfully to say, 'I am satisfied with my job.'" In this definition, the underlying assumption is that "it is possible for [a worker] to balance the specific satisfactions against the specific dissatisfactions and thus to arrive at a composite satisfaction with the job as a whole." We shall discuss the implications of defining satisfaction in this way later in the chapter, when we survey some of the different methods which have been developed to measure a worker's reactions of liking and disliking for his vocation.[1]

Contemporary Concepts of Vocational Satisfaction. One of the most influential current conceptual schemata for vocational satisfaction has been proposed by Ginzberg et al. (1951), who have identified three different types of satisfaction in work. First, there are the *intrinsic* satisfactions which come from two sources: (1) the pleasure which is derived from engaging in work activity ("function pleasure"), and (2) the sense of accomplishment which is experienced from meeting social standards of success and personal realization of abilities through achievement. Second, there are the *concomitant* satisfactions which are associated with the physical and psychological conditions of a person's work. These would include working in a clean, air-conditioned plant, having many fringe benefits, enjoying congenial co-workers, being employed by a company with a "worker orientation," etc. And, third, there are the *extrinsic* satisfactions which are the tangible rewards of work, i.e., pay and bonuses. Ginzberg et al. (1951, p. 217) point out, however, that the critical consideration is not the absolute amount of these satisfactions "but the amount in relation to expectations, which in turn, is a function of values and goals."

Although not as widely known as Ginzberg's analysis of vocational satisfaction, two other contemporary definitions of the concept should be mentioned. Viewing vocational satisfaction within the context of the work organization or social system, Bullock (1953, p. 5) has defined it as:

> ... an attitude which results from a balance and summation of many specific likes and dislikes experienced in connection with the job. This attitude manifests itself in evaluations of the job and of the employing organization. These evaluations may rest largely upon one's own success or failure in the achievement of personal objectives and upon the perceived contributions of the job and employing organization to these ends. Thus a worker may like certain aspects of his work yet thoroughly dislike others.

In this respect, Bullock's concept of vocational satisfaction is much like Hoppock's. The former goes on to add, however, that:

[1] For an historical review of the meanings of vocational satisfaction in different eras, see Balchin (1947).

> The factors molding or shaping . . . [satisfaction] are to be found in the social pressures and influences of the formal organizational structure, its culture and status systems; the informal structure of the work group, its culture and its status systems; and in the community associations of the employee [Bullock, 952, p. 5].

A similar but more comprehensive concept of vocational satisfaction has been formulated by Smith, P. C. (1963) and her associates at Cornell University. This group begins by making the observation that:

> Satisfaction is a product of other variables, rather than a cause in itself. It may even be regarded as only an epiphenomenon—it is possible that feelings of satisfaction or dissatisfaction occur only when a question is asked of the individual, or when circumstances pose potential alternatives (favorable or unfavorable) to him which require him to make an evaluation. The feelings of an individual about various aspects of his job are not absolute, but relative to the alternatives available to him.

On the basis of this assumption, vocational satisfaction is defined as an affective state which is "a function of the worker's present job, on the one hand, and his frame of reference and his adaptation level on the other."

Concepts Related to Vocational Satisfaction. In order to sharpen the definition of vocational satisfaction, it is important to distinguish it from several closely related concepts. Among these, the two with which satisfaction is most often confused are *job attitudes* and *morale*. The former is usually considered to be a worker's positive or negative reactions to the specific aspects of his work, e.g., adequacy of tools, work load, co-workers, vacations, etc. Herzberg et al. (1957) have classified 134 specific job aspects, which were studied in approximately 150 investigations, into the following 10 major job-factor categories: (1) intrinsic aspects of job; (2) supervision; (3) working conditions; (4) wages; (5) opportunity for advancement; (6) security; (7) company and management; (8) social aspects of job; (9) communications; and (10) benefits. In contrast to definitions of satisfaction, job attitudes are *not* conceptualized as being general in nature. They refer only to the components of work and the environment in which it is performed. Sometimes satisfaction is conceived of as the composite of various job attitudes (e.g., Smith), but the latter are still defined as responses to the several aspects of the job.

In contrast, morale is usually seen as a more comprehensive concept than satisfaction, including it as one element among others, which together provide "an index of the extent to which the individual perceives a probability of satisfying his own motives through cooperation with the group" (Stagner, 1958, p.

64). Guion (1958, p. 62) has defined morale as "the extent to which an individual's needs are satisfied and the extent to which the individual perceives that satisfaction as stemming from his total job situation," which is very similar to some concepts of satisfaction (e.g., Schaffer, 1953), but typically morale has involved an emphasis upon the individual's relationship to his work group and employing organization. Thus, Katz (1951, p. 76) has enumerated the following dimensions of morale: (1) intrinsic job satisfaction; (2) involvement in the immediate work group; (3) identification with the company; (4) relationship to supervisor; (5) extraoccupational satisfactions; and (6) identification with an occupational system, e.g., thinking of oneself as a "railroader" rather than the employee of a specific railroad. In addition to job attitudes and morale, vocational satisfaction is occasionally defined in terms of absenteeism, accidents, grievances, and job tenure or turnover (e.g., Kilbridge, 1961), but since these variables are operationally independent of the usual procedures for measuring satisfaction, it is probably more accurate to consider them different phenomena.

One further distinction should be made in defining what we mean by the concept of vocational satisfaction. The adjective "vocational" has been used rather than "job" to designate the individual's satisfaction with his "life's work," not just the particular position he holds at a given point in time. It is certainly legitimate, and it may also be quite useful theoretically and empirically, to ask a worker what his *job* satisfaction is at any given moment, but such a question may not necessarily indicate his *vocational* satisfaction. He may be dissatisfied with his job, because of certain situational factors, such as an incompetent supervisor, but be satisfied with his vocation—the work for which he has trained and in which he has gained experience. In other words, he might want to change his job but not his vocation. Smith, P. C. (1963, p. 9) has elaborated upon this distinction with reference to the type of question which is used to elicit expressions of satisfaction:

> The manner in which a question is posed is likely to affect the alternatives which the individual is considering when he answers. Summary evaluations, such as "all in all, how do you feel about your job?" are likely to bring out long-term factors to a greater extent than specific questions such as "Is the cafeteria service adequate?" Answers to long-term questions should be expected to be related to long-term rather than short-term behavior, and vice versa.

It is the long-term behavior which is of interest to us in the study of the development of vocational behavior, and consequently we shall focus more upon *vocational* than job satisfaction in the remainder of this chapter, although both concepts will be dealt with. It should be noted that, in addition to the type of question used to elicit statements of satisfaction, vocational satisfaction can be defined as an individual's average job satisfaction over an extended period of time, i.e., so that two or more jobs are included.[2]

Theories of Vocational Satisfaction. Thus far we have discussed the definition of vocational satisfaction, but not its relationship to other variables, which is a matter for theory. Brophy (1959) has classified theories of vocational satisfaction into four types: need, expectation, role, and self. Examples of each of these will be presented as well as one theory which does not directly fit any of Brophy's types.[3]

1. *Need theory.* Two need theories of satisfaction have been proposed—one by Schaffer (1953), which is discussed at length further on in the chapter (see "Recent Studies"), and the other by Morse (1953), which is summarized here. In brief, the latter's theory states that the amount of vocational satisfaction experienced by a worker is a function of two factors: "(1) how much his needs are fulfilled by being in a particular situation, i.e., how much his need-tension-level is reduced, and (2) how much his needs remain unfulfilled." Expressed in equation form this theory would be as follows: S (satisfaction) $= f(T_1 - T_2) - (T_2)$, where T_1 is the worker's initial tension level and T_2 is his tension level after being exposed to his vocation. For example: if a worker's initial need-tension level (T_1) before he enters his vocation is 10, and if his need-tension level after working for a period of time (T_2) is 2, then his satisfaction (S) would equal $(10 - 4)$ or 6. Morse introduces the correction factor T_2 into the satisfaction function in order to account for individual differences in need levels prior to occupational entry. Thus, two individuals in the same work environment may differ in their satisfaction, despite equivalent reductions in tension levels, because the needs of one were initially stronger than those of the other.

2. *Expectation theory.* The type of theory of satisfaction which Brophy (1959, p. 270) includes in this category is based upon the hypothesis that "an individual's degree of satisfaction with an activity leading toward a goal is an inverse function of the level of his perceived probability of attaining the goal, both in situations when the goal is attained and in situations when it is not

[2] Harmon (1966) has conducted the only study which has been located on the distinction between vocational and job satisfaction, but rather than intercorrelating her measures of these two variables, in order to determine whether they were the same or different, she related them to changes in vocation and job after occupational entry as "external criteria" of differential satisfaction. In other words, instead of investigating the interrelationship of vocational and job satisfaction, she analyzed the relationship between two different ways of defining or measuring the same variables. Consequently, the empirical correlation between vocational and job satisfaction remains to be determined.

[3] For an interesting discussion of vocational satisfaction from the psychoanalytic point of view, but one which cannot be considered a "theory," see Ginsberg (1956).

attained." A theory of satisfaction which generally corresponds to this model is the one by Katzell (1964), which was summarized in Chapter 9. The propositions in it which directly pertain to satisfaction are the following (Katzell, 1964, p. 342):

> 1. The events or conditions experienced by a person in his job or occupation arouse, among other responses, feelings or affect which he can verbalize on a continuum of "like-dislike," "pleasant-unpleasant," or "satisfactory-unsatisfactory," or similar evaluative or hedonic dimensions.
> 2. People differ markedly in degree of job satisfaction. In addition to errors of measurement, the variance in job satisfaction may be attributed to (*a*) differences in stimuli, i.e., features of jobs (such as pay or supervision), and (*b*) differences in the job incumbents.
> 3. The intra-individual sources of job satisfaction (*2b* above) may be accounted for largely in terms of the concept of adaptational levels or the related concept of personal values. . . . The feeling or affective response evoked is, according to this view, directly proportional to the discrepancy between the stimulus and its corresponding adaptation level, and inversely proportional to the adaptation level.

It is apparent that Katzell's concept of adaptation level is very similar to Morse's notion of tension level, i.e., both are defined in terms of the difference between what the worker wants and what he gets. The two theories are dissimilar, however, in that Katzell hypothesizes that satisfaction is a *multiplicative* function of these variables, whereas Morse concludes that it is a *subtractive* function.

3. *Role theory*. Brophy (1959) distinguishes between two kinds of role theories of satisfaction—sociological and psychological. The former is exemplified by Bullock's (1953) concept of vocational satisfaction as a function of the organizational context within which the individual works. Bullock operationally defines satisfaction in terms of the discrepancies which exist between either (1) the worker's ideal role expectations and those of society or (2) the worker's ideal role and his real role. Brophy (1959, p. 272, italics in original) notes that there are three characteristics of such a sociological role theory of satisfaction:

> First, it involves an evaluation of the environment from a viewpoint external to the individual, rather than from the individual's own phenomenological frame of reference. Second, it considers an aggregate of individual positions as a single position. . . . Third, it focuses on *people in general* within the broadly defined position and the expectations made of them, rather than upon a single person and his interaction with the environment.

In contrast, psychological role theories of satisfaction are more ideographic in nature, their basic proposition being that "satisfaction with a position is determined by the degree of compatibility between one's perceived imposed role and his concept of ideal role for the position" (Brophy, 1959, p. 273). Here, it is the individual's perception of his own position which is considered to be the most important factor in determining his vocational satisfaction.

4. *Self theory.* Although Brophy's (1959) theory of satisfaction incorporates concepts and propositions from all the different types of theories, it probably resembles a self theory of satisfaction more than any other. His theory consists of 10 hypotheses on both general life satisfactions and vocational satisfactions, but only the latter are listed here (Brophy, 1959, pp. 280–281):

> *Hypothesis 4.* There is an inverse relationship between vocational satisfaction and the magnitude of the discrepancy between self concept and imposed occupational role.
>
> *Hypothesis 5.* There is an inverse relationship between vocational satisfaction and the magnitude of the discrepancy between concept of ideal occupational role and imposed occupational role.
>
> *Hypothesis 6.* There is an inverse relationship between vocational satisfaction and the magnitude of the discrepancy between self concept and concept of ideal self. . . .
>
> *Hypothesis 9.* There is a positive relationship between vocational satisfaction and occupational role acceptance.
>
> *Hypothesis 10.* There is a positive relationship between vocational satisfaction and general satisfaction.

As can be discerned from reading these hypotheses, they are all based upon the general assumption that vocational satisfaction is a function of agreement among the worker's self-concepts, both real and ideal, and the occupational roles he perceives or plays in the world of work.

5. *Cognitive theory.* Following Brophy's (1959) enumeration of satisfaction theories, Vroom (1964) proposed his so-called "cognitive" theory which represents still another approach to the analysis and explanation of why workers are satisfied or dissatisfied with their jobs or vocations. This theory has already been discussed in Chapter 9, but it may be worthwhile, in this context, to highlight that part of it which is directly relevant to satisfaction. Vroom begins with the assumption that vocational satisfaction is conceptually equivalent to the worker's valence for his job or vocation, where "valence" is defined as the attraction which the outcomes of two alternative courses of action have for a person. Satisfaction (or valence) is then conceived to be a function of the extent to which the worker can attain his goals through his job and the strength of his expectancy that he will be able to remain in it. (For a complete statement of Vroom's hypotheses on satisfaction, see Chapter 9.)

Unresolved Issues and Problems in Conceptualizing Vocational Satisfaction. There are several questions about the concept of vocational satisfaction which remain unanswered and which should be mentioned. What research has been done on them will be summarized, but it has not been extensive.

1. *Is general satisfaction with life related to vocational satisfaction?* There have been three independent studies of this problem, and all three have found a relationship. Weitz (1952) devised a measure of General Satisfaction which, for a sample of 168 life insurance agents, correlated .39 with "a number of items concerning their job [sic] as sources of satisfaction or dissatisfaction." Using the Weitz test as well as the Rundquist-Sletto Morale Scale as measures of general satisfaction and the Brayfield-Rothe Job Satisfaction Index and SRA Employee Inventory as measures of vocational satisfaction, Brayfield, Wells, and Strate (1957) obtained similar results, but only for males. The correlations for 41 men employed in office jobs were: Brayfield-Rothe versus Weitz, 32; Brayfield-Rothe versus Rundquist-Sletto, .49; SRA versus Weitz, .68; and SRA versus Rundquist-Sletto, .67. None of the correlations for 52 women office workers was significant (with the exception of Rundquist-Sletto versus Weitz, 43). Finally, Brophy (1959) has reported an r of .50 between general and vocational satisfaction for a group of 81 female nurses. It can be concluded, therefore, that general and vocational satisfaction are related, although further study of possible sex differences in the relationship is needed.

2. *Is there an optimal degree of vocational satisfaction?* Hoppock (1935b, pp. 51–52) early proposed that: "What we seek is an *optimum* satisfaction which will release us from the tension of a frantic and persistent urge to be doing something else, but leave us dissatisfied enough to have something left to work for." Similarly, Hoppock and Super (1950, p. 126) have observed that:

> We all want a reasonable degree of satisfaction. Sometimes we think life would be wonderful if we could have everything we want. At other times we realize that that would mean satiety, a state of existence only temporarily pleasant. What is best for us, probably, is a condition somewhere between complete satisfaction and complete dissatisfaction, one that would leave us enough unrealized desires to keep us at work with active interest, but would relieve us of an urge to run away from our present troubles.

Whether there is an optimal degree of vocational satisfaction, which is, by some criterion, "best" for the worker has not been established empirically. To the contrary, most of the evidence which has accumulated over the years on the distribution of satisfaction in the labor force indicates that most workers are satisfied with their jobs. The possibility of optimal satisfaction should not be overlooked, however, particularly in the study of satisfaction in relation to other variables. For example: if satisfaction is related to motivation, as the

Model for Vocational Adjustment specifies (Chapter 8), and if there is an optimal degree of satisfaction, then the relationship between satisfaction and motivation should be a *non*linear rather than linear one, with the optimally satisfied workers being more highly motivated than either the highly satisfied or dissatisfied workers.

3. *Does vocational satisfaction fluctuate from day to day?* Hoppock (1935b, p. 5) has suggested that "the degree of satisfaction may vary from day to day," as has Thomas, L. G. (1956, p. 197), who observes that "a given job may be quite satisfying to a worker today but found dull or thoroughly disliked by the same worker tomorrow." Research data on this hypothesis, however, are lacking, although Hoppock attempted unsuccessfully to collect some. He writes that:

> Each subject was also asked to keep a record of his daily attitude toward his job for a period of three weeks, on a graphic rating scale provided for the purpose. Some declined to do so on the ground that there would be no difference from day to day. Of those who did take the blanks only a few returned them [Hoppock, 1935b, p. 56].

4. *Is vocational satisfaction conscious or unconscious?* The concept of vocational satisfaction proposed by Fisher and Hanna (1931), which has been discussed, implies that satisfaction, or more accurately dissatisfaction, is largely unconscious because the worker "does not know" why he dislikes his job. Likewise, Young (1940, pp. 615–616) has concluded that: "The individual does not know why he is unhappy or dissatisfied or unsuccessful, and it is not uncommon for him to project blame for his maladjustment upon his job and the working situation." In contrast, Schaffer (1953, p. 2) has defined dissatisfaction as "a conscious recognition of a state of tension." Because of the definitional and methodological problems involved in studying consciousness or awareness (Adams, J. K., 1957), it may not be possible to resolve this issue. Certainly, further research and conceptualization, e.g., Levy's (1963, pp. 21–24) discussion of the unconscious as a hypothetical construct, is indicated.

Comment. It is apparent from a review of early and contemporary concepts and theories of vocational satisfaction that this phenomenon has been defined in various ways, and, as a consequence, its meaning has become confused. In order to clarify the definition of vocational satisfaction, it would seem necessary to specify more precisely the referent which is being considered. If it is some specific aspect of the job, such as duties and tasks or working conditions, then the concept which is defined would be *job attitudes.* If it is the overall job in which the individual is presently employed, then the concept would be *job satisfaction.* If it is the type of work in which the individual has been trained and/or has gained experience in several jobs (two or more), then the concept would be *vocational satisfaction*. And, if the referent includes the work group and/or employing organization, as well as job or vocational satisfaction, the concept would be *morale*. Defining these concepts in this manner might then lead to more meaningful tests of the theories of vocational satisfaction which have been proposed, since some of them may be confirmable only if a particular variable is used in their propositions. The best theory, of course, would be the one that is most generally applicable, i.e., to job attitudes, job satisfaction, vocational satisfaction, and morale. Whether such a theory will ever be devised remains to be seen, but the studies on the relationship of general to vocational satisfaction, particularly the one by Brayfield et al. (1957), are promising. It appears that these two variables are correlated, irrespective of the measures which are used. Whether they also enter into other relationships, such as those hypothesized by Katzell (1964), Vroom (1964), and others, is a problem for further research.

The Measurement of Vocational Satisfaction

Given the conceptual definition of vocational satisfaction as the individual's overall liking/disliking for the type of work he has been trained for and employed in (for a period of time), we can now turn to some of the operational procedures which have been devised to measure satisfaction. We shall not go into any detail on the methodological problems involved in assessing satisfaction (e.g., Decker, 1955; England & Stein, 1961; Rosen, R. A. H., & Rosen, H., 1955; and Weitz & Nuckols, 1953), but some mention should be made of the desiderata which have been suggested for measures of satisfaction, in order to have a baseline for evaluating those which will be reviewed here. Brayfield and Rothe (1951) have enumerated seven desirable characteristics of any index of satisfaction:

1. It should give an index to "over-all" job satisfaction rather than to specific aspects of the job situation.
2. It should be applicable to a wide variety of jobs.
3. It should be sensitive to variations in attitude.
4. The items should be of such a nature (interesting, realistic, and varied) that the scale would evoke cooperation from both management and employees.
5. It should yield a reliable index.
6. It should yield a valid index.
7. It should be brief and easily scored.

Smith, P. C. (1963, pp. 4–5) has introduced a somewhat different emphasis by suggesting that measures of satisfaction "should be sensitive not only to individual differences (in background, non-work situations, etc.) but also to differences in the work situation" and "should be provided for each of the major discriminably different aspects of the job. . . ." This last requirement, in particular, represents a difference in orientation which is reflected in measures of satisfaction. Some elicit generalized, undifferentiated evaluations of the job or vocation, whereas others ask for reactions to specific aspects of the work situation which are then summated to obtain an overall index of liking/disliking. These global-versus-summation approaches to the measurement of satisfaction will become clearer as we discuss each of the following instruments: (1) Hoppock Job Satisfaction Blank; (2) Kerr Tear Ballot for Industry; (3) Brayfield-Rothe Index of Job Satisfaction; (4) SRA Employee Inventory; and (5) Cornell Job Descriptive Index. In addition, certain other methods of measuring satisfaction, such as the interview, will be briefly described.

The Hoppock Job Satisfaction Blank (JSB). The best-known and most widely used measure of satisfaction is the JSB, which is also the oldest. First developed by Hoppock (1935b) in the mid-thirties, this blank has gone through five different forms, the last of which consists of the questions shown in Table 11-1. As is apparent from its content, the JSB represents the "global" approach to the measurement of satisfaction. It is assumed that the worker summates his likes and dislikes for his job or vocation and, in responding to the questions, weights them subjectively according to their importance to him. His score can be expressed in either a weighted "index of satisfaction," based upon standard-deviation values for each item multiplied by the response percentages of a norm group, or a simple average or total of the values assigned to each foil. Since the two scoring methods correlated .997, the latter seems preferable because of its greater simplicity and ease of computation.

The internal consistency of the JSB is quite high for an instrument of this type. The split-half reliability of the first and third questions versus the second and fourth is .87, corrected by Spearman-Brown to .93 ($N = 301$). Hoppock also correlated the JSB with a composite score based upon 257 questions about satisfaction with specific aspects of the job, e.g., "Is there too much noise where you work?", and obtained an r of .67. From this relationship between the two major types of instruments used to measure satisfaction, Hoppock (1935b, p. 274) concluded: "In other words, the mere summation of satisfaction with various aspects of the job is not equivalent to satisfaction with the job as a whole." He attributes this inequivalence to the fact that the worker assigns weights to his responses in the global approach, whereas the investigator does this in the summation procedure. Because the latter method does not take into consideration individual differences between workers in the assignment of weights, Hoppock prefers the global measure.

Table 11-1. The Job Satisfaction Blank *(From Hoppock, 1935, p. 243)*

1. Choose the *one* of the following statements which best tells how well you like your job. Place a check mark (√) in front of that statement:
   ______ I hate it.
   ______ I dislike it.
   ______ I don't like it.
   ______ I am indifferent to it.
   ______ I like it.
   ______ I am enthusiastic about it.
   ______ I love it.

2. Check one of the following to show *how much of the time* you feel satisfied with your job:
   ______ All of the time.
   ______ Most of the time.
   ______ A good deal of the time.
   ______ About half of the time.
   ______ Occasionally.
   ______ Seldom.
   ______ Never.

3. Check the *one* of the following which best tells how you feel about changing your job:
   ______ I would quit this job at once if I could get anything else to do.
   ______ I would take almost any other job in which I could earn as much as I am now earning.
   ______ I would like to change both my job and my occupation.
   ______ I would like to exchange my present job for another job in the same line of work.
   ______ I am not eager to change my job, but I would do so if I could get a better job.
   ______ I cannot think of any jobs for which I would exchange mine.
   ______ I would not exchange my job for any other.

4. Check one of the following to show how you think you compare with other people:
   ______ No one likes his job better than I like mine.
   ______ I like my job much better than most people like theirs.
   ______ I like my job better than most people like theirs.
   ______ I like my job about as well as most people like theirs.
   ______ I dislike my job more than most people dislike theirs.
   ______ I dislike my job much more than most people dislike theirs.
   ______ No one dislikes his job more than I dislike mine.

The Kerr Tear Ballot for Industry (TBI). In contrast to the JSB, this instrument exemplifies the summation approach to the measurement of vocational satisfaction. The TBI, which is so named because the worker tears the edge of the answer sheet opposite the foil he wants to endorse, is made up of the 10 statements about the various aspects of the job and work situation shown in Table 11-2. Scores are computed by simply adding the values which correspond to the "torn" foils, the highest possible score being 50 and the

Table 11-2. The Tear Ballot for Industry (From Kerr, 1944)

ANSWER BY TEARING!

Tear Ballot For Industry

By WILLARD A. KERR
Illinois Institute of Technology

DEAR EMPLOYEE: It is the obligation of each of us in this company to try to improve the happiness and welfare of others. You are one of the large random sample of employees being asked to cooperate in this sincerely constructive scientific survey of opinions. No one will ever try or be able to connect your name with this ballot. You don't sign your name - in fact, you are not even required to expose your handwriting on this new type of opinion ballot! Only a sincere and honest expression of your opinion is requested.

DIRECTIONS: *Check one answer to each question by* **TEARING THE ARROWHEAD**

1. Does the company make you feel that your job is reasonably secure as long as you do good work?
   1. Yes, job seems wholly secure
   2. Usually
   3. About half the time
   4. Rarely
   5. No, job seems very insecure

2. In your opinion, how does this company compare with others in its interest in the welfare of employees?
   1. It's tops, shows more interest than any other
   2. Slightly above average
   3. It is average
   4. Slightly below average
   5. Poor, shows less interest than other plans

3. How does your immediate superior compare with other managers, foremen, or section leaders as to supervisory ability?
   1. Among the best
   2. Slightly above average
   3. Average
   4. Slightly below average
   5. Among the worst

4. Considering your work, are your working conditions comfortable and healthful?
   1. Yes, excellent
   2. Slightly above average
   3. Average for type of work
   4. Slightly below average
   5. No, very bad

5. Are most of the workers around you the kind who will remember you when you pass them on the street?
   1. Yes, they are very friendly
   2. Yes, usually
   3. About half the time
   4. Rarely
   5. No, they are unfriendly

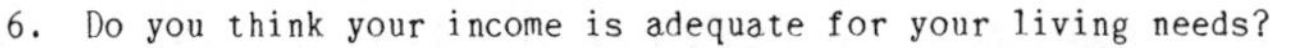

6. Do you think your income is adequate for your living needs?
   1. Yes, enough for enough luxuries
   2. Slightly above average
   3. Just enough for average comfort
   4. Barely enough to get by on
   5. Much less than enough to get along on

Over

Copyright 1944 by **INDUSTRIAL OPINION INSTITUTE**
All rights reserved. Printed in U.S.A.

This scale is copyrighted. The reproduction of any part of it by mimeograph, or in any other way, whether the reproductions are sold or are furnished free for use, is a violation of the copyright law. For origin and first use of the tearing method, see *Kerr, W. A., Where They Like To Work.* - JOURNAL OF APPLIED PSYCHOLOGY, 1943, 27, 438-442.

Table 11-2. The Tear Ballot for Industry *(From Kerr, 1944) (Continued)*

7. Do you feel that you have proper opportunity to present a problem, complaint or suggestion to the management?
   1. Yes, always
   2. Usually
   3. On occasion
   4. Rarely
   5. No, never

8. Do you have confidence in the *good intentions of the management*?
   1. Yes, it is sincere
   2. Usually
   3. Half the time
   4. Not often
   5. No, it is insincere

9. Do you have confidence in the *good sense of the management?*
   1. Yes, it is capable and efficient
   2. It is usually efficient
   3. Half the time
   4. It is often inefficient
   5. No. it is stupid and inefficient

10. What effect is your experience with the company having upon your personal happiness?
    1. Improves it greatly
    2. Slightly beneficial
    3. Little or no effect
    4. Slightly disturbing
    5. Extremely harmful

11. Special problems: Please indicate any or all of the following problems which are really sources of frequent annoyance to you:

    NOTE: *We can all imagine problems that don't exist. Just report the facts.*

    1. Inconvenient or undependable transportation
    2. Unfairness in promotion policy
    3. Lack of time to take care of personal business
    4. Lack of attention to employee recreation
    5. Broken promises on part of supervisors
    6. Family troubles at home
    7. Poor housing conditions or excessive rents

WE SHALL APPRECIATE YOUR PROPERLY TEARING each of the following tabulation items:

12. Your sex: *Male* / *Female*

13. Your present work: *Office* / *Non-Office*

14. Are you a supervisor or foreman? *Yes* / *No*

15. Your hours of work *(chiefly)*: *Day shift* / *Swing shift* / *Night shift* / *Rotation shift system*

16. Your age *(tear nearest)*:

    15 20 25 30 35 40 45 50 55 60 65 70 75 80

Industrial Opinion Institute
PSYCHOMETRIC AFFILIATES
Box 1625 Chicago 90, Illinois

lowest 10. There are no reported test-retest stability estimates for the TBI, but its internal consistency coefficients range from .65 to .88, with a mean of .83, as determined in several samples (Kerr, 1952). Studies of the relationships of the TBI to other variables have been summarized by Kerr (1952, p. 105)[4] as follows:

> In New Orleans it was shown to be significantly related to past personal turnover rates of a sample of wage earners. In a Chicago factory it was found to be significantly related with the per cent hearing loss of personnel (age constant). It was a highly significant predictor of sociometric status in a study of building trades workers. It was substantially correlated with chemical workers' satisfaction with their collective bargaining agency and its achievements. It was significantly related with the empathic ability of a sample of craftsmen. It discriminated between personnel in a financially sound firm and one in bankruptcy receivership. It revealed sensitivity in reflecting the change in group morale resulting from sociometric regrouping in a construction industry experiment. It was related with a spontaneous grievance criterion in two small shops.

Although it would be informative to know the relationship of the TBI to the JSB, no data are presently available on the correlation between these two instruments.

The Brayfield-Rothe Index of Job Satisfaction (IJS). Brayfield and Rothe (1951) constructed this scale in order to meet as many of the specifications for an ideal measure of satisfaction as possible. Thus, they started with a large pool of 1,075 statements about workers' general reactions to their jobs, edited and revised these, reducing them to a total of 246 items, and had 77 judges sort the latter according to Thurstone's equal-interval scaling procedures. A preliminary scale of 18 items was constructed which (1) represented the entire satisfaction-dissatisfaction continuum, (2) consisted of statements with high interjudge agreement in the sorting, (3) had only items referring to the job in general instead of its specific aspects, and (4) was acceptable to both management and employees. Next, the scale was administered to 10 female office workers, and its internal consistency was determined by computing the rank-order correlations between the odd and even items, the resulting *rho* being .48 (corrected by Spearman-Brown). Brayfield and Rothe concluded that this internal consistency coefficient was too low and that perhaps the scaling and scoring procedures for the scale should be changed. Accordingly, they decided to use Likert-type scales, ranging from 1 to 5, for responding to the 18 items. The final version of the IJS, with this modification, is reproduced in Table 11-3. For a group of 231 female office employees the corrected odd-even inter-

[4] See this article for references to articles on the TBI.

Table 11-3. The Index of Job Satisfaction *(From Brayfield & Rothe, 1951, p. 309)*

Some jobs are more interesting and satisfying than others. We want to know how people feel about different jobs. This blank contains eighteen statements about jobs. You are to cross out the phrase below each statement which best describes how you feel about your present job. There are no right or wrong answers. We should like your honest opinion on each one of the statements. Work out the sample item numbered (0).

0. There are some conditions concerning my job that could be improved.
   STRONGLY AGREE AGREE UNDECIDED DISAGREE STRONGLY DISAGREE
1. My job is like a hobby to me.
   STRONGLY AGREE AGREE UNDECIDED DISAGREE STRONGLY DISAGREE
2. My job is usually interesting enough to keep me from getting bored.
   STRONGLY AGREE AGREE UNDECIDED DISAGREE STRONGLY DISAGREE
3. It seems that my friends are more interested in their jobs.
   STRONGLY AGREE AGREE UNDECIDED DISAGREE STRONGLY DISAGREE
4. I consider my job rather unpleasant.
   STRONGLY AGREE AGREE UNDECIDED DISAGREE STRONGLY DISAGREE
5. I enjoy my work more than my leisure time.
   STRONGLY AGREE AGREE UNDECIDED DISAGREE STRONGLY DISAGREE
6. I am often bored with my job.
   STRONGLY AGREE AGREE UNDECIDED DISAGREE STRONGLY DISAGREE
7. I feel fairly well satisfied with my present job.
   STRONGLY AGREE AGREE UNDECIDED DISAGREE STRONGLY DISAGREE
8. Most of the time I have to force myself to go to work.
   STRONGLY AGREE AGREE UNDECIDED DISAGREE STRONGLY DISAGREE
9. I am satisfied with my job for the time being.
   STRONGLY AGREE AGREE UNDECIDED DISAGREE STRONGLY DISAGREE
10. I feel that my job is no more interesting than others I could get.
    STRONGLY AGREE AGREE UNDECIDED DISAGREE STRONGLY DISAGREE
11. I definitely dislike my work.
    STRONGLY AGREE AGREE UNDECIDED DISAGREE STRONGLY DISAGREE
12. I feel that I am happier in my work than most other people.
    STRONGLY AGREE AGREE UNDECIDED DISAGREE STRONGLY DISAGREE
13. Most days I am enthusiastic about my work.
    STRONGLY AGREE AGREE UNDECIDED DISAGREE STRONGLY DISAGREE
14. Each day of work seems like it will never end.
    STRONGLY AGREE AGREE UNDECIDED DISAGREE STRONGLY DISAGREE
15. I like my job better than the average worker does.
    STRONGLY AGREE AGREE UNDECIDED DISAGREE STRONGLY DISAGREE
16. My job is pretty uninteresting.
    STRONGLY AGREE AGREE UNDECIDED DISAGREE STRONGLY DISAGREE
17. I find real enjoyment in my work.
    STRONGLY AGREE AGREE UNDECIDED DISAGREE STRONGLY DISAGREE
18. I am disappointed that I ever took this job.
    STRONGLY AGREE AGREE UNDECIDED DISAGREE STRONGLY DISAGREE

nal consistency estimate of this scale was .87. In a study of the validity of the IJS, it was found that its total score differentiated significantly between adult students in a night personnel psychology class who were employed in personnel and nonpersonnel jobs. Those in the former were more satisfied, presumably because they were engaged in occupations consistent with their manifest interest in learning more about personnel psychology. The IJS was also correlated with the JSB in this group, and the *r* was .92.

The SRA Employee Inventory (EI).[5] Although the EI is basically a measure of job attitudes, it does yield a total score, and there is some evidence (see "Dimensions" to follow) that its items load on a general satisfaction factor; consequently, it will be briefly described here. It consists of 78 items divided into 15 scales, one of which elicits reactions to the inventory. The various attitudinal scales and illustrative items are as follows:

1. *Job demands:* "My job is often dull and monotonous."
2. *Working conditions:* "I have the right equipment to do my work."
3. *Pay:* "I'm paid fairly as compared with other employees."
4. *Employee benefits:* "Compared with other companies, employee benefits here are good."
5. *Friendliness and cooperation of fellow employees:* "The people I work with are very friendly."
6. *Supervisor-employee interpersonal relations:* "My boss ought to be friendlier toward employees."
7. *Confidence in management:* "Management ignores our suggestions and complaints."
8. *Technical competence of supervision:* "My boss has the work well organized."
9. *Effectiveness of administration:* "Management fails to give clear-cut orders and instructions."
10. *Adequacy of communication:* "You can say what you think around here."
11. *Security of job and work relations:* "You can get fired around here without much cause."
12. *Status and recognition:* "Sometimes I feel that my job counts for very little in this organization."
13. *Identification with the company:* "I really feel a part of this organization."

[5] Now called the SRA Attitude Surveys, which include not only the original 78 items developed by the Industrial Relations Center of the University of Chicago but also 21 additional items on the company and 31 items on personnel.

14. *Opportunity for growth and advancement:* "I can learn a great deal on my present job."

The number of items per scale varies from two to eight, and, as can be seen from these samples, the items express both positive and negative attitudes toward the job. The worker responds to the items by marking boxes labeled "Agree," "?," and "Disagree" on a rudimentary Likert-type scale.

This response format and scoring system were selected on the basis of a study conducted by Baehr (1953) of a preliminary 64-item form of the EI. She found that unweighted, 3-point scales, with items categorized according to specific job aspects, i.e., job demands, working conditions, etc., yielded score profiles which were essentially the same as those produced by the possible combinations of inventories with categorized or randomized items, 3- or 5-point scales, and weighted or unweighted response percentages, e.g., a weighted 5-point scale with randomized items. In another study, Ash (1954) has reported additional data on the psychometric characteristics of the EI. He obtained internal consistency coefficients for the 14 job-attitude categories which ranged from .60 to .84, with a median of .68; for the total score, the estimate was .96. Baehr (1954) has also reported test-retest reliabilities for an interval of 1 week, the coefficients for two groups of workers ranging from .60 to .80. With respect to the validity of the EI, Ash (1954, pp. 337–338) found that it was related to some variables but not to others:

> Management, supervisory and union estimates of employee morale, as reflected in the kinds of items included in the Inventory, did not agree very closely with Inventory scores based on employee responses.
>
> The picture of employee morale that is obtained from the Inventory agreed in only a limited way with what a sample of employees said in interviews. The main emphases seem to be similar in both, however.
>
> The attitudes of people towards their jobs did not seem to be correlated to a significant extent with personal factors such as age, sex, marital and dependency status, intelligence or similar factors. . . .
>
> Employee attitudes were related to some extent to measures of job performance, but the data involved were too limited to afford firm conclusions.

Data from factor analyses of the EI are not included here, but are discussed at length in the next section.

The Cornell Job Descriptive Index (JDI). One of the most comprehensive programs of research on the measurement of satisfaction, the only possible exception being Hoppock's (1935b) pioneer studies, was initiated by Smith, P. C. (1963) and others at Cornell University during the early 1960s. The primary purpose of this project was to construct a measure of satisfaction which would be valid according to the "multi-trait–multi-method" model for test development proposed by Campbell, D. T., and Fiske (1959). More specifically, two criteria had to be met: (1) several different aspects of satisfaction with the job, i.e., pay, supervision, promotion, had to be identified (discriminant validity), and (2) several different measures of these areas of satisfaction had to agree in what they measured (convergent validity). In other words, these criteria would be satisfied, if in a cluster or factor analysis, two or more clusters or factors were identified *and* measures of the same variables clustered together or loaded on the same factor.

In general, the findings of a number of studies supported both the discriminant and convergent validity of the instruments which Smith and her associates used to assess satisfaction (Kendall, Smith, Hulin, & Locke, 1963; Locke, Smith, Kendall, Hulin, & Miller, 1964). Among these measures was the Job Descriptive Index (JDI), which was especially devised for the project in order to overcome some of the shortcomings of previous interview, rating scale, and other methods (Smith, P. C., 1963). In its final form, after its having been developed through a series of item analyses and scoring procedures (Locke, Smith, Hulin, & Kendall, 1963), the JDI consists of 72 items divided into five scales which measure satisfaction with: work, pay, promotions, supervision, and people. A total score can also be computed from the unweighted average of the scale scores. The latter are based upon the worker's responses of "Yes," "?," and "No" to such job-descriptive adjectives and phrases as "*Work:* dull, varied, tense" and "*Pay:* poor, barely enough, good."

The internal consistency coefficients of the JDI scales, corrected by Spearman-Brown, were all in the .80s for a sample of 80 male electronics workers (Locke et al., 1963). A study of the effects of "scale order" upon JDI scores produced negative findings, indicating that it evidently does not make any difference which scale is presented first in administering the questionnaire. Similarly, response sets, as measured by the number of "Yes's" checked on the Holland Vocational Preference Inventory, do not appear to affect scores on the JDI, since "Partialling out response set [from the VPI] had no significant effect on the convergent validities of the [JDI] scales as determined by their correlations with interview ratings" (Locke et al., 1963, p. 7). The intercorrelations of the JDI scales for several different samples range from .10 to .70, with most of the *r*'s in the .30s and .40s. They appear to have some variance in common, as factor analyses have demonstrated, but they also clearly measure unique aspects of satisfaction with the job.

Other Measures of Vocational Satisfaction. In addition to those measures of satisfaction already mentioned, a number of other techniques have been tried out to elicit a worker's reactions to his job. Some of these might be more accurately classified as measures of job attitudes rather than vocational satisfaction, but most of them either yield a total score, which is indicative of overall satisfaction, or they load on a general satisfaction factor. One of these is a *questionnaire* called the Triple Audit of Industrial Relations, which is comprised of 76 items scored for such variables as working conditions, compensation, and co-workers (Carlson, Dawis, England, & Lofquist, 1962). Another paper-and-pencil inventory, which is quite similar, consisting of 99 statements about physical and mental exertion, relations with employer, interest in, liking for, and emotional involvement in the job, etc., has been constructed by Johnson, G. H. (1955). A third measure of this type, but more similar to the Hoppock JSB than the others, is the Job-Satisfaction Scale developed by Bullock (1952). The *incomplete-sentences* technique has been used by Friesen (1952) to measure attitude toward working situation, attitude toward work, attitude toward self, and attitude toward leisure. Probably the most novel approach to the measurement of satisfaction is one which was conceived by the Employee Relations Staff of General Motors Corporation and called My Job Contest (Evans & Laseau, 1950). Prizes were given for the best letter written by a worker on the topic, "My Job and Why I Like It," and analyses were made of a host of variables, such as fair treatment, building a good job, and seniority, which were identified as significant in a worker's job satisfaction. Finally, *interviews* have been employed by Heron (1952a; 1954) and Morse (1953) to survey workers' satisfaction with their jobs, and Marriott and Denerley (1955a; 1955b) have conducted methodological studies of the usefulness of the interview for this purpose.

Comment. If one point is clear from this review of measures of vocational satisfaction, it is that no one instrument or technique is sufficient to assess an individual's attitudes and feelings about his work. Or, put somewhat differently, certain measures are better for some purposes than are others. Still, some choice does exist between similar measures. The Hoppock JSB is preferable to the Brayfield-Rothe IJS for the assessment of *vocational* satisfaction, not only because it is conceptually more relevant, but also because it is more reliable and more heavily researched, i.e., has been shown to correlate with more independently defined variables. The JSB might also be preferred to all the summation instruments, if individual differences in the way job aspects are weighted in arriving at an overall estimate of satisfaction is of concern. In general, however, the Kerr TBI, the SRA EI, and the Cornell JDI would seem to be more appropriate for the measurement of the components of job satisfaction. These inventories provide both part and total scores which can be analyzed either separately or together. Of these three, the JDI would appear to have the most promise as the "measure of job satisfaction of the future" because of its sophisticated conceptualization and its "discriminant and convergent" validity. Furthermore, it covers more aspects of the job and has more general applicability than the TBI, and its scales are generally more internally consistent than those of the EI. The less objective techniques—incomplete sentences, the My Job Contest, and the interview—are good for survey research, but difficult to use in theoretical or applied research, where variables must be quantified.

The Dimensions of Vocational Satisfaction

There are many unanswered questions about what the dimensions of vocational satisfaction are—more than with either vocational motivation or vocational success—and most of these involve unresolved issues in the application and interpretation of factor-analytic methods. For many years controversy has raged over such problems as what values to use in the diagonal of the intercorrelation matrix which is to be factor-analyzed and whether "second order" or general factors should be extracted during the rotations (Wolfle, 1940). The factor analyses of vocational satisfaction which we shall review in this section reflect these methodological problems, but do not offer any solutions to them. Thus, their findings are open to alternative interpretations, and the best we can do in drawing conclusions from them is to present a point of view which best seems to "fit" not only the data from the factor analyses, but also observations of workers' reactions to their vocations. To highlight the effects of methodology upon interpreation, a series of factor analyses of the SRA Employee Inventory are summarized first, and then several studies with other instruments are discussed, from which some implications for conducting future research on the dimensions of vocational satisfaction are derived.

Factor Analyses of the SRA Employee Inventory. Five factor analyses of this instrument have been reported. The first two were independent, but complementary, studies conducted by Baehr (1954) and Ash (1954). The third was a "re-rotation" of the Baehr and Ash data by Wherry (1954). The fourth, performed on inter-item rather than interscale matrices, was done by Dabas (1958). And, the fifth was a reanalysis and comparison of all the studies by Wherry (1958):

1. Baehr (1954) ran two factor analyses of the SRA Employee Inventory *scales*, one on a group of 134 Subjects from predominantly white-collar jobs and one on a sample of 163 factory and production workers. Test-retest reliability coefficients were used for the diagonal cell entries in the intercorrelation matrices, which were factor-analyzed by the complete centroid method. From the rotated factor solutions, four factors emerged which were common to both samples: Immediate Supervision, Job Satisfaction, Integration in the Organization, and Friendliness and Cooperation of Fellow Employees. In addi-

tion, there were seven other factors which were unique to one group or the other. Although Baehr's factor matrix was oblique, she did not extract a "second order" or general factor.

2. Ash (1954) administered the SRA Employee Inventory to 142 Subjects, mainly in production or maintenance jobs (see foregoing section), and factor-analyzed its scales along with those of the Thurstone Temperament Schedule and the total score from the Brayfield-Rothe IJS. Using the complete centroid method, he rotated to an *oblique* simple structure and obtained six interpretable factors: Personality Integration, Job Rewards, Management Effectiveness, Immediate Supervision, General Job Satisfaction, and a bipolar factor with negative loadings on the Thurstone Emotional Stability scale and SRA Friendliness and Cooperation of Fellow-Employees scale and with positive loadings on the Thurstone Active and Reflective scales. No "second order" or general factor was identified.

3. Wherry (1954) objected to Baehr's use of reliabilities rather than communalities in the diagonals of her factor analysis and to the oblique rotations employed by both Baehr and Ash; consequently, he "re-rotated" the data from these studies with communalities as the diagonal entries and solved for an orthogonal simple structure. He found that a "second order" or general factor of overall job satisfaction could be posited which had significant loadings on all 14 scales of the SRA EI as well as a high loading (.55) on the Brayfield-Rothe IJS. In addition, he identified four group factors: Working Conditions and Requirements, Financial Rewards, Immediate Supervision, and Effective Management and Administration.

4. Dabas (1958) criticized the use of the SRA scales rather than items as the variables in the Baehr, Ash, and Wherry factor analyses, because a scale might load on a factor as a result of only one or two item interrelationships and hence lead to the erroneous conclusion that the entire scale represented a factor. Accordingly, he factor-analyzed the items of the SRA EI for a group of 996 Subjects in a variety of jobs throughout the country. It should be noted, however, that he did *not* compute the actual inter-item correlations. Rather, using the Wherry-Winer (1952) method for factoring large numbers of items, which necessitates that the items be categorized or grouped in some way, he correlated each item with each SRA scale. From these data, he derived a general job satisfaction factor; five "sub-general" factors, which he named Over-all Opinion of Working Conditions, General Satisfaction with Financial Reward for Effort, Over-all Confidence in Management, Over-all Opinion about Immediate Supervisor, and Over-all Satisfaction with Self-Development; and seven group factors, which he called Work Load, Environmental Setting, Fringe Benefits, General Satisfaction with Fellow Workers, Belief in Justice and Interest of Management, and General Satisfaction with Personnel Actions.

5. Finally, Wherry (1958) has compared the results of the several factor

analyses, using a technique which yields "invariance" values for the factors, in order to determine their generality. He concluded that the various studies agree in identifying a general Job Satisfaction factor and five group factors: Working Conditions, Financial Reward, Supervision, Management, and Personal Development. These factors and their interrelationships are represented graphically in Figure 11-1, where the values on the lines are the average factor loadings of the lower on the higher-order factors and the values in the boxes are the average specific loadings of the factors.

Whether the diagram in Figure 11-1 accurately represents the factorial structure of vocational satisfaction depends, in part at least, upon the procedures which are followed in a factor analysis. In an exchange of papers on the factor analyses of the SRA Employee Inventory, Baehr (1956) and Wherry (1956) have argued about the appropriate procedures for investigating the dimensions of vocational satisfaction. As Baehr (1956, p. 81) points out, "the central issue of the dispute concerns the use of oblique as opposed to orthogonal factors in the final rotated matrix, which is the end point of the calculations in the factorial solution and the beginning of the interpretation of the factors." She contends that, if the purpose of a study is to condense test data, then orthogonal factors should be sought; if it is to identify "underlying functional unities" which determine test performance, however, then oblique factors may best represent the data. She maintains that the values entered in the diagonal cells of the intercorrelation matrix should also be determined by the objectives of an investigation:

> If the purpose is to account for the complete variance of each test, then unity should be recorded in the diagonal cells. When the purpose of the study is limited to the study of the common factors (i.e., when the factor matrix is intended to account only for the common-factor variance of the tests in the battery), then the communality is recorded in the diagonal cells. When the purpose of the analysis is to account for both the common and the specific factor variance then the reliability (which represents the sum of the common and specific variance) is recorded in the diagonal cells [Baehr, 1956, p. 86].

In short, then, Baehr's position is that decisions about orthogonal versus oblique factors and diagonal cell entries should be made in terms of the purposes of the factor analysis.

Wherry (1956, p. 98) agrees with Baehr that the "main issue is whether or not there is a large general factor which explains a large part of the variance of the original [SRA Employee Inventory] sub-tests," but he reaches the opposite conclusion that such a factor is necessary to fit the data in a psychologically meaningful way. He argues that he did not "introduce" the general factor into his rerotation of the Baehr and Ash matrices, but that it was there

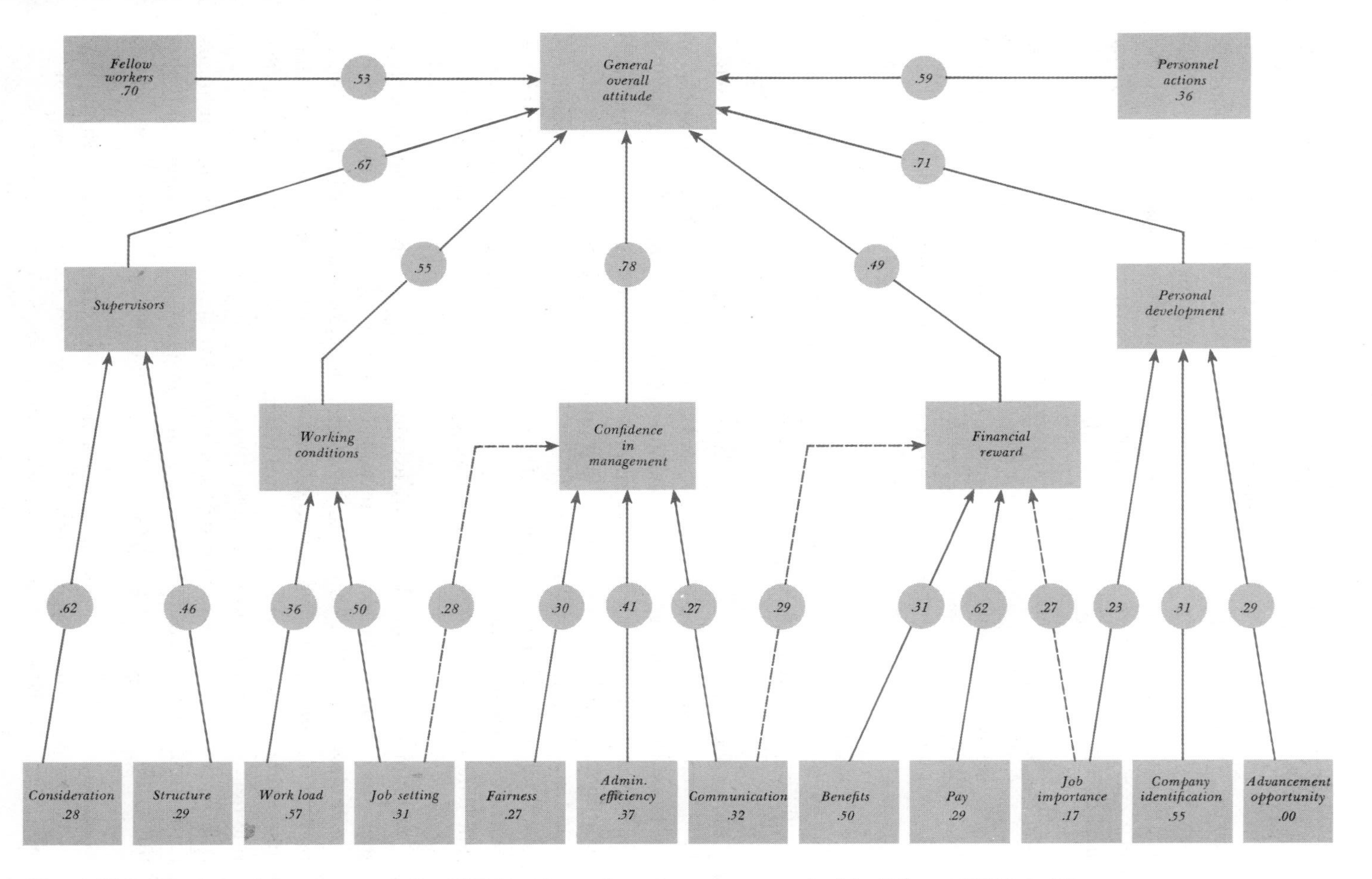

***Figure 11-1. The factorial structure of the SRA Employee Inventory as summarized by Wherry** (1958, p. 86).*

and that he "did not choose to ignore" it. What Wherry is saying is that, following the criterion of simple structure, he found four *oblique* factors, from which he extracted the second-order factor by factoring the primary reference vectors. In other words, with the exception of using reliabilities in the diagonals, Wherry conducted exactly the same initial analysis as Baehr, but he supplemented it with a further analysis of the relationships among the primaries. With respect to the values in the diagonal cells of the correlation matrix, Wherry (1956, p. 97) reasons as follows:

> Reliability coefficients, unlike the inter-correlations, require certain assumptions or procedures I would not want to use in any main study. Test-retest coefficients involve quotidian variability apt to be high in morale or interest studies. Internal consistency estimates assume a single factor which is contrary to the assumption of multiple factors which led to the study. Hence I would not trust reliability coefficients.

He adds that, if specific variance is assumed for each test, then reliabilities would be too high to use for the diagonal values.

Other Studies. Of the other factor analyses of vocational satisfaction which have been located, one directly supports Wherry's contentions (Clarke & Grant, 1961), two can be interpreted as favorable (Schreiber, Smith, & Harrell, 1952; Carlson et al., 1962),[6] one is indeterminate (Friedlander, 1963), and one tends to support Baehr's position (Twery, Schmid, & Wrigley, 1958):

1. Using the Wherry-Winer method, Clarke and Grant (1961) found evidence for a "hierarchical" model of vocational satisfaction, with a general-satisfaction factor, two or more subgeneral factors, and several group factors. The data they report are only illustrative, however, and they do not name or interpret the factors.

2. From the intercorrelations of five job satisfaction scales—adjustment to job, supervision, participation-expression, working conditions, and incentives —Schreiber et al. (1952) obtained one factor of "wide scope," which had loadings on all but one of the variables and which they named Job Satisfaction, and another factor more restricted in nature, which was comprised of information items and which they called Knowledge of Employee Benefits.

3. Carlson et al. (1962) also factor-analyzed five scales—working conditions, supervision, compensation, co-workers, and general job satisfaction—but they did so for each of eight groups of workers classified as "control" or "handi-

[6] From two communality cluster analyses of attitude items, Harrison (1960; 1961) has concluded that his results support Wherry's analysis of the SRA Employee Inventory, but the method he used did not provide for the extraction of a general factor.

capped," "blue-collar" or "white-collar," and "skilled" or "non-skilled." In five of the eight groups, they identified two factors, and in all but one of these the general job satisfaction scale loaded significantly on both factors.

4. In Friedlander's (1963) study, three factors—Social and Technical Environment, Intrinsic Self-Actualizing Work Aspects, and Recognition through Advancement—emerged from his analysis of 17 "source of satisfaction" items, and there were no differences in general job satisfaction among groups of Subjects which were high on each factor and satisfied with it. This does not mean, however, that the two variables, i.e., overall satisfaction with the job and satisfaction with its various components, are necessarily related.

5. Twery et al. (1958) found a "General Attitude to Job" factor, using both unities and communalities as diagonal cell entries, which appeared to be more of a group than a general factor, although they note that it was "factorially complex," with appreciable loadings on at least one other factor.

Comment. There are two questions which need to be answered about the dimensions of vocational satisfaction: (1) How many dimensions are there and (2) what are they? As we have seen from the results of factor analyses of the SRA EI and other measures of vocational satisfaction, the answer to the first question is far from clear-cut. Depending upon the method of factor analysis which is used and the assumptions which are made in rotating to a final solution, the factorial structure of vocational satisfaction would appear to be made up of either (1) group factors or (2) group factors *plus* a second-order general factor. The decision between these alternatives must ultimately be made in terms of the relationships of the two models to other, independently defined, variables not within the "closed system" of factor analysis. Theoretically, it would seem that the "hierarchical" model might have greater potential heuristic value, since it is difficult to conceive of highly satisfied or dissatisfied workers as being differentially satisfied with the various aspects of their vocations. But it may be that those of moderate overall job satisfaction *are* more satisfied with certain features of their work than with others.

The answer to the second question also remains to be resolved, since, aside from the general job satisfaction factor which has emerged from the studies already mentioned, there is no consistent pattern of substantive dimensions which has been firmly established. Friedlander (1963) has suggested that his factors correspond most closely to Ginzberg et al.'s (1951) intrinsic, concomitant, and extrinsic sources of vocational satisfaction, and the findings on the SRA EI, as summarized by Wherry (1958), would roughly fit into such a conceptual schema; but an equally plausible hypothesis is that the dimensions will vary from one occupation to another, as functions of different situational determinants and work requirements (Smith, P. C., 1963). Again, additional research is indicated in order to clarify the nature of the dimensions of vocational satisfaction.

STUDIES OF VOCATIONAL SATISFACTION

To provide an historical perspective on the studies which have been conducted on vocational satisfaction, we shall begin this review of research with a summary of a classic study that still has considerable import for work in this area. We shall then consider, in some detail, two more recent studies which have set the stage for conceptualizations and investigations of vocational satisfaction since the mid-1950s. And, finally, we shall present both an overview of 35 years of research on vocational satisfaction and a review of findings on selected problems which have been intensively studied in the past or which suggest new lines of inquiry for the future.

A Classic Study

The pioneer research on vocational satisfaction which has been the touchstone for all later studies of this phenomenon was conducted by Hoppock (1935b) in the early 1930s and reported in his classic work, *Job Satisfaction,* which was published under the sponsorship of the National Occupational Conference in the midst of the Depression.[7] It is notable, if not surprising, that Hoppock launched a study of vocational satisfaction during this period when, for most workers, the major concern of the day was not whether they liked their jobs, but rather whether they could find jobs. The extent to which unemployment introduced bias into Hoppock's findings, however, was probably negligible, as the accumulated research on the incidence of dissatisfaction in the labor force since 1935 has brought out. The percentage of dissatisfied workers has always been relatively low and has changed very little in the past 30 years (see discussion to follow). In this regard, then, as in several others, we can have considerable confidence in Hoppock's results. Although his methodology and statistical analyses do not meet modern standards, they were, nevertheless, fairly sophisticated, and they yielded what have proved to be stable (replicable) data on vocational satisfaction. We shall now summarize what Hoppock found from the three studies which he conducted, one on employed and unemployed adults, a second on satisfied and dissatisfied teachers, and a third on the extent of vocational dissatisfaction in an entire community.

Employed and Unemployed Adults. This particular study was the least rigorous one in the series and is more in the nature of a case study than it is an empirical investigation. What Hoppock did was to interview 40 employed

[7] See also Hoppock (1935a; 1937).

and 40 unemployed adults according to a semistructured schedule of questions which included the following: "What are the things about your work that you like, that cause you to feel partly or entirely satisfied with it?"; "Have you ever thought seriously about changing your present job?"; and, "Is there any relation between your leisure activity and your interest in your job?" He concluded that:

> From the results of these interviews no conclusions have been drawn except that what happened in these cases can happen; but the comments of the subjects suggested that, among the factors related to job satisfaction, there may be found the following: relative status of the individual within the social and economic group with which he identifies himself, relations with superior and associates on the job, nature of the work, earnings, hours of work, opportunities for advancement, variety, freedom from close supervision, visible results, the satisfaction of doing good work; opportunities for service to others, environment, freedom to live where one chooses, responsibility, vacations, excitement, opportunity for self-expression, competition, religion, opportunity for or necessity of traveling, fatigue, appreciation or criticism, security, and ability to adjust oneself to unpleasant circumstance [Hoppock, 1935b, pp. 70 71].

If we were to draw a general conclusion from this statement, it most likely would be that the determinants of vocational satisfaction are *multiple*. It should be remembered, however, that the data for this conclusion are impressionistic, *not* empirical, and that it should be qualified accordingly.

Satisfied and Dissatisfied Teachers. In contrast to the first study, all the Subjects in this one were employed, but they did differ from each other in the extent to which they were satisfied with their vocations. Hoppock administered the first form of his blank to 500 teachers in and around the metropolitan New York area and then selected the 100 most and 100 least satisfied for purposes of comparison on their job attitudes. As mentioned previously, only a small percentage (10 percent) of this sample actually indicated that they disliked or were dissatisfied with their work; consequently, the "dissatisfied" group is more accurately described as the "less satisfied" group. There were 215 job attitude items to which each Subject responded and on which the two groups were compared. Again, in contrast to the first study, Hoppock reports the raw data and tests for differences between percentages of response for each of the 215 items.

He summarized his findings as follows (Hoppock, 1935b, pp. 26–40):

> 1. The satisfied showed fewer indications of emotional maladjustment.

2. The satisfied were more religious.
3. The satisfied enjoyed better human relationships with superior and associates.
4. More of the satisfied were teaching in cities larger than 10,000 population.
5. The satisfied earned about the same as the dissatisfied.
6. The satisfied *felt* more successful.
7. Familial relationships and social status were more favorable among the satisfied.
8. More of the satisfied actively "selected" their vocations rather than getting into them by "chance."
9. No teacher "disliked" children, and four-fifths of the dissatisfied found their work "interesting."
10. The dissatisfied reported monotony and fatigue more often.
11. The satisfied were 7.5 years older.

With the possible exception of the fourth, fifth, and ninth findings, it might be concluded that the major dimension along which the satisfied and dissatisfied were differentiated was *general adjustment status*. The former were better adjusted emotionally, had better interpersonal relationships, felt more successful, had more satisfactory relationships with their parents, and were less subject to monotony and fatigue. Taken together, these characteristics would seem to indicate better overall adjustment and would jibe with Fisher and Hanna's (1931) hypothesis, already mentioned, that vocational dissatisfaction and emotional maladjustment are related.

Community Survey of Vocational Satisfaction. In what must have been the first survey of its kind, Hoppock conducted a door-to-door census of vocational satisfaction among all the inhabitants of New Hope, Pennsylvania, during the summer of 1933. Each of the 351 gainfully employed adults out of a total population of 1,113 (in 1930) was asked to fill out a Job Satisfaction Blank, and 309, or approximately 88 percent, complied. Most of the Subjects were native-born whites (92 percent), but their jobs cut across the occupational hierarchy, so that both high and low skill levels were represented in the sample. In only this respect, however, can the sample be considered as representative of the labor force in general. What Hoppock found from the survey was that most workers were satisfied with their vocations: 66 percent reported "high" satisfaction, 12 percent indicated they were "indifferent," and only 22 percent were "dissatisfied." There was a tendency for the less skilled workers to be more dissatisfied, and there was a trend for the older workers to be more satisfied. From these findings, Hoppock (1935b, p. 12) concluded that "most persons, in some hit-or-miss manner, succeed eventually in effecting job adjustments which are reasonably harmonious with their abilities, ambitions, and affections." This seems to be an overinterpretation of the data, however, since there were no measures of "abilities, ambitions, and affections" or indices of "harmonious job adjustments." A more accurate conclusion would be that, to the extent that vocational satisfaction is a component of vocational adjustment, it can be said that most workers (approximately two-thirds in this study) are adjusted to their vocations.

Recent Studies

Two other studies on vocational satisfaction which are of major proportions have been done since Hoppock completed his classic work in 1935.[8] Both of these investigations represent somewhat new departures in research on satisfaction, one being primarily concerned with the relationship of personality and adjustment to vocational satisfaction, although it also studied the associations of these variables with interests, and the other being an analysis of the extent to which vocational satisfaction and need satisfaction are related in work activities. The first study, conducted by Kates in 1950, has not led directly to any further research, but it has occupied a prominent place in some theoretical speculations about the role of personality factors in vocational satisfaction (e.g., Roe, 1956). In contrast, the second study, completed by Schaffer in 1953, has not only emerged as the precursor of a series of investigations on the occupation as a need satisfier (Blai, 1964; Froehlich & Wolins, 1960; Kuhlen, 1963; Ross & Zander, 1957), but it has also been frequently cited in theoretical statements on vocational satisfaction (e.g., Katzell, 1964). The reviews of these studies which follow summarize their (1) hypotheses, (2) procedures, (3) results, and (4) conclusions, along with a critical comment on the inferences which can be drawn from them. In addition, a second study by Kates has been included here rather than in the next section, because its problem and methodology are quite similar to those in his first study, despite differences between the occupational groups investigated.

Kates's Studies. The more comprehensive study of the two conducted by Kates (1950a, pp. 2–3) was designed to test the following hypotheses on the relationships among (1) Rorschach personality and adjustment variables, (2)

[8] A study which might have been included in this section is Reynolds and Shister's (1949) investigation of the relationship of job satisfaction to labor mobility. It was not reviewed in detail for several reasons: It is a nontechnical report, written for the layman, and consequently it presents little data for evaluation; it cuts across many topics, such as "The Worker's Choice of a Job" and "Movement up the Occupational Ladder," which span most of the work years in vocational development; and it is essentially nonpsychological in its approach and interpretations.

inventoried interests, and (3) vocational satisfaction in a group of clerical workers:

1. Job satisfaction in clerical work bears a significant positive relationship to scores on the clerical scale of the Strong Vocational Interest Blank. Those clerks who possess interests similar to those of successful office workers tend to be more satisfied.
2. Job satisfaction in clerical work is not related to Rorschach signs of maladjustment. The degree of job satisfaction of clerical workers is independent of the number of Rorschach signs of maladjustment.
3. The work dissatisfaction of routine clerical workers who possess the interests of successful office workers is not related to the number of Rorschach signs of maladjustment.
4. Certain Rorschach responses, evidenced in the records of routine clerical workers, are significantly associated with their possession of vocational interests similar to those of successful office workers.

These hypotheses were deduced from observations made by several different theorists on the interrelationships of personality, interest, and satisfaction (e.g., Fisher & Hanna, 1931; Schaffer, 1936; Young, 1940).

To test the hypotheses he had formulated, Kates chose the Rorschach, the SVIB, and the Hoppock blank to measure personality, interest, and satisfaction, respectively. The Subjects were 100 male routine clerical workers employed by a governmental agency. Their mean age was 29.7 years; their mean educational level was 12.1 years of schooling; and their salaries ranged from $2,300 to $2,850 per annum at the time of the study. All Subjects had been on their jobs for a period of at least 6 months. Their duties and tasks varied from one job to another, but in general they involved processing forms, issuing authorizations for supplies, maintaining personnel records, typing, and filing. The primary statistical procedure employed in the analyses of data was zero-order correlation; it was supplemented by chi-square and analysis of variance tests, when extreme groups were compared, and by multiple correlation, when more than one variable was used to predict another.

Because two of the hypotheses stated that *no relationships* would obtain between adjustment and vocational satisfaction, the results of Kates's study appear to be more positive than they actually are. There was a low positive correlation of .21 between the SVIB clerical scale and the JSB, which was significant at the .05 level, but this relationship could not be established when Subjects were cross-classified according to whether they had high or low letter ratings on clerical interest and whether they were "dissatisfied," "indifferent," or "satisfied" with respect to their jobs. The χ^2 value for this analysis was 2.89, which was not significant at the .05 level. Similarly, the relationships of vocational satisfaction to the two measures of adjustment were nonsignificant: the Hoppock blank correlated −.16 with the Davidson List of Signs and .02 with the Munroe Inspection Technique. A supplementary analysis of variance of categorized Hoppock and Munroe scores was also negative, as was a correlational analysis of the relationship of the Hoppock to scoring determinants on the Munroe list. The only significant association which was found was between adjustment and interest. The SVIB clerical scores correlated −.54 with the Davidson, which, because of the way the latter is keyed, means that Subjects with interests similar to office workers were more maladjusted, and .33 with the Munroe, which indicates the same type of relationship. Additional analyses of clerical interest in relation to specific Munroe scoring categories revealed that the former is related to CF:FC, FC, FM:M, M, and Popular Responses, the multiple R being .72 (.70 when corrected for shrinkage). Thus, there seems to be a substantial relationship between vocational interests and adjustment-personality, but not between these variables and vocational satisfaction.

These findings were not replicated, however, in Kates's (1950b) second study, in which the Subjects were 25 New York City policemen. Using essentially the same measuring instruments and statistical analyses, Kates obtained an r of .47 between the Hoppock blank and the Munroe Inspection Technique total score. Furthermore, the Hoppock blank was correlated −.51 with Popular Responses and .52 with Total Color in the Munroe scoring categories. These r's were significant at only the .05 level, but they do indicate the possibility of relationships among these variables. Additional findings in this study were: an r of −.51 between the Hoppock blank and the Occupational Level score of the SVIB, which was significant at the .01 level; an r of .35 between the Hoppock blank and the SVIB policeman interest scale, which was nonsignificant; and an r of .19 between the latter measure and the Munroe total score, which was also nonsignificant. In short, then, satisfaction with police work was found to be positively related to maladjustment, i.e., the more satisfied policemen were more maladjusted, and it was found to be negatively associated with level of occupational interest, i.e., the more satisfied had interests on the lower occupational levels.

Comment. Kates's studies represent a bold attempt to investigate the interest and personality factors which may play an important part in vocational satisfaction, but his findings must be interpreted with caution. Despite its widespread use, the Rorschach still has questionable validity as a personality assessment device (Zubin, Eron, & Schumer, 1965), and only scant data are available on the meaning of the Davidson and Munroe adjustment scores. It can legitimately be asked: How well do they correlate with other indexes of adjustment status? Also, in the second study the N was extremely small for the statistical procedures used, and thus little confidence can be had in the stability of the *r*'s which were reported. Correlation coefficients based on *N*'s less than 100 often fluctuate greatly when they are replicated. These are considerations of measurement and methodology, and, although they are important, they are not as critical as the theoretical shortcomings of Kates's analysis of vocational satisfaction. He does not explicate the logical "links" which presumably exist among the variables he studied. More specifically, why select these variables to intercorrelate unless there is some theoretical reason for doing so? And why predict that some of them, e.g., satisfaction and maladjustment, will *not* intercorrelate? Much more conceptual work must be done before these questions can be answered adequately. Perhaps it is for this reason that Kates's studies have not led to further research on a problem which is central to a comprehensive understanding of vocational satisfaction.

Schaffer's Study. In contrast to Kates, Schaffer (1953) attempted to link his study of vocational satisfaction to a more general theory of behavior or personality. He took as his conceptual starting point Hendrick's (1943b, p. 311) *instinct to master:* "Work is not primarily motivated by sexual need or associated aggression, but by the need for efficient use of the muscular and intellectual tools, regardless of what secondary needs—self-preservative, aggressive, or sexual—a work performance may also satisfy."[9] In order to deduce a testable hypothesis from this principle, Schaffer (1953, p. 2) restated it as a proposition which stipulates that:

> For any individual in any given situation the amount of tension or dissatisfaction generated is determined by (*a*) the strength of his needs or drives, and (*b*) the extent to which he can perceive and utilize opportunities in the situation for the satisfaction of those needs.

This proposition led, then, to the following hypothesis, which was the central one of Schaffer's (1953, p. 3) study:

> Over-all job satisfaction will vary directly with the extent to which those needs of an individual which can be satisfied in a job are actually satisfied; the stronger the need, the more closely will job satisfaction depend on its fulfillment.

To test this hypothesis Schaffer constructed a questionnaire, consisting of five parts, which was designed to measure the three variables of interest: (1) job satisfaction, (2) need strength, and (3) need satisfaction. He used the already available Hoppock JSB to measure job satisfaction. To assess need

[9] See Chap. 8 for a discussion of Hendrick's concepts in relation to classical psychoanalytic theory.

strength he wrote 11 items, of varying types, for each of 12 needs in Murray's (1938) theory of personality, as shown in Table 11-4. Two kinds of scores were derived from this measure of need strength: (1) a total for each need based upon the sum of ratings on 5-point scales for the 11 items keyed to a given need and (2) the rank assigned to the totals for a given individual. In other words, the total score expresses differences between individuals on each need, whereas the rank reflects differences between needs for each individual. This distinction is a critical one for the evaluation of Schaffer's study, since he chose to use ranks in his analyses, but it can be argued that he should have utilized total scores (see "Comment" to follow). Finally, need satisfaction was measured by 24 items, two for each need, which Subjects rated on a 5-point continuum. Thus, for the statement "On my job when I do a piece of work I know that I'll get enough praise and recognition for it," which is keyed to the need for Approbation and Recognition, Subjects indicated their degree of satisfaction on the following scale: (1) *completely* satisfied, (2) *very well* satisfied, (3) *well* satisfied, (4) *slightly* satisfied, and (5) *not at all* satisfied.

The Subjects of the study were 72 employed males who were contacted through several different business concerns and vocational guidance agencies. The analyses were largely correlational in nature, although they were supplemented by some group-difference statistics. The major finding was that overall job satisfaction correlated .44 with need satisfaction (mean of the 12 need-satisfaction scores for each Subject), *irrespective of need strength.* When the latter was taken into account by multiplying need-strength ranks and corresponding need-satisfaction scores, the correlation went up to only .48, an increase which was not significant. However, when this same relationship was determined for successive numbers of needs in order of strength, i.e., for the strongest need, then the two strongest needs, three strongest needs, etc., through to all 12 needs, the *r*'s ranged from a high of .54 (the strongest need) to .44 (all 12 needs). Two additional findings, both of which bear upon the interpretation of Schaffer's study, should be mentioned. First, he intercorrelated the need-strength ranks across all Subjects, and out of 66 *r*'s, 41 had negative signs. Second, he related need strength to need satisfaction on the hypothesis that were they associated, "it would cast some doubt on the validity of the need-strength measures" (Schaffer, 1953, p. 15), but he found in two analyses that they were unrelated. On the basis of all his results, Schaffer (1953, p. 18) concluded that they were "consistent with the theoretical framework upon which the study was based."

Comment. Some question can be raised, however, about whether this conclusion can legitimately be drawn. First, it is apparent that by using ranks instead of total scores for the need-strength scales, Schaffer canceled out all

Table 11-4. The Need Strength Questionnaire *(After Schaffer, 1953, pp. 21–29)*

Need	*Sample item*
Recognition and approbation	"The nice thing about this job is that when you do something well you know that you're going to *get the credit for it.*"
Affection and interpersonal relationships	"When you work as closely as we do it sometimes is difficult to prevent arguments. But I wouldn't trade it for anything. I've been working with this bunch for quite a few years and I think that's about the best thing here—the fact that I have *so many close friends.*"
Mastery and achievement	"Yes, I sometimes work pretty hard even when I don't have to. But that's just so I can know I did a good job. It's important for me to do a *good job according to my own standards.*"
Dominance	"I like being supervisor. There is a good feeling of satisfaction that comes with being able to give the orders rather than having to take them."
Social welfare	"When I think of the number of people that are benefited as a direct result of my work I really feel swell. I wouldn't be doing anything else. *Doing work like this that gives me a chance to help those who need it is very important to me.*"
Self-expression	"I like to be myself. That may sound funny, but just think of all the times when you have to act in a way that's different from what you know you are. None of that for me. I always like to act just as I think of myself."
Socioeconomic status	"The reason I moved into this neighborhood is that here I can own one of the nicest houses on the block. If I moved into a higher-class community I would probably be living in a house that was far from being the nicest. I like the place I live in to be at least as nice as most around."

individual differences between Subjects on these measures. Since a rank of 1 for individual X on *n* Dominance may be equal to a total score of 32 on the scale which measures the strength of this need, whereas a rank of 1 for individual Y may be equal to a total score of 20, the ranks are not equivalent and cannot properly be used in correlational analyses. In effect, the ranks are *ipsative* scores, and, because they are, the intercorrelations of the need-strength scales are mostly (about two-thirds) negative (Guilford, 1952). It may also be for this same reason that Schaffer obtained no appreciable increase in the correlation between job satisfaction and need satisfaction when the latter was weighted by need-strength ranks.

Second, Schaffer does not make clear why he thought a relationship between need strength and need satisfaction would invalidate the measures of the former. It might be argued that, other things being equal, such as the opportunities for the Subjects to satisfy the 12 needs selected for this study in their work, a low to moderate *negative* correlation might be expected between need

Need	*Sample item*
Moral value scheme	"I get my ideas of right and wrong from the Bible. Others may get theirs from other sources maybe; but just so long as you do have some set of rules by which you live, you're O.K. *It's important to have your life governed by something 'higher' like that.*"
Dependence	"I refused the chance for promotion for just one reason. Here my work is laid out for me and *I know just what is expected of me.* I'm working under the supervision of one of the best guys in the outfit. I like working for a guy like that—I know I'll get all the help and advice I need."
Creativity and challenge	"It may give you an uncomfortable feeling to have to try something new on your own, something that hasn't been done before, *but I really like it.*"
Economic security	"What keeps me here at this place is that I know my job is permanent. I may not move ahead very rapidly or get such big salary increases, but I know that this company is here to stay and so is my job. That's what I need to feel comfortable—the knowledge that *my job is always going to be here for me.*"
Independence	"Well, it's just that I don't like anybody telling me how to do things. Sure I take advice and orders from my bosses, but I don't particularly like it. *I mostly like to do things on my own,* without having somebody telling me how."

strength and need satisfaction. In other words, given essentially equivalent opportunities for satisfying their needs in work, Subjects with many strong needs would most likely experience less need satisfaction than Subjects with fewer strong needs. Again, Schaffer's results may have been affected by his use of ranks rather than total scores for need strength. It would be interesting to find out what the correlation of need-strength *scores* with need-satisfaction scores is. In fact, it would be worthwhile to do the study over again, conducting all the analyses with scores rather than ranks. The results might be more positive and easier to interpret. As they stand now, it can only be concluded that they do *not* support Schaffer's hypothesis.

Other Studies

The number of studies on vocational satisfaction is legion. It would be impossible to review them all here, and it would be inadvisable, since many of them are quite old and only of historical interest; others are commentaries which deal with neither theory nor research; and a large number are methodologically unsound. An overview of these studies is essential, however, in order to gain a perspective on the research which has been conducted on satisfaction over the years and to draw any conclusions which appear to be justified. Fortunately, since his classic study in 1935, Hoppock and his associates have compiled yearly reviews of the literature on satisfaction from which a summary of fact and opinion can be made. In addition, there are certain topics of special interest which we should consider in greater detail, not only because of their prominence in the study of satisfaction in the past, but more importantly because of their salience for future research. Accordingly, in this section we shall discuss (1) Hoppock's reviews of the literature on vocational satisfaction and (2) research on the correlates of vocational satisfaction.

Hoppock's Reviews.[10] These compilations of vocational satisfaction research have followed roughly the same format since their inception, and it can be conveniently used to summarize their findings and conclusions:

1. Each review has reported the "percent dissatisfied" for previous years. These percentages have been brought together for all years of the reviews in Table 11-5. Here it can be seen that, although the percentages of dissatisfaction were somewhat higher during the earlier years of the reviews, they have stabilized for the last decade at 12 to 13 percent. There is no readily apparent reason for the higher percentages in the period preceding 1953, unless it might be that increased fringe benefits in recent years have had the effect of reducing dissatisfaction. This hypothesis would be consistent with the conclusions of Herzberg et al. (1959) (see Chapter 9), who have argued that it is the job-context factors which are the critical ones in producing dissatisfaction. Whatever the explanation of the figures in Table 11-5, however, it can be concluded from them that a relatively small percentage of the labor force—at least that part of it which has been included in satisfaction studies, and this would appear to be fairly sizable—experiences job dissatisfaction. This conclusion would appear to be justified, even if allowance is made for the way in which satisfaction (or dissatisfaction) is measured. Herzberg et al. (1957) have pointed out that questions which ask whether a worker would choose the same job again and which provide a Likert-type rating scale for responding usually

[10] The references to these reviews are as follows: Hoppock and Spiegler (1938); Hoppock and Odom (1940); Hoppock and Schaffer, R. H. (1943); Hoppock and Hand (1945); Hand, Hoppock, and Zlatchin (1948); Hoppock, Robinson, H. A., and Zlatchin (1948); Hoppock and Robinson, H. A. (1949; 1950; 1951); Robinson, H. A. and Hoppock (1952); Robinson, H. A. (1953; 1954; 1955; 1956; 1957; 1958a; 1958b); Robinson, H. A., and Connors (1960; 1961; 1962; 1963); Robinson, H. A., Connors, and Robinson, A. H. (1964); Robinson, H. A., Connors, and Whitacre (1966).

***Table 11-5. Cumulative Median Percentages of Vocational Dissatisfaction 1938–1963** (From Hoppock Reviews)*

Year	*Percent dissatisfied*	*Year*	*Percent dissatisfied*
1935–1937	70/111 < 33⅓*	1953	13
1938–1939	73/117 < 33⅓*	1954	12
1940–1941	79/126 < 33⅓*	1955	13
1942–1943	25	1956	12
1944–1945	†	1957	12
1946–1947	21	1958	13
1948	19	1959	13
1949	19	1960	13
1950	19	1961	13
1951	18	1962	13
1952	15	1963	13

* During these years cumulative median percentages were not reported. The entries refer to the number of percentages (numerator) out of the total number reported (denominator) in a given year, which were less than 33⅓ percent.

† A median percentage was not reported for this period.

yield higher percentages of dissatisfaction. This question corresponds, conceptually, more closely to vocational aspiration (see discussion to follow) than it does satisfaction, however, and consequently it measures a somewhat different variable than the typical job satisfaction blank or questionnaire. And rating scales yield essentially the same data as dichotomous-response formats (i.e., "Yes" or "No" answers to the question "Are you satisfied with your job?"), if the extreme categories on the scales are combined (Hoppock, 1935b).

More important than these methodological considerations in the interpretation of the findings on the extent of vocational satisfaction (or dissatisfaction) among workers is the evidence on occupational differences in satisfaction. In one of the first studies of this phenomenon, Super (1939) found that percentage of satisfaction varied markedly from one occupational *level* to another. Professional and managerial workers were more satisfied than commercial, skilled, and semiskilled workers, but the relationship was not a wholly linear one. Skilled and semiskilled workers were more satisfied than commercial workers, which led Super (1939, p. 550) to conclude that there may be two occupational scales of satisfaction, a *white-collar* scale, "with Professional workers at the top, the Proprietary-Managerial group . . . next, and the Commercial and Sub-Professional . . . groups at the bottom," and a *manual* scale, consisting of the "Skilled, Semi-Skilled, and . . . Unskilled groups." In the other major study of occupational level and satisfaction, Centers (1948) obtained similar results, except that in his sample skilled workers were even more satisfied than professional workers. The percentages of satisfied workers by level were as follows:

Large Business, 100; Professional, 82; Small Business, 91; White Collar, 82; Skilled Manual, 84; Semi-Skilled, 76; and Unskilled, 72.

A possible explanation for these findings, which suggest a nonlinear relationship between occupational level and vocational satisfaction, comes from a study by Form and Geschwender (1962), in which they argue from reference-group theory that manual workers assess their satisfaction relative to the occupational positions their parents and brothers hold and not by some absolute standard of their status in the hierarchy. More specifically, these investigators tested the following four hypotheses (Form & Geschwender, 1962, pp. 229–230):

> 1. There will be no association between job satisfaction of the subject and his occupational level relative to his parents' occupational aspirations for him.
> 2. There will be a positive association between job satisfaction and occupational level of the subject relative to that of his father.
> 3. There will be a positive association between job satisfaction and occupational level of the subject relative to that of his brothers.
> 4. There will be a positive association between job satisfaction and generational occupational mobility of the subject relative to that of all those of similar origin, i.e., those whose father's occupation was similar to that of the subject's father (generational occupational mobility score, GOMS).

The first of these hypotheses is an "anchor" or control for the others, in the sense of eliminating parental aspiration as a point of reference for satisfaction. Actually, the way the data turned out, it was not possible to test this hypothesis directly, because 80 percent of the 595 manual workers in the study reported that their parents had no aspirations for them, which is a remarkable finding in itself. The results on the other hypotheses generally supported them, leading Form and Geschwender (1962, p. 237) to draw the following conclusion:

> Thus it is the *normal* condition for most manual workers not to expect great upward mobility and for them not to internalize strongly the ideology of opportunity. Lacking the ideology of opportunity they tend to use peer groups and the male members of their family of orientation as social references in evaluating their occupational positions.

This appears to be an overinterpretation of their data, i.e., there was no evidence that manual workers have not strongly internalized the ideology of opportunity, but their findings can be interpreted to explain the manual and white-collar scales of satisfaction found by Super (1939). Manual workers may feel more satisfied with their jobs than white-collar workers because they use their parents and brothers as reference groups rather than occupational groups on the professional and managerial levels.

Research on differences between occupational *fields* in vocational satisfaction is even more limited than that on occupational level. Wrenn (1934), Paterson and Stone (1942), and Inlow (1951) have reported differences between fields, but not with level controlled. In other words, they compared occupations, such as sales and engineering, in which field and level were confounded. There is a suggestion in these studies that occupations at the same level do differ in satisfaction, but in what ways and to what extent are unknown. Further investigation of this problem is needed.

2. In most of the Hoppock reviews, an attempt has been made to extrapolate the major emphases or foci of the research which was conducted during a given year. These trends have been summarized in Table 11-6 for the period from 1950 to 1963. Several different topics or problems have been predominant in research on vocational satisfaction, but a few appear to be recurring. There has been a persistent concern with the *definition* of vocational satisfaction. It has been difficult to differentiate satisfaction, not only from attitudes and morale but also from general satisfaction, job success, and vocational adjustment. Another long-term problem has been the *measurement* of satisfaction. As has been discussed, there have been a great number of different instruments used to quantify satisfaction, with little or no effort having been expended on their standardization. Vroom (1964, p. 100) observes that: "This practice greatly restricts the comparability of different studies and results in relatively little attention to problems of scaling and of reliability or validity." A third major emphasis in studies of vocational satisfaction has been upon the identification of its *correlates*. Interest in this problem has been partly theoretical, but mostly it has been practical. If the factors which contribute to satisfaction could be isolated, the conditions of the work environment could be changed so as to eliminate much of the discontent which leads to industrial conflict.

The Correlates of Vocational Satisfaction. Because of this focus upon the specific aspects of work which might affect satisfaction, however, most of the studies of its correlates have dealt more with the worker's satisfaction with such variables as supervision, wages, hours of work, etc., than with his vocation. As Vroom (1964, p. 104) points out:

> The reasons for this are simple. If one is interested in the effects of a specific work role variable, such as amount of wages, on job satisfaction, it is likely that these effects will be more evident on workers' reports of their satisfaction with their wages than on their reports of their satisfaction with their job as a whole or with other aspects of their jobs.

Table 11-6. Emphases in Research on Vocational Dissatisfaction 1950–1963 *(From Hoppock Reviews)*

Year	*Emphasis*
1950	Trend toward refinement of measures of vocational satisfaction.
1951	Search for individual and group adjustment correlates of vocational satisfaction.
1952	Concern with the definition of vocational satisfaction and the factors related to the concept.
1953	Continued analysis of vocational satisfaction as a concept; criticism of measuring instrument; focus upon the relationship of vocational to general satisfaction with other life activities.
1954	Measurement of vocational satisfaction; differentiation from closely related concepts, e.g., morale and job attitudes; two viewpoints espoused on best method for measuring vocational satisfaction: ask worker to express his feelings toward various specific aspects of his job, and determine extent to which job satisfies worker's needs.
1955	Interest in relationship of automation to vocational satisfaction; association of such factors as supervision, age, education, etc., with vocational satisfaction; validation of measures of vocational satisfaction.
1956	Increasing number of studies on satisfaction with teaching; follow-ups of the vocational satisfaction of school and college graduates; use of questionnaires to measure vocational satisfaction.
1957	Re-examination of vocational satisfaction as a concept; is satisfaction synonymous with success and adjustment? is it different for men and women? what needs are satisfied in vocations?
1958	Factor analysis of vocational satisfaction; use of more sophisticated statistical methodology in studies of vocational satisfaction.
1959	Relationships of aspirations, expectations, and status to vocational satisfaction; influence of the work group upon the prestige of the worker as a factor in vocational satisfaction.
1960	Relationship of self-concept, recognition, and status to vocational satisfaction.
1961	Factor analysis of measures of vocational satisfaction and correlated variables.
1962	Many studies of satisfaction with teaching; also, research on aspirations in relation to achievement, opportunities for self-expression, and interactions among members of the work group as correlates of vocational satisfaction.
1963	Satisfaction with teaching; focus upon morale in relation to vocational satisfaction.

It might still be possible to draw inferences about the correlates of overall vocational satisfaction from the correlates of job attitudes, if it is assumed that the latter are components of the former. From their comprehensive review of "Factors Related to Job Attitudes," Herzberg et al. (1957, p. 81) have concluded, however, that such extrapolations are probably not justified: "If we are able to determine how the employee feels about each of the identified and defined job factors, can we then predict how he feels about his job in general? There is very little direct evidence to indicate that such prediction will be possible." We are left, therefore, with only a few isolated studies on the correlates of overall *vocational* satisfaction.

All the articles cited in Hoppock's reviews, which supposedly dealt with this problem, were read and evaluated according to the following criteria: (1) Did they report *empirical* findings; (2) was a measure of vocational satisfaction, e.g., Hoppock's JSB, used to collect the data; and (3) was the study reasonably sound methodologically? Out of a total of over 3,000 references, only a handful of studies was culled which met the criteria.[11] Many of these have already been reviewed in the section, "The Measurement of Vocational Satisfaction," e.g., Ash (1954), Kerr (1952), etc., and the remainder will be summarized here, with the exception of those on age (see Chapter 12), under the following rubrics: (1) need satisfaction in relation to vocational satisfaction; (2) vocational aspiration and vocational satisfaction; and (3) the relationship of vocational interests to vocational satisfaction.

1. *Need satisfaction in relation to vocational satisfaction.* Although Schaffer's (1953) research stimulated considerable interest in the occupation as a need satisfier, only one investigation has been found in which his hypothesis on the relationship of need satisfaction to vocational satisfaction has been directly tested.[12] In this study, which was conducted by Kuhlen (1963, p. 56), Schaffer's original formulation was refined and extended to encompass three predictions: "Those individuals whose measured needs are relatively stronger than the potential of the occupation for satisfying those needs (as they perceived this potential) will tend to be frustrated and hence to be less well satisfied with their occupation."

[11] The writer is indebted to Mrs. Diane Seldon Hill, who took major responsibility for conducting this extensive and laborious survey.

[12] For related studies, which deal only indirectly, however, with the relationship between need and vocational satisfaction, see: Froehlich and Wolins (1960) and Ross and Zander (1957). An investigation by Blai (1964) is also relevant, although it used Maslow's theory of needs as a conceptual framework. He found a correlation of .58 between a "Hoppock type" measure of job satisfaction and a weighted need-satisfaction score much like Schaffer's. So few data are reported on these scores, however, that it is difficult to evaluate them.

This "relationship will hold to a greater degree among men than among women," since the occupation is a major source of need satisfaction for the former.

Because the achievement need is vocationally relevant, i.e., can be satisfied directly through work, the "satisfaction of this need would be particularly important for (i.e., more highly related to) occupational satisfaction."

With 203 (108 males, 95 females) teachers-in-service as Subjects, Kuhlen collected data pertinent to these propositions with three instruments: (1) the Edwards Personal Preference Schedule (EPPS); (2) an 11-point rating scale of vocational satisfaction; and (3) a questionnaire called "Personality Types and Occupations," which was constructed to elicit perceptions of the need-satisfaction potential of the occupation of teaching. The ratings of vocational satisfaction correlated .25 and .02, respectively, for men and women, with discrepancy scores between the EPPS and the questionnaire, thus confirming the first two hypotheses. The third hypothesis was supported only for women, however, and only at the .05 level of significance. Thus, Kuhlen's findings lend some support to Schaffer's hypothesis that need satisfaction is related to vocational satisfaction, but two qualifications should be noted: First, the relationship holds only for men, presumably because the occupation is more important to them as a source of need satisfaction than it is to women; and, second, as Kuhlen points out, vocational satisfaction was correlated with perceived, not actual, satisfaction of needs in the occupation.

2. *Vocational aspiration and vocational satisfaction.* Earlier in this chapter theories of vocational satisfaction proposed by Morse (1953), Katzell (1964), and Brophy (1959) were discussed, in which one of the central propositions was that satisfaction is inversely related to the discrepancy between vocational aspiration and vocational attainment. Or, stated differently, the more satisfied worker has achieved more of what he wants. There are several studies which have tested this hypothesis:

a. Super (1939) related expressions of dissatisfaction to the degree of discrepancy between aspiration and achievement in vocation for 270 employed men and found that the percentage dissatisfied increased as the discrepancy increased, with the exception of one discrepancy level where the numbers of satisfied and dissatisfied Subjects were equal. He concluded that: "men who aspire to occupational levels above those at which they find themselves tend to be dissatisfied with their work, and that the greater the discrepancy between aspiration and achievement the greater will be the proportion of dissatisfaction" (Super, 1939, p. 554).

b. Although they did not use a measure of overall *vocational* satisfaction, Centers and Cantril (1946) have reported data on *income* satisfaction in relation to income aspiration which may nevertheless be of interest in this context.

These investigators asked a representative sample ($N = 1{,}165$) of the national population over 18 years of age what the weekly average income of their immediate families was and how much more money they would need to make their families happier or more comfortable. From the responses which were made to these questions, Centers and Cantril (1946, p. 65; italics and capitals in original) drew the following conclusion:

> *The higher a person's income is, the more likely is he to be satisfied with it and the smaller is the PROPORTION of present income desired in addition, except in the case of persons in the upper income group where those who are dissatisfied want a relatively large increase.*

The explanation proposed for the upper-income group's deviation from the general trend was that this group, which was composed largely of professional people, i.e., physicians, lawyers, and college professors, wanted to compete for social status with persons far above them in income, e.g., business executives. Consequently, even though they were at a high income level, they were disproportionately dissatisfied.

c. Mann (1953, p. 902) tested the hypothesis that "satisfactions of nonsupervisory employees with certain aspects of their occupational status are inversely related to the level of education they have attained, when type of work, job skill level, length of service, and sex are held constant." Here the reasoning is that, other things being equal (i.e., time on the job and sex), within a given work and skill class those workers with more education will be less satisfied. In other words, educational level becomes an index of vocational aspiration and thus would vary negatively with satisfaction, which is largely what Mann found. For blue-collar men, amount of education was inversely associated with (1) overall satisfaction with company and job, (2) satisfaction with job responsibility, and (3) satisfaction with promotional opportunities. For white-collar men, it was related only to satisfaction with promotional opportunities, and for white-collar women only to satisfaction with job responsibility. Thus, although some of the expected relationships between education and satisfaction were confirmed, they appear to be specific to the status and sex of the worker.[13]

d. Finally, as part of a series of studies on the status and satisfaction of a group of mental-health workers, including psychiatrists, clinical psychologists, social workers, etc., Rettig, Jacobsen, and Pasamanick (1958) and Jacobsen, Rettig, and Pasamanick (1959) gathered data on two related hypotheses: First, workers whose objective status is low, but who overestimate their status, will be as satisfied as workers whose objective status is high, and who do *not* overestimate it. A corollary to this hypothesis was that the overestimators would be more satisfied than accurate estimators of the same objective status. Both the primary and secondary hypotheses were substantiated: Apparently status overestimation serves a compensatory function in raising a worker's satisfaction above its expected level. In other words, by distorting his actual level of attainment, the worker "closes the gap" between it and his level of aspiration and hence feels more satisfied. Second, the prediction was made that satisfaction would be negatively correlated with the discrepancy between expected and aspired status. The findings confirmed this hypothesis only for clinical psychologists who worked in state institutions, and not for those employed in other agencies. No explanation was offered concerning why this difference occurred.

To summarize this research on vocational aspiration and vocational satisfaction we can say that it is mostly positive, indicating that the more a worker fulfills his aspirations, the more satisfied he will be. Thus, there is some substantiation for those theories of satisfaction which state that the discrepancy between vocational aspiration and attainment is inversely related to satisfaction, but there is also evidence that they might be revised to take cognizance of the fact, as established by Rettig et al. (1958), that aspirations may be fulfilled *either* in reality *or* in imagination.

3. *The relationship of vocational interests to vocational satisfaction.* Since the early days of interest measurement, it has been hypothesized that vocational interests are related to vocational satisfaction. In his classic volume on the SVIB, Strong (1943, p. 384) wrote that: "The criterion of a vocational-interest test should be whether or not the person will be satisfied in the career to which it directs him, other factors than interest being disregarded." Similarly, in their review of vocational and educational satisfaction, Hoppock and Super (1950, p. 129) note that: "Discrepancies between the interest of the man and the nature of the work are a primary cause of dissatisfaction with one's job. The better the placement, in terms of suitability of work with respect to interests, the greater the resultant satisfaction and the better the emotional adjustment." Probably the most explicit statement on the relationship of interests to satisfaction has been made by Darley and Hagenah (1955, p. 12; italics in original), who conceptualize the following continuum of jobs, along which interests and satisfactions presumably vary:

> At one end are essentially intrinsic and self-perpetuating satisfactions (the man creatively engrossed and in love with his job); then comes a band of jobs that provide a nice balance between intrinsic and extrinsic satisfactions (the man whose job is preponderantly satisfying but who attains outside his job other wanted ends of status, security, and a moderately satisfying life style); finally there is a large

> block of jobs that are admittedly highly important to the economy but provide within themselves mainly subsistence outcomes, leaving to extrinsic factors and sources the satisfactions of those needs for *social* meaning and integrity that are important to all men.

Although these various statements of the interest-satisfaction hypothesis differ in detail, they have in common the assumption that *if* a worker is interested in his job, *then* he will be satisfied with it.

By and large, the empirical results on this hypothesis have tended to confirm it. In one of the first studies designed to test it, Sarbin and Anderson (1942) concluded that 82 percent (62 out of 76 Subjects) of a group of male workers, who had applied for vocational counseling because of dissatisfaction with their jobs, did not have primary interest patterns on the SVIB which were congruent with their current employment.[14] Much the same finding was obtained by Jacobs and Traxler (1954), but with the KPR-V as the measure of interests. These investigators found that satisfied accountants scored higher on the computational and clerical scales, and lower on the artistic and outdoor scales, than dissatisfied accountants, which is what might be expected in terms of the nature of the work performed by accountants. Three other studies have also demonstrated that a relationship between interests and satisfaction exists: Gadel and Kreidt (1952) have reported an r of .44 between interest in IBM machine operation and job satisfaction; Strong (1955) correlated two ratings of satisfaction with SVIB interests on two occasions, the tetrachoric r's being .23 and .30 on the first testing and .38 and .30 on the second testing (all were significant at the .01 level); and Thorpe and Campbell (1965) have obtained r's of .21 and .25 between satisfaction, on the one hand, and the SVIB and expressed interests, respectively, on the other.[15] Only one study has been located in which the results were negative. Schletzer (1966) followed up 185 graduates of professional schools at the University of Minnesota, who had taken the SVIB in the twelfth grade, with another SVIB and three measures of satisfaction, among which were the Hoppock JSB and the Brayfield-Rothe IJS. She

[14] Although it does not substantially change this conclusion, a discrepancy in Sarbin and Anderson's (1942, p. 28) data should be noted. In Table 1 of their article, they report that 33 of the 76 Subjects in their total group did *not* express dissatisfaction with their occupation, yet they were included in computing the percentage cited. When the data are corrected accordingly, 81 percent (35 out of 43 Subjects) were actually dissatisfied and also lacked primary interest in their occupations.

[15] Still another study has been reported by Geist (1963), in which he found some extremely high r's (e.g., .999) between his Picture Interest Inventory and a modified JSB, but Campbell (1965) has questioned these results, pointing out that correlations in the .70s and .80s were obtained with scales that had standard deviations of 0.0. Geist (1965) replied that the high r's were possible, but before they can be accepted without qualification they should be replicated upon another sample.

classified both early and late interests according to whether they were congruent with present occupation and then correlated them with the satisfaction scores. Only one *r* out of 56 was significant.

With the exception of Schletzer's study, then, the *conclusion* we can draw from the research which has accumulated on the interest-satisfaction hypothesis is that there is a low positive correlation between these variables. Why Schletzer's data did not yield more than one significant *r* is difficult to understand. One possible explanation is that the range on the satisfaction variables in her study was restricted. She reports means and standard deviations for the Hoppock JSB and Brayfield-Rothe IJS which indicate that her Subjects were generally highly satisfied with their vocations. This homogeneity of the sample with respect to satisfaction may have attenuated the correlations with interests. Strong (1943; 1955; 1958) has suggested several other factors which might also affect the relationship between interests and satisfaction, e.g., inadequacy of measures of satisfaction, and has concluded that these two variables do not "express the same aspects of behavior." But his concern has been almost exclusively with the problem of establishing a criterion for the SVIB and demonstrating its predictive validity; consequently, he interprets *r*'s in the .20s and .30s between interests and satisfaction as being too low to have any practical value. Theoretically, however, they are meaningful, since they indicate at least some tendency for interests and satisfaction to vary together: the worker who likes what he does feels pleased with what he does. The reason the relationship is not greater than it is probably arises from the fact that many other factors are related to both interests and satisfaction, such as the nature of the work performed (Darley & Hagenah, 1955), and tend to obscure or reduce it. If these extraneous variables were held constant, it is quite possible that the correlation between interests and satisfaction would be considerably higher, i.e., in the .40s and .50s.

VOCATIONAL SATISFACTION IN RELATION TO VOCATIONAL SUCCESS

Now that we have reviewed separately the theory and research which has accumulated on vocational satisfaction and vocational success, we can consider the question of whether these phenomena are related to each other. As was noted at the end of Chapter 8, vocational satisfaction and success have been viewed as distinct, but not wholly independent, components of vocational adjustment. One of the first to argue for this point of view was Lurie (1942, pp. 9–10) who contended that "the concept of occupational adjustment as a psychological entity should be supplanted by a concept of occupational adjustment as a complex of factors . . . one [of which] has to do with job satisfaction and one with ease of obtaining employment, in addition to others not as yet identified." By "ease of obtaining employment," Lurie meant success in getting and holding a job. Lurie and Weiss (1942) have elaborated upon the conception of vocational adjustment as a composite of satisfaction, success, and other variables, as have Gellman (1953) and Heron (1952a; 1952b; 1954). Similarly, Brayfield and Crockett (1955) have observed that the literature of industrial and vocational psychology is replete with statements about the *assumed* relationship between satisfaction and success. Whether this relationship *actually* exists, however, has not been as extensively documented. In this section we shall (1) review what evidence has been gathered on the relationship between vocational satisfaction and success, (2) summarize the theoretical speculations which have been prompted by it, and (3) outline some of the research which has recently been done on the problem.

Reviews of Research on the Relationship between Vocational Satisfaction and Vocational Success

For their review of "employee attitudes and employee performance," Brayfield and Crockett (1955) classified the literature according to several criteria. First, they distinguished between "performance on the job," as measured by productivity, supervisors' ratings, etc., and "withdrawal from the job," as indicated by absences, accidents, and employment stability. Second, they dealt separately with analyses based upon the attitudes of individuals and those conducted on the attitudes of groups. And, third, they differentiated between "studies in which a single index of attitudes either as a single item or as a summation of items was used and those few in which multiple indices were used." The conclusions which they drew were as follows (Brayfield & Crockett, 1955, pp. 402–408):

1. Performance on the job
   a. Individual analyses: "The prototype study used a single overall index of employee attitudes variously titled job satisfaction or morale. . . . When 14 homogeneous occupational groups and one large sample of assorted hourly factory workers were studied statistically significant low positive relationships between job satisfaction and job performance were found in two of the 15 comparisons."
   b. Group analyses: "The results from the study design which we have described in this section are substantially in agreement with the previous findings of minimal or no relationship between employee attitudes and performance."
2. Withdrawal from the job (individual and group analyses): "With respect to withdrawal from the job, then, there is some evidence, mainly from the

group design studies, of a significant but complex relationship between employee attitudes and absences. The investigations reviewed here also lend some support to the assumption that employee attitudes and employment stability are positively related. The data on accidents and attitudes are extremely limited, but they do not support any significant relationships."

In short, Brayfield and Crockett concluded that, largely irrespective of type of analysis or measure, only absences and employment stability were related to satisfaction.

A quite different interpretation of the research on satisfaction in relation to success was reached by Herzberg et al. (1957), despite the fact that they reviewed many of the same studies as Brayfield and Crockett. The conclusion of this second review, with respect to "performance on the job," was that: "The preponderance of the data adds up to the following picture: in approximately half of the studies reported workers with positive job attitudes outproduced workers with negative job attitudes" (Herzberg et al., 1957, p. 111). Similarly, the conclusion on "withdrawal from the job" was that:

> Positive job attitudes were more unequivocally related to the worker's tendency to stay with the job, either in the day-to-day decisions as to whether to report to work in the face of a minor illness or family crisis, or in the more important decisions to be made about job termination. There is some evidence to show that workers with positive job attitudes have fewer accidents and fewer psychosomatic illnesses. Insufficient data were available on the role of attitudinal factors in the frequency and quality of grievances and complaints. In general, it was noted that the critical employee is not always a poorer producer than an uncritical employee [Herzberg et al., 1957, p. 111].

Thus, Herzberg and his fellow reviewers (1957, p. 112) consider that "the consensus of industrial psychologists and management that positive job attitudes are a tremendous asset to industry is supported by much of the experimental evidence now available."

Since this conclusion almost directly contradicts that of Brayfield and Crockett, it is important to speculate on why there is such a disparity between the two reviews. Katzell (1957, p. 244) has suggested that there are probably several reasons, among which two stand out: First, Brayfield and Crockett accepted only statistically significant findings as confirmatory of a relation between satisfaction and success, whereas Herzberg et al. interpreted "suggestive" trends in the data; and, second, "Brayfield and Crockett state their generalization prior to their consideration of the parameters involved in the relationships between attitudes and performance, whereas Herzberg et al. more appropriately take such influence into account in arriving at their over-all judgment." Perhaps the most cogent and parsimonious explanation of all, however, is that the studies were not clear-cut and definitive enough to be subject to only one interpretation. If they had been less equivocal, there presumably would have been greater agreement between the two reviews.

The third review which has appeared on the relationship between satisfaction and success is more circumscribed, dealing only with three studies, but nonetheless important, since these investigations were broad in scope and based upon large *N*'s, characteristics of research in this area which have generally been wanting. Kahn (1960) has summarized these studies, which were conducted by the Survey Research Center at the University of Michigan over a period of several years, one in an insurance company, another on a railroad, and a third in a group of implement and tractor manufacturers. In each of these studies, a measure of intrinsic job satisfaction, among others, such as satisfaction with company and supervision, was related to some index of productivity, for either the individual or work group, but none of the relationships was significant. Confronted with these negative findings, Kahn (1960, pp. 275; 285–286) and his co-workers were led to conclude that "productivity and job satisfaction do not necessarily go together" and that "we should abandon, in our future research, the use of satisfaction or morale indexes as variables intervening between supervisory and organizational characteristics on the one hand, and productivity on the other."

More recently, Vroom (1964) has reviewed the relationship between satisfaction and success, but with no substantial change in the conclusions which had been reached earlier. He summarizes the findings as follows:

> 1. There is a consistent negative relationship between job satisfaction and the probability of resignation. . . .
> 2. There is a less consistent negative relationship between job satisfaction and absences. . . .
> 3. There is some indication of a negative relationship between job satisfaction and accidents. . . .
> 4. There is no simple relationship between job satisfaction and job performance [Vroom, 1964, p. 186].

For 20 studies which had been completed in the last decade and a half, Vroom found that the median correlation between satisfaction and success was .14, with a range from −.31 to .86 (most of the *r*'s, however, were very close to the median). Whether the analyses were for individuals or groups apparently made no appreciable difference, since the respective *r*'s were .135 and .14. In light of these findings, Vroom (1964, p. 187) closes his review with the comment that:

> The absence of a marked or consistent correlation between job satisfaction and performance casts some doubt on the generality or intensity of either effects of satisfaction on performance or perfor-

> mance on satisfaction. It also suggests that the conditions which determine a person's level of job satisfaction and his level of job performance are not identical. Some conditions may produce high satisfaction and low performance, others low satisfaction and high performance, and still others high satisfaction and high performance or low satisfaction and low performance.

Finally, in a review covering the period since Brayfield and Crockett's (1955) survey of the literature, Fournet, Distefano, and Pryer (1966) draw much the same conclusions as those already mentioned. Following Brayfield and Crockett, they comment that:

> Production is seldom a goal in itself but is more commonly a means of goal attainment. High satisfaction and high production can be expected to occur together when productivity is perceived as a means to certain important goals, and when these goals are achieved. Under other conditions the relationship may be negative or there may be none at all [Fournet et al., 1966, p. 176].

Thus, with the exception of Herzberg et al. (1957), the general consensus among those who have reviewed the accumulated findings on the relationship between satisfaction and success is that these two variables are not consistently and systematically associated with each other. Rather, the relationship which obtains between them, if indeed there is one, is complex and contingent upon the presence or absence of other factors.

Theoretical Speculations about the Relationship between Vocational Satisfaction and Vocational Success

Brayfield and Crockett (1955) have proposed that the most salient conditions which may affect the relationship between satisfaction and success are those which are found in the worker's social environment. Following Katz and Kahn (1952), they enumerate four social systems within which the individual may establish and seek achievement of his goals: (1) outside the plant, (2) relations with co-workers in the plant, (3) the union structure, and (4) the company structure. Goals differ in each of these social systems, and productivity on the job may or may not be a means of achieving them. If it is, then productivity and satisfaction should be positively related, on the assumption that goal achievement results in satisfaction. If it is not, then productivity and satisfaction should be either unrelated or even negatively related, under certain conditions.

Let us consider an instance of each possible relationship to illustrate how the particular social system can affect the covariation between productivity (success) and satisfaction. *Outside the plant,* a worker's goal may be to improve his status, to be "upward mobile," and increased productivity may be the means, through the additional income or prestige or authority it brings, for realizing this objective. In this case, high productivity would most likely go with high satisfaction derived from attaining the goal of enhanced social status. *Inside the plant,* these variables might be negatively correlated, however, if the worker's goal is acceptance by his work group, and low or average productivity is a *sine qua non* for such acceptance. In other words, a low producer is highly satisfied with his job because he is accepted by his work group, which sets low productivity as a condition for membership. *In the union,* much the same situation exists, since high productivity is seldom rewarded by advancement in the union. *In the company,* the motivation of a worker to produce more, and thereby improve his position, may stem from dissatisfaction with his present job, in which case productivity would again be negatively related to satisfaction. There are other possibilities which might be enumerated, such as the irrelevancy of productivity for achievement of extraoccupational goals in organizational and recreational pursuits, but these examples should suffice to illustrate Brayfield and Crockett's reasoning on how the relationship between satisfaction and success may be a function of the social systems within which the worker pursues his goals.

Morse (1953) has also posited a third variable in order to account for what kind of relationship might obtain between satisfaction and success, but rather than the worker's social systems she invokes the concept of "strength of needs." She points out that many factors are necessary to predict job satisfaction and success, particularly the latter, but that one factor, strength of needs, is common to both. It follows that, if the other predictors of satisfaction and success are held constant, it should be possible to specify the nature of the relationship between these variables under different intensities or magnitudes of strength of needs. Accordingly, Morse (1953, p. 126) extrapolates the following predictions:

> When individuals have strong needs which are predictably related to productivity and where the environmental return from the job is high, they will be both satisfied with their job and high in production. In other words, in such situations we would predict that there would be a positive relationship between amount of satisfaction and productivity, since a high need level will result in both higher productivity and higher satisfaction. In situations where the environmental return is low, those with high needs will be more productive but will be less satisfied, since their behavior does not lead to need-satiation or fulfillment.

By "environmental return" she means the probability that behavior will be followed by tension reduction; in short, environmental return is roughly equivalent to reward. Thus, Morse is hypothesizing that, if a worker's job is rewarding, and if he has strong needs, then he will be productive and satisfied. If his job is not rewarding, however, his strong needs will make him productive, but he will be dissatisfied.

Triandis (1959) has formulated the most sophisticated and refined analysis of the possible relationships between satisfaction and success, on the one hand, and a third variable, on the other, but instead of social systems or strength of needs he conceptualizes the latter as "pressure for high production." He depicts the effects of this factor graphically as shown in Figure 11-2, where *X* is output or productivity, $+Y$ is satisfaction, and $-Y$ is dissatisfaction. As pressure for high production increases from point *A* to point *G* on the curve, various possible relationships between satisfaction (*Y*) and success (*X*) can obtain. At *A* satisfaction is at a maximum, and success (output) is at a minimum; at *C* both satisfaction and success are high; but then satisfaction decreases until at *D* the worker is indifferent and produces only enough to "get

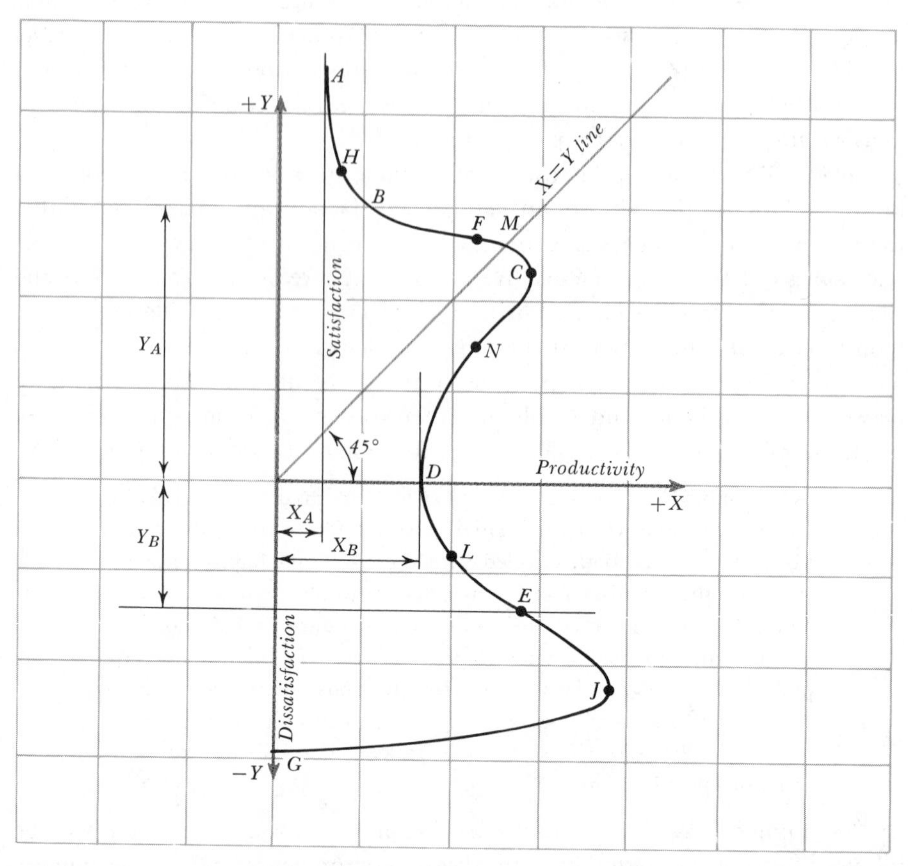

Figure 11-2. "Pressure for production" in relation to vocational satisfaction. *(From Triandis, 1959, p. 310.)*

by"; at *J* high dissatisfaction is accompanied by high productivity, but only so long as the worker has to remain in his job; finally, at *G* dissatisfaction is so great effective job performance is reduced to zero.

Along this curve, then, the relationship between satisfaction and success may be positive or negative or nonexistent, depending upon what the pressure for production is. Although the conditions represented by point *J*, for example, are unlikely today, they have been observed in the past. Brayfield and Crockett (1955, p. 416) cite a study by Goode and Fowler (1949), in which management threatened marginal workers with discharge if they fell below a standard of high production. Since the workers could not secure employment elsewhere, they remained on their jobs, producing at a high level, but were very dissatisfied. What the optimal pressure for production might be has been worked out mathematically by Triandis (1959) and is represented by point *M* in Figure 11-2. At this point, success (X) equals satisfaction (Y), i.e., $Z = F(X, Y)$ is a maximum, and the relationship between success and satisfaction is theoretically as high as it can possibly be.

In contrast to the "third variable" conceptual schemata of Brayfield and Crockett, Morse, and Triandis, Katzell (1964) has adopted what might be called a "functional" approach to the explanation of the relationship between satisfaction and success, the latter being defined both as participation in the job, i.e., the obverse of withdrawal from the job, and performance on the job. With respect to participation, the individual decides whether to be present or absent at work and whether to stay in a job or change to another. More generally, the choice between these alternatives can be expressed in the equation:

$$P_A = f_A S_A - f_B S_B$$

where P_A stands for the extent to which a worker will select alternative *A*, as opposed to *B*, and S_A and S_B are the net degrees of satisfaction associated with these choices. Similarly, net amount of productive behavior (E) can be defined as:

$$E = f_P S_P - f_N S_N$$

where *P* and *N* refer to net satisfactions derived from productive and nonproductive behavior, respectively. From this function, it follows that "production has no necessary correlation with job satisfaction, for the $f_P S_P$ term would be positively correlated with production, whereas the $f_N S_N$ term would be negatively correlated with production, and the two might combine in various ways" (Katzell, 1964, p. 354). Thus, Katzell views job participation and performance as functions of the differences between the satisfactions associated with alternative courses of action which the worker might follow.

The last explanation of the relationship between satisfaction and success which we shall consider here stems from Vroom's (1964) "cognitive theory" of vocational motivation, which was described in detail in Chapter 9 and which was briefly summarized earlier in this chapter. It will be recalled that Vroom conceives of satisfaction as the valence which a worker's job has for him—that is, the extent to which he thinks he can attain his goals through his job. From this concept of satisfaction, it can be deduced that: "The more satisfied a worker, the stronger the force on him to remain in his job and the less the probability of his leaving it voluntarily" (Vroom, 1964, p. 165), either temporarily (absences) or permanently (turnover). In other words, Vroom proposes that the correlations between satisfaction and these "withdrawal" behaviors should be negative. Unlike some theorists (e.g., Hill & Trist, 1953), however, Vroom does not include accidents in the class of "withdrawal" behaviors, since, following Stagner, Flebbe, and Wood (1952), he reasons that accidents probably lead to dissatisfaction, because the worker sees his job as unsafe, rather than that dissatisfaction results in accidents. Consequently, he would expect a negative correlation between these variables when accidents precede dissatisfaction but not when dissatisfaction precedes accidents. Finally, Vroom (1964, p. 187) takes the position that satisfaction and success are "both conceptually and empirically separable outcomes of the person-work role relationship." Not only is the relationship between them affected by the influence of satisfaction upon performance and performance upon satisfaction, but it is also a function of "third variables."

Recent Research on the Relationship between Vocational Satisfaction and Vocational Success

There is a handful of studies on satisfaction versus success which have appeared since the reviews by Vroom (1964) and Fournet et al. (1966) or which were not covered by them. These include two investigations in which "withdrawal from the job" was used as the index of success or job performance, and two others in which the criterion was a measure of effectiveness:

1. For a group of 110 employees (not otherwise described), Svetlik, Prien, and Barrett (1964) obtained *r*'s of .29 and .27, both significant at the .01 level, between overall job satisfaction and (1) job tenure in years and (2) company tenure in years, respectively. Satisfaction also correlated .24 (.05 level) with salary. Similarly, Hulin and Smith (1965) found that, for 185 male and 75 female workers, the Job Descriptive Index (JDI) was related to both job tenure and company tenure, but they do not report the actual *r*'s. Their interest was in showing that the relationships were linear rather than curvilinear, as hypothesized by Herzberg et al. (1957), and consequently they used a different type of statistical analysis. They concluded, incidentally, that the linear model probably better fits the data on the relationship of satisfaction to tenure than the nonlinear model.

2. In one of the studies of job performance, Miller and Muthard (1965) correlated a shortened version of Johnson's, G. H. (1955) Job Satisfaction Inventory with several criteria of success, including co-worker ratings, supervisor's ratings, state agency ratings, case velocity, average case load, and average closures, for 143 male and female vocational rehabilitation counselors. Only verbal descriptions of the correlations were given, i.e., no *r*'s were reported, so that it is difficult to evaluate their findings. There appeared to be some relationships which would be expected, but the most notable finding was that they were different for the male and female counselors. In the other study of job performance, Kirchner (1965) computed *r*'s between several attitude scales of the Likert-type, as well as the Brayfield-Rothe Index of Job Satisfaction (IJS), and (1) net-sales points and (2) net-total points of 72 outdoor advertising salesmen. He found that the IJR correlated .42 and .46, respectively, with these performance criteria.

Thus, recent findings on the relationship of satisfaction to success are much like those reviewed in past years and necessitate no major changes in the conclusions previously drawn: satisfaction is consistently related to job tenure (or its obverse, job turnover) but only infrequently associated with success (as indicated by various measures of job performance).

Some new lines of inquiry have been opened up, however, which may yield different findings on the relationship between satisfaction and success. Katzell, Barrett, and Parker (1961) investigated the relationship of certain work situational characteristics to job attitudes and performance, using the following theoretical orientation:

> Our review of extant research and theory on the subject has led us to a general model in which the work situation is regarded as a system having as separate outputs employee job satisfaction and performance, and as inputs characteristics both of the working environment and of the employees. Various of the inputs may be expected to affect either or both of the two sets of outputs via their effects on employee motivation, ability, or both. Furthermore, the inputs may be interactive in their effects.

To test the hypotheses generated by this conceptual framework, the investigators correlated three sets of variables with each other: (1) work situation: size of work force, city size, wage rate, unionization, and percentage of male workers; (2) job performance: quantity, quality, profitability, product-value, and turnover; and (3) job attitudes: 47 multiple-choice items on worker satisfactions. They also performed two factor analyses on the interrelationships of the work situation and job performance variables.

The correlational analyses revealed that, in general, both job performance and job attitudes are negatively related to the work situational factors included in the study. From the first factor analysis, the authors interpreted the latter as representing an "urbanization" dimension, which means that workers in less highly urbanized areas are more productive and satisfied. The second factor analysis, which used an oblique rather than orthogonal solution, produced different results, however, and led the authors to this revised conclusion (Cureton & Katzell, 1962, p. 230):

> In summary, the oblique factor solution indicates that the nonurban culture pattern previously reported may be thought of as comprising two positively correlated facets: one reflects small size of plant and community and is associated with relatively high production and profitability; the other reflects relatively low wages, proportionately few male employees and the absence of a union, and is associated with relatively high turnover.

Again, the method of factor analysis which is used becomes a critical consideration in the interpretation of the results. About the most we can conclude from this study is that the work situation is related to both satisfaction and success, as the authors' model would suggest, but the nature of the relationship is not clear. Furthermore, since partial correlations were not computed, we do not know whether the work situation is related independently to satisfaction and success, or whether it is, in part or whole, producing the correlation between them.

The other set of input variables, employee characteristics, which Katzell, Barrett, and Parker (1961) specified in their model, but did not study, were related to job performance and job attitudes by Harding and Bottenberg (1961) in a sample of 376 airmen. The statistical analysis was designed to determine whether various combinations of attitude and biographical variables contributed more or less to the multiple correlation with job performance criteria. In all, there were four sets of variables: (1) attitudes: e.g., satisfaction with supervisor, interest and pride in job, general morale, etc.; (2) biographical: rank, career intention, length of service, kind of work performed, and number of months in squadron; (3) interaction between rank and attitude: scores for attitudes held at certain ranks; and (4) job performance: supervisor's rating, supervisor's ranking, and estimated absences. The R's for the first three sets of variables, i.e., attitudes and biographical and interaction, as the predictors, versus the fourth set, as the criterion variables, were moderately high, being .43, .42, and .38, respectively, for ratings, rankings, and absences. When a test was made for the unique contribution of the biographical variables to the prediction of job performance, it was found that these variables added significant unique variance over and above that associated with attitudes, but only for ratings and rankings and not for absences. It was *not* found, however, that either attitude or interaction variables improved upon the correlations of biographical data with the criteria.

To investigate further the question of whether employee characteristics influence the relationship between satisfaction and success, Lawler (1966) tested the hypothesis that job performance = f (ability × motivation), where performance was the equivalent of success, and motivation (as he measured it) was the equivalent of satisfaction. In other words, Lawler proposed that success is a *multiplicative* function of ability and satisfaction. He predicted, therefore, that "attitudes which are measures of an individual's motivational level, as contingency [the extent to which an employee thinks his pay depends upon his ability] attitudes appear to be, will be more highly related to job performance measures for high than for low ability employees" (Lawler, 1966, p. 154). Why he expected this particular difference for the high- and low-ability Subjects was not spelled out, but it was what he found. That is, ability and attitudes were significantly correlated for the former group, but not for the latter. Whether the r's for the two groups differed statistically, however, was not determined. Better evidence for Lawler's hypothesis comes from a two-way analysis of variance he conducted, in which the results indicated main effects for ability and attitudes upon job performance (superior's rankings), as well as an interaction effect of ability and attitudes. With the exception of the ability main effect, the same findings were obtained with the employee's self-ratings of his job performance. Because most of Lawler's results were of borderline significance (.05 level), they can be considered only as suggestive, but they are promising enough that further research on the multiplicative model should be encouraged.

Finally, a series of laboratory experiments reported by Locke (1965) represent an important new approach to the analysis of the relationship between satisfaction and success. Each experiment was designed to test the hypothesis that success with a task leads to satisfaction with it and that the relationship between task success and task satisfaction is linear:

1. In Experiment I, the task was to unscramble words of varying lengths within a given period of time. After the task was completed, Subjects were asked to rate their liking for the words of different lengths on a 9-point scale. When these ratings were plotted against proportion of successes on the task, the function was clearly a linear one, the r between the two variables being .49 ($p < .01$).

2. Experiment II required Subjects to work toward standards for listing objects which could be described by a given adjective (e.g., "heavy"). Satisfaction with the task was measured by both a 7-point "liking" scale and the Work scale of the Cornell Job Descriptive Index (JDI). Again, the results confirmed a linear relationship between task success and task satisfaction, as measured

by the scale and the JDI, the correlations being .41 and .43 ($p < .01$), respectively.

3. Experiment III was much like the preceding one, except that the task involved giving uses for objects. The function between task success and task satisfaction was linear, and the r's between task success and the rating scale and JDI, respectively, were .42 and .41 ($p < .01$).

4. In Experiment IV, a pursuit-rotor learning task was used, and only the 7-point "liking" scale was administered. The findings were substantially the same as before: the relationship between task success and task satisfaction was linear, and its magnitude was moderate positive ($r = .42$, $p < .05$).

Thus we can agree with Locke (1965, pp. 384 385) that:

> The findings of the four experiments reported here lend strong support to the generality of a linear relationship between degree of task success and degree of liking for and satisfaction with the task. The findings were replicated over a number of different *S*s, across two different measures of satisfaction, and over several different situations and tasks. . . . In conclusion, this research supports the notion that task success is an important source of effective attitudes toward the task or work.

Comment

Locke's study highlights a logical issue which runs through all the theory and research on the relationship of satisfaction to success and which remains essentially unresolved. It is this: which comes first, satisfaction or success? Since the Western Electric studies, in which it was established that motivation and morale are related to productivity (see Chapter 9), industrial and personnel psychologists have assumed that the more satisfied worker will be the more productive worker. In other words, satisfaction precedes success. Similarly, in the early conceptualizations of the Survey Research Center, satisfaction was viewed as an antecedent to success, although both were seen as dependent upon supervisory practices and organizational structures (Kahn, 1960).

Vroom (1964, p. 187) points out, however, that a more reasonable case can be made for the temporal, if not causal, priority of success over satisfaction:

> It has been argued by some writers that greater satisfaction should result in higher performance and by others that higher performance should result in greater satisfaction. With respect to the former, there is no obvious theoretical basis for assuming that an increase in the valence of the work role should result in greater performance. In order for this to occur, one must assume that the increased valence of the work role generalizes to other objects and events, e.g., recognition from management, the attainment of which is contingent

> on performance. On the other hand, effects of performance on satisfaction are somewhat more plausible and would be expected to occur when effective performance brings with it greater rewards, at not appreciably greater cost, than ineffective performance. When workers are highly motivated to perform effectively, their success in attaining effective performance might be expected to affect the attractiveness of their job.

If we follow this logic, it would tend to explain the inconsistent results which have been found on the relationship between satisfaction and success: in studies where no relationship was obtained, it may have been because success on the job was not achieved (or experienced) before satisfaction was measured. In any case, the implication seems clear: we need more systematic and highly controlled research, such as that initiated by Locke, on the *conditions* under which vocational satisfaction and vocational success are related, before we can draw any definitive conclusions.

12

DEVELOPMENTAL ASPECTS OF VOCATIONAL ADJUSTMENT

In Chapter 8, it was noted that the Model for Vocational Adjustment can be viewed not only cross-sectionally but also longitudinally. In other words, the components in the process of adjusting to work—motives, thwarting conditions, adjustment mechanisms, and outcomes (success and satisfaction)—can be thought of as changing as the worker grows older. Whether such a conceptualization of vocational adjustment is supported by empirical evidence, however, needs to be determined. The purpose of this chapter, therefore, is to review and summarize the relevant research on the developmental aspects of vocational adjustment. It can be organized into four topics: (1) developmental stages in vocational adjustment, (2) career patterns and vocational adjustment, (3) developmental trends in vocational success, and (4) developmental trends in vocational satisfaction. Another subject which might have been discussed is occupational mobility. It was not included for two reasons: First, it has been dealt with comprehensively and extensively in occupational sociology texts, such as Caplow (1954); and, second, it does not seem as directly related to vocational psychology as career patterns, which is covered in the chapter.

DEVELOPMENTAL STAGES IN VOCATIONAL ADJUSTMENT

We have previously discussed the various stages which have been proposed as occurring in the process of choosing a vocation during the adolescent years (see Chapter 5). These stages represented discernible periods of time, each with its beginning and end points, through which the adolescent passed as he attempted to solve the problem of vocational choice. Now, we return to this developmental process, and the stages which have been identified in it, later in the individual's life as he strives to adjust to the vocation he has committed himself to in the world of work. Unlike the earlier part of his vocational development, once he enters an occupation the individual can expect to develop through, not just one, but several stages of vocational adjustment, which, taken collectively, comprise most of his work life. Each stage can be defined by the criteria of discreteness, dominance, and irreversibility, which were enumerated in Chapter 5. In brief, a stage is delimited by differentiable vocational behaviors and/or tasks, which are predominant over others during a given period of time in vocational development, and which, once established, have a persistent ("irreversible") effect upon the course of vocational development. Given this conceptual definition of a stage, we can ask: What are the stages which have been delineated in the process of vocational adjustment? What vocational behaviors and/or tasks characterize each stage? And, what empirical evidence has accumulated on the stages? These and related questions are dealt with in the following discussion of the (1) hypothesized stages in vocational adjustment and (2) research on the stages in vocational adjustment.

Hypothesized Stages in Vocational Adjustment

Super's Establishment, Maintenance, and Decline Stages. According to Super (1957; Super et al., 1963), the first stage in vocational adjustment is Establishment, a period during which the neophyte worker takes his first full-time job and attempts to advance in it. The actual beginning of this stage is difficult to determine exactly, not only because individuals enter the world of work at different ages, and with different amounts of education and training, but also because Establishment, as a process, encompasses certain aspects of the "transition from school to work" (see Chapter 5), e.g., "committing" oneself to a particular vocation, which are part of the Exploratory stage. Super (1963) has recently designated this early phase of Establishment the "trial (commitment) and stabilization" substage. It is distinct from the preceding "trial (little commitment)" substage of the Exploratory stage, because of the individual's greater investment and involvement in the vocation he has decided to pursue. Moreover, the vocational developmental tasks of the stages and substages are different: in the Exploratory stage they are crystallizing, specifying, and implementing a vocational preference, whereas in the Establishment stage they are stabilizing, consolidating status, and advancing in a vocation. When the worker has substantially completed these latter tasks, the Establishment stage comes to a close, and he moves into the Maintenance stage, the onset of which varies between individuals and occupations but which usually occurs at approximately age 35.

During the Maintenance stage, Super (1957) states that the primary task of the worker is "preserving or being nagged by the self-concept." No longer does the individual dream of fulfilling the lofty vocational aspirations which he held in years past—either he has achieved his earlier goals in large part, or he has resigned himself to the futility of ever fully realizing them. "As middle age is reached there is a tendency to keep on doing the kind of thing which helped one to get established, which one knows how to do well" (Super, 1957, p. 147). This does not mean that the worker in the Maintenance stage is no longer productive. He is. But: "The pioneering is done by younger men who are now in the establishment stage, who have the motivation and recent training which make it easier for them to make new syntheses of knowledge, to combine creatively ideas picked up from various elders with whom they have worked and to generate new ideas of their own" (Super, 1957, p. 147). Furthermore, it should be recognized that there are often considerable occupational differences in both the onset and the significance of the Maintenance stage. At the lower levels of the occupational hierarchy, this period of vocational development usually occurs earlier and lasts longer than at the upper strata.

Super (1957) has termed the last part of the work life the Decline stage, which he divides into two substages, deceleration and retirement: "The former is a period of tapering off of activities, of slowing down and cutting out; the latter is one in which considerable cutting has been done, and major readjustments have to be made to curtailed activity, including the finding of substitute activities" (Super, 1957, p. 154). The major vocational developmental task of this stage is "adjustment to a new self." Not only must the worker cope with the increasing limitations which are placed upon him by his advanced age, and the ailments and infirmities it brings, but he must begin to conceive of himself as a "nonworker," a person who will no longer regularly engage in a full-time job. Adjustment to retirement involves, in effect, formulating and implementing a new way of life, in which work does not play a central part. It is true that some retired people appear to be working as long and as hard, as ever, but eventually they must fill their days more and more with nonwork activities. The Decline stage ends, of course, with death, which, for the typical individual, brings to a close a span of vocational development embracing more than half a century of preparation for and participation in the world of work.

Miller and Form's Trial, Stable, and Retirement Periods. Miller, D. C., and Form (1951; 1964) view the trial work period, from approximately age 18 to 34, as a "social experience," during which the individual strives to find a place for himself in the world of work by trying out different jobs, reality-testing his abilities and interests, and estimating his chances for advancement. The trial period is defined as one of "job transition beginning when the worker seeks his first full-time job and continuing until he has secured a work position in which he remains more or less permanently (Three years or more)" (Miller, D. C., & Form, 1951, p. 637; 1964, p. 554). During this period, six different types of career orientation, each with its own pattern of work progression, have been identified by Miller, D. C., and Form (1947; 1949) from studies of the job histories of large numbers of workers in Ohio, Michigan, and Washington. These career orientations and progressions are presented in Table 12-1, where it can be seen that some, the ambitious and fulfilled, repre-

Table 12-1. Six Types of Career Orientations and Progressions *(From Miller, D. C., & Form, 1951, p. 638)*

CAREER ORIENTATION	AMBITIOUS	RESPONSIVE	FULFILLED
Character of Aspiration	Feeling of hope and confidence that higher occupational goals can be attained.	Feeling of acceptance with job progression which parents or relatives expect worker to follow.	Feeling of satisfaction upon attainment of desired occupational goal.
CAREER ORIENTATION	CONFUSED	FRUSTRATED	DEFEATED
Character of Aspiration	Feeling of uncertainty regarding past and present work progress and indecision regarding further moves.	Feeling of being thwarted in occupational aspiration but desirous of moving toward another goal.	Feeling of resignation and hopelessness with work progress.
KIND OF WORK PROGRESSION	RISING	REPEATING AND PARALLELING	COMPLETED
Identified by:	Evidence of movement involving successive increase of income or status or both.	Evidence of acceptance of a job previously followed by a parent or relative. Evidence that steps are planned more or less in advance by others, usually parents or relatives.	Evidence that desired occupational goal was attained and the holder is now satisfied to remain in the occupation and at the level he has attained.
KIND OF WORK PROGRESSION	ERRATIC	BLOCKED	REGRESSIVE
Identified by:	Evidence of erratic horizontal and vertical occupational mobility.	Evidence that desired occupational goal was not attained and that holder is now unable, temporarily at least, to move to another goal.	Evidence of movement involving successive loss of income or status or both.

sent more satisfactory vocational adjustments than others, the frustrated and defeated. Miller and Form observe, however, that for all young workers this is a period of stress and strain, accentuated by the necessity of having to acquire new attitudes and habits and giving up old ones.

Once the individual has established himself in the world of work, he is usually about 35 years old, the age which Miller and Form designate for the onset of the stable work period. They define this segment of the work life as "a period of job persistence beginning when the worker finds a work position in which he remains more or less permanently (three years or more) and continuing until retirement, death, or until he enters another trial period" (Miller, D. C., & Form, 1951, p. 701). Careers are stabilized in these middle years of vocational development by myriad factors: (1) realization or rationalization of the trial-period goal: (2) seniority in one's job; (3) increasing age and decreasing employability; (4) greater income; (5) financial responsibilities associated with marriage and family; (6) home ownership; (7) friendship ties on the job; (8) institutional ties in the community; and (9) identification with work plant and community, i.e., company loyalty and civic pride. But there are also certain conditions, both in the marketplace and the worker's personal life, which may disrupt careers: (1) cyclical and seasonal unemployment; (2) technological unemployment; (3) sickness and physical disability; (4) divorce; and (5) chance risks of life, e.g., business failure, war, etc. As a consequence of the influence of these factors, Miller and Form observe that all workers must usually cope with one or more of the following adjustment problems during the stable period: (1) redefinition of vocational goals to be consistent with successes and failures; (2) development of tolerance for the frustrations involved in waiting to be promoted, particularly when ability exceeds job specifications; (3) resolution of conflicts over life and work values; and (4) reappraisal of one's responsibilities and roles in the family and community with advancing age, changing interests, and growing conservatism in politics and economics.

The last period in Miller and Form's schema of the work life is the retired work period, which begins when the worker leaves his full-time employment and ends when he dies. The age at which most workers retire varies considerably, but it is typically 65. Miller, D. C., and Form (1951, p. 770) point out, however, that "Most workers do not retire. They either die on the job or suffer a physical breakdown on the job which leads to death." In the years to come, this trend will probably be reversed because of the increasing tendency to release workers at younger ages. As this happens, the social and vocational adjustment problems of the retired worker will become accentuated and intensified. Miller, D. C., and Form (1951, pp. 774–777) enumerate these as follows: (1) shift from work plant to home interests; (2) changes in status; (3) reduced comrade relationships; (4) problems of old-age security; and (5) declining health and energy. How the older person handles these problems will depend in large part upon his attitudes toward retirement. He may accept retirement as part of the natural course of vocational development and be content with channelling his energies into nonwork activities. He may stop working only because he has to and reject retirement. He may have to continue working, in order to meet financial obligations, but wish to be retired. Or he may stay on the job as long as he can because of his negative attitudes toward retirement. Eventually, however, all workers must give up their jobs, and, when they do, Miller, D. C., and Form (1951, pp. 781–784) note that their primary adjustment problems are financial and familial.

Havighurst's Becoming, Maintaining, and Contemplating Stages. Havighurst (1964) has synthesized Erikson's (1959) work on the crises and stages in the development of the healthy personality with Super's (1957) enumeration of vocational life stages to delineate three stages in the process of vocational adjustment. The first of these is what he calls "Becoming a Productive Person." It corresponds to the period between ages 25 and 40 and entails the achievement of two vocational developmental tasks: mastering the skills of one's occupation, and moving up the ladder within one's occupation. The second stage is that of "Maintaining a Productive Society." It encompasses the years between 40 and 70, and also involves the accomplishment of two tasks. One is to become more socially oriented, to assume civic responsibilities associated with the job, and to engage in a greater range of activities. "Emphasis shifts toward the societal and away from the individual aspect of the worker's role" (Havighurst, 1964, p. 216). The other is to help initiate younger workers into the earlier stages of vocational adjustment, to assist them in acquiring an occupational identity and in getting established. The last stage is termed "Contemplating a Productive and Responsible Life," which extends from age 70 to death. Havighurst (1964, p. 216) describes the individual in this period as follows: "He looks back over his work life with satisfaction, sees that he has made his social contribution, and is pleased with it. While he may not have achieved all of his ambitions, he accepts his life and believes in himself as a productive person." Thus, the main theme which runs through Havighurst's conceptualization of the stages in vocational adjustment is the *productive* role which society expects the individual to play in the world of work and the extent to which he can fulfill this expectation.

Summary. For purposes of comparison and contrast, Figure 12-1 presents the stages and periods in vocational adjustment delineated by Super (1957; Super et al., 1963), Miller, D. C., and Form (1951; 1964), and Havighurst (1964). The

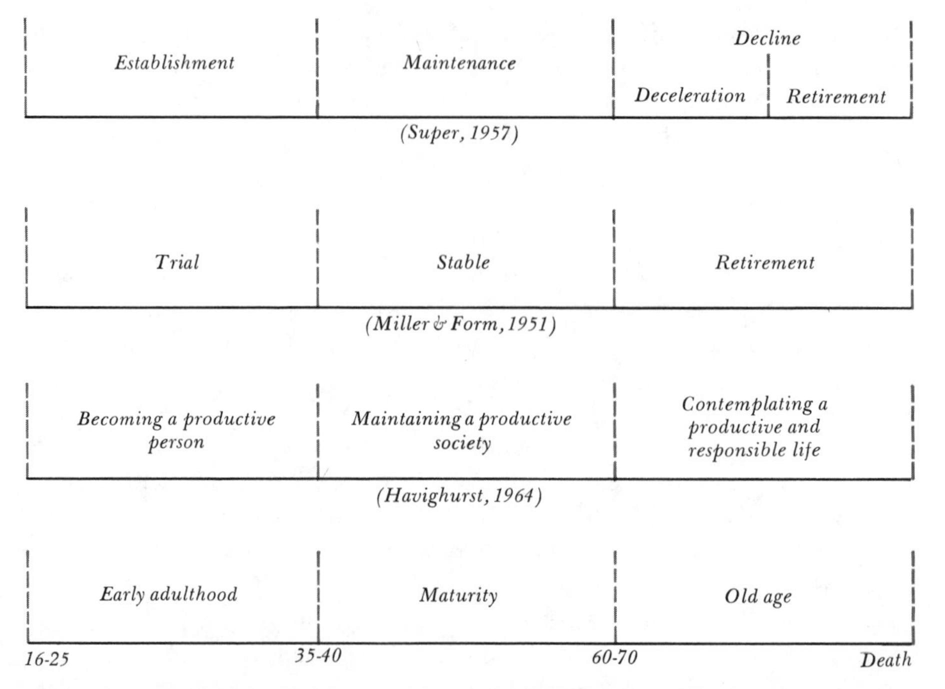

***Figure 12-1. Developmental stages in vocational adjustment as proposed by Super** (1957; Super et al., 1963), **Miller, D. C., and Form** (1951; 1964), **and Havighurst** (1964).*

ages which delimit the various stages are quite similar, but the names which have been given to them reflect some differences among the three conceptualizations. Super has drawn heavily upon self-concept theory to characterize the predominant thema of the Exploratory, Maintenance, and Decline stages, the trend in vocational development being from the implementation of the self-concept in an occupational role, through the preserving of the self-concept in one's life work, to adjustment to a new self-concept in retirement. In contrast, Miller and Form focus upon the social adjustments which the individual must make within the work organization as he progresses through the Trial, Stable, and Retired periods. Finally, Havighurst's schema represents a partial synthesis of these two frameworks, the one primarily psychological and the other sociological, in that he formulates a psychosocial interpretation of the stages through which the worker passes to become a productive person not only as an individual, but also as a member of society.

Research on the Stages in Vocational Adjustment

Although no one has directly set out to substantiate the stages in vocational adjustment we have discussed, there is a handful of studies which are relevant to vocational adjustment from the time the individual enters the world of work until he leaves it:

1. In one of several surveys of life-time worry patterns (Dykman, Heimann, & Kerr, 1952; Kerr, Newman, & Sadewic, 1949), Kerr and his associates (Van Zelst & Kerr, 1951, pp. 151–152) found four discernible "stages" in the retrospective worries of 236 building-trades leaders who were 40 or older:

> 1. An early personal worry cluster—appearance, sexual relations, religious-philosophical convictions, peace of mind, morality of self, and marital difficulties.
> 2. A vocational success worry cluster in the thirties—meeting people, envy of others, giving up major ambitions, work associates, and politics.
> 3. A mid-life stress worry cluster (39–40)—peace of mind, morality of self, sexual relations, marital difficulties, and religious-philosophical.
> 4. A declining years worry cluster—loss of work efficiency, death, health, and giving up major ambitions.

2. Kuhlen and Johnson (1952, pp. 3–4) have reported definite age trends in the goals of single and married women and married men teachers, drawing the following conclusion about the latter: "Emphasis up to age 50 among married men seems to be on vocational advancement; thereafter wish to stay on the same job is more frequently mentioned than other jobs or promotion.... After 50 the typical hope (or expectation) is that the next ten years will bring retirement."

3. Saleh (1964; Saleh & Otis, 1963) has tested the hypothesis, stemming from Herzberg's (1959) theory of vocational motivation (see Chapter 9), that preretirees, ages 60 to 65, would report motivators as greater sources of satisfaction in the middle years of vocational adjustment (ages 30 to 55) and hygienes in the later years. This is exactly what he found for a sample of 85 male employees at the managerial level. He reasoned that this reversal in the salience of motivators and hygienes for satisfaction with increasing age might be attributable to either the prepotency of safety and security needs in the preretirement period or the general unavailability of motivators in work, e.g., promotion possibilities, in this late stage of vocational development.

4. Friedmann and Havighurst (1954) have compared the meanings of work and retirement among steelworkers, coal miners, retail salespersons, skilled craftsmen, and physicians, and have concluded that the higher the worker is in the occupational hierarchy, the more he perceives his vocation as intrinsically satisfying and an end in itself. The higher-level worker prefers to continue his vocation and *not* to retire at age 65. He views his work as a way of life rather than merely a way to earn a living.

These studies are far from conclusive, but they do suggest that vocational-adjustment behaviors change as the worker grows older and that these changes may be delineated into stages. The need for further research, however, is apparent, particularly the collection of longitudinal data on the stages in vocational adjustment.

CAREER PATTERNS AND VOCATIONAL ADJUSTMENT

Whereas life stages designate the periods which can be delineated in the individual's vocational adjustment, career patterns trace his job movement, whether it is progression or regression, through the world of work. The concept of career patterns has its historical roots in the sociologist's interest in social mobility. To determine the extent to which a society is "open," i.e., how much opportunity its members have for changing their station in life, the sociologist has extensively studied occupational mobility, horizontal as well as vertical. For example, in his classic treatise on social mobility, which has provided much of the conceptual background for subsequent research on career patterns, Sorokin (1927) discussed such phenomena as interoccupational and intraoccupational stratification, fluctuation of the occupational composition of the population, occupational ascent and descent, occupational transmission from father to son, occupational recruiting from different social strata, etc. It was not until considerably later, however, that Davidson, P. E., and Anderson (1937) introduced the concept of career patterns in order to depict the work history of an individual over an extended period of time. The effect of this innovation has been to conceptualize the career pattern more as a phenomenon of vocational development than simply as an index of social mobility. As a developmental variable, it has distinctive characteristics and properties which we shall summarize in the following discussion of (1) definitions of career patterns, (2) classifications of career patterns, and (3) studies of career patterns.[1]

Definitions of Career Patterns

Different definitions of career patterns have reflected somewhat varying emphases, depending upon whether the definition was cast within a predomi-

[1] There is an extensive sociological literature, most of it nonempirical, on careers which it is not possible to include here. It has just been reviewed, however, by Slocum (1966), who cites most of the pertinent references. Those which he does not cover are given in the List of References. Also, for additional analytical and descriptive articles, in which either empirical data are not reported or they are not treated statistically, see Beall and Bordin (1964); Slocum (1965); Hubbard (1965); and Strauss (1965). Finally, of possible interest as a juxtapose to conventional interpretations of careers is Lyon's (1965) proposed *serial* career model, in which greater allowance is made for the effects of cultural determinants upon the course of vocational development.

nantly sociological or psychological framework, but there has nevertheless been a common theme which has run through them. They all conceptualize the career pattern as a sequence of related events over time in the work history of the individual. Davidson, P. E., and Anderson (1937, p. 367) defined a worker's career pattern as "the number of occupations followed and the duration of each." As Miller, D. C., and Form (1947, p. 367) have noted, however, Davidson and Anderson analyzed the relationship between only the first and last jobs of the worker, rather than all his jobs. To correct for this shortcoming, the former (Form & Miller, 1949) have used the total number of jobs held by the worker to define career patterns along two dimensions: the abscissa representing the time spent in a job, and the ordinate denoting its socioeconomic level, as determined by Edwards's scale. A less operational, but more comprehensive, definition of career pattern has been proposed by Becker (1952, p. 470), who views it as a "patterned series of adjustments" which the individual makes to the "network of institutions, formal organizations, and informal relationships" he finds in the world of work. Much the same emphasis has been given by Super (1954) to the analysis of career patterns by what he calls the "thematic-extrapolative" method. The career pattern of an individual is inferred from the thema which run through his work history, such as security, marginality, regression, etc. In contrast to the more or less objective defining rules used by Miller and Form, Super's approach is more subjective and relies heavily upon the expertise of judges to extrapolate career thema from the work history.

Classifications of Career Patterns

Career patterns have been classified in several different ways, as Nosow and Form (1962, p. 284) have observed:

> In some occupations a career pattern represents orderly movement from one occupational level to another. . . . A second pattern is one among unskilled workers, which entails movement from one job to another, with jobs having no apparent relationship with one another. A third type involves a series of job moves which are not closely related but which do form a coherent pattern. . . . Still a fourth pattern is found wherein occupations themselves change over a period of time.

A more specific classification of career patterns has been suggested by Miller, D. C., and Form (1947, pp. 370–371), based upon the possible combinations of initial, trial, and stable jobs listed in Table 12-2. As is shown in this table, they identify six different types of career patterns (Miller, D. C., & Form, 1951, p. 712), each with its major defining characteristics. They have further categorized these into *secure* and *insecure* career patterns, depending upon whether

Table 12-2. Classification of Career Patterns (After Miller, D. C., & Form, 1947; 1951)

SECURE	Stable	Stable Initial-Stable-Trial-Stable Stable-Trial-Stable Initial-Stable
	Conventional	Initial-Trial-Stable Initial-Trial-Stable-Trial-Stable Trial-Stable
INSECURE	Unstable	Trial-Stable-Trial Initial-Trial-Stable-Trial
	Trial	Initial-Trial Trial
	Disestablished	Stable-Trial Initial-Stable-Trial
	Multiple Trial	Trial-Trial-Trial-Trial

the last job in the sequence is a stable or trial job. Super (1957) has proposed a revision of Miller and Form's sixfold classification schema, which condenses it to the following four types of career patterns: (1) stable, (2) conventional, (3) unstable, and (4) multiple trial. Although he does not cite his reasons for this simplification, Super evidently considers the single trial and disestablished patterns to be special cases of the multiple trial and unstable patterns, respectively. Super (1957, pp. 77–78) has also devised a classification of women's career patterns, which includes seven different types: (1) stable homemaking, (2) conventional, (3) stable working, (4) double-track, (5) interrupted, (6) unstable, and (7) multiple-trial.

Studies of Career Patterns

A Classic Study. The first investigation in which empirical data on career patterns were collected was conducted by Davidson, P. E., and Anderson (1937) toward the end of the Depression years in San Jose, California. In this community of approximately 17,745 gainfully employed male workers, they surveyed the employment histories of 1,242 Subjects, which constituted almost exactly a 7 percent sample. Data on the number, kind, and variety of previous occupational experiences, as well as amount of schooling, vocational training, and income, were gathered on each Subject by means of a paper-and-pencil "schedule," supplemented by an interview for those who were illiterate. Analyses of the data were largely descriptive, involving mostly the computation of percentages for various categorizations and stratifications of the sample, but some significance tests for between-group comparisons were run, and, in general, the statistical treatment of the data was sophisticated for the era during which the study was conducted. Because of Davidson and Anderson's primary interest in the sociological problem of social mobility, as posed by Sorokin (1927) and others, they analyzed their data not only to establish trends in career patterns, but also, more generally, to draw conclusions about such phenomena as occupational inheritance, occupational mobility, and geographical migration, which might be related to how much "equality of opportunity" actually exists for workers to get ahead, regardless of their backgrounds. We shall summarize, however, only their findings on (1) the number and duration of occupations followed by workers and (2) their career patterns at different occupational levels.

First, with respect to the *number* of regular occupations held, 64 percent of the sample, for which data were available (1,165 out of 1,242), reported that they had had only one occupation; 20 percent had been in three occupations. Second, *duration* in regular occupation was related to age, as might be expected, since older workers have had a longer period of time in which to establish themselves. The average number of years in a regular occupation was 28.3 for 55-year-olds, in contrast to 2.2 for 20 to 34-year-olds. It was also found that 22 percent of the sample had been in their regular occupations for more than 20 years; 23 to 67 percent, depending upon occupational level, had pursued their regular occupations for 10 years or less. Finally, results on the proportion of the *working life* spent in a regular occupation indicated that, of 1,124 respondents, 14 percent had been in their regular occupations one-fourth or less of their employed lives; 28 percent, from one-half to three-fourths; and 32 percent, more than three-fourths (Davidson, P. E., & Anderson, 1937, p. 80). The average or typical worker had spent about 57 percent of his working life in his regular occupation. Davidson, P. E., and Anderson (1937, p. 83) drew a conclusion from these findings which has a direct implication for research on vocational development: "The occupation regarded by a worker at any given time as his regular one can scarcely be considered as giving a complete picture of his working career." Clearly, more than one occupation—ideally, the whole career pattern—should be used in developmental studies of vocational adjustment.

Unfortunately, in their analysis of career patterns, Davidson and Anderson did not observe this principle. As was mentioned previously, they used only the worker's first and last occupations to plot his career pattern. They classified these occupations according to Edwards's scale, and then related them to two other variables: (1) the father's regular occupation and (2) the amount of schooling attained by the son. Their results indicated that there are marked differences in the career patterns and backgrounds of workers on different occupational levels. In general, the tendency is for the last occupation to be on the same level as the first and to be consistent with amount of schooling. At the professional and proprietor levels, the trend is for the last occupation to be on essentially the same level as the father's regular occupation, but this is less true for the clerical level and obtains even less so on the skilled, semiskilled, and unskilled levels. In fact, the latter are more accurately characterized by downward occupational mobility: the largest percentages of paternal occupations are on levels *higher than* those of the sons.

Although Davidson and Anderson do not discuss it, a possible explanation for this phenomenon may be that the "proprietor" level in Edwards's classification system includes farm owners and tenants, and consequently their sons, who follow occupations of a skilled, semiskilled, or unskilled type, possibly in order to leave the farm, end up on a level lower than that of their fathers, according to the occupational scale which was used, but not necessarily by other criteria, such as father's educational level. Whatever the reason, however, it does not seem justified to conclude, as Davidson, P. E., and Anderson (1937, p. 113) did, that heredity and environment, in combination, "produce a very considerable rigidity and consequent stratification of occupations on the several levels of the pyramid of labor that confines the movement of workers largely within a single occupational level." If anything, their findings on career patterns appear to show that there *is* intergenerational mobility within the occupational hierarchy, but it is primarily *downward,* at least at the lower levels. Certainly, further research on this issue is needed before a definitive conclusion can be reached, and it should not obscure the value of Davidson and Anderson's classic work on the concept of the career pattern, which they introduced and which has led to considerable subsequent research.

A Recent Study. One of the most comprehensive studies of career patterns which has stemmed from the early work of Davidson and Anderson is the "Ohio Study" conducted by Miller, D. C., and Form (1947; 1949). These investigators selected a stratified representative sample of 276 workers from gainfully employed males in Ohio and interviewed them to gather data on their occupational histories. The Subjects were asked to recall every job that they had held, from the time they started to work, and the amount of time they had spent in each. These data were analyzed first to classify each job according to whether it was an initial, trial, or stable job. To briefly summarize the definitions of these terms, which were discussed earlier in the section on "Developmental Stages in Vocational Adjustment," an *initial* job is one which is held while the individual is still completing his formal education; a *trial* job is one pursued for a period of 3 years or less, after the individual's formal education has been terminated; and a *stable* job is one which lasts for 3 or more years. Miller, D. C., and Form (1947, p. 365) note that the defining criteria for classifying jobs into these categories can be applied by judges with a high degree of agreement. Two judges agreed on 95 percent of the jobs they classified, the disagreement arising in determining whether a job was an initial or trial one, since in some instances it was difficult to decide when a person's formal education had been completed. Thus, these procedures for defining career patterns appear to be highly objective and reliable. Miller, D. C., and Form (1947, p. 365; italics in original) conclude that their classification schema allows the measurement of "the *continuity,* the *stability,* and the *security* evident within various occupational levels, as well as the 'deviation' patterns for each occupational level."

To study each of these phenomena, i.e., the continuity, stability, and security of career patterns, Miller, D. C., and Form (1947) established three hypotheses for testing:

1. "Occupational careers of all workers tend to remain on the same occupational level from the first part-time job to the last job held" (p. 367). Results from a chi-square analysis, in which the distributions of initial and trial jobs were compared with those for last permanent jobs across occupational levels, indicated that "once started on an occupational level, a worker tends to remain on that level" (p. 368). The contingency coefficients for initial and trial jobs versus last jobs, for example, were moderate to high, being .54 and .71, respectively, where the highest possible C was .926.

2. "Job stability is associated with the white-collar workers; job instability, with manual workers" (p. 368). Although no statistical tests were made on their data, which were the median number of years spent in initial, trial, and stable jobs at each occupational level, Miller, D. C., and Form (1947, p. 369) concluded that, in general, the hypothesis was supported. The higher occupational levels spent less time in initial and trial jobs, and more time in stable jobs, whereas the opposite was true of the lower occupational levels. There were some notable exceptions to this trend, however, for professional and skilled workers. The former held their initial jobs for a disproportionately long period of time, given their occupational level, and the latter did the same for their stable jobs.[2]

3. "Job security is associated with the white-collar workers; job insecurity is associated with manual workers" (p. 370). Using the classification of "secure" and "insecure" career patterns shown in Table 12-2, Miller, D. C., and Form (1947, p. 371; italics in original) found that: *"Seventy-three percent of the pat-*

[2] Whether a stable career pattern *necessarily* indicates good vocational adjustment may be contingent, however, on why a worker stays in his job as well as how long he persists in it. Shoben (1952, p. 290) makes the point that: "Stability sometimes may represent responsibility, persistence, and a sensible orientation with respect to goals, whereas sometimes it may reflect only a fear of change or an unrealistic and defensive appraisal of one's own attributes."

terns of the white-collar group were in the secure categories as opposed to forty-six per cent of manual workers." The major exception to a linear relationship between occupational level and security of career pattern was the skilled-worker group, which had a higher percentage of secure patterns than clerical and kindred workers. Thus, Miller and Form's three hypotheses were largely confirmed. It was primarily the skilled workers who did not conform to expectations, much as Super (1939) found in his study of occupational level and job satisfaction. There is increasing evidence that skilled workers are more like professionals, proprietors, managers, etc., than they are like clerical workers.

In another report of their study, Form and Miller (1949) further analyzed their data on the security of career patterns. Their purpose was to determine the years spent in the initial, trial, and stable work periods for each occupational level, regardless of the work sequence. To do this they devised a "security index," which expressed the "*ratio of the mean years in the stable work period* ($\overline{Y}_s$) *to the sum of the mean years in the initial* ($\overline{Y}_i$) *and trial work periods* ($\overline{Y}_t$)" (Form & Miller, 1949, p. 320; italics in original), or:

$$I_s = \frac{\overline{Y}_s}{\overline{Y}_i + \overline{Y}_t}$$

The assumption underlying this index is that "the initial and trial work periods [are] unstable, relatively insecure, occupationally mobile years in which the worker is struggling to establish himself" (Form & Miller, 1949, p. 320). Index values were obtained for each occupational level, and it was found that, with one exception, they corresponded exactly to Edwards's scale. The only deviation was the coefficient for the unskilled workers, which ranked them above, instead of below, the semiskilled level.

These findings have been depicted graphically in Figures 12-2 and 12-3, where high- and low-security career patterns are also shown in relationship to three other variables: (1) father's education, (2) father's occupation, and (3) son's education. It is clear from these diagrams that the career patterns of the upper occupational levels are considerably more secure than those of the lower levels. Furthermore, it is apparent that background factors are associated with the security of career patterns. As Form and Miller (1949, p. 329) point out, "There is a strong tendency for the children of white-collar persons to inherit their father's occupation or climb above it. Children of manual workers inherit their father's occupation or fall below it." This is the same trend which was noted in Davidson and Anderson's data. Why it exists should be an interesting problem for future research. As suggested previously, it may be, in part, an artifact of the occupational classification schema which has been used to determine the level of the paternal occupation.

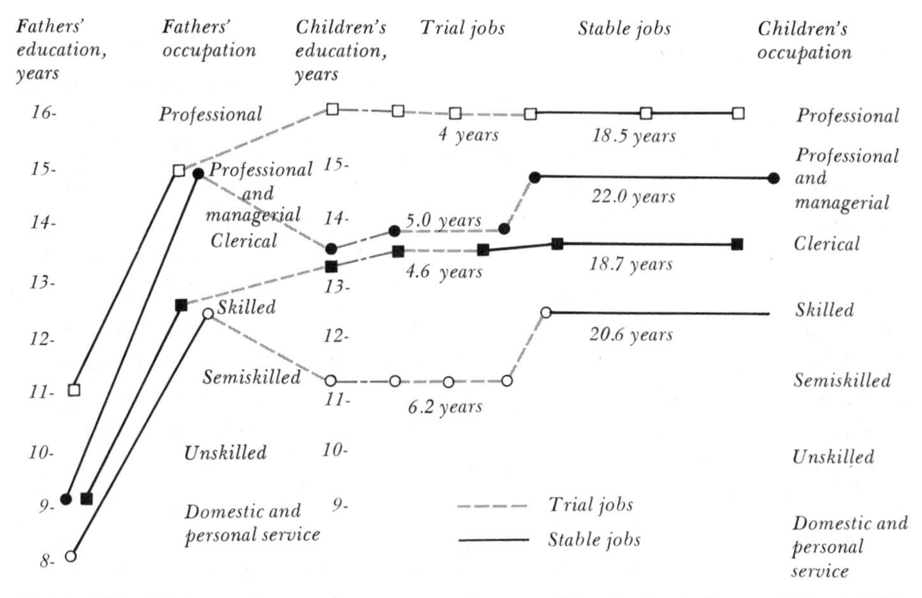

Figure 12-2. High-security career patterns. *(From Miller, D. C., & Form, 1944, p. 327.)*

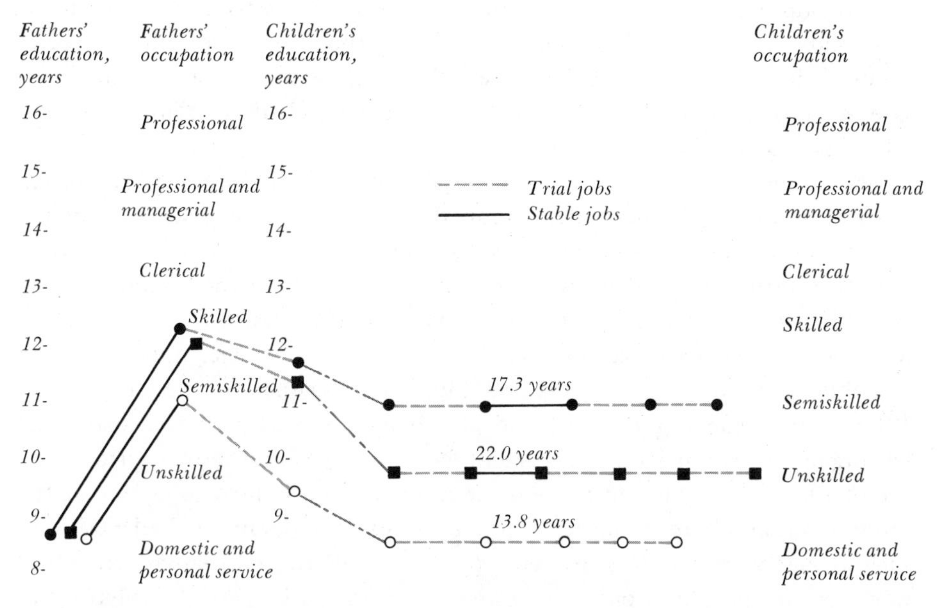

Figure 12-3. Low-security career patterns. *(From Miller, D. C., & Form, 1949, p. 327.)*

Other Studies. In addition to the investigations by Davidson and Anderson and by Miller and Form, there have been several other studies of career patterns which it is important to review. Four of these have been on the career patterns of specific occupational groups, and three have dealt with the correlates of career patterns. Brief summaries of the more significant findings of the group studies are given first, followed by summaries of the correlate studies:[3]

1. In a survey type of investigation of the medical profession, Hall, O. (1948) found that four stages in the careers of physicians could be identified. The first of these was what he termed "generating an ambition," in which the aspiring young doctor is either aided or not in his initial steps toward a career in medicine by his family and friends. If the novice doctor comes from a professional background, the chances are much greater that he will progress more rapidly and successfully with his career than if he comes from a nonprofessional stratum. The second stage of "incorporation into the institutions of medicine" is much the same as the first, in that career progression depends largely upon some external agent for certain enabling actions. In this instance, it is gaining acceptance for an appointment on a hospital staff for intern training. The third stage, called "acquiring a clientele," comes when the physician has completed his training and attempts to establish himself in the community. He will be more or less successful in his efforts to the extent that he is able to become a specialist, which is more prestigious and remunerative, and to gain access to hospital facilities, which are essential for the conduct of a specialty. The last stage of being accepted by the "inner fraternity" involves sponsorship by a member of the "core" of physicians which controls and regulates medical practice in a community. As Hall, O. (1948, p. 336) points out, "The sponsored protegé must be assisted and vouched for at each step in his career." Thus, the career patterns of physicians, from the initial to the terminal stages, are largely dependent upon the informal social machinery of the medical profession. This is not nearly as true of other occupational groups.

2. In a rather unusual study of the career patterns of professional athletes, Bookbinder (1955) was interested in discovering what happens vocationally to major league baseball players after they "retire"—at an age, usually around 35, which is very young as compared with other occupations. For a group of 121 former major leaguers, who had played for an average of 13.2 years, had left organized ball at an average age of 35.1, and had been retired for an average of 19.3 years, he found that (*a*) the most frequently held jobs were at the professional and managerial level, usually in other types of baseball positions, such as managers, coach, scout, etc.; (*b*) almost all the jobs entered involved working with people in one way or another, principally through athletics and sales work, in which their baseball fame could be used to advantage; (*c*) job changing was infrequent, the most stable post-baseball occupation being farming; and (*d*) there appeared to be little relationship between father's occupa-

[3] Not included here are two studies which may be of general interest but which are based upon retrospective data and which only indirectly deal with careers: Anderson, D. (1966) and Beilin (1954).

tion and the later occupations of the ballplayers. These findings on the career patterns of former major leaguers suggest, then, that they generally remain on the same level and in the same field throughout their work lives, which indicates considerably more stability than is usually thought of for individuals who are associated with athletics or entertainment.

3. A group of 315 machinists was followed up by Kouble and Rothney (1956), after a period of 12 to 13 years of employment, to determine (*a*) extent of unemployment, (*b*) occupational changes, (*c*) first-job assignments, (*d*) current job assignments, (*e*) income advancement, (*f*) company mobility, (*g*) effects of company mobility, and (*h*) geographic mobility. The conclusions which could be drawn about these various aspects of the career patterns of machinists indicated the following: All but three had maintained steady employment since the completion of their trade-school training. Only 15 percent left the occupation for another which was not directly related to their training. Over 90 percent were assigned to first jobs, such as machine operator or assembler, which were below the level of their qualifications. Only after considerable time on the job were they promoted to more all-around specialties, such as tool-and-die maker, or first-line management positions. Increases in wages appeared to be directly related to advancement from highly specialized jobs, through all-around classifications, to supervisory responsibilities. Changing from one company to another was infrequent, but when it occurred it resulted more often in promotions to all-around duties rather than foreman rank. Those machinists who remained with their original employer were twice as likely to be advanced to the managerial level as those who moved to another company. Finally, there seemed to be very little geographic mobility of the machinists studied: four out of five changes of company were made within the same labor market. To summarize these results, it might be said that the outstanding characteristic of the career patterns of machinists is their stability, security, and success: they progress in an orderly and systematic fashion to higher income and skill/responsibility levels with a low degree of horizontal and geographical mobility.

4. Guest (1955) has reported data on the careers of assembly-line workers which contrast sharply with those on higher-level occupations. The Subjects of this study were 202 line workers who performed a highly repetitive assembly task, which was completed within a time cycle of approximately 1 to 2 minutes. These men held 54 different job-classification titles, but fell into only 8 pay groups. Actually, 95 percent were in 4 pay groups, the differential for most of them (60 percent) being 10 cents. In short, the opportunity for advancement in pay was extremely restricted. Over a period of 12 to 15 years, the average per-hour wage increase was only *5 cents,* the equivalent of one job class. Some of the production workers advanced to supervisory positions, but most of them remained on the lower echelons for the entire span of their work lives. Guest (1955, p. 156) sums up the lot of the assembly-line laborer as follows:

> Since differences in pay in industrial occupations are generally related to differences in skill, it is not difficult to understand why auto assembly jobs fall into a relatively narrow pay range and why, even among men with several years' experience, any upward change in job status within production departments is hardly discernible.

As Miller and Form found in their study, and as is corroborated by this and the other studies of specific occupational groups, career patterns vary markedly from one level of skill and responsibility to another.

Whether career patterns are also related to other variables has been the problem of three investigations, all of which have yielded largely negative results. Bendix, Lipsett, and Malm (1954) attempted to trace the relationship of father's occupation and educational attainment to the career patterns of a sample of 935 male workers and found only equivocal or weak associations among the variables. The data on father's occupation showed that it was consistently related to percentage of time spent by the son in occupations on the paternal level, but not on others. Educational attainment tended to be correlated with the percentage of time spent in a worker's highest-level job. Youmans (1956) studied several factors which might be associated with the careers of 380 male and female federal management interns and concluded that only college major (public administration versus others) was contributory to advancement. Such factors as urban-rural background, socioeconomic status, physical health, military service, educational level, mental ability (above selection cutoff), authoritarianism (California *F* scale), and psychological stress were unrelated to vertical career mobility. Finally, Doyle (1965) has reported quite similar results for 488 male college graduates from a small Catholic college. He found that only 4 out of 41 variables were correlated with career patterns classified as stable, conventional, and unsettled. These variables, which were related to the patterns in the order given, were (1) initial job tenure, (2) current job tenure, (3) total number of jobs held, and (4) initial job aspiration. Only the last variable, however, was experimentally independent of the procedures used to operationally define the career patterns, so that actually there was just this one correlate which was identified out of the 41 studied. In other words, those with more definite vocational aspirations when they graduated from college had more stable career patterns after they entered the world of work.

DEVELOPMENTAL TRENDS IN VOCATIONAL SUCCESS

In Chapter 10, we discussed the definition, study, and prediction of vocational success, but not its status as a developmental phenomenon. Here, we shall pose the question of whether there are developmental trends in vocational success and survey some of the answers which have emerged from the accumulated research on the problem. We shall present first a fairly detailed account of a classic study of age and achievement conducted by Lehman, which is the precursor of many subsequent investigations. Next, we shall review some of the recent studies which his pioneer research stimulated and attempt to draw conclusions which are consistent with both earlier and later findings. Finally, we shall summarize the results from other studies on systematic changes in vocational success with increasing age and evaluate what their salience for vocational development theory and research may be.

A Classic Study

Over a period of several years, from 1936 to 1951, Lehman published many articles on the relationship of chronological age to creativity and productivity, which he subsequently compiled into his classic work entitled *Age and Achievement* (Lehman, 1953). This book reports a mass of data on developmental trends in vocational success, classified according to the following topics: (1) age and achievement in specific fields of endeavor, including science, medicine, philosophy, music, art, and literature; (2) the quality versus quantity of productivity; (3) the range of the creative years; and (4) the interrelationships of past, present, and future achievements. Lehman's procedure was usually to use an anthology or history in a field to identify what were considered to be the outstanding works or "significant" contributions of workers in the field. In other words, his criterion of vocational success was whether the product of an individual, e.g., a scientific discovery or musical composition, was cited or listed in one of the field's reference sources. Thus, for chemists, Lehman consulted Hilditch's (1911) *A Concise History of Chemistry,* which lists the names of several hundred noted chemists and the dates when they made their significant contributions to chemistry. He then found out the individual's date of birth and determined his age at the time of his achievement. The next step was to calculate the mean number of outstanding accomplishments for age intervals of (usually) 5 years, the mean being computed, rather than using N, because younger individuals were more numerous in Lehman's samples. Finally, graphs were drawn, such as the one in Figure 12-4, which depicted the trends in significant achievements across age levels. Similar analyses were made of total achievements, not just significant ones, and some correlational analyses of quality versus quantity of production were conducted.

It is difficult to summarize the voluminous findings obtained by Lehman. Perhaps an overview of them can be gained, however, by presenting some illustrative data and then enumerating his general conclusions. Figure 12-4 provides an example of the age-versus-achievement trend which seemed to characterize most of the occupational groups which were studied. As is apparent in

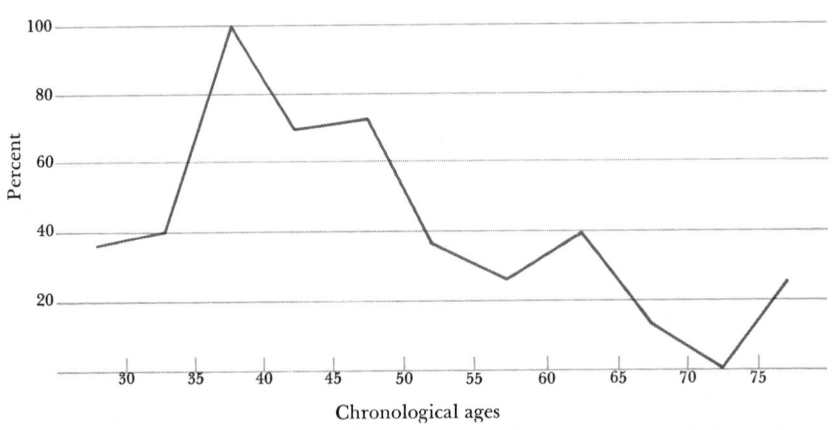

Figure 12-4. The relationship of age to achievement for psychologists. *(From Lehman, 1953, p. 30.)*

this graph, which is based upon data for 50 psychologists who made a total of 85 significant contributions, there is a precipitous increase in creativity during the first two age intervals, with the peak (mode) in the 35 to 40 range, and then a marked decline throughout the remaining years of the work life. Much the same curve was found for other occupations, the most noteworthy variations being in the modal age interval. Chemists, certain musical composers, and athletes generally attained their fame in their twenties, whereas educational, governmental, and religious leaders reached their highest offices in their fifties and sixties. As Lehman (1953, p. 309) notes, however, the overall results indicate that "the golden decade for achievement is the thirties." Furthermore, achievement in this period of vocational development is related to greater total output than achievement later on. In other words, if an individual makes an outstanding contribution early in his career, the chances are that *quantitatively* he will produce more than a person who achieves success at an older age. But this does not mean that quality and quantity of output are highly related. Lehman (1953, p. 62) points out that "*quantity of output* tends to sustain itself at the upper age levels much better than does *quality of output*." Finally, some incidental but interesting findings were that (1) the ages of greatest success and maximum income are correlated but not highly;[4] (2) the peaks of athletic and intellectual performance closely coincide as far as age level is concerned; and (3) as compared with previous centuries, contemporary leaders in education, politics, and religion are considerably older.

The major conclusion which Lehman drew from his study of age and achievement was that the outstanding contributions of workers in a variety of occupational fields come relatively early in their careers, i.e., typically during

[4] Lehman does not report an r for this relationship.

the Establishment stage of vocational development. He also observes that "very superior achievement seems most likely to occur during a relatively narrow age-range, and the more noteworthy the performance, the more rapidly does the resultant age-curve descend after it has attained its peak" (Lehman, 1953, p. 70). In short, not only do notable accomplishments appear early in the work life, but, for most occupations, they are usually made within a period of a few years. It is important to note that this phenomenon is characteristic of *significant* achievements only; it is not the case with total productivity. The latter tends to follow more of a bell-shaped distribution in contrast to the positively skewed distribution of the former.

Lehman (1953, pp. 328–329) enumerates several different reasons concerning why the distribution of distinguished accomplishments is skewed toward the younger age levels, some of which are:

1. Decline in physical vigor, energy, and resistance to fatigue
2. Diminution in sensory capacity and motor precision
3. Serious illness, poor health, and bodily infirmities
4. Unhappy marriages and sexual maladjustment
5. Too easy, too great, or too early fame, which leads to complacency

To these might be added at least one more which was suggested to Lehman by a botanist who had read one of his articles on "man's most creative years": he proposed that a worker's subsequent achievements may be limited by his first success, for which he gained renown, much as the terminal bud on a branch precludes the development of other buds (the principle in botany of "inhibition of pre-formed parts"). Whatever the explanation, the import of Lehman's study is that the greatest achievements in work are made early in life.

Comment. Whether this inference can legitimately be drawn from Lehman's data, however, depends upon whether the trends he found in achievement are attributable to age—or, more accurately, to age-related events. Dennis (1954; 1956a; 1958) has argued that they are *not* for several reasons: First, Lehman combined data on Subjects with different longevities, so that it is unknown whether short-lived men might not have made a more significant contribution later on had they lived longer. Second, there is the possibility of sampling errors due to small *N*'s and Lehman's use of different age intervals for different occupational fields. Third, standards of excellence change within a person's lifetime, so that his earlier works may be judged by different criteria than his later ones. Fourth, because of the growth of most fields in recent years, the competition for making a significant contribution has increased. Thus, in 1900 the best psychologist was selected from among a group of about 100 psychologists in the country; today, there are well over 20,000 psychologists in America. Finally, and most important in Dennis's opinion, there may have been biases of two sorts in the sources from which Lehman gathered his data. One of these biases is what Dennis considers to be the reluctance of anthologists and historians to cite an individual's most recent productions, which typically come later in life. Rather, he contends, they single out an early work, usually one which represents a pioneering effort, for recognition. The other bias is in the percentage of significant contributions which are cited in anthologies and histories, relative to the total number of publications in a field. Dennis (1958, p. 457) has established, for example, that "the proportion of scientific work cited decreases from decade to decade of time and that, hence, among men born at a specified time the probability of citation of their works declines from decade to decade of life." He goes on to conclude that: "This circumstance results in a spurious finding of an age decrement in the output of significant works."

Lehman (1956) has joined the issues raised by Dennis in a point-by-point rebuttal, in which he defends the existence of age trends in outstanding achievements. Among his counterarguments are these: First, with respect to the differing longevities of his Subjects, Lehman (1956, p. 334) replies: "My data are pretty convincing that, even if *all* of the creative workers had been long-lived, the relative creative production rate of the oldsters would not have been as great as that of the younger men." Second, on sampling errors and age intervals, Lehman (1956, p. 335) states: "The sharpness of some of the peaks in my age-curves is certainly due in part to the manner in which I chose my age intervals. . . . But when one, by this means, can obtain the same sharply pointed peaks in age-curve after age-curve, surely something other than chance factors must be operating." Third, pertaining to Dennis's comment that citation sources may "contain systematic errors somewhat favoring a man's early work at the expense of his later products," Lehman (1956, p. 336) answers: "This statement is purely speculative. Nor do I see how the validity of this point could be proved." And he adds: "I tried in my investigation only to ascertain the ages at which the most significant creative contributions were made. I did *not* attempt to ascertain how many years it took the contributor to sell his great idea to his colleagues." Finally, Lehman (1956, p. 336) dismisses Dennis's observation that standards for evaluating contributions are changing with the comment that: "It seems to me that this question had best be left to specialists within the various fields of endeavor to decide. It is not a question that can be settled by Dennis and/or Lehman." As regards the increased competition for recognition in recent years, because of the growth of the creative occupations, Lehman did not offer a rejoinder.

Recent Studies

The controversy between Dennis and Lehman fortunately did not end with this interchange of pros and cons on the relationship of age to achievement. It led to further studies by both men, in an effort to clarify the issues which had been raised in their debate. In a series of five papers, Lehman (1958; 1960; 1962a; 1962b; 1966) has presented data gathered to refute Dennis's criticism or to elaborate upon his original findings:

First, he dealt with the problem of the effects of individual differences in longevity upon creativity and productivity and found that for two groups of 109 chemists, one of which was short-lived and the other long-lived, the age curves for achievement were quite similar (Lehman, 1958). In fact, at the few points where they deviated from each other, the curve for the short-lived chemists declined later than that for the long-lived chemists, which is exactly opposite to what would be expected, if unequal longevities had biased Lehman's data as Dennis maintained they did.

Second, with respect to Dennis's (1958) finding, already mentioned, that the ratio of citations to total publications has gone down in recent decades, thus indicating bias in anthologies and histories, Lehman (1960, p. 129; italics in original) argued that an equally likely interpretation is that "the progressive decline in Dennis' index of citation means only that *really great* contributions to science have been increasing at a slower rate than have run-of-the-mine contributions." He supports this argument both logically and empirically with new data from 44 references which yielded essentially the same curves as his original sources.

Third, Lehman (1962a) compared living with deceased mathematicians and scientists to test Dennis's contention that recency of publication might affect age of outstanding contributions and found that the peak years of achievement were almost exactly the same for the two groups (ages 30 to 39), although the rate of decrement was steeper for those who were still living.

Fourth, Lehman (1966, p. 368) replicated these findings on living and deceased psychologists, leading him to conclude that "the historian's inability 'to see so near his face' [as Dennis had proposed] is relatively unimportant in so far as my age curves for still-living contributors is concerned."

Finally, in a review article, Lehman (1962b) has suggested some possible reinterpretations of his findings, in particular his earlier conclusion (Lehman, 1953) that contributors born prior to 1775 attained their maximum production rates about 10 years later than those born after this date. He is convinced now that this discrepancy is attributable to such factors as reluctance to publish during the earlier era and the present emphasis upon "publish or perish" in the academic world (Caplow & McGee, 1958), rather than intergenerational differences in the ability to achieve at a young age.

In contrast to Lehman's focus upon outstanding accomplishments, Dennis (1954; Dennis & Girden, 1954; 1956b) has been concerned more with total career productivity. Because of this difference in emphasis, his findings do not necessarily contradict those of Lehman and, in some instances, actually support and corroborate them. What Dennis found first was that the publications of scientists, after the early years of their careers, reach a certain level and remain there well into old age. Thus, he (Dennis, 1956b) reports the data presented in Table 12-3, which show the low point in productivity to be in the twenties with only a slight "tailing off" in the later decades of life for two groups of scientists, one which lived to their seventies and the other to their eighties. In this same study, he also determined that only (about) 50 percent of the groups' total output had been achieved by the time they were in their fifties. Furthermore, in an analysis of the octogenarians alone, he found that in the 10 years before they turned 80 they averaged an additional 13.1 papers. Overall, the mean number of articles per year for the entire sample was almost 2.0 between ages 30 and 60. Dennis's (Dennis & Girden, 1954; 1956b) other major finding was the trend in the correlations between publications from one decade of a scientist's career to another. In general, the *r*'s are highest between consecutive decades, the range being from approximately .50 to .85. The poorest predictions of later productivity are made from the twenties, presumably because "publication seldom begins before the late 20s, and for that reason the samples of productivity obtained from the 20s are small ones" (Dennis & Girden, 1954, pp. 465–466).

In commenting upon these results as compared with Lehman's, Dennis (1954, p. 467) says:

> Readers who are acquainted with Lehman's data may be surprised at the figures presented above, since most of Lehman's figures show a drop in productivity after age 50. However, the majority of the data compiled by Lehman refer only to outstanding works, whereas our data refer to total publications. It would seem that there is a

***Table 12-3. Mean Number of Papers Published by Scientists per Decade** (Dennis, 1956b, p. 724)*

Decade	*20s*	*30s*	*40s*	*50s*	*60s*	*70s*
70-year group	9.1	20.1	21.8	23.8	18.1	
80-year group	6.9	21.9	24.7	18.5	17.0	13.1
Combined groups	8.1	20.7	22.9	21.9	17.7	

marked difference between the age trends for works of greatest value and age trends in total works.

It would appear, then, that part of the original difference in interpretation and opinion between Dennis and Lehman can be resolved by distinguishing between outstanding and total achievements, but, as will be pointed out in the conclusions we shall draw after reviewing other relevant studies, some additional considerations must be made before we can state what the developmental trends in vocational success are.

In another study on age and achievement, Bromley (1956) tested several hypotheses either directly or indirectly implied by Lehman's research. The hypotheses were as follows:

1. Quantity of output declines slowly.
2. Quality of output declines faster than quantity.
3. The peak years for both quality and quantity of output occur at a relatively young age.
4. Output of very high quality declines faster than output of lesser merit.
5. Quality and quantity of output are positively correlated.
6. No sex differences exist in connection with any association between age and creative intellectual output.
7. The decline with age of quantity and quality of output is not associated with the decline with age of general intelligence.

To measure "creative achievement" Bromley used a modified version of the Shaw Test (Howson, 1948), which consists of four wooden blocks that can be arranged in 15 different series, according to height, weight, position of notch, etc. Responses are graded as "good," "fairly good," "fairly poor," or "poor." To assess intelligence the Wechsler-Bellevue (Form I) was administered, and both IQs and EQs (efficiency quotients) were determined for each Subject. The sample was made up of 256 Subjects, equally divided by sex, and distributed into four age groups (17 to 35, 35 to 51, 51 to 66, and 66 to 82), each with 32 males and 32 females. The analyses were largely inspectional ones, although some statistics were reported. Bromley's findings confirmed all his research hypotheses (1 to 5) and one of his null hypotheses (6) but disconfirmed the other (7). In short, he obtained results in support of Lehman's interrelationships among quality of output, quantity of output, and age; but, in addition, he found that, in contrast to Lehman's (1953, p. 328) opinion that declining intelligence is a relatively unimportant factor in waning achievements, age decrements in both quality and quantity of output (on the Shaw Test) are strongly associated with reduced intellectual efficiency in older individuals.

The most recent research on Lehman's findings, and the issues they have raised, has served only to further perpetuate some of the confusions and misunderstandings, however, which characterized the difference in opinion between Lehman and Dennis. Using a criterion of rankings of "present value" to the company, Oberg (1960) has reported that research and development personnel in a manufacturing concern reach their peak before the age of 40 and then go into a decline in their later years, but that engineers continue to increase in their performance through to the 56 to 60 period. From the former finding, he concludes that his study corroborates Lehman's results. In a thoroughgoing analysis of Oberg's investigation, Kirchner (1961) has identified several shortcomings in it which make any conclusions suspect. Of these, the most serious was that Oberg did not conduct statistical tests to determine whether there were reliable differences between his age groups. It might be noted, too, that he used a criterion different from Lehman's: present value to company, not most significant achievement. This difference in criteria has been continually overlooked. Thus, Stewart and Sparks (1966) have challenged Lehman's conclusions with a well-designed study of the patent productivity of chemists, which showed that output does not fall off in the later years of the work life, but these investigators report no data, such as Lehman's, on the years of the most outstanding achievements of their Subjects. The relevance of their findings, therefore, is for Dennis's research on total productivity, which receives support from them, and not for Lehman's work on when the apogee of vocational success is attained.

Other Studies

Two additional kinds of studies, in contrast to those already reported, are relevant for the analysis of developmental trends in vocational success: (1) comparisons of older and younger workers in terms of their relative productivity, employability, rated success, and work characteristics; and (2) changes in salary over time.

The research on *older workers* has shown, almost without exception, that most of them can work efficiently and productively much longer than typical retirement practices and policies allow:

1. A host of studies has been conducted on the *productivity* of older workers,[5] and the weight of the evidence strongly indicates that they perform just as well on their jobs as do younger workers (Breen & Spaeth, 1960; Clay, 1956; Department of Labor, 1957; Greenberg, 1962; King, 1956; Mark, 1956). Breen and Spaeth (1960, p. 68), for example, made numerous comparisons of older and younger workers on the means and variances of objective job-performance indices, and concluded that: "It is clear that chronological age is not related to productivity among these workers."

[5] See Odell (1958) for an extensive list of references on the productivity of the older worker.

2. The *employability, availability,* and *promotability* (merit wage increases) of older part-time workers, as compared with younger ones, was investigated by Stanton (1951), who found that older workers were being hired, many for the first time, after they had reached an age of 60; that they averaged 212 days out of the year when they were available for work, in contrast to 103 days for younger workers; and that they were given wage increases *more often* than younger workers, the percentages for the two groups being 57 and 11, respectively. From these findings, Stanton concluded that older workers, in part-time employment, are every bit as successful as their younger counterparts—if not more so.[6]

3. Of three studies which have reported data on *ratings of success* in relation to age, all indicated that older workers—in each instance, the Subjects were salesmen—compared favorably with those who were younger. Cover and Pressey (1950) found that older route salesmen were rated higher than their younger co-workers on truck operation and handling customer credit, although their total sales were less, presumably because they did not have as much physical stamina to make as many house calls. Maher (1955, p. 451) concluded from his findings on supervisory and sales personnel in a large manufacturing concern, which showed that the older employees were either equal to or better than the younger on several criteria of success, e.g., ratings by superiors, forced-choice rankings, and sales records, that "the sales area of the company would seem to be one in which older men may operate more efficiently than younger ones." And, Kirchner, McElwain, and Dunnette (1960) have obtained age curves for sales effectiveness which reveal that the peak period occurs in the age range of 30 to 45 years, but that the decrement in subsequent years is not large, the eta for the two variables (sales versus age) being only .26. These investigators comment: "It cannot be overemphasized . . . that great individual differences exist and that many older salesmen are ranked extremely high in sales effectiveness" (Kirchner et al., 1960, p. 93).

4. There have been at least three comparisons of the *characteristics* of older and younger workers, the common implication of which has been that, although they did not learn or perform their jobs as rapidly, the former were more stable than the latter. Smith, M. W. (1952; 1953) gathered data on males and females and on skilled, unskilled, and clerical workers which established that not only are desirable worker traits relatively unaffected by aging but older workers are less often discharged as incompetent, are less likely to quit because of dissatisfaction or family situations, and receive as many above-average ratings in ability, attendance, and attitude as younger workers. These findings led Smith, M. W. (1953, p. 21) to conclude that:

[6] For studies of attitudes toward older workers, see Kirchner, Linbam, and Paterson (1952); Tuckman and Lorge (1952); and Kirchner and Dunnette (1954).

> Few traits show great change with age; fewer still show consistent age changes for all three work groups [i.e., skilled, unskilled, and clerical]. Speed does seem consistently to decrease with age; ability to learn, a little less so. But steadiness increases, and so somewhat does ability to work without supervision. That in none of these types of work was efficiency considered to decrease with age suggests the overall value of the "slow but steady" older man.

Similarly, Bowers (1952) obtained relatively small differences in such abilities and traits as promotion possibilities, work without supervision, job satisfaction, thoroughness, and initiative between age groups, but did find that older workers had better attendance records, were steadier, and were more conscientious.

In contrast to the extensive research on older workers, only two studies have been found on *changes in salary* with age. Hilton and Dill (1962) related annual salary growth rate, computed according to the conventional formula for compound interest, for 143 engineers who entered industry between 1950 and 1957, to their first-year salaries and their 1957 salaries. They found that first-year salary was negatively correlated with salary growth ($r = -.78$) and that 1957 salary was positively associated with salary growth ($r = .62$). Because the relationship between first-year salary and salary growth was partially artifactual, because of its part-whole nature, and because the correlation between first-year salary and 1957 salary was an r of .00, they concluded that the relationship of first-year salary to salary growth was a spurious one. They accounted for it by noting that first-year salaries vary not only from year to year, but also between individuals in any given year. This means that higher initial salaries may be followed by a slow rate of salary growth. Using salary alone, rather than salary growth, however, Brenner and Lockwood (1965) have reported consistently high correlations between salaries at different points in time, the best predictions being in adjacent years. Thus, the research on developmental trends in salary is not only limited, but it is inconclusive.

DEVELOPMENTAL TRENDS IN VOCATIONAL SATISFACTION

Despite the vast empirical literature on vocational satisfaction which has accumulated over the years (see Chapter 11), there has been relatively little attention given to the study of developmental trends in satisfaction. What studies have been done are mostly cross-sectional, rather than longitudinal, and consequently suffer from the shortcomings of point-in-time data on developmental phenomena. They do support some conclusions in which we can have confidence, however, and suggest some further lines of inquiry on the changes which occur in satisfaction with increasing age. Most of the research on this problem has to do with the so-called "satisfaction cycle," which will be discussed first, but there are also other studies of age and satisfaction, as well as adjustment in the retirement period, which will be reviewed.

The "Satisfaction Cycle"

There is considerable, reliable evidence from several studies that the relationship of satisfaction to age is curvilinear. Hoppock and Super (1950, p. 130) observe that: "The development of job satisfaction may be cyclical." Similarly, Herzberg et al. (1957, pp. 5–6) note that satisfaction "is high among young workers. It tends to go down during the first few years of employment. The low point is reached when workers are in their middle and late twenties, or early thirties. After this period [satisfaction] climbs steadily with age." The first studies in which this trend was investigated systematically were conducted by Super (1939; 1941), who obtained the results shown in Table 12-4 between age ranges and satisfaction. It will be noted that there are decided "dips" in satisfaction in the age ranges of 25 to 34, 45 to 54, and 65 up. As will be brought out later, some of this fluctuation could be accounted for by age differences in occupational levels, but some of it is apparently attributable to development. Super also attempted to establish that satisfactions derived from avocations likewise vary with age, but he was not able to confirm this hypothesis.

Hull, R. L., and Kolstad (1942) found a somewhat similar curve, but with morale and length of service as the variables. They concluded that:

> In general, employees with less than one year's service have had relatively higher average scores than have those with from one year to five years of service. The trend then reverses at about the five-year point, with employees of more than five or ten years' service having scores somewhat above the average for the entire group [Hull, R. L., & Kolstad, 1942, p. 357].

Table 12-4. Vocational Satisfaction in Different Age Ranges *(Super, 1939, p. 556)*

Age	*Satisfied*		*Dissatisfied*		*Total*
20–24	28	71.80%	11	28.20%	39
25–34	49	48.04	53	51.96	102
35–44	50	74.63	17	25.37	67
45–54	28	65.12	15	34.88	43
55–64	15	88.21	2	11.79	17
65 up	4	80.00	1	20.00	5
Total	174		99		237

NOTE: $\chi^2 = 31.41$; $df = 5$; $p < .01$.

Again, with morale rather than strictly satisfaction data, Benge and Copell (1947) have documented the "satisfaction cycle," as it is shown in Figure 12-5. Bernberg (1954) has also corroborated this phenomenon, on different Subjects with different measures, and has also established, as did Hull, R. L., and Kolstad (1942), that the relationship of morale to age exists even when length of service is held constant. Finally, Herzberg et al. (1957) have reviewed several other studies (e.g., Kessler, 1954; Lazarsfeld, 1931; Mann, 1953; Neilson, 1951; and Stagner, Rich, & Britten, 1941) of narrower age ranges, which further tend to support the cyclical nature of satisfaction in relation to age.

Why satisfaction is not linearly or monotonically related to age, but instead is associated in a cyclical fashion, has been explained in two different ways. First, using Buehler's, C. (1933) delineation of life stages as a conceptual framework, Super (1939, p. 557) has reasoned that:

> Younger men, just getting a start in the world, are exploring its possibilities, glad to have almost any job, and confident of their ability to get ahead. Then, after about age 25, comes a period of dissatisfaction with the old job, of wanting to get ahead more rapidly. Additional effort is expended . . . and increasing age brings greater achievement and greater satisfaction. Again, after 45, there is a relative increase in dissatisfaction, due to a change in the emphasis of interest: work loses some of its attractions and other types of satisfactions have not yet been developed. After a period of readjustment,

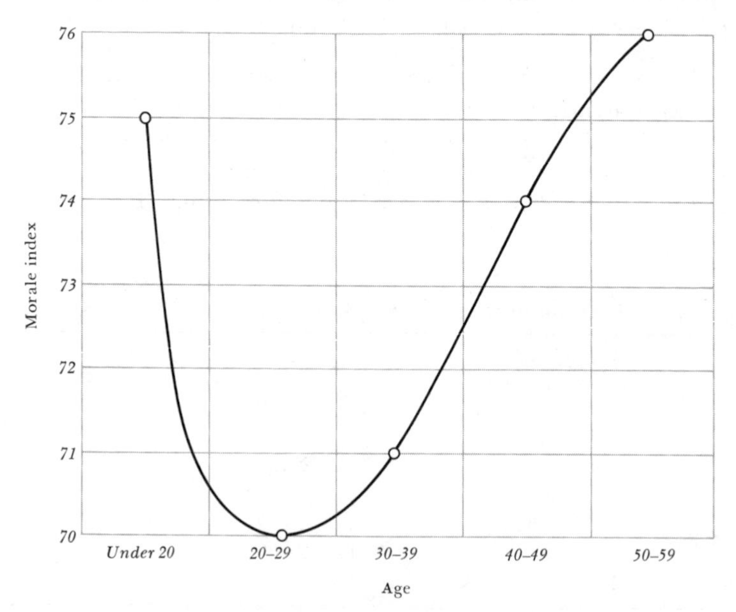

Figure 12-5. The relationship of vocational satisfaction (morale) to age. *(From Benge & Copell, 1947, pp. 19–22.)*

> new, nonvocational sources of enjoyment are found and the improved general adjustment is shown in increased job satisfaction.

In support of this interpretation, Super cites his findings on the relationship of satisfaction to age and level of occupational attainment. In general, as Table 12-5 shows, younger workers tend to "move up" in the occupational hierarchy as they grow older, with the exception of the "backsliding" in the 45 to 54 age range, where the percentage in commercial occupations increases and that in the professions decreases. It is during this period, however, that there is a corresponding "trough" in the satisfaction cycle, thus suggesting a possible relationship between the worker's success in "getting ahead" and his satisfaction with his vocation.

The second explanation of the satisfaction cycle has been formulated by Herzberg et al. (1957, pp. 8–9), who pose the question of what causes the neophyte's initial high level of satisfaction to wane and answer that: "The decline in the beginning worker's morale beyond the first year has been attributed to his growing difficulties with the contrast between the work regimen and that of school, his major previous experience." Miller, D. C., and Form (1951, p. 622), for example, have enumerated the value differences (see Table 12-6) which often exist between the nonmonetary and monetary worlds and which make the transition from the one to the other wrought with frustration and tension. It is not improbable, therefore, that the young worker becomes increasingly discouraged and dissatisfied as he attempts to adjust not only to a new job but also to a new way of life, predicated upon unfamiliar values. He copes with this situation in two ways, according to Herzberg et al. (1957, p. 9):

> One is that dissatisfied younger workers change jobs or even occupations until they find a slot into which they can fit with high morale. The other is that there are actual changes in the worker's total situation as he ages which would lead to increased job satisfaction in any job or occupation.

The upswing in the satisfaction cycle comes as the individual matures and his interests broaden:

> This in itself may lead to more general satisfaction which . . . is closely linked to the worker's attitude toward his job. One specific factor in job satisfaction which is ranked as the most important by a great many workers is security. This actually does increase in most cases with age for those workers who remain with one company and so develop seniority rights [Herzberg et al., 1957, p. 10].

Which of these accounts of the satisfaction cycle better fits the data, and will lead to new data, remains to be determined. Both are reasonable, and, in

Table 12-5. Occupational Level Attained in Different Age Ranges *(Super, 1939, p. 557)*

Age	Number and occupational level										Total
	Semiskilled		*Skilled*		*Commercial*		*Managerial*		*Professional*		
20–24	9	24.32%	5	13.51%	17	45.95%	3	8.11%	3	8.11%	37
25–34	8	8.00	17	17.00	34	34.00	8	8.00	33	33.00	100
35–44	3	4.48	8	11.94	16	23.88	12	17.97	28	41.79	67
45–54	1	2.23	4	9.30	14	32.56	9	20.93	15	34.89	43
55–64	0		0		4	23.53	4	23.53	9	52.94	17
65 up	0		0		1	20.00	2	40.00	2	40.00	5
Total	21		34		86		38		90		269

NOTE: $\chi^2 = 82.90$; $df = 20$; $p < .01$.

Table 12-6. Differences in Values between the School and Workplace *(From Miller, D. C., & Form, 1951, p. 622)*

	Patterns and emergent values within the nonmonetary work plants of home, school, and church	Patterns and emergent values within the monetary work plants of factory, office, and store
1.	PATTERN: Nonoptional membership VALUE: Each person belongs permanently to the group	PATTERN: Optional membership VALUE: Each worker must be free to enter or leave employment of any employer; each employer must be free to accept or reject any worker (upon cause) from his employment
2.	PATTERN: Sympathetic cooperation VALUE: Each person should try to help the others	PATTERN: Competitive striving VALUE: Every worker guards his self-interest if he wishes to hold his job or get ahead
3.	PATTERN: Uniform moral code VALUE: Each person should do what is considered right	PATTERN: Ethical neutrality VALUE: Each person should be free to lead his own life without dictation from his employer or fellow workers
4.	PATTERN: Personality growth VALUE: Each person should have an opportunity to develop to his fullest capacity	PATTERN: Work persistence VALUE: Each person should learn to stick on a job
5.	PATTERN: Status devaluation VALUE: Each person should be evaluated for what he is and what he can do as a person	PATTERN: Status evaluation VALUE: Each person can be evaluated by his class, education, race, nationality, and religion

some ways, not very different. It may be possible, and more parsimonious, to combine them into one theoretical statement about developmental trends in satisfaction which will have greater subsumptive and predictive value than either has separately.

Other Studies

In addition to the research which has accumulated on the satisfaction cycle, there have been several other studies on the relationship of satisfaction to age, as well as two on the attitudes and adjustments of older workers and one on the methodological problems involved in obtaining longitudinal data on satisfaction. Each of these is briefly summarized as follows:

1. Based upon data from his first study of job satisfaction (see Chapter 11), Hoppock (1936) obtained a correlation of .21 between his JSB and age for 286 Subjects. He suggested three reasons why this relationship might obtain: First, some dissatisfied workers resign to take other jobs and thus improve their status and increase satisfaction as they grow older (this hypothesis is quite similar to the one proposed by Herzberg); second, some who are dissatisfied eventually accept their "lot in life" and become at least less dissatisfied if not more satisfied; and, third, workers may experience greater satisfaction as a result of increasing proficiency and familiarity with their work.

2. As an incidental finding in a study of the relationship between hearing loss and the Tear Ballot for Industry, Zintz and Kerr (1951) computed an r of .34 between age and satisfaction. They did not discuss this correlation, except to note that when it was partialled out of the relationship between hearing loss and satisfaction, the r for the latter changed from $-.25$ to $-.42$.

3. In two analyses of age-group differences in satisfaction, Inlow (1951) and Vollmar and Kinney (1955) have reported data which further corroborate the curvilinear relationship between these two variables. Inlow's mean satisfaction scores for five age ranges were as follows: 2.45 (22 to 27 years), 1.88 (28 to 33 years), 2.10 (34 to 39 years), 2.05 (40 to 45 years), and 2.17 (46 years and over). Again, we see that the low points in the satisfaction cycle occur toward the middle of the Establishment stage and near the middle of the Maintenance stage. Similarly, Vollmar and Kinney found that satisfaction varies nonlinearly with age, but they also determined that the relationship is not the same for different educational levels. Thus, the low point in satisfaction for workers with a grammar school education comes in the 40 to 49 age range, whereas for college graduates it occurs in the 30 to 39 years. Vollmar and Kinney conclude, much as Super (1939) did about occupational level, that educational level affects the relationship between satisfaction and age.

4. Saleh and Otis (1964, p. 426) hypothesized that "the level of stated job satisfaction will increase with age to the pre-retirement period and, within that period will show a decline." They reasoned that, as workers contemplate growing older in their jobs and as the pace becomes more burdensome for them, they will become more dissatisfied with their vocations. They asked 80 male managers of a manufacturing firm, who were in the 60 to 65 age range, and 38 others, who were about 10 years younger, to rank the following five periods according to the satisfaction they experienced in them: (1) up to 29; (2) 30 to 39; (3) 40 to 49; (4) 50 to 59; and (5) 60 and over. For both groups of Subjects, satisfaction increased through the fourth period, and for the older group it went down in the last period. Saleh and Otis concluded that these findings supported their hypothesis, but two qualifications should be taken into account: First, their data were retrospective and were subject to the dis-

tortions of recall, which usually result in past experiences being viewed as more positive than present ones; and, second, the interval of "up to 29" cut across the usual first two periods in the "satisfaction cycle," so that any differences between them were obscured. Thus, the data of this study must be interpreted with caution: they *may* indicate a "tailing off" of satisfaction in the Decline stage of vocational development, but they do *not* contradict the curvilinear trend in vocational satisfaction in earlier stages.

5. There have been three follow-up studies of the satisfaction of workers, but only one of them has been longitudinal, i.e., satisfaction having been assessed on two or more occasions:

a. Hoppock (1960) contacted 23 out of 40 persons in his 1935 study, who had expressed their satisfaction at that time, and asked them to indicate again, 27 years later, how satisfied they were with their jobs. Of the 23, 17 reported greater satisfaction on the follow-up. Moreover, those who increased the most in their satisfaction were those who had changed jobs, a finding which led Hoppock (1960, p. 492) to pose the question: "Could it be that the person who dislikes his job needs to change his job more than he needs to change himself?"

b. In their follow-up of clinical psychologists, who had been participants in the University of Michigan Veterans Administration assessment project (Kelly, E. L., & Fiske, 1951), Kelly, E. L., and Goldberg (1959) suggest an indirect answer to Hoppock's question. These investigators report that in response to the item "If I had my life to live over again (knowing what I now know), I would try to end up in . . . ," only three out of five Ph.D. clinicians indicated that they would enter their present occupation again. In other words, 40 percent of these clinical psychologists were saying that they would like to try something different (change jobs), if they had the chance to relive their work lives. It should be noted, however, that this does *not* mean that they are necessarily dissatisfied with clinical psychology. As was discussed in Chapter 11, the type of question used by Kelly and Goldberg does not yield the same results as those in standard measures of satisfaction, such as the Hoppock JSB and Kerr TBI.

c. The third study, which was conducted by Lipsett and Wilson (1954), is mentioned here, not so much because of its direct relevance for the relationship of satisfaction to age, but because of its uniqueness as one of the few (only?) follow-up studies on the assumption, which is central to the Matching Men and Jobs approach, that "suitable" interests and ability lead to vocational satisfaction. For 224 former clients at the Rochester Counseling Center, they found that those who either disliked their jobs or were indifferent toward them had *both* interests and ability which were "unsuitable" for their current occupations. Thus, there is some evidence to substantiate the proposition (see

Chapter 8) that "vocational adjustment varies directly with the extent of agreement between worker characteristics and work demands."

6. Although not directly concerned with vocational satisfaction, two surveys of the attitudes and adjustments of older workers by Melzer (1958; 1963) are of interest because of the dearth of research on the retirement stage of vocational development. In the earlier study, he found that specific attitudes toward pay, working conditions, co-workers and supervisors became more favorable with increasing age, and in the later study he obtained the following results: (1) Older workers feel they have a greater "share of happiness" from life, but not necessarily a greater "share of recognition"; (2) for older workers, spare-time activities have *less* significance than work; and (3) older workers value steady work more than they do advancement.

7. Finally, a methodological note: in an attempt to establish the utility of a quasilongitudinal design for the study of satisfaction over time, Hardin (1965, p. 367) compared perceived (retrospective) with actual changes in satisfaction and concluded that:

> Perceived change is a poor predictor of computed change. . . . Unless ways can be found to improve the validity of perceived change responses, a genuinely longitudinal design should probably be used, despite its cost and frequent malfunction, by research workers interested in actual changes in job satisfaction.

In short, there does not appear to be any substitute for the bona fide follow-up study in extrapolating developmental trends in vocational satisfaction (cf. Schaie, 1965).

IV
CONCLUSION

13

RESEARCH IN VOCATIONAL PSYCHOLOGY

The preceding chapters have been devoted primarily to a review and synthesis of the empirical research which has accumulated over the years on vocational choice and adjustment. The findings have come from many sources and have been the product of diverse disciplines. As a result, they have not been formally synthesized into a body of scientific knowledge which might serve as a base for further conceptualization and investigation. Rather, different fields of study, notably industrial psychology and occupational sociology, have pursued research interests which have impinged upon those of vocational psychology and each other but which have not been explicitly interrelated. One purpose of this chapter, therefore, is to summarize the subject matter of vocational psychology as it currently exists and thereby achieve some degree of codification of it. Another purpose is to extrapolate from this summary what some of the major research needs in the field are and to suggest what directions might be followed in fulfilling them. To discuss these topics the chapter has been organized into four sections: (1) a summary of research in vocational psychology; (2) a survey of research needs in vocational psychology; (3) a review of new longitudinal designs and analyses for developmental research in vocational psychology; and (4) a proposal for experimental research in vocational psychology.

SUMMARY OF RESEARCH IN VOCATIONAL PSYCHOLOGY

To provide a baseline for identifying research needs in the field of vocational psychology this section presents a general summary of what is known about vocational choice and adjustment. No attempt will be made to go into detail; this has already been done in the preceding parts of the book. The purpose of the following discussion is to recapitulate—to bring together in one place the conclusions which can legitimately be drawn from vocational research. To do this, a modified outline format has been used, in which the divisions are:

(1) vocational behaviors, e.g., vocational maturity or vocational success; (2) conceptual definitions of these vocational behaviors; (3) measures which have been constructed or devised to operationalize them; (4) related concepts or behaviors; (5) normative characteristics of the vocational behaviors, i.e., their distributions, central tendencies, dispersions, etc.; (6) dimensions of the vocational behaviors; (7) developmental trends in the vocational behaviors; and (8) correlates of the vocational behaviors. Choice behaviors are outlined first, and then adjustment behaviors are reviewed. A summary of the research on the correlates of occupational membership (occupational differences in traits and factors) was given in Chapter 2 and will not be repeated here.

Summary of Research on Vocational Choice

The vocational choice behaviors which have been selected for the following summary are those which have been studied extensively enough that some conclusions about them can be drawn. This does not mean that research on them is definitive or that it is not open to varying interpretations, but only that it encompasses sufficient empirical work that a summary seems justified. The vocational behaviors which are thus included below are: (1) vocational choice; (2) vocational choice attitudes and competencies; (3) indices of vocational maturity; (4) indecision in vocational choice; and (5) unrealism in vocational choice.

I. Vocational Choice

- **A.** Conceptual definitions
  - **1.** The occupations which the individual *says* he will probably enter.
  - **2.** Operationally, "An individual, X, makes a vocational choice if he expresses an intention to enter a particular occupation."
- **B.** Measures
  - **1.** Interview, open-ended question, and questionnaire
  - **2.** For most purposes, the open-ended question is the best measure of vocational choice. Its reliability is in the .70s to .80s, and its validity relationships to several variables have been established empirically.
- **C.** Related concepts
  - **1.** There is considerable evidence that measures of vocational choice elicit responses different from those elicited by measures of vocational *preferences, aspirations,* and *interests.*
    - **a.** Of these concepts, choice is most "reality-based." It indicates what the individual thinks he probably will do.
    - **b.** Preference is what he would like to do, if reality conditions would permit.

c. Aspiration is what he fantasies about doing.
d. Interests are similar to preferences, except that they are usually more realistic because they are related to membership and/or persistence in an occupation.

2. Although these concepts are operationally independent, they are nevertheless empirically related to each other.

D. Normative characteristics

1. Vocational choice is systematic, not chance, behavior. There are reliable individual differences in choice, and there are statistically significant relationships between it and other variables (see "Correlates").
2. The most popular choices over the years have been engineering, medicine, and teaching. When choices are classified by both field and level, it is apparent that field and level are related. Moreover, choices on the highest level appear to be less realistic than those on lower levels.

E. Dimensions

Vocational choice is a *variable,* not a construct, and consequently it does not have "dimensions."

F. Developmental trends

1. Vocational choice is a *process,* a series of related behavioral events, but it is not wholly continuous. There is at least one *discontinuity* in it between ages 14 and 16, when there is, first, indecision and, then, indiscriminateness in choice.
2. After 16, the choice process becomes more and more *exclusive,* as negative decisions are made, and the relationships among choice, preference, aspiration, and interest change.
3. That there are *stages* in the choice process seems apparent, but their limits are not well established empirically, with the possible exception of the Fantasy stage, which probably begins about age 9 and ends around age 13. Crystallization and specification of choice appear to occur between ages 18 and 21 in the Realistic stage, during which there is also a trend toward greater realism in choice.

G. Correlates

1. Stimulus variables
   a. *Culture* influences choice, but the effects are not uniform from one social class to another.
   b. *Social class* is related to choice independently of other variables, viz., culture and intelligence.
   c. *Race* affects choices: Negroes tend to choose more "people-oriented" than "thing-oriented" occupations.

d. *Geographic region* is associated with choice, the main differences being between urban and rural areas.
e. Community: Data on *peer* and *ethnic* groups in relation to choice are observational or inconclusive but suggest that relationships exist.
f. Family: *Father's occupation* and choice are related but not as highly as usually assumed; *parental identification* is related to interests and presumably choice, although the latter has not been conclusively established; evidence on *familial relationships* and choice is either largely negative or equivocal.
g. *School:* Data on the relationship of educational experiences to choice are limited but suggest that the school may be a significant agent of vocationalization.
h. *Church:* essentially unrelated to choice.

2. Organismic variables
a. *Endocrine glands:* Findings suggest a relationship to choice, but they are not definitive.
b. *Physique:* fragmentary evidence indicates a low-order relationship between body type and choice.
c. *Heredity:* inconclusive data from studies of twins are open to alternative interpretations and thus conclusions are not possible.

3. Response variables
a. *General aptitude:* Intelligence is related not only to choice but also to preference and aspiration, the estimated correlations being in the .30 to .40 range.
b. *Interests:* the correlations of choice and expressed interests with inventoried interests are in the .40s; they are somewhat higher (.50s) for estimated, ranked, and rated interests in relation to inventoried interests. The relationships vary somewhat, however, with the type of inventory used to measure interests. Also, the agreement between choice and interests is usually higher for females than for males.
c. *Personality:* there is increasing evidence that the self-concept is related to vocational choice, which generally supports Super's theory of the association between these two variables; there is also some research which indicates that ego processes, self-evaluation, utility for risk, values, and life goals are related to choice, but it is not as conclusive as the work on the self-concept.

II. Vocational Choice Attitudes and Competencies

A. Conceptual definitions

1. *Choice attitudes:* those dispositional response tendencies which are manifested in involvement in the choice process, orientation to-

ward work, independence in decision making, preference for job factors, and conceptions of the choice process.

2. *Choice competencies:* those cognitive or ego functions which involve such mental processes as assimilating information about self and reality, resolving conflicts between alternative courses of action, establishing future goals, and relating means to ends through planning.

B. Measures

1. *Choice attitudes:* the Attitude Scale of the Vocational Development Inventory, which consists of 50 age- and grade-related items scored for a total vocational maturity (VM) score.
2. *Choice competencies:* the Competence Tests of the Vocational Development Inventory, including measures of Planning, Goal Selection, Occupational Information, Self-knowledge, and Problem Solution.

C. Related concepts

Vocational choice attitudes and competencies are conceptually related to Super's dimensions of vocational maturity in adolescence and Gribbons and Lohnes's construct of Readiness for Vocational Planning. There are no empirical data on the interrelationships of these variables, however, so that it is not possible to state the extent to which they define the same or different choice attitudes and competencies.

D. Normative characteristics

1. The Attitude Scale of the Vocational Development Inventory differentiates the responses of fifth through twelfth graders, all of its items being monotonically related to age and grade, with which the total VM score correlates .46. There is about 35 percent overlap in total scores between adjacent grades. The test-retest stability coefficient for 1 year is .70.
2. Preliminary data have been collected on the Competence Tests of the Vocational Development Inventory, for the purpose of constituting a universe of item content, but they have not as yet been standardized.

E. Dimensions

Vocational choice attitudes and competencies have been conceived of as dimensions of the more global construct of vocational maturity in adolescence, which includes consistency and wisdom of vocational choice as well. As yet, there are no data on the interrelationships of these variables, other than Super and Overstreet's factor analysis of the vocational maturity indices and Gribbons and Lohnes's discriminant analysis of the Readiness for Vocational Planning scales. The results of both these studies are consistent with a hierarchical model of vocational maturity, with one general and several group and specific factors representing the dimensions.

F. Developmental trends

1. There is a trend for responses to the Attitude Scale to shift from predominantly "True" endorsements in the lower grades to mostly "False" ones in the upper grades.
2. There are distinct stages in the trends, with the "breaks" being primarily at the transition points between grades 6 and 7 and between grades 9 and 10, which correspond to the divisions in the educational structure among the elementary, junior high school, and senior high school levels.

G. Correlates

1. The maturity of choice attitudes is related to both indecision and unrealism in vocational choice. Adolescents who are undecided or unrealistic in their career decision making are less mature in their choice attitudes.
2. The social desirability of mature choice attitudes does not appear to affect their relationships to choice indecision and unrealism.
3. At present, data on the correlates of choice competencies are not available.

III. Indices of Vocational Maturity

A. Conceptual definitions

1. One definition of vocational maturity is: "the life stage in which the individual actually is, as evidenced by the developmental tasks with which he is dealing, in relation to the life stage in which he is expected to be, in terms of his age" (Super & Overstreet, 1960, p. 8).
2. Another definition of vocational maturity is: the maturity of an individual's vocational behavior "in the actual life stage (regardless of whether it is expected life stage), as evidenced by the behavior shown in dealing with developmental tasks of the actual life stage compared with the behavior of other individuals who are dealing with the same developmental tasks" (Super & Overstreet, 1960, p. 9).

B. Measures

A variety of indices of vocational maturity have been constructed, most of them being ratings of interview protocols. The major variables which have been quantified are: orientation to vocational choice; information and planning about preferred occupation; consistency of vocational preferences; crystallization of traits; and wisdom of vocational preferences.

C. Related concepts

The most closely related concepts are those of vocational choice attitudes and competencies, which, together with the indices, can be conceived of as constituting the construct of vocational maturity. This construct has been conceptualized within a hierarchical model, in which a general factor is "degree of vocational development"; several group factors represent the VM indices and choice attitudes and competencies, and various specific factors define vocational behaviors which mature during the adolescent period.

D. Normative characteristics

1. Most of the reliabilities for the indices of vocational maturity are based upon interjudge agreement in rating interview protocols, and are high, being usually in the .80s and .90s. For many of the indices, however, reliability estimates could not be determined.
2. No normative data have been reported on differences between age or grade groups for the indices.

E. Dimensions

1. A factor analysis of the VM indices at the ninth-grade level has yielded a primary dimension called "orientation toward planning for the future" and secondary dimensions of "anticipation of immediate, intermediate, and remote vocational developmental tasks."
2. A correlational analysis of the relationship between ninth- and twelfth-grade VM indices has suggested that a dimension which spans this period is "Occupational Information—Training and Educational Requirements."

F. Developmental trends

No developmental trends in the VM indices have been identified, other than the increase in occupational information about training and educational requirements already mentioned. There are several relationships between certain demographic and status variables at the ninth and twelfth grades and later vocational adjustment at age 25, but there are no demonstrated associations between adolescent and adult vocational maturity.

G. Correlates

In general, the indices of vocational maturity, both within and between points in time, have correlated more highly with intellective than with nonintellective variables. The expected relationships of vocational maturity with personality remain to be established.

IV. Indecision in Vocational Choice

A. Conceptual definitions

1. Indecision in vocational choice has been defined as "the inability

of the individual to select, or commit himself to, a particular course of action which will eventuate in his preparing for and entering a specific occupation.

2. Operationally, "An individual, X, has 'no choice,' if he cannot discriminate among occupations, either because he rejects them all or accepts them all."

B. Measures

Choice indecision is measured by the same instruments as are used to elicit choice, but the individual either does not respond to them or says that he is "undecided."

C. Related concepts

The concept most closely associated with indecision is *indecisiveness.* The distinction between these two concepts is that indecision is specific to vocational choice and can usually be resolved by changing the conditions for decision making, i.e., information about choice supply, incentive to choose, and freedom to choose, whereas indecisiveness is a more generalized personality attribute and persists even when the conditions for choice are optimal.

D. Normative characteristics

In the last year of high school and the first year of college, the percentage "undecided" is in the 20 to 30 percent range, becoming somewhat less as the individual progresses from the secondary to the higher educational levels.

E. Dimensions

Like vocational choice, indecision is a variable, not a construct, and consequently it does not have "dimensions."

F. Developmental trends

The principal trend in indecision during the adolescent years appears to be the one identified by Gesell et al. (1956), who found that indecision is great at about age 10, diminishes to age 13, recurs at age 14, then declines again through age 16.

G. Correlates

Indecision appears to be slightly related to intelligence, the decided individual being the brighter, and possibly to scholastic achievement, although there is some contrary evidence on the latter relationship. Farm youth tend to be more undecided than those in urban areas, and college-bound high school students are slightly more decided than those not headed for college.

V. Unrealism in Vocational Choice

A. Conceptual definitions

The occupation the individual has selected as the one he intends to enter is not consistent, in some way, with reality, usually as defined by his aptitudes and interests, but also by the availability of training facilities, military obligations, parental financial support, etc.

B. Measures

1. Unrealism is usually measured by determining discrepancies between choice and reality factors, such as aptitudes and interests.
2. It has also been judged from interview and case-record data, and comparisons of choices with distributions of workers in occupations have been made.

C. Related concepts

There are no concepts which are directly related to unrealism, which generally means that an individual has less of some trait or resource than is necessary to implement his choice. It may also refer, however, to making a choice which will not fulfill one's capacities or potentialities, or to being coerced into a choice which is not in one's area of interest.

D. Normative characteristics

What reliable evidence there is on unrealism in vocational choice indicates that about 20 to 30 percent of late adolescents are unrealistic. Studies in which comparisons of choice and occupational distributions have been made have yielded higher percentages, whereas those in which ratings have been used have produced lower percentages.

E. Dimensions

Unrealism is similar to vocational choice and indecision, in that it is a variable rather than a construct, and thus it has no "dimensions."

F. Developmental trends

Although there is the generally held hypothesis that unrealism decreases as the individual grows older, there are few longitudinal data to support it.

G. Correlates

1. Intelligence appears to be a correlate of unrealism, although this relationship may be partly artifactual, because the higher the level of intelligence, the less the possibility of not possessing sufficient ability for an occupation and hence being unrealistic in choosing it.
2. As was noted, there is evidence that immaturity in choice attitudes is related to unrealism in choice.

Conclusions. It is clear from this summary of research on vocational choice that we know considerably more about the choice act per se than we do about the related phenomena of choice attitudes and competencies, indices of vocational maturity, and indecision and unrealism in choice. There are probably two principal reasons why this is the case: First, research on the choice act dates back to the beginning of the Matching Men and Jobs approach in vocational psychology, whereas studies of the development of vocational behavior are relatively recent in origin, most of them having been launched since 1950. The results of the latter are only now appearing in the literature, and many of them are still incomplete and unreplicated. Thus, in contrast to the choice act, our knowledge of vocational development is uncertain and uncodified. And, second, most of the research in the field has been on *normal* choice behaviors. What fragmentary evidence we have on indecision and unrealism has come largely from counseling studies, in which comparisons of individuals who have these problems with those who do not have been rare.

Summary of Research on Vocational Adjustment

The research on each component in the Model of Vocational Adjustment proposed in Chapter 8 has been summarized in the following outline. Motivation is dealt with first, success next, and then satisfaction. A final section is devoted to overall vocational adjustment. Developmental trends in these behaviors have been reviewed where appropriate, rather than as a separate topic.

I. Vocational Motivation

  A. Conceptual definitions

    1. One concept of vocational motivation is that the worker has certain wants or *needs* which he strives to fulfill through his work. In other words, he is motivated by the lack or deprivation of what he wants. Maslow's hierarchy of prepotent needs, e.g., safety, information, self-actualization, is an example of this concept of vocational motivation.
    2. Another concept of vocational motivation is that the worker is stimulated to action by the presence, rather than the absence, of certain conditions. Thus, Viteles defines motives as *states of tension* aroused in the worker by incentives; Katzell equates motives with *job values* which evoke higher levels of job satisfaction; and Vroom proposes that the motivation to work is a function of the *force* impinging upon an individual to follow one course of action rather than another.

  B. Measures

    1. Several paper-and-pencil inventories designed to assess vocational motivation have been constructed: Super's Work Values Inventory, Ghiselli's Initiative Scale, the Minnesota Need Questionnaire, Hammond's Occupational Attitude Rating Scales, Bendig and Stillman's Job Incentive Rankings, and Astin's Work Satisfaction Questionnaire. In addition, several other scales have been devised and a projective technique called the Vocational Apperception Test has been developed.

2. Of these various measures, only the Minnesota Need Questionnaire (with the possible exception of the Vocational Apperception Test) has been based upon the concept of vocational motivation as deprivation. The others stem from the concept of vocational motivation as "drive" or persistent stimulation.

C. Related concepts

1. Vocational motives are sometimes confused with the stimuli and responses from which they are inferred, such as *incentives* and *attitudes*, respectively. Motives are usually thought of, however, as "intervening" between these two sides of the behavioral equation.
2. Another closely related concept is vocational satisfaction, which is conceived of as the hedonic response to drive reduction or need fulfillment. The distinction here is between vocational motivation as the instigator of behavior and vocational satisfaction as the outcome of behavior.
3. Also, there is the widely held hypothesis that vocational interests *are* vocational motives, but the empirical evidence is equivocal and hence subject to conflicting interpretations. A strong argument can be made, however, that to the extent interests direct and energize the individual's responses they are motives. The large body of research on the relationship of interests to field of choice, occupational membership, and persistence in an occupation after entry would support this conclusion.

D. Normative characteristics

There has been no large-scale descriptive research on the distributions of vocational motives in the working population. The only relevant data are from Centers's studies, in which he found that the higher occupational strata are motivated primarily by the intrinsic aspects of work (opportunity for self-expression, independence, interesting job functions) and the lower levels by the extrinsic components (security, pay, co-workers).

E. Dimensions

1. Several independent factor analyses with different measures of vocational motivation have yielded comparable findings. The major dimensions appear to be: material security, job freedom, personal status, social service, behavior control, system, and structure.
2. In addition, there is some suggestion from a factorial study of the Minnesota Need Questionnaire, that, at least with this type of measure, which is based upon the concept of vocational motivation as deprivation, there may be a general "vocational need" dimension as well as the more specific ones.

F. Developmental trends

No research has been found on how vocational motives change with increasing age. The work on interest development, which indicates generally that older individuals are more socially oriented and prefer more sedentary activities, might be cited, but it provides only indirect evidence at best.

G. Correlates

1. One well-established correlate of vocational motives is *vocational interests*. In particular, the bipolar interest dimension of Things versus People is related to several vocational motivation factors.
2. Despite the methodological flaws in the Hawthorne studies, they strongly suggested, and subsequent research has confirmed, that the interpersonal relationships established in the *work group* act as motivators for productivity and related job behaviors.
3. The relationship of vocational motivation to *satisfaction*, however, is not as clear-cut. Herzberg has hypothesized that job-content factors contribute to satisfaction and job-context factors to dissatisfaction, but studies of this two-factor theory of vocational motivation have been inconclusive.
4. A variable which may be confounded with those of primary interest in this research on Herzberg's hypotheses is *occupational level*, which Centers has found to be related to vocational motivation, as has been indicated. The relationships of vocational motivation to satisfaction and dissatisfaction may vary from one level of the occupational hierarchy to another, just as the salience of job-content and context factors differs for workers on the upper and lower strata.

II. Vocational Success

A. Conceptual definitions

1. Success has been defined in many different ways, depending upon the frame of reference used. Generally, it refers to how well a worker performs the duties and tasks of his job. If he does well, usually as evaluated by external criteria, he is rewarded with increased pay, bonuses, promotion, special recognition, etc. Because individuals differ in their levels of vocational aspiration, what may be success to one worker may be failure to another.
2. Operationally, vocational success can be defined as "the probability that a worker's behavior will achieve a particular goal in a given work environment."

B. Measures

1. The most frequently used criterion of vocational success has been

the rating scale. In approximately two-thirds of the studies reviewed on success it was the criterion measure. Typically, supervisors were asked to rate subordinates, but without consensual validation (interrater agreement) of their judgments.

2. The second most commonly applied criterion of vocational success has been output or productivity. This index of success has usually been a quantitative one, i.e., how much has a worker turned out, rather than a qualitative one, i.e., how well has he done it.

C. Related concepts

Some British vocational psychologists, notably Stott, have argued that the worker's perception and evaluation of his job performance should be included in any meaningful and comprehensive concept of success, but the predominant viewpoint is that such an expression would be satisfaction rather than success and that the two should be kept distinct. If success and satisfaction are considered to be complementary components of overall vocational adjustment, this issue becomes less important.

D. Normative characteristics

Large-scale, representative data on vocational success are not available, other than unemployment figures, which may vary considerably from one season to another but which are close to 5 percent of the labor force. Presumably, a larger percentage of workers than this who hold regular jobs are unsuccessful by other criteria. But, what this percentage is has not been systematically determined.

E. Dimensions

1. Because of the lack of comparability of factorial methodologies, it is difficult to draw any firm conclusions about the dimensions of vocational success. If factor-analytic techniques are used, however, which allow the extraction of a general factor from the data, it has usually appeared in studies of success criteria. Moreover, there is also evidence of group and specific factors, thus suggesting that a hierarchical model might best represent the dimensions of vocational success.

2. This conclusion must be qualified, however, to the extent that the content (but not the structure) of the dimensions probably varies from one occupation to another, at least on the group and specific factor levels.

F. Developmental trends

1. The most notable trend in vocational success over time is for outstanding achievements, largely irrespective of field, to be made early in the career, usually in the period between ages 35 and 40.

2. Contrary to general belief, the productivity of older workers is not necessarily less than their younger colleagues. The latter may learn new tasks more rapidly, but they are less efficient and reliable.

G. Correlates

1. Intelligence is related to success in attainment on the occupational scale, i.e., workers at the higher occupational levels are, on the average, brighter than those on the lower levels, but it is not consistently associated with success within occupations.
2. Interests are correlated with success in some occupations, such as life insurance sales, but not in others.
3. Personality does not appear to be directly related to success in most occupations, but there is some evidence that it may be indirectly related as a "moderator" variable, which either facilitates or interferes with the successful performance of job functions.
4. Most of the research on the prediction of vocational success, including the large-scale studies by the Thorndikes, have yielded negative results. Ghiselli has launched a new attack on this old problem by trying to identify moderator variables which will improve the prediction of success, but his research is still in too early a stage to evaluate its promise.

III. Vocational Satisfaction

A. Conceptual definitions

1. Although satisfaction has been defined in various ways, a common theme which runs through them is the worker's reactions of pleasantness-unpleasantness to what he is doing: in other words, his evaluation of the *hedonic tone* of his vocation along a continuum of liking-disliking. In this definition, *vocational* satisfaction is distinguished from *job* satisfaction, the referent for the former being the occupation the worker is trained or qualified for and the latter being his current employment.
2. A widely used classification schema for the different types of satisfaction which can be derived from one's vocation has been conceived by Ginzberg et al. (1951), who delineate three kinds of vocational satisfaction: *extrinsic, intrinsic,* and *concomitant.*

B. Measures

1. In general, measures of vocational satisfaction are one of two types: they elicit a global reaction of the worker toward his vocation, in which he subjectively "weights" his likes and dislikes for it; or they evoke specific responses to various aspects of the vocation, which are then summated, typically with unit weights, and expressed in a total score.
2. Among the many measures which have been constructed to assess

vocational satisfaction, the most thoroughly studied are these: Hoppock Job Satisfaction Blank; Kerr Tear Ballot for Industry; Brayfield-Rothe Index of Job Satisfaction; SRA Employee Inventory; and Cornell Job Descriptive Index.

C. Related concepts

1. In contrast to vocational satisfaction, *job attitudes* refer to the positive-negative reactions the individual has towards the specific aspects of his work, such as supervision, company policies, benefits, etc., instead of his overall evaluation of it.
2. On the other hand, *morale* is generally viewed as a more comprehensive concept than vocational satisfaction, including the latter along with an appraisal of the individual's relationship to his work group and employing organization.

D. Normative characteristics

1. Because of the large number of studies which have been conducted, some confidence can be had in the percentages of dissatisfaction which Hoppock's reviews have reported over the years since 1935. These have leveled off and have remained quite stable for the past decade and a half at approximately 13 percent of the labor force.
2. There is almost equally as good evidence, however, that the percentage dissatisfied varies from one occupational level to another—but not in a linear fashion. There appear to be two "satisfaction hierarchies," one for white-collar workers and another for manual workers, with a range of overlap between them. The reason for this apparent anomaly may be that workers at the skilled level and below take members of their families as points of reference for assessing their vocational satisfaction rather than higher-strata occupational groups.

E. Dimensions

1. The interpretation of factor analyses of vocational satisfaction is wrought through with methodological problems, in particular whether it is justified to extract a general factor when different kinds of diagonal entries are used in the intercorrelation matrix.
2. If a procedure is used which allows the identification of a general factor, it usually is found, along with several group and specific factors. Thus, as with vocational success, a hierarchical model would seem to best fit the data on vocational satisfaction, although other conceptualizations should be entertained until greater agreement is reached on methodological issues in factor analysis.

F. Developmental trends

1. There is considerable empirical evidence, although it is largely cross-sectional, which supports the existence of a "satisfaction cycle"

during the years of vocational adjustment. It begins at a high point with occupational entry, hits its lowest point in the middle of the Establishment stage (approximately age 25), rises again to its peak at the start of the Maintenance stage (about age 35), and then levels off or goes into an incipient decline as retirement approaches.

2. What the "dynamics" of this trend in vocational satisfaction are have not been determined in research as yet, but there are some findings which indicate that they may be affected by educational and occupational level. These two factors apparently influence the course which the "satisfaction cycle" takes, but in unknown ways.

G. Correlates

1. There have been numerous studies of workers' satisfaction with specific aspects of the job, but few of the correlates of his overall vocational satisfaction. What studies have been done, however, confirm that vocational satisfaction is related to the following variables, although the correlations are sometimes low: need satisfaction, vocational aspiration, and vocational interests.
2. In contrast, the accumulated research of many years fail to substantiate a relationship between vocational satisfaction and vocational success, defined as job performance or productivity, although it does support a low-order association between the former and job tenure (or turnover).

IV. Vocational Adjustment

A. Conceptual definitions

1. Because of the centrality of work in the life and history of man, many concepts of vocational adjustment have been expounded. These have ranged from the religious and economic to the sociological and psychological. Among the latter, the most prominent have been the concepts of vocational fitness, self-realization in work, and mastery of vocational developmental tasks.
2. Problems in vocational adjustment have been conceptualized in terms of the thwarting conditions which the worker encounters on his job. These are of two kinds: conflict and frustration, the former being within the individual and the latter between the individual and the environment.

B. Measures

1. Only a few measures of overall vocational adjustment have been constructed, and these have not been extensively studied. Friend and Haggard, for example, used a rating schedule to obtain vocational adjustment scores, and there is one scale on the Bell Adjustment Inventory which yields a score for vocation, but most

studies have measured success and satisfaction rather than vocational adjustment.

2. Similarly, little work has been done on the measurement of work-adjustment mechanisms. The Forer Vocational Survey might be adapted for this purpose, but it is only partially applicable.

C. Related concepts

1. Vocational adjustment has often been considered to be merely a specific aspect of general adjustment, but it has also been argued that the two are not the same. A worker may be poorly adjusted in other areas of his life, yet on the job he may be well adjusted, possibly because what he does is supportive of his otherwise aberrant personality.
2. Work-adjustment mechanisms are much like those used in adjusting to other areas of life activities; but they differ in that their substantive characteristics are peculiar to the work situation.

D. Normative characteristics

Because so few instruments have been constructed to measure vocational adjustment, no research has been located which provides data on what percentage of the labor force is poorly adjusted to their jobs. Estimates of the extent of work alienation are high, but research shows that only about 15 percent of the workers studied were alienated from their jobs. A more likely hypothesis is that most workers in our society are *indifferent* to their jobs.

E. Dimensions

The two major dimensions, or components, of vocational adjustment which have been hypothesized and studied are success and satisfaction, but, as the research summarized indicates, these two variables are not lawfully related to each other. Consequently, they cannot be conceived of as dimensions of vocational adjustment, although they can be thought of as independent outcomes of the vocational adjustment process.

F. Developmental trends

1. Research on the stages in vocational adjustment has been indirect and fragmentary. It consists of a few cross-sectional analyses of lifetime worry patterns and vocational goals, based mostly upon retrospective data of questionable validity.
2. Studies of career patterns have established that there are differential sequences of movement through the world of work. These patterns of advancement vary from one occupational level to another, with greater stability and security being associated with professional and managerial status.

G. Correlates

That there is a low to moderate positive correlation between vocational adjustment, on the one hand, and the various aspects (personal, social, familial, etc.) of general adjustment, on the other, has been demonstrated in many studies. The factors which affect or produce this relationship, however, have not as yet been identified, although there is some observational evidence that the occupation may play a part in determining the magnitude and direction of the association between vocational and general adjustment.

Conclusions. This summary of research on vocational adjustment reflects both the strengths and weaknesses of the studies which have been conducted on vocational motivation, success, satisfaction, and adjustment. The strengths lie in the great number of investigations which have been made of most of these phenomena, particularly success and satisfaction; the weaknesses appear in the often expedient and nontheoretical nature of the studies. The result is that, although there may be a large body of empirical data on certain aspects of vocational adjustment, there is little or none on others. Moreover, that which is available is difficult to fit into a psychologically meaningful conceptual schema. When an attempt is made to do this, as with the Model of Vocational Adjustment proposed in Chapter 8, the lacuna in our knowledge and understanding of how and why workers adjust to their jobs as they do become painfully apparent. In the next section, we shall turn our attention to what some of these gaps are, with respect to both vocational choice and vocational adjustment.

RESEARCH NEEDS IN VOCATIONAL PSYCHOLOGY

Implicit in the foregoing summary of research on vocational choice and adjustment are some of the problems and phenomena which need further investigation. To organize these research needs in a manner which may lead to new lines of inquiry, a classification schema adopted from Edwards and Cronbach (1952) and Edwards (1954) has been used. They have proposed that there are four kinds of research which can be conducted, depending upon what the purpose of a study is:

1. *Survey research:* to discover relevant variables for more systematic study and to establish the parameters of known variables.
2. *Technique research:* to develop methods, whether test or nontest, for making observations which are quantifiable.

3. *Theoretical research:*[1] to test hypotheses which have been deduced from theories or which have been formulated to account for empirical laws.
4. *Applied research:* to determine what course of action should be taken.

Although the first three types of research have implications for the fourth, applied research will not be included in the discussion which follows, since it deals primarily with the effects of counseling, training, and similar programs upon vocational behavior and development, and consequently is more appropriately the subject matter of personnel psychology and vocational guidance than it is vocational psychology (see Chapter 1). Our concern here is with those research problems which can be investigated in (1) survey, (2) technique, and (3) theoretical studies of vocational choice and adjustment.

Survey Research

This type of research is designed to provide the vocational psychologist with new information about vocational choice and adjustment. Its primary purpose is to identify variables of interest which may be more systematically studied in subsequent research. Thus, its modes of data collection and analysis are descriptive and exploratory, rather than inferential and confirmatory. A commonly used method for gathering survey data is the unstructured or open-ended interview, and another is the biographical inventory or questionnaire, with primer items worded to elicit extensive ("bandwidth"), as contrasted with intensive ("fidelity"), information on vocational behavior and development. Often tests, either standardized or tailor-made, will be administered in order to establish base rates for phenomena which have been observed with less objective techniques. Descriptive statistics (central tendencies, dispersions, etc.) based upon such test data are usually considered to be a product of survey research. Likewise, correlational and factorial analyses are sometimes classified as survey research, if they are made to open up new lines of inquiry. Following Tucker (1955), Bechtoldt (1961) has pointed out, for example, that factor analysis may be *exploratory* or *confirmatory*. The distinction rests upon what is known about an area of investigation: "The exploratory factor analysis, being the first, is used to generate hypotheses while a confirmatory factor analysis is designed subsequently to test these hypotheses" (Bechtoldt, 1961, p. 407). Unfortunately, this distinction is frequently overlooked, not only in factorial analyses but in other kinds as well. If vocational psychology is to be built upon a reliable body of scientific knowledge, it cannot be too strongly

[1] This category of research was originally labelled "critical" by Edwards and Cronbach (1952) and Edwards (1954), but "theoretical" seems to describe it more accurately.

emphasized that survey research should not be interpreted *as if* it is confirmatory.

Comprehensive cross-sectional surveys of many vocational choice and adjustment phenomena are badly needed in order to suggest hypotheses for more formal testing. Some of the questions which might serve as the foci of such studies are these:

1. What are the "necessary and sufficient" conditions for making vocational choices?
2. What are the "dynamics" of the compromise process in career decision making? Do all individuals make compromises, or is it only those whose vocational development is delayed or impaired?
3. What are the background or etiological factors which lead to problems in vocational choice? What circumstances or experiences accentuate or ameliorate their effects?
4. What are the problems which workers encounter in adjusting to their vocations? What adjustment mechanisms do they use in solving them? How are these solutions related to vocational motivation, satisfaction, and success?
5. What are the factors which contribute to success after occupational entry? Why do workers fail in their vocations? What are the base rates for failure and success in the labor force?

In addition to inquiries along these lines, interview and questionnaire studies might be made of those individuals who "deviate" from the established norms and regressions for choice and adjustment variables. Why is it, for example, that some workers enter occupations at a level considerably below their general intelligence and others are successful in occupations above their level of intelligence? Cross-sectional survey research on these and similar questions should serve not only to suggest new studies but also to extend and elaborate upon work which has already been started.

Survey research of longitudinal design is even more critically needed than cross-sectional analyses of vocational behavior. Commenting upon what we actually know about the nature and course of vocational development, Borow (1961, p. 24) has noted that: "Our lack of first-rate descriptions and of normative data is most serious." The reviews of the literature in Chapter 5 ("The Development of Vocational Choice") and Chapter 12 ("Developmental Aspects of Vocational Adjustment") have underscored the paucity of empirical evidence on such questions as these:

1. To what extent is vocational development a process? That is, what earlier vocational behaviors are *necessary* for the appearance or occurrence of later vocational behaviors?
2. Is vocational development a continuous process, or are there discontinuities in it? If there are discontinuities, when do they take place, and what effect do they have on the process of decision making and work adjustment?
3. What are the empirical limits of the stages in vocational development? What factors, such as the life spans of occupations, affect these boundries? Are there individual differences in them? If there are, how do they influence subsequent vocational development. For example: Are adolescents who crystallize their choices after the end of the Exploratory stage any less well adjusted vocationally once they enter the world of work?
4. What are the relationships of success and satisfaction to career patterns over extended periods of time? Does the relationship between success and satisfaction differ from one type of career pattern to another?
5. Why are outstanding achievements typically accomplished early in the work life? Why does satisfaction follow a cyclical curve over the span of the work years? What part does "involvement in work" play in both success and satisfaction at different points in the career?

These are only a few of the directions which longitudinal surveys of vocational development might take; others have been suggested by Borow (1964a), Brayfield (1964), Crites (1965), Super (1954), and Super et al. (1957). The main point is that the process of vocational development must be much more adequately and completely described before it can be more meaningfully understood.

Technique Research

There are three general classes of techniques to quantify vocational variables on which research of this type is conducted: (1) tests, (2) scales, and (3) experimental procedures. By far the most common technique research in vocational psychology has been on the construction and validation of tests to measure such variables as choice, aspiration, interests, motivation, and satisfaction. Two approaches have been followed in vocational test construction, the rational and the empirical, both of which have had shortcomings. Rationally constructed tests, e.g., Super's Work Values Inventory (WVI), often have limited validity, because their a priori scoring keys fail to correlate with other variables. In contrast, empirically devised tests, e.g., the Strong Vocational Interest Blank (SVIB), are usually valid but have little theoretical relevance, because their scales do not correspond to the concepts and terms of theories of vocational behavior and development. To resolve this dilemma, the writer (Crites, 1965) has proposed a combined "rational-empirical" approach to the construction of vocational tests, in which item content is derived from descriptions of theoretical variables [Underwood's (1957) "literary definitions" of concepts] and scoring keys are comprised from those items which differentiate appropriate criterion groups. The Vocational Development Inventory (VDI) is being constructed in this manner. As indicated in Chapter 10, scaling techniques have been used primarily for assessing vocational success, but seldom have they been applied as they should be, in order to determine their internal consistency, reliability, and other psychometric characteristics (Guilford, 1954; Torgerson, 1958). Even less attention has been devoted to the conceptualization and development of experimental procedures to define and quantify both independent and dependent variables for laboratory studies of vocational behavior.

Needed technique research on both vocational choice and adjustment measures falls into two categories: (1) the development of new tests, scales, and experimental procedures, and (2) the refinement of already existing instruments. Foremost among the choice behaviors which have not been quantified as yet are the concepts of *compromise* and *synthesis* in Ginzberg's (1951) and Super's (1957) theories of vocational development, respectively. Also, experimental designs for distinguishing between *indecision* and *indecisiveness*, such as the one presented in the last section of this chapter, must be tried out empirically to determine their usefulness. Other variables of major theoretical import, which have not been operationally defined and quantified, include: coping mechanisms (Bordin et al., 1963); ego functions (Ginzberg et al., 1951); kinds of needs (Roe, 1956); differentiation and integration (Tiedeman & O'Hara, 1963); and conflict and dissonance in decision making (Hilton, 1962). Further work also needs to be done on most of the techniques which are presently available for measuring choice behaviors, either because they were not thoroughly enough studied when they were first introduced or because research on their psychometric characteristics has not been completed. Included in this category would be the following: the reliability of Trow's (1941) questions; the validity of Crowley's (1959) questionnaire; the Career Pattern Study's indices of vocational maturity; Starishevsky and Matlin's (Super et al., 1963) model for the translation of self-concepts into vocational terms; and Crites's (1965) Vocational Development Inventory and vocational problem classification system.

Of the variables in the Model of Vocational Adjustment proposed in Chapter 8, work-adjustment problems and mechanisms stand out as the ones which have not been previously measured. New techniques, based upon sound survey research, need to be constructed to operationalize them. The other variables in the model have been quantified, but often in only superficial ways. Researchers interested in the study of vocational motivation are confronted with the problem of demonstrating empirically that they are measuring variables which have motivational properties and not just associative attributes (Brown, J. S., 1961). The assessment of vocational success also poses some complex problems, which have been accentuated by the relatively unsystematic and unsophisticated research conducted on them. There is a critical need for a large-scale project designed to develop general measures of success, to establish base rates for success in the working population, and to gather other data on the parameters and correlates of success. In contrast, the measurement of satisfaction is considerably more advanced, the major problem for future research being the "operational identification" and "stimulus variable elaboration" of existing instruments. There have been no studies, for example, of the relationships between global and summation measures of satisfaction. Finally, despite the cogency of the career pattern as both a theoretical and criterion variable during the years of the work life, few studies have been conducted on ways of defining and quantifying it since Miller and Form's work in the early 1950s. Future research might focus upon such problems as the optimal number of years which should be used to define a stable position, criteria other than the duration and level of jobs which should be taken into consideration in delineating types of career patterns, and the merits of the "thematic-extrapolative" method (Super, 1954) as a technique for analyzing career patterns.

Theoretical Research

More than any other type, theoretical research has dominated vocational psychology since 1950; yet there remains much to be done before the gap which has developed between theory construction and the establishment of empirical laws during the past decade can be closed. Theories of vocational choice have been more extensively tested than theories of vocational adjustment, but none of the theories has been thoroughly enough studied that it has emerged as more promising or useful than the others. Not only are there major propositions in most of the theories which have not been empirically evaluated, but some theories, notably those on vocational adjustment, have not been researched at all.

There are undoubtedly many reasons for this state of affairs in theoretical research, but two stand out as particularly salient: First, as will be discussed at greater length in the next chapter, many of the theories of both choice and adjustment have been formulated and stated in language which is extremely difficult to reduce to empirical referrents for the purpose of testing hypotheses. And, second, so many theories have been proposed in such a short span of time that research on them has been largely diffused and unsystematic. Comprehensive programs of theoretical research on vocational behavior and development have been the exception rather than the rule and have been relatively recent in origin (see Chapter 5). Instead, the focus of theoretical research in the field has been upon tests of isolated hypotheses from several theories, thus resulting in a disparate and fractionated body of knowledge which is practically impossible to integrate and synthesize. What is needed is theoretical research founded upon what Campbell, D. T. (1957) has called "transition" studies, which are designed to both replicate and extend previous experiments and investigations. Such research not only yields more reliable results, but it is also *incremental* (Brayfield, 1964): one study builds upon another until a fund of empirical evidence accumulates which is extensive and stable enough to appraise the value of theoretical statements with some confidence.

Of the theories of vocational choice reviewed in Chapter 3, those which have received the least attention in theoretical research are the decision-making models (Gelatt, 1962; Hilton, 1962; Hershenson & Roth, 1966). Yet, it would appear from their substance and structure that they may have the most promise for integrating field and laboratory research on vocational behavior and development, whether it is of cross-sectional or longitudinal design. Not only are they comprehensive enough to encompass most of the variables which other theories have proposed as the critical ones in the process of vocational choice, but they are more readily translatable into operational terms and hence more susceptible to empirical test. Similarly, the "conceptual framework" for choice and entry outlined by Blau et al. (1956) lends itself to the formulation of specific hypotheses about decision making and selection at the time when the individual is on the threshold of the world of work, but it has not been directly studied in theoretical research. The most relevant findings are those on job applicants and employers summarized in Chapter 5.

Other theories of vocational choice which are likely to produce considerable theoretical research are those of Bordin et al. (1963), Holland (1966b), Super et al. (1963), and Tiedeman and O'Hara (1963). Roe's (1957) hypotheses on the relationship of parental attitudes to field of choice have been extensively studied as they are now formulated, with largely negative results; but if they are revised to account for the effects of other variables, possibly along the lines suggested in Chapter 14, they may again be the focus of theoretical research. And certain aspects of Ginzberg's (1951) theory should not be overlooked as sources of provocative hypotheses on the factors which affect choice. In particular, his discussion of the work and pleasure orientations of the adolescent in relation to his active or passive involvement in the choice process warrants appropriate theoretical research.

Theoretical research on vocational adjustment is in an even less advanced stage than that on vocational choice. With the exception of the recent interest in testing hypotheses derived from Herzberg's (1959) two-factor theory of vocational motivation, most of the studies which have been conducted on vocational adjustment phenomena have been largely atheoretical. Yet, there are several theories which might profitably be investigated. Both Katzell (1964) and Vroom (1964) have proposed hypotheses which could be tested with only a minimum of prior conceptualization and instrumentation. The various theories of vocational satisfaction are good bets for theoretical research, as are the hypotheses on the conditions and variables which influence the relationship of satisfaction to success. Another potentially productive line of inquiry, which was opened up by Roe's (see Chapter 10) studies of eminent scientists, is the role played by "involvement in work" as a factor in vocational success. Also, Rothe's (see Chapter 10) research on output curves should be pursued to further clarify and test his hypotheses on "ineffectiveness of incentivation" and "restriction of output." Super (1954) has outlined what amounts to a program of research on the correlates of career patterns, which should be given high priority in studies of the developmental aspects of vocational adjustment. Finally, mention should be made of the Model of Vocational Adjustment presented in Chapter 8 as a possible schema for theoretical research on the dynamics of how and why workers adjust to their jobs as they do. Such research presumes, however, that adequate measures of the variables in the model have been developed, which, as was brought out in the discussion of technique research, is not the case.

Comment. As was mentioned in the discussion of the writer's Vocational Development Project in Chapter 5, survey, technique, and theoretical research should not be conducted independently of each other. They should be the interrelated components or phases of an overall *program* of research on vocational behavior and development. By programmatic research is meant "the sustained efforts of an investigator or research team to clarify a specific issue or problem, or a set of related problems, within a more or less limited field through a series of investigations" (Brayfield, 1964, p. 316). Depending upon how much is known about a field of study, survey research typically precedes the other types, since it is necessary first to identify which variables are of interest and potential significance for further investigation. Once they have been selected, technique research is initiated to measure them: tests are constructed, scales are devised, apparatus is built, etc. It is at this stage of programmatic research that operational definitions are given to the variables under study. Next, assuming that the technique research has served its purpose, theoretical research can be pursued to test hypotheses about expected relationships among the variables of interest.

If a program of research is to yield interpretable results, this temporal sequence in the conduct of survey, technique, and theoretical research must be observed and maintained. Too frequently survey research is reported and interpreted *as if* it were theoretical research, yet insufficient technique research has been completed to measure the variables adequately and the same data are drawn upon to formulate *and* test hypotheses. Similarly, the findings of theoretical research are often taken as evidence for *both* the validity of the instruments which were used to measure variables and the confirmability of the hypotheses which were investigated. Such confusions and confoundings of one type of research with another can only lead to findings which are equivocal and inconclusive.

DEVELOPMENTAL RESEARCH IN VOCATIONAL PSYCHOLOGY

With the increasing emphasis upon and commitment to Vocational Development theory in the field since 1950, the need for developmental research on choice and adjustment phenomena has become more and more acute. Cross-sectional analyses of presumably developmental variables have been made, such as Tiedeman and O'Hara's (1959) study of the vocational self-concept in adolescence (see Chapter 5), but they have been criticized as less than adequate (Schaie, 1965). The ideal design for developmental research has been the longitudinal analysis of vocational behavior over prolonged periods of time, as exemplified by the projects described in Chapter 5. There are two major drawbacks to the longitudinal approach, however, which seriously circumscribe its usefulness: First, it is woefully inefficient with regard to the time which must pass in order to collect data and the cost of following up Subjects in order to keep the sample intact. And, second, it is considerably less precise and powerful logically and statistically than has usually been assumed. As will be brought out below, there are other models and methods of analysis than the conventional longitudinal design which are superior to it. These are discussed in this section under the following headings: (1) modified longitudinal designs, (2) Markov chain analyses, and (3) a general developmental research model.

Modified Longitudinal Designs

One problem with the traditional longitudinal study is that the vocational behavior of a sample may be affected and altered simply by virtue of its being interviewed or tested or subjected to whatever measurement procedure is used. In other words, the measures may be what Campbell, D. T. (1957, p. 299) terms *reactive:* they modify "the phenomenon under study, which changes the very thing that one is trying to measure." To assess the possible effects of such reactive measures, the Career Pattern Study (Super & Overstreet, 1960, pp. 28–29) compared their core group with a control group of 173 boys who were one grade ahead of the study sample on variables such as age and intelligence scores, which were available on both groups from school records. Admittedly, this design is limited to a comparison of the core and control groups on existing data, but it does provide an analysis that is not typically made in longitudinal studies.

Another modification in designing developmental research, which the writer has used in the Vocational Development Project (Crites, 1964; 1965), is depicted in Figure 13-1. In this diagram, it can be seen that the core samples, on which repeated measurements are obtained for the duration of the study, are supplemented by cross-sectional samples, in order to increase N for certain types of analyses, viz., correlations between demographic and developmental variables. This sampling design can also be followed to gather all the necessary data for the various analyses which can be made in Schaie's (1965) general model which will be discussed later.

Still another design which has been proposed is the one conceived by Cooley (1964b) and summarized in Chapter 5 for the study of scientific careers. Not only does it telescope the total span of a longitudinal study into a shorter period of time, by using overlapping samples [cf. Schaie's (1965) "time-sequential" design], but, as Cooley (1964b, p. 91) notes, it allows selective sampling of age or grade levels, so that specific educational or vocational groups can be

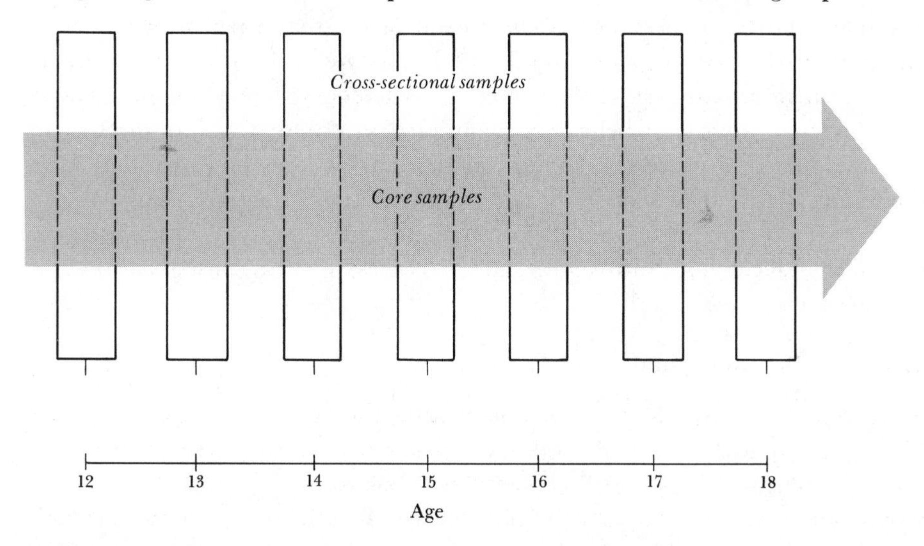

Figure 13-1. Sampling design for the Vocational Development Project. *(From Crites, 1965, p. 10.)*

investigated over long time spans rather than in a particular developmental stage.

Markov Chain Analyses

Mathematical models have not been used in vocational psychology to conceptualize and explain choice and adjustment phenomena (see Chapter 14), but this does not mean that they are inapplicable. Lohnes (1965) has explicated how a particular type of stochastic model, viz., Markov chains, can be applied to data on vocational developmental processes. Although there are several varieties of Markov chains, the one he describes is appropriate for nominal or ordinal categorical (discrete variable) data with a small number of classes, preferably between two and seven. These data are cast in a table the first row of which represents the first point in time of a developmental process and the first column the second point in time. Thus, the intersecting cell gives the probability of Subjects being classified in the same category on two successive occasions.

To illustrate, Gribbons, Halperin, and Lohnes (1966) have reported Markov chain analyses for selected data gathered with the Readiness for Vocational Planning (RVP) scales (see Chapter 5). The results from one of these analyses are reproduced in Table 13-1 for the development of coping mechanisms between the eighth and tenth grades. As can be seen from the notations in the table, the Subjects classified into Group 1 were judged to be coping less adequately with the vocational developmental tasks of this period than those in Group 2. The probabilities in the stationary transition matrix indicate, for example, that the chances were about 67 out of 100 that a person who was in Group 1 in the eighth grade would still be in Group 1 in the tenth grade. Markov analyses can establish, therefore, whether systematic contingencies exist between vocational behaviors manifested at different points in time in the developmental process. Like most models of this type, however, they have their limitations: they span only two points in time; they are designed primarily for the treatment of categorical data; and they may necessitate the grouping of behaviors into more general classes, with a consequent loss of information.

A General Developmental Research Model

More comprehensive than either the modified longitudinal designs or the Markov chain analyses is a general developmental research model proposed by Schaie (1965), which provides a potential framework for the study of many vocational choice and adjustment phenomena. It is based upon the proposition that a response which develops is "a function of the age of the organism, the cohort [group or sample] to which the organism belongs, and the time at

Table 13-1. A Markov Chain Analysis of Transitional Coping Behavior *(From Gribbons, Halperin, & Lohnes, 1966, p. 405)*

Markov	COPING BEHAVIORS		N-110
Group 1	floundering, stagnation		
Group 2	trial, instrumentation, establishment		
	INITIAL PROBABILITIES		
Group 1	.64		Group 2 .36
	TRANSITION MATRIX 1 (1958–1961) (frequencies in brackets)		
	Group 1	1961	Group 2
Group 1	.63 (44)		.37 (26)
1958			
Group 2	.30 (12)		.70 (28)
	TRANSITION MATRIX 2 (1961–1963)		
	Group 1	1963	Group 2
Group 1	.66 (37)		.34 (19)
1961			
Group 2	.39 (21)		.61 (33)
	TRANSITION MATRIX 3 (1963–1965)		
	Group 1	1965	Group 2
Group 1	.74 (43)		.26 (15)
1963			
Group 2	.37 (19)		.64 (33)
	STATIONARY TRANSITION MATRIX		
	Group 1		Group 2
Group 1	.674		.326
Group 2	.356		.644
Stationarity hypothesis $\chi^2_4 = 2.7, p \approx .61$			
Order zero versus order one $\chi^2_1 = 33., p < .001$			
Order one versus order two $\chi^2_2 = 1.8, p \approx .41$			
	LIMITING MATRIX (EQUILIBRIUM AT 6TH POWER)		
Group 1	.522		.478
Group 2	.522		.478

which measurement occurs" (Schaie, 1965, p. 93). Schaie points out that the problem with conventional cross-sectional and longitudinal designs is that these factors (age, cohort, and time of measurement) are confounded in one combination or another, and hence it is not possible to draw unequivocal conclusions from data analyzed in them. His solution is to derive methods which allow for the control or analysis of the confounded sources of variance, so that, given certain assumptions, the effects of each can be estimated.

Schaie (1965, p. 107) proposes that the most efficient design for a developmental study would involve the following steps:

1. Draw a random sample from each cohort over the age range to be investigated, and measure at Time k (Score A).
2. Get a second measurement on all subjects tested at Time k at Time l (Score B).
3. Draw a random sample from each cohort in the range tested at Time k plus one cohort below that range, and test at Time l (Score C).

With data collected in this manner, it would be possible to conduct several different kinds of analyses. The traditional cross-sectional and longitudinal analyses could be made from comparisons of Scores B and C and Scores A and B, respectively, but in addition to these the design provides for what Schaie calls "time-lag" analyses through comparisons of Scores A and C. Space does not permit a full exposition of these comparisons and the statistical procedures used with them, which Schaie outlines in detail. Suffice it to say that the logic of his model is to formulate a research strategy based upon the collection of data at a minimum of two points in time which can be analyzed to determine whether response functions are simple or complex and whether they are affected by practice on previous occasions.

Comment. In a symposium on research methodology at an American Psychological Association convention (Chicago, 1965), Donald T. Campbell made an observation about the value of statistical and experimental designs which is seldom recognized: They have to be tried out empirically to see whether they "work," every bit as much as a new piece of apparatus or a new test. Too often what appear to be elegant methodologies and designs are accepted uncritically and put to use before they have been properly evaluated against established criteria, such as the known parameters of a set of data as determined by traditional statistical techniques. Caution should be exercised, therefore, in utilizing the designs and models we have discussed here until more is known about them. They do seem to have considerable promise, however, for increasing the precision with which the development of vocational behavior can be investigated.

EXPERIMENTAL RESEARCH IN VOCATIONAL PSYCHOLOGY

Developmental research is conducted almost exclusively in the field, although it is conceivable that it might also be pursued in the laboratory. As primarily field research, however, it is basically descriptive rather than explanatory. It provides data on the parameters of vocational phenomena and the relationships which obtain among them, but it is seldom well enough controlled to draw inferences about *why* these phenomena exist as they do. In the field, the vocational psychologist is essentially an observer: he can enumerate and record the factors which seem to affect or influence the nature and course of vocational development, but he usually cannot directly manipulate them to determine their effects. Nor is he typically in a position to hold constant other factors which may also be related to the variables of interest. In the laboratory, however, he is an experimenter: he can exert greater control over the circumstances of his research, and he can manipulate the conditions which he hypothesizes may be associated with the development of vocational behavior. In short, he can more closely approximate the ideal of the univariate experiment—"that all factors are held constant except one, and this one is varied in some manner to determine whether or not it influences the phenomenon" (Underwood, 1966, p. 10). That few experimental studies have been conducted in vocational psychology is apparent from our review of the literature in the preceding chapters, but this does not mean that such research is impossible to design or carry out. To illustrate how the experimental approach might be followed in the analysis of a vocational problem, a paradigm for the study of indecision and indecisiveness follows.

An Experimental Analysis of Vocational Indecision and Indecisiveness

Tyler (1953, p. 239) has noted that: "The distinction between indecision in a limited area and indecisiveness based upon severe personal conflicts is not an easy one to make and probably can never be made with complete accuracy." Goodstein (1965, p. 158) draws a similar conclusion when he observes that the critical diagnostic consideration in differentiating indecision and indecisiveness is "the assessment of the role of anxiety in the etiology of the problem." He proposes that the inability to make a vocational choice may be linked with either one of two quite different antecedent conditions. As is shown in Figure 13-2, what has been called "indecision" is seen as being related to a "limitation of experience" in the vocational development of the individual, which has restricted his opportunities to acquire or learn the responses necessary to make a choice. Because his "coping" behavior, as Super (1963) terms it, is inadequate or nonadaptive, the individual fails in accomplishing the vocational developmental task of choosing an occupation, and experiences anxiety as a result. Goodstein (1965, p. 156) states that "the anxiety evidenced by the [individual] is seen as a consequent of [his] failure to have developed the appropriate skills. The anxiety is seen as playing a rather minor role in the etiology of the problem, being primarily responsible for the [individual's] not availing himself of the . . . resources available for problem-solving." The implication is that if the individual is exposed to the appropriate experiences—the ones he somehow missed earlier in his vocational development—he not only will feel less anxious but he will also be able to make a vocational choice.

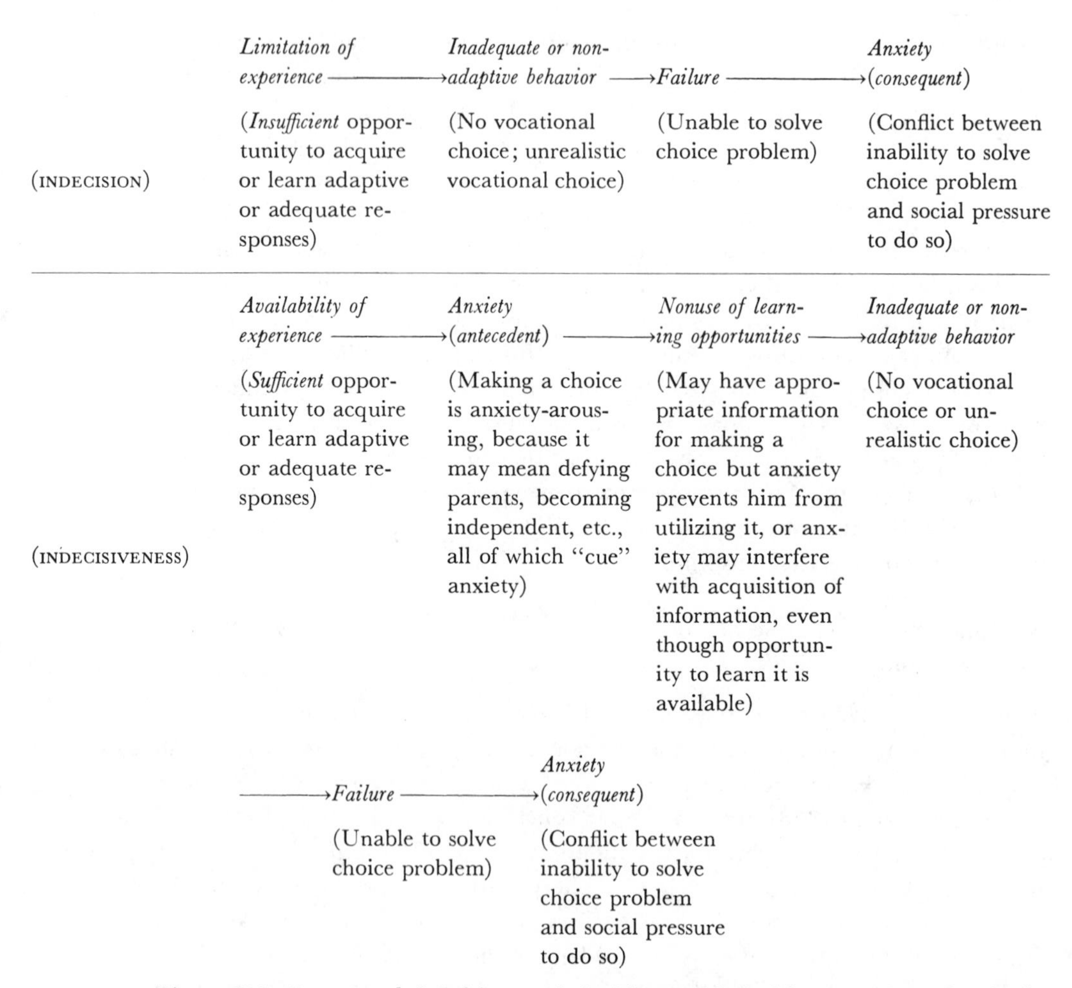

Figure 13-2. Conceptual definitions of indecision and indecisiveness. *(After Goodstein, 1965, et passim).*

In contrast, "indecisiveness" is viewed by Goodstein as being directly related to antecedent anxiety. The individual has had sufficient opportunities in his previous vocational development to learn the responses which would allow him to cope with the problem of vocational choice, and to solve it successfully, but because of interfering anxiety, aroused by the necessity of having to make a decision, he has either not acquired the responses or, if he has, he is unable to act appropriately. Goodstein (1965, pp. 156–157) concludes that:

> Thus the [individual] who is vocationally uncommited is undecided not simply because of lack of information either about himself or the world of work but because making a decision or commitment is

> strongly anxiety arousing.... For example, making a vocational decision may involve breaking away from parents or defying them; it may represent an act of independence for which the [individual] is not ready; it may mean a commitment to an academic career for which the [individual] may feel inadequate, and so on. In each of these hypothetical examples the [individual] avoids the anxiety by avoiding making a decision.

This stratagem is ultimately self-defeating, however, not only because the individual fails to make a vocational choice but also because not having a choice is, in itself, anxiety arousing. The implication is that, because of the role of anxiety in the etiology of indecisiveness, the provision of current opportunities for learning will have little effect upon the individual's ability to make a vocational choice. In fact, they may increase his anxiety because they reactivate the conflicts associated with decision making.

From Goodstein's theoretical analyses of indecision and indecisiveness, it is possible to formulate what Marx (1951) and Underwood (1957) have referred to, respectively, as "E/C" or "S-R, E/C" operational definitions of these concepts. The paradigm for this type of definition is the comparison of the effect upon behavior of a zero amount of a treatment with that of some finite amount. "If there is a reliable difference in behavior resulting from these two conditions, the procedures used to derive it define the phenomenon. The symbols, E/C, refer to experimental and control conditions; the experimental condition is the one having a finite amount of a given stimulus condition, the control condition, zero amount" (Underwood, 1957, p. 69).

Figure 13-3 shows how such a design might be used to define indecision and indecisiveness. A group of Subjects is administered a standard inventory, e.g., Trow's (1941), to elicit their vocational choices. Those who have no choice, i.e., they state that they are "undecided," are then randomly assigned to experimental and control groups. Next, the experimental group is exposed to some "informational experience," such as being given the results of a battery of vocational tests or presented occupational information, while the control group receives no information. Finally, both groups are retested with the

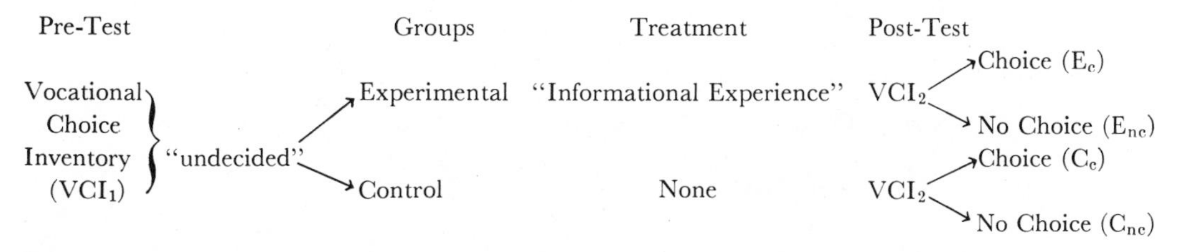

Figure 13-3. Experimental design for operationally defining indecision and indecisiveness.

choice inventory, and Subjects are classified according to whether they are decided or not. In order to define indecision and indecisiveness from the results of this experiment, two outcomes must obtain: First, the number of choices in the experimental group must be significantly greater upon retest than in the control group. If it is not, then changes from no choice to choice between test and retest would have to be attributed to error variance in the choice inventory or some factor other than the effects of the experimental treatment. Second, within the experimental group, there would have to be some Subjects who were able to make a choice upon retest and some who were not. The former would be those who had had problems of indecision, but were able to solve them given the appropriate information, whereas the latter would be those with problems of indecisiveness, since they were unable to declare a choice, even though they had the relevant information.

In defining indecision and indecisiveness in this way, the assumption has been made that the reason some Subjects in the experimental group cannot make a vocational choice, despite their exposure to the "informational experience," is that anxiety produces counteracting effects. To test this hypothesis empirically, the design depicted in Figure 13-4 can be used, which is much the same as that for defining indecision and indecisiveness, with one modification. After the "informational experience," all Subjects, in both the experimental and control groups, are tested with the Taylor Manifest Anxiety Scale and the Attitude Scale of the Vocational Development Inventory. Also, half of the Subjects in the two groups are tested with these scales *before* the experimental treatment, in order to assess the possible "reactive effects" of the pretest upon the dependent variable (Campbell, D. T., 1957). Simply taking the MAS and the VDI may produce changes in choice, either independently or in combination with the "informational experience." This can be determined with this

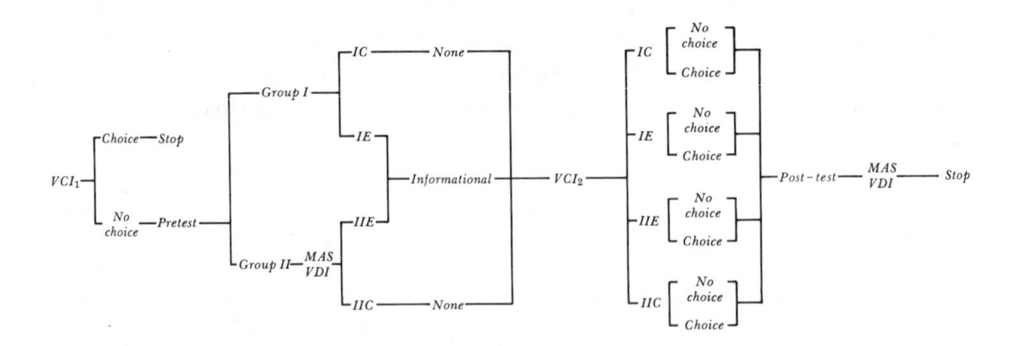

Figure 13-4. Experimental design for studying the relationship of manifest anxiety and vocational maturity to indecision and indecisiveness.

procedure by an analysis of variance of the main and interaction effects of pretesting and no pretesting for the experimental and control groups.

If the pretesting is not reactive, the predictions diagrammed in Figure 13-5 can be tested directly. Because the status of the experimental and control groups on pretest is unknown at present, the "indecision" Subjects are depicted as being either equal to or less than the "indecisive" Subjects on both the MAS and VDI. On post-test, however, the former should be lower on MAS and higher on VDI, and the latter should be somewhat higher on MAS, because of the anxiety-arousing effects of the "informational experience" and decision-making situation, and about the same on VDI. Using a Type I analysis of variance (Lindquist, 1953), the theoretical expectations about the role of anxiety in indecision and indecisiveness would be supported, if the interaction effects were significant. The main effects across groups would most likely be

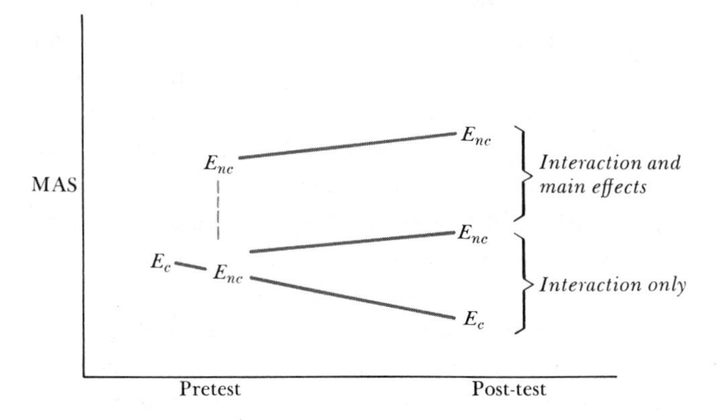

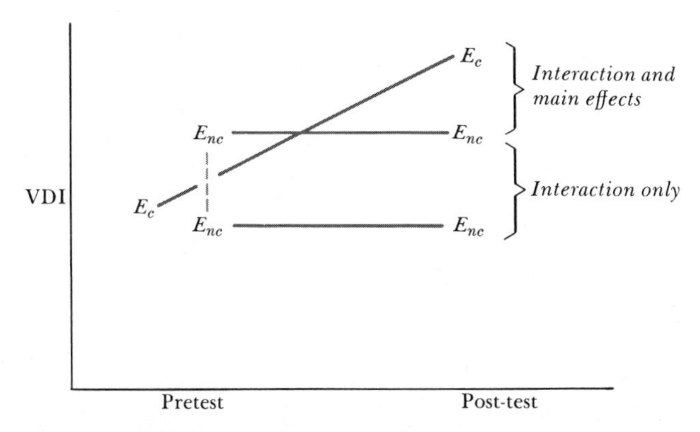

Figure 13-5. Predicted differences between indecision and indecisive groups in manifest anxiety and vocational maturity.

found, in addition, if the "indecision" and "indecisive" Subjects differed in MAS and VDI.

Comment. Whether the results of this experiment will be as predicted remains to be determined; it has not as yet been conducted, although it is planned as part of the theoretical research of the Vocational Development Project (see Chapter 5). It has been described here to illustrate one type of laboratory study which might be made on vocational behavior. Another approach might be to select Subjects on some behavioral dimension, as in the Iowa studies of anxiety and learning (Taylor, J. A., & Spence, 1952; Spence & Farber, 1953), and then make differential predictions from theory concerning the status of Highs and Lows on various dependent variables (Hall, D. W., 1963). Whatever methodological tactic is employed, the point is that an experimental research strategy in vocational psychology is not only needed but is also feasible (Brayfield, 1964). It should be pursued, however, in conjunction with relevant field studies, so as to minimize as much as possible the artificiality and sterility which too frequently characterizes laboratory-centered research (Borow, 1964a). This can be accomplished by selecting as one of the variables in an experiment a vocational behavior which has been thoroughly studied in the field, thus providing a link between the two research settings. In the illustrative experiment we have described, for example, normative data from the field are available on both Trow's vocational choice inventory and the writer's Vocational Development Inventory. If vocational psychology is to mature as a field of scientific inquiry, it must be based upon experimental as well as descriptive research, and the two must be meaningfully interrelated.

14

THEORY CONSTRUCTION IN VOCATIONAL PSYCHOLOGY

During the past decade, vocational psychologists have devoted considerable time to and have expended much energy in the spinning of theories of vocational choice and adjustment. As indicated in previous chapters, however, these theories are only partially related to the accumulated findings of the field before midcentury. Theory construction has struck out in new directions, with its emphasis upon the developmental nature of vocational behavior, and has left much of the Matching Men and Jobs approach behind. The effect has been to accentuate the widening gap between opinion and fact, and to pose as a recurring question how useful the theories are. It is to this question that the present chapter is addressed. An overview of theory construction in the field is presented first, and then an evaluation of its current status is made, in order to assess what remains to be done. Finally, the future of theory construction in vocational psychology is considered, and some possible schemata for more self-conscious and articulate theorizing are outlined.

AN OVERVIEW OF THEORY CONSTRUCTION IN VOCATIONAL PSYCHOLOGY

Throughout this book, we have discussed several different theories of vocational choice and adjustment individually but have not yet viewed them from the same frame of reference. It is the purpose of this section, therefore, to present an overview of theory construction in vocational psychology by (1) describing its early development, (2) providing a summary of the major theoretical orientations in the field, and (3) making an analysis of some of the formal characteristics of the theories which have been proposed.

Early Theory Construction in Vocational Psychology

To gain an historical perspective on the enterprise of theory construction in vocational psychology and to place it in an appropriate context for analysis and evaluation, it may be worthwhile to trace the chronology of explanation in the field. It is all too brief, as will soon become apparent, because theory building by vocational psychologists is a relatively recent endeavor. There are some earlier theoretical efforts, however, which are notable exceptions and which are the precursors of current attempts to explain vocational behavior and development. All these were the products of psychological orientations, and all of them were published after 1940, but they had roots in the more distant past, and consequently the *Zeitgeist* of the early years of conceptualization in vocational psychology also needs to be recounted. Accordingly, the history of theory construction which follows is divided into three periods: (1) the pre-1940s, (2) the 1940s, and (3) the 1950s.

The years *prior to the 1940s* were marked by outstanding achievements in occupationology and psychometrics (see Chapters 1 and 2) but few contributions to the construction of formal theories of vocational behavior. This was the era of "dustbowl empiricism," when the foremost question in the field was "Which occupation is the best one for this individual?", *not* "Why did he choose this occupation instead of another?" Likewise, Freud discussed the role of work in the life of the individual only incidentally and usually in footnotes to other topics, but he did observe that satisfying and satisfactory *Arbeiten* were one of the hallmarks of maturity in adulthood. Similarly, economists and sociologists gave scant attention to the problem of explaining vocational choice and adjustment, other than to recognize these variables as possible instances of phenomena of more central interest, such as the occupational distribution of workers and social mobility. Mayo and his associates cast their analysis of the results from the Hawthorne studies more in theorylike terms than any investigators before them, but still their discourse was less a theory of vocational behavior than it was a commentary on the social problems of industry. Thus, the approach to vocational phenomena in this period was largely atheoretical, but in it can be discerned several of the antecedents of later theory construction: vocational choice as a problem-solving process, vocational adjustment as an aspect of personality development, and work as an interpersonal situation.

The *1940s* witnessed the emergence of the first interest expressed by vocational psychologists in formulating theoretical statements about vocational behavior and development, probably because it was not until this time that there was anything to "theorize" about. Theories are seldom spawned from armchair speculation alone: "Explanatory work proper starts, and can start, only after the empirical constructs have been laid down. And this work, of course, consists in nothing else but finding the *empirical laws,* i.e., the functional relationships between the variables" (Spence, 1960, p. 6; italics in original). Perhaps the most important legacy of the pre-1940 period, then, was less the rough-and-ready propositions it passed on than it was the fund of empirical research which Yerkes, Strong, Paterson, and others accumulated, for it was upon this foundation, especially the studies of interests, that the first theories in vocational psychology were constructed.

From the findings of the California Adolescent Growth Study, Carter (1940) framed a paper on the development of vocational "attitudes" (interests) which has since become a classic and which has served as the conceptual cornerstone of contemporary self theories of vocational development, particularly as formulated by Super (see Chapter 3). From Carter's (1940, p. 186) central idea that "The pattern of vocational interests which gradually forms [in adolescence] becomes closely identified with the self," Super (1949; 1951a) formulated the hypothesis that "In choosing an occupation one is, in effect, choosing a means of implementing a self concept." Also reflected in Super's thinking about the self in relation to vocational behavior and development is Bordin's (1943) theory of interests as "dynamic phenomena," which has the distinction of being the only strictly deductive theory ever proposed in vocational psychology. That is, Bordin postulated a basic proposition about the relationship of the self-concept to interest formation, and from it he deduced a set of hypotheses which could be tested empirically. The 1940s were marked with significant theoretical activity, therefore, but because it was of more restricted scope than that of the next decade, it has generally been erroneously assumed that theory construction in vocational psychology did not begin until after midcentury.

In the early *1950s,* at a convention of the American Personnel and Guidance Association, Ginzberg perpetuated this misconception when he told the assemblage of vocational counselors and personnel workers that they were counseling without an explicitly formulated theory of how vocational choices are made. Yet, in addition to the conceptualizations of the 1940s, Dysinger (1950) had published his paper, "Maturation and Vocational Guidance," in which he not only argued that vocational decision making is a developmental process, but also outlined the stages through which adolescents pass in arriving at a career choice. In one sense, though, Ginzberg was correct in his appraisal, since there was no denying the fact that the orientation of pre-1950 vocational psychologists was predominantly applied, not theoretical. The contributions of Carter, Super, and Bordin notwithstanding, it was not until the catalytic effect of Ginzberg's (1951) book pervaded the field that vocational psychology awakened to the need for theory construction which had gone unfulfilled for so long. Within the decade after Ginzberg's work appeared, however, no less than 15 "theories" were published, and more were on their way. The consequence was twofold: First, the theories were poorly constructed, in a formal sense, because few vocational psychologists had any background or training in philosophy of science; and, second, a notable schism developed between theory and research, as increasing time and effort were expended on the former at the expense of the latter.

Summary of Theory Construction in Vocational Psychology

It would be neither possible nor profitable to summarize the content of all the theories of vocational behavior and development which have been discussed in this book. It might prove to be informative, however, to review in broad outline the central ideas of the major theoretical orientations which have been formulated in vocational psychology and related fields, in order to identify the phenomena and factors they underemphasize as well as to highlight those they stress. For this purpose, Table 14-1 was prepared, in which are enumerated the major nonpsychological, psychological, and general theoretical orientations cross-classified by vocational choice and vocational adjustment. The summary which follows is organized around this table:

1. *Nonpsychological theories of vocational choice.* As the designation of these theories indicates, they place primary emphasis upon factors which are

Table 14-1. Classification of Major Theories of Vocational Choice and Adjustment by Orientation

	Theories of	
Orientation	*Vocational choice*	*Vocational adjustment*
NONPSYCHOLOGICAL	Accident	Historical
	Economic	Economic
	Classical	Sociological
	Neoclassical	
	Cultural and sociological	
PSYCHOLOGICAL	Trait-and-factor	Trait-and-factor
	Psychodynamic	"Square peg"
	Psychoanalytic	Vocational fitness
	Need	Psychodynamic
	Self	Psychoanalytic
	Developmental	Need
	Decision	Self
		Developmental
GENERAL	Interdisciplinary	Reinforcement
	(Blau et. al., 1956)	(Dawis, England, &
	General developmental	Lofquist, 1964)
	(Super & Bachrach, 1957)	Motivation-satisfaction
	Typological	(Herzberg, Mausner, &
	(Holland, 1966)	Syderman, 1959)

external to the individual as the main determinants of his vocational choices. They view the individual as a "linear passive" system, with little or no effect upon the relationship between input and output. In other words, they postulate a proportional function between stimulus and response: what goes in, comes out. Thus, economic theories of vocational choice see the individual as directly responsive to the "whole of the advantages and disadvantages" of the labor market, however these are defined. Similarly, sociological theories attribute negligible significance to the individual as an agent or variable in the choice process, focusing as they do upon the various aspects of the social system as the salient factors in decision making. And, accident theory goes so far as to state that even the conditions which are external to the individual cannot be related to choice—that choice is not a reliable behavior which is associated with an identifiable circumstance of the environment or characteristic of the individual. As will be brought out below, however, it can be argued that accident theory is, in effect, no theory and consequently cannot be considered as an explanation of vocational choice.

2. *Nonpsychological theories of vocational adjustment.* Again, the focus of this theoretical orientation is less upon the individual per se than it is upon the work he performs. The questions about vocational adjustment for which answers have been sought through the ages are those which concern the meaning of work as an earthly and religious activity. Is it an end in itself, or is it a means to other ends? Is it drudgery, or must man work to realize his humanness? Is it not his work with tools which sets him off (above?) from the rest of the animal kingdom? And, how does he cope with work which is *infra dignitate?* Running through these and similar questions is a common theme which typifies nonpsychological interpretations of vocational adjustment: it is a concern with the cosmic and societal significance of work. Thus, the economist probes for the causes of unemployment, and the sociologist asks how it is that the modern worker has become increasingly alienated from his work and hence from the social context in which it takes place. Conspicuous by its absence from these nonpsychological orientations, however, is an interest in what motivates the individual to work, once his basic physiological and security needs have been satisfied. For, if the worker is seen as a "linear passive" system, in which output is proportional to input, then there is no reason to introduce motivational constructs as mediating variables.

3. *Psychological theories of vocational choice.* Within this theoretical orientation, we have considered essentially four different approaches to the conceptualization and explanation of vocational choice: the trait-and-factor, psychodynamic, developmental, and decision-making. All these theories have the same locus—the individual. They begin and end with him as the prime factor in the choice process. The input or stimulus side of the behavioral equation

($R = fS$) is either wholly omitted or dealt with in only a general way. The principal explanatory concepts in these theories have to do with the personal characteristics of the individual or the functioning of his personality. They generally minimize the effects of prior experience and emphasize the present status of the individual or the world as he sees it from his phenomenal field. Most of them recognize that the individual develops as he grows older, but the changes in his vocational behavior are usually dealt with descriptively, as in the delineation of life stages, rather than theoretically, as explanatory principles. Thus, psychological theories of vocational choice tend to be "one-sided": they focus almost exclusively upon the individual's behavior and the "dynamics" which underlie it.

4. *Psychological theories of vocational adjustment.* Although decision-making models have not been applied to vocational adjustment, the other psychological orientations have been used, with basically the same emphases which were evident in their analyses of vocational choice. Whether the theory stems from the trait-and-factor, psychodynamic, or developmental frame of reference, it stresses the role of the individual in the process of adjustment to work. Particular attention is given to motivational variables and the satisfactions which are derived from fulfilling needs or implementing the self-concept in a compatible occupational role. It is surprising, therefore, that these psychological theories do not draw more heavily upon the psychology of adjustment for appropriate constructs and behavioral principles in conceptualizing vocational adjustment, but they have largely neglected this area of study and have adopted a more developmental approach.[1] As a result, there have been few unifying schemata proposed, such as the Model of Vocational Adjustment outlined in Chapter 8, for interrelating the various aspects—motivation, frustration and conflict, coping and defense mechanisms, success, and satisfaction—of the process of vocational adjustment. What is needed is a synthesis of adjustment and developmental psychology which will be explanatory as well as descriptive.

5. *General theories of vocational choice.* The outstanding characteristic of this theoretical orientation is its comprehensiveness. General theories of choice have been constructed to embrace as many of the determinants of decision making as possible. They are also developmental, in that they have incorporated the principle that choice is a process which takes place over an extended period of time. The "conceptual schema" of Blau and his associates traces the parallels between the individual and the environment from birth to occupational entry; Super and Bachrach make a near-exhaustive enumeration of the

[1] This bias may reflect a more general lack of discourse between adjustment and developmental psychology. Even a cursory perusal of the subject indexes of both older and newer texts in these two fields reveals few cross-references.

tasks an individual must master at each stage of his vocational development; and Holland outlines the course of the life and work history in terms of interactions between personal orientations and model environments. What these theories gain in comprehensiveness by being so general, however, they lose in the cohesiveness of their propositions. They are loosely integrated aggregates of assumptions, concepts, and hypotheses, which are seldom logically related to each other, except in an intuitive way. Holland calls such theories "heuristic," in the sense that they implicitly suggest possible relationships among variables, but they do not explicitly state what they are. That general or heuristic theories are provocative can hardly be questioned; but, simply because they are so general, these theories can usually be interpreted so as to "catch the data whichever way they fall."

6. *General theories of vocational adjustment.* There is only the theory by Dawis and his associates which properly belongs in this category, although Herzberg's motivation-hygiene theory might also be included. In neither case, however, are these theories as loosely formulated as the general theories of vocational choice. The MSVR theory of work adjustment consists of a series of interrelated, explicit propositions about the factors which affect the individual's vocational satisfaction and success, and Herzberg's theory stands in direct contrast to traditional hypotheses about the nature of work satisfaction. In short, determinate (nonequivocal) empirical tests of hypotheses deduced from both theories can be made.

Comment. Of the theoretical orientations we have summarized, the nonpsychological has had the least impact upon explanatory efforts in vocational psychology. It has had its most prominent expression in theories like Roe's on the relationship of family factors to choice, and it has been drawn upon in the general theories to enumerate the stimulus conditions which influence vocational development, but otherwise the nonpsychological theories have not gained widespread acceptance in the field. Similarly, the general theories have been viewed more as summary statements, which they largely are, and have not aroused much interest as explanations of vocational phenomena. Clearly, the most influential theories have been the psychological, and, of these, at least since 1950, the predominant ones have been the self and developmental theories, or a combination of them. Based upon a sampling of the number of citations in the literature, as well as the number of studies it has stimulated (see discussion to follow), Super's self theory of vocational development has dominated the field's thinking about choice, followed closely by Roe's and Holland's theories, and Herzberg's motivation-hygiene theory of satisfaction has had a comparable effect upon conceptualizations of vocational adjustment. Probably the most obvious omission in theory construction in vocational psychology has been the formulation of a theory based upon the principles of learning. Aside from a few passing references to concepts like reinforcement (e.g., in Dawis, England, and Lofquist's theory of work adjustment) and Goodstein's analysis of the circumscribed problem of the role of anxiety in choice indecision (see Chapter 13), learning theory has not been systematically applied in explaining vocational behavior and development.

Analysis of Theory Construction in Vocational Psychology

There are any number of ways in which theories of vocational behavior and development might be analyzed, so that their formal characteristics can be identified. Those which have been selected for discussion here are those which seem most appropriate for the present stage of development of theory construction in vocational psychology. Since theory building in this field is relatively new and unsophisticated, a general rather than detailed analysis of the forms it has taken is called for. Accordingly, the following two methods of analysis have been chosen: (1) modes of theory construction and (2) characteristics of concepts.

Marx (1963, pp. 14–19) has described four different *modes of theory construction* which have been used in psychology: (1) model, (2) deductive, (3) inductive, and (4) functional. These approaches to theorizing are defined by the directions which can obtain between the conceptual (theory-language) and empirical (data-language) levels, as shown in Figure 14-1. The *model* provides an analogue to which data can be fitted. The usefulness of a model as a theory depends upon the extent to which the relationships among variables specified in it are isomorphic to those in the data (Brodbeck, 1957). The most prevalent application of models in psychology today is in the explanation of learning phenomena (e.g., Estes, 1959). The *deductive* theory is usually based upon already-established empirical laws, but its essence resides in the logical deduction of theorems (testable hypotheses) from axioms (postulates), so that the direction of inference in this mode of theory construction is primarily from the conceptual to the data level. The most notable example of this type of theory is Hull's (1940) hypothetico-deductive theory of learning. The *induc-*

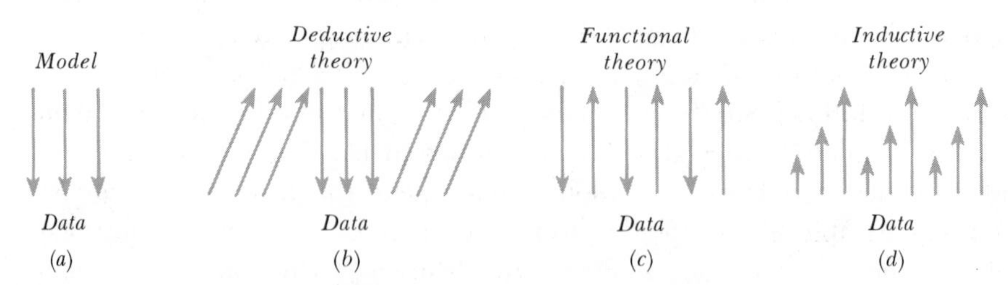

Figure 14-1. Four modes of theory construction. *(From Marx, 1963, p. 14.)*

tive theory proceeds in exactly the opposite direction, from data to summary statements of empirical relationships, supposedly without resort to deductive reasoning. Even in the most strictly positivistic approach, however, such as is exemplified by Skinner (1950), it can be argued that some kind of conceptualization or deduction is used, if only in the choice of an experimental problem or design (Marx, 1963, p. 18). Finally, the *functional* theory involves a continuous interaction between the conceptual and data levels. Hypotheses are formulated; they are tested empirically; they are accepted, rejected, or modified; and further hypotheses are developed as indicated. This mode of theory construction is probably most representative of the explanatory process engaged in by psychologists.

Although vocational psychologists have not adhered strictly to any of the various modes of theory construction, general instances of the use of each can be found. Most of the conceptualization of vocational development has been accomplished by following models borrowed from developmental psychology. For example, Beilin (1955) has shown how several principles of development, e.g., differentiation and integration, pace, and growth toward independence, can be applied to data on vocational phenomena. Developmental tasks, life stages, vocational maturity quotients: all these concepts have been used as models for theorizing about vocational development. How isomorphic they are to data on the latter, however, is another matter and will be discussed in the next section. Deductive theories are scarce in vocational psychology. As previously mentioned, about the only one which qualifies as truly deductive is Bordin's theory of "interests as dynamic phenomena." A case might be made for the theory of work adjustment proposed by Dawis, England, and Lofquist, but the hypotheses formulated in it are more declarative statements than they are inferences deduced from a set of postulates. In contrast to other fields of psychology, the most frequently constructed theory in vocational psychology appears to be the inductive, possibly because this field is in an earlier stage of theory building than most others. For, it is less complex and demanding to make summary statements of empirical relationships, which is the sum substance of inductive theories, than it is to undertake any of the other modes of theory construction. Thus, Stefflre (1966) entitled his inductive theory of vocational development, "Ten Propositions in Search of a Theory." The last type of theory, the functional, is best exemplified by Holland (1966b), who has continually moved back and forth between the theory- and data-language levels in the process of developing and testing hypotheses.

Which of these modes of theory construction will prove to be the best is difficult to say. Perhaps the question should not even be posed, since the several approaches to theorizing may be suited to different purposes, depending upon their relationship to the nature of the research which is being conducted on vocational behavior and development. If the research is experimental and laboratory-based, then the model and deductive modes may be the most appropriate. They typically lend themselves to the generation of hypotheses which are difficult to test anywhere other than under the highly controlled conditions of the laboratory. An example is provided by the hypotheses deduced from learning theory on the role of anxiety in indecision and indecisiveness and the corresponding experimental design outlined in Chapter 13. If the research is exploratory and in the field, however, theorizing of the inductive and functional types may be more useful. These modes are more "open-ended" and allow for the formulation of hypotheses which are less formal and more tentative. Ginzberg's survey of vocational choice illustrates how an inductive theory can be derived from field research designed to explore how career decisions are made at different points in adolescence. If and when research in vocational psychology becomes more experimental, there will probably be a shift in the modes of theory construction which are most widely used, from the less to the more formal. But even then, inductive theorizing will have its place in opening up new lines of inquiry and codifying existing empirical knowledge.

Another way of analyzing theory construction has been suggested by Underwood (1957), who distinguishes among five different kinds of *concepts* which can be used in building a theory, each concept being at a successively higher level of abstraction:

Level 1 concepts are operational definitions of stimulus variables. They refer to the external environment, which can be manipulated or measured by the investigator; they do not refer to the behavior of the organism. Examples of concepts on this level are deprivation time, room temperature, cortical lesion, etc.

In contrast, Level 2 concepts are operational definitions which identify phenomena—that is, they specify in a "point-at-able" way the behaviors of the organism to which the theorist (or investigator) has reference. These may range from eye blinks elicited by air puffs to scores on paper-and-pencil tests. Underwood notes that at this level the phenomenon is only identified; no inferences are made about what produced or "caused" it.

Level 3 concepts have the same operational definitions as those on Level 2, but, in addition, the psychologist infers from these procedures that some factor or process, *x*, has caused the behavior he observes. Thus, from the administration of an intelligence test to an individual, he may conclude that the individual's score reflects a capacity (*x*), which "really" exists within him, to comprehend the meaning of words or to solve problems with symbols.

Level 4 concepts go one step further: they postulate some causal condition or variable rather than simply inferring it from the defining operations for a phenomenon. "The scientist, in postulating the process, brings under a single explanatory idea or principle several independently defined phenomena" (Underwood, 1957, p. 214). To do this, however, without engaging in unnecessary abstraction and possible circularity of reasoning, he must (according to Underwood) tie or link up the postulated process with a stimulus variable. An example is the process of inhibition, which is postulated to account for weak responses to standard stimulus variations.

Level 5 concepts are little more than summary statements of Level 4 concepts: "They summarize the interaction of other postulated processes in an explanatory system" (Underwood, 1957, p. 223). An illustration is Hull's concept of effective reaction potential, which synthesizes the Level 4 concepts of reaction potential, reactive inhibition, and conditioned inhibition in his theory of learning.

In vocational psychology, Level 1 concepts are best exemplified by the classification and measurement techniques used to categorize and quantify occupations, which have constituted the principal stimulus dimension of interest in the field, particularly in the Matching Men and Jobs approach. Other, less widely investigated, Level 1 concepts include: socioeconomic status, father's occupation, educational level, place of residence (urban-rural), parental attitudes, and developmental tasks. Level 2 concepts are represented by all the various methods which have been used to measure vocational behavior *and* which have not been given "surplus meaning" by inferring from them the causal processes producing the behavior. Outstanding among these are vocational choice, as elicited by open-ended questions like Trow's (see Chapter 4), and job performance (success), as defined by supervisor's ratings or indices of productivity (see Chapter 10). Most concepts in vocational psychology, however, are of the Level 3 type, in which some inference is made from the defining procedures about what is causing individual differences in responses. Vocational interest is the most obvious example of a Level 3 concept, where it is generally assumed that "interests are motives" (see Chapter 9). In other words, it is reasoned that individuals differ in their likes and dislikes, as assessed by an interest inventory, *because* they differ in their motives.

Strictly speaking, Level 4 concepts have not been extensively formulated in vocational psychology, not because causal processes have not been postulated, but because they typically have not been linked to stimulus variables. In short, what we have in the field is a large number of concepts which fall between Levels 3 and 4. The most notable of these is the self-concept, which has been postulated to explain vocational behavior and development in several theories (e.g., Super and Tiedeman), but which has not been related systematically to the stimulus side of the behavioral equation (a fuller discussion of this point to follow). Needless to say, Level 5 concepts have not been developed, since there are no Level 4 concepts for them to summarize. If the dimensions of the self in Super's (1963) theory were linked to appropriate stimulus dimensions, however, then his concepts of the metadimensions and systems of the self might approximate what Underwood has defined as Level 5 concepts.

The value of analyzing vocational theories in terms of the levels of abstraction characteristic of the concepts in them lies in making explicit what has and has not been accomplished toward the end of formulating meaningful and useful explanations of vocational behavior and development. The emphasis thus far has been almost entirely upon Level 2 and 3 concepts, which means that little work has been done on relating stimulus dimensions to response variables. Even Holland (1966b), who, more than any other theorist, has attempted to link environmental and behavioral variables, has not introduced Level 4 concepts which would possibly serve to "mediate" the low-order, but significant, relationships he has found between these two classes of variables. That there are distinct logical as well as heuristic advantages in theorizing with Level 4 rather than Level 3 concepts will be brought out in the next section.

AN EVALUATION OF THEORY CONSTRUCTION IN VOCATIONAL PSYCHOLOGY

Many criteria for the evaluation of theory construction have been proposed in both writings on philosophy of science (e.g., Brodbeck, 1957; Feigl & Brodbeck, 1953) and psychology (e.g., Marx, 1963; Underwood, 1957), but no general agreement has been reached on which of these are the most important. The problem here is to select those criteria which seem to have the most relevance to theory construction in vocational psychology, given its present stage of development. A prime consideration would appear to be the appraisal of theories of vocational behavior and development in a constructive way, so that new directions in theorizing stemming from what has already been done might be indicated, rather than a sweeping condemnation of our first efforts at explanation. Consequently, the discussion which follows has as its focus a statement of where we currently are in building theories in vocational psychology and where we might head in the future. It is organized into three parts: (1) comments on theory construction in vocational psychology by those who have been most involved in this enterprise; (2) status of theory construction in vocational psychology, as assessed with reference to a conceptual schema proposed by Marx (1963); and (3) other criteria for evaluating theory construction in vocational psychology.

Comments upon Theory Construction in Vocational Psychology

Evaluations of theory building in vocational psychology have been neither extensive nor systematic. Usually, they have been made in connection with discussions of broader topics or as background for the development of a new thesis. Some of the first observations on theorizing about vocational behavior which have been found were those of Darley and Hagenah (1955) on Super's (1949; 1953) early conceptualizations of interest formation and vocational development. Of the former, in which Super (1949, p. 406) proposes that "Interests are the product of interaction between inherited aptitude and endocrine factors, on the one hand, and opportunity and social evaluation on the other," Darley and Hagenah (1955, p. 159) observe:

> This statement is an interesting descriptive listing of all the possible causal, contingent, or conditional factors associated with the origin and development of interests. It would be difficult, however, to derive a specific set of hypotheses to guide research or to account for existing research findings on the basis of Super's summary, as was possible in Bordin's theory.

Similarly, they state that Super's (1953) theory of vocational development (see Chapter 3) "is a more orderly presentation of [his] views," but that "it still embraces primarily in descriptive terms a great range of factors—genetic, endocrine, maturational, sociological, and personalistic—as determinants of the behavior with which we are concerned" (Darley & Hagenah, 1955, p. 101). In Darley and Hagenah's opinion, then, Super's first attempts at theory construction had descriptive or subsumptive value but not predictive value (see discussion to follow).

Similarly, Super (1953, pp. 186–187) criticized Ginzberg's theory, but for different reasons:

> First, it does not build adequately on previous work: for example, the extensive literature on the nature, development, and predictive value of inventoried interests is rather lightly dismissed.
>
> Second, "choice" is defined as preference rather than as entry or some other implementation of choice, and hence means different things at different age levels. . . .
>
> A third defect in Ginzberg's theory emerges from these different meanings of the term "choice" at different ages: it is the falseness of the distinction between "choice" and "adjustment" which he and his research team make. . . .
>
> Finally, a fourth limitation in the work of the Ginzberg team lies in the fact that, although they set out to study the process of occupational choice, and although they properly concluded it is one of compromise between interests, capacities, values, and opportunities, they did not study or describe the compromise process [Super, 1953, pp. 186–187].

In short, Super's criticisms focus primarily upon Ginzberg's definitions of terms, not upon the propositions in his theory.[2]

[2] For other critiques of Ginzberg's theory, see: Kitson (1951) and Tiedeman (1952).

As a preface to the first formulation of his theory of vocational choice, Holland (1959, p. 35) commented that:

> Previous theories of vocational choice appear to have two serious deficiencies: they are either too broad or too specialized. Some theories—for example, Ginzberg's theory and Super's theory of vocational development (1951a, 1957)—are so general in statement that they are of negligible value for integrating present knowledge or stimulating further research. In contrast, other writers (Bordin, 1943; Hoppock, 1957; Roe 1957) have concentrated on more limited aspects of vocational choice with more explicit theories, but these are incomplete in that they are self-concept–centered, need-centered, or etiologically-oriented, although there is an extensive literature implying that all of these divergent emphases are probably of importance in vocational choice.

Wrenn (1959, p. 94; italics in original) has pointed out, however, that:

> The value of a theory lies not only in its psychological or other rationale, perhaps not mainly in this at all, but in its capacity to generate research.... The theory which synthesizes several common sense observations so that it sounds good, may be merely strengthening our biases, supporting our wishful thinking. We need theories which will help us in the process of *ordering* our observations and *testing* our inferences from them.

Responding to both Holland and Wrenn, Super (1963, p. 4; italics in original) has contended that they have missed two important points about the process of theory-building:

> First, early in the development of a field of knowledge facts are scarce, scattered, unconnected, and ill-established. Any attempt to organize them in a meaningful way (that is, to construct a theory) is bound to result in something vague, general, and highly tentative, or in segmental, limited theories which may be so limited and so unconnected as to seem unworthy of the name of theory. But if research is to be something more than trial and error, such vague or limited theorizing must be done to provide a basis for further work. Second, the vague, segmental theories pertaining to self concepts in vocational development *have* generated research, and some of these researches have confirmed while others have led to the refinement of various elements of the theory.

Precisely because of these and similar considerations, some vocational psychologists have preferred not to call their explanatory productions "theories." Blau et al. (1956, pp. 531–532) reason as follows:

> It should be stressed that we are proposing a conceptual framework, not a theory of occupational choice and selection. A scientific theory must, in our opinion, be derived from systematic empirical research.... In general, theory is concerned with the order among various determinants, that is, the interconnections between direct and more remote ones. The function of a conceptual scheme of occupational choice and selection is to call attention to different kinds of antecedent factors, the exact relationships between which have to be determined by empirical research before a systematic theory can be developed.

Likewise, Tiedeman and O'Hara (1963, pp. v–vi) state that their conceptualization of career development is not a theory:

> Neither is it an eclectic statement of available theories of career development. Nor is it solely a review of empiric investigations. Rather it is a concatenation of concepts that seem to be needed as primitive terms in a science of career development relating personality and career through the mechanisms of differentiation and integration as a chooser chooses and experiences in the evolution of his life problem.

Also, Holland's (1963; 1964a; 1966b) statements about his "theory" might be cited here, since he considers it heuristic rather than formal in character, the distinction being in the extent to which the propositions in it are logically related to each other. Thus, he defines a heuristic theory as one that "stimulates research and investigation by its suggestive character rather than by its logical or systematic structure" (Holland, 1966b, pp. 8–9).

In a series of papers over a period of years, Borow (1960; 1961; 1964a; 1966) has traced the progress of theory construction in vocational psychology from its precursors in the 1940s, through its infancy in the 1950s, to its present stage of development. Some of his observations are as follows:

> Emphasis is upon the generation of hypothetical constructs and the consequent use of explanatory principles and causal connections rather than exclusively upon the invention and use of intervening variables in the testing of response-response laws [Borow, 1960, p. 63].

> We must distinguish much more sharply between axiomatic statements about career development and testable assumptions and propositions about career development [Borow, 1961, p. 23].

> We must learn to make a much clearer separation between observation terms and hypothetical terms in talking about career development. In this connection, we shall have to strive soon to erect some

> workable coordinating definitions that will link data-based variables to non-instantial variables as, for example, the link between verbally expressed vocational indecision and inferred role conflict [Borow, 1961; p. 24].
>
> It is a weakness of much current theory making and research in vocational guidance and occupational psychology that data from conventional and conceptually rootless tests are erroneously treated as dynamic variables and used as "explanations" of behavior [Borow, 1964a, p. 380].
>
> Current work on occupational behavior suffers from premature and pretentious attempts at broad-scope theory building. Some theories use ad hoc models. . . . Other theories are modeled rather rigidly and uncritically on specialized theories designed to serve other purposes (e.g., self-concept theory, psychoanalytic theory, decision theory). Such theories are compelled to make implicit or explicit assumptions about occupational behavior which are often highly questionable [Borow, 1964a, p. 381].

Despite these drawbacks of contemporary theories, however, Borow (1966, p. 398) sees definite values accruing from them:

> First, by offering broadly integrative models, they bring the study of youth in vocational development into the mainstream of behavioral science and allow readier access to the insights and *modus operandi* of related disciplines. . . . Secondly, the newer and broader conceptual systems have suggested a wide-ranging assortment of promising research issues, a condition that has unmistakably revitalized psychological research on occupational behavior.

To summarize, Borow is critical of the vocational psychologist's lack of an analytical attitude in his theory building, which results in a blurring of essential distinctions between opinion and fact, but is optimistic about the prospects for future research on vocational behavior and development emanating from the newly formulated theories.

Comment. If as many general criticisms as possible could be extrapolated from these comments on theory construction in vocational psychology, they would probably be these:

1. Theories of vocational choice and adjustment have been either too broadly or too narrowly conceived.
2. They have been more descriptive than predictive in nature.
3. And, they have not adequately related the theory- and data-language levels.

Upon closer analysis, it is apparent that these criticisms are not unrelated. Most theories in the field have been constructed by borrowing concepts and principles from other areas (see previous discussion), primarily personality theory and developmental psychology. Whether comprehensive or specific in their focus, few of their terms have been given operational meaning when applied to vocational phenomena. Theory building with them has been largely by analogy rather than definition. Borow (1964a, p. 380) describes what has happened as follows:

> The unverified (hypothetical) statements are introduced into the system to connect existing knowledge in a meaningful way and to go beyond what is known in a suggestive way to give a more nearly complete, though tentative, account of behavior. Such unverified but testable propositions have heuristic value in pointing directions for research or in leading the skeptical student to devise alternate hypothetical interpretations. When, however, as is frequently true, these statements are accepted either as a priori knowledge or as confirmed propositions, the cause of a science of occupational man is poorly served.

Unfortunately, the latter has more often been the case than not. The major task which must be accomplished now, before further theory construction is indicated, is to establish the necessary "rules of correspondence" between the conceptual and empirical levels of existing theories of vocational behavior and development.

Status of Theory Construction in Vocational Psychology

These comments upon theory building in vocational psychology have often been insightful and penetrating, but they have been made with respect to one theory or another and consequently do not provide a systematic evaluation of all theories of vocational choice and adjustment. To assess the current status of theory construction in the field, such a comprehensive appraisal is needed. A particularly appropriate conceptual schema which can be used for this purpose has been formulated by Marx (1963, p. 11) and is shown in Figure 14-2. Marx delineates three dimensions along which the progress of a field of study toward becoming a science can be evaluated. The most important of these is the control of the observations which provide a discipline with its subject matter. These observations may vary along a continuum from informal, personalistic ones, usually made in the field, to highly rigorous, objective ones, as typically found in the laboratory. The more a field's observations approximate the latter, the more scientific it is, although, as Marx (1963, p. 11) notes, its

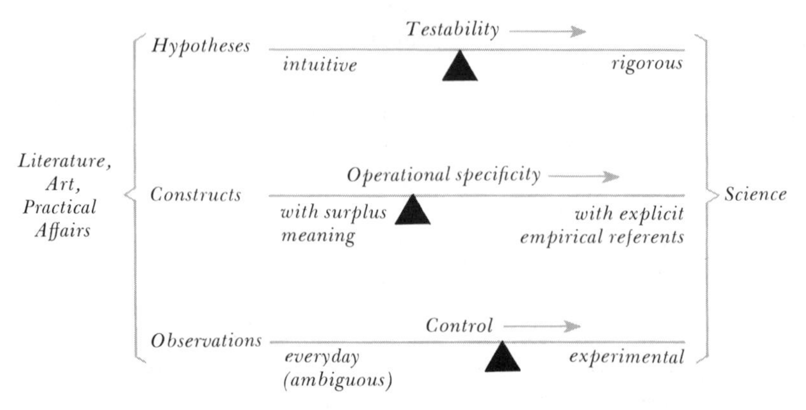

Figure 14-2. Three dimensions of scientific theory construction. *(From Marx, 1963, p. 11.)*

concepts may become less natural and lifelike.[3] The second dimension of scientific development is the translation of the variables of interest in a field into operational terms. Concepts can be studied more or less scientifically, depending upon the extent to which their empirical referents have been specified. If they have surplus meanings, which vary from one context and occasion to another, they are essentially unanalyzable and hence without the realm of science. Finally, there is the dimension of the testability of hypotheses, by which is meant two things: to be within the province of science, not only must a hypothesis be stated in such a way that scientific procedures can be used to test it, but it must also be specific enough so that it can be disconfirmed. In other words, it cannot be so general that it will "catch the data whichever way they fall." We shall now consider what the status of theory construction in vocational psychology is on each of these dimensions.

Control of Observations. The degree to which theories of vocational choice and adjustment have been constructed upon a foundation of controlled observations has ranged from one extreme of this dimension to the other. Illustrative of theories built upon data obtained from largely uncontrolled sources are those which have been based upon interviews, such as Ginzberg's (1951) and Herzberg's (1959). Likewise the theories of Bordin, Nachmann, and Segal (1963) and Roe (1957) have been derived from mostly informal observations or responses to projective techniques. Super's (1953; 1957; 1963) theory rests partly upon objective measurements and partly upon interview data, as do most of the sociological schemata of vocational behavior and development (e.g., Chinoy, 1952; Miller, D. C., & Form, 1951; Wilensky, 1964). Farther along the continuum of control of observations are the theories of Holland

[3] See Pratt (1939) for a discussion of this problem.

(1966b) and Dawis, England, and Lofquist (1964), both of which have been formulated almost exclusively from test data. Probably the exemplar of this position, however, has been the trait-and-factor approach to choice and adjustment, which has been synonymous with the standardization of the conditions under which behavior is measured, at least in field situations. Since there have been very few experimental studies conducted in vocational psychology, it is not surprising that theories of vocational behavior have seldom been built upon laboratory-controlled observations. Vroom's (1964) cognitive theory of vocational motivation probably comes closer to this ideal than any other at present. The decision-making models of choice hold considerable promise for future experimental work, possibly along the lines of Festinger's (1957; 1964) studies of cognitive dissonance, but research with them is only now beginning.

Operational Specificity of Constructs. As has been mentioned, one of the major shortcomings of recent theory construction in vocational psychology which has become increasingly apparent is the disjunction which exists in most theories between the theory- and data-language levels. Concepts have been introduced and used in explanation, without specifying what their empirical referents are or without relating them logically to other concepts which have been operationally defined. Foremost among the central concepts in vocational theories which have not been given empirical meaning are: compromise (Ginzberg et al., 1951); psychoanalytic coping mechanisms (Bordin et al., 1963); differentiation and integration (Tiedeman & O'Hara, 1963); fusion process (Bakke, 1953); and most of the "need" constructs. Some questionnaire-type inventories of the latter, particularly those in Maslow's theory, have been devised (e.g., Porter, L. W., 1962), but whether they actually assess variables with motivational properties is debatable (see Chapter 9). Considerable progress has been made, however, in the operational definition of the phenomenal, as contrasted with the trait-and-factor, self by Super and his associates (1963), and two parallel inventories to quantify the parental attitudes in Roe's (1957) theory have been developed (Brunkan & Crites, 1963; Roe & Siegelman, 1964). Also, the writer (Crites, 1965) has been working on complementary scales and tests to measure some of the attitude and competence variables in the construct of vocational maturity, but much more technique research on these and other concepts is needed (see Chapter 13) before the constructs of vocational psychology will be adequately defined both rationally and empirically.

Testability of Hypotheses. The extent to which hypotheses are testable and disconfirmable is largely a matter of the language in which they are cast. At one extreme of this dimension, there are hypotheses which are extremely difficult, if not impossible, to test scientifically, because they are stated in largely literary or metaphorical terms. An example is Super's (1951b) proposition that "In choosing an occupation one is, in effect, choosing a means of implementing a self-concept." In testing this hypothesis, the key word is "implementing," yet it is not directly translatable into any methodological or statistical procedures which would allow it to be studied empirically. Similarly, many of the hypotheses in the other theories of vocational behavior and development are essentially untestable, unless unwarranted assumptions about the equivalency of terms are made, because they are not "research-directed" (Ackoff, 1953). At the other extreme of this dimension, there are the highly specific hypotheses of such theorists as Katzell (1964), Morse (1953), and Vroom (1964), who have stated precisely what the expected relationships are among the variables with which they have dealt. Thus, Katzell (1964; see Chapter 9), for example, proposes that vocational dissatisfaction is a direct function of job characteristics and an inverse function of job values. When hypotheses are worded in this way, they can usually be expressed as equations, which can be tested simply by substituting the appropriate empirical values for the variables in them. Most of the hypotheses in vocational theories, however, have not been so rigorously formulated. They tend to be more intuitive than logical, and hence their testability is less.

Comment. If we were to estimate the status of theory construction in vocational psychology on each of these three dimensions—control of observations, operational specificity of constructs, and testability of hypotheses—it might be as shown in Figure 14-2. It should be understood that these estimated positions on the continua represent "averages" of approximately how much progress has been made toward scientific theory building in the field. From this profile, it is apparent that we are most advanced in the control of the observations we make, primarily because of the traditional trait-and-factor emphasis upon standardized measuring instruments. The next step on this dimension would appear to be the systematic observation of vocational behavior under laboratory conditions. The testability of hypotheses in vocational theories is about average, or slightly below, because theorists so often use "literary" rather than "scientific" language in formulating them. There is no reason why hypotheses cannot be stated in terms which are reducible to the methodological and statistical procedures used to test them. Nothing is lost by phrasing them more systematically, except possibly literary style, and greater testability is gained. Finally, much the same problem exists, except to a greater degree, in increasing the operational specificity of constructs in theories of vocational behavior and development. Just as greater testability of hypotheses can be achieved by phrasing them procedurally rather than metaphorically, so greater operational specificity of constructs can be attained by closing the gap between their literary definitions and empirical referents. To do this, Borow (1961, p. 24) proposes that: "We need . . . instruments based on a theory of test scores which has meaning for a theory of behavior in *nontest* situations." The writer (Crites, 1965) has outlined a "rational-empirical" approach to test construction which is designed to meet this need, but considerable work must be done with it before its worth can be determined.

Other Criteria for Evaluating Theory Construction in Vocational Psychology

In addition to Marx's dimensions, there are other criteria which are often used to evaluate theories, but which are more specific and therefore not equally applicable to all theories. Five of these, each of which will be defined in the section to follow, have been selected to appraise theory construction in vocational psychology. Expressed in question form, they are: (1) How well does a theory account for already-existing data? In other words, what is its *subsumptive* value? (2) How *parsimonious* is a theory? Other things being equal, does it require fewer or more explanatory propositions than rival theories? (3) Are the propositions in a theory *internally consistent?* That is, are they logically related to each other so that they are not contradictory? (4) How provocative or *heuristic* is a theory in stimulating new research? And (5) what is a theory's *predictive* value in identifying new phenomena? In the following discussion, the major theories of vocational choice and adjustment are evaluated by these criteria.

Subsumptive Value. This criterion has two aspects: First, it requires of a theory that it account for what is already known about the phenomena of interest; and, second, it requires that it be consistent with any new data which become available. As indicated throughout this book, and as summarized in the last chapter (see section entitled "Theoretical Research"), theoretical propositions and empirical findings in vocational psychology seldom jibe wholly, but they have probably been less congruent for one theory than for any other. This is Roe's (1957; Roe & Siegelman, 1964) theory of the effects of parental attitudes upon the origins of choice and interests. Although Roe formulated her theory largely from observations she made in studying the personal and work histories of eminent scientists, and despite the intuitive appeal of her hypotheses, the accumulated evidence on the relationships between familial interpersonal atmosphere and vocational behavior is mostly negative. Why has this been the case? Roe's theory is an etiological or genetic theory, in the tradition of psychoanalytic explanations of adult behavior in terms of infantile experiences, and, as such, it essentially ignores the intervening years of development, not to mention differential demographic and status variables, as salient factors in the determination of vocational choice. In this sense, Roe makes the "linear passive" assumption so prominent in the nonpsychological theories of vocational behavior and, in effect, excludes the personality of the individual as a "mediator" between stimulus input and response output. It is true not only of Roe, but also other vocational psychologists that they have not used the "intervening variable" construct in their theorizing to explain disproportionalities in the behavioral equation (see next section for a fuller discussion of this point). The consequence has been that their theories have had less subsumptive, as well as predictive (see discussion to follow), value than was initially anticipated.

Parsimony. Theories of vocational choice and adjustment vary considerably in the number of assumptions and propositions which comprise them, but this does not necessarily mean that those with the greater number are less parsimonious. The test of a theory's parsimony is whether it can account for the same phenomena as another theory but with fewer explanatory principles. Such tests can rarely be made, however, because two or more theories are seldom constructed to explain *exactly* the same data (Cohen, M. R., & Nagel, 1934, pp. 219–221). In vocational psychology, this is as true as it is in other fields, but some discriminations can be made in the parsimony of theories devised to explain choice as contrasted with adjustment phenomena. In general, the least parsimonious vocational theories are those which interpret the choice process within a developmental framework. These are what might be called "omnibus" theories which invoke a variety of propositions to encompass as many aspects of vocational development as possible. Super's (1953; Super & Bachrach, 1957) theories are of this type, as are most of the "need" theories, although to a lesser extent. The principal drawback to such theory building, as elucidated by Darley and Hagenah's (1955, p. 161) comment on Super's earlier theory (see foregoing discussion), is that it does not get far enough "above the data" to have other than a rather limited descriptive or summary value. It typically does not, for example, allow the deduction of hypotheses which lead to further research. In contrast, most of the theories of vocational motivation and satisfaction, such as Katzell's (1964), Vroom's (1964), Morse's (1953), and Herzberg's (1959), are not only more parsimonious than the choice theories, but they also generally have greater predictive power, primarily because the propositions in them are statements about the *functional relationships* which are expected to obtain among different classes of variables. If the developmental and need theories of vocational choice were revised accordingly, i.e., stated in terms of hypothesized functional relationships, they would gain in both parsimony and predictive value.

Internal Consistency. A theory is internally consistent if it fulfills two logical requirements: (1) all its propositions are related to each other, and (2) none of its propositions is contradictory of another one. Again, it is the developmental theories of vocational choice which are deficient. Although none of them contains propositions which are contradictory, i.e., one proposition negates another, few of them have been constructed so that their propositions are systematically interrelated. Rather, they tend to be listings of essentially independent propositions. Thus, the elements in Ginzberg's (1951) theory, viz., "choice is a process," "the process is largely irreversible," and "the process eventuates in a compromise between needs and reality," are logically independent. That is, the truth or falsity of one does not *necessarily* imply the truth or falsity of the others. As a result, it is not possible to combine these propositions syllogistically, so that their implications can be tested. In effect, these and similar theories, in which the propositions are not part of a logical network, are "dead-end" theories: they lead nowhere, other than possibly to repeated tests and modifications of the original propositions. The theory which most closely approximates the ideal of an "internally consistent" theory is the one formulated by Dawis et al. (1964) on work adjustment. Not only do they enumerate corrollaries which follow from several of their major propositions, but they combine propositions and deduce their implications. To increase the internal consistency of vocational theories, and thereby enhance their predictive usefulness, the logical connections among the propositions in them must be explicated.

Heuristic Value. The more research a theory stimulates, the more heuristic value it has. A theory which provokes no studies to test its propositions has only limited utility as a mode of scientific explanation. Of those vocational theories which have appeared since 1950, many have not generated related research. These include the theories by Dysinger (1950), Blau et al. (1950), Hoppock (1957), Gelatt (1962), Hilton (1962), Katzell (1964), Vroom (1964), Fletcher (1966), and Stefflre (1966), as well as some others of lesser scope (e.g., Lo Cascio, 1964). Even Ginzberg's (1951) theory, which had such a pervasive effect upon recentering the thinking of the field, has resulted in only a handful of studies which are directly relevant to its central propositions. There are several theories, however, which have produced considerable research, either because their originators and other interested investigators have conducted it or because they have been controversial. Among the former, those which stand out are the theories by Super, Roe, and Holland, each of which has led to from 5 to 10 studies. Bordin's (1963) theory has been fairly extensively followed up, but almost exclusively by his students. The most controversial theory in the field has been Herzberg's (1959), which has aroused more discussion and disagreement, in both opinion and fact, than any work on vocational motivation since the Hawthorne studies. It should be apparent, therefore, that the heuristic value of a theory is not *necessarily* an index of its popularity as an explanation of behavioral phenomena, but only an indication of the amount of research activity it has stimulated. Thus, Roe's theory has been widely studied but with largely negative results.

Predictive Value. Throughout much of the preceding discussion, there has been the implication that, if a theory has limited subsumptive and heuristic value, and if it is not parsimonious and internally consistent, then it will have little or no predictive value. That such is the case can be illustrated by most theories of vocational choice and adjustment. Because they are largely inductive theories, i.e., summary statements of empirical relationships, they lack the cohesiveness and cogency which is characteristic of more rigorously formulated deductive and functional theories. It is difficult, if not impossible, to trace the logical inferences and implications from data through propositions to predictions in these theories. The self theories of vocational development, for example, notably those of Super (1963) and Tiedeman and O'Hara (1963), are essentially R-R theories, in which behavior is not functionally related to stimulus variables (Crites, 1966b). Thus, as they are presently formulated, these theories can posit relationships only among variables of equal status, i.e., response variables; they cannot generate predictions from independent to dependent variables. In this sense, then, they are "closed systems," which are ultimately circular in their logic (Spence, 1944). Similarly, Holland's (1966b) theory has limited predictive value. It can only "suggest" further relationships among variables which are instances of the general classes of variables already in it. Because Holland has eschewed formulating a logical internal structure for his theory, he has no so-called "composition rules" (Spence, 1960, p. 378) by which propositions can be combined and predictions of new phenomena can be made. Likewise, Roe's (1957) theory lacks predictive power, as has been mentioned, because she has not made provision in it for the effects of variables which intervene between early familial experiences and later vocational development. More generally, it can be said of all these theories that their predictive value would be greatly enhanced if they used intervening variable constructs to make the needed conceptual linkages between stimulus and response variables.

Comment. When the criteria of theory construction considered in this section are applied to vocational theories, it is clear that we are in a relatively early stage of conceptualization and explanation in vocational psychology. Our theories are primitive ones, ones which need considerable rethinking and revision. This does not mean, however, that the enterprise of theory building should be abandoned, as some of its critics might conclude. Spence's (1960, p. 32) comment on the theoretical problems encountered in the field of learning is apropos here: "That theory construction has not always been intelligently pursued . . . is no reason for doing without theory." The problem is to determine what has been the major obstacle to the construction of more sophisticated theories of vocational behavior and development. The foregoing analysis and evaluation suggests that we have not given sufficient attention to the relationships which we might expect to exist between stimulus variables, on the one hand, and response variables, on the other. There are two reasons for this state of affairs: either our theories have focused almost exclusively upon R-R relationships, to the neglect of S variables, or, if they have included the latter, they have not linked them conceptually, by means of intervening variables, to vocational behavior. The task now is to make explicit how, and under what conditions, this can be done.

THE FUTURE OF THEORY CONSTRUCTION IN VOCATIONAL PSYCHOLOGY

"The past is prologue": what lies ahead for theory construction in vocational psychology will be largely determined by what has already been accomplished and not accomplished. As indicated in the foregoing discussion of the status of theory building in the field, the most obvious lacuna in our explanations of vocational behavior and development has been the lack of conceptualization of the intervening variables which link stimulus with response variables in the behavioral equation. In addition to the reasons already given for this omission in our theorizing, another may be that vocational psychologists, having been traditionally trained in differential and test psychology, which are highly response-oriented, are not familiar with the intervening-variable construct, which was introduced by Tolman (1936) in experimental psychology to account for disproportionalities in S-R functions. The theoretical problems which led to this development in experimental psychology, however, are much the same as those faced by vocational psychology now. A discussion of why, when, and how intervening variables should be used in theory construction, therefore, might suggest some new directions for future explanatory efforts in vocational psychology. In this last section of the chapter, and of the book, then, a possible model for theory construction in the field is presented, which explicates the use of the intervening-variable construct as well as other principles in the explanatory process. Some general considerations and issues, upon which the model is predicated, are dealt with first, and finally some implications of the model for the construction of a comprehensive theory of vocational behavior and development are extrapolated.

General Considerations and Issues in Theory Construction

It should be understood that the model for constructing vocational theories, which will be discussed, is based upon certain assumptions about the nature and function of theory, upon which there is often less than general agreement among philosophers of science and psychologists alike. In order to provide as explicit a rationale for the model as possible, it is necessary, therefore, to indicate what these assumptions are and why they have been made. The issues involved can be stated as the following questions: (1) Why construct theories? (2) What is a "theory"? And (3) what are the functions of theories?

To Theorize or Not to Theorize. That theorizing is necessarily a valued activity in science has been questioned by the so-called "ultrapositivists," who contend that it either serves no useful purpose or that it may actually constitute an obstacle to the conduct of significant research. For example, Woodrow (1942) has proposed that general mathematical laws of behavior may be formulated without introducing theoretical constructs, such as the intervening variable, by fitting an equation to several different empirical curves. But, as Spence (1960, p. 34) has pointed out, such an approach, despite its apparent subsumptive value, lacks comprehensiveness: "Its defect is not that the factors *within* the subject are not specified, but rather that it fails to give any indication whatever of the conditions or variables even *outside* the subject which determine these parameters. . . . [It] provides us with very little more information than we had when he started."

Another critic of theory building has been Skinner (1950, p. 194) who has questioned its supposed heuristic value: "That a theory generates research does not prove its value unless the research is valuable. Much useless experimentation results from theories, and much energy and skill are absorbed by them." He prefers to proceed in his research without using inferential terms, but, as Marx (1963, p. 18) has noted, this does not mean that he and other ultrapositivists do not engage in some kind of informal theorizing, if only in their selection of problems to investigate. Likewise, Super et al. (1957, p. 21) have observed that "No modern scientist approaches a problem tabula rasa. To some degree, relevant classificatory schemes, theories, and general research precedents are usually available." Even the trait-and-factor theorist, who most closely resembles the ultrapositivist in vocational psychology, operates on the basis of a rather elaborate set of theorylike assumptions in his research (cf. Cooley, 1964b).

Actually, the "theory versus no theory" issue is not an alive one in vocational psychology today; an almost universal commitment has been made in the field to theory building. The issue has been examined here, however, partly because it is still an unresolved one in other areas of psychology, but mostly because by posing it some of the disadvantages and excesses of unbridled theory construction may be brought into sharper focus. The most important of these is that theorizing may be the single most obstructive factor to the production of solid empirical research.

The Definition of Theory. Thus far in this chapter (and throughout the book) we have discussed theory without formally defining it. The principal reason for this circumvention is that, although psychologists generally understand what is meant by theory, they do not agree on specific definitions. Underwood (1957, pp. 177–180) has extensively documented the various ways in which the term has been defined and the many uses to which it has been put. Suffice it to say here that his solution to the problem is to consider theory as one method of explanation, the purpose of which he says is "to account for the greatest number of facts or observations with the fewest number of principles or assumptions. . . . The ultimate in explanation would be two comprehensive principles from which all the relationships of the universe logically stemmed" (Underwood, 1957, p. 180).

Similarly, in considering definitions of theory as (1) the conceptual versus the empirical aspects of science, (2) any generalized explanatory principle, and (3) a summary statement of empirical laws, Marx (1963, p. 9) points out that the preferred definition is that theory refers "to a group of logically organized (deductively related) laws." Pursuing the intent of these definitions one step further, the writer (Crites, 1966a, p. 16) has attempted to specify more explicitly what constitutes the *sine qua non* of a "theory": "The necessary elements of a theory are considered to be two empirical laws, with at least three operationally defined concepts, which can be related to each other logically in the form of an hypothetical syllogism ('if-if, then' deduction)." Note that there are three specifications in this definition of a theory: (1) There must be no less than two propositions about relationships between variables, otherwise it would be impossible to deduce hypotheses from the theory; (2) there must be a minimum of three concepts or terms which have explicit empirical referents, in order to relate the theory to the data-language level; and (3) there must be one of these concepts (variables) which is common to the two propositions, so that they can be related deductively.[4]

The Functions of Theory. Any number of functions which theory fulfills have been enumerated in the literature on theory construction, many of which have already been discussed, viz., to summarize empirical laws, to generate research, to predict new phenomena, etc. But, seldom have analyses been made of the conditions under which theory building is and is not appropriate. As a consequence, it is too frequently engaged in indiscriminately, i.e., theories are spun when they are not needed. It may be worthwhile, therefore, to identify those situations in which theory can serve a useful purpose.

Two general cases can be delineated: The first arises when, as has been mentioned in this chapter and in Chapter 6, there is a disproportionality in the

[4] For a fuller explanation and an example of this requirement, see the section headed "A Model for Theory Construction in Vocational Psychology."

relationship between stimulus and response. More specifically, there may be observed (1) a weak R to a strong S, (2) a strong R to a weak S, (3) variation in R with no variation in S, (4) no variation in R with variation in S, and (5) variation in R with variation in S on one occason but not on another (Underwood, 1957; Spence, 1960; Brown, J. S., 1961). In contrast, whenever the organism is "linear passive," then theory is not necessary. It is sufficient to explain variation in R by proportional variation in S. The second case is logically similar to the first, but it concerns the unpredicted variance in R-R relationships rather than disproportionalities in S-R functions. To the extent that the correlation between two R variables is less than 1.00, given attenuation due to such factors as errors of measurement, restriction in range, etc., it is often informative to ask why certain Subjects deviate from the regression for the total sample. Thus, theory building in this instance may suggest antecedent or concomitant variables which "moderate" or otherwise influence the relationship between the variables of interest, as in the prediction of vocational success (see Chapter 10). Ultimately, it should be noted, these "third" variables must either be S variables or chained to them conceptually, in order to avoid circular reasoning in the theory. If they are exclusively R variables, they all have equal behavioral status, and it cannot be said which is a function of which.[5]

Comment. Let it be clear that there are no right or wrong conclusions which can be drawn about (1) whether or not to theorize, (2) how best to define theory, and (3) what the functions of theory are. On the basis of the present status of theory construction in vocational psychology, however, there do appear to be some preferred alternative courses of action. One of these is to continue theory building, but to be aware of the pitfalls it entails, especially the deterrent it may constitute to progress in new research on vocational behavior and development. A second is to recognize that a theory must meet certain standards in order for it to be useful in explaining and predicting vocational phenomena. And a third is to formulate theories only when they are needed —when there are disproportionalities in S-R relationships and when there is unpredicted variance in R-R correlations.

A Model for Theory Construction in Vocational Psychology

The model for theory building which is proposed here for vocational psychology was originally formulated by Margenau (1950) to describe the explanatory process in the physical sciences and was subsequently adapted by Torgerson

[5] It is assumed here that all responses are elicited or measured at the same point in time. If there is a time interval, and one response is used to predict another, then it is sometimes said that the later response is a function of the earlier one.

(1958), with some modifications, for the social and behavioral sciences. It is the latter's version of the model which is reproduced in Figure 14-3.

In this diagram, the shaded vertical line on the right represents the data-language level—the observable, empirical phenomena of a science, such as the choice act and occupational entry in vocational psychology. Moving to the left, the double lines stand for what Torgerson calls "rules of correspondence" or what are more commonly known as operational definitions. These are the quantitative or measurement procedures which are specified and followed to assign classificatory or scalar values to the observed phenomena. The circles which are connected to the double lines are the constructs so defined. Thus, a vocational psychologist may measure the vocational success of a worker by asking his supervisor to summarize and evaluate the worker's job performance on a rating scale or adjective checklist like those described in Chapter 10.

In the next section of the figure, the dotted lines have been used by Torgerson to indicate that these operationally defined constructs, at least in the social and behavioral sciences, are not necessarily the same as their theoretical counterparts. He writes: "In these sciences [as contrasted with the physical sciences] we often have the concept as one thing *and* a measure of it as another" (Torgerson, 1958, p. 7). On this distinction, however, there is a wide divergence of opinion. The logical positivist, for example, maintains that the theoretical concept and its operational definition are equivalent, and thus he eliminates any surplus meaning which may be attributed to the former. He also circumvents the dilemma which arises when tests of a theory are negative.

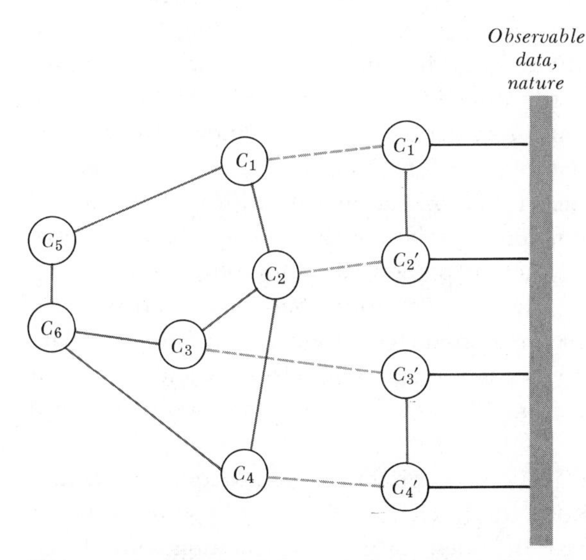

Figure 14-3. A model for theory construction in vocational psychology. *(From Torgerson, 1958, p. 5.)*

If a distinction is made between theoretical and operationally defined concepts, then the researcher may "conclude that the operationally defined variables are, after all, not really measures of the corresponding constitutively [theoretically] defined variables, but are only presumed to be related to them, and hence, that the theory may still be correct and the experiments simply inappropriate" (Torgerson, 1958, p. 7). The model may accommodate both points of view, although the dotted lines would have to be eliminated in order to represent accurately the logical positivist's position.

Finally, the single curved line depicts a correlation between two operationally defined constructs, and the solid straight lines indicate the logical relationships which may be deduced among the constructs of a theory (regardless of whether they are theoretical, operational, or both).

The value of this model is that it illustrates schematically what the structure of a well-developed theory is. First, it includes operationally defined concepts (at least three) which anchor it in observable behavioral data. Second, it has an internally consistent network of logical relationships among constructs which orders and summarizes empirical laws. And, third, because of these two attributes, it allows the deduction of hypotheses about new phenomena which can be tested in further research. In short, a theory constructed in accordance with this model would meet all the criteria for a "good" theory previously mentioned. Moreover, any of the modes of theory construction delineated by Marx (1963) might be used to pattern a theory after the model, although the mode of choice would appear to be the functional approach. Because it involves a continuous interaction between the theory- and data-language levels, a theory could be formulated by this mode either by proceeding from left to right or from right to left in the model. Most likely, once some basic empirical laws were established, the latter direction would be preferred, because the theory could then be built upon a foundation of reliable knowledge. Following the model in this way and using the functional mode, then, the steps in constructing a theory would be: (1) the operational definition of theoretical constructs, (2) the logical deduction of relationships among the constructs, and (3) the empirical testing of these hypothesized relationships. Intervening variables would be introduced as needed, i.e., to mediate disproportionalities in S-R functions and to account for unpredicted variance in R-R correlations, and the theory would gradually become more comprehensive and useful for explanatory and heuristic purposes alike as new phenomena were subsumed and predicted by it.

To illustrate the model and the process of theory construction which may be followed with it, consider Roe's (1957, Chapters 3 and 6) hypotheses on the interrelationships of (1) parental attitudes, (2) major orientation toward persons and nonpersons, and (3) field of vocational choice. There are three theoretical constructs, each of which has been operationally defined, and two propositions implicit in Roe's conceptualization (see the circumplex on p. 89, Chapter 3) about their relationships to each other; but these have not been related logically in the "if-if, then" form. To do this, let us first state the propositions: "Parental attitudes of acceptance, avoidance, and concentration are related to major orientation toward persons and nonpersons," and "major orientation toward persons and nonpersons is related to field of vocational choice." Next, if it is assumed or demonstrated in research that these propositions are "true," i.e., are confirmed by empirical evidence, then they can be related to each other syllogistically as follows:

If "Parental attitudes of acceptance, avoidance, and concentration are related to major orientation toward persons and nonpersons" *and*

If "Major orientation toward persons and nonpersons is related to field of vocational choice,"

Then "Parental attitudes of acceptance, avoidance, and concentration are related to field of vocational choice."

To deduce the latter proposition, it is assumed, as Roe does, that parental attitudes influence the development of major orientation, which, in turn, determines vocational choice. In other words, there is an etiological and functional priority which is postulated among these variables, so that their interclass relationships are inclusive.[6] Finally, to complete the cycle of theory building, the proposition or hypothesis, as it is more commonly called, which has been deduced from the major and minor premises must now be put to empirical test to determine its confirmability.[7]

Toward a Comprehensive Theory of Vocational Behavior and Development

As we have noted, intervening variables might be used in conjunction with the model for theory construction, but Torgerson's schema does not make explicit provision for them, although the single straight lines might be construed to represent them. Nor does the model depict the time dimension, which is criti-

[6] It is important to note that it is not necessary to invoke the concept of "cause" in this line of reasoning to explain the interrelationships among the variables. See Brodbeck (1957, pp. 433–435) for a fuller discussion of this point.

[7] In logical argument, it is assumed that the premises are the only antecedents of the consequent, and hence the latter follows *necessarily* from the former, but in an empirically based science, the number of possible antecedents is usually indeterminate, so that the consequent must be verified on the data-language level. For a more extended analysis of this problem, see: Brodbeck (1963) and Johnson, H. M. (1954).

cal in a field like vocational psychology for the conceptualization of developmental phenomena. A diagram (Figure 14-4) conceived by Spence (1960, p. 50), however, portrays both of these factors and can be used to supplement the theory model as well as to explicate the empirical and hypothetical laws which can be formulated within it. He discusses the variables and relationships shown in Figure 14-4 as follows:

> The environment or world situation at three different time intervals is represented by St − n (past), St = 0 (present), and St + n (future). These S's and also the R's represent empirical variables. I have also represented the class of experimental neurophysiological variables of the first figure by the symbol 0, to the left of the rectangle. The four classes of empirical laws, listed at the right side of the figure, are represented by the solid curved lines. The guessed-at or postulated laws relating the hypothetical state [intervening] variables (I_b, I_b, etc.) to the various experimental variables are represented by the dotted lines. Thus, No. 5 type of "law" defines or introduces the intervening variables in terms of past events; No. 6 type relates them to the present environmental variables and No. 7 to time; No. 8 "laws" present inter-relations assumed between these intervening variables, and, finally, the relations represented by No. 9 relate the intervening variables to the response variables [Spence, 1960, pp. 49–50].

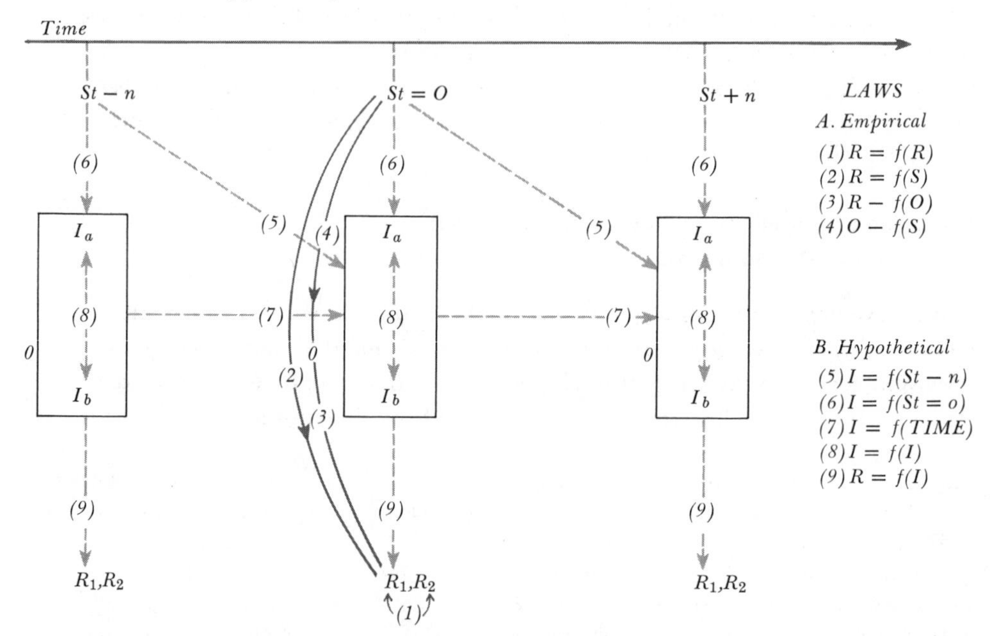

Figure 14-4. Diagram showing relationships between empirical and hypothetical laws along the time dimension. *(From Spence, 1960, p. 50.)*

Together, the Torgerson model and the Spence diagram provide the necessary schemata for the construction of a comprehensive theory of vocational behavior and development.

How such a theory might be formulated can be illustrated by continuing the analysis of Roe's hypotheses previously begun. We left it at the point where the hypothesis that "parental attitudes are related to vocational choice" was ready for empirical test. Actually, as the research reviewed in Chapter 6 indicates, several tests of this hypothesis, and those from which it was deduced, have been made, and the results substantiate only the relationship between major orientation and choice. In other words, for some reason, there is a disproportionality in the predicted S-R function: certain parental attitudes are *not* systematically related to either major orientation or choice. It is at this point that the theorist may introduce intervening variables to explain the deviation from expectation.

Suppose he questions first why no relationship between parental attitudes and major orientation has been found, on the assumption, of course, that one really exists, but may be obscured by other variables. He may propose that a likely intervening variable may be intelligence. He may reason, for example, that bright and dull children may react to the same parental attitudes in different ways. The bright child may use the freedom afforded by parental attitudes of loving acceptance to try out new ways of solving problems, to experiment much as the creative and curious scientist does, and, ultimately, to develop a major orientation toward nonpersons. In contrast, the dull child may respond to the same parental attitude by becoming dependent upon interpersonal support for the accomplishment of any task, by seeking activities which are not problem-oriented, and, eventually, by assuming a major orientation toward persons. Thus, because of the possible differential effects of intelligence, Roe's hypothesized linear relationship between parental attitudes and major orientation "breaks down," and, presumably as a result, the relationship between parental attitudes and vocational choice also "breaks down." By introducing intelligence as an intervening variable, however, which is linked to both the stimulus and response variables in Roe's theory, it may be possible to demonstrate empirically that parental attitudes, major orientation, and vocational choice are interrelated.

Constructing a theory of vocational behavior and development in this manner involves a series of successive approximations. Each link in the chain of inference must be established empirically and/or logically. And no theory is ever complete, but it may become more and more comprehensive as it encompasses a greater number and variety of empirical and hypothetical relationships. The future of theory construction in vocational psychology may well depend upon the tolerance of vocational psychologists for the painstaking and often fruitless work which useful conceptualization and explanation demands.

REFERENCES

ABELSON, R. P. Sex differences in predictability of college grades. *Educational and Psychological Measurement,* 1952, **12**, 638–644.

ACHILLES, P. S. Vocational motives in college: Career decisions among undergraduates. *Occupations,* 1935, **13**, 624–628.

ACKOFF, R. L. *The design of social research.* Chicago: University of Chicago Press, 1953.

ADAMS, J. K. Laboratory studies of behavior without awareness. *Psychological Bulletin,* 1957, **54**, 383–405.

ADAMS, J. S., & ROSENBAUM, W. B. The relationship of worker productivity to cognitive dissonance about wage incquities. *Journal of Applied Psychology,* 1962, **46**, 161–164.

ADAMS, S. Trends in the occupational origins of physicians. *American Sociological Review,* 1953, **18**, 404–409.

ADAMS, S. Trends in the occupational origins of business leaders. *American Sociological Review,* 1954, **19**, 541–548.

ALLEN, E. P., & SMITH, P. *The value of vocational tests as aids to choice of employment.* Birmingham, England: City of Birmingham Education Committee, 1932; 1940.

ALLEN, P. J. Childhood backgrounds and success in a profession. *American Sociological Review,* 955, **20**, 186–190.

ALLPORT, G. W. *Personality: A psychological interpretation.* New York: Holt, 1937.

ALLPORT, G. W. The trend in motivational theory. *Journal of Orthopsychiatry,* 1953, **23**, 107–119.

ALLPORT, G. W. Traits revisited. *American Psychologist,* 1966, **21**, 1–10.

ALPERT, R. Anxiety in academic achievement situations: Its measurement and relation to aptitude. (Doctoral dissertation, Stanford University) Ann Arbor, Mich.: University Microfilms, 1957. No. 25–365.

AMERICAN EDUCATIONAL RESEARCH ASSOCIATION. Report of the Committee on the Criteria of Teacher Effectiveness. *Review of Educational Research,* 1952, **22**, 238–253.

AMERICAN EDUCATIONAL RESEARCH ASSOCIATION. Second report of the Committee on Criteria of Teacher Effectiveness. *Journal of Educational Research,* 1953, **46**, 641–658.

AMERICAN PERSONNEL AND GUIDANCE ASSOCIATION. *The use of multifactor tests in guidance.* Washington, D.C.: American Personnel and Guidance Association, 1958.

AMERICAN PSYCHOLOGICAL ASSOCIATION. *A career in psychology*. Washington, D.C.: American Psychological Association, 1963.

AMMONS, R. B., BUTLER, N., & HERZIG, S. A. Manual for the *Vocational Apperception Test.* Missoula, Mont.: Psychological Test Specialists, 1949.

AMMONS, R. B., BUTLER, M., & HERZIG, S. A. A projective test for vocational research and guidance at the college level. *Journal of Applied Psychology,* 1950, **34**, 198–205.

ANASTASI, A. The nature of psychological "traits." *Psychological Review,* 1948, **55**, 127–138.

ANASTASI, A. *Differential psychology.* (3rd ed.) New York: Macmillan, 1958.

ANASTASI, A. *Fields of applied psychology*. New York: McGraw-Hill, 1964.

ANDERSON, D. What a high school class did with fifty years of life. *Personnel and Guidance Journal,* 1966, **45**, 116–123.

ANDERSON, R. G. Rorschach test results and efficiency ratings of machinists. *Personnel Psychology,* 1949, 2, 513–524.

ANDERSON, T. B., & OLSON, L. C. Congruence of

self and ideal-self and occupational choices. *Personnel and Guidance Journal,* 1965, **44**, 171–176.

ANDERSON, V. V. *Psychiatry in industry.* New York: Harper, 1929.

ANDERSON, W. A. Some social factors associated with the vocational choices of college men. *Journal of Educational Sociology,* 1932, **6**, 100–113.

ANDERSON, W. A. The occupational attitudes of college men. *Journal of Social Psychology,* 1934, **5**, 435–466.

ANDERSON, W. F., & DIPBOYE, W. J. Occupational values and post-high school plans. *Vocational Guidance Quarterly,* 1959, **8**, 37–40.

ANDERSON, B. E., & NILSSON, S. G. Studies in the reliability and validity of the critical incident technique. *Journal of Applied Psychology,* 1964, **48**, 398–403.

ANGYAL, A. *Foundations for a science of personality.* New York: Commonwealth Fund, 1941.

APOSTAL, R. A. Two methods of evaluating vocational counseling. *Journal of Counseling Psychology,* 1960, **7**, 171–175.

APOSTAL, R. A., & MILLER, J. G. A manual for the use of a set of diagnostic categories. University of Missouri Testing and Counseling Service Research Report, 1959.

ARENDT, H. *The human condition.* Chicago: University of Chicago Press, 1958.

ARGYLE, M. The relay assembly test room in retrospect. *Occupational Psychology,* 1953, **27**, 98–103.

ARISTOTLE. *Politics.* New York: Modern Library, 1943.

ARMSTRONG, F. G. An experimental study of a structured interview for determining vocational interests. (Doctoral dissertation, Temple University) Ann Arbor, Mich.: University Microfilms, 1957. No. 19–609.

ARSENIAN, S. Own estimate and objective measurement. *Journal of Educational Psychology,* 1942, **33**, 291–302.

ASH, P. The SRA Employee Inventory—a statistical analysis. *Personnel Psychology,* 1954, **7**, 337–364.

ASHBY, J. O., WALL, H. W., & OSIPOW, S. H. Vocational certainty and indecision in college freshmen. *Personnel and Guidance Journal,* 1966, **44**, 1037–1041.

ASTIN, A. W. Dimensions of work satisfaction in the occupational choices of college freshmen. *Journal of Applied Psychology,* 1958, **42**, 187–190.

ASTIN, A. W. Further validation of the Environmental Assessment Technique. *Journal of Educational Psychology,* 1963, **54**, 217–226.

ASTIN, A. W. Criterion-centered research. *Educational and Psychological Measurement,* 1964, **24**, 807–822.

ASTIN, A. W. Effect of different college environments on the vocational choices of high aptitude students. *Journal of Counseling Psychology,* 1965, **12**, 28–34.

ASTIN, A. W., & HOLLAND, J. L. The Environmental Assessment Technique: A way to measure college environment. *Journal of Educational Psychology,* 1961, **52**, 308–316.

ASTIN, A. W., & NICHOLS, R. C. Life goals and vocational choice. *Journal of Applied Psychology,* 1964, **48**, 50–58.

ATKINSON, J. W. Motivational determinants of risk-taking behavior. *Psychological Review,* 1957, **64**, 359–372.

ATKINSON, J. W. *Motives in fantasy, action, and society.* Princeton: Van Nostrand, 1958.

ATKINSON, J. W., & LITWIN, G. H. Achievement motive and test anxiety conceived as motive to approach success and motive to avoid failure. *Journal of Abnormal and Social Psychology,* 1960, **60**, 52–63.

BACHRACH, P. B. Research notes from here and there. *Journal of Counseling Psychology,* 1957, **4**, 71–74.

BAEHR, M. E. A simplified procedure for the measurement of employee attitudes. *Journal of Applied Psychology,* 1953, **37**, 163–167.

BAEHR, M. E. A factorial study of the SRA Employee Inventory. *Personnel Psychology,* 1954, **7**, 319–339.

BAEHR, M. E. A reply to Robert J. Wherry concerning an orthogonal rerotation of the Baehr and Ash studies of the SRA Employee Inventory. *Personnel Psychology,* 1956, **9**, 81–91.

BAKKE, E. W. *The fusion process.* New Haven, Conn.: Labor and Management Center, Yale University, 1953.

BALCHIN, N. Satisfactions in work. *Occupational Psychology,* 1947, **21**, 125–134.

BALDWIN, A. L. The role of an "ability" construct in a theory of behavior. In D. C. McClelland, A. L. Baldwin, U. Bronfenbrenner & F. L. Strodtbeck (Eds.), *Talent and society.* Princeton: Van Nostrand, 1958, Pp. 195–232.

BARNETT, G. J., HANDELSMAN, I., STEWART, L. H., & SUPER, D. E. The occupational level scale as a measure of drive. *Psychological Monographs,* 1952, **66** (10, Whole No. 342).

BARNETT, G. J., STEWART, L. H., & SUPER, D. E. Level of occupational interest: deadweight or dynamism? *Educational and Psychological Measurement,* 1953, **13**, 193–208.

BARNETTE, W. L., JR. Occupational aptitude pattern research. *Occupations,* 1950, **29**, 5–12.

BARNETTE, W. L., JR. An occupational aptitude pattern for engineers. *Educational and Psychological Measurement,* 1951, **11**, 52–66. (a)

BARNETTE, W. L., JR. Occupational aptitude patterns of selected groups of counseled veterans. *Psychological Monographs,* 1951, **65** (5, Whole No. 322). (b)

BARUCH, D. W. Why they terminate. *Journal of Consulting Psychology,* 1944, **8**, 35–46.

BASS, B. M. *Organizational psychology.* Boston: Allyn and Bacon, 1965.

BASS, B. M., & WURSTER, C. R. Effects of company rank on LGD performance of oil refinery supervisors. *Journal of Applied Psychology,* 1953, **37**, 100–104.

BATEMAN, R. M. The effect of work experience on high school students' vocational choice. *Occupations,* 1949, **27**, 453–456.

BAUDLER, L., & PATERSON, D. G. Social status of women's occupations. *Occupations,* 1948, **26**, 421–424.

BAUERNFEIND, R. H. The matter of "ipsative scores." *Personnel and Guidance Journal,* 1962, **41**, 210–217.

BAYLEY, N. On the growth of intelligence. *American Psychologist,* 1955, **10**, 805–818.

BEALL, L., & BORDIN, E. S. The development and personality of engineers. *Personnel and Guidance Journal,* 1964, **43**, 23–32.

BEARDSLEE, D. C., & O'DOWD, D. D. The college-student image of the scientist. *Science,* 1961, **133**, 907–1001.

BEARDSLEE, D. C., & O'DOWD, D. D. Students and the occupational world. In N. Sanford (Ed.), *The American college.* New York: Wiley, 1962. Pp. 597–626.

BECHTOLDT, H. P. Problems in establishing criterion measures. In D. B. Stuit (Ed.), *Personnel research and test development in the Bureau of Naval Personnel.* Princeton: Princeton University Press, 1947. Pp. 357–379.

BECHTOLDT, H. P. Selection. In S. S. Stevens (Ed.), *Handbook of experimental psychology.* New York: Wiley, 1951. Pp. 1237–1266.

BECHTOLDT, H. P. Construct validity: A critique. *American Psychologist,* 1959, **14**, 619–620.

BECHTOLDT, H. P. An empirical study of the factor analysis stability hypothesis. *Psychometrika,* 1961, **26**, 405–432.

BECKER, H. S. The career of the Chicago public school teacher. *American Journal of Sociology,* 1952, **57**, 470–477.

BECKMAN, R. O. To what extent are vocations inherited? *Vocational Guidance Magazine,* 1929, **8**, 9–11.

BECKMAN, R. O. A new scale for gauging occupational rank. *Personnel Journal,* 1934, **13**, 255–233.

BEDFORD, T. The ideal work curve. *Journal of Industrial Hygiene,* 1922, **4**, 235–245.

BEESON, M. F., & TOPE, R. E. A study of vocational preferences of high school students. *Vocational Guidance Magazine,* 1928, **7**, 115–119.

BEGELMAN, J. Relation of body build, physical performance, intelligence, and recreational interests to occupational choice. Unpublished doctoral dissertation, University of Michigan, 1951.

BEILIN, H. The mobility and achievement of a 1926 class of high school graduates. *Journal of Counseling Psychology,* 1954, **1**, 144–148.

BEILIN, H. The application of general developmental principles to the vocational area. *Journal of Counseling Psychology,* 1955, **2**, 53–57.

BELL, F. O., HOFF, A. L., & HOYT, K. B. A comparison of three approaches to criterion measurement. *Journal of Applied Psychology,* 1963, **47**, 416–418.

BELL, H. M. *Youth tell their story.* Washington, D.C.: American Council on Education, 1938.

BELL, H. M. *Matching youth and jobs.* Washington, D.C.: American Council on Education, 1940.

BELL, H. M. Ego-involvement in vocational decisions. *Personnel and Guidance Journal,* 1960, **38**, 732–736.

BELLOWS, R. M. Procedures for evaluating vocational criteria. *Journal of Applied Psychology,* 1941, **25**, 499–513.

BENDER, J. F. Emotional adjustment of workers. *Personnel Journal,* 1944, **22**, 301–307.

BENDIG, A. W., & STILLMAN, E. Dimensions of job incentives among college students. *Journal of Applied Psychology,* 1958, **42**, 367–371.

BENDIX, R., LIPSETT, S. M., & MALM, F. T. Social

origins and occupational career patterns. *Industrial Labor Relations Review,* 1954, **7**, 246–261.

BENGE, E. J., & COPELL, D. F. Employee morale survey. *Modern Management,* 1947, **12**, 19–22.

BERDIE, R. F. Can factors in vocational choice be weighed? *Personnel and Guidance Journal,* 1943, **22**, 43–46.

BERDIE, R. F. Factors related to vocational interests. *Psychological Bulletin,* 1944, **41**, 137–157. (a)

BERDIE, R. F. Prediction of college satisfaction and achievement. *Journal of Applied Psychology,* 1944, **28**, 239–245. (b)

BERDIE, R. F. Scores on the Strong Vocational Interest Blank and the Kuder Preference Record in relation to self ratings. *Journal of Applied Psychology,* 1950, **34**, 42–50.

BERDIE, R. F. Validities of the Strong Vocational Interest Blank. In W. L. Layton (Ed.), *The Strong Vocational Interest Blank: Research and uses.* Minneapolis: University of Minnesota Press, 1960. Pp. 18–61.

BERDIE, R. F. Intra-individual variability and predictability. *Educational and Psychological Measurement,* 1961, **21**, 663–676.

BEREZIN, A. G. The development and use of a system of diagnostic categories in counseling. (Doctoral dissertation, University of Missouri) Ann Arbor, Mich.: University Microfilms, 1957. No. 24–213.

BERG, I. A. Personality structure and occupational choice. *Personnel and Guidance Journal,* 1953, **32**, 151–154.

BERGMANN, G. Theoretical psychology. *Annual Review of Psychology,* 1953, **4**, 435–458.

BERGMANN, G. *The philosophy of science.* Madison, Wisconsin: University of Wisconsin Press, 1957.

BERGMANN, G., & SPENCE, K. W. Operationalism and theory in psychology, *Psychological Review,* 1941, **48**, 1–14.

BERNARDIN, A. C., & JESSOR, R. A construct validation of the Edwards Personal Preference Schedule with respect to dependency. *Journal of Consulting Psychology,* 1957, **21**, 63–67.

BERNBERG, R. E. Socio-psychological factors in industrial morale. III. Relation of age to morale. *Personnel Psychology,* 1954, **7**, 395–399.

BERNSTEIN, A. J. Absence of primary interest patterns in adolescent boys. Doctoral dissertation, Columbia University, 1953.

BETZ, E., WEISS, D. J., DAWIS, R. V., ENGLAND, G. W., & LOFQUIST, L. H. *Seven years of research on work adjustment.* Minneapolis: Industrial Relations Center, University of Minnesota, 1966.

BILLS, M. A. Relation of scores in Strong's Interest Blank to success in selling casualty insurance. *Journal of Applied Psychology,* 1938, **22**, 97–104.

BINET, A., & HENRI, V. La psychologie individuelle. *Année psychologie,* 1895, **2**, 411–463.

BINET, A., & SIMON, T. *A method of measuring the development of the intelligence of young children.* Chicago: Chicago Medical Book Co., 1915.

BINGHAM, W. V., & DAVIS, W. T. Intelligence test scores and business success. *Journal of Applied Psychology,* 1924, **8**, 1–22.

BINGHAM, W. V., & FREYD, M. *Procedures in employment psychology.* Chicago: Shaw, 1926.

BLAI, B., JR. Occupational study of job satisfaction and need satisfaction. *Journal of Experimental Education,* 1964, **32**, 383–388.

BLAU, P. M., GUSTAD, J. W., JESSOR, R., PARNES, H. S., & WILCOCK, R. C. Occupational choice: A conceptual framework. *Industrial Labor Relations Review,* 1956, **9**, 531–543.

BLISS, E. F., JR. Earnings of machine tenders and of bench workers. *Personnel Journal,* 1931, **10**, 102–107.

BLOCHER, D. H., & SCHUTZ, R. A. Relationships among self-descriptions, occupational stereotypes, and vocational preferences. *Journal of Counseling Psychology,* 1961, **8**, 314–317.

BLOCK, J., LEVINE, L., & MC NEMAR, Q. Testing for the existence of psychometric patterns. *Journal of Abnormal and Social Psychology,* 1951, **46**, 356–359.

BLOOM, B. S. *Stability and change in human characteristics.* New York: Wiley, 1964.

BLUM, S. H. The desire for security: An element in the vocational choice of college men. *Journal of Educational Psychology,* 1961, **52**, 317–321.

BODIN, A. M. A proposal for new bibliographic tools for psychologists. *Journal of Counseling Psychology,* 1963, **10**, 193–197.

BOGARD, H. M. Union and management trainees—a comparative study of personality and occupational choice. *Journal of Applied Psychology,* 1960, **44**, 56–63.

BOLANOVICH, D. J. Statistical analysis of an industrial rating chart. *Journal of Applied Psychology,* 1946, **30**, 23–31.

BOLING, J., & FINE, S. A. Cues used by raters in the rating of temperament requirements of jobs. *Journal of Applied Psychology,* 1959, **43**, 102–108.

BOOKBINDER, H. Work histories of men leaving a short life span occupation. *Personnel and Guidance Journal,* 1955, **34**, 164–167.

BORDIN, E. S. A theory of vocational interests as dynamic phenomena. *Educational and Psychological Measurement,* 1943, **3**, 49–65.

BORDIN, E. S. Diagnosis in counseling and psychotherapy. *Educational and Psychological Measurement,* 1946, **6**, 169–184.

BORDIN, E. S., NACHMANN, B., & SEGAL, S. J. An articulated framework for vocational development. *Journal of Counseling Psychology,* 1963, **10**, 107–116.

BORDIN, E. S., & WILSON, E. H. Change of interest as a function of shift in curricular orientation. *Educational and Psychological Measurement,* 1953, **13**, 297–307.

BORING, E. G. *Sensation and perception in the history of experimental psychology.* New York: Appleton-Century-Crofts, 1942.

BORING, E. G. *A history of experimental psychology.* (2nd ed.) New York: Appleton-Century-Crofts, 1950.

BOROW, H. Research programs in career development. *Journal of Counseling Psychology,* 1960, **7**, 62–70.

BOROW, H. Vocational development research: Some problems of logical and experimental form. *Personnel and Guidance Journal,* 1961, **40**, 21–25.

BOROW, H. Information retrieval: A definition and a conference report. *Journal of Counseling Psychology,* 1962, **9**, 360–363.

BOROW, H. Information retrieval, Part II: Simple and complex systems. *Journal of Counseling Psychology,* 1963, **10**, 88–93.

BOROW, H. An integral view of occupational theory and research. In H. Borow (Ed.), *Man in a world at work.* Boston: Houghton Mifflin, 1964. Pp. 364–386. (a)

BOROW, H. Milestones: A chronology of notable events in the history of vocational guidance. In H. Borow (Ed.), *Man in a world at work,* Boston: Houghton Mifflin, 1964. Pp. 45–64. (b)

BOROW, H. Development of occupational motives and roles. In L. W. Hoffman and M. L. Hoffman (Eds.), *Review of child development research.* Vol. 2, New York: Russell Sage, 1966. Pp. 373–422.

BORRESEN, A. M. Counselor influence on diagnostic classification of client problems. *Journal of Counseling Psychology,* 1965. **12**, 252–258.

BOWERS, W. H. An appraisal of worker characteristics as related to age. *Journal of Applied Psychology,* 1952, **36**, 296–300.

BOYNTON, P. L. The vocational preferences of school children. *Journal of Genetic Psychology,* 1936, **49**, 411–425.

BRADLEY, W. A., JR. Correlates of vocational preferences. *Genetic Psychology Monographs,* 1943, **28**, 99–169.

BRAYFIELD, A. H. Vocational counseling today. In E. G. Williamson (Ed.), *Vocational counseling: A reappraisal in honor of Donald G. Paterson.* Minneapolis: University of Minnesota Press, 1961. Pp. 22–58.

BRAYFIELD, A. H. Research on vocational guidance: Status and prospect. Part I: A critical examination of research issues. In H. Borow (Ed.), *Man in a world at work.* Boston: Houghton Mifflin, 1964. Pp. 310–323.

BRAYFIELD, A. H., & CROCKETT, W. H. Employee attitudes and employee performance. *Psychological Bulletin,* 1955, **52**, 396–424.

BRAYFIELD, A. H., KENNEDY, C. E., JR., & KENDALL, W. E. Social status of industries. *Journal of Applied Psychology,* 1954, **38**, 213–215.

BRAYFIELD, A. H., & ROTHE, H. F. An index of job satisfaction. *Journal of Applied Psychology,* 1951, **35**, 307–311.

BRAYFIELD, A. H., WELLS, R. V., & STRATE, M. W. Interrelationships among measures of job satisfaction and general satisfaction. *Journal of Applied Psychology,* 1957, **41**, 201–205.

BRAZZIEL, W. F., JR. Occupational choice in the Negro college. *Personnel and Guidance Journal,* 1961, **39**, 739–742.

BREEN, L. Z., & SPAETH, J. L. Age and productivity among workers in four Chicago companies. *Journal of Gerontology,* 1960, **15**, 68–70.

BRENDER, M. Toward a psychodynamic system of occupational classification. *Journal of Counseling Psychology,* 1960, **7**, 96–100.

BRENNER, M. H., & LOCKWOOD, H. C. Salary as a predictor of salary: A 20-year study. *Journal of Applied Psychology,* 1965, **49**, 295–298.

BREWER, J. M. Causes for discharge. *Personnel Journal,* 1927, **6**, 171–172. (a)

BREWER, J. M. Reasons for discharge. Washington, D.C.: Federal Board for Vocational Education, Bulletin No. 45, 1927. (b)

BREWER, J. M. Religion and vocational success. *Religious Education,* 1930, **25**, 1–3.

BREWER, J. M. *History of vocational guidance.* New York: Harper, 1942.

BRIGANTE, T. R. Fromm's marketing orientation and the values of the counselor. *Journal of Counseling Psychology,* 1958, **5**, 83–87.

BRILL, A. A. *Basic principles of psychoanalysis.* New York: Doubleday, 1949.

BRINKER, P. A. Supervisors' and foremen's reasons for frustration. *Personnel Journal,* 1955, **34**, 101–103.

BRODBECK, M. The philosophy of science and educational research. *Review of Educational Research,* 1957, **27**, 427–440.

BRODBECK, M. Logic and scientific method in research on teaching. In N. L. Gage (Ed.), *Handbook of research on teaching.* Chicago: Rand McNally, 1963. Pp. 44–93.

BRODMAN, K. Absenteeism, working efficiency, and emotional maladjustments. *Industrial Medicine,* 1945, **15**, 1–5.

BROGDEN, H. E. The primary personal values measured by the Allport-Vernon test, "A study of values." *Psychological Monographs,* 1952, **66** (16, Whole No. 348).

BROGDEN, H. E., & TAYLOR, E. K. The dollar criterion: Applying the cost accounting concept to criterion construction. *Personnel Psychology,* 1950, **3**, 133–154. (a)

BROGDEN, H. E., & TAYLOR, E. K. The theory and classification of criterion bias. *Educational and Psychological Measurement,* 1950, **10**, 159–186. (b)

BROMLEY, D. B. Some experimental tests of the effect of age on creative intellectual output. *Journal of Gerontology,* 1956, **11**, 74–82.

BROPHY, A. L. Self, role, and satisfaction. *Genetic Psychology Monographs,* 1959, **59**, 263–308.

BROWER, D. The relation between intelligence and Minnesota Multiphasic Personality scores. *Journal of Social Psychology,* 1947, **25**, 243–245.

BROWN, J. S. *The motivation of behavior.* New York: McGraw-Hill, 1961.

BROWN, M. N. Expressed and inventoried interests of veterans. *Journal of Applied Psychology,* 1951, **35**, 401–403.

BRUNER, J. S., GOODNOW, J. J., & AUSTIN, G. A. *A study of thinking.* New York: Wiley, 1956.

BRUNKAN, R. J. Perceived parental attitudes and parental identification in relation to field of vocational choice. *Journal of Counseling Psychology,* 1965, **12**, 39–47.

BRUNKAN, R. J. Perceived parental attitudes and parental identification in relation to problems in vocational choice. *Journal of Counseling Psychology,* 1966, **13**, 394–402.

BRUNKAN, R J., & CRITES, J. O. A Family Relations Inventory to measure perceived parental attitudes. *Journal of Counseling Psychology,* 1964, **11**, 3–12.

BUEHLER, C. *Der menschliche Lebenslauf als psychologisches Problem.* Leipzig: Hirzel, 1933.

BUEHLER, K. *Der Krise der Psychologie.* Jena, Austria: G. Fischer, 1929.

BUEL, W. D. The validity of behavioral rating scale items for the assessment of individual creativity. *Journal of Applied Psychology,* 1960, **44**, 407–412.

BUEL, W. D. Biographical data and the identification of creative research personnel. *Journal of Applied Psychology,* 1965, **49**, 318–321.

BUEL, W. D., ALBRIGHT, L. E., & GLENNON, J. R. A note on the generality and cross-validity of personal history for identifying creative research scientists. *Journal of Applied Psychology,* 1966, **50**, 217–219.

BUEL, W. D., & BACHNER, V. M. The assessment of creativity in a research setting. *Journal of Applied Psychology,* 1961, **45**, 353–358.

BULLOCK, R. P. *Social factors relating to job satisfaction: A technique for the measurement of job satisfaction.* Res. Monogr. No. 70. Bur., Business Res., Ohio State University, 1952.

BULLOCK, R. P. Position, function, and job satisfaction in the social system of a modern hospital. *Nursing Research,* 1953, **2**, 4–14.

BURCHARD, W. H. Role conflicts of military chaplains. *American Sociological Reveiew,* 1954, **19**, 528–535.

BURKE, R. J. Are Herzberg's motivators and hygienes unidimensional? *Journal of Applied Psychology,* 1966, **50**, 317–321.

BURNSTEIN, E. Fear of failure, achievement motivation, and aspiring to prestigeful occupations. *Journal of Abnormal and Social Psychology,* 1963, **67**, 189–193.

BUROS, O. K. *The fourth mental measurements yearbook.* Highland Park, N.J.: Gryphon Press, 1953.

BURT, C. *The marks of examiners.* London: Macmillan, 1936.

BURT, C. The differentiation of intellectual ability. *British Journal of Educational Psychology,* 1954, **24**, 76–90.

BYRNE, R. H. Proposed revisions of the Bordin-Pepinsky diagnostic constructs. *Journal of Counseling Psychology,* 1958, **5**, 184–187.

BYRNS, R. Relation of vocational choice to mental ability and occupational opportunity. *School Review,* 1939, **47**, 101–109.

CALLIS, R. Diagnostic classification as a research tool. *Journal of Counseling Psychology,* 1965, **12**, 238–243.

CALLIS, R., ENGRAM, W. C., & MC GOWAN, J. F. Coding the Kuder Preference Record–Vocational. *Journal of Applied Psychology,* 1954, **38**, 359–364.

CAMPBELL, D. P. The Center for Interest Measurement Research. *Journal of Counseling Psychology,* 1964, **11**, 395–399.

CAMPBELL, D. P. A critical note on Geist's "Work satisfaction and scores on a picture interest inventory." *Journal of Applied Psychology,* 1965, **49**, 74.

CAMPBELL, D. T. Factors relevant to the validity of experiments in social settings. *Psychological Bulletin,* 1957, **54**, 297–312.

CAMPBELL, D. T., & FISKE, D. W. Convergent and discriminant validation by the multitrait-multimethod matrix. *Psychological Bulletin,* 1959, **56**, 81–105.

CAMPBELL, N. R. *Symposium: Measurement and its importance for philosophy.* Aristotelian Society, Supplement Vol. 17. London: Harrison, 1938.

CAMPBELL, R. E. The prestige of industries. *Journal of Applied Psychology,* 1960, **44**, 1–5.

CANTER, R. R. Intelligence and the social status of occupations. *Personnel and Guidance Journal,* 1956, **34**, 258–260.

CANTONI, L. J. Men, emotions, and jobs. *School and Society,* 1955, **81**, 40–41.

CAPLAN, S. W., RUBLE, R. A., & SEGEL, D. A theory of educational and vocational choice in junior high school. *Personnel and Guidance Journal,* 1963, **42**, 129–135.

CAPLOW, T. *The sociology of work.* Minneapolis: University of Minnesota Press, 1954.

CAPLOW, T., & MC GEE, R. J. *The academic marketplace.* New York: Basic Books, 1958.

CARKHUFF, R. R., & DRASGOW, J. The confusing literature on the OL scale of the SVIB. *Journal of Counseling Psychology,* 1963, **10**, 283–288.

CARLIN, L. O. Vocational decisions and high school experiences. *Vocational Guidance Quarterly,* 1960, **8**, 168–170.

CARLSON, R. E., DAWIS, R. V., ENGLAND, G. W., & LOFQUIST, L. H. *Minnesota Studies in Vocational Rehabilitation: XIII. The measurement of employment satisfaction.* Minneapolis: Industrial Relations Center, University of Minnesota, 1962.

CARP, F. M. High school boys are realistic about occupations. *Occupations,* 1949, **28**, 97–99.

CARROLL, S. J., JR. Relationship of various college graduate characteristics to recruiting decisions. *Journal of Applied Psychology,* 1966, **50**, 421–423.

CARRUTHERS, J. B. Tabular summary showing relation between clerical test scores and occupational performance. *Occupations,* 1950, **29**, 40–50.

CARTER, H. D. Twin similarities in occupational interests. *Journal of Educational Psychology,* 1932, **23**, 641–655.

CARTER, H. D. The development of vocational attitudes. *Journal of Consulting Psychology,* 1940, **4**, 185–191.

CARTER, H. D. Vocational interests and job orientation. *Applied Psychology Monographs,* 1944, No. 2.

CARTER, H. D., & JONES, M. C. Vocational attitude patterns in high school students. *Journal of Educational Psychology,* 1938, **29**, 321–334.

CARTER, H. D., TAYLOR, K. VON F., & CANNING, L. B. Vocational choices and interest test scores of high school students. *Journal of Psychology,* 1941, **11**, 297–306.

CASE, H. M. Two kinds of crystallized occupational choice behavior: A problem in delineation and relationship. *American Sociological Review,* 1954, **19**, 85–87.

CATTELL, J. M. Mental tests and measurements. *Mind,* 1890, **15**, 373–381.

CATTELL, R. B. Occupational norms of intelligence. *British Journal of Psychology,* 1934, **25**, 1–28.

CATTELL, R. B. *The description and measurement of personality.* Yonkers, N.Y.: World, 1946.

CAUTELA, J. R. The factor of psychological need in occupational choice. *Personnel and Guidance Journal,* 1959, **38**, 46–48.

CENTERS, R. Motivational aspects of occupational stratification. *Journal of Social Psychology,* 1948, **28**, 187–217.

CENTERS, R. *The psychology of social classes.* Princeton, N.J.: Princeton University Press, 1949.

CENTERS, R., & BUGENTAL, D. E. Intrinsic and extrinsic job motivations among different segments of the working population. *Journal of Applied Psychology,* 1966, **50**, 193–197.

CENTERS, R., & CANTRIL, H. Income satisfaction and income aspiration. *Journal of Abnormal and Social Psychology,* 1946, **41**, 64–69.

CHAMPNEY, H. The measurement of parent behavior. *Child Development,* 1941, **12**, 131–166.

CHARRON, L. Increasing employees' job interest. *Proceedings: The fifth annual training conference of educational directors in industry and commerce.* Montreal, Canada: Canadian Industrial Trainers Association, 1951, 53–62.

CHERNOW, H. M. The effects of personal adjustment counseling upon the reality of vocational choice. (Doctoral dissertation, New York University) Ann Arbor, Mich.: University Microfilms, 1956. No. 16–586.

CHILD, I. The judging of occupations from printed photographs. *Journal of Social Psychology,* 1936, **7**, 117–118.

CHINOY, E. The tradition of opportunity and the aspirations of automobile workers. *American Journal of Sociology,* 1952, **57**, 453–459.

CHRISTENSEN, T. E. The dictionary classification of AGCT scores for selected civilian occupations. *Occupations,* 1946, **25**, 97–101.

CLARK, C. D., & GIST, N. P. Intelligence as a factor in occupational choice. *American Sociological Review,* 1938, **3**, 683–694.

CLARK, H. F. *Economic theory and correct occupational distribution.* New York: Teachers College Bureau of Publications, 1931.

CLARK, H. F. Life earnings as a criterion. In R. Hoppock (Ed.), *Criteria of vocational success.* New York: National Occupational Conference, 1936. Pp. 931–932.

CLARK, H. F. *Life earnings in selected occupations.* New York: Harper, 1937.

CLARK, K. E. *The vocational interests of nonprofessional men.* Minneapolis: University of Minnesota Press, 1961.

CLARK, K. E., & CAMPBELL, D. P. Manual for the *Minnesota Vocational Interest Inventory.* New York: Psychological Corporation, 1965.

CLARK, R. E. Psychoses: Income and occupational prestige. *American Journal of Sociology,* 1949, **54**, 433–440.

CLARK, R. E. Psychoses, income, and occupational prestige. In R. Bendix and S. M. Lipset (Eds.), *Class status and power.* Glencoe, Ill.: Free Press, 1953. Pp. 333–340.

CLARKE, A. V., & GRANT, D. L. Application of a factorial method in selecting questions for an employee aptitude survey. *Personnel Psychology,* 1961, **14**, 131–139.

CLAY, H. A study of performance in relation to age at two printing works. *Journal of Gerontology,* 1956, **11**, 417–424.

COHEN, A. Sociological studies of occupations as a "way of life." *Personnel and Guidance Journal,* 1964, **43**, 267–272.

COHEN, J. The ideas of work and play. *British Journal of Sociology,* 1953, **4**, 312–322.

COHEN, M. R., & NAGEL, E. *An introduction to logic and scientific method.* New York: Harcourt, Brace & World, 1934.

COMBS, A. W., & SNYGG, D. *Individual behavior.* (Rev. ed.) New York: Harper & Row, 1959.

COOLEY, W. W. *Career development of scientists.* Cambridge, Mass.: Graduate School of Education, Harvard University, 1963. (a)

COOLEY, W. W. Predicting choice of a career in scientific research. *Personnel and Guidance Journal,* 1963, **42**, 21–28. (b)

COOLEY, W. W. A computer-measurement system for guidance. *Harvard Educational Review,* 1964, **34**, 559–572. (a)

COOLEY, W. W. Current research on the career development of scientists. *Journal of Counseling Psychology,* 1964, **11**, 88–95. (b)

COREY, L. G. Psychological adjustment and the worker role: An analysis of occupational differences. *Journal of Applied Psychology,* 1959, **43**, 253–255.

COTTLE, W. C. A factorial study of the Multiphasic, Strong, Kuder, and Bell inventories using a population of adult males. *Psychometrika,* 1950, **15**, 25–47.

COTTON, J. O., & STOLZ, R. E. The general applicability of a scale for rating research productivity. *Journal of Applied Psychology,* 1960, **44**, 276–277.

COUNTS, G. S. The social status of occupations: A problem in vocational guidance. *School Review,* 1925, **33**, 16–27.

COUTU, W. The relative prestige of twenty professions as judged by three groups of professional students. *Social Forces,* 1936, **14**, 522–529.

COVER, C. B., & PRESSEY, S. L. Age and route sales efficiency. *Journal of Applied Psychology,* 1950, **34**, 229–231.

COXE, W. W. Reliability of vocational choices of

high school students. *School and Society*, 1930, **32**, 816–818.

CRANE, D. Scientists at major and minor universities: A study of productivity and recognition. *American Sociological Review*, 1965, **30**, 699–714.

CRAWFORD, A. B., & CLEMENT, S. H. (Eds.) *The choice of an occupation*. New Haven: Yale University Press, 1932.

CREAGER, J. A., & HARDING, F. D., JR. A hierarchical factor analysis of foreman behavior. *Journal of Applied Psychology*, 1958, **42**, 197–203.

CRITES, J. O. Vocational maturity and vocational adjustment. Paper presented at the meeting of the American Personnel and Guidance Association, St. Louis, March, 1958.

CRITES, J. O. Ego-strength in relation to vocational interest development. *Journal of Counseling Psychology*, 1960, **7**, 137–143.

CRITES, J. O. Factor analytic definitions of vocational motivation. *Journal of Applied Psychology*, 1961, **45**, 330–337. (a)

CRITES, J. O. A model for the measurement of vocational maturity. *Journal of Counseling Psychology*, 1961, **8**, 255–259. (b)

CRITES, J. O. An interpersonal relations scale for occupational groups. *Journal of Applied Psychology*, 1962, **46**, 87–90. (a)

CRITES, J. O. Parental identification in relation to vocational interest development. *Journal of Educational Psychology*, 1962, **53**, 262–270. (b)

CRITES, J. O. Research on vocational motivation factors. Paper presented at the meeting of the American Psychological Association, Philadelphia, August 31, 1963. (a)

CRITES, J. O. Symposium: New research in vocational development. *Personnel and Guidance Journal*, 1963, **41**, 766–786. (b)

CRITES, J. O. Vocational interest in relation to vocational motivation. *Journal of Educational Psychology*, 1963, **54**, 277–285. (c)

CRITES, J. O. Proposals for a new criterion measure and research design. In H. Borow (Ed.), *Man in a world at work*. Boston: Houghton Mifflin, 1964. Pp. 324–340.

CRITES, J. O. Measurement of vocational maturity in adolescence: I. Attitude Test of the Vocational Development Inventory. *Psychological Monographs*, 1965, **79** (2, Whole No. 595).

CRITES, J. O. Programmatic research on vocational development. Unpublished manuscript, University of Iowa, 1966. (a)

CRITES, J. O. Self theories of vocational development. Paper presented at the meeting of the American Personnel and Guidance Association, Washington, D.C., April, 1966. (b)

CRONBACH, L. J. Statistical methods applied to Rorschach scores: A review. *Psychological Bulletin*, 1949, **9**, 149–171.

CRONBACH, L. J. The two disciplines of scientific psychology. *American Psychologist*, 1957, **12**, 671–684.

CRONBACH, L. J., & GLESER, G. Assessing similarity between profiles. *Psychological Bulletin*, 1953, **50**, 456–473.

CRONBACH, L. J., & MEEHL, P. E. Construct validity in psychological tests. *Psychological Bulletin*, 1955, **52**, 281–302.

CROSBY, R. C., & WINSOR, A. L. The validity of student estimates of their interests. *Journal of Applied Psychology*, 1941, **25**, 408–414.

CROWLEY, F. J. The goals of male high school seniors. *Personnel and Guidance Journal*, 1959, **37**, 488–492.

CULVER, B. F. When students choose careers. *Personnel Journal*, 1935, **14**, 64–70.

CUNLIFFE, R. B. Whither away and why: Trends in the choice of vocation in Detroit. *Personnel Journal*, 1927, **6**, 25–28.

CURETON, E. E. Validity. In E. F. Lindquist (Ed.), *Educational measurement*. Washington, D.C.: American Council on Education, 1951. Pp. 621–694.

CURETON, E. E., & KATZELL, R. A. A further analysis of the relations among job performance and situational variables. *Journal of Applied Psychology*, 1962, **46**, 230.

CURLE, A. Incentives to work: An anthropological appraisal. *Human Relations*, 1949, **2**, 41–47.

DABAS, Z. S. The dimensions of morale: An item factorization of the SRA employee inventory. *Personnel Psychology*, 1958, **11**, 217–234.

DALTON, M. Informal factors in career achievement. *American Journal of Sociology*, 1951, **56**, 407–415.

DANSKIN, D. G. Occupational sociology in occupational exploration. *Personnel and Guidance Journal*, 1955, **34**, 134–136.

DANSKIN, D. G. Studies in the sociological aspects of specific occupations. *Personnel and Guidance Journal*, 1956, **36**, 104–111.

DARLEY, J. G. *Clinical aspects and interpretation of the Strong Vocational Interest Blank.* New York: Psychological Corporation, 1941.

DARLEY, J. G., & HAGENAH, T. *Vocational interest measurement.* Minneapolis: University of Minnesota Press, 1955.

DARLEY, J. G., & WILLIAMS, C. T. Clinical records of individual student problems. In A. H. Brayfield (Ed.), *Readings in modern methods of counseling.* New York: Appleton-Century-Crofts, 1950. Pp. 97–101.

DASHIELL, J. F. *Fundamentals of general psychology.* (3rd ed.) Boston: Houghton Mifflin, 1949.

DAVIDSON, H. H. *Personality and economic background.* New York: Kings Crown, 1943.

DAVIDSON, H. H. A measure of adjustment obtained from Rorschach protocols. *Journal of Projective Techniques,* 1950, **14**, 31–38.

DAVIDSON, P. E., & ANDERSON, H. D. *Occupational mobility in an American community.* Palo Alto: Stanford University Press, 1937.

DAVIES, J. G. W. What is occupational success? *Occupational Psychology,* 1950, **24**, 7–17.

DAVIS, A., GARDNER, B. B., & GARDNER, M. R. *Deep south.* Chicago: University of Chicago Press, 1941.

DAVIS, D. A., HAGAN, N., & STROUF, J. Occupational choice of twelve-year-olds. *Personnel and Guidance Journal,* 1962, **40**, 628–629.

DAVIS, E. W. A functional pattern technique for classification of jobs. *Teachers College Contributions to Education,* 1942, 844.

DAVIS, J. A. *Great aspirations: The graduate school plans of America's college seniors.* Chicago: Aldine, 1964.

DAVIS, J. A. *Undergraduate career decisions.* Chicago: Aldine, 1965.

DAVIS, J. A., & BRADBURN, N. Great aspirations: The career plans of America's June 1961 college graduates. *Vocational Guidance Quarterly,* 1962, **10**, 137–142.

DAWIS, R. V., ENGLAND, G. W., & LOFQUIST, L. H. *Minnesota studies in vocational rehabilitation: XV. A theory of work adjustment.* Minneapolis: Industrial Relations Center, University of Minnesota, 1964.

DAY, S. R. Teacher influence on the occupational preferences of high school students. *Vocational Guidance Quarterly,* 1966, **14**, 215–219.

DEARBORN, W. F., & ROTHNEY, J. W. M. Scholastic, economic, and social backgrounds of unemployed youth. *Harvard Bulletin in Education,* 1938, No. 20.

DECKER, R. L. A study of three specific problems in the measurement and interpretation of employee attitudes. *Psychological Monographs,* 1955, **69** (16, Whole No. 401).

DEEG, M. E., & PATERSON, D. G. Changes in social status of occupations. *Occupations,* 1947, **25**, 205–208.

DENNIS, W. Predicting scientific productivity in later maturity from records of earlier decades. *Journal of Gerontology,* 1954, **9**, 465–467.

DENNIS, W. Age and achievement. A critique. *Journal of Gerontology,* 1956, **11**, 331–333. (a)

DENNIS, W. Age and productivity among scientists. *Science,* 1956, **123**, 724–725. (b)

DENNIS, W. The age decrement in outstanding scientific contributions: Fact or artifact? *American Psychologist,* 1958, **13**, 457–460.

DENNIS, W., & GIRDEN, E. Current scientific activities of psychologists as a function of age. *Journal of Gerontology,* 1954, **9**, 175–178.

DEPARTMENT OF LABOR, BUREAU OF LABOR STATISTICS. *Comparative job performance by age: Large plants in the men's footwear and household furniture industries.* Bulletin No. 1223, November, 1957.

DEPARTMENT OF LABOR, BUREAU OF LABOR STATISTICS. *Comparative job performance by age: Office workers.* Bulletin No. 1273, February, 1960.

DEPARTMENT OF LABOR, BUREAU OF LABOR STATISTICS. *Occupational outlook handbook.* (1965 ed.) Washington, D.C.: Government Printing Office, 1965.

DICKINSON, C. How college seniors preferences compare with employment and enrollment data. *Personnel and Guidance Journal,* 1954, **32**, 485–488. (a)

DICKINSON, C. Ratings of job factors by those choosing various occupational groups. *Journal of Counseling Psychology,* 1954, **1**, 188–189. (b)

DICKINSON, C. What employers look for in the college graduate. *Personnel and Guidance Journal,* 1955, **33**, 460–464.

DICKINSON, W. J. The Hawthorne plan of personal counseling. *American Journal of Orthopsychiatry,* 1945, **15**, 343–347.

Dictionary of occupational titles. Vols. I and II. Washington, D.C.: Government Printing Office, 1965.

DILLEY, J. S. Decision-making ability and vocational maturity. *Personnel and Guidance Journal,* 1965, **44**, 423–427.

DIPBOYE, W. J., & ANDERSON, W. F. The ordering of occupational values by high school freshmen and seniors. *Personnel and Guidance Journal,* 1959, **38**, 121–124.

DIPBOYE, W. J., & ANDERSON, W. F. Occupational stereotypes and manifest needs of high school students. *Journal of Counseling Psychology,* 1961, **8**, 293–304.

DODGE, A. F. *Occupational ability patterns.* New York: Teachers College Bureau of Publications, 1935.

DODGE, A. F. What are the personality traits of the successful salesperson? *Journal of Applied Psychology,* 1938, **22**, 229–238.

DODGE, A. F. What are the personality traits of the successful clerical worker? *Journal of Applied Psychology,* 1940, **24**, 576–586.

DODGE, A. F. What are the personality traits of the successful teacher? *Journal of Applied Psychology,* 1943, **27**, 325–337.

DODGE, A. F. A study of personality traits of successful teachers. *Occupations,* 1948, **27**, 107–112.

DOLE, A. A. Educational choice is not vocational choice. *Vocational Guidance Quarterly,* 1963, **12**, 30–35.

DORCUS, R. M., & JONES, M. H. *Handbook of employee selection.* New York: McGraw-Hill, 1950.

DOYLE, R. E. Career patterns of male college graduates. *Personnel and Guidance Journal,* 1965, **44**, 410–415.

DRAKE, L. E. MMPI patterns predictive of underachievement. *Journal of Counseling Psychology,* 1962, **9**, 164–167.

DRASGOW, J. Occupational choice and Freud's principle of overdetermination. *Vocational Guidance Quarterly,* 1957, **6**, 67–68.

DRESDEN, K. W. Vocational choices of secondary pupils. *Occupations,* 1948, **27**, 104–106.

DRESSEL, P. L. Research in counseling: A symposium. Some approaches to evaluation. *Personnel and Guidance Journal,* 1953, **31**, 284–287.

DUBIN, R. Industrial workers' worlds: A study of the "central life interests" of industrial workers. *Social Problems,* 1955, **3**, 131–142.

DUBIN, R. *The world of work.* Englewood Cliffs, N.J.: Prentice-Hall, 1958.

DU BOIS, P. H. (Ed.) The classification program. Washington, D.C.: U.S. Government Printing Office, 1947. (*AAF Aviation Psychology Program Research Report,* No. 2)

DUFTY, N. F. Occupational status, job satisfaction and levels of aspiration. *British Journal of Sociology,* 1960, **11**, 348–355.

DU MAS, F. M. The coefficient of profile similarity. *Journal of Clinical Psychology,* 1949, **5**, 123–131.

DUNNETTE, M. D. Factor structures of unusually satisfying and unusually dissatisfying job situations for six occupational groups. Paper presented at the meeting of the Midwestern Psychological Association, Chicago, April, 1965.

DVORAK, B. J. Differential occupational ability patterns. *Bulletin of Employment Stability Research Institution,* 1935, No. 8. University of Minnesota.

DYER, J. R. Sources and permanence of vocational interest of college men—101 cases over five year period. *Journal of Applied Psychology,* 1932, **16**, 233–240.

DYER, W. G. Parental influence on the job attitudes of children from two occupational strata. *Sociology and Social Research,* 1958, **42**, 203–206.

DYKMAN, R. A., HEIMANN, E. K., & KERR, W. A. Lifetime worry patterns of three diverse adult cultural groups. *Journal of Social Psychology,* 1952, **35**, 91–100.

DYNES, R. R., CLARKE, A. C., & DINITZ, S. Levels of occupational aspiration: Some aspects of family experience as a variable. *American Sociological Review,* 1956, **21**, 212–214.

DYSINGER, W. S. Maturation and vocational guidance. *Occupations,* 1950, **29**, 198–201.

EARLE, F. M. *Methods of choosing a career.* London: Harrap, 1931.

EARLE, F. M. *Psychology and the choice of a career.* London: Methven, 1933.

EATON, W. H. Hypotheses related to worker frustration. *Journal of Social Psychology,* 1952, **35**, 59–68.

EDGERTON, H. A., & KOLBE, L. E. The method of minimum variation for the coordination of criteria. *Psychometrika,* 1936, **1**, 185–187.

EDWARDS, A. L. Experiments: Their planning and execution. In G. Lindzey (Ed.), *Handbook of social psychology.* Vol. I. Cambridge, Mass.: Addison-Wesley, 1954. Pp. 259–288.

EDWARDS, A. L., & CRONBACH, L. J. Experimental design for research in psychotherapy. *Journal of Clinical Psychology,* 1952, **8**, 51–59.

EDWARDS, A. M. *Comparative occupational statistics for the United States, 1870–1940.* Washington, D.C.: Government Printing Office, 1943.

EDWARDS, W. The theory of decision making. *Psychology Bulletin,* 1954, **51**, 380–417.

EDWARDS, W. Behavioral decision theory. *Annual Review of Psychology,* 1961, **12**, 473–499.

EILBERT, L. R. A study of emotional immaturity utilizing the critical incident technique. *University of Pittsburgh Bulletin,* 1953, **49**, 199–204.

EMPEY, L. T. Social class and occupational aspiration: A comparison of absolute and relative measurement. *American Sociological Review,* 1956, **21**, 703–709.

ENDICOTT, F. S. What qualities do employers seek? *Occupations,* 1944, **23**, 205–206.

ENGLAND, G. W., & STEIN, C. I. The occupational reference group—a neglected concept in employee attitude studies. *Personnel Psychology,* 1961, **14**, 299–304.

ENGLANDER, M. E. A psychological analysis of vocational choice: Teaching. *Journal of Counseling Psychology,* 1960, **7**, 257–264.

ENGLANDER, M. E. *Q* sort: A means to explore vocational choice. *Educational and Psychological Measurement,* 1961, **21**, 597–605.

ENGLISH, H. B., & ENGLISH, A. C. *A comprehensive dictionary of psychological and psychoanalytical terms.* New York: McKay, 1958.

ERAN, M. Relationship between self-perceived personality traits and job attitudes in middle management. *Journal of Applied Psychology,* 1966, **50**, 424–430.

ERIKSON, E. H. *Childhood and society.* New York: Norton, 1950.

ERIKSON, E. H. Identity and the life cycle. *Psychological issues,* 1959, **1**, 1–171.

ESTES, W. K. Component and pattern models with Markovian interpretations. In R. R. Bush & W. K. Estes (Eds.), *Studies in mathematical learning theory.* Stanford: Stanford University Press, 1959. Pp. 9–52.

EVANS, C. E., & LASEAU, L. N. My job contest. *Personnel Psychology Monograph,* 1950, No. 1.

EWART, E., SEASHORE, S. E., & TIFFIN, J. A factor analysis of an industrial merit scale. *Journal of Applied Psychology,* 1941, **25**, 481–486.

EWEN, R. B. Some determinants of job satisfaction: A study of the generality of Herzberg's theory. *Journal of Applied Psychology,* 1964, **48**, 161–163.

EWEN, R. B., SMITH, P. G., HULIN, C. G., & LOCKE, E. A. An empirical test of the Herzberg two-factor theory. *Journal of Applied Psychology,* 1966, **50**, 544–550.

EYSENCK, H. J. *Dimensions of personality.* London: Routledge, 1947.

EYSENCK, H. J. *The structure of personality.* New York: Wiley, 1953.

FAGIN, W. B. Constitutional factors in vocational interests. Doctoral dissertation, Columbia University, 1950.

FARBER, I. E. The role of motivation in verbal learning and performance. *Psychological Bulletin,* 1955, **52**, 311–327.

FARIS, R. E. L. Ecological factors in human behavior. In J. McV. Hunt (Ed.), *Personality and the behavior disorders.* New York: Ronald, 1944. Pp. 736–760.

FEIGL, H., & BRODBECK, M. (Eds.), *Readings in the philosophy of science.* New York: Appleton-Century-Crofts, 1953.

FEINGOLD, G. A. The relation between the intelligence and vocational choices of high school pupils. *Journal of Applied Psychology,* 1923, **7**, 143–156.

FESTINGER, L. *A theory of cognitive dissonance.* Stanford, Calif.: Stanford University Press, 1957.

FESTINGER, L. *Conflict decision, and dissonance.* Palo Alto, Calif.: Stanford University Press, 1964.

FIELD, F. L., KEHAS, C. D., & TIEDEMAN, D. V. The self-concept in career development: A construct in transition. *Personnel and Guidance Journal,* 1963, **41**, 767–770.

FINE, S. A. A structure of worker functions. *Personel and Guidance Journal,* 1955, **34**, 66–73.

FINE, S. A. USES occupational classification and Minnesota Occupational Rating Scales. *Journal of Counseling Psychology,* 1957, **4**, 218–223.

FINE, S. A. Matching job requirements and worker qualifications. *Personnel,* 1958, **34**, 52–58.

FINE, S. A., & HEINZ, C. A. The functional occupational classification structure. *Personnel and Guidance Journal,* 1958, **37**, 180–192.

FIRTH, R. Anthropological background to work. *Occupational Psychology,* 1948, **22**, 94–102.

FISHER, V. E., & HANNA, J. V. *The dissatisfied worker.* New York: Macmillan, 1931.

FISKE, D. W. Values, theory and the criterion

problem. *Personnel Psychology,* 1951, **4,** 93–98.

FISKE, D. W. The constraints of intra-individual variability in test response. *Educational and Psychological Measurement,* 1957, **17,** 317–337. (a)

FISKE, D. W. An intensive study of variability scores. *Educational and Psychological Measurement,* 1957, **17,** 453–465. (b)

FISKE, D. W., & RICE, L. Intra-individual response variability. *Psychological Bulletin,* 1955, **52,** 217–250.

FLANAGAN, J. C. The aviation psychology program in the Army Air Forces. Washington, D.C.: U.S. Government Printing Office, 1947. (*AAF Aviation Psychology Program Research Report,* No. 1)

FLANAGAN, J. C. The critical incident technique. *Psychological Bulletin,* 1954, **51,** 327–358.

FLANAGAN, J. C., & COOLEY, W. W. *Project Talent: One-year follow-up studies.* Pittsburgh: School of Education, University of Pittsburgh, 1966.

FLANAGAN, J. C., & DAILEY, J. T. Project Talent—the identification, development, and utilization of human talents. *Personnel and Guidance Journal,* 1960, **38,** 504–505.

FLANAGAN, J. C., DAILEY, J. T., SHAYCOFT, M. F., GORHAM, W. A., ORR, D. B., & GOLDBERG, I. *Design for a study of American youth.* Boston: Houghton Mifflin, 1962.

FLEEGE, U. H., & MALONE, H. J. Motivation in occupational choice among junior-senior high school students. *Journal of Educational Psychology,* 1946, **37,** 77–86.

FLETCHER, F. M. Concepts, curiosity, and careers. *Journal of Counseling Psychology,* 1966, **13,** 131–138.

FOLLEY, J. D., JR. Development of a list of critical requirements for retail sales personnel from the standpoint of customer satisfaction. Master's thesis, University of Pittsburgh, 1953.

FOLSON, W. W., & SOBOLEWSKI, E. L. Income and social status of occupations. *Personnel and Guidance Journal,* 1957, **36,** 277–278.

FORD, A. *A scientific approach to labor problems.* New York: McGraw-Hill, 1931.

FORER, B. R. Personality factors in occupational choice. *Educational and Psychological Measurement,* 1953, **13,** 361–366.

FORER, B. R. Manual for the *Forer Vocational Survey.* Los Angeles: Western Psychological Services, 1957.

FORM, W. H., & GESCHWENDER, J. A. Social reference basis of job satisfaction: The case of manual workers. *American Sociological Review,* 1962, **27,** 228–237.

FORM, W. H., & MILLER, D. C. Occupational career pattern as a sociological instrument. *American Journal of Sociology,* 1949, **54,** 317–329.

FORREST, A. L. Persistence of vocational choice of the Merit Scholarship winners. *Personnel and Guidance Journal,* 1961, **39,** 466–471.

FOURNET, G. P., DISTEFANO, M. K., JR., & PRYER, M. W. Job satisfaction: Issues and problems. *Personnel Psychology,* 1966, **19,** 165–184.

FRASER, R., BUNBURY, E., DANIELL, B., BARLING, M., WALDRON, F., KEMP, P., & LEE, I. The incidence of neurosis among factory workers. Medical Research Council, *Industrial Health Research Board, Report No. 90.* London: H. M. Stationary Office, 1947.

FREDERICKSEN, N., & GILBERT, A. C. F. Replication of a study of differential predictability. *Educational and Psychological Measurement,* 1960, **20,** 759–767.

FREDERICKSEN, N., & MELVILLE, S. D. Differential predictability in the use of test scores. *Educational and Psychological Measurement,* 1954, **14,** 647–656.

FRENCH, J. R. P., KAHN, R. L., & MANN, F. C. Work, health, and satisfaction. *Journal of Social Issues,* 1962, **17,** 1–127.

FRENCH, W. L. Can a man's occupation be predicted? *Journal of Counseling Psychology,* 1959, **6,** 95–101.

FRENKEL-BRUNSWICK, E. Adjustments and reorientations in the course of the life span. In R. G. Kuhlen & G. G. Thompson (Eds.), *Psychological studies of human development.* New York: Appleton-Century-Crofts, 1952. Pp. 94–104.

FREUD, S. *Civilization and its discontents.* New York: Norton, 1962.

FRIEDLANDER, F. Underlying sources of job satisfaction. *Journal of Applied Psychology,* 1963, **47,** 246–250.

FRIEDLANDER, F. Job characteristics as satisfiers and dissatisfiers. *Journal of Applied Psychology,* 1964, **48,** 388–392.

FRIEDLANDER, F. Comparative work value systems. *Personnel Psychology,* 1965, **18,** 1–20.

FRIEDLANDER, F. Motivations to work and organizational performance. *Journal of Applied Psychology,* 1966, **50,** 143–152.

FRIEDLANDER, F., & WALTON, E. Positive and negative motivations toward work. *Administrative Science Quarterly,* 1964, **9**, 194–207.

FRIEDMANN, E. A., & HAVIGHURST, R. J. *The meaning of work and retirement.* Chicago: University of Chicago Press, 1954.

FRIEND, J. G., & HAGGARD, E. A. Work adjustment in relation to family background. *Applied Psychology Monographs,* 1948, No. 16.

FRIESEN, E. P. The incomplete sentence technique as a measure of employee attitudes. *Personnel Psychology,* 1952, **5**, 329–345.

FROEHLICH, H. P., & WOLINS, L. Job satisfaction as need satisfaction. *Personnel Psychology,* 1960, **13**, 407–420.

FROMM, E. *Man for himself.* New York: Rinehart, 1947.

FROMM, E. *The art of loving.* New York: Harper Colophon Books, 1962.

FROOMKIN, J. Jobs, skills, and realities. *Columbia University Forum,* 1964, **7**, 30–33.

FRYER, D. Occupational intelligence standards. *School and Society,* 1922, **16**, 273–277.

FRYER, D. *The measurement of interests.* New York: Holt, 1931.

FRYER, D., & SPARLING, E. J. Intelligence and occupational adjustment. *Occupations,* 1934, **12**, 55–63.

GADDIS, W. H. Current influences in the development of a concept of vocational interest. *Personnel and Guidance Journal,* 1959, **38**, 198–201.

GADEL, M. S., & KRIEDT, P. H. Relationships of aptitude, interest, performance and job satisfaction of IBM operators. *Personnel Psychology,* 1952, **5**, 207–212.

GAHAGAN, L. Judgment of occupations from printed photographs. *Journal of Social Psychology,* 1933, **4**, 128–134.

GALINSKY, M. D. Personality development and vocational choice of clinical psychologists and physicists. *Journal of Counseling Psychology,* 1962, **9**, 299–305.

GALINSKY, M. D., & FAST, I. Vocational choice as a focus of the identity search. *Journal of Counseling Psychology,* 1966, **13**, 89–92.

GALLER, E. H. Influence of social class on children's choices of occupations. *Elementary School Journal,* 1951, **51**, 439–445.

GALTON, F. *Hereditary genius: An inquiry into its laws.* New York: Appleton, 1870.

GALTON, F. *Inquiries into human faculty and its development.* London: Macmillan, 1883.

GARRETT, H. E. A developmental theory of intelligence. *American Psychologist.* 1946, **1**, 372–378.

GARRETT, H. E. *Statistics in psychology and education.* (5th ed.) New York: Longmans, 1958.

GARVEY, W. D., & GRIFFITH, B. C. The APA project on scientific information exchange in psychology. *Journal of Counseling Psychology,* 1963, **10**, 297–302.

GAUDET, F. J., & KULICK, W. Who comes to a vocational guidance center? *Personnel and Guidance Journal,* 1954, **33**, 211–215.

GAUDET, S., & CARLI, A. R. Why executives fail. *Personnel Psychology,* 1957, **10**, 7–22.

GEIST, H. *The Geist Picture Interest Inventory, General, Male.* Missoula, Mont.: Psychological Test Specialists, 1959.

GEIST, H. Work satisfaction and scores on a picture interest inventory. *Journal of Applied Psychology,* 1963, **47**, 369–373.

GEIST, H. Reply to Campbell. *Journal of Applied Psychology,* 1965, **49**, 74–75.

GELATT, A. B. Decision-making: A conceptual frame of reference for counseling. *Journal of Counseling Psychology,* 1962, **9**, 240–245.

GELLMAN, W. Components of vocational adjustment. *Personnel and Guidance Journal,* 1953, **31**, 536–539.

GESELL, A., ILG, F. L., & AMES, L. B. *Youth: The years from ten to sixteen.* New York: Harper & Row, 1956.

GETZELS, J. W., & GUBA, E. G. Role, role conflict, and effectiveness. *American Sociological Review,* 1954, **19**, 164–175.

GHISELLI, E. E. A scale for the measurement of initiative. *Personnel Psychology,* 1955, **8**, 156–164.

GHISELLI, E. E. Correlates of initiative. *Personnel Psychology,* 1956, **9**, 311–320. (a)

GHISELLI, E. E. Differentiation of individuals in terms of their predictability. *Journal of Applied Psychology,* 1956, **40**, 374–377. (b)

GHISELLI, E. E. Dimensional problems of criteria. *Journal of Applied Psychology,* 1956, **40**, 1–4. (c)

GHISELLI, E. E. Differentiation of tests in terms of the accuracy with which they predict for a given individual. *Educational and Psychological Measurement,* 1960, **20**, 675–684. (a)

GHISELLI, E. E. The prediction of predictability. *Educational and Psychological Measurement,* 1960, **20**, 3–8. (b)

GHISELLI, E. E. Moderating effects and differential reliability and validity. *Journal of Applied Psychology,* 1963, **48**, 81–86.

GHISELLI, E. E. Maturity of self-perception in relation to managerial success. *Personnel Psychology,* 1964, **17**, 41–48.

GHISELLI, E. E. *The validity of occupational aptitude tests.* New York: Wiley, 1966.

GHISELLI, E. E., & BARTHOL, R. P. The validity of personality inventories in the selection of employees. *Journal of Applied Psychology,* 1953, **37**, 18–20.

GHISELLI, E. E., & BARTHOL, R. P. Role perceptions of successful and unsuccessful supervisors. *Journal of Applied Psychology,* 1956, **40**, 241–244.

GHISELLI, E. E., & HAIRE, M. The validation of selection tests in the light of the dynamic character of criteria. *Personnel Psychology,* 1960, **13**, 225–231.

GIELE, J., & ROE, A. Bibliography on careers. Unpublished manuscript, Center for Research in Careers, Graduate School of Education, Harvard University, 1964.

GILBERT, W. M. Comment. *Journal of Counseling Psychology,* 1958, **5**, 187–188.

GILGER, G. A., JR. Declarations of vocational interests. *Occupations,* 1942, **20**, 276–279.

GILMER, B. VON H. *Industrial psychology.* (2nd ed.) New York: McGraw-Hill, 1966.

GINSBERG, A. Hypothetical constructs and intervening variables. *Psychological Review,* 1954, **61**, 119–131.

GINSBERG, S. W. Work and its satisfactions. *Journal of the Hillside Hospital,* 1956, **5**, 301–311.

GINZBERG, E. *Grass on the slag heaps: The story of the Welsh miners.* New York: Harper & Row, 1942.

GINZBERG, E. The occupational adjustment of 1000 selectees. *American Sociological Review,* 1943, **8**, 256–263.

GINZBERG, E. Perspectives on work motivation. *Personnel,* 1954, **31**, 43–49.

GINZBERG, E. Man and his work. *California Management Review,* 1962, **5**, 21–28.

GINZBERG, E., & BERMAN, H. *The American worker in the twentieth century.* New York: Free Press, 1963.

GINZBERG, E., GINSBURG, S. W., AXELRAD, S., & HERMA J. L. *Occupational choice.* New York: Columbia University Press, 1951.

GIRSHICK, M. A. An elementary survey of statistical decision theory. *Review of Educational Research,* 1954, **24**, 448–466.

GLICK, P., JR. Anticipated occupational frustration. *Vocational Guidance Quarterly,* 1963, **11**, 91–95.

GLICK, P., JR. Occupational values and anticipated occupational frustration of agricultural college students. *Personnel and Guidance Journal,* 1964, **42**, 674–679.

GLICK, P., JR. Anticipated occupational frustration: A follow-up report. *Vocational Guidance Quarterly,* 1965, **14**, 62–66. (a)

GLICK, P., JR. Three-dimensional classification of the occupations of college graduates. *Vocational Guidance Quarterly,* 1965, **14**, 130–135. (b)

GONYEA, G. G. Dimensions of job perceptions. *Journal of Counseling Psychology,* 1961, **8**, 305–312.

GONYEA, G. G. Job perceptions in relation to vocational preference. *Journal of Counseling Psychology,* 1963, **10**, 20–26.

GONYEA, G. G., & LUNNEBORG, C. E. A factor analytic study of perceived occupational similarity. *Journal of Applied Psychology,* 1963, **47**, 166–172.

GOODE, W. J., & FOWLER, I. Incentive factors in a low morale plant. *American Sociological Review,* 1949, **14**, 618–624.

GOODENOUGH, F. L., & ANDERSON, J. E. *Experimental child study.* New York: Appleton-Century, 1931.

GOODMAN, N. A classified bibliography on careers. Unpublished manuscript, Center for Research in Careers, Graduate School of Education, Harvard University, 1966.

GOODSTEIN, L. D. Behavior theoretical views of counseling. In B. Stefflre (Ed.), *Theories of counseling.* New York: McGraw-Hill, 1965. Pp. 140–192.

GOODSTEIN, L. D., CRITES, J. O., HEILBRUN, A. B., JR., & REMPEL, P. P. The use of the California Psychological Inventory in a university counseling service. *Journal of Counseling Psychology,* 1961, **8**, 147–153.

GORDON, G. G. The relationship of "satisfiers" and "dissatisfiers" to productivity, turnover, and morale. Paper read at the meeting of the American Psychological Association, Chicago, September, 1965.

GORDON, O. J. A factor analysis of human needs and industrial morale. *Personnel Psychology,* 1955, **8**, 1–18.

GORDON, T. The airline pilot's job. *Journal of Applied Psychology,* 1949, 33, 122–131.

GORDON, T. The development of a method of

evaluating flying skill. *Personnel Psychology,* 1950, **3**, 71–84.

GRAEN, G. B. Addendum to "An empirical test of the Herzberg two-factor theory." *Journal of Applied Psychology,* 1966, **50**, 551–555. (a)

GRAEN, G. B. Motivator and hygiene dimensions for research and development engineers. *Journal of Applied Psychology,* 1966, **50**, 563–566. (b)

GRANGER, S. G. Psychologists' prestige rankings of 20 psychological occupations. *Journal of Counseling Psychology,* 1959, **6**, 183–188.

GRANT, D. L. A factor analysis of managers' ratings. *Journal of Applied Psychology,* 1955, **39**, 283–286.

GRAY, S. The vocational preference of Negro school children. *Journal of Genetic Psychology,* 1944, **64**, 239–247.

GREEN, L. B., & PARKER, H. J. Parental influence upon adolescents' occupational choice: A test of an aspect of Roe's theory. *Journal of Counseling Psychology,* 1965, **12**, 379–385.

GREENBERG, L. Productivity of older workers. *Gerontologist,* 1962, **1**, 38–41.

GRIBBONS, W. D. Changes in readiness for vocational planning from the eighth to the tenth grade. *Personnel and Guidance Journal,* 1964, **41**, 908–913.

GRIBBONS, W. D., HALPERIN, S., & LOHNES, P. R. Applications of stochastic models in research on career development. *Journal of Counseling Psychology,* 1966, **13**, 403–408.

GRIBBONS, W. D., & LOHNES, P. R. Relationships among measures of readiness for vocational planning. *Journal of Counseling Psychology,* 1964, **11**, 13–19. (a)

GRIBBONS, W. D., & LOHNES, P. R. Validation of vocational planning interview scales. *Journal of Counseling Psychology,* 1964, **11**, 20–26. (b)

GRIBBONS, W. D., & LOHNES, P. R. Predicting five years of development in adolescents from readiness for vocational planning scales. *Journal of Educational Psychology,* 1965, **56**, 244–253. (a)

GRIBBONS, W. D., & LOHNES, P. R. Shifts in adolescents' vocational values. *Personnel and Guidance Journal,* 1965, **44**, 248–252. (b)

GRIBBONS, W. D., & LOHNES, P. R. *Career development.* Weston, Mass.: Regis College, 1966. (a)

GRIBBONS, W. D., & LOHNES, P. R. Occupational preferences and measured intelligence. *Vocational Guidance Quarterly,* 1966, **15**, 211–214. (b)

GRIGG, A. E. Childhood experience with parental attitudes: A test of Roe's hypothesis. *Journal of Counseling Psychology,* 1959, **6**, 153–156.

GROSS, E. The worker and society. In H. Borow (Ed.), *Man in a world at work.* Boston: Houghton Mifflin, 1964. Pp. 67–95.

GRUNES, W. F. On perception of occupations. *Personnel and Guidance Journal,* 1956, **34**, 276–279.

GRUNES, W. F. Looking at occupations. *Journal of Abnormal and Social Psychology,* 1957, **54**, 86–92.

GUERTIN, W. H., FRANK, G. H., & RABIN, A. I. Research with the Wechsler-Bellevue Intelligence Scales: 1950–1955. *Psychological Bulletin,* 1956, **53**, 235–257.

GUERTIN, W. H., RABIN, A. I., FRANK, G. H., & LADD, C. E. Research with the Wechsler Intelligence Scales for Adults: 1955–60. *Psychological Bulletin,* 1962, **59**, 1–26.

GUEST, R. H. Work careers and aspirations of automobile workers. *American Sociological Review,* 1955, **19**, 155–163.

GUILFORD, J. P. Some lessons from aviation psychology. *American Psychologist,* 1948, **3**, 3–11.

GUILFORD, J. P. When not to factor analyze. *Psychological Bulletin,* 1952, **49**, 26–37.

GUILFORD, J. P. *Psychometric methods.* (2nd. ed.) New York: McGraw-Hill, 1954.

GUILFORD, J. P. *Personality.* New York: McGraw-Hill, 1959.

GUILFORD, J. P., CHRISTENSEN, P. R., BOND, N. A., JR., & SUTTON, M. A. A factor analysis study of human interests. *Psychological Monographs,* 1954, **68** (4, Whole No. 375).

GUION, R. M. Industrial morale (a symposium): 1. The problem of terminology. *Personnel Psychology,* 1958, **11**, 59–64.

GUION, R. M. Criterion measurement and personnel judgments. *Personnel Psychology,* 1961, **14**, 141–149.

GUNN, B. Children's conceptions of occupational prestige. *Personnel and Guidance Journal,* 1964, **42**, 558–563.

GURIN, G. Work satisfactions. *Industrial Medicine and Surgery,* 1963, **32**, 212–214.

GUSFIELD, J. R., & SCHWARTZ, M. The meanings of occupational prestige: Reconsideration of the NORC scale. *American Sociological Review,* 1963, **28**, 265–271.

GUTTMAN, L. The basis for scalogram analysis. In S. A. Stouffer, et al., *Measurement and prediction*. Princeton, N. J.: Princeton University Press, 1950. Pp. 60–90.

GUTTMAN, L. A new approach to factor analysis: The radex. In P. F. Lazarfeld (Ed.), *Mathematical thinking in the social sciences*. Glencoe, Ill.: Free Press, 1954. Pp. 258–348.

HADLEY, R. G., & LEVY, W. V. Vocational development and reference groups. *Journal of Counseling Psychology*, 1962, **9**, 110–114.

HAGEN, D. Careers and family atmosphere: A test of Roe's theory. *Journal of Counseling Psychology*, 1960, **7**, 251–256.

HAHN, M. E., & MC LEAN, M. S. *Counseling psychology*. New York: McGraw-Hill, 1955.

HAIRE, M. Psychology and the study of business: Joint behavioral sciences. In R. A. Dahl, M. Haire, & P. F. Lazarsfeld, *Social science research on business: Product and potential*. New York: Columbia University Press, 1959. Pp. 45–98.

HAIRE, M. *Psychology in management*. (2nd ed.) New York: McGraw-Hill, 1964.

HALL, C. S., & LINDZEY, G. *Theories of personality*. New York: Wiley, 1957.

HALL, C. W. Social prestige values of a selected group of occupations. *Psychological Bulletin*, 1938, **35**, 696.

HALL, D. W. A study of the interrelationships among manifest anxiety, vocational choice certainty, and choice behavior. (Doctoral dissertation, University of Iowa) Ann Arbor, Mich.: University Microfilms, 1963. No. 63–8006.

HALL, O. The stages of a medical career. *American Journal of Sociology*, 1948, **53**, 327–336.

HALLIDAY, R. W. Problems involved in the classification of professional occupations. *Occupations*, 1949, **27**, 530–534.

HALPERN, G. Relative contributions of motivator and hygiene factors to overall job satisfaction. Paper read at the meeting of the American Psychological Association, Chicago, September, 1965.

HALPERN, G. Relative contributions of motivator and hygiene factors to overall job satisfaction. *Journal of Applied Psychology*, 1966, **50**, 198–200.

HAMBURGER, M. Realism and consistency in early adolescent aspirations and expectations. (Doctoral dissertation, Columbia University) Ann Arbor, Mich.: University Microfilms, 1958. No. 58–2588.

HAMMOND, M. Occupational attitude rating scales. *Personnel and Guidance Journal*, 1954, **32**, 470–474.

HAMMOND, M. Motives related to vocational choices of college freshmen. *Journal of Counseling Psychology*, 1956, **3**, 257–261.

HAMMOND, M. Attitudinal changes of "successful" students in a college of engineering. *Journal of Counseling Psychology*, 1959, **6**, 69–71.

HANCOCK, J. W. Why workers feel insecure. *Personnel Journal*, 1949, **28**, 177–179.

HAND, T., HOPPOCK, R., & ZLATCHIN, P. J. Job satisfaction: Researches of 1944 and 1945. *Occupations*, 1948, **26**, 425–431.

HARDIN, E. Perceived and actual change in job satisfaction. *Journal of Applied Psychology*, 1965, **49**, 363–367.

HARDING, F. D., & BOTTENBERG, R. A. Effect of personal characteristics on relationships between attitudes and job performance. *Journal of Applied Psychology*, 1961, **45**, 428–430.

HARMON, H. H. *Modern factor analysis*. Chicago: University of Chicago Press, 1960.

HARMON, L. W. Occupational satisfaction—a better criterion? *Journal of Counseling Psychology*, 1966, **13**, 295–299.

HARRELL, T. W. *Industrial psychology*. (Rev. ed.) New York: Rinehart, 1958.

HARRELL, T. W., & HARRELL, M. S. Army General Classification Test scores for civilian occupations. *Educational and Psychological Measurement*, 1945, **5**, 229–240.

HARREN, V. A. The vocational decision-making process among college males. *Journal of Counseling Psychology*, 1966, **13**, 271–277.

HARRIS, D. B. Work and the adolescent transition to maturity. *Teachers College Record*, 1961, **63**, 146–153.

HARRISON, R. Sources of variation in managers' job attitudes. *Personnel Psychology*, 1960, **13**, 425–434.

HARRISON, R. Cumulative communality cluster analysis of workers' job attitudes. *Journal of Applied Psychology*, 1961, **45**, 123–125.

HART, H. Work as integration. *Medical Records*, 1947, **160**, 735–739.

HARTMAN, G. W. The prestige of occupations. *Personnel Journal*, 1934, **13**, 144–152.

HARTMANN, G. W. The relative social prestige of representative medical specialties. *Journal of Applied Psychology*, 1936, **20**, 659–663.

HARTMANN, H. The mutual influence in the development of ego and id. In Anna Freud, et al. (Ed.), *The psychoanalytic study of the child. Vol. I.* New York: International University Press, 1945. Pp. 11–30.

HATT, P. K. Occupation and social stratification. *American Journal of Sociology,* 1950, **55**, 533–545.

HAVIGHURST, R. J. *Human development and education.* New York: Longmans, 1953.

HAVIGHURST, R. J. Youth in exploration and man emergent. In H. Borow (Ed.), *Man in a world at work.* Boston: Houghton Mifflin, 1964. Pp. 215–236.

HAY, E. N. Predicting success in machine bookkeeping. *Journal of Applied Psychology,* 1943, **27**, 483–493.

HAY, J. E. Self-ideal congruence among engineering managers. *Personnel and Guidance Journal,* 1966, **44**, 1084–1088.

HEBB, D. O. *The organization of behavior.* New York: Wiley, 1949.

HELSON, H. Adaptation-level as a basis for a quantitative theory of frames of reference. *Psychological Review,* 1948, **55**, 297–313.

HELSON, H. Adaptation-level theory. In S. Koch (Ed.), *Psychology: A study of a science. Vol. I. Sensory, perceptual, and physiological foundations.* New York: McGraw-Hill, 1959. Pp. 565–621.

HENDRICK, I. The discussion of the "instinct to master." *Psychoanalytic Quarterly,* 1943, **12**, 561–565. (a)

HENDRICK, I. Work and the pleasure principle. *Psychoanalytic Quarterly,* 1943, **12**, 311–329. (b)

HENRY, W. E. The business executive: The psychodynamics of a social role. *American Journal of Sociology,* 1949, **54**, 286–291.

HERON, A. *Why men work.* Palo Alto: Stanford University Press, 1948.

HERON, A. The establishment for research purposes of two criteria of occupational adjustment. *Occupational Psychology,* 1952, **26**, 78–85. (a)

HERON, A. A psychological study of occupational adjustment. *Journal of Applied Psychology,* 1952, **36**, 385–387. (b)

HERON, A. Satisfaction and satisfactoriness: Complementary aspects of occupational adjustment. *Occupational Psychology,* 1954, **28**, 140–153.

HERON, A. Personality and occupational adjustment: A cross-validation study. *Canadian Journal of Psychology,* 1955, **9**, 15–20.

HERSEY, R. Case study of a successful man. In R. Hoppock (Ed.), *Criteria of vocational success.* New York: National Occupational Conference, 1936. Pp. 921–925.

HERSEY, R. Zest for work—gone or hiding? *Mental Hygiene,* 1954, **38**, 12–27.

HERSEY, R. *Zest for work.* New York: Harper & Row, 1955.

HERSHENSON, D. B., & ROTH, R. M. A decisional process model of vocational development. *Journal of Counseling Psychology,* 1966, **13**, 368–370.

HERTZMAN, M., & PEARCE, J. Personal meaning of the human figure in the Rorschach Test. *Psychiatry,* 1947, **10**, 413–422.

HERZBERG, F. The motivation to work among Finnish supervisors. *Personnel Psychology,* 1965, **18**, 393–402.

HERZBERG, F. *Work and the nature of man.* New York: World, 1966.

HERZBERG, F., MAUSNER, B., PETERSON, R. O., & CAPWELL, D. F. *Job attitudes: Review of research and opinion.* Pittsburgh: Psychological Service of Pittsburgh, 1957.

HERZBERG, F., MAUSNER, B., & SNYDERMAN, B. B. *The motivation to work.* New York: Wiley, 1959.

HEWER, V. H. What do theories of vocational choice mean to a counselor? *Journal of Counseling Psychology,* 1963, **10**, 118–125.

HEWER, V. H. Evaluation of a criterion: Realism of vocational choice. *Journal of Counseling Psychology,* 1966, **13**, 289–294.

HILDITCH, T. P. *A concise history of chemistry.* New York: Van Nostrand, 1911.

HILL, J. M. M., & TRIST, E. L. A consideration of industrial accidents as a means of withdrawal from the work situation. *Human Relations,* 1953, **6**, 357–380.

HILLS, J. R. Controlled association scores and engineering success. *Journal of Applied Psychology,* 1958, **42**, 10–13.

HILLS, J. R. Decision theory and college choice. *Personnel and Guidance Journal,* 1964, **43**, 17–22.

HILTON, T. L. Career decision-making. *Journal of Counseling Psychology,* 1962, **9**, 291–298.

HILTON, T. L., & DILL, W. R. Salary growth as a criterion of career progress. *Journal of Applied Psychology,* 1962, **46**, 153–158.

HIRT, M. Interests and aptitudes. *Vocational Guidance Quarterly,* 1959, **7**, 171–173.

HOLDFN, G. S. Scholastic aptitude and the relative persistence of vocational choice. *Personnel and Guidance Journal,* 1961, **40**, 36–41.

HOLLAND, J. L. A personality inventory employing occupational titles. *Journal of Applied Psychology,* 1958, **42**, 336–342.

HOLLAND, J. L. A theory of vocational choice. *Journal of Counseling Psychology,* 1959, **6**, 35–44.

HOLLAND, J. L. Some explorations with occupational titles. *Journal of Counseling Psychology,* 1961, **8**, 82–85.

HOLLAND, J. L. Some explorations of a theory of vocational choice: I. One and two-year longitudinal studies. *Psychological Monographs,* 1962, **76**, (26, Whole No. 545).

HOLLAND, J. L. Explorations of a theory of vocational choice and achievement: II. A four-year prediction study. *Psychological Reports,* 1963, **12**, 537–594 (a).

HOLLAND, J. L. Explorations of a theory of vocational choice. Part I: Vocational images and choice. *Vocational Guidance Quarterly,* 1963, **11**, 232–239. (b)

HOLLAND, J. L. Exploration of a theory of vocational choice. Part II: Self-descriptions and vocational preferences. *Vocational Guidance Quarterly,* 1963, **12**, 17–21. (c)

HOLLAND, J. L. Exploration of a theory of vocational choice. Part III: Coping behavior and vocational preferences. *Vocational Guidance Quarterly,* 1963, **12**, 21–24. (d)

HOLLAND, J. L. Explorations of a theory of vocational choice. Part IV: Vocational daydreams. *Vocational Guidance Quarterly,* 1963, **12**, 93–97. (e)

HOLLAND, J. L. *Explorations of a theory of vocational choice: V. A one-year prediction study.* Moravia, N.Y.: Chronicle, Guidance Professional Service, 1964. (a)

HOLLAND, J. L. Major programs of research of vocational behavior. In H. Borow (Ed.), *Man in a world at work.* Boston: Houghton Mifflin, 1964, Pp. 259–284. (b)

HOLLAND, J. L. A psychological classification scheme for vocations and major fields. *Journal of Counseling Psychology,* 1966, **13**, 278–288. (a)

HOLLAND, J. L. *The psychology of vocational choice: A theory of personality types and environmental models.* New York: Ginn, 1966. (b)

HOLLAND, J. L., KRAUSE, A. H., NIXON, M., & TREMBOTH, M. F. The classification of occupations by means of Kuder interest profiles: I. The development of interest groups. *Journal of Applied Psychology,* 1953, **37**, 263–269.

HOLLAND, J. L., & NICHOLS, R. C. The development and validation of an indecision scale: The natural history of a problem in basic research. *Journal of Counseling Psychology,* 1964, **11**, 27–34. (a)

HOLLAND, J. L., & NICHOLS, R. C. Explorations of a theory of vocational choice: III. A longitudinal study of change in major field of study. *Personnel and Guidance Journal,* 1964, **43**, 235–242. (b)

HOLLINGSHEAD, A. B. *Elmtown's youth.* New York: Wiley, 1949.

HOLLINGWORTH, H. L. *Vocational psychology and character analysis.* New York: Appleton, 1931.

HOMANS, G. C. The Western Electric researches. In S. D. Hoslett (Ed.), *Human factors in management.* New York: Harper & Row, 1951. Pp. 210–240.

HOPPOCK, R. Occupational ability patterns. *Occupations,* 1934, **12**, 47–48.

HOPPOCK, R. Comparisons of satisfied and dissatisfied teachers. *Psychological Bulletin,* 1935, **32**, 681. (a)

HOPPOCK, R. *Job satisfaction.* New York: Harper & Row, 1935. (b)

HOPPOCK, R. Age and job satisfaction. *Psychological Monographs,* 1936, **47**, No. 212.

HOPPOCK, R. Job satisfaction of psychologists. *Journal of Applied Psychology,* 1937, **21**, 300–303.

HOPPOCK, R. *Occupational information.* New York: McGraw-Hill, 1957.

HOPPOCK, R. A twenty-seven year follow-up on job satisfaction of employed adults. *Personnel and Guidance Journal,* 1960, **38**, 489–492.

HOPPOCK, R. *Occupational information.* (2nd ed.) New York: McGraw-Hill, 1963.

HOPPOCK, R., & HAND, T. J. Job satisfaction researches of 1942–1943. *Occupations,* 1945, **23**, 412–415.

HOPPOCK, R., & ODOM, C. L. Job satisfaction: Researches and opinions of 1938–1939. *Occupations,* 1940, **19**, 25–28.

HOPPOCK, R., & ROBINSON, H. A. Job satisfaction researches of 1948. *Occupations,* 1949, **28**, 153–161.

HOPPOCK, R., & ROBINSON, H. A. Job satisfaction researches of 1949. *Occupations,* 1950, **29**, 13–18.

HOPPOCK, R., & ROBINSON, H. A. Job satisfaction researches of 1950. *Occupations,* 1951, **29**, 572–578.

HOPPOCK, R., ROBINSON, H. A., & ZLATCHIN, P. J. Job satisfaction researches of 1946–1947. *Occupations,* 1948, **27**, 167–175.

HOPPOCK, R., & SHAFFER, R. H. Job satisfaction: Researches and opinions of 1940–1941. *Occupations,* 1943, **21**, 457–463.

HOPPOCK, R., & SPIEGLER, S. Job satisfaction: Researches of 1935–1937. *Occupations,* 1938, **16**, 636–643.

HOPPOCK, R., & SUPER, D. E. Vocational and educational satisfaction. In D. H. Fryer, & E. R. Henry, (Eds.) *Handbook of applied psychology.* New York: Rinehart, 1950. Vol. I. Pp. 126–134.

HORNEY, K. *The neurotic personality of our time.* New York: Norton, 1937.

HORNEY, K. Inhibitions in work. *American Journal of Psychoanalysis,* 1947, **7**, 18–25.

HORNEY, K. *Neurosis and human growth.* New York: Norton, 1950.

HORST, P. Obtaining a composite measure from different measures of the same attribute. *Psychometrika,* 1936, **1**, 53–60.

HOTELLING, H. The most predictable criterion. *Journal of Educational Psychology,* 1935, 26, 139–142.

HOWSON, J. D. Intellectual impairment associated with brain-impaired patients as revealed by the Shaw Test of Abstract Thought. *Canadian Journal of Psychology,* 1948, **2**, 125–133.

HOYT, D. P. *The relationship between college grades and adult achievement: A review of the literature.* Iowa City, Iowa: American College Testing Program, ACT Research Reports, September, 1965, No. 7.

HOYT, D. P., & NORMAN, W. T. Adjustment and academic predictability. *Journal of Counseling Psychology,* 1954, **1**, 96–99.

HOYT, K. B. The specialty oriented student: A challenge to vocational guidance. *Vocational Guidance Quarterly,* 1963, **11**, 192–198.

HOYT, K. B. High school guidance and the Specialty Oriented Student research program. *Vocational Guidance Quarterly,* 1965, **13**, 229–236.

HSU, F. L. K. Incentives to work in primitive communities. *American Sociological Review,* 1943, **8**, 638–642.

HUBBARD, H. G. Career choices of successful business executives. *Personnel and Guidance Journal,* 1965, **44**, 147–152.

HUGHES, E. C. *Men and their work.* Glencoe, Ill.: Free Press, 1958.

HULIN, C. L. The measurement of executive success. *Journal of Applied Psychology,* 1962, **46**, 303–306.

HULIN, C. L. A second look at the motivation of industrial supervisors. *Personnel Psychology,* 1963, **16**, 249–254.

HULIN, C. L., & SMITH, P. C. A linear model of job satisfaction. *Journal of Applied Psychology,* 1965, **49**, 209–216.

HULL, C. L. *Aptitude testing.* New York: World, 1928.

HULL, C. L., HOVLAND, C. I., ROSS, R. T., HALL, M., PERKINS, D. T., & FITCH, F. B. *Mathematico-deductive theory of role learning.* New Haven: Yale University Press, 1940.

HULL, R. L., & KOLSTAD, A. Morale on the job. In G. Watson (Ed.), *Civilian morale.* Boston: Houghton Mifflin, 1942. Pp. 349–364.

HUNT, E. G., & SMITH, G. Vocational psychology and choice of employment. *Occupational Psychology,* 1945, **19**, 109–116.

HUNT, E. P., & SMITH, P. Vocational guidance research: Ten years work by the Birmingham Education Committee. *Occupational Psychology,* 1938, **12**, 302–307.

HUNT, H. C. Why people lose their jobs or aren't promoted. *Personnel Journal,* 1936, **14**, 227.

HURLOCK, E. G., & JANSING, C. The vocational attitudes of boys and girls of high-school age. *Journal of Genetic Psychology,* 1934, **44**, 175–191.

HUTSON, P. W. Vocational choices: 1930 and 1961. *Vocational Guidance Quarterly,* 1962, **10**, 218–222.

HYTE, C. Occupational interests of Negro high school boys. *School Review,* 1936, **44**, 34–40.

ICHEISER, G. On certain conflicts in occupational life. *Occupational Psychology,* 1940, **14**, 107–111.

INKELES, A., & ROSSI, P. H. National comparisons of occupational prestige. *American Journal of Sociology,* 1956, **61**, 329–339.

INLOW, G. M. Job satisfaction of liberal arts graduates. *Journal of Applied Psychology,* 1951, **35**, 175–181.

IVEY, A. E. Interests and work values. *Vocational Guidance Quarterly,* 1963, **11**, 121–128.

JACKSON, J. M. A simple and more rigorous technique for scale analysis. In *A manual for scale analysis.* Part II. Montreal: McGill University, 1949. (Mimeographed)

JACOBS, R., & TRAXLER, A. E. Use of the Kuder in counseling with regard to accounting as a career. *Journal of Counseling Psychology,* 1954, **1**, 153–158.

JACOBSON, F. N., RETTIG, S., & PASAMANICK, B. Status, job satisfaction, and factors of job satisfaction of state institution and clinic psychologists. *American Psychologist,* 1959, **14**, 144–150.

JAMES, F., III. Comment on Hilton's model of career decision-making. *Journal of Counseling Psychology,* 1963, **10**, 303–304.

JAMES, F., III. Occupational choice and attitude change. *Journal of Counseling Psychology,* 1965, **12**, 311–315.

JAQUES, E., & CROOK, I. The personality make-up of emotionally unstable soldiers in relation to occupational adjustments. *Journal of Clinical Psychology,* 1946, **2**, 221–230.

JAY, R., & COPES, J. Seniority and criterion measures of job proficiency. *Journal of Applied Psychology,* 1957, **41**, 58–60.

JENNINGS, J. R., & STOTT, M. B. A fourth follow-up of vocationally advised cases. *Human Factor,* 1936, **10**, 165–174.

JENSEN, B. T., COLES, G., & NESTOR, B. The criterion problem in guidance research. *Journal of Counseling Psychology,* 1955, **2**, 58–61.

JENSON, P. G., & KIRCHNER, W. K. A national answer to the question, "Do sons follow their fathers' occupations?" *Journal of Applied Psychology,* 1955, **39**, 419–421.

JERSILD, A. T. *Child development and the curriculum.* New York: Teachers College Bureau of Publications, 1946.

JOHNSON, D. M. *The psychology of thought and judgment.* New York: Harper & Row, 1955.

JOHNSON, G. H. An instrument for the measurement of job satisfaction. *Personnel Psychology,* 1955, **8**, 27–37.

JOHNSON, H. M. On verifying hypotheses by verifying their implicates. *American Journal of Psychology,* 1954, **67**, 723–727.

JOHNSON, R. W. Number of interviews, diagnosis and success of counseling. *Journal of Counseling Psychology,* 1965, **12**, 248–251.

JONES, E. S. Relation of ability to preferred and probable occupation. *Educational Administrative Supervisor,* 1940, **26**, 220–226.

JONES, K. J. Occupational preference and social orientation. *Personnel and Guidance Journal,* 1965, **43**, 574–579.

JURGENSEN, C. E. What job applicants look for in a company. *Personnel Psychology,* 1948, **1**, 433–445.

JURGENSEN, C. E. Overall job success as a basis for employee ratings. *Journal of Applied Psychology,* 1950, **34**, 333–337.

KAHL, J. A. Educational and occupational aspirations of "common man" boys. *Harvard Educational Review,* 1953, **23**, 186–203.

KAHN, R. L. Productivity and job satisfaction. *Personnel Psychology,* 1960, **13**, 275–287.

KAHN, R. L. Job factors, attitudes, and effects. *Contemporary Psychology,* 1961, **6**, 9–10.

KAHNEMAN, D., & GHISELLI, E. E. Validity and nonlinear heteroscedastic models. *Personnel Psychology,* 1962, **15**, 1–11.

KAHOE, R. D. Motivation-hygiene aspects of vocational indecision and college achievement. *Personnel and Guidance Journal,* 1966, **44**, 1030–1036.

KAISER, H. F. The application of electronic computers to factor analysis. *Educational and Psychological Measurement,* 1960, **20**, 141–151.

KAPLAN, O. Age and vocational choice. *Journal of Genetic Psychology,* 1946, **68**, 131–134.

KATES, S. L. Rorschach responses related to vocational interests and job satisfaction. *Psychological Monographs,* 1950, **64** (3, Whole No. 309). (a)

KATES, S. L. Rorschach responses, Strong Blank scales and job satisfaction among policemen. *Journal of Applied Psychology,* 1950, **34**, 249–254. (b)

KATZ, D. Survey Research Center: An overview of the human relations program. In H. Guetzleow (Ed.), *Groups, leadership, and men.* Pittsburgh: Carnegie Press, 1951. Pp. 68–85.

KATZ, D., & KAHN, R. L. Some recent findings in human relations research in industry. In G. E. Swanson, T. M. Newcomb, & E. L. Hartley (Eds.), *Readings in social psychology.* New York: Holt, 1952. Pp. 650–665.

KATZ, M. *Decisions and values: A rationale for secondary school guidance.* New York: College Entrance Examination Board, 1963.

KATZ, M. A model of guidance for career decision-making. *Vocational Guidance Quarterly,* 1966, **15**, 2–10.

KATZELL, R. A. Industrial psychology. In *Annual review of psychology.* Palo Alto: Annual Reviews, 1957. Pp. 243–244.

KATZELL, R. A. Personal values, job satisfaction, and job behavior. In H. Borow (Ed.), *Man in a world at work*. Boston: Houghton Mifflin, 1964. Pp. 341–363.

KATZELL, R. A., BARRETT, R. S., & PARKER, T. C. Job satisfaction, job performance, and situational characteristics. *Journal of Applied Psychology,* 1961, **45**, 65–72.

KEFAUVER, G. N., NOLL, V. H., & DRAKE, C. E. *The secondary-school population,* Monograph No. 4, National Survey of Secondary Education. Washington, D.C.: Office of the Commissioner of Education, 1932.

KELLEY, T. L. *Crossroads in the mind of man*. Palo Alto: Stanford University Press, 1928.

KELLEY, T. L. *Talents and tasks*. Harvard Education Papers, No. 1, July, 1940.

KELLY, E. L., & FISKE, D. W. The prediction of success in the V.A. training program in clinical psychology. *American Psychologist,* 1950, **5**, 395–406.

KELLY, E. L., & FISKE, D. W. *The prediction of performance in clinical psychology*. Ann Arbor, Mich.: University of Michigan Press, 1951.

KELLY, E. L., & GOLDBERG, L. R. Correlates of later performance and specialization in psychology. *Psychological Monographs,* 1959, **73** (12, Whole No. 482).

KELLY, G. A. *The psychology of personal constructs*. New York: Norton, 1955.

KELSO, D. F. A study of occupational stereotypes reflected in the Strong Interest test. Master's thesis, State College of Washington, 1948.

KENDALL, L. M., SMITH, P. C., HULIN, C. L., & LOCKE, E. A. Cornell studies of job satisfaction: IV. The relative validity of the Job Descriptive Index and other methods of measurement of job satisfaction. Unpublished manuscript, Cornell University, 1963.

KENDALL, W. E. The occupational level key of the Strong Vocational Interest Blank for Men. *Journal of Applied Psychology,* 1947, **31**, 283–287.

KERR, W. A. Summary of validity studies of the Tear Ballot. *Personnel Psychology,* 1952, **5**, 105–113.

KERR, W. A., NEWMAN, H. L., & SADEWIC, A. R. Lifetime worry patterns of American psychologists. *Journal of Consulting Psychology,* 1949, **8**, 377–380.

KERR, W. D., & WILLIS, W. K. Interest and ability: Are they related? *Vocational Guidance Quarterly,* 1966, **15**, 197–200.

KESSLER, M. S. Job satisfaction of veterans rehabilitated under Public Law 16. *Personnel and Guidance Journal,* 1954, **33**, 78–81.

KIBRICK, A. K., & TIEDEMAN, D. V. Conception of self and perception of role in schools of nursing. *Journal of Counseling Psychology,* 1961, **8**, 62–69.

KILBRIDGE, M. O. Turnover, absence, and transfer rates as indicators of employee dissatisfaction with repetitive work. *Industrial and Labor Relations Review,* 1961, **15**, 21–32.

KILZER, L. R. Vocational choices of high school seniors. *Educational Administration and Supervisors,* 1935, **21**, 576–581.

KING, H. F. An attempt to use production data in the study of age and performance. *Journal of Gerontology,* 1956, **11**, 410–416.

KINNANE, J. F., & BANNON, M. M. Perceived parental influence and work-value orientation. *Personnel and Guidance Journal,* 1964, **43**, 273–279.

KINNANE, J. F., & GAUBINGER, J. R. Life values and work values. *Journal of Counseling Psychology,* 1963, **10**, 362–366.

KINNANE, J. F., & PABLE, M. W. Family background and work value orientation. *Journal of Counseling Psychology,* 1962, **9**, 320–325.

KINNANE, J. F., & SUZIEDELIS, A. Work value orientation and inventoried interests. *Journal of Counseling Psychology,* 1962, **9**, 144–148.

KIRCHNER, W. K. Critique of Oberg's "Age and achievement—and the technical man." *Personnel Psychology,* 1961, **14**, 53–58.

KIRCHNER, W. K. Relationships between general and specific attitudes toward work and objective job performance for outdoor advertising salesmen. *Journal of Applied Psychology,* 1965, **49**, 455–457.

KIRCHNER, W. K., & DUNNETTE, M. D. Attitudes toward older workers. *Personnel Psychology,* 1954, **7**, 257–265.

KIRCHNER, W. K., LINBAM, T. L., & PATERSON, D. G. Attitudes toward the employment of older people. *Journal of Applied Psychology,* 1952, **36**, 154–156.

KIRCHNER, W. K., MC ELWAIN, C. S., & DUNNETTE, M. D. A note on the relationship between age and sales effectiveness. *Journal of Applied Psychology,* 1960, **44**, 92–93.

KIRK, B. A. Classifying the literature in counseling psychology. *Journal of Counseling Psychology,* 1958, **5**, 89–97.

KITSON, H. D. *The psychology of vocational adjustment.* Philadelphia: Lippincott, 1925.

KITSON, H. D. Can we predict vocational success? *Occupations,* 1948, **26**, 539–541.

KITSON, H. D. Review of Ginzberg, E., Ginsburg, S. W., Axelrad, S. & Herma, J. L., *Occupational choice: An approach to a general theory. Personnel and Guidance Journal,* 1951, **29**, 611–613.

KITSON, H. D. Psychology in vocational adjustment. *Personnel and Guidance Journal,* 1958, **36**, 314–319.

KLEIN, S. M., & MAHER, J. R. Education level and satisfaction with pay. *Personnel Psychology,* 1966, **19**, 195–208.

KLEINMUNTZ, B. (Ed.) *Problem solving.* New York: Wiley, 1966.

KLINE, M. V., & SCHNECK, J. M. An hypnotic experimental approach to the genesis of occupational interests and choice. *British Journal of Medical Hypnotism,* 1950, **1**, 2–11.

KLOPFER, B., AINSWORTH, M. D., KLOPFER, W. G., & HOLT, R. R. *Developments in the Rorschach Technique. Vol. I. Theory and technique.* New York: World, 1954.

KLOPFER, B., & KELLEY, D. M. *The Rorschach Technique.* Yonkers-on-Hudson, New York: World, 1942.

KLUCKHOHN, F. R. Dominant and variant value orientations. In C. Kluckhohn & H. A. Murray (Eds.), *Personality in nature, society, and culture.* (2nd ed.) New York: Knopf, 1953. Pp. 342–357.

KNAUFT, E. B. Vocational interests and managerial success. *Journal of Applied Psychology,* 1951, **35**, 160–163.

KOHN, N., JR. Trends and development of the vocational and other interests of veterans at Washington University. *Educational and Psychological Measurement,* 1947, **7**, 631–637.

KOHOUT, V. A., & ROTHNEY, J. W. M. A longitudinal study of consistency of vocational preferences. *American Educational Research Journal,* 1964, **1**, 10–21.

KOPP, T., & TUSSING, L. The vocational choices of high school students as related to scores on vocational interest inventories. *Occupations,* 1947, **25**, 334–339.

KORMAN, A. K. Self-esteem variable in vocational choice. *Journal of Applied Psychology,* 1966, **50**, 479–486.

KORNER, A. G. Origin of impractical or unrealistic vocational goals. *Journal of Consulting Psychology,* 1946, **10**, 328–334.

KORNHAUSER, A. Mental health of factory workers. *Human Organization,* 1962, **21**, 43–47.

KORNHAUSER, A. *Mental health of the industrial worker: A Detroit study.* New York: Wiley, 1965.

KOUBLE, C. E., & ROTHNEY, S. W. M. A follow-up study of machinist journeymen. *Personnel and Guidance Journal,* 1956, **35**, 24–29.

KOYAMA, Y. The mobility of occupations. *Research Bulletin of the Takaoka Community College,* 1931, No. 3, 203–243.

KRIESBERG, L. The retail furrier: Concepts of security and success. *American Journal of Sociology,* 1952, **57**, 478–485.

KRIESBERG, L. The bases of occupational prestige: The case of dentists. *American Sociological Review,* 1962, **27**, 238–244.

KRIPPNER, S. The occupational experiences and vocational preferences of 351 upper middle class junior high school pupils. *Vocational Guidance Quarterly,* 1962, **10**, 167–170.

KRIPPNER, S. Junior high school students' vocational preferences and their parents' occupational levels. *Personnel and Guidance Journal,* 1963, **41**, 590–595.

KROGER, R., & LOUTTIT, C. The influence of father's occupation on the vocational choices of high school boys. *Journal of Applied Psychology,* 1935, **19**, 203–212.

KUDER, G. F. Manual for the *Kuder Preference Record—Vocational.* Chicago: Science Research Associates, 1960.

KUHLEN, R. G. *Psychology of adolescent development.* New York: Harper & Row, 1952.

KUHLEN, R. G. Needs, perceived need satisfaction opportunities, and satisfaction with occupation. *Journal of Applied Psychology,* 1963, **47**, 56–64.

KUHLEN, R. G., & JOHNSON, G. H. Changes in goals with increasing adult age. *Journal of Consulting Psychology,* 1952, **16**, 1–4.

KUNDE, T. A., & DAWIS, R. V. Comparative study of occupational prestige in three Western cultures. *Personnel and Guidance Journal,* 1959, **37**, 350–352.

KURTZ, A. B. The simultaneous prediction of a number of criteria by use of a unique set of weights. *Psychometrika,* 1937, **2**, 95–101.

LAMOURIA, L. H., & HARRELL, T. W. An approach to an objective criterion for research managers. *Journal of Applied Psychology,* 1963, **47**, 353–357.

LAMPMAN, R. J. On choice in labor markets. *Industrial Labor Relations Review,* 1956, **9**, 629–636.

LANDIS, C., & PHELPS, L. W. The prediction from photographs of success and of vocational aptitude. *Journal of Experimental Psychology,* 1928, **11**, 313–324.

LATHAM, A. J. Job appropriateness: A one-year follow-up of high school graduates. *Journal of Social Psychology,* 1951, **34**, 55–68.

LAWLER, E. E., III. Ability as a moderator of the relationship between job attitudes and job performance. *Personnel Psychology,* 1966, **19**, 153–164.

LAWRENCE, P. F. Vocational aspirations of Negro youth in California. *Journal of Negro Education,* 1950, **19**, 47–56.

LAYTON, W. L. (Ed.) *The Strong Vocational Interest Blank: Research and uses.* Minneapolis: University of Minnesota Press, 1960.

LAZARSFELD, P. F. *Jugend and beruf.* Jena, Austria: G. Fischer, 1931.

LAZARSFELD, P. F., & GAUDET, H. Who gets a job? *Sociometry,* 1941, 4, 64–77.

LEE, M. C. Interactions, configurations, and nonadditive models. *Educational and Psychological Measurement,* 1961, **21**, 797–805.

LEHMAN, H. C. *Age and achievement.* Princeton, N.J.: Princeton University Press, 1953.

LEHMAN, H. C. Reply to Dennis' critique of *Age and achievement. Journal of Gerontology,* 1956, **11**, 333–337.

LEHMAN, H. C. The influence of longevity upon curves showing man's creative production rate at successive age Levels. *Journal of Gerontology,* 1958, **13**, 187–191.

LEHMAN, H. C. The age decrement in outstanding scientific creativity. *American Psychologist,* 1960, **15**, 128–134.

LEHMAN, H. C. The creative production rates of present versus past generations of scientists. *Journal of Gerontology,* 1962, **17**, 409–417. (a)

LEHMAN, H. C. More about age and achievement. *Gerontologist,* 1962, **2**, 141–148. (b)

LEHMAN, H. C. The psychologist's most creative years. *American Psychologist,* 1966, **21**, 363–369.

LEHMAN, H. C., & WITTY, P. A. Constancy of vocational interest. *Personnel Journal,* 1929, **8**, 153–165.

LEHMAN, H. C., & WITTY, P. A. Further study of the social status of occupations. *Journal of Educational Sociology,* 1931, **5**, 101–112. (a)

LEHMAN, H. C., & WITTY, P. A. One more study of permanence of interest. *Journal of Educational Psychology,* 1931, **22**, 481–492. (b)

LEHMAN, H. C., & WITTY, P. A. A study of vocational attitudes in relation to pubescence. *American Journal of Psychology,* 1931, **43**, 93–101. (c)

LESTER, R. A. Comment. *Industrial Labor Relations Review,* 1956, **9**, 641–642.

LEVIN, M. M. Status anxiety and occupational choice. *Educational and Psychological Measurement,* 1949, **9**, 29–38.

LEVY, L. H. *Psychological interpretation,* New York: Holt, 1963.

LEWIN, K. *A dynamic theory of personality.* New York: McGraw-Hill, 1935.

LEWIN, K. Psychology of success and failure. In R. Hoppock (Ed.), *Criteria of vocational success.* New York: National Occupational Conference, 1936. Pp. 926–930.

LEWIS, D. *Quantitative methods in psychology.* New York: McGraw-Hill, 1960.

LINDQUIST, E. F. *Design and analysis of experiments in psychology and education.* Boston: Houghton Mifflin, 1953.

LINK, H. C. Limiting the problem. In R. Hoppock (Ed.), *Criteria of vocational success.* New York: National Occupational Conference, 1936. Pp. 933–935.

LIPSET, S. M., BENDIX, R., & MALM, F. T. Job plans and entry into the labor market. In Nosow, S., & Form, W. H. (Eds.), *Man, work, and society.* New York: Basic Books, 1962. Pp. 297–306.

LIPSETT, L. Social factors in vocational development. *Personnel and Guidance Journal,* 1962, **40**, 432–437.

LIPSETT, L., & WILSON, J. W. Do "suitable" interests and mental ability lead to job satisfaction? *Educational and Psychological Measurement,* 1954, **14**, 373–380.

LO CASCIO, R. Delayed and impaired vocational development: A neglected aspect of vocational development theory. *Personnel and Guidance Journal,* 1964, **42**, 885–887.

LOCKE, E. A. The relationship of task success to task liking and satisfaction. *Journal of Applied Psychology,* 1965, **49**, 379–385.

LOCKE, E. A., SMITH, P. C., HULIN, C. L., & KENDALL, L. M. Cornell studies of job satisfaction: V. Scale characteristics of the Job Descriptive Index. Unpublished manuscript, Cornell University, 1963.

LOCKE, E. A., SMITH, P. C., KENDALL, L. M., HULIN, C. L., & MILLER, A. M. Convergent and discriminant validity for areas and methods of rating job satisfaction. *Journal of Applied Psychology,* 1964, **48**, 313–319.

LOCKWOOD, W. V. Realism of Vocational Preference. *Personnel and Guidance Journal,* 1958, **37**, 98–106.

LODAHL, T. M. Patterns of job attitudes in two assembly technologies. *Administrative Science Quarterly,* 1964, **8**, 482–519.

LODAHL, T. M., & KEJNER, M. The definition and measurement of job involvement. *Journal of Applied Psychology,* 1965, **49**, 24–33.

LOHNES, P. R. Markov models for human development research. *Journal of Counseling Psychology,* 1965, **12**, 322–327.

LONG, W. F. A job preference survey for industrial applicants. *Journal of Applied Psychology,* 1952, **36**, 333–337.

LORGE, I. Criteria for guidance. In R. Hoppock (Ed.), *Criteria of vocational success.* New York: National Occupational Conference, 1936. Pp. 958–962.

LORGE, I., & BLAU, R. Broad occupational groupings by intelligence levels. *Occupations,* 1942, **20**, 419–423.

LURIE, W. A. A study of Spranger's value-types by the method of factor analysis. *Journal of Social Psychology,* 1937, **8**, 17–37.

LURIE, W. A. Estimating the level of vocational aspiration. *Journal of Social Psychology,* 1939, **10**, 467–473.

LURIE, W. A. The concept of occupational adjustment. *Educational and Psychological Measurement,* 1942, **2**, 3–14.

LURIE, W. A. Character formation and vocational needs. *Jewish Social Service Quarterly,* 1954, **30**, 363–372.

LURIE, W. A., & WEISS, A. Analyzing vocational adjustment. *Occupations,* 1942, **21**, 138–142.

LYON, R. Beyond the conventional career: Some speculations. *Journal of Counseling Psychology,* 1965, **12**, 153–158.

MAC CORQUODALE, K., & MEEHL, P. E. On a distinction between hypothetical constructs and intervening variables. *Psychological Review,* 1948, **55**, 95–107.

MACK, R. W., MURPHY, R. J., & YELLIN, S. The Protestant ethic, level of aspiration, and social mobility: An empirical test. *American Sociological Review,* 1956, **21**, 295–300.

MACKAYE, D. L. The fixation of vocational interest. *American Journal of Sociology,* 1927, **33**, 353–370.

MACRAE, A. A target for critics. *Occupations,* 1934, **13**, 21–29.

MACRAE, A., JENNINGS, J. R., & STOTT, M. B. A follow-up of vocationally advised cases. *Human Factor,* 1937, **11**, 16–26.

MAHER, H. Age and performance of two work groups. *Journal of Gerontology,* 1955, **10**, 448–451.

MAHONE, C. H. Fear of failure and unrealistic vocational aspirations. *Journal of Abnormal and Social Psychology,* 1960, **60**, 253–261.

MAIER, N. R. F. *Psychology in industry.* (2nd ed.) Boston: Houghton Mifflin, 1955.

MALLINSON, G. G., & CRUMRINE, W. M. An investigation of the stability of interests of high school students. *Journal of Educational Research,* 1952, **45**, 369–383.

MALINOVSKY, M. R., & BARRY, J. R. Determinants of work attitudes. *Journal of Applied Psychology,* 1965, **49**, 446–451.

MANN, F. C. A study of work satisfaction as a function of the discrepancy between inferred aspirations and achievement. (Doctoral dissertation, University of Michigan) Ann Arbor, Mich.: University Microfilms, 1953. No. 5701.

MANN, F. C., & HOFFMAN, L. R. *Automation and the worker.* New York: Holt, 1960.

Manual for the Differential Aptitude Tests. New York: The Psychological Corporation, 1966.

MARGENAU, H. *The nature of physical reality.* New York: McGraw-Hill, 1950.

MARK, J. A. Measurement of job performance and age. *Monthly Labor Review,* December, 1956, **79**, 1410–1414.

MARLOWE, M., & BARBER, L. The effect of psychological handicap in two factory groups. *British Journal of Industrial Medicine,* 1952, **9**, 221–226.

MARLOWE, M., & BARBER, L. Psychological handicap in relation to productivity and occupational adjustment. *British Journal of Industrial Medicine,* 1953, **10**, 125–131.

MARR, E. Some behaviors and attitudes relating

to vocational choice. *Journal of Counseling Psychology,* 1965, **12**, 404–408.

MARRIOTT, R., & DENERLEY, R. A. A method of interviewing used in studies of workers' attitudes: I. Effectiveness of the questions and of interviewer control. *Occupational Psychology,* 1955, **29**, 1–14. (a)

MARRIOTT, R., & DENERLEY, R. A. A method of interviewing used in studies of workers' attitudes: II. Validity of the method and discussion of the results. *Occupational Psychology,* 1955, **29**, 69–81. (b)

MARX, K. Estranged labour. In C. W. Mills (Ed.), *Images of man.* New York: Braziller, 1960. Pp. 496–507.

MARX, M. H. (Ed.) *Psychological theory.* New York: Macmillan, 1951.

MARX, M. H. (Ed.) *Theories in contemporary psychology.* New York: Macmillan, 1963.

MASLOW, A. H. *Motivation and personality.* New York: Harper & Row, 1954.

MASON, W. S., & GROSS, N. Intra-occupational prestige differentiation: The school superintendency. *American Sociological Review,* 1955, **20**, 326–331.

MATHEWSON, R. H., & ORTON, J. W. Vocational imagery and vocational maturity of high school students. *Journal of Counseling Psychology,* 1963, **10**, 384–388.

MCARTHUR, C., & STEVENS, L. B. The validation of expressed interests as compared with inventoried interests: A fourteen-year follow-up. *Journal of Applied Psychology,* 1955, **39**, 184–189.

MCCABE, S. P. Occupational stereotypes as studied by the Semantic Differential. *American Psychologist,* 1960, **15**, 454.

MCCLELLAND, D. C. *The achieving society.* Princeton: Van Nostrand, 1961.

MCCLELLAND, D. C., ATKINSON, J. W., CLARK, R. A., & LOWELL, B. L. *The achievement motive.* New York: Appleton-Century-Crofts, 1953.

MCCORMACK, T. H. The druggists' dilemma: Problems of a marginal occupation. *American Journal of Sociology,* 1956, **61**, 308–315.

MCCORMICK, E. J., FINN, R. H., & SCHEIPS, C. O. Patterns of job requirements. *Journal of Applied Psychology,* 1957, **41**, 358–364.

MCGILL, K. H. The school-teacher stereotype. *Journal of Education and Sociology,* 1931, **4**, 642–650.

MCGUIRE, C., & BLOCKSMA, D. D. The background of vocational choice. *Research paper in human development,* No. 10. Austin, Texas: Department of Educational Psychology, University of Texas, 1953.

MCNAUGHTON, W. L. Attitudes of ex-employees at intervals after quitting. *Personnel Journal,* 1956, **35**, 61–63.

MCNEMAR, Q. *Psychological statistics.* (2nd ed.) New York: Wiley, 1955.

MCQUEEN, L. J., & TYLER, L. E. Standardization of the Tyler Choice Pattern Test for use with high school students. *American Psychologist,* 1961, **16**, 371.

MCQUITTY, L. L., WRIGLEY, C., & GAIER, E. L. An approach to isolating dimensions of job success. *Journal of Applied Psychology,* 1954, **38**, 227–232.

MEAD, G. H. *Mind, self, and society.* Chicago: University of Chicago Press, 1934.

MEAD, M., & METRAUX, R. Image of the scientist among high school students. *Science,* 1957, **126**, 384–390.

MEADOW, L. Toward a theory of vocational choice. *Journal of Counseling Psychology,* 1955, **2**, 108–112.

MEHENTI, P. M. Agreement between vocational preference and inventoried interest in relation to some presumed indices of vocational maturity. (Doctoral dissertation, Columbia University) Ann Arbor, Mich.: University Microfilms, 1954. No. 8732.

MELCHER, R. D. Getting the facts on employee resignations—an exit interview program. *Personnel,* 1955, **31**, 504–514.

MELTON, A. W. Learning. In W. S. Monroe (Ed.), *Encyclopedia of educational research.* New York: Macmillan, 1941. Pp. 667–686.

MELTZER, H. Frustration, expectation and production in industry. *American Journal of Orthopsychiatry,* 1945, **15**, 329–342.

MELTZER, H. Personality problems in managerial groups. *Industrial Medicine,* 1946, **15**, 429–434.

MELTZER, H. Age differences in work attitudes. *Journal of Gerontology,* 1958, **13**, 74–81.

MELTZER, H. Age differences in happiness and life adjustments of workers. *Journal of Gerontology,* 1963, **18**, 66–70.

MELTZER, L., & SALTER, J. Organization structure and the performance and job satisfaction of physiologists. *American Sociological Review,* 1962, **27**, 351–362.

MENGER, C. The social status of occupations for

women. *Teachers College Record,* 1932, **33,** 696–704.

MENNINGER, K. A. Work as a sublimation. *Bulletin of Menninger Clinic,* 1942, **6,** 170–182.

MENNINGER, W. C. Men, machines and mental health. *Mental Hygiene,* 1952, **36,** 184–196.

MERWIN, J. C., & D. VESTA, F. J. A study of need theory and career choice. *Journal of Counseling Psychology,* 1959, **6,** 302–308.

MIERZWA, J. A. Comparison of systems of data for predicting career choice. *Personnel and Guidance Journal,* 1963, **42,** 29–34.

MILLER, C. H. Age differences in occupational values of college men. *Journal of Counseling Psychology,* 1954, **1,** 190–192.

MILLER, C. H. Occupational choice and values. *Personnel and Guidance Journal,* 1956, **35,** 244–246.

MILLER, D. C. Industry and the worker. In H. Borow (Ed.), *Man in a world at work.* Boston: Houghton Mifflin, 1964. Pp. 96–124.

MILLER, D. C., & FORM, W. H. Measuring patterns of occupational security. *Sociometry,* 1947, **10,** 362–375.

MILLER, D. C., & FORM, W. H. *Industrial sociology.* New York: Harper & Row, 1951.

MILLER, D. C., & FORM, W. H. *Industrial sociology.* (2nd ed.) New York: Harper & Row, 1964.

MILLER, I. W., & HALLER, A. O. A measure of level of occupational aspiration. *Personnel and Guidance Journal,* 1964, **42,** 448–455.

MILLER, L. A., & MUTHARD, J. E. Job satisfaction and counselor performance in state rehabilitation agencies. *Journal of Applied Psychology,* 1965, **49,** 280–283.

MILLER, N. E. Psychological research on pilot training. Washington, D.C.: U.S. Government Printing Office, 1947. (*AAF Aviation Psychology Program Research Report* No. 8)

MILLIKEN, R. L. Realistic occupational appraisal by high school seniors. *Personnel and Guidance Journal,* 1962, **40,** 541–544.

MINER, J. B., & ANDERSON, J. K. The postwar occupational adjustment of emotionally disturbed soldiers. *Journal of Applied Psychology,* 1958, **42,** 317–322.

MINOR, C., & NEEL, R. G. The relationship between achievement motive and occupational preference. *Journal of Counseling Psychology,* 1958, **5,** 39–43.

MITCHELL, C. Pupils' vocational choices. *Vocational Guidance Magazine,* 1933, **11,** 363–367.

MOFFIE, D. J. The validity of self-estimated interests. *Journal of Applied Psychology,* 1942, **26,** 606–614.

MONTESANO, N., & GEIST, H. Differences in occupational choice between ninth and twelfth grade boys. *Personnel and Guidance Journal,* 1964, **43,** 150–154.

MOORE, H. Basic needs of industrial workers. *Personnel Journal,* 1949, **27,** 344–348.

MOORE, W. E. Current issues in industrial sociology. *American Sociological Review,* 1947, **12,** 651–657.

MOORE, W. E. Industrial sociology: status and prospects. *American Sociological Review,* 1948, **7,** 382–400.

MOORE, W. E. *Economy and society.* Random House, 1955.

MORE, O. M. A note on occupational origins of health service professions. *American Sociological Review,* 1960, **25,** 403–404.

MORRIS, J. L. Propensity for risk-taking as a determinant of vocational choice. *Journal of Personality and Social Psychology,* 1966, **3,** 328–335.

MORRISON, R. F., OWENS, W. A., GLENNON, J. R., & ALBRIGHT, L. E. Factored life history antecedents of industrial research performance. *Journal of Applied Psychology,* 1962, **46,** 281–284.

MORRISON, R. L. Self-concept implementation in occupational choices. *Journal of Counseling Psychology,* 1962, **9,** 255–260.

MORSE, N. C. *Satisfactions in the white-collar job.* Ann Arbor, Mich.: University of Michigan, 1953.

MOSEL, J. N., FINE, S. A., & BOLING, J. The scalability of estimated worker requirements. *Journal of Applied Psychology,* 1960, **44,** 156–160.

MOSER, H. P., DUBIN, W., & SHELSKY, I. A proposed modification of the Roe Occupation Classification. *Journal of Counseling Psychology,* 1956, **3,** 27–31.

MOSER, W. E. Vocational preference as related to mental ability. *Occupations,* 1949, **27,** 460–461.

MOWSESIAN, R., HEATH, B. R. G., & ROTHNEY, J. W. M. Superior students' occupational preferences and their fathers' occupations. *Personnel and Guidance Journal,* 1966, **45,** 238–242.

MUNROE, R. L. The Inspection Technique: A method of rapid evaluation of the Rorschach protocol. *Rorschach Research Exchange,* 1944, **8**, 46–69.

MUNSTERBERG, H. *Psychology and life.* Boston: Houghton Mifflin, 1899.

MUNSTERBERG, H. *Psychology and industrial efficiency.* Boston: Houghton Mifflin, 1913.

MURPHY, G. *Historical introduction to modern psychology.* New York: Harcourt, Brace & World, 1949.

MURRAY, H. A. *Explorations in personality.* New York: Oxford University Press, 1938.

MYERS, S. M. Who are your motivated workers? *Harvard Business Review,* 1964, **42**, 73–88.

MYERS, W. E. High school graduates choose vocations unrealistically. *Occupations,* 1947, **25**, 332–333.

NACHMANN, B. Childhood experience and vocational choice in law, dentistry, and social work. *Journal of Counseling Psychology,* 1960, **7**, 243–250.

NAGLE, B. F. Criterion development. *Personnel Psychology,* 1953, **6**, 271–289.

NATIONAL OPINION RESEARCH CENTER. Jobs and occupations: A popular evaluation. *Opinion News,* 1947, **9**, 3–13.

NEEL, R. G. Nervous stress in the industrial situation. *Personnel Psychology,* 1955, **8**, 405–415.

NEFF, W. S. Problems of work evaluation. *Personnel and Guidance Journal,* 1966, **44**, 682–688.

NEFF, W. S., & HELFAND, A. A Q-sort instrument to assess the meaning of work. *Journal of Counseling Psychology,* 1963, **10**, 139–145.

NEILSON, W. R. A study of the "painfully employed." Unpublished manuscript, University of Pittsburgh, 1951.

NELSON, A. G. Vocational maturity and client satisfaction. *Journal of Counseling Psychology,* 1956, **3**, 254–256.

NELSON, E. Fathers' occupations and student vocational choices. *School and Society,* 1939, **50**, 572–576.

NELSON, E., & NELSON, N. Students' attitudes and vocational choices. *Journal of Abnormal and Social Psychology,* 1940, **35**, 279–282.

NELSON, J. O. The source of eagerness in daily work. *Vocational Guidance Quarterly,* 1963, **11**, 162–166.

NELSON, R. C. Early versus developmental vocational choice. *Vocational Guidance Quarterly,* 1962, **11**, 23–30.

NELSON, R. C. Knowledge and interests concerning sixteen occupations among elementary and secondary school students. *Educational and Psychological Measurement,* 1963, **23**, 741–754.

NEVINS, C. I. An analysis of reasons for the success or failure of bookkeepers in sales companies. Master's thesis, University of Pittsburgh, 1949.

NEWMAN, J., & FINE, S. A. Validity of job descriptions for physical requirements and work condition information. *Personnel Psychology,* 1957, **10**, 181–189.

NICK, E. W. High school boys choose vocations. *Occupations,* 1942, **20**, 264–269.

NORRELL, G., & GRATER, H. Interest awareness as an aspect of self-awareness. *Journal of Counseling Psychology,* 1960, **7**, 289–292.

NORTON, J. L. Patterns of vocational interest development and actual job choice. *Journal of Genetic Psychology,* 1953, **82**, 235–262.

NORTON, J. L. A study of the "Estimates of Worker Trait Requirements." *Personnel and Guidance Journal,* 1962, **41**, 59–61.

NASOW, S., & FORM, W. H. (Eds.) *Man, work, and society.* New York: Basic Books, 1962.

OBERG, W. Age and achievement—and the technical man. *Personnel Psychology,* 1960, **13**, 245–259.

OBERNDORF, C. P. Psychopathology of work. *Bulletin of Menninger Clinic,* 1951, **15**, 77–84.

Occupational outlook handbook. Washington, D.C.: Government Printing Office, 1966.

O'CONNOR, J. P., & KINNANE, J. F. A factor analysis of work values. *Journal of Counseling Psychology,* 1961, **8**, 263–267.

ODELL, C. E. Productivity of the older worker. *Personnel and Guidance Journal,* 1958, **37**, 288–291.

O'HARA, R. P. Talk about self. The results of a pilot series of interviews in relation to Ginzberg's theory of occupational choice. Unpublished manuscript, Graduate School of Education, Harvard University, 1959.

O'HARA, R. P. Acceptance of vocational interest areas by high school students. *Vocational Guidance Quarterly,* 1962, **10**, 101–105.

O'HARA, R. P., & TIEDEMAN, D. V. Vocational self-concept in adolescence. *Journal of Counseling Psychology,* 1959, **6**, 292–301.

OLSHANSKY, S. S. The concept of success in our culture. *Personnel and Guidance Journal,* 1953, **32**, 355–356.

OPPENHEIMER, E. A. The relationship between certain self constructs and occupational preferences. *Journal of Counseling Psychology,* 1966, **13**, 191–197.

ORLANSKY, H. Infant care and personality. *Psychological Bulletin,* 1949, **46**, 1–48.

OSGOOD, C. E., & STAGNER, R. Analysis of a prestige frame of reference by a gradient technique. *Journal of Applied Psychology,* 1941, **25**, 275–290.

OSIPOW, S. H. Perceptions of occupations as a function of titles and descriptions. *Journal of Counseling Psychology,* 1962, **9**, 106–109.

OSIPOW, S. H. Consistency of occupational choices and Roe's classification of occupations. *Vocational Guidance Quarterly,* 1966, **15**, 285–286.

OSIPOW, S. H., ASHBY, J. D., & WALL, H. W. Personality types and vocational choice: A test of Holland's theory. *Personnel and Guidance Journal,* 1966, **45**, 37–42.

OSTROM, S. R. The OL key of the Strong Vocational Interest Blank for men and scholastic success at college freshmen level. *Journal of Applied Psychology,* 1949, **33**, 51–54. (a)

OSTROM, S. R. The OL key of the Strong test and drive at the twelfth grade level. *Journal of Applied Psychology,* 1949, **33**, 240–248. (b)

OTIS, J. L. The criterion. In W. H. Stead, et al., *Occupational counseling techniques.* New York: American Book, 1940. Pp. 73–94.

OTIS, J. L., & SMITH, K. R. Job psychographs in job analysis. *Occupations,* 1934, **12**, 47–54.

OVERS, R. P., & DEUTSCH, E. C. Sociological studies of occupations. *Personnel and Guidance Journal,* 1966, **44**, 711–714.

PACE, R. W. Oral communication and sales effectiveness. *Journal of Applied Psychology,* 1962, **46**, 321–324.

PAINE, F. T., CARROL, S. J., JR., & LEETE, B. A. Need satisfactions of managerial level personnel in a government agency. *Journal of Applied Psychology,* 1966, **50**, 247–249.

PALMER, D. L., PURPUS, E. R., & STOCKFORD, L. O. Why workers quit. *Personnel Journal,* 1944, **23**, 111–119.

PALMER, G. L. *Labor mobility in six cities.* New York: Social Science Research Council, 1954.

PANTON, J. H. MMPI code configurations as related to measures of intelligence among a state prison population. *Journal of Social Psychology,* 1960, **51**, 403–407.

PARNES, H. S. *Research on labor mobility.* New York: Social Science Research Council, 1954.

PARSONS, F. *Choosing a vocation.* Boston: Houghton Mifflin, 1909.

PATCHEN, M. The effect of reference group standards on job satisfactions. *Human Relations,* 1958, **11**, 303–314.

PATERSON, D. G. *Physique and intellect.* New York: Appleton-Century-Crofts, 1930.

PATERSON, D. G. A target for critics. *Occupations,* **13**, 1934, 18–21.

PATERSON, D. G. Vocational interest inventories in selection. *Occupations,* 1946, **25**, 152–153.

PATERSON, D. G., & DARLEY, J. G. *Men, women, and jobs.* Minneapolis: University of Minnesota Press, 1936.

PATERSON, D. G., GERKEN, C. D'A., & HAHN, M. E. *The Minnesota Occupational Rating Scales.* Chicago: Science Research Associates, 1941.

PATERSON, D. G., GERKEN, C. D'A., & HAHN, M. E. *Revised Minnesota Occupational Rating Scales.* Minneapolis: University of Minnesota Press, 1953.

PATERSON, D. G., & STONE, C. H. Dissatisfaction with life work among adult workers. *Occupations,* 1942, **21**, 219–221.

PEARLIN, L. I. Alienation from work: A study of nursing personnel. *American Sociological Review,* 1962, **27**, 314–326.

PEEL, E. A. Prediction of a complex criterion and battery reliability. *British Journal of Psychology* (Statistical Section), 1948, **1**, 84–94.

PENNOCK, G. A. Industrial research at Hawthorne. *Personnel Journal,* 1930, **8**, 296–299.

PEPINSKY, H. B. The selection and use of diagnostic categories in clinical counseling. *Applied Psychology Monographs,* 1948, No. 15.

PEPINSKY, H. B., & PEPINSKY, P. N. *Counseling: Theory and practice.* New York: Ronald, 1954.

PERRONE, P. A. Factors influencing high school seniors' occupational preferences. *Personnel and Guidance Journal,* 1964, **42**, 976–980.

PINNEY, M. The influence of home and school in the choice of a vocation. *Journal of Educational Research,* 1932, **25**, 286–290.

POND, M. Success of the factory worker. In R. Hoppock (Ed.), *Criteria of vocational success.* New York: National Occupational Conference, 1936, Pp. 940–944.

POND, M., & BILLS, M. A. Intelligence and clerical jobs. *Personnel Journal,* 1933, **12**, 41–56.

POOL, D. A. A note on the vocational aspirations

of the emotionally disturbed. *Vocational Guidance Quarterly,* 1965, **13**, 207–208.

PORTER, A. A longitudinal research program for predicting executive success of college students. *Personnel and Guidance Journal,* 1963, **42**, 160–165.

PORTER, J. K. Predicting the vocational plans of high school senior boys. *Personnel and Guidance Journal,* 1954, **33**, 215–218.

PORTER, L. W. Differential self-perceptions of management personnel and line workers. *Journal of Applied Psychology,* 1958, **42**, 105–108.

PORTER, L. W. Perceived trait requirements in bottom and middle management jobs. *Journal of Applied Psychology,* 1961, **45**, 232–236. (a)

PORTER, L. W. A study of perceived need satisfactions in bottom and middle management. *Journal of Applied Psychology,* 1961, **45**, 1–10 (b)

PORTER, L. W. Job attitudes in management: I. Perceived deficiencies in need fulfillment as a function of job level. *Journal of Applied Psychology,* 1962, **46**, 375–384.

PORTER, L. W. Job attitudes in management: II. Perceived importance of needs as a function of job level. *Journal of Applied Psychology,* 1963, **47**, 141–148. (a)

PORTER, L. W. Job attitudes in management: III. Perceived deficiencies in need fulfillment as a function of line versus staff type of job. *Journal of Applied Psychology,* 1963, **47**, 267–275. (b)

PORTER, L. W. Job attitudes in management: IV. Perceived deficiencies in need fulfillment as a function of size of company. *Journal of Applied Psychology,* 1963, **47**, 386–397. (c)

PORTER, L. W. *Organizational patterns of managerial job attitudes.* New York: American Foundations of Management Research, 1964.

PORTER, L. W., & HENRY, M. M. Job attitudes in management: V. Perceptions of the importance of certain personality traits as a function of job level. *Journal of Applied Psychology,* 1964, **48**, 31–36. (a)

PORTER, L. W., & HENRY, M. M. Job attitudes in management: VI. Perceptions of the importance of certain personality traits as a function of line versus staff type of job. *Journal of Applied Psychology,* 1964, **48**, 305–309. (b)

PORTER, L. W., & LAWLER, E. E., III. Properties of organization structure in relation to job attitudes and job behavior. *Psychological Bulletin,* 1965, **64**, 23–51.

PORTER, T. L., & COOK, T. E. A comparison of student and professional prestige ranking of jobs in psychology. *Journal of Counseling Psychology,* 1964, **11**, 385–387.

PRADOS, M. Rorschach studies on artists-painters: I. Quantitative results. *Journal of Projective Techniques,* 1944, **8**, 178–183.

PRATT, C. C. *The logic of modern psychology.* New York: Macmillan, 1939.

PRIEN, E. P. Dynamic character of criteria: Organization change. *Journal of Applied Psychology,* 1966, **50**, 501–504.

PROCTOR, W. M. A 13-year follow-up of high school pupils. *Occupations,* 1937, **15**, 306–310.

PRUETTE, L., & FRYER, D. Affective factors in vocational maladjustment. *Mental Hygiene,* 1923, **7**, 102–118.

RABIN, I. The use of the Wechsler-Bellevue scales with normal and abnormal persons. *Psychological Bulletin,* 1945, **42**, 410–422.

RABIN, I., & GUERTIN, W. H. Research with the Wechsler-Bellevue test: 1945–1950. *Psychological Bulletin,* 1951, **48**, 211–248.

RADCLIFFE, J. A. Some properties of ipsative score matrices and their relevance for some current interest tests. *Australian Journal of Psychology,* 1963, **15**, 1–11.

RAPOPORT, R., & RAPOPORT, R. Work and family in contemporary society. *American Sociological Review,* 1965, **30**, 381–394.

RASCHE, W. F. Empirical criteria. In R. Hoppock (Ed.), *Criteria of vocational success.* New York: National Occupational Conference, 1936. Pp. 936–939.

RASKIN, E. Comparison of scientific and literary ability: A biological study of eminent scientists and men of letters of the nineteenth century. *Journal of Abnormal and Social Psychology,* 1936, **31**, 20–35.

RECKLESS, W. C., DINITZ, S., & MURRAY, E. The "good" boy in a high delinquency area. *Journal of Criminal Law and Criminology,* 1957, **48**, 18–25.

REEVES, J. W. What is occupational success? *Occupational Psychology,* 1950, **24**, 153–159.

REMSTAD, R., & ROTHNEY, J. W. M. Occupational classification and research results. *Personnel and Guidance Journal,* 1958, **36**, 465–472.

RETTIG, S. Status and job satisfaction of the professional: A factor analysis. *Psychological Reports,* 1960, **6**, 411–413.

RETTIG, S., JACOBSON, F. N., & PASAMANICK, B. Status overestimation, objective status, and job satisfaction among professions. *American Sociological Review,* 1958, **23**, 75–81.

REYNOLDS, L. G., & SHISTER, J. The worker's view of job opportunity. *Advanced Management,* 1948, **13**, 170–177.

REYNOLDS, L. G., & SHISTER, J. *Job horizons: A study of job satisfaction and labor mobility.* New York: Harper & Row, 1949.

RICHARDS, L. S. *Vocophy.* Marlboro, Mass.: Pratt Brothers, 1881.

RICHARDS, J. M., JR., TAYLOR, C. W., PRICE, P. B., & JACOBSEN, T. L. An investigation of the criterion problem for one group of medical specialists. *Journal of Applied Psychology,* 1965, **49**, 79–90.

RICHARDSON, L. A., JR., Perceived monetary value of job type, company size, and location among college seniors. *Journal of Applied Psychology,* 1966, **50**, 412–416.

RICHARDSON, M. W. The combination of measures. In P. Horst, *The prediction of personal adjustment.* New York: Social Science Research Council, 1941. Pp. 377–401.

RICHEY, R. W., FOX, W. H., & FAUSET, C. E. Prestige ranks of teaching. *Occupations,* 1951, **30**, 33–36.

RIEGER, A. F. The Rorschach test in industrial selection. *Journal of Applied Psychology,* 1949, **33**, 569–571.

RIESMAN, D. *The lonely crowd.* New Haven, Conn.: Yale University Press, 1950.

ROACH, D. E. Factor analysis of rated supervisory behavior. *Personnel Psychology,* 1956, **9**, 487–498.

ROBBINS, B. S. Neurotic disturbances in work. *Psychiatry,* 1939, **2**, 333–342.

ROBINSON, F. P. *Principles and procedures in student counseling.* New York: Harper & Row, 1950.

ROBINSON, F. P. Modern approaches to counseling "diagnosis." *Journal of Counseling Psychology,* 1963, **10**, 325–333.

ROBINSON, H. A. Job satisfaction researches of 1952. *Personnel and Guidance Journal,* 1953, **32**, 22–26.

ROBINSON, H. A. Job satisfaction researches of 1953. *Personnel and Guidance Journal,* 1954, **33**, 26–29.

ROBINSON, H. A. Job satisfaction researches of 1954. *Personnel and Guidance Journal,* 1955, **33**, 520–523.

ROBINSON, H. A. Job satisfaction researches of 1955. *Personnel and Guidance Journal,* 1956, **34**, 565–568.

ROBINSON, H. A. Job satisfaction researches of 1956. *Personnel and Guidance Journal,* 1957, **36**, 34–37.

ROBINSON, H. A. Job satisfaction researches of 1957. *Personnel and Guidance Journal,* 1958, **37**, 55–60. (a)

ROBINSON, H. A. Job satisfaction researches of 1958. *Personnel and Guidance Journal,* 1959, **37**, 669–673. (b)

ROBINSON, H. A., & CONNORS, R. P. Job satisfaction researches of 1959. *Personnel and Guidance Journal,* 1960, **39**, 47–52.

ROBINSON, H. A., & CONNORS, R. P. Job satisfaction researches of 1960. *Personnel and Guidance Journal,* 1961, **40**, 373–377.

ROBINSON, H. A., & CONNORS, R. P. Job satisfaction researches of 1961. *Personnel and Guidance Journal,* 1962, **41**, 240–246.

ROBINSON, H. A., & CONNORS, R. P. Job satisfaction researches of 1962. *Personnel and Guidance Journal,* 1963, **42**, 136–142.

ROBINSON, H. A., CONNORS, R. P., & ROBINSON, A. H. Job satisfaction researches of 1963. *Personnel and Guidance Journal,* 1964, **43**, 360–366.

ROBINSON, H. A., CONNORS, R. P., & WHITACRE, G. H. Job satisfaction researches of 1964–65. *Personnel and Guidance Journal,* 1966, **45**, 371–379.

ROBINSON, H. A., & HOPPOCK, R. Job satisfaction researches of 1951. *Occupations,* 1952, **30**, 594–598.

ROE, A. Alcohol and creative work. *Quarterly Journal of Studies of Alcohol,* 1946, **7**, 415–467. (a)

ROE, A. Painting and personality. *Rorschach Research Exchange,* 1946, **10**, 86–100. (b)

ROE, A. The personality of artists. *Educational and Psychological Measurement,* 1946, **6**, 401–408. (c)

ROE, A. Artists and their work. *Journal of Personality,* 1946, **15**, 1–40. (d)

ROE, A. A Rorschach study of a group of scientists and technicians. *Journal of Consulting Psychology,* 1946, **10**, 317–327. (e)

ROE, A. Psychological examinations of eminent biologists. *Journal of Consulting Psychology,* 1949, **13**, 225–246. (a)

ROE, A. Analysis of Group Rorschachs of biologists. *Journal of Projective Techniques,* 1949, **13**, 25–43. (b)

ROE, A. Analysis of Group Rorschachs of physical scientists. *Journal of Projective Techniques,* 1950, **14,** 385–398.

ROE, A. A psychological study of eminent biologists. *Psychological Monographs,* 1951, **65** (14, Whole No. 331). (a)

ROE, A. Personality and vocation. *Transactions of New York Academy of Science,* 1947, **9,** 257–267.

ROE, A. A psychological study of eminent physical scientists. *Genetic Psychology Monographs,* 1951, **43,** 121–239. (b)

ROE, A. Psychological tests of research scientists. *Journal of Consulting Psychology,* 1951, **15,** 492–495. (c)

ROE, A. A study of imagery in research scientists. *Journal of Personality,* 1951, **19,** 459–470. (d)

ROE, A. Analysis of Group Rorschachs of psychologists and anthropologists. *Journal of Projective Techniques,* 1952, **16,** 212–224. (a)

ROE, A. Group Rorschachs of university faculties. *Journal of Consulting Psychology,* 1952, **16,** 18–22. (b)

ROE, A. A psychological study of eminent psychologists and anthropologists, and a comparison with biological and physical scientists. *Psychological Monographs,* 1953, **67,** (2, Whole No. 352) . (a)

ROE, A. *The making of a scientist.* New York: Dodd, Mead, 1953. (b)

ROE, A. A new classification of occupations. *Journal of Counseling Psychology,* 1954, **1,** 215–220.

ROE, A. *The psychology of occupations.* New York: Wiley, 1956.

ROE, A. Early determinants of vocational choice. *Journal of Counseling Psychology,* 1957, **4,** 212–217.

ROE, A. Comment. *Journal of Counseling Psychology,* 1959, **6,** 157–158.

ROE, A. Vocational development: A lifelong process. Paper read at the annual convention of the American Personnel and Guidance Association, Chicago, April, 1962.

ROE, A., HUBBARD, W. D., HUTCHINSON, T., & BATEMAN, T. Studies of occupational history. Part I: Job changes and the classification of occupations. *Journal of Counseling Psychology,* 1966, **13,** 387–393.

ROE, A., & MIERZWA, J. The use of the Rorschach in the study of personality and occupations. *Journal of Projective Techniques,* 1960, **24,** 282–289.

ROE, A., & SIEGELMAN, M. *Origin of interests.* APGA Inquiry Studies—No. 1. Washington D.C.: American Personnel and Guidance Association, 1964.

ROETHLISBERGER, F. J., & DICKSON, W. J. *Management and the worker.* Cambridge, Mass.: Harvard University Press, 1939.

ROGERS, C. R. *Counseling and psycotherapy.* Boston: Houghton Mifflin, 1942.

ROGERS, C. R. *Client-centered therapy: Its current practice, implications, and theory.* New York: Houghton Mifflin, 1951.

RONAN, W. W. A factor analysis of eleven job performance measures. *Personnel Psychology,* 1963, **16,** 255–268.

ROSE, A. W., & WALL, M. C. Social factors in prestige ranking of occupations. *Personnel and Guidance Journal,* 1957, **35,** 420–423.

ROSE, W. Comparison of relative interest in occupational groupings and activity interest as measured by the Kuder Preference Record. *Personnel and Guidance Journal,* 1948, **26,** 302–308.

ROSEN, H. Occupational motivation of research and development personnel. *Personnel Administration,* 1963, **26,** 37–43.

ROSEN, H., & MCCALLUM, E. F. Correlates of productivity. *Personnel Psychology,* 1962, **15,** 429–439.

ROSEN, H., & WEAVER, C. G. Motivation in management: A study of four managerial levels. *Journal of Applied Psychology,* 1960, **44,** 386–392.

ROSEN, R. A. H., & ROSEN, H. A suggested modification in job satisfaction surveys. *Personnel Psychology,* 1955, **8,** 303–314.

ROSENBERG, M. *Occupations and values.* Glencoe, Ill.: Free Press, 1957.

ROSS, I. C., & ZANDER, A. Need satisfaction and employee turnover. *Personnel Psychology,* 1957, **10,** 327–338.

ROSS, W. F., & ROSS, G. Backgrounds of vocational choice: An Apache study. *Personnel and Guidance Journal,* 1957, **35,** 270–275.

ROSSI, P. H., & INKELES, A. Multidimensional ratings of occupations. *Sociometry,* 1957, **20,** 234–251.

ROTHE, H. F. Output rates among butter wrappers: I. Work curves and their stability. *Journal of Applied Psychology,* 1946, **30,** 199–211. (a)

ROTHE, H. F. Output curves among butter wrappers: II. Frequency distributions and an hypothesis regarding the restriction of output. *Journal of Applied Psychology,* 1946, **30,** 320–327. (b)

ROTHE, H. F. Output rates among machine operators: I. Distributions and their reliability. *Journal of Applied Psychology,* 1947, **31**, 484–489.

ROTHE, H. F. Matching men to job requirements. *Personnel Psychology,* 1951, **4**, 291–301. (a)

ROTHE, H. F. Output rates among chocolate dippers. *Journal of Applied Psychology,* 1951, **35**, 94–97. (b)

ROTHE, H. F., & NYE, C. T. Output rates among coil winders. *Journal of Applied Psychology,* 1958, **42**, 182–186.

ROTHE, H. F., & NYE, C. T. Output rates among machine operators: II. Consistency related to methods of pay. *Journal of Applied Psychology,* 1959, **43**, 417–420.

ROTHE, H. F., & NYE, C. T. Output rates among machine operators: III. A nonincentive situation in two levels of business activity. *Journal of Applied Psychology,* 1961, **45**, 50–54.

ROTTENBERG, S. On choice in labor markets. *Industrial Labor Relations Review,* 1956, **9**, 183–199.

RULON, P. J., TIEDEMAN, D. V., TATSUOKA, M. M., & LANGMUIR, C. R. *Multivariate statistics for personnel classification.* New York: Wiley, 1967.

RUSALEM, H., & COHEN, J. S. Occupational prestige rankings by institutionalized and noninstitutionalized retarded students. *Personnel and Guidance Journal,* 1964, **42**, 981–986.

RUSH, C. H., JR. A factorial study of sales criteria. *Personnel Psychology,* 1953, **6**, 9–24.

RYANS, D. G. A study of criterion data: A factor analysis of teacher behaviors in the elementary school. *Educational and Psychological Measurement,* 1952, **12**, 333–444.

RYANS, D. G. Notes on the criterion problem in research, with special reference to the study of teacher characteristics. *Journal of Genetic Psychology,* 1957, **9**, 33–61.

SALEH, S. D. A study of attitude change in the preretirement period. *Journal of Applied Psychology,* 1964, **48**, 310–312.

SALEH, S. D., & OTIS, S. L. Sources of job satisfaction and their effects on attitudes toward retirement. *Journal of Industrial Psychology,* 1963, **1**, 101–106.

SALES, S. M. Supervisory style and productivity: Review and theory. *Personnel Psychology,* 1966, **19**, 275–286.

SAMLER, J. Psycho-social aspects of work: A critique of occupational information. *Personnel and Guidance Journal,* 1961, **39**, 458–465.

SAMSON, R., & STEFFLRE, B. Like father . . . like son? *Personnel and Guidance Journal,* 1952, **31**, 35–39.

SANBORN, M. P. Vocational choice, college choice, and scholastic success of superior students. *Vocational Guidance Quarterly,* 1965, **14**, 161–168.

SARBIN, T. R. Role theory. In G. Lindzey (Ed.), *Handbook of social psychology.* Vol. I. Cambridge, Mass.: Addison-Wesley, 1954. Pp. 223–258.

SARBIN, T. R., & ANDERSON, H. C. A preliminary study of the relation of measured interest patterns and occupational dissatisfaction. *Educational and Psychological Measurement,* 1942, **2**, 23–36.

SARBIN, T. R., & JONES, D. S. An experimental analysis of role behavior. *Journal of Abnormal and Social Psychology,* 1955, **51**, 236–241.

SAUNDERS, D. R. Moderator variables in prediction. *Educational and Psychological Measurement,* 1956, **16**, 209–222.

SCHACHTER, S., WILLERMAN, B., FESTINGER, L., & HYMAN, R. Emotional disruption and industrial productivity. *Journal of Applied Psychology,* 1961, **45**, 201–213.

SCHAIE, K. W. A general model for the study of developmental problems. *Psychological Bulletin,* 1965, **64**, 92–107.

SCHAFFER, R. H. Job satisfaction as related to need satisfaction in work. *Psychological Monographs,* 1953, **67** (14, Whole No. 364)

SCHLETZER, V. M. SVIB as a predictor of job satisfaction. *Journal of Applied Psychology,* 1966, **50**, 5–8.

SCHLETZER, V. M., DAWIS, R. V., ENGLAND, G. W., & LOFQUIST, L. H. *Minnesota studies in vocational rehabilitation: VII. Factors related to employment success.* Minneapolis: Industrial Relations Center, University of Minnesota, 1959.

SCHMID, J., & LEIMAN, J. M. The development of hierarchical factor solutions. *Psychometrika,* 1957, **22**, 53–61.

SCHMIDT, J. L., & ROTHNEY, J. W. M. Variability of vocational choice of high school students. *Personnel and Guidance Journal,* 1955, **34**, 142–146.

SCHNEIDER, E. V. *Industrial sociology.* New York: McGraw-Hill, 1957.

SCHNEIDER, S. F. The prediction of certain aspects of the psychotherapeutic relationship from Rorschach's test: An empirical and exploratory study. (Doctoral dissertation, University of Michigan) Ann Arbor, Mich.: University Microfilms, 1953. No. 5725.

SCHREIBER, R. J., SMITH, R. G., & HARRELL, T. W. A factor analysis of employee attitudes. *Journal of Applied Psychology,* 1952, **36**, 247–250.

SCHUH, A. J. Use of the Semantic Differential in a test of Super's vocational adjustment theory. *Journal of Applied Psychology,* 1966, **50**, 516–522.

SCHULTZ, D. G., & SIEGEL, A. I. Generalized Thurstone and Guttman scales for measuring technical skills in job performance. *Journal of Applied Psychology,* 1961, **45**, 137–142.

SCHULTZ, D. G., & SIEGEL, A. I. The analysis of job performance by multi-dimensional scaling techniques. *Journal of Applied Psychology,* 1964, **48**, 329–335.

SCHUTZ, R. A., & BLOCHER, D. H. Self-concepts and stereotypes of vocational preferences. *Vocational Guidance Quarterly,* 1960, **8**, 241–244.

SCHUTZ, R. A., & BLOCHER, D. H. Self-satisfaction and level of occupational choice. *Personnel and Guidance Journal,* 1961, **39**, 595–598.

SCHUTZ, R. A., & MAZER, G. E. A factor analysis of the occupational choice motives of counselors. *Journal of Counseling Psychology,* 1964, **11**, 267–271.

SCHWARTZ, M. M., JENUSAITIS, E., & STARK, H. Motivational factors among supervisors in the utility industry. *Personnel Psychology,* 1963, **16**, 45–54.

SCIENCE RESEARCH ASSOCIATES. *The American College Testing Program: Technical report 1960–61 edition.* Chicago: Science Research Associates, 1960.

SCOTT, T. B., DAWIS, R. V., ENGLAND, G. W., & LOFQUIST, L. H. *Minnesota studies in vocational rehabilitation: X. A definition of work adjustment.* Minneapolis: Industrial Relations Center, University of Minnesota, 1960.

SCOTT, W. D., & CLOTHIER, R. C. *Personnel management.* New York: Shaw, 1925.

SCOTT, W. D., CLOTHIER, R. C., & SPRIEGEL, W. R. *Personnel management,* (5th ed.) New York: McGraw-Hill, 1954.

SEAGOE, M. V. Prediction of in-service success in teaching. *Journal of Educational Research,* 1946, **39**, 658–663.

SEARS, J. B. Occupation of fathers and occupational choices of 1,039 boys in grades 7 and 8 of the Oakland schools. *School and Society,* 1915, **1**, 750–756.

SEASHORE, S. E., INDIK, B. P., & GEORGOPOULOS, B. S. Relationships among criteria of job performance. *Journal of Applied Psychology,* 1960, **44**, 195–202.

SEEMAN, M. On the meaning of alienation. *American Sociological Review,* 1959, **24**, 783–791.

SEGAL, S. J. The role of personality factors in vocational choice: A study of accountants and creative writers. (Doctoral dissertation, University of Michigan) Ann Arbor, Mich.: University Microfilms, 1954. No. A54–1031.

SEGAL, S. J. A psychoanalytic analysis of personality factors in vocational choice. *Journal of Counseling Psychology,* 1961, **8**, 202–210.

SEGAL, S. J., & SZABO, R. Identification in two vocations: Accountants and creative writers. *Personnel and Guidance Journal,* 1964, **43**, 252–255.

SEGEL, D. Construction and interpretation of differential ability patterns. *Journal of Experimental Education,* 1934, **3**, 203–287.

SEWELL, W. H., HALLER, A. O., & STRAUSS, M. A. Social status and educational and occupational aspiration. *American Sociological Review,* 1957, **22**, 67–73.

SHAFFER, L. F., & SHOBEN, E. J., JR. *The psychology of adjustment.* (2nd ed.) Boston: Houghton Mifflin, 1956.

SHARTLE, C. L. Developments in occupational classification. *Journal of Consulting Psychology,* 1946, **10**, 81–84.

SHARTLE, C. L. *Occupational information.* (3rd ed.) Englewood Cliffs, N.J.: Prentice-Hall, 1959.

SHARTLE, C. L. Occupational analysis, worker characteristics, and occupational classification systems. In H. Borow (Ed.), *Man in a world at work.* Boston: Houghton Mifflin, 1964. Pp. 285–309.

SHARTLE, C. L., DVORAK, B. J., et al. Occupational analysis activities in the War Manpower Commission. *Psychological Bulletin,* 1943, **40**, 701–713.

SHARTLE, C. L., DVORAK, B. J., HEINZ, C. A., et al. Ten years of occupational research. *Occupations,* **22**, 1944, 387–446.

SHELDON, W. H. *The varieties of human physique: An introduction to constitutional psychology*. New York: Harper & Row, 1940.

SHELDON, W. H. *The varieties of temperament: A psychology of constitutional differences.* New York: Harper & Row, 1942.

SHEPHERD, R. E. The relation of counseling and student problems to graduation. *Journal of Counseling Psychology,* 1965, **12**, 244–247.

SHOBEN, E. J., JR. Some problems in evaluating criteria of effectiveness. *Personnel and Guidance Journal,* 1952, **31**, 287–294.

SHOBEN, E. J., JR. Work, love, and maturity. *Personnel and Guidance Journal,* 1956, **34**, 326–332.

SHOBEN, E. J., JR. Toward a concept of the normal personality. *American Psychologist,* 1957, **12**, 183–189.

SHOEMAKER, W. L. Rejection of vocational interest areas. *Vocational Guidance Quarterly,* 1959, **8**, 72–74.

SIEGEL, A. I., & PFEIFFER, M. G. Factorial congruence in criterion development. *Personnel Psychology,* 1965, **18**, 267–279.

SIEGEL, L. *Industrial psychology*. Homewood, Ill.: Irwin, 1962.

SIMON, H. A. A behavioral model of rational choice. *Quarterly Journal of Economics,* 1955, **49**, 99–118.

SIMONS, J. B. An existential view of vocational development. *Personnel and Guidance Journal,* 1966, **44**, 604–610.

SIMMONS, D. D. Children's rankings of occupational prestige. *Personnel and Guidance Journal,* 1962, **41**, 332–336.

SIMS, V. M. *The measurement of socioeconomic status*. Bloomington, Ill.: Public School Publishing, 1928.

SIMS, V. M. *Sims SCI Occupational Rating Scale.* Yonkers-on-Hudson, N.Y.: World, 1952.

SINGER, J. O. Delayed gratification and ego-development: Implications for clinical and experimental research. *Journal of Consulting Psychology,* 1955, **19**, 259–266.

SINGER, S. L., & STEFFLRE, B. Age differences in job values and desires. *Journal of Counseling Psychology,* 1954, **2**, 89–91. (a)

SINGER, S. L., & STEFFLRE, B. Sex differences in job values and desires. *Personnel and Guidance Journal,* 1954, **32**, 483–484. (b)

SINGH, T. N., & BAUMGARTEL, H. Background factors in airline mechanics' work motivation: A research note. *Journal of Applied Psychology,* 1966, **50**, 357–359.

SINNETT, E. R. Some determinants of agreement between measured and expressed interests. *Educational and Psychological Measurement,* 1956, **16**, 110–118.

SISSON, E. D. Vocational choice of college students. *School and Society,* 1937, **46**, 765–768.

SISSON, E. D. An analysis of the occupational aims of college students. *Occupations,* 1938, **17**, 211–215. (a)

SISSON, E. D. The predictive value of vocational choices of college students. *School and Society,* 1938, **47**, 646–648. (b)

SISSON, E. D. Vocational choices of students from cities, towns, and farms. *School and Society,* 1941, **54**, 94–96.

SKINNER, B. F. Are theories of learning necessary? *Psychological review,* 1950, **57**, 193–216.

SLOAN, T. J., & PIERCE-JONES, J. The Bordin-Pepinsky diagnostic categories: Counselor agreement and MMPI comparisons. *Journal of Counseling Psychology,* 1958, **5**, 189–195.

SLOCUM, W. L. Occupational careers in organizations: A sociological perspective. *Personnel and Guidance Journal,* 1965, **43**, 858–866.

SLOCUM, W. L. *Occupational careers.* Chicago: Aldine, 1966.

SLUCKIN, W. Combining criteria of occupational success: Part I. *Occupational Psychology,* 1956, **30**, 20–26. (a)

SLUCKIN, W. Combining criteria of occupational success: Part II. *Occupational Psychology,* 1956, **30**, 57–68. (b)

SMALL, L. A theory of vocational choice. *Vocational Guidance Quarterly,* 1952, **1**, 29–32.

SMALL, L. Personality determinants of vocational choice. *Psychological Monographs,* 1953, **67**, (1, Whole No. 351)

SMALL, L., SWEAT, L. G., & VON ARNOLD, B. *Personality needs as determinants of vocational choice and their relationship to school and work achievement.* New York: Vocational Advisory Service, 1955. Mimeographed.

SMIGEL, E. O. Occupational sociology. *Personnel and Guidance Journal,* 1954, **32**, 536–539.

SMIGEL, E. O. (Ed.) *Work and leisure.* New Haven, Conn.: College and University Press, 1963.

SMIT, J. A study of the critical requirements for instructors of general psychology courses. *University of Pittsburgh Bulletin,* 1952, **48**, 279–284.

SMITH, A. *An inquiry into the nature and causes*

of the wealth of nations. New York: Random House, 1937.

SMITH, F. J., & KERR, W. A. Turnover factors as assessed by the exit interview. *Journal of Applied Psychology,* 1953, **37**, 352–355.

SMITH, K. U. *Work theory and economic behavior*. Bloomington, Ind.: Foundation for Economic and Business Studies, 1962.

SMITH, M. Proposals for making a scale of status of occupations. *Sociology and Social Research,* 1935, **20**, 40–49.

SMITH, M. The temperament factor in industry. *Human Factor,* 1936, **10**, 301–314.

SMITH, M. An empirical scale of prestige status of occupations. *American Sociological Review,* 1943, **8**, 185–192.

SMITH, M. W. Evidences of potentialities of older workers in a manufacturing company. *Personnel Psychology,* 1952, **5**, 11–18.

SMITH, M. W. Older worker's efficiency in jobs of various types. *Personnel Journal,* 1953, **32**, 19–23.

SMITH, P. C. Cornell studies of job satisfaction: I. Strategy for the development of a general theory of job satisfaction. Unpublished manuscript, Cornell University, 1963.

SMITH, W. J., ALBRIGHT, L. E., GLENNON, J. R., & OWENS, W. A. The prediction of research competence and creativity from personal history. *Journal of Applied Psychology,* 1961, **45**, 59–62.

SNOW, C. E. A discussion of the relation of illumination intensity to productive efficiency. *The Technical Engineering News,* 1927.

SOLBY, B. The role concept in job adjustment. *Sociometry,* 1944, **7**, 222–229.

SOLLENBERGER, R. T. Some relationships between the urinary excretion of male hormone by maturing boys and their expressed interests and attitudes. *Journal of Psychology,* 1940, **9**, 179–189.

SOROKIN, P. *Social mobility*. New York: Harper, 1927.

SPARLING, E. J. Do college students choose vocations wisely? *Teachers College Contributions to Education,* 1933, No. **561**.

SPEARMAN, C. "General intelligence" objectively determined and measured. *American Journal of Psychology,* 1904, **15**, 201–293.

SPENCE, K. W. The nature of theory construction in contemporary psychology. *Psychological Review,* 1944, **51**, 47–68.

SPENCE, K. W. *Behavior theory and learning: Selected papers*. Englewood Cliffs, N.J.: Prentice-Hall, 1960.

SPENCE, K. W., & FARBER, I. E. Conditioning and extinction as a function of anxiety. *Journal of Experimental Psychology,* 1953, **45**, 116–119.

SPIKER, C. C., & MCCANDLESS, B. R. The concept of intelligence and the philosophy of science. *Psychological Review,* 1954, **61**, 255–266.

SPRECHER, T. B. A study of engineers' criteria for creativity. *Journal of Applied Psychology,* 1959, **43**, 141–148.

SPRINTHALL, N. A. Work values and academic achievement. *Vocational Guidance Quarterly,* 1966, **15**, 52–56.

SRA Employee Inventory. Chicago: Science Research Associates, 1951.

STAGNER, R. The relation of personality to academic aptitude and achievement. *Journal of Educational Research,* 1933, **26**, 648–660.

STAGNER, R. Stereotypes of workers and executives among college men. *Journal of Abnormal and Social Psychology,* 1950, **45**, 743–748.

STAGNER, R. Motivational aspects of industrial morale. *Personnel Psychology,* 1958, **11**, 64–70.

STAGNER, R., FLEBBE, D. R., & WOOD, E. F. Working on the railroad: A study of job satisfaction. *Personnel Psychology,* 1952, **5**, 293–306.

STAGNER, R., RICH, J. M., & BRITTON, R. H. Job attitudes: I. Defense workers. *Personnel Journal,* 1941, **20**, 90–97.

STANTON, J. E. Part-time employment for the older worker. *Journal of Applied Psychology,* 1951, **35**, 418–421.

STEAD, W. H., & MASINCUP, W. E. *The occupational research program of the United States Employment Service*. Chicago: Public Administration Service, 1941.

STEAD, W. H., & SHARTLE, C. L. *Occupational counseling techniques*. New York: American Book, 1940.

STEFFLRE, B. Vocational aspiration and level of interest scores on the Lee Thorpe Occupational Interest Inventory. *Personnel and Guidance Journal,* 1955, **33**, 385–388.

STEFFLRE, B. Analysis of the interrelationships of rankings of occupations. *Personnel and Guidance Journal,* 1959, **37**, 435–438.

STEFFLRE, B. Vocational development: Ten propositions in search of a theory. *Personnel and Guidance Journal,* 1966, **44**, 611–616.

STEPHENSON, R. M. Status achievement and the occupational pyramid. *Social Forces,* 1952, **31**, 75–77.

STEPHENSON, R. M. Realism of vocational choice: A critique and an example. *Personnel and Guidance Journal,* 1957, **35**, 482–488.

STEPHENSON, R. R. A new pattern analysis technique for the SVIB. *Journal of Counseling Psychology,* 1961, **8**, 355–362. (a)

STEPHENSON, R. R. Occupational choice as a crystallized self concept. *Journal of Counseling Psychology,* 1961, **8**, 211–216. (b)

STERN, G. G., MASLING, J., DENTON, B., HENDERSON, J., & LEVIN, R. Two scales for the assessment of unconscious motivations for teaching. *Educational and Psychological Measurement,* 1960, **20**, 9–29.

STEVENS, R. B. The attitudes of college women toward women's vocations. *Journal of Applied Psychology,* 1940, **24**, 615–627.

STEVENS, S. S. (Ed.) *Handbook of experimental psychology.* New York: Wiley, 1951.

STEWART, N. AGCT scores of Army personnel grouped by occupation. *Occupations,* 1947, **26**, 5–41.

STEWART, N., & SPARKS, W. J. Patent productivity of research chemists as related to age and experience. *Personnel and Guidance Journal,* 1966, **45**, 28–36.

STOCKIN, B. G. A test of Holland's occupational level formulation. *Personnel and Guidance Journal,* 1964, **42**, 599–602.

STOLZ, R. E. Development of a criterion of research productivity. *Journal of Applied Psychology,* 1958, **42**, 308–310.

STOLZ, R. E. Subordinates' perceptions of the productive engineer. *Journal of Applied Psychology,* 1959, **43**, 306–310.

STONE, C. H., & KENDALL, W. E. *Effective personnel selection procedures.* Englewood Cliffs, N.J.: Prentice-Hall, 1956.

STONE, L. A. The relationship of utility for risk to college year, sex, and vocational choice. *Journal of Counseling Psychology,* 1962, **9**, 87.

STONE, V. W. Measured vocational interests in relation to intra-occupational proficiency. *Journal of Applied Psychology,* 1960, **44**, 78–82.

STOTT, M. B. Criteria used in England. In R. Hoppock (Ed.), *Criteria of vocational success.* New York: National Occupational Conference, 1936. Pp. 953–957.

STOTT, M. B. Occupational success. *Occupational Psychology,* 1939, **13**, 126–140.

STOTT, M. B. What is occupational success? *Occupational Psychology,* 1950, **24**, 105–112.

STOTT, M. B. Follow-up problems in vocational guidance, selection, and placement. *Occupational Psychology,* 1956, **30**, 137–152.

STRAUSS, S. Career choices of scholars. *Personnel and Guidance Journal,* 1965, **44**, 153–159.

STRONG, E. K., JR. *Change of interest with age.* Palo Alto: Stanford University Press, 1931.

STRONG, E. K., JR. *Vocational interests of men and women.* Palo Alto: Stanford University Press, 1943.

STRONG, E. K., JR. Amount of change of occupational choice of college freshmen. *Educational and Psychological Measurement,* 1952, **12**, 677–690.

STRONG, E. K., JR. Validity of occupational choice. *Educational and Psychological Measurement,* 1953, **13**, 110–121.

STRONG, E. K., JR. *Vocational interests 18 years after college.* Minneapolis: University of Minnesota Press, 1955.

STRONG, E. K., JR. Interests of fathers and sons. *Journal of Applied Psychology,* 1957, **41**, 284–292.

STRONG, E. K., JR. Satisfaction and interests. *American Psychologist,* 1958, **13**, 449–456.

STRONG, E. K., JR. An eighteen-year longitudinal report on interests. In W. L. Layton (Ed.), *The Strong Vocational Interest Blank: Research and uses.* Minneapolis: University of Minnesota Press, 1960. Pp. 3–17.

STRUENING, E. L., & EFRON, H. Y. The dimensional structure of opinions about work and the social context. *Journal of Counseling Psychology,* 1965, **12**, 316–321.

STRUNK, O., JR. Theological students: A study in perceived motives. *Personnel and Guidance Journal,* 1958, **36**, 320–322.

STUBBINS, J. Lack of realism in vocational choice. *Occupations,* 1948, **26**, 410–418.

STUBBINS, J. The relationship between level of vocational aspiration and certain personal data: A study of some traits and influences bearing on the prestige level of vocational choice. *Genetic Psychology Monographs,* 1950, **41**, 327–408.

STUDDIFORD, W. S. A functional system of occupational classification. *Occupations,* 1951, **30**, 37–42.

SUPER, D. E. Occupational level and job satisfaction. *Journal of Applied Psychology,* 1939, **23**, 547–564.

SUPER, D. E. *Avocational interest patterns.* Palo Alto: Stanford University Press, 1940.

SUPER, D. E. Avocation and vocational adjustment. *Character and Personality,* 1941, **10**, 51–61.

SUPER, D. E. *The dynamics of vocational adjustment.* New York: Harper & Row, 1942.

SUPER, D. E. Vocational interest and vocational choice. *Educational and Psychological Measurement,* 1947, **7**, 375–384.

SUPER, D. E. *Appraising vocational fitness.* New York: Harper & Row, 1949.

SUPER, D. E. The criteria of vocational success. *Occupations,* 1951, **30**, 5–8. (a)

SUPER, D. E. Vocational adjustment: Implementing a self-concept. *Occupations,* 1951, **30**, 88–92. (b)

SUPER, D. E. A theory of vocational development. *American Psychologist,* 1953, **8**, 185–190.

SUPER, D. E. Career patterns as a basis for vocational counseling. *Journal of Counseling Psychology,* 1954, **1**, 12–20.

SUPER, D. E. The dimensions and measurement of vocational maturity. *Teachers College Record,* 1955, **57**, 151–163.

SUPER, D. E. Vocational development: The process of compromise or synthesis. *Journal of Counseling Psychology,* 1956, **3**, 249–253.

SUPER, D. E. *The psychology of careers.* New York: Harper & Row, 1957.

SUPER, D. E. The multifactor tests: Summing up. In *The use of multifactor tests in guidance.* Washington, D.C.: American Personnel and Guidance Association, 1958. Pp. 88–91.

SUPER, D. E. The critical ninth grade: Vocational choice or vocational exploration. *Personnel and Guidance Journal,* 1960, **39**, 106–109.

SUPER, D. E. Consistency and wisdom of vocational preference as indices of vocational maturity in ninth grade. *Journal of Educational Psychology,* 1961, **52**, 35–43. (a)

SUPER, D. E. Some unresolved issues in vocational development research. *Personnel and Guidance Journal,* 1961, **40**, 11–14. (b)

SUPER, D. E. The structure of work values in relation to status, achievement, interests, and adjustment. *Journal of Applied Psychology,* 1962, **46**, 231–239.

SUPER, D. E. The definition and measurement of early career behavior: A first formulation. *Personnel and Guidance Journal,* 1963, **41**, 775–780.

SUPER, D. E., & BACHRACH, P. B. *Scientific careers and vocational development theory.* New York: Teachers College Bureau of Publications, 1957.

SUPER, D. E., & CRITES, J. O. *Appraising vocational fitness.* (Rev. ed.) New York: Harper & Row, 1962.

SUPER, D. E., CRITES, J. O., HUMMEL, R. C., MOSER, H. P., OVERSTREET, P. L., & WARNATH, C. F. *Vocational development: A framework for research.* New York: Teachers College Bureau of Publications, 1957.

SUPER, D. E., & OVERSTREET, P. L. *The vocational maturity of ninth grade boys.* New York: Teachers College Bureau of Publications, 1960.

SUPER, D. E., STARISHEVSKY, R., MATLIN, N., & JORDAAN, J. P. *Career development: self-concept theory.* Princeton, N.J.: College Entrance Examination Board, 1963.

SVETLIK, B., PRIEN, E., & BARRETT, G. Relationships between job difficulty, employee's attitude toward his job, and supervisory ratings of the employee effectiveness. *Journal of Applied Psychology,* 1964, **48**, 320–324.

SWITZER, D. K., GRIGG, A. E., MILLER, J. S., & YOUNG, R. K. Early experiences and occupational choices: A test of Roe's hypothesis. *Journal of Counseling Psychology,* 1962, **9**, 45–48.

SYMONDS, P. M. *The ego and the self.* New York: Appleton-Century-Crofts, 1951.

TAFT, R., & MULLINS, A. Who quits and why. *Personnel Journal,* 1946, **24**, 300–307.

TAUSSIG, F. W. *Principles of economics.* Vol. 2. New York: Macmillan, 1939.

TAYLOR, C. W., PRICE, P. B., RICHARDS, J. M., JR., & JACOBSEN, T. L. An investigation of the criterion problem for a medical school faculty. *Journal of Applied Psychology,* 1964, **48**, 294–301.

TAYLOR, C. W., PRICE, P. B., RICHARDS, J. M., JR., & JACOBSEN, T. L. An investigation of the criterion problem for a group of medical general practitioners. *Journal of Applied Psychology,* 1965, **49**, 399–406.

TAYLOR, J. A., & SPENCE, K. W. The relationship of anxiety level to performance in serial learning. *Journal of Experimental Psychology,* 1952, **44**, 61–64.

TECHNICAL COMMITTEE ON INDUSTRIAL CLASSIFICATION, BUREAU OF THE BUDGET, *Standard industrial classification manual.* Washington, D.C.: Government Printing Office, 1950.

TERMAN, L. M. *Genetic studies of genius.* Vol. I. Palo Alto: Stanford University Press, 1925.

TERMAN, L. M. Scientists and nonscientists in a group of 800 gifted men. *Psychological Monographs,* 1954, **68**, (Whole No. 378).

TERWILLIGER, J. S. Dimensions of occupational preference. *Educational and Psychological Measurement,* 1963, **23**, 525–542.

TEST SERVICE BULLETIN, *Aptitude, intelligence and achievement.* No. 51. New York: Psychological Corporation, 1956.

THOMAS, L. G. *The occupational structure and education,* Englewood Cliffs, N.J.: Prentice-Hall, 1956.

THOMAS, R. M., & SOEPARMAN. Occupational prestige: Indonesia and America. *Personnel and Guidance Journal,* 1963, **41**, 430–437.

THOMPSON, A. S., & DAVIS, J. A. What workers mean by security. *Personnel Psychology,* 1956, **9**, 229–241.

THOMPSON, O. E. Occupational values of high school students. *Personnel and Guidance Journal,* 1966, **44**, 850–853.

THOMSON, G. H. An analysis and comparison of certain techniques for weighting criterion data. *Educational and Psychological Measurement,* 1954, **14**, 449–458.

THORNDIKE, E. L. *Prediction of vocational success.* New York: Commonwealth Fund, 1934.

THORNDIKE, E. L. Rebounds from the target: More about the "Prediction of vocational success." *Occupations,* 1935, **13**, 329–333.

THORNDIKE, R. L. Problems in determining an adequate criterion. Washington, D.C.: U.S. Government Printing Office, 1947. (*AAF Aviation Psychology Program Research Report,* No. 3.)

THORNDIKE, R. L. *Personnel selection.* New York: Wiley, 1949.

THORNDIKE, R. L. The prediction of vocational success. *Vocational Guidance Quarterly,* 1963, **11**, 179–187.

THORNDIKE, R. L., & HAGEN, E. *10,000 careers.* New York: Wiley, 1959.

THORNDIKE, R. L., & HAGEN, E. *Measurement and evaluation in psychology and education.* (2nd ed.) New York: Wiley, 1961.

THORPE, R. P., & CAMPBELL, D. P. Expressed interests and worker satisfaction. *Personnel and Guidance Journal,* 1965, **44**, 238–243.

THRELKELD, H. The educational and vocational plans of college seniors. *Teachers College Contributions to Education,* 1935, No. 639.

THURSTONE, L. L. A multiple factor study of vocational interests. *Personnel Journal,* 1931, **10**, 198–205.

THURSTONE, L. L. *Primary mental abilities. Psychometric Monographs,* No. 1. Chicago: University of Chicago Press, 1938.

THURSTONE, L. L. *Multiple-factor analysis.* Chicago: University of Chicago Press, 1947.

TIEDEMAN, D. V. Review of Ginzberg, E., Ginsburg, S. W., Axelrad, S., & Herma, J. L., *Occupational choice: An approach to a general theory. Harvard Educational Review,* 1952, **22**, 184–190.

TIEDEMAN, D. V. A model for the profile problem. *Proceedings, 1953 invitational conference on testing problems.* Princeton, N.J.: Educational Testing Service, 1954. Pp. 54–75.

TIEDEMAN, D. V. Decision and vocational development: A paradigm and its implications. *Personnel and Guidance Journal,* 1961, **40**, 15–20.

TIEDEMAN, D. V. Career development through liberal arts and work. *Vocational Guidance Quarterly,* 1965, **14**, 1–7.

TIEDEMAN, D. V., & O'HARA, R. P. The Harvard Studies in Career Development: A current view in retrospect and in prospect. Unpublished manuscript, Graduate School of Education, Harvard University, 1960.

TIEDEMAN, D. V., & O'HARA, R. P. *Career development: Choice and adjustment.* Princeton, N.J.: College Entrance Examination Board, 1963.

TIEDEMAN, D. V., & PANDIT, J. L. On identity and level of occupational aspiration. Unpublished manuscript, Harvard Studies in Career Development, Harvard University, 1958.

TIFFIN, J. *Industrial psychology.* New York: Prentice-Hall, 1942.

TIFFIN, J., & MC CORMICK, E. J. *Industrial psychology.* (4th ed.) New York: Prentice-Hall, 1958.

TIFFIN, J., & MCCORMICK, E. J. *Industrial psychology.* (5th ed.) Englewood Cliffs, N.J.: Prentice-Hall, 1965.

TILGHER, A. Work through the ages. In S. Nosow and W. H. Form (Eds.), *Man, work, and society.* New York: Basic Books, 1962. Pp. 11–24.

TIRYAKIN, E. A. The prestige evaluation of occupations in an underdeveloped country: The Phillippines. *American Journal of Sociology,* 1958, **63**, 390–399.

TOLMAN, E. C. Operational behaviorism and current trends in psychology. *Proceedings of the 25th Aniversary Celebration of the Inauguration of Graduate Studies.* Los Angeles: University of Southern California Press, 1936.

TOLMAN, E. C. Cognitive maps in rats and men. *Psychological Review,* 1948, **55**, 189–208.

TOLMAN, E. C. Discussion. In J. S. Bruner, & D. Krech, *Perception and personality*. Durham, N.C.: Duke University Press, 1950.

TOMKINS, S. S. *The Thematic Apperception Test: The theory and technique of interpretation.* New York: Grune & Stratton, 1947.

TOOPS, H. A. The criterion. *Educational and Psychological Measurement,* 1944, **4**, 271–293.

TOOPS, H. A. Some concepts of job families and their importance in placement. *Educational and Psychological Measurement,* 1945, **5**, 195–215.

TOOPS, H. A. A research utopia in industrial psychology. *Personnel Psychology,* 1959, **12**, 189–226.

TORGERSON, W. S. Theory and methods of scaling. New York: Wiley, 1958.

TRABUE, M. R. Occupational ability patterns. *Personnel Journal,* 1933, **11**, 344–351.

TRABUE, M. R. Graphic representation of measured characteristics of successful workers. *Occupations,* 1934, **12**, 40–45.

TRABUE, M. R. Functional classification of occupations. *Occupations,* 1936, **15**, 127–131.

TRATTNER, M. H., FINE, S. H., & KUBIS, J. F. A comparison of worker requirement ratings made by reading job descriptions and by direct observation. *Personnel Psychology,* 1955, **8**, 183–194.

TRIANDIS, H. C. A critique and experimental design for the study of the relationships between productivity and job satisfaction. *Psychological Bulletin,* 1959, **56**, 309–312.

TROW, W. D. Phantasy and vocational choice. *Occupation,* 1941, **20**, 89–93.

TROXELL, J. P. Elements in job satisfaction. *Personnel,* 1954, **31**, 199–205.

TUCCI, M. A. College freshmen and vocational choice. *Vocational Guidance Quarterly,* 1963, **12**, 27–29.

TUCKER, L. R. The objective definition of simple structure in linear factor analysis. *Psychometrika,* 1955, **20**, 209–225.

TUCKMAN, J. Social status of occupations in Canada. *Canadian Journal of Psychology,* 1947, **1**, 71–74.

TUCKMAN, J. Rankings of women's occupations according to social status, earnings, and working conditions. *Occupations,* 1950, **28**, 290–294.

TUCKMAN, J. Rigidity of social status rankings of occupations. *Personnel and Guidance Journal,* 1958, **36**, 534–537.

TUCKMAN, J., & LORGE, I. Attitudes toward older workers. *Journal of Applied Psychology,* 1952, **36**, 149–153.

TURNER, W. W. Dimensions of foreman performance: A factor analysis of criterion measures. *Journal of Applied Psychology,* 1960, **44**, 216–223.

TWERY, R., SCHMID, J., & WRIGLEY, C. Some factors in job satisfaction: A comparison of three methods of analysis. *Educational and Psychological Measurement,* 1958, **18**, 189–202.

TYLER, L. E. The relationship of interests to abilities and reputation among first-grade children. *Educational and Psychological Measurement,* 1951, **11**, 255–264.

TYLER, L. E. *The work of the counselor.* New York: Appleton-Century-Crofts, 1953.

TYLER, L. E. The development of "vocational interests": The organization of likes and dislikes in ten-year-old children. *Journal of Genetic Psychology,* 1955, **86**, 33–44.

TYLER, L. E. *The Psychology of human differences.* (2nd ed.) New York: Appleton-Century-Crofts, 1956.

TYLER, L. E. Theoretical principles underlying the counseling process. *Journal of Counseling Psychology,* 1958, **5**, 3–10.

TYLER, L. E. Distinctive patterns of likes and dislikes over a twenty-two year period. *Journal of Counseling Psychology,* 1959, **6**, 234–237. (a)

TYLER, L. E. Toward a workable psychology of individuality. *American Psychologist,* 1959, **14**, 75–81. (b)

TYLER, L. E. Research explorations in the realm of choice. *Journal of Counseling Psychology,* 1961, **8**, 195–201. (a)

TYLER, L. E. *The work of the counselor.* (2nd ed.) New York: Appleton-Century-Crofts, 1961. (a)

TYLER, L. E. The antecedents of two varieties of interest pattern. *Genetic Psychology Monographs,* 1964, **70**, 177–227.

TYLER, L. E. *The psychology of human differences.* (3rd ed.) New York: Appleton-Century-Crofts. 1965.

ULRICH, G., HECHLIK, J., & ROEBER, E. C. Occupational stereotypes of high school students. *Vocational Guidance Quarterly,* 1966, **15**, 169–174.

UNDERWOOD, B. J. *Experimental psychology.* New York: Appleton-Century-Crofts, 1949.

UNDERWOOD, B. J. *Psychological research.* New York: Appleton-Century-Crofts, 1957.

UNDERWOOD, B. J. *Experimental psychology.* (2nd ed.) New York: Appleton-Century-Crofts, 1966.

U.S. BUREAU OF THE BUDGET, DIVISION OF STATISTICAL STANDARDS. *Standard industrial classification.* Washington, D.C.: Government Printing Office, 1957.

U.S. DEPARTMENT OF LABOR. *Guide to the use of the General Aptitude Test Battery.* Washington, D.C.: Government Printing Office, 1962.

U.S. DEPARTMENT OF LABOR, BUREAU OF EMPLOYMENT SECURITY. *Estimates of worker trait requirements for 4,000 jobs as defined in the Dictionary of Occupational Titles.* Washington, D.C.: Government Printing Office, 1956.

UTTON, A. C. Recalled parent-child relations as determinants of vocational choice. *Journal of Counseling Psychology,* 1962, **9**, 49–53.

VALLANCE, T. R., GLICKMAN, A. S., & SUCI, G. J. Criterion rationale for a personnel research program. *Journal of Applied Psychology,* 1953, **37**, 429–431.

VAN KLEECK, M. Towards an industrial sociology. *American Sociological Review,* 1946, **5**, 501–505.

VAN ZELST, R. H., & KERR, W. A. Reported lifetime worry experience of Illinois building trades union leaders. *Personnel Psychology,* 1951, **4**, 151–159.

VERNON, P. E. Classifying high-grade occupational interests. *Journal of Abnormal and Social Psychology,* 1949, **44**, 85–96.

VERNON, P. E. *The structure of human abilities.* London: Methuen, 1950.

VITELES, M. S. *Industrial psychology.* New York: Norton, 1932.

VITELES, M. S. A dynamic criterion. In R. Hoppock (Ed.), *Criteria of vocational success.* New York: National Occupational Conference, 1936, Pp. 963–967.

VITELES, M. S. *Motivation and morale in industry.* New York: Norton, 1953.

VITELES, M. S., & SMITH, K. R. The prediction of vocational aptitude and success from photographs. *Journal of Experimental Psychology,* 1932, **15**, 615–629.

VOLLMAR, H. M., & KINNEY, J. A. Age, education, and job satisfaction. *Personnel,* 1955, **32**, 38–43.

VROOM, V. A. *Work and motivation.* New York: Wiley, 1964.

WAGMAN, M. Sex and age differences in occupational values. *Personnel and Guidance Journal,* 1965, **44**, 258–262.

WAGNER, R. F. A study of the critical requirements for dentists. *University of Pittsburgh Bulletin,* 1950, **46**, 331–339. (Abstract)

WAGNER, R. F. Using critical incidents to determine selection test weights. *Personnel Psychology,* 1951, **4**, 373–381.

WALKER, C. R., & GUEST, R. H. *The man on the assembly line.* Cambridge, Mass.: Harvard University Press, 1952.

WALKER, K. F. A study of occupational stereotypes. *Journal of Applied Psychology,* 1958, **42**, 122–124.

WALLACE, W. L. The relationship of certain variables to discrepancy between expressed and inventoried vocational interest. Unpublished doctoral dissertation, University of Michigan, 1949.

WALSH, R. P. The effect of needs on responses to job duties. *Journal of Counseling Psychology,* 1959, **6**, 194–198.

WALTHER, R. H. The functional occupational classification project: A critical appraisal. *Personnel and Guidance Journal,* 1960, **38**, 698–706.

WALTON, E. What makes engineers move—and remain? *Personnel Administration,* 1960, **23**, 22–26.

WARNATH, C. F. Comment. *Journal of Counseling Psychology,* 1960, **7**, 101.

WARNER, W. L., MEEKER, M., & EELLS, K. *Social class in America.* Chicago: Science Research Associates, 1949.

WARREN, J. R. Self concept, occupational role expectation, and change in college major. *Journal of Counseling Psychology,* 1961, **8**, 164–169.

WATLEY, D. J. Time of decision to study engineering. *Personnel and Guidance Journal,* 1965, **44**, 63–67.

WEBB, W. B. Occupational indecision among college students. *Occupations,* 1949, **27**, 331–332.

WECHSLER, D. Cognitive, conative, and non-intellective intelligence. *American Psychologist,* 1950, **5**, 78–83.

WEIDER, A., & MITTELMANN, B. Personality and psychosomatic disturbances among industrial personnel. *American Journal of Orthopsychiatry,* 1946, **16**, 631–639.

WEINSTEIN, E. Children's conception of occupational stratification. *Sociological and Social Research,* 1958, **42**, 278–284.

WEINSTEIN, M. S. Personality and vocational choice. Unpublished doctoral dissertation, Western Reserve University, 1953.

WEISS, D. J., DAWIS, R. V., ENGLAND, G. W., & LOFQUIST, L. H. *Minnesota studies in vocational rehabilitation: XVI. The measurement of vocational needs.* Minneapolis: Industrial Relations Center, University of Minnesota, 1964.

WEITZ, J. A neglected concept in the study of job satisfaction. *Personnel Psychology,* 1952, **5**, 201–205.

WEITZ, J. Criteria for criteria. *American Psychologist,* 1961, **16**, 228–231.

WEITZ, J., & NUCKOLS, R. C. The validity of direct and indirect questions in measuring job satisfaction. *Personnel Psychology,* 1953, **5**, 487–494.

WELCH, M. K. The ranking of occupations on the basis of social status. *Occupations,* 1948, **27**, 237–241.

WERNIMONT, P. F. Intrinsic and extrinsic factors in job satisfaction. *Journal of Applied Psychology,* 1966, **50**, 41–50.

WERTS, C. Social class and initial career choice of college freshmen. *Sociology of Education,* 1966, **39**, 74–85.

WESLEY, S. M., COREY, D. Q., & STEWART, M. The intra-individual relationship between interest and ability. *Journal of Applied Psychology,* 1950, **34**, 193–197.

WEST, E. D. The significance of interpersonal relationships in job performance. *Occupations,* 1951, **29**, 438–440.

WHEELER, W. M. Rorschach indices of male homosexuality. *Rorschach Research Exchange,* 1949, **13**, 97–126.

WHERRY, R. J. An approximation method for obtaining a maximized multiple criterion. *Psychometrika,* 1944, **9**, 263–266.

WHERRY, R. J. *The control of bias in ratings, VII. A theory of rating.* Columbus, Ohio: The Ohio State University Research Foundation, PRB Report 922, 1952.

WHERRY, R. J. An orthogonal re-rotation of the Baehr and Ash studies of the SRA Employee Inventory. *Personnel Psychology,* 1954, **7**, 365–380.

WHERRY, R. J. A rejoinder to Baehr's reply on rotation of the SRA Employee Inventory studies. *Personnel Psychology,* 1956, **9**, 93–99.

WHERRY, R. J. The past and future of criterion evaluation. *Personnel Psychology,* 1957, **10**, 1–5.

WHERRY, R. J. Factor analysis of morale data: Reliability and validity. *Personnel Psychology,* 1958, **11**, 78–89.

WHERRY, R. J., & WINER, B. J. A method for factoring large numbers of items. *Psychometrika,* 1952, **18**, 161–179.

WHITE, R. W. *Lives in progress.* New York: Holt, 1952.

WHITE, R. W. Motivation reconsidered: The concept of competence. *Psychological Review,* 1959, **66**, 297–333.

WHYTE, W. H. *The organization man.* New York: Simon & Schuster, 1956.

WICKERT, F. Psychological research on problems of redistribution. Washington, D.C.: U.S. Government Printing Office, 1947. *(AAF Aviation Psychology Program Research Report,* No. 14.)

WILDER, J. R., & RIGGS, L. Employers' attitudes toward college graduates. *Personnel and Guidance Journal,* 1948, **26**, 235–239.

WILENSKY, H. L. Varieties of work experience. In H. Borow (Ed.), *Man in a world at work.* Boston: Houghton Mifflin, 1964. Pp. 125–154.

WILKS, S. S. Weighting systems for linear functions of correlated variables when there is no dependent variable. *Psychometrika,* 1938, **3**, 23–40.

WILLIAMS, F. J., & HARRELL, T. W. Predicting success in business. *Journal of Applied Psychology,* 1964, **48**, 164–167.

WILLIAMS, G., & KELLMAN, S. The Rorschach technique in industrial psychology. In B. Klopfer et al., *Developments in the Rorschach Technique. Vol. II. Fields of application,* New York: World, 1956. Pp. 545–581.

WILKINSON, F. Social distance between occupations. *Sociology & Social Research,* 1929, **13**, 234–244.

WILLIAMSON, E. G. Scholastic motivation and the choice of a vocation. *School and Society,* 1937, **46**, 353–357.

WILLIAMSON, E. G. The clinical method of guidance. *Review of Educational Research,* 1939, **9**, 214–217. (a)

WILLIAMSON, E. G. *How to counsel students.* New York: McGraw-Hill, 1939. (b)

WILLIAMSON, E. G. *Vocational counseling.* New York: McGraw-Hill, 1964.

WILLIAMSON, E. G., & DARLEY, J. G. Trends in the occupational choices of high school seniors. *Journal of Applied Psychology,* 1935, **19**, 361–370.

WILLIAMSON, E. G., & DARLEY, J. G. *Student personnel work.* New York: McGraw-Hill, 1937.

WILSON, A. B. Residential segregation of social classes and aspirations of high school boys. *American Sociological Review,* 1959, **24**, 836–845.

WILSON, W. E. Veterans' vocational objectives. *Occupations,* 1948, **26**, 359–360.

WINFIELD, D. The relationship between IQ scores and Minnesota Multiphasic Personality Inventory. *Journal of Social Psychology,* 1953, **38**, 299–300.

WITTY, P., GARFIELD, S., & BRINK, W. A comparison of the vocational interests of Negro and white high-school students. *Journal of Educational Psychology,* 1941, **32**, 124–132.

WITTY, P. A., & LEHMAN, H. C. A study of vocational attitude and intelligence. *Elementary School Journal,* 1931, **31**, 735–746.

WOLFBEIN, S. L. Labor trends, manpower, and automation. In H. Borow (Ed.), *Man in a world at work.* Boston: Houghton Mifflin, 1964. Pp. 155–173.

WOLFE, D. Factor analysis to 1940. *Psychometric Monographs,* No. 3. Chicago: University of Chicago Press, 1940.

WOODROW, H. The problem of general quantitative laws in psychology. *Psychological Bulletin,* 1942, **39**, 1–27.

WOOLEY, H. T. *An experimental study of children at work and in school between the ages of fourteen and eighteen years.* New York: Macmillan, 1926.

WRENN, C. G. Vocational satisfaction of Stanford graduates. *Personnel Journal,* 1934, **13**, 21–24.

WRENN, C. G. Intelligence and the vocational choices of college students. *The Educational Record,* 1935, **16**, 217–219

WRENN, C. G. Vocational choice theory—an editorial comment. *Journal of Counseling Psychology,* 1959, **6**, 94.

WRENN, C. G. Human values and work in American life. In H. Borow (Ed.), *Man in a world at work.* Boston: Houghton Mifflin, 1964. Pp. 24–44.

WRIGHT, H. A. Personal adjustment in industry. *Occupations.* 1940, **18**, 500–505.

WRIGLEY, C. The prediction of a complex aptitude. *British Journal of Psychology,* (Statistical Section), 1952, **5**, 93–104.

WRIGLEY, C. F., CHERRY, C. N., LEE, C., & MCQUITTY, L. L. Use of the square-root method to identify factors in the job performance of aircraft mechanics. *Psychological Monographs,* 1957, **71** (1, Whole No. 430).

WRIGLEY, C. F., & MCQUITTY, L. L. The square root method of factor analysis: A re-examination and a shortened procedure. *USAF Personnel Training Research Bulletin,* in press.

WYATT, F. The scoring and analysis of the Thematic Apperception Test. *Journal of Psychology,* 1947, **24**, 319–330.

WYLIE, R. C. *The self-concept: A review of the literature.* Lincoln, Neb.: University of Nebraska Press, 1961.

YERKES, R. M. (Ed.) Psychological examining in the U.S. Army. *Memoirs of the National Academy of Sciences,* 1921, Vol. 15.

YODER, D. *Personnel management and industrial relations.* New York: Prentice-Hall, 1942.

YODER, D., HENEMAN, H. G., & CHEIT, E. F. *Triple Audit of Industrial Relations.* Industrial Relations Center Bulletin 11, University of Minnesota, 1951.

YODER, D., PATERSON, D. G., HENEMAN, H. G., STONE, C. H., *et al. Local labor market research: A case study of the St. Paul labor market.* Minneapolis: University of Minnesota Press, 1948.

YOUMANS, E. G. Federal management intern career patterns. *Public Personnel Review,* 1956, **17**, 71–78.

YOUNG, K. *Personality and problems of adjustment.* New York: Croft, 1940.

ZILLER, R. C. Vocational choice and utility for risk. *Journal of Counseling Psychology,* 1957, **4**, 61–64.

ZINTZ, F. R., & KERR, W. A. Hearing loss and worker morale. *Journal of Applied Psychology,* 1951, **35**, 92–93.

ZUBIN, J., ERON, L. D., & SCHUMER, F. *An experimental approach to projective techniques.* New York: Wiley, 1965.

ZURCHER, L. A., JR., MEADOW, A., & ZURCHER, S. L. Value orientation, role conflict, and alienation from work: A cross-cultural study. *American Sociological Review,* 1965, **30**, 539–548.

ZYTOWSKI, D. G. Avoidance behavior in vocational motivation. *Personnel and Guidance Journal,* 1965, **43**, 746–750.

NAME INDEX

SUBJECT INDEX

This book was set in Baskerville by Monotype Composition Company, Inc., and printed on permanent paper and bound by The Maple Press Company. The designer was Elliot Epstein; the drawings were done by Textart Service, Inc. The editors were Walter Maytham and Sonia Sheldon. Adam Jacobs supervised the production.